T0271049

IFRS Essentials

IFRS Essentials

Dieter Christian Norbert Lüdenbach

A John Wiley & Sons, Ltd., Publication

This edition first published 2013

Registered office
John Wiley & Sons Ltd, The Atrium, Southern Gate, Chichester, West Sussex, PO19 8SQ, United Kingdom

For details of our global editorial offices, for customer services and for information about how to apply for permission to reuse the copyright material in this book please see our website at www.wiley.com.

Library of Congress Cataloging-in-Publication Data

A catalogue record for this book is available from the British Library.

ISBN 978-1-118-49471-4 (paperback) ISBN 978-1-118-50134-4 (ebk)
ISBN 978-1-118-50138-2 (ebk) ISBN 978-1-118-50137-5 (ebk)

Typeset in 10/11pt Times by Aptara Inc., New Delhi, India
Printed in Great Britain by TJ International Ltd, Padstow, Cornwall

CONTENTS

PREFACE

There are several IFRS commentaries that exceed several thousands of pages. The reading and utilization of such commentaries requires the investment of large amounts of time as well as previous knowledge to be able to understand and apply the information. Such publications are of particular relevance for experts. However, their content goes far beyond the needs of students and most readers. Alternatively, the IFRS book market also includes books that promise to convey an understanding of IFRS in several days. These books do not and cannot have the depth that many readers need.

Consequently, the authors have aimed at striking a balance between the two: this book does not include every single detail because such an approach would overload the book with information not relevant for most readers. Therefore, this book is not an encyclopedia. However, it does convey an understanding of IFRS that gives students and readers an in-depth introduction to the topics. It illustrates the **essentials of IFRS** relevant to the audience described above.

The workbook is characterized by a balanced ratio of "theory" (**explanation of the rules**) and "practice" (illustration of the application of the rules by means of **examples**). It aims to capture problems and their solutions by using explanations that are short, simple, and easy to understand. Obscure language and incomplete illustrations are avoided.

The book can be used by lecturers at **universities** and **other educational institutions**. Students as well as auditing trainees will gain access into IFRS in a fast and comprehensive manner. However, the book is also suitable, among others, for **employees** in the areas of accounting and auditing in order to develop their skills and deepen their knowledge of IFRS. Due to the extensive explanations of the rules and solutions in each of the examples, the book is also suitable for **self-study**.

The **German edition** of the book can be ordered at www.nwb.de.

Finally, we would like to thank Ms Kathryn Crotzer for the linguistic review of the entire book.

Vienna and Düsseldorf, June 2012
Dieter Christian and Norbert Lüdenbach

ABBREVIATIONS

AG	Application Guidance (for an accounting standard)
AICPA	American Institute of Certified Public Accountants
APB	Accounting Principles Board (of the AICPA, predecessor of the FASB)
BC	Basis for Conclusions (for an accounting standard)
bp	Basis points
CAD	Canadian dollar
CAPM	Capital asset pricing model
CEO	Chief executive officer
CFO	Chief financial officer
CGU(s)	Cash-generating unit(s)
CNY	Chinese yuan renminbi
CODM	Chief operating decision maker
CPI	Consumer price index
Cr	Credit record
CU	Currency unit(s)
Dr	Debit record
EBIT	Earnings before interest and taxes
EBITDA	Earnings before interest, taxes, depreciation, and amortization
ED	Exposure Draft
EDP	Electronic data processing
e.g.	Exempli gratia (for example)
etc.	Et cetera
EU	European Union
F	Conceptual Framework
FASB	Financial Accounting Standards Board in the US
FIFO	First-in, first-out
GAAP	Generally accepted accounting principles/practices
i	Interest rate
IAS(s)	International Accounting Standard(s)
IASB	International Accounting Standards Board
ICAEW	Institute of Chartered Accountants in England and Wales
i.e.	Id est (that is)
IE	Illustrative Examples (for an accounting standard)
IFRIC	International Financial Reporting Interpretations Committee
IFRS(s)	International Financial Reporting Standard(s)
IG	Implementation Guidance (for an accounting standard)
IN	Introduction (for an accounting standard)
JPY	Japanese yen
m	Million
NCI	Non-controlling interest(s)
OB	see Section 2 of the first chapter ("The objective of general purpose financial reporting") on the Conceptual Framework
OCI	Other comprehensive income
p.	Page
p.a.	Per annum

P/L	Profit or loss
PiR	Praxis der internationalen Rechnungslegung (IFRS journal in German language)
PoC-method	Percentage of completion method
PPI	Producer price index
PVIFA	Present value interest factor of annuity
QC	Chapter 3 ("Qualitative characteristics of useful financial information") of the Conceptual Framework
ROI	Return on investment
SAR(s)	Share appreciation right(s)
SIC	Standing Interpretations Committee
SPE(s)	Special purpose entity (entities)
t	Tax rate
UL	Useful life (for tax purposes)
US	United States of America
USA	United States of America
vs.	Versus
WACC	Weighted average cost of capital
WPI	Wholesale price index

THE CONCEPTUAL FRAMEWORK FOR FINANCIAL REPORTING

1 INTRODUCTION

The Conceptual Framework sets out the concepts that underlie the preparation and presentation of financial statements for external users (Conceptual Framework, Section "Purpose and status"). The relationship between the Conceptual Framework and individual IFRSs can be described as follows.

- In the **absence of regulation**, management has to develop an accounting policy. That accounting policy has to be compatible with the Conceptual Framework if there are no requirements in IFRSs which deal with similar and related issues (IAS 8.11).
- In a limited number of cases, there may be a **conflict between the Conceptual Framework and the requirements of an IFRS**. In such cases, the requirements of the IFRS prevail over those of the Conceptual Framework (Conceptual Framework, Section "Purpose and status").

2 THE OBJECTIVE OF GENERAL PURPOSE FINANCIAL REPORTING

The objective of general purpose financial reporting is to provide **financial information** about the reporting entity that is **useful** to existing and potential investors, lenders, and other creditors **in making decisions** about providing resources to the entity (e.g. providing loans to the entity or buying equity instruments of the entity) (OB2).

Existing and potential investors, lenders, and other creditors are the **primary users** to whom general purpose financial reports are directed (OB5). They require useful information in order to be able to assess the future cash flows of the entity they are evaluating. Normally, general purpose financial reports are not primarily prepared for use by management, regulators or other members of the public, although they may also find those reports useful (OB9-OB10).

General purpose financial reports are not designed to show the value of a reporting entity. Instead, they help the primary users to estimate such value (OB7).

Changes in the reporting entity's economic resources and claims against the entity result from that entity's **financial performance** and from **other events or transactions** such as issuing debt or equity instruments. To properly assess the entity's future cash flow prospects, users need to be able to distinguish between both of these changes (OB15).

Accrual accounting is applied when preparing the financial statements. Accrual accounting depicts the effects of transactions and other events and circumstances on the reporting entity's economic resources and claims against the entity in the periods in which those effects occur, even if the resulting cash receipts and payments occur in a different period (OB17). However, the statement of cash flows is not prepared on an accrual basis (IAS 7).

3 GOING CONCERN

The financial statements are normally prepared on the assumption that the entity is a going concern and will continue in operation for the foreseeable future. Thus, it is assumed that the entity has neither the intention nor the need to liquidate or curtail materially the scale of its operations. However, if such an intention or need exists, the financial statements may have to be prepared on a different basis and, if so, the basis used is disclosed (F.4.1).

4 QUALITATIVE CHARACTERISTICS OF USEFUL FINANCIAL INFORMATION

4.1 Introduction

The objective of general purpose financial reporting (see Section 2) is a very broad concept. Consequently, the IASB provides guidance on how to make the judgments necessary to achieve that overall objective. The qualitative characteristics of useful financial information described subsequently identify the types of information that are likely to be most useful to the existing and potential investors, lenders, and other creditors for making decisions about the reporting entity on the basis of information in its financial report (QC1). The following chart represents an overview of the qualitative characteristics.[1]

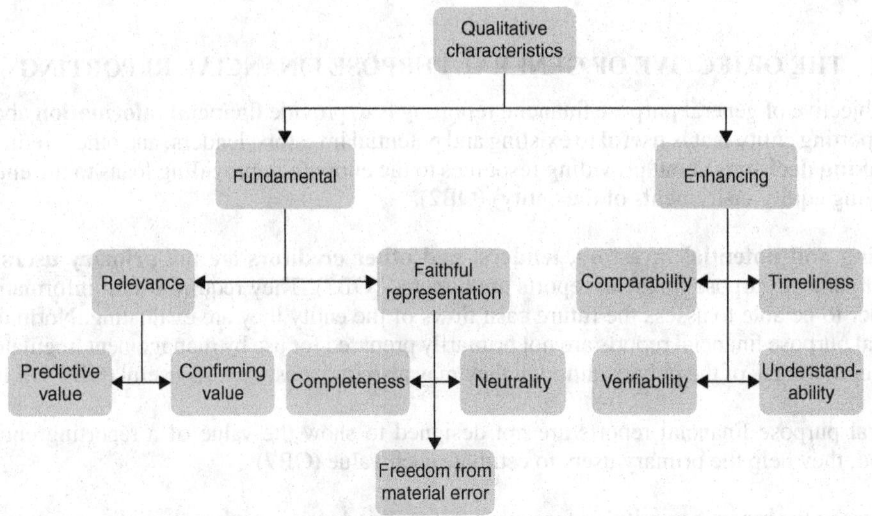

4.2 Fundamental Qualitative Characteristics

Financial information must be both relevant and faithfully represented if it is to be useful (QC4 and QC17).

[1] *See KPMG, Briefing Sheet,* Conceptual Framework for Financial Reporting*: Chapters 1 and 3, October 2010, Issue 213.*

4.2.1 Relevance Financial information is relevant if it is **capable of making a difference** in the decisions made by users (QC6). Financial information is capable of making a difference in decisions if it has predictive value, confirmatory value, or both (QC7).

Predictive value means that the financial information can be used as an input to processes employed by users to predict future outcomes. Financial information need not be a prediction or forecast itself in order to have predictive value. Instead, financial information with predictive value is employed by users in making their own predictions (QC8). **Confirmatory value** means that the financial information provides feedback about (i.e. confirms or changes) previous evaluations (QC9).

The predictive value and confirmatory value are interrelated. Financial information that has predictive value often also has confirmatory value (QC10).

Financial information about a specific reporting entity is material if omitting it or misstating it could influence the decisions of users. In other words, **materiality** is an entity-specific aspect of relevance based on the magnitude or nature, or both, of the items to which the information relates in the context of an individual entity's financial report. Hence, the IASB cannot specify a uniform quantitative threshold for materiality or predetermine what could be material in a particular situation (QC11).

4.2.2 Faithful Representation A faithful representation of economic phenomena would have three characteristics. It would be complete, neutral, and free from error. The IASB intends to maximize those qualities to the extent possible (QC12).

A **complete** depiction includes all information necessary for a user to understand the economic phenomenon being depicted. That information includes the necessary numerical information, descriptions, and explanations (QC13).

A **neutral** depiction is without bias in the selection or presentation of information. A neutral depiction is not slanted, weighted, emphasized, de-emphasized or otherwise manipulated in order to increase the probability that the information will be received favorably or unfavorably by users (QC14).

Free from error means that there are no errors or omissions in the description of an economic phenomenon, and the process used to produce the reported information has been selected and applied with no errors in the process. Nevertheless, free from error does not mean perfectly accurate in all respects. For example, there is always some uncertainty when estimating an unobservable price or value (QC15).

Faithful representation **excludes prudence** because it was considered to be in conflict with neutrality (FBC3.19 and BC3.27–BC3.28).

In the Conceptual Framework, **substance over form** does not represent a separate component of faithful representation because it would be redundant. This is because representing a legal form that differs from the economic substance of the underlying economic phenomenon could not result in a faithful representation. Consequently, faithful representation implies that financial information represents the substance of an economic phenomenon rather than merely representing its legal form (FBC3.19 and BC3.26). This means that substance over form is an important principle in IFRS. The following are examples for applying the principle of substance over form with regard to the issue of revenue recognition when selling goods.

- The assessment of when to recognize revenue is based on the transfer of beneficial ownership and not on the transfer of legal title or the passing of possession (IAS 18.15). For example, when goods are sold under **retention of title**, the seller recognizes revenue when the significant risks and rewards of ownership have been transferred, the seller retains neither effective control nor continuing managerial involvement to the degree usually associated with ownership, and the general criteria (the revenue and the costs can be measured reliably and it is probable that the economic benefits will flow to the seller) are met (IAS 18.14). This means that revenue is recognized by the seller and the goods are recognized by the buyer when beneficial ownership is transferred.
- In an **agency relationship**, an agent may sell goods of the principal in his own name. The **agent** receives a commission from the principal as consideration. In the agent's statement of comprehensive income, the amounts collected by the agent on behalf of the principal do not represent revenue. Instead, **revenue** of the agent is the **amount of commission** (IAS 18.8). This procedure results from the application of the principle "substance over form." Moreover, the agent does not recognize the goods received from the principal in his statement of financial position because beneficial ownership is not transferred to the agent. The **principal** recognizes revenue and derecognizes the goods when he loses beneficial ownership as a result of the sale of the goods to a third party (IAS 18.IE2c and IAS 2.34).
- In an agency relationship in which an agent sells goods of his principal, the accounting treatment described above applies. However, in some cases **determining whether an entity is acting as a principal or as an agent** is not straightforward. That determination requires judgment and consideration of all relevant facts and circumstances. An entity is **acting as a principal** when it has exposure to the significant risks and rewards associated with the sale of the goods. Features that indicate that an entity is acting as a principal include (IAS 18.IE21):
  - The entity has the **primary responsibility** for fulfilling the order, for example by being responsible for the acceptability of the goods.
  - The entity has **inventory risk** before or after the customer order, during shipping or on return.
  - The entity has **latitude in establishing prices**, either directly or indirectly (e.g. by providing additional goods or services).
  - The entity **bears the customer's credit risk** for the amount receivable from the customer.

One feature indicating that an entity is **acting as an agent** is that the amount the entity earns is predetermined (being either a fixed fee per transaction or a stated percentage of the amount billed to the customer).

4.3 Enhancing Qualitative Characteristics

The enhancing qualitative characteristics enhance the usefulness of information that is relevant and faithfully represented. However, they cannot make information useful if that information is irrelevant or not faithfully represented. They may also help to determine which of two ways should be used to depict an economic phenomenon if both are considered equally relevant and faithfully represented (QC19 and QC33).

Enhancing qualitative characteristics should be maximized to the extent possible. However, one enhancing qualitative characteristic may have to be diminished in order to maximize another qualitative characteristic (QC33–QC34).

4.3.1 Comparability Information about a reporting entity is more useful if it can be compared with similar information about the **same entity for another period** or another date and with similar information about **other entities** (QC20).

Consistency, although related to comparability, is not the same. Consistency refers to the use of the same methods for the same items, either in a single period across entities or from period to period, within the reporting entity. Comparability is the goal whereas consistency helps to achieve that goal (QC22).

The IASB also notes that permitting **alternative accounting methods** for the same economic phenomenon diminishes comparability (QC25).

4.3.2 Verifiability Verifiability means that different knowledgeable and independent observers could reach consensus although not necessarily complete agreement that a particular depiction constitutes a faithful representation (QC26).

Quantified information need not be a single point estimate in order to be verifiable. A range of possible amounts and the related probabilities can also be verified (QC26).

It may not be possible to verify some explanations and forward-looking information until a future period, if at all. To help users decide whether they want to use that information, it is normally necessary to disclose the underlying assumptions, the methods of compiling the information and other factors, and circumstances that support the information (QC28).

4.3.3 Timeliness Timeliness means having information available to decision-makers in time to be capable of influencing their decisions. Normally, the older the information is the less useful it is (QC29).

4.3.4 Understandability Information is made understandable by classifying, characterizing and presenting it clearly and concisely (QC30).

Financial reports are prepared for users who have a reasonable knowledge of business and economic activities and who review and analyze the financial information diligently. Sometimes even well-informed and diligent users may need to seek the aid of an adviser to understand information about complex phenomena (QC32).

5 THE COST CONSTRAINT ON USEFUL FINANCIAL REPORTING

Cost is a pervasive constraint on the information that can be provided by financial reporting. Reporting information imposes **costs** and it is important that those costs are justified by the **benefits** of reporting that information (QC35). Hence, when applying the cost constraint in developing an IFRS, the IASB assesses whether the benefits of reporting particular information are likely to justify the costs incurred to provide and use that information (QC38).

6 THE ELEMENTS OF FINANCIAL STATEMENTS

6.1 Definitions

The elements directly related to the measurement of **financial position** are defined as follows in the Conceptual Framework (F.4.4):

- An **asset** is a resource which is controlled by the entity as a result of past events and from which future economic benefits are expected to flow to the entity.
- A **liability** is a present obligation of the entity that arises from past events, the settlement of which is expected to result in an outflow from the entity of resources embodying economic benefits.
- **Equity** is the residual interest in the assets of the entity after deducting all its liabilities.

Assets and liabilities (as defined above) are not always recognized in the statement of financial position. This is because recognition in the statement of financial position requires that the recognition criteria (see Section 6.2) are met (F.4.5).

Furthermore, the elements of **performance** are defined in the Conceptual Framework as follows (F.4.25):

- **Income** encompasses increases in economic benefits during the period in the form of inflows or enhancements of assets or decreases of liabilities that result in increases in equity, other than those relating to contributions from equity participants.
- **Expenses** are decreases in economic benefits during the period in the form of outflows or depletions of assets or incurrences of liabilities that result in decreases in equity, other than those relating to distributions to equity participants.

Income and expenses (as defined above) are not always recognized in the statement of comprehensive income. This is because recognition in the statement of comprehensive income requires that the recognition criteria (see Section 6.2) are met (F.4.26).

Income encompasses both **gains** (e.g. from the disposal of non-current assets) and **revenue** (e.g. from the sale of merchandise). Similarly, expenses encompass **losses** as well as **other expenses** (F.4.29–4.35).

6.2 Recognition

Recognition is the process of incorporating an element (see Section 6.1) in the statement of financial position or in the statement of comprehensive income (F.4.37).

An **asset** is recognized in the statement of financial position when it is probable that the future economic benefits associated with the asset will flow to the entity and the asset has a cost or value that can be measured reliably (F.4.44).

A **liability** is recognized in the statement of financial position when it is probable that an outflow of resources which embody economic benefits will result from the settlement of a present obligation and the amount at which the settlement will take place can be measured reliably (F.4.46).

The so-called **matching principle** applies to the recognition of income and expenses in the statement of comprehensive income. Expenses are recognized in the statement of comprehensive income on the basis of a direct association between the costs incurred and the earning of specific items of income. This means that expenses and income that result directly and jointly from the same transactions or other events are recognized simultaneously or combined. For example, the costs of goods sold are recognized at the same time as the income derived from the sale of the goods. However, the application of the matching principle does not allow the recognition of items in the statement of financial position that do not meet the definition of assets or liabilities (F.4.50).

6.3 Measurement

The measurement of the items recognized in the statement of financial position items is defined in the individual standards. The description of different types of measurement in F.4.55 is of no importance in practice.

7 EXAMPLES WITH SOLUTIONS

Example 1

Relevance: Predictive value and confirmatory value

Entity E discloses revenue information for 01 in its financial statements as at Dec 31, 01.

Required

Assess whether E's revenue information is relevant within the meaning of the Conceptual Framework.

Hints for solution

In particular Section 4.2.1.

Solution

Predictive value means that the financial information can be used as an input to processes employed by users to predict future outcomes. Financial information need not be a prediction or forecast itself in order to have predictive value. Instead, financial information with predictive value is employed by users in making their own predictions. E's revenue information for the current period (01) can be used as the basis for predicting revenues in future periods. Consequently, it has predictive value (QC8 and QC10).

Confirmatory value means that the financial information provides feedback about (i.e. confirms or changes) previous evaluations (QC9). E's revenue information for the current period (01) can be compared with revenue predictions for 01 that were made in past periods. Hence, it also has confirmatory value (QC9–QC10).

Financial information is **relevant** if it has predictive value, confirmatory value or both (QC6–QC7). Since E's revenue information has predictive value as well as confirmatory value, it is relevant within the meaning of the Conceptual Framework.

Example 2

Substance over form – retention of title

On Dec 31, 01, wholesaler W delivers merchandise under retention of title to retailer R. On that date, the significant risks and rewards of ownership are transferred. W retains neither effective control nor continuing managerial involvement to the degree usually associated with ownership. The carrying amount of the merchandise in W's statement of financial position is CU 4. They are sold for CU 5.

Required

Prepare all necessary entries in the financial statements as at Dec 31, 01 of (a) W and (b) R.

Hints for solution

In particular Section 4.2.2.

Solution

General aspects

Irrespective of the retention of title, beneficial ownership is transferred from W to R on Dec 31, 01. This is because the significant risks and rewards of ownership have been transferred and W retains neither effective control nor continuing managerial involvement to the degree usually associated with ownership. Moreover, it can be assumed that the criterion "probability of the inflow of economic benefits" is met because there are no indications to the contrary. In addition, it is obvious that the revenue and the costs can be measured reliably (IAS 18.14).

(a) W's perspective

On Dec 31, 01, W loses beneficial ownership. Therefore, the criteria for revenue recognition are met. The carrying amount of the merchandise sold has to be recognized as an expense in the period in which the related revenue is recognized, i.e. in 01 (IAS 2.34):

Dec 31, 01	Dr	Cash	5	
	Cr	Revenue		5
Dec 31, 01	Dr	Cost of sales	4	
	Cr	Merchandise		4

(b) R's perspective

R recognizes the merchandise in its statement of financial position when obtaining beneficial ownership:

Dec 31, 01	Dr	Merchandise	5	
	Cr	Cash		5

Example 3

Determining whether the entity is acting as a principal or as an agent

Entity E operates an internet business. E's customers pay via credit card. After a credit card check, the order is automatically sent to producer P who immediately sends the goods to the final customer.

E is responsible for any defects of P's products to the final customers. However, E and P have stipulated that all claims of final customers are forwarded to and resolved by P at P's cost.

E receives commission of 10% of the amount billed to the final customer for each sale. The selling prices and the conditions of sales are determined by P alone.

On Dec 07, 01, E sells goods to the final customer in the amount of CU 50. All payments are carried out on the same day.

Required

Assess whether E is acting as a principal or as an agent and prepare all necessary entries in E's financial statements as at Dec 31, 01.

Hints for solution

In particular Section 4.2.2.

Solution

E considers the following criteria when assessing whether it acts as a principal or as an agent (IAS 18.IE21):

- E is responsible for any defects of P's products to the final customers. However, E and P have stipulated that all claims of final customers are forwarded to and resolved by P at P's cost. This means that, in fact (i.e. when applying the principle "substance over form"), E does not have any obligations with regard to defective goods.
- E has no inventory risk, i.e. no risk of a decline in value of the goods.
- The selling prices and the conditions of the sales are determined by P alone. Hence, E has no latitude in establishing prices.
- The amount that E earns is predetermined, being a stated percentage of the amount billed to the final customer.
- Since the final customers have to pay via credit card, E does not bear the customers' credit risk.

According to the characteristics of E's business, E is acting as an agent. Consequently, E's revenue is the amount of commission:

Dec 07, 01	Dr	Cash	5	
	Cr	Revenue		5

Example 4

Is recognition of an intangible asset in the statement of financial position appropriate?

In Jun 01, entity E spent CU 100 for employee training. E's management believes that its employees will make a more competent impression on E's clients as a result of the training which will then increase E's revenue.

Required

Assess whether the expenses for employee training have to be recognized as an intangible asset in E's statement of financial position. In doing so, also discuss the impact of the matching principle (F.4.50).

Hints for solution

In particular Sections 6.1 and 6.2.

Solution

Considering the matching principle (F.4.50) would suggest the following procedure: the expense of CU 100 is at first recognized as an intangible asset in E's statement of financial position. It affects profit or loss in the same periods in which the related increases in revenue occur. According to that procedure, the increases in revenue would be recognized in profit or loss in the same periods as the training costs that are necessary for creating the higher revenue.

However, the application of the matching principle does not allow the recognition of items in the statement of financial position that do not meet the definition of assets or liabilities (F.4.50), or of items that are assets but do not meet the recognition criteria.

Consequently, the procedure described above (capitalization of the training costs initially and subsequent recognition in profit or loss when the related increases in revenue occur) cannot be applied because the training costs do not represent an intangible asset that meets the recognition criteria (IAS 38.69b). Consequently, they are recognized in profit or loss in Jun 01.

IAS 1 PRESENTATION OF FINANCIAL STATEMENTS

1 INTRODUCTION AND SCOPE

IAS 1 primarily addresses the presentation of financial statements and can be divided into three large areas:

- General guidelines going beyond presentation issues (e.g. going concern).
- General principles relating to presentation (e.g. offsetting, consistency of presentation, and comparative information).
- Structure and content of the financial statements and most of its components (statement of financial position, statement of comprehensive income, separate income statement, statement of changes in equity, and notes).

With regard to recognition and measurement, IAS 1 refers to other IFRSs (IAS 1.3).

2 GOING CONCERN

When preparing financial statements, management has to make an assessment of the entity's ability to continue as a going concern. Financial statements are prepared on a going concern basis unless management either **intends to liquidate the entity** or to **cease trading**, or has **no realistic alternative but to do so**. When management is aware, in making its assessment, of material uncertainties related to events or conditions that may cast significant doubt upon the entity's ability to continue as a going concern, those uncertainties have to be disclosed. When financial statements are not prepared on a going concern basis, that fact has to be disclosed, together with the basis on which the financial statements were prepared and the reason why the entity is not regarded as a going concern. In assessing whether the going concern assumption is appropriate, management takes into account all available information about the future, which is at least, but is not limited to, 12 months from the end of the reporting period (IAS 1.25–1.26).

3 FAIR PRESENTATION OF THE FINANCIAL STATEMENTS AND COMPLIANCE WITH IFRSs

Financial statements have to **present fairly** the financial position, financial performance, and cash flows of an entity. It is generally presumed that the application of IFRSs, with additional disclosure when necessary, results in financial statements that achieve such fair presentation (IAS 1.15).

In extremely rare circumstances, compliance with a requirement in an IFRS may conflict with the principle of fair presentation. In such a case, it is generally necessary to depart from that requirement (**overriding principle**) (IAS 1.19). In the case of such a departure, it is necessary to disclose, among others, how the assets, profit or loss, etc. would have been reported in complying with the requirement (IAS 1.20d). In practice, the overriding principle is hardly ever applied.

An entity whose financial statements comply with IFRSs has to disclose an explicit and unreserved statement of such compliance in the notes (**statement of compliance**). Disclosing such a statement requires that the entity has complied with all the requirements of IFRSs (IAS 1.16).

4 GENERAL PRINCIPLES RELATING TO PRESENTATION

4.1 Materiality and Aggregation

Items of a dissimilar nature or function have to be presented separately, unless they are immaterial. The materiality threshold that applies to the notes is generally lower than the threshold that applies to the other components of the financial statements. This means, for example, that items which are not itemized in the statement of financial position because they are immaterial in that statement may have to be shown in the notes (IAS 1.29–1.31).

4.2 Offsetting

Offsetting is **generally prohibited** (IAS 1.32). This means that in general an entity cannot offset assets and liabilities, or income and expenses. However, in certain situations, offsetting may be required or permitted by an IFRS. Regarding the separate income statement or the single statement of comprehensive income, the scope of the prohibition to offset is not straightforward.

4.3 Frequency of Reporting

The financial statements (including comparative information) have to be presented at least annually, i.e. the normal reporting period is 12 months. When an entity changes its balance sheet date (e.g. from Dec 31 to Mar 31), the transition period can be longer or shorter than one year (IAS 1.36). However, this choice may be restricted by national laws.

4.4 Comparative Information

Comparative information regarding the **preceding period** for all amounts reported in the current period's financial statements has to be presented except when IFRSs permit or require otherwise. This means that, as a minimum, two of each of the components of the financial statements[1] have to be presented, as well as related notes (IAS 1.10(ea), 1.38, and 1.38A).

It is necessary to present an additional statement of financial position (i.e. a **third balance sheet**) as at the beginning of the preceding period, if (IAS 1.10f and 1.40A–1.40D):

- an accounting policy is applied retrospectively, a retrospective restatement is made, or when items are reclassified and
- this has a material effect on the information in the statement of financial position at the beginning of the preceding period.

If the presentation or classification of items in the financial statements is changed, the comparative amounts have to be reclassified unless reclassification is impracticable (IAS 1.41).

---

[1] *See Section 5.*

4.5 Consistency of Presentation

The presentation and classification of items in the financial statements have to be retained from one period to the next (consistency of presentation) unless (IAS 1.45):

- it is apparent that another presentation or classification would result in reliable and more relevant information (IAS 8.7–8.12), or
- a new or amended IFRS requires a change in presentation.

5 COMPONENTS OF THE FINANCIAL STATEMENTS

An entity's financial statements consist of the following components (IAS 1.10):

- A **statement of financial position (balance sheet)**. (In some cases it is necessary to present an additional statement of financial position as at the beginning of the preceding period.[2])
- Either:[3]
  - a single statement of comprehensive income (one statement approach), or
  - a separate income statement and a statement of comprehensive income (two statement approach).
- A statement of changes in equity.
- A **statement of cash flows**.
- **Notes**: The notes contain information supplementary to that which is presented in the other components of the financial statements (IAS 1.7).

6 STRUCTURE AND CONTENT OF THE COMPONENTS OF THE FINANCIAL STATEMENTS[4]

6.1 Statement of Financial Position (Balance Sheet)

Apart from an exception that is generally relevant only for financial institutions, **current** and **non-current** assets and current and non-current liabilities have to be presented as separate classifications in the statement of financial position (IAS 1.60). Deferred tax assets and deferred tax liabilities must not be classified as current (IAS 1.56).

Assets and liabilities are classified as **current** when one of the following conditions is met (IAS 1.66 and 1.69):

---

[2] *See Section 4.4.*

[3] *An amendment to IAS 1 issued in June 2011 changed the titles of the statements presenting profit or loss, other comprehensive income, and total comprehensive income. In the new version of the standard, the terms "statement of profit or loss and other comprehensive income" and "statement of profit or loss" are used. However, the standard also permits using different titles for these statements (IAS 1.10). Therefore, the titles "statement of comprehensive income" and "separate income statement," which are preferred by the authors of this book, are used in this book. These are the titles that were used in IAS 1 before the amendment in June 2011.*

[4] *The effects of non-current assets or disposal groups held for sale and of discontinued operations are discussed in the chapter on IFRS 5. With regard to the statement of cash flows, we refer to the chapter on IAS 7.*

- It is expected to realize the asset or intended to sell or consume it during the normal operating cycle. In the case of a liability, it must be expected to settle the liability in the normal operating cycle.
- The asset or liability is held primarily for the purpose of trading.
- It is expected to realize the asset or the liability is due to be settled within 12 months after the reporting period. In the case of a liability, it is sufficient if the creditor has the right to demand settlement within 12 months after the reporting period, even if this is not expected.
- The asset is cash or a cash equivalent (as defined in IAS 7.6).[5]

In the case of a manufacturing company, the operating cycle is the time between the acquisition of materials that are processed during production, and the realization of the finished goods in cash or cash equivalents. Sometimes (e.g. in the building industry), the operating cycle may be longer than 12 months. When the normal operating cycle of an entity is not clearly identifiable, it is assumed to be 12 months (IAS 1.68 and 1.70).

Normally the rules of IAS 1.54 result in the minimum structure of the statement of financial position shown below. The order of the items is not prescribed.

ASSETS	*EQUITY AND LIABILITIES*
Non-current assets	**Equity**
Intangible assets	Issued capital and reserves
Property, plant, and equipment	Non-controlling interests
Investment property	
Investments accounted for using the equity method	**Non-current liabilities**
Other non-current financial assets	Non-current financial liabilities
Deferred tax assets	Long-term provisions
	Government grants related to assets
Current assets	Deferred tax liabilities
Inventories	
Trade and other receivables	**Current liabilities**
Other current financial assets	Trade and other payables
Current tax assets	Other current financial liabilities
Other non-financial assets	Short-term provisions
Cash and cash equivalents	Current tax liabilities
Total assets	**Total equity and liabilities**

When an entity **breaches a provision of a long-term loan arrangement** on or before the end of the reporting period with the effect that the liability becomes payable on demand, the entire liability has to be classified as current (IAS 1.74).

6.2 Statement of Comprehensive Income and Separate Income Statement

6.2.1 Profit or Loss, Other Comprehensive Income and How They Interrelate Total comprehensive income includes all components of profit or loss and of other comprehensive income (IAS 1.7).

Other comprehensive income includes the following components (IAS 1.7):

(a) Changes in revaluation surplus (within the meaning of IAS 16 and IAS 38).

[5] *See the chapter on IAS 7, Section 1.*

(b) Actuarial gains and losses on defined benefit plans recognized in other comprehensive income (IAS 19.93A).
(c) Exchange differences on translating the financial statements of foreign operations according to the current rate method (IAS 21).
(d) Gains and losses on equity instruments measured at fair value through other comprehensive income (IFRS 9).[6]
(e) The effective portion of gains and losses on hedging instruments in a cash flow hedge (IAS 39).
(f) Changes in credit risk of certain liabilities (IFRS 9).[7]

Reclassification adjustments are amounts reclassified to profit or loss in the current period that were recognized in other comprehensive income in the current or previous periods (IAS 1.7).

Reclassification adjustments **may occur** in the case of components (c) and (e) of other comprehensive income (see the list at the beginning of this section) (IAS 1.95–1.96). This means that such income or expense is first recognized in other comprehensive income and increases or decreases the appropriate reserve. At a later date it may be necessary to reclassify that amount to profit or loss ("Dr Other comprehensive income (reserve) Cr Profit or loss" or "Dr Profit or loss Cr Other comprehensive income (reserve)") (IAS 1.93). Reclassification adjustments arise, for instance, upon disposal of a **foreign operation** that has been translated according to the current rate method (IAS 21) and when a **hedged forecast transaction** affects profit or loss (IAS 39) (IAS 1.95).[8]

Reclassification adjustments **do not occur** in the case of components (a), (b), (d), and (f) of other comprehensive income (see the list at the beginning of this section) (IAS 1.96):

- **Changes in revaluation surplus** may be transferred to retained earnings in subsequent periods as the asset is used or when it is derecognized, but they are not reclassified to profit or loss.
- **Actuarial gains and losses** are included in retained earnings in the period that they are recognized as other comprehensive income (IAS 19.93D).
- An entity may make an irrevocable election at initial recognition to present subsequent changes in the fair value of an **equity instrument** within the scope of IFRS 9 that is not

[6] *See the chapter on IFRS 9/IAS 39, Section 2.3.7 for more information with regard to the election to measure equity instruments at fair value through other comprehensive (IFRS 9.5.7.1b and 9.5.7.5). Under the "old" version of IAS 39 (i.e. under the version of IAS 39 before the consequential amendments resulting from IFRS 9), fair value gains and losses on financial assets classified as "available for sale" were also recognized in other comprehensive income. However, there were exceptions to that rule (see the chapter on IFRS 9/IAS 39, Section 3.2 with regard to the category "available for sale").*

[7] *See the chapter on IFRS 9/IAS 39, Section 2.3.7. This component of other comprehensive income did not exist under the "old" version of IAS 39.*

[8] *When an entity still applies the "old" version of IAS 39 (i.e. the version of IAS 39 before the consequential amendments resulting from IFRS 9), the classification of financial assets as "available for sale" can also result in reclassification adjustments. This is because IAS 39 requires reclassification of amounts relating to available-for-sale financial assets that were previously recognized in other comprehensive income to profit or loss in particular situations (see the chapter on IFRS 9/IAS 39, Section 3.2). In IFRS 9, the category "available for sale" no longer exists.*

held for trading in other comprehensive income (IFRS 9.5.7.1b and 9.5.7.5). Amounts presented in other comprehensive income must not be subsequently transferred to profit or loss, i.e. not even when the equity instrument is derecognized. However, the entity may transfer the cumulative gain or loss within equity, e.g. to retained earnings (IFRS 9.B5.7.1 and 9.BC5.25b).

- It may be necessary to present the **fair value change** of a financial liability which is **attributable to changes in the liability's credit risk** in other comprehensive income. Amounts presented in other comprehensive income must not be subsequently transferred to profit or loss. However, the cumulative gain or loss may be transferred within equity (e.g. to retained earnings) (IFRS 9.B5.7.9).

6.2.2 Preparation of the Statement(s) The items of income and expense are presented in one of the following ways (IAS 1.10A, 1.81A, and 1.82A):

(a) Presentation in a **single statement of comprehensive income** which includes all components of profit or loss and of other comprehensive income.
(b) Presentation in **two statements**:
  (i) **Separate income statement**: This statement displays the components of profit or loss.
  (ii) **Statement of comprehensive income**: This statement begins with profit or loss, displays the items of other comprehensive income (including the share of the OCI of associates and joint ventures accounted for using the equity method), and is presented immediately after the separate income statement.

The items of **other comprehensive income** presented are classified by nature and grouped into those that (in accordance with other IFRSs) (IAS 1.82A and 1.IN18):

- **will not be reclassified**[9] subsequently to profit or loss, and
- are **potentially reclassifiable** to profit or loss subsequently (i.e. will be reclassified when specific conditions are met).

Operating expenses which are recognized in **profit or loss** are presented in one of the following ways (IAS 1.99, 1.102, and 1.103):

- **Nature of expense method**: This is a classification based on the nature of the expenses (e.g. employee benefits expense, depreciation, and amortization expense, etc.).
- **Function of expense method** (also called **cost of sales method**): According to this method, expenses are classified based on their function within the entity as part of cost of sales or, for example, as part of distribution costs or administrative expenses.

It is necessary to choose the method (i.e. either the nature of expense method or the function of expense method) that provides information that is reliable and more relevant (IAS 1.99). A combination of both methods is not allowed, i.e. it is not possible to present operating expenses partly according to their nature and partly according to their function in the same statement.

[9] *See Section 6.2.1 with regard to reclassification adjustments.*

The statement shown below is an example of a **single statement of comprehensive income according to the function of expense method** in which non-controlling interests are ignored. This statement includes some disclosures which could also be presented in the notes (IAS 1.97–1.105) because in practice, they are usually made in the single statement of comprehensive income (or separate income statement).[10]

STATEMENT OF COMPREHENSIVE INCOME (for the year 01)	
PROFIT OR LOSS SECTION	
Revenue	XX
Cost of sales	XX
Gross profit	**XX**
Distribution costs	XX
Administrative expenses	XX
Other operating income	XX
Other operating expenses	XX
Results of operating activities	**XX**
Share of the profit or loss of associates	XX
Other finance income	XX
Other finance expenses	XX
Results of financing activities	**XX**
Profit before tax	**XX**
Income tax	XX
PROFIT FOR THE YEAR	**XX**
OCI SECTION	
Items that will not be reclassified to profit or loss (OCI I):	
Gains on property revaluation	XX
Share of the gain (loss) on property revaluation of associates	XX
Actuarial gains and losses on defined benefit plans	XX
Designated equity instruments[11]	XX
Changes in credit risk of certain liabilities[12]	XX
Income tax relating to items that will not be reclassified	XX
Items that may be reclassified subsequently to profit or loss (OCI II):	
Cash flow hedges	XX
Exchange differences on translating foreign operations according to the current rate method	XX
Income tax relating to items that may be reclassified	XX
OTHER COMPREHENSIVE INCOME (net of tax)	**XX**
TOTAL COMPREHENSIVE INCOME	**XX**

[10] *Due to the consequential amendment of IAS 1 by IFRS 9, the single statement of comprehensive income or the separate income statement also has to include the following separate line items if they are material: (a) gains and losses arising from the derecognition of financial assets measured at amortized cost and (b) the gain or loss arising on the reclassification of a financial asset measured at amortized cost into the fair value category (IAS 1.82(aa) and (ca) and IAS 8.8).*

[11] *When an entity still applies the "old" version of IAS 39 (i.e. the version of IAS 39 before the consequential amendments resulting from IFRS 9), this line item would be titled "available-for-sale financial assets" and included in OCI II (see the chapter on IFRS 9/IAS 39, Section 3.2).*

[12] *When an entity still applies the "old" version of IAS 39 (i.e. the version of IAS 39 before the consequential amendments resulting from IFRS 9), there is no such line item in the statement.*

If the entity had presented the **single statement of comprehensive income according to the nature of expense method**, only the first part of that statement would have been different (to the results of operating activities), whereas the rest would have stayed the same:

Revenue
Changes in inventories of finished goods and work in progress
Work performed by the entity and capitalized
Other operating income
Raw materials and consumables used
Employee benefits expense
Depreciation and amortization expense
Other operating expenses
Results of operating activities

The items shown below have to be disclosed in the single statement of comprehensive income (IAS 1.81B). In such a statement, they are presented below total comprehensive income.

(a) Profit or loss attributable to owners of the parent.
(b) Profit or loss attributable to non-controlling interests.
(c) Total comprehensive income attributable to owners of the parent.
(d) Total comprehensive income attributable to non-controlling interests.

If a separate income statement is presented, items (a) and (b) are presented in that statement whereas items (c) and (d) are presented in the statement of comprehensive income (IAS 1.81B).

Additional line items, headings, and subtotals are presented in the statement of comprehensive income and the separate income statement (if presented) when such presentation is relevant to an understanding of the entity's financial performance (IAS 1.85).

IAS 1 does not require presentation of the subtotal **"results of operating activities."** However, this subtotal is often presented in practice. If presented, the amount disclosed has to be representative of activities that would normally be regarded as operating. For example, it would not be appropriate to exclude items clearly related to operations (such as inventory write-downs and restructuring expenses) because they occur irregularly or infrequently or are unusual in amount. Similarly, it would not be appropriate to exclude items because they do not involve cash flows, such as depreciation and amortization expenses (IAS 1.BC56).

In the single statement of comprehensive income or in the separate income statement, **finance income** and **finance expenses** are presented separately. They are only offset to the extent that they represent (a) profit or loss or (b) other comprehensive income of investments accounted for using the equity method (IAS 1.82 and 1.82A). Items of income or expense must not be presented as **extraordinary** items. This applies to the statement of comprehensive income, the separate income statement (if presented), and the notes (IAS 1.87).

If the **"function of expense method"** is applied, additional information on the nature of expenses (including depreciation and amortization expense and employee benefits expense) is disclosed (IAS 1.104).

In the example of a statement of comprehensive income presented above, the **items of other comprehensive income** are presented **before tax** and two amounts are shown for the tax relating to those items: (a) income tax relating to items that will not be reclassified and (b) income tax relating to items that may be reclassified. This procedure ensures that the items of profit or loss and other comprehensive income are presented in the same way, i.e. before tax. However, it would also be possible to present each item of other comprehensive income net of tax in the statement of comprehensive income (IAS 1.91 and 1.IG).

The disclosures described below can be made either in the notes or in the statement of comprehensive income. We prefer disclosure in the notes in order to avoid overloading the statement of comprehensive income.

- The amount of income tax relating to each item of other comprehensive income (including reclassification adjustments[13]) (IAS 1.90).
- Reclassification adjustments[14] relating to components of other comprehensive income (IAS 1.92 and 1.94).

6.3 Statement of Changes in Equity

The following statement is an example of a statement of changes in equity for the reporting period and the comparative period.

	Issued capital	*Capital reserve*	*Retained earnings*	*Accumulated OCI I*	*Accumulated OCI II*	*Subtotal: Equity attributable to owners of the parent*	*Non-controlling interests*	*Total equity*
Balance as at Jan 01, 01								
Changes in accounting policies								
Correction of prior period errors								
Adjusted balance as at Jan 01, 01								
Capital increase								
Dividends								
Total comprehensive income								
Transfers								
Balance as at Dec 31, 01								
Dividends								
Total comprehensive income								
Transfers								
Balance as at Dec 31, 02								

[13] *See Section 6.2.1.*

[14] *See Section 6.2.1.*

Explanations relating to the statement of changes in equity presented previously:

- **Retained earnings** represent in particular (a) the accumulated amounts of profit or loss attributable to owners of the parent less distributions to owners of the parent and (b) amounts transferred to retained earnings from accumulated OCI without affecting OCI or profit or loss.[15] For example, an entity may transfer the revaluation surplus relating to a piece of land (i.e. accumulated OCI relating to revaluations of that land) to retained earnings when that land is sold ("Dr Revaluation Surplus Cr Retained earnings").[16] In the above statement, such direct transfers within equity which neither affect OCI nor profit or loss are shown in the **line "Transfers"**.
- The column "**Accumulated OCI I**" represents items that will not be reclassified subsequently to profit or loss.[17] An example for OCI I is the other comprehensive income resulting from the revaluation of land (see the explanations previously).
- The column "**Accumulated OCI II**" represents items that may be reclassified subsequently to profit or loss.[18] For example, in the case of a foreign operation that has been translated according to the current rate method, reclassification of exchange differences previously recognized in OCI ("Dr Profit or loss Cr OCI" or "Dr OCI Cr Profit or loss") takes place when the foreign operation is sold (IAS 21.48).[19]

If the statement of changes in equity is presented as in the example above, additional disclosures have to be made in the **notes** (IAS 1.106A, 1.107, and 1.BC74A–BC75).

If an entity decides to present **actuarial gains and losses** arising on defined benefit plans in other comprehensive income (IAS 19.93A–19.93D), the presentation of the statement of changes in equity has to be modified. This is dealt with in the chapter on IAS 19/IAS 26 (Section 2.3.3.4 and Example 4).

7 EXAMPLES WITH SOLUTIONS[20]

References to Other Chapters

With regard to the effects of changes in accounting policies and corrections of prior period errors to the statement of financial position, the separate income statement and the statement of changes in equity, we refer to the chapter on IAS 8 (Examples 3–6). Example 4 of the chapter on IAS 19/IAS 26 illustrates the presentation of the statement of comprehensive income and of the statement of changes in equity if actuarial gains and losses are recognized in other comprehensive income.

---

[15] *See Section 6.2.1.*

[16] *See the chapter on IAS 16, Section 4.1.*

[17] *See Section 6.2.*

[18] *See Section 6.2.*

[19] *See the chapter on IAS 21, Section 4.2.*

[20] *Tax effects are ignored in these examples.*

7.1 Examples that can be Solved Without the Knowledge of Other Chapters of the Book

Example 1

Nature of expense method vs. function of expense method

Entity E operates in retail sales, i.e. E purchases merchandise from wholesalers and resells to customers. The following table presents the expenses from the year 01 according to their nature and function:

	Cost of sales	*Administrative expenses*	*Distribution costs*	*Total*
Raw materials and consumables used	18	1	1	**20**
Employee benefits expense	5	2	2	**9**
Depreciation and amortization	3	1	1	**5**
Other operating expenses	2	1	6	**9**
Total	**28**	**5**	**10**	**43**

Revenue for the year 01 is CU 50.

Required

E prepares its first financial statements according to IFRS as at Dec 31, 01. E decides to prepare a separate income statement (two statement approach). E's chief financial officer would prefer to present the items of the results of operating activities as shown below if possible. In this statement, cost of sales, administrative expenses, and distribution costs would be presented excluding an allocation of depreciation and amortization. Depreciation and amortization expense would therefore be shown as a separate line item:

Revenue	**50**
Cost of sales	–25
Gross profit	**25**
Administrative expenses	–4
Distribution costs	–9
Depreciation and amortization expense	–5
Results of operating activities	**7**

Assess whether this presentation of the results of operating activities in E's separate income statement is possible. If not, prepare new versions for E's separate income statement which correspond with IFRS.

For simplification purposes, comparative figures are ignored in this example. It is not intended to shift information to the notes.

Hints for solution

In particular Section 6.2.2.

Solution

The separate income statement above is a mixture between a presentation of expenses according to their function and their nature. Such a mixed presentation is not possible according to IFRS. The chief financial officer can choose between the following two presentations, provided that both of them are reliable and equal in terms of relevance (IAS 1.99).

Function of expense method:

Revenue	**50**
Cost of sales	–28
Gross profit	**22**
Administrative expenses	–5
Distribution costs	–10
Results of operating activities	**7**

Nature of expense method:

Revenue	**50**
Raw materials and consumables used	–20
Employee benefits expense	–9
Depreciation and amortization expense	–5
Other operating expenses	–9
Results of operating activities	**7**

The solution of this example (presentation of the items of the results of operating activities) would have been the same if E had decided to present a single statement of comprehensive income.

Example 2

Current vs. non-current liabilities

On Dec 31, 01, the remaining time to maturity of a loan taken up by entity E is 18 months. E's normal operating cycle is 12 months.

Required

Assess for each of the following versions, whether the liability has to be classified as current or as non-current in E's statement of financial position as at Dec 31, 01:

(a) No further events took place with regard to the liability.
(b) On Dec 31, 01, E breaches a covenant under which E is required to maintain a certain equity ratio. This breach entitles the lender to demand immediate repayment of the entire loan. Irrespective of the breach, the lender declares on Jan 03, 02 its willingness not to exercise the right of immediate repayment and not to change the terms of the loan. However, the right of the lender to demand immediate payment does not expire due to the declaration.
(c) The situation is the same as in (b). However, the lender declares its willingness not to exercise the right of immediate repayment and not to change the terms of the loan on Dec 31, 01, i.e. before the end of the reporting period.

(d) The situation is the same as in (b). However, on Jan 05, 02, the lender signs an agreement in which it waives its right to demand immediate repayment of the entire loan.
(e) The situation is the same as in (d). However, the agreement described in (d) is signed on Dec 31, 01.

Hints for solution

In particular Section 6.1.

Solution

Version (a)

The liability, which is payable after Dec 31, 02, is presented as a non-current liability.

Version (b)

E does not have the unconditional right to defer settlement of the liability for at least 12 months after Dec 31, 01. Thus, the liability is presented as a current liability (IAS 1.74).

Version (c)

In this version, the lender declares its willingness not to exercise the right of immediate repayment and not to change the terms of the loan before the end of the reporting period. However, the right of the lender to demand immediate payment does not expire due to the declaration. This means that E does not have an unconditional right to defer settlement of the liability for at least 12 months after the balance sheet date. Hence, the liability is presented as current (IAS 1.74).

Version (d)

On Dec 31, 01, E does not have the unconditional right to defer settlement of the liability for at least 12 months after Dec 31, 01. The lender signed the agreement in which it waives its right to demand immediate repayment of the entire loan after Dec 31, 01. Thus, the liability is presented as a current liability (IAS 1.74).

Version (e)

The agreement in which the lender waives its right to demand immediate repayment of the loan is signed before the end of E's reporting period. This means that E has an unconditional right to defer settlement of the liability for at least 12 months after the balance sheet date. Hence, the liability is presented as non-current (IAS 1.74).

Example 3

Overriding principle – continuation of Example 2(d)

The situation is the same as in Example 2(d). However, E believes that the application of IAS 1.74 and the resulting classification of the liability as current would not lead to a fair presentation of its financial statements and would be so misleading that it would conflict with the objective of financial statements set out in the Conceptual Framework. Therefore, E wants to apply the overriding principle and classify the liability as non-current.

Required

Assess whether the procedure suggested by E is possible in E's statement of financial position as at Dec 31, 01.

Hints for solution

In particular Section 3.

Solution

The procedure suggested by E is not possible. Thus, the liability has to be presented as current in accordance with IAS 1.74. This is because the overriding principle can hardly ever be applied in financial statements according to IFRS.

When assessing whether the overriding principle can be applied, E has to consider, among others, how its circumstances differ from those of other entities that comply with IAS 1.74. If other entities in similar circumstances comply with IAS 1.74, there is a rebuttable presumption that E's compliance with the requirement would not be so misleading that it would conflict with the objective of financial statements set out in the Conceptual Framework (IAS 1.24b). Consequently, the prevailing view is that it is hardly ever possible to apply the overriding principle according to IFRS.

Example 4

Going concern

(a) On Dec 31, 01, it is intended to liquidate entity in A in 18 months. Nevertheless, A intends to prepare its financial statements on a going concern basis because IAS 1.26 mentions a period of 12 months from the end of the reporting period as a reference point.
(b) With regard to entity B's financial statements as at Dec 31, 01, there is significant doubt about B's ability to continue as a going concern. Nevertheless, B intends to prepare its financial statements on a going concern basis.

Required

Assess whether it is appropriate to prepare A's and B's financial statements as at Dec 31, 01 on a going concern basis.

Hints for solution

In particular Section 2.

Solution (a)

A is not allowed to prepare its financial statements as at Dec 31, 01 on a going concern basis. This is because the 12 month period (mentioned in IAS 1.26) for considering an entity's future is a minimum requirement and A intends to cease operations 18 months from the end of its reporting period.[21]

Solution (b)

B prepares its financial statements as at Dec 31, 01 on a going concern basis. This is because the existence of significant doubts about B's ability to continue as a going concern is not a sufficient reason to depart from preparing B's financial statements on a going concern basis. Financial statements are prepared on a going concern basis unless management either intends to liquidate the entity or to cease trading, or has no realistic alternative but to do so (IAS 1.25).[22]

Example 5

Presentation of a deferred tax liability in the statement of financial position

On Dec 31, 01, entity E recognizes a provision relating to a lawsuit. The carrying amount of the provision is CU 26 according to IFRS and CU 34 for tax purposes.

According to IAS 12, E also recognizes a deferred tax liability in the amount of CU 2 relating to the provision (= CU 8 · E's tax rate of 25%).[23]

E's lawyers think it is highly probable that the lawsuit will be settled until May 02 and that the decision of the court will be accepted by the parties to the dispute.

Required

Assess whether the deferred tax liability has to be presented as a current liability or as a non-current liability in E's statement of financial position as at Dec 31, 01.

Hints for solution

In particular Section 6.1.

Solution

Since it is highly probable that the dispute will be settled until May 02, the temporary difference of CU 8 will reverse within the year 02. However, IAS 1.56 prohibits classification of deferred tax assets and deferred tax liabilities as current. Hence, the deferred liability of CU 2 is presented as a non-current liability in E's statement of financial position.

7.2 Examples that Require Knowledge of Other Sections of the Book

Before trying to solve the following examples, it is recommended to work through the chapters on IAS 16, IAS 19, IAS 21, and IFRS 9/IAS 39 first.

[21] *See PwC,* Manual of Accounting, IFRS 2011, *4.25.*

[22] *See PwC,* Manual of Accounting, IFRS 2011, *4.25.*

[23] *See the chapter on IAS 12 with regard to deferred tax.*

Example 6A

Statement of comprehensive income and statement of changes in equity – equity instruments measured at fair value through other comprehensive income according to IFRS 9[24]

On Jan 01, 01, entity E acquires shares for CU 10 and elects irrevocably to present changes in their fair value in other comprehensive income (IFRS 9.5.7.1b and 9.5.7.5). On Dec 31, 01, fair value of these shares is CU 18. On May 01, 02, E sells the shares for CU 18. On derecognition, E transfers the amount recognized in other comprehensive income and accumulated in the fair value reserve to retained earnings (IFRS 9.B5.7.1).

Required

(a) Prepare any necessary **entries** in E's financial statements as at Dec 31 for the years 01 and 02.
(b) Illustrate the effects of the entries on E's **single statements of comprehensive income** for the years 01 and 02.
(c) Illustrate the effects of the entries on E's **statement of changes in equity** as at Dec 31, 02.

In 01 and 02, the carrying amount of E's issued capital is CU 100 and the carrying amount of E's capital reserve is CU 20.

Hints for solution

In particular Sections 6.2 and 6.3.

Solution

Jan 01, 01	Dr	Shares	10	
	Cr	Cash		10
Dec 31, 01	Dr	Shares	8	
	Cr	OCI I		8

The amount of OCI I of CU 8 is accumulated in the fair value reserve.

May 01, 02	Dr	Cash	18	
	Cr	Shares		18

At the date of derecognition, the gains of CU 8 recognized in other comprehensive income in 01 must not be reclassified to profit or loss. E decides to transfer that amount to retained earnings instead (IFRS 9.B5.7.1). This entry does not affect profit or loss, or other comprehensive income.

[24] *See the chapter on IFRS 9/IAS 39, Section 2.3.7 with regard to equity instruments accounted for at fair value through other comprehensive income.*

May 01, 02	Dr	Fair value reserve (accumulated OCI I)	8	
	Cr	Retained earnings		8

These entries have the following effects on the **statement of comprehensive income**:

	02	*01*
PROFIT OR LOSS SECTION		
Other finance income	0	0
Results of financing activities	**0**	**0**
PROFIT FOR THE YEAR	**0**	**0**
OCI SECTION		
Items that will not be reclassified to profit or loss (OCI I):		
Designated equity instruments	0	8
Subtotal	**0**	**8**
OTHER COMPREHENSIVE INCOME	**0**	**8**
TOTAL COMPREHENSIVE INCOME	**0**	**8**

The entries have the following effects on the **statement of changes in equity**:

	Issued capital	*Capital reserve*	*Retained earnings*	*Accumulated OCI I*	*Total equity*
Balance as at Jan 01, 01	**100**	**20**	**0**	**0**	**120**
Total comprehensive income	–	–	0	8	8
Balance as at Dec 31, 01	**100**	**20**	**0**	**8**	**128**
Total comprehensive income	–	–	0	0	0
Transfer to retained earnings	–	–	8	–8	0
Balance as at Dec 31, 02	**100**	**20**	**8**	**0**	**128**

Example 6B

Statement of comprehensive income and statement of changes in equity – shares classified as "available for sale" according to the "old" version of IAS 39[25]

On Jan 01, 01, entity E acquires shares for CU 10 and classifies them as "available for sale" (IAS 39.9). On Dec 31, 01, fair value of these shares is CU 18. On May 01, 02, E sells the shares for CU 18.

Required

Complete the same exercises as in Example 6A.

Hints for solution

In particular Sections 6.2 and 6.3.

[25] *The "old" version of IAS 39 is the version before IFRS 9 and its consequential amendments. See the chapter on IFRS 9/IAS 39, Section 3.2 with regard to equity instruments classified as "available for sale."*

Solution

Jan 01, 01	Dr	Shares	10	
	Cr	Cash		10
Dec 31, 01	Dr	Shares	8	
	Cr	OCI II		8

The amount of OCI II of CU 8 is accumulated in the fair value reserve.

May 01, 02	Dr	Cash	18	
	Cr	Shares		18

At the date of derecognition, the gain of CU 8 recognized in other comprehensive income in 01 is reclassified to profit or loss:

May 01, 02	Dr	OCI II	8	
	Cr	Finance income		8

These entries have the following effects on the **statement of comprehensive income**:

	02	*01*
PROFIT OR LOSS SECTION		
Other finance income	8	0
Results of financing activities	**8**	**0**
PROFIT FOR THE YEAR	**8**	**0**
OCI SECTION		
Items that may be reclassified subsequently to profit or loss (OCI II):		
Available-for-sale financial assets	−8	8
Subtotal	**−8**	**8**
OTHER COMPREHENSIVE INCOME	**−8**	**8**
TOTAL COMPREHENSIVE INCOME	**0**	**8**

The entry "Dr OCI II Cr Finance income CU 8" in 02 represents a reclassification adjustment within the meaning of IAS 1.7 (IAS 1.93 and 1.95) because other comprehensive income is reclassified to profit or loss. If other comprehensive income of CU 8 had been presented in 01 and finance income of CU 8 (in profit or loss) in 02, total comprehensive income for both years would have been CU 16. This would not be appropriate because the shares were acquired for CU 10 and sold for CU 18, which means that there has been income of CU 8. Thus, the following procedure is prescribed:

- 01: Other comprehensive income of CU 8 is recognized.
- 02: Finance income (profit or loss) of CU 8 and other comprehensive income of CU −8 are recognized. This results in total comprehensive income for 02 of zero.
- Hence, total comprehensive income for 01 and 02 is CU 8, which corresponds with the actual situation.

The entries have the following effects on the **statement of changes in equity**:

	Issued capital	*Capital reserve*	*Retained earnings*	*Accumulated OCI II*	*Total equity*
Balance as at Jan 01, 01	**100**	**20**	**0**	**0**	**120**
Total comprehensive income	–	–	0	8	8
Balance as at Dec 31, 01	**100**	**20**	**0**	**8**	**128**
Total comprehensive income	–	–	8	–8	0
Balance as at Dec 31, 02	**100**	**20**	**8**	**0**	**128**

In 02, an amount of CU 8 is presented at the crossing of the column "Retained earnings" and the line "Total comprehensive income". This corresponds with profit or loss of CU 8 presented in the statement of comprehensive income for the year 02.

Example 7

Statement of comprehensive income and statement of changes in equity – revaluation of property, plant, and equipment[26]

On Jan 01, 01, entity E acquires land for CU 10 which is held as property, plant, and equipment. On Dec 31, 01, the fair value of the land is CU 14. E sells the land on Aug 10, 02 for CU 14.

Required

Complete the same exercises as in Example 6A. Land is accounted for by E according to the revaluation model of IAS 16. E transfers revaluation surplus to retained earnings when the corresponding item of property, plant, and equipment is derecognized (IAS 16.41).

Hints for solution

In particular Sections 6.2 and 6.3.

Solution

Jan 01, 01	Dr	Land	10	
	Cr	Cash		10
Dec 31, 01	Dr	Land	4	
	Cr	OCI I		4

The amount of OCI I of CU 4 is accumulated in revaluation surplus.

Aug 10, 02	Dr	Cash	14	
	Cr	Land		14

[26] *See the chapter on IAS 16, Section 4.1 with regard to the accounting treatment of revalued land.*

Upon derecognition of the land (i.e. on Aug 10, 02), E transfers the revaluation surplus directly to retained earnings (IAS 16.41). This is not a reclassification adjustment because revaluation surplus is not transferred to profit or loss (IAS 1.7 and 1.96).

Aug 10, 02	Dr	Revaluation surplus (accumulated OCI I)	4	
	Cr	Retained earnings		4

These entries have the following effects on the **statement of comprehensive income**:

	02	*01*
PROFIT OR LOSS SECTION		
PROFIT FOR THE YEAR	**0**	**0**
OCI SECTION		
Items that will not be reclassified to profit or loss (OCI I):		
Changes in revaluation surplus	0	4
Subtotal	**0**	**4**
OTHER COMPREHENSIVE INCOME	**0**	**4**
TOTAL COMPREHENSIVE INCOME	**0**	**4**

The entry "Dr Revaluation surplus (accumulated OCI I) Cr Retained earnings CU 4" in 02 does not represent a reclassification adjustment within the meaning of IAS 1.7 (IAS 1.96). Consequently, in 02, the line "Changes in revaluation surplus" does not include an amount of CU –4 (IAS 1.IG).

The entries have the following effects on the **statement of changes in equity**:

	Issued capital	*Capital reserve*	*Retained earnings*	*Accumulated OCI I*	*Total equity*
Balance as at Jan 01, 01	**100**	**20**	**0**	**0**	**120**
Total comprehensive income	–	–	0	4	4
Balance as at Dec 31, 01	**100**	**20**	**0**	**4**	**124**
Total comprehensive income	–	–	0	0	0
Transfer to retained earnings	–	–	4	–4	0
Balance as at Dec 31, 02	**100**	**20**	**4**	**0**	**124**

Example 8

Statement of comprehensive income and statement of changes in equity – exchange differences[27]

On Jan 01, 02, entity E sells a foreign operation to which the current rate method has been applied in its entirety. Until that sale, the foreign operation has been a wholly-owned subsidiary of E. The cumulative amount of exchange differences relating to that foreign operation recognized in other comprehensive income is CU +5 as at Dec 31, 01, and CU +3 as at Dec 31, 00.

[27] *See the chapter on IAS 21, Sections 4.1 and 4.2.*

Required

Complete the same exercises as in Example 6A.

Hints for solution

In particular Sections 6.2 and 6.3.

Solution

In 01, an amount of CU +2 was recognized in other comprehensive income (credit entry). Reclassification adjustments may occur relating to exchange differences when translating foreign operations according to the current rate method, similar to available-for-sale financial assets according to the "old" version of IAS 39 (see Example 6B) (IAS 1.7 and 1.95). Consequently, the accounting treatment in the case of reclassifications is conceptionally the same. In the case of the disposal of a foreign operation that has been translated according to the current rate method, reclassification takes place when the gain or loss on disposal is recognized (IAS 21.48).

Jan 01, 02	Dr	OCI II	5	
	Cr	Profit or loss		5

Effects on the **statement of comprehensive income**:

	02	*01*
PROFIT OR LOSS SECTION		
Income	5	0
Results of operating activities	**5**	**0**
PROFIT FOR THE YEAR	**5**	**0**
OCI SECTION		
Items that may be reclassified subsequently to profit or loss (OCI II):		
Exchange differences	−5	2
Subtotal	**−5**	**2**
OTHER COMPREHENSIVE INCOME	**−5**	**2**
TOTAL COMPREHENSIVE INCOME	**0**	**2**

Effects on the **statement of changes in equity**:

	Issued capital	*Capital reserve*	*Retained earnings*	*Accumulated OCI II*	*Total equity*
Balance as at Jan 01, 01	**100**	**20**	**0**	**3**	**123**
Total comprehensive income	–	–	0	2	2
Balance as at Dec 31, 01	**100**	**20**	**0**	**5**	**125**
Total comprehensive income	–	–	5	−5	0
Balance as at Dec 31, 02	**100**	**20**	**5**	**0**	**125**

In 02, an amount of CU 5 is presented at the crossing of the column "Retained earnings" and the line "Total comprehensive income". This corresponds with the profit for the year 02 presented in the statement of comprehensive income.

IAS 2 INVENTORIES

1 SCOPE

IAS 2 prescribes the accounting treatment for inventories. **Inventories** comprise the following assets (IAS 2.6):

- Assets held for sale in the ordinary course of business (i.e. **finished goods and merchandise**).
- Assets in the process of production for such sale (**work in progress**).
- Assets to be consumed in the production process or in the rendering of services (**materials and supplies**).

As soon as revenue is recognized for **service contracts** (IAS 18.20–18.28), it is included in the scope of IAS 18 (IAS 2.8) and is generally accounted for according to the **stage of completion**. This applies similarly to **construction contracts** within the meaning of IAS 11.

Among others, **financial instruments** are not included in the scope of IAS 2 (IAS 2.2).

2 MEASUREMENT

2.1 Measurement at Recognition

At recognition, inventories are measured at **cost** (IAS 2.9 and 2.1), which comprises all costs of purchase, costs of conversion, and other costs incurred in bringing the inventories to their present location and condition (IAS 2.10).

The **costs of purchase** include the purchase price, import duties and other taxes that are not recoverable, and transport, handling, and other costs directly attributable to the purchase. Trade discounts, rebates, and other similar items are deducted in determining the costs of purchase (IAS 2.11).

When an arrangement contains a **financing element** (e.g. a difference between the purchase price for normal credit terms and the amount paid), the element is not part of the costs of purchase. It is instead recognized as **interest expense** over the period of the financing (IAS 2.18).

The **costs of conversion** comprise costs **directly related** to the units of production (i.e. direct labor and direct materials). They also include a systematic allocation of **fixed production overheads** (e.g. depreciation and the cost of factory management) and **variable production overheads** (e.g. indirect materials and indirect labor) (IAS 2.12). **Other costs** are included in the costs of conversion to the extent that they are incurred in bringing the inventories to their present location and condition. For example, it may be appropriate to include non-production overheads or the costs of designing products for specific customers in determining the cost of inventories (IAS 2.15). In limited cases, which are identified in IAS 23, the costs of conversion also include **borrowing costs** (IAS 2.17).

The amount of fixed overheads allocated to each unit of production is not increased as a result of the **actual level of production** (i.e. the quantity produced or the time of production during a period) in a period being **significantly lower than normal capacity**. Otherwise, the carrying amount of a unit of production would increase while the actual level of production decreases. By contrast, if the actual level of production **significantly exceeds normal capacity**, fixed overheads allocated to each unit of production are decreased so that inventories are not measured above cost. **Variable overheads** are allocated to each unit of production on the basis of the actual use of the production facilities (IAS 2.13).

The following are examples of costs not included in the costs of purchase or conversion (IAS 2.16):

- Abnormal amounts of wasted materials or labor.
- Storage costs (unless they are necessary in the production process before a further production stage).
- Administrative overheads that do not contribute to bringing the inventories to their present location and condition.
- Selling costs.

Techniques to measure the cost of inventories, such as the standard cost method or the retail method, may be used if the results approximate cost. **Standard costs** are determined on the basis of normal levels of materials and supplies, labor, efficiency, and capacity utilization (IAS 2.21). According to the **retail method**, the cost of the inventory is calculated by deducting the appropriate percentage gross margin from the sales value of the inventory (IAS 2.22).

The cost of inventories that are not ordinarily interchangeable and goods or services produced and segregated for specific projects have to be assigned by using **specific identification** of their individual costs. This means that each item is measured on the basis of its individual costs of purchase or conversion. By contrast, the costs of purchase or conversion of other inventories have to be assigned by using the **FIFO** (first in, first out) or **weighted average cost formula**. In the latter case, the average may by calculated on a periodic basis or as each additional shipment is received, depending upon the circumstances of the entity (IAS 2.23–2.27).

2.2 Measurement after Recognition

After recognition (i.e. at the first balance sheet date after the purchase or conversion and also at following balance sheet dates), inventories are measured at the **lower amount of (a) costs of purchase or conversion and (b) net realizable value** (IAS 2.9 and 2.1). This principle may lead to a write-down or to a reversal of a write-down.

Net realizable value is the estimated selling price in the ordinary course of business less the estimated costs necessary to make the sale, less the estimated costs of completion (IAS 2.6). The **estimated costs of completion** are relevant in the case of work in progress. They represent the costs of conversion not incurred until the end of the reporting period. They comprise the same items of cost that are included in measuring the costs of conversion and therefore also include **fixed costs**.

Inventories are usually written down **item by item**. However, in some circumstances it may be appropriate **to group similar or related items**. There is a certain degree of discretion in determining the group. It may be appropriate to group similar or related items of inventory if they relate to the same product line, have similar purposes or end uses, are produced and marketed in the same geographical area, and cannot be practicably evaluated separately from other items in that product line. However, it is not possible, for example, to regard all finished goods or all inventories of a particular operating segment as a group. In the case of services, each service is generally treated as a separate item (IAS 2.29).

Materials and supplies are not written down below cost if the finished goods in which they will be incorporated are expected to be sold at or above cost. However, when a decrease in the price of materials indicates that the cost of the finished goods exceeds net realizable value, the materials are written down. In such cases the replacement cost of the raw materials will often be the best available measure of their net realizable value (IAS 2.32).

3 PRESENTATION AND DERECOGNITION

Inventories may be presented only as a single amount in the statement of financial position (IAS 1.54g). If so, it is usually necessary to explain the composition of the inventories (finished goods, merchandise, materials and supplies, and work in progress) in the notes (IAS 2.36b).

The presentation of changes in the carrying amount of inventories in profit or loss depends on the form in which the analysis of expenses is presented:

- If the reporting entity presents its expenses according to the **function of expense method (= cost of sales method)** (IAS 1.99, 1.102, and IAS 1.IG), the following applies: The carrying amount of inventories that are sold is recognized as cost of sales in the period in which the related revenue is recognized. A write-down increases cost of sales, whereas a reversal of a write-down leads to a reduction in cost of sales (IAS 2.34).[1]
- If the reporting entity presents its expenses according to the **nature of expense method**, the following applies: The cost of the merchandise sold is recognized in the line item "cost of merchandise sold." The difference between the carrying amount of finished goods and work in progress at the end of the reporting period and the corresponding amount at the end of the previous period is presented in the line item "changes in inventories of finished goods and work in progress." A write-down and a reversal of a write-down are included in the appropriate line item mentioned above (IAS 2.34 and IAS 1.IG).

4 EXAMPLES WITH SOLUTIONS

Example 1

Costs of conversion of finished goods

In 01, entity E started the production of product P. The production of P required direct materials of CU 100 and 10,000 hours in the cost unit "manufacturing" in 01. The following additional information is given (in CU):

[1] *See KPMG,* Insights into IFRS, *6th edition, 3.8.440.70.*

	Material cost center	*Production cost center*
Direct materials	1,000	
Direct labor		1,250
Various overheads	600	2,500

60% of the costs presented as "various overheads" in the table above represent fixed costs and 40% of them represent variable costs. Normal capacity of the production cost center is 100,000 hours p.a.

Posting status:

The costs mentioned above have been recognized as "cost of sales."

Required

Prepare any necessary entries in E's financial statements as at Dec 31, 01. Assume that the actual level of production in the production cost center in 01 is (a) 125,000 hours and (b) 75,000 hours.

Hints for solution

In particular Section 2.1.

Solution (a)

Regarding the **material cost center**, the "various overheads" of CU 600 are expressed as a percentage of direct materials. This percentage is needed later when calculating the costs of conversion (where the percentage is applied to the direct materials of CU 100 for P).

Various overheads	600
Direct materials	1,000
Percentage	**60%**

However, for the **production cost center**, an hourly rate is calculated. This is necessary because it is known that the production of P caused 10,000 hours in the production cost center and when calculating the costs of conversion of P these 10,000 hours will be multiplied by the hourly rate. The hourly rate must also include direct labor.

Moreover, the actual level of production in 01 significantly exceeds normal capacity. Consequently, fixed overheads allocated to each unit of production have to be decreased. This is achieved by dividing fixed costs (just as variable costs) by 125,000 hours (IAS 2.13):

Direct labor	1,250
Various overheads	2,500
Total	**3,750**
Hours	125,000
Hourly rate	**0.03**

At this point it is possible to calculate the costs of conversion of P:

Direct materials	100
+ 60% (in order to take the various overheads in the material cost center into account)	60
+ Production costs *(10,000 hours · CU 0.03)*	300
= Costs of conversion	**460**

Dec 31, 01	Dr	Finished goods	460	
	Cr	Cost of sales		460

Solution (b)

Regarding the **material cost center**, the calculation of the percentage is the same as in (a).

Generally the same considerations as in (a) apply to the calculation of the hourly rate for the **production cost center**. However, in contrast to (a), the actual level of production in 01 is significantly lower than normal capacity. Capacity utilization of the production cost center is 75% (75,000 hours: 100,000 hours). Therefore, only variable costs are included on the basis of the actual level of production (i.e. on the basis of the costs actually incurred). Direct labor represents variable costs. The amount of fixed costs allocated to each unit of production must not be increased as a result of the actual level of production being significantly lower than normal capacity (IAS 2.13).

Direct labor	1,250
Variable overheads *(40% of CU 2,500)*	1,000
Fixed overheads *(60% of CU 2,500) · 75%*	1,125
Total	**3,375**
Hours	75,000
Hourly rate	**0.045**

In the calculation above, fixed overheads included are CU 0.015 per hour [(60% · CU 2,500 · 75%) : 75,000 hours]. If the actual level of production were equal to normal capacity, fixed overheads included would also be CU 0.015 per hour (CU 1,500 : 100,000 hours). Consequently, fixed overheads allocated to each unit of production are not increased as a result of the low production, as IAS 2.13 requires.

At this point it is possible to calculate the costs of conversion of P:

Direct materials	100
+ 60% (in order to take the various overheads in the material cost center into account)	60
+ Production costs (10,000 hours · CU 0.045)	450
= Costs of conversion	**610**

Dec 31, 01	Dr	Finished goods	610	
	Cr	Cost of sales		610

Example 2

Costs of purchase – financing element

Entity E purchases merchandise on Nov 01, 01. Delivery takes place on the same day. In the case of (normal) deferred settlement terms of one month, the purchase price would be CU 200. However, E and its supplier stipulate that payment has to be made on Nov 30, 02, but at an amount of CU 212 (CU 200 plus interest of 6% for one year).

Required

Prepare any necessary entries in E's financial statements as at Dec 31, 01. Should it be necessary to recognize interest expense, assume that E recognizes interest expense on a straight-line basis due to materiality considerations.

Hints for solution

In particular Section 2.1.

Solution

Nov 01, 01	Dr	Merchandise	200	
	Cr	Trade payables		200

Interest for the period from Dec 01, 01 to Nov 30, 02 (length of the financing) must not be capitalized. It is instead recognized as interest expense. Interest amounts to CU 1 per month (CU 200 · 6% p.a. : 12 months). Consequently interest expense of CU 1 has to be recognized in 01 (i.e. for December 01) (IAS 2.18):

Dec 31, 01	Dr	Interest expense	1	
	Cr	Trade payables		1

Example 3

Measurement of merchandise

On Dec 31, 01, entity E owns 100 units of merchandise M. The purchase took place on Oct 15, 01. Settlement in cash and delivery took place on the same date. The costs of purchase were CU 1 per unit. On Dec 31, 01, the net realizable value amounts to CU 0.9 per unit.

On Jul 10, 02, 90 units of M were sold to a customer for CU 95. Settlement in cash and delivery took place on the same date.

On Dec 31, 02 there are still 10 units of M in the warehouse of E which could not be sold yet. At that date, net realizable value amounts to CU 1.1 per unit.

Required

Prepare any necessary entries in E's financial statements as at Dec 31, for the years 01 and 02.

Hints for solution

In particular Sections 2.2 and 3.

Solution

Nov 15, 01	Dr	Merchandise	100	
	Cr	Cash		100

On Dec 31, 01, the inventories have to be measured at the lower of cost (CU 100) and net realizable value (CU 90) (IAS 2.9). This results in a write-down of CU 10:

Dec 31, 01	Dr	Cost of sales	10	
	Cr	Merchandise		10
Jul 10, 02	Dr	Cash	95	
	Cr	Revenue		95

On Dec 31, 01, the inventories were written down to the net realizable value of CU 0.9 per unit, which means that CU 0.9 became the new carrying amount. Thus, the carrying amount of the 90 units sold is CU 81 (CU 0.9 · 90 units). The carrying amount of the inventories that are sold is recognized as an expense in the period in which the related revenue is recognized (IAS 2.34):

Jul 10, 02	Dr	Cost of sales	81	
	Cr	Merchandise		81

The following table illustrates the measurement of the 10 remaining units of M on Dec 31, 02:

	Per unit	*Units (Dec 31, 02)*	*Total*
Current carrying amount	0.9	10	**9**
Measurement on Dec 31, 02			
Cost (1)	1.0		
Net realizable value (2)	1.1		
Lower amount of (1) and (2) (IAS 2.9)	1.0	10	**10**
Reversal of the write-down			**1**

Dec 31, 02	Dr	Merchandise	1	
	Cr	Cost of sales		1

Example 4

Measurement of raw materials

In Nov 01, entity E decided to start producing product P in 02. Production of P requires raw material R, which is incorporated in P. Thus, E purchased 100 units of R in Nov 01. The costs of purchase were CU 12 per unit. Settlement in cash and delivery took place in Nov 01. E expects that the costs of conversion for one unit of P will be CU 20.

On Dec 31, 01, the costs of purchase of R have decreased to CU 7 per unit. These replacement costs are the best available measure of R's net realizable value. Due to the decrease in the price of R, E expects that it will be able to sell P for only CU 18.

Required

Prepare any necessary entries in E's financial statements as at Dec 31, 01.

Hints for solution

In particular Sections 2.2 and 3.

Solution

Nov 01	Dr	Raw materials	1,200	
	Cr	Cash		1,200

The raw materials have to be written down to their net realizable value (replacement costs) because a decline in the price of the materials indicates that the cost of the finished goods exceeds their net realizable value (IAS 2.32):

Dec 31, 01	Dr	Cost of sales	500	
	Cr	Raw materials		500

Example 5

Measurement of work in progress

On Dec 31, 01, there were 100 units of a work in progress in entity E's warehouse:

Estimated selling price	20
Costs of conversion incurred until Dec 31, 01	10
Variable costs of conversion that will be incurred after Dec 31, 01	4
Fixed costs of conversion that will be incurred after Dec 31, 01	5
Estimated selling costs that will be incurred after Dec 31, 01	2

Posting status:

Dec 31, 01	Dr	Work in progress	10	
	Cr	Cost of sales		10

Required

Prepare any necessary entries in E's financial statements as at Dec 31, 01.

Hints for solution

In particular Sections 2.2 and 3.

Solution

In determining net realizable value, the fixed costs of conversion that will be incurred after Dec 31, 01 are also considered:

Estimated selling price	20
Variable costs of conversion that will be incurred after Dec 31, 01	−4
Fixed costs of conversion that will be incurred after Dec 31, 01	−5
Estimated selling costs that will be incurred after Dec 31, 01	−2
Net realizable value	**9**
Carrying amount before recognition of the write-down	**10**
(= costs of conversion incurred until Dec 31, 01)	
Write-down	**−1**

Dec 31, 01	Dr	Cost of sales	1	
	Cr	Work in progress		1

IAS 7 STATEMENT OF CASH FLOWS

1 INTRODUCTION

A **statement of cash flows** is a mandatory part of the financial statements (IAS 1.10(d) and IAS 7.1). **Cash flows** are inflows and outflows of cash and cash equivalents. **Cash** comprises demand deposits and cash on hand. **Cash equivalents** are short-term, highly liquid investments which are readily convertible to known amounts of cash and which are subject to an insignificant risk of changes in value (IAS 7.6). Thus, an investment normally qualifies as a cash equivalent only when it has a short maturity of, say, three months or less, from the date of acquisition. Equity investments are normally excluded from cash and cash equivalents (IAS 7.7). Bank overdrafts that are repayable on demand are included as cash and cash equivalents to the extent that they form an integral part of the entity's cash management (IAS 7.8).[1]

The statement of cash flows aims to give insights to the users of financial statements about the actual **cash inflows and cash outflows** during a period. By contrast, **income and expenses** are sometimes of a non-cash nature.

In the statement of cash flows, the cash flows arising during the period are classified according to the **activities of the entity** (IAS 7.6, 7.10, and 7.13–7.17):

- **Operating activities**: These are the principal revenue-producing activities of the entity and other activities which are not investing or financing activities. Examples are cash outflows for the purchase and cash inflows from the sale of merchandise, wages of employees, etc.
- **Investing activities** are the acquisition and disposal of long-term assets and other investments not included in cash equivalents (e.g. cash payments to acquire property, plant, and equipment). Only expenditures that result in a recognized asset in the entity's statement of financial position are eligible for classification as investing activities (IAS 7.16).
- **Financing activities**: These activities result in changes in the size and composition of the contributed equity and borrowings of the entity. Examples are cash proceeds from issuing shares or loans, as well as cash repayments of amounts borrowed.

The following table illustrates basic relations:

Cash and cash equivalents as at Jan 01		**10**
Cash flows from operating activities	**5**	
Cash flows from investing activities	**−9**	
Cash flows from financing activities	**2**	
Cash flows		**−2**
Cash and cash equivalents as at Dec 31		**8**

[1] *See KPMG,* Insights into IFRS, *5th edition, 2.3.10.60.*

2 PREPARATION OF THE STATEMENT OF CASH FLOWS

2.1 Operating Activities

Cash flows from operating activities have to be reported using either (IAS 7.18):

- the **direct method**, whereby major classes of gross cash receipts and gross cash payments are disclosed; or
- the **indirect method**, whereby the entity's profit or loss is adjusted in order to derive the cash flows from operating activities.

Although the IASB encourages entities to use the direct method (IAS 7.19), the **indirect method** is normally used in practice. Therefore, this method is described more precisely, subsequently. It can be summarized as follows:

	Profit or loss
+	Non-cash expenses (e.g. depreciation and amortization)
–	Non-cash income (e.g. reversals of impairment losses)
+/–	Entries which affect cash but not profit or loss (e.g. "Dr Merchandise Cr Cash")
+/–	Reclassifications to the other activities presented
=	**Cash flows from operating activities**

Non-cash expenses (e.g. depreciation of a building) were deducted in determining profit for the year. When determining cash flows from operating activities, this deduction has to be reversed by adding these expenses. Another example of non-cash expenses is recognizing provisions because the entry "Dr Expense Cr Provision" affects profit or loss but does not affect cash. Instead, the payment is effected when the obligation is settled. These considerations apply to **non-cash income** (e.g. reversals of impairment losses) vice versa.

Afterwards, **entries that affect cash but not profit or loss** are taken into account. For example, the entry "Dr Merchandise Cr Cash" does not affect profit or loss. However, the purchase of merchandise has to be taken into account in the statement of cash flows since it results in a reduction of cash.

Finally, income and expenses arising from transactions that affect profit or loss but do not constitute operating activities have to be **reclassified**. For example, the sale of an item of property, plant, or equipment may give rise to a gain that is included in profit or loss. Such a gain has to be eliminated when calculating the cash flows from operating activities because the cash inflows arising from the sale of an item of property, plant, or equipment represent investing activities and not operating activities (IAS 7.14 and IAS 1.34a).

2.2 Investing and Financing Activities

For both investing and financing activities, the **direct method** is **mandatory**. Major classes of gross cash receipts and gross cash payments have to be reported separately. However, in some cases the cash flows may be reported on a net basis (IAS 7.21–7.24).

Investing and financing transactions that do not require the use of cash or cash equivalents (**non-cash investing and financing transactions**) have to be excluded from the statement of cash flows. An example is the acquisition of a machine by means of a finance lease (IAS 7.43–7.44).

3 SPECIAL TOPICS

3.1 Interest and Dividends

The standard requires **separate disclosure** of each of the following cash flows (IAS 7.31) in the statement of cash flows:[2]

- Interest received
- Interest paid
- Dividends received
- Dividends paid

Entities that are not financial institutions can classify each of interest and dividends paid either as operating or financing activities and each of interest and dividends received as operating or investing activities (IAS 7.31–7.34):[3]

	Interest		*Dividends*	
	Received	*Paid*	*Received*	*Paid*
Operating activities	X	X	X	X
Investing activities	X		X	
Financing activities		X		X

The classification has to be **consistent** from period to period (IAS 7.31).

Interest paid, which has to be disclosed separately in the statement of cash flows, also comprises interest capitalized according to IAS 23 (IAS 7.32).

3.2 Income Taxes

Cash flows arising from income taxes have to be disclosed separately in the statement of cash flows. They have to be classified as cash flows from operating activities unless it is practicable to identify them with, and therefore classify them as, financing or investing activities (IAS 7.35–7.36).[4]

4 CONSOLIDATED STATEMENTS OF CASH FLOWS

4.1 Introduction

The consolidated statement of cash flows reflects only the cash flows into and out of the group and not cash flows that are internal to the group (such as intra-group sales revenues, management charges, interest, and financing arrangements). This means that consolidated cash flows are presented as those of a single economic entity.[5] The consolidated statement of financial position and the amount of consolidated profit or loss are the basis for preparing the consolidated statement of cash flows.

---

[2] *See KPMG,* Insights into IFRS, *7th edition, 2.3.50.10.*

[3] *See KPMG,* Insights into IFRS, *7th edition, 2.3.50.20.*

[4] *See KPMG,* Insights into IFRS, *7th edition, 2.3.50.10 and 2.3.50.20.*

[5] *See Ernst & Young,* International GAAP 2011, *p. 2806.*

4.2 Acquisitions and Disposals of Subsidiaries

The following amounts must be presented **separately** (i.e. **offsetting is prohibited**) in the statement of cash flows and classified as investing activities (IAS 7.39 and 7.41):

- Aggregate cash flows arising from obtaining control of subsidiaries
- Aggregate cash flows arising from losing control of subsidiaries

In the statement of cash flows, the aggregate amount of cash paid (received) as consideration for obtaining (losing) control of subsidiaries is reported net of the subsidiaries' cash, which is acquired (disposed of) as part of such transactions (IAS 7.42).

4.3 Associates

When applying the equity method, cash flows as well as cash and cash equivalents of the associate are not included in the consolidated statement of cash flows. Only the cash flows between the group and the associate are included in the consolidated statement of cash flows (e.g. dividends paid by the associate to the group and cash received by the group due to the sale of goods to the associate). The share of the profit or loss of an associate as well as an impairment loss on the carrying amount of the investment in an associate are not included because they are of a non-cash nature (IAS 7.37–7.38).

5 EXAMPLES WITH SOLUTIONS

Example 1

Introductory example – non-cash expenses

On Jan 01, 01, entity E acquires a machine and pays the purchase price of CU 10. The machine is available for use on the same day. Its useful life is 10 years.

Required

Assess which payments and expenses result from the situation described above from E's perspective.

Hints for solution

In particular Section 2.1.

Solution

In each of the years 01–10, a depreciation expense of CU 1 is recognized relating to the machine. This means that the payment of CU 10 is allocated over the machine's useful life in E's statement of comprehensive income.

However, a cash outflow (CU 10) only takes place at the beginning of 01. Hence, the payment of CU 10 is presented in E's statement of cash flows for 01 in its entirety as a cash outflow in E's investing activities.

Example 2

Introductory example – gain on disposal of an item of property, plant, or equipment

On Dec 31, 01, entity E sells a machine for CU 10. Payment is effected in cash on the same day. On the same day, the machine's carrying amount is CU 9. This results in the following entry in which the gain on disposal is recognized on a net basis (IAS 1.34a):

Dec 31, 01	Dr	Cash	10	
	Cr	Machine		9
	Cr	Gain on disposal		1

E's profit for 01 (which includes the gain on disposal of the machine) is CU 100.

Required

Illustrate the effects of the disposal of the machine on E's statement of cash flows. E presents its cash flows from operating activities according to the indirect method. Ignore tax effects.

Hints for solution

In particular Sections 2.1 and 1.

Solution

The gain on disposal of the machine has increased E's profit for 01 to CU 100. The gain represents an inflow of cash. Nevertheless, it has to be eliminated (i.e. deducted) when calculating E's cash flows from operating activities. This is because the sale of an item of property, plant, or equipment is presented as part of investing activities and not in E's operating activities. Investing activities are ultimately increased by the entire sales proceeds of CU 10.

Profit for 01	100
Gain on disposal	–1
Cash flows from operating activities	**99**
Proceeds from the sale of property, plant, and equipment	10
Cash flows from investing activities	**10**
Cash flows	**109**

Example 3

Introductory example – cash flows from operating activities

In 01, entity E recognizes a depreciation expense relating to property, plant, and equipment in the amount of CU 60 and purchases merchandise for CU 40 (payment in cash). E's profit for 01 is CU 100.

Required

Illustrate the effects of the depreciation as well as of the purchase of the merchandise on E's statement of cash flows. E presents its cash flows from operating activities according to the indirect method.

Hints for solution

In particular Section 2.1.

Solution

The reduction in E's profit by the depreciation of CU 60 has to be reversed because depreciation represents a non-cash expense. The purchase of the merchandise is recognized by means of the entry "Dr Merchandise Cr Cash CU 40." Consequently, the purchase does not affect E's profit. However, it leads to a cash outflow of CU 40 that has to be taken into account when determining E's cash flows from operating activities.

Profit for 01	100
Depreciation expense	60
Purchase of merchandise in cash	−40
Cash flows from operating activities	**120**

Example 4

Preparation of a statement of cash flows[6]

Entity E's statement of financial position as at Dec 31, 01 is presented as follows:

	ASSETS	*Dec 31, 01*	*Dec 31, 00*		*EQUITY AND LIABILITIES*	*Dec 31, 01*	*Dec 31, 00*
(a)	Building 1	290	0	(e)	Share capital	260	160
(b)	Building 2	0	40		Profit for year	40	0
(c)	Truck	20	0	(c)	Lease liability	20	0
(d)	Merchandise	50	100	(f)	Trade payable	20	0
	Cash	40	20	(g)	Provision	10	0
				(h)	Loan liability	50	0
	Total	**400**	**160**		**Total**	**400**	**160**

E's **separate income statement** for 01 is presented as follows (the line item **"other expenses"** relates to E's operating activities and only includes expenses that were paid in cash in 01):

	01
Sales revenue	450
Gain on the disposal of building 2	10
Cost of the merchandise sold	−300
Depreciation expense	−10
Recognition of the provision	−10
Other expenses	−100
Profit for 01	**40**

[6] *The statement of financial position as well as the separate income statement are illustrated in a simplified way in this example.*

Remarks on the statement of financial position:

(a) On Jan 01, 01, E acquired **building 1** (which represents an item of property, plant, and equipment) for CU 300 (payment in cash). The building was available for use on the same day. Its useful life is 30 years.
(b) On Jan 01, 01, E sold **building 2** (which represented an item of property, plant, and equipment) for CU 50 (payment in cash). The building's carrying amount as at Dec 31, 00 was CU 40.
(c) On Dec 31, 01, a **truck** (property, plant, and equipment) was acquired by means of a finance lease. The carrying amount of the truck as at Dec 31, 01 is CU 20, which is equal to the carrying amount of the lease liability.
(d) The carrying amount of the **merchandise** was CU 100 on Dec 31, 00 and is CU 50 on Dec 31, 01. In 01, new merchandise was purchased for CU 250. Thereof, CU 230 was paid in cash ("Dr Merchandise Cr Cash CU 230") and CU 20 was purchased on credit ("Dr Merchandise Cr Trade payable CU 20"). In 01, merchandise with a carrying amount of CU 300 was sold for CU 450 ("Dr Cost of the merchandise sold Cr Merchandise 300" and "Dr Cash Cr Sales revenue 450").
(e) In 01, E **issued shares** ("Dr Cash Cr Share capital CU 100").
(f) The carrying amount of the **trade payables** was CU 0 on Dec 31, 00 and is CU 20 on Dec 31, 01 (see (d)).
(g) On Dec 31, 01 a **provision** is recognized **for warranties** in the amount of CU 10.
(h) On Dec 31, 01 E took out a **loan** in the amount of CU 50 from its bank.

Required

Prepare E's statement of cash flows for the year 01. E's financial statements are prepared as at Dec 31. E presents its cash flows from operating activities according to the indirect method.

Hints for solution

In particular Section 2.

Solution

(1)	Profit or loss	40
(2)	Depreciation expense	10
(3)	Expense for the recognition of a provision	10
(4)	Merchandise	70
(5)	Gain on the disposal of property, plant, and equipment	−10
	Cash flows from operating activities	**120**
(6)	Acquisition of property, plant, and equipment	−300
(7)	Disposal of property, plant, and equipment	50
	Cash flows from investing activities	**−250**
(8)	Increase in share capital	100
(9)	Taking up of the loan	50
	Cash flows from financing activities	**150**
	Cash flows	**20**
Check:		
	Cash as at Dec 31, 00	20
	Cash flows in 01	20
	Cash as at Dec 31, 01	**40**

Remarks on the statement of cash flows:

In the statement of cash flows, only the transactions that result in inflows and outflows of cash are taken into account. Some of these transactions are already included in profit for the year (e.g. the sale of the merchandise for CU 450).

(1) Under the indirect method, the entity's profit or loss is reconciled to the cash flows from operating activities (IAS 7.18b). Consequently, profit or loss is the starting point.

(2 and 3) Depreciation expense does not affect cash (non-cash expense). It was deducted in determining profit for the year 01. Consequently, when determining cash flows from operating activities this deduction has to be reversed by adding depreciation. The same applies to the expense for the recognition of the provision.

(4) The amount of CU 70 consists of two components:
- Merchandise is purchased in the amount of CU 250. Thereof, only CU 230 was paid in cash ("Dr Merchandise Cr Cash CU 230") and CU 20 was purchased on credit ("Dr Merchandise Cr Trade payable CU 20"). Hence, the total effect in 01 of the purchase of the merchandise on cash is CU –230.
- The cost of the merchandise sold of CU 300 (carrying amount of the merchandise that was recognized as an expense when the merchandise was sold) represents a non-cash expense. Hence, it is treated in the same way as the depreciation expense and the expense for the recognition of the provision (see remarks 2 and 3).

(5) The gain on the disposal of building 2 that has been included in profit or loss has to be reclassified from operating activities to investing activities.

(6) CU 300 had to be paid for the acquisition of property, plant, and equipment.

(7) The cash inflow arising from the sale of building 2 (which represented an item of property, plant, and equipment) amounts to CU 50.

(8) The cash inflow of CU 100 results from the increase in share capital.

(9) The cash inflow of CU 50 results from taking up the loan.

Example 5

Interest, issue, and redemption of a bond[7]

On Jan 01, 01, entity E issues a bond. On the same day, E receives CU 100 for issuing the bond. No interest is explicitly stipulated. However, E has to pay CU 121 on Dec 31, 02 in order to settle its obligations under the bond. E measures the bond at amortized cost, i.e. according to the effective interest method. The effective interest rate is 10% p.a. (CU 121 : 1.1^2 = CU 100).

[7] *See the chapter on IFRS 9/IAS 39, Section 2.3.5 and Examples 5–9 with regard to the effective interest method.*

(Correct) posting status:

Jan 01, 01	Dr	Cash	100	
	Cr	Liability		100
Dec 31, 01	Dr	Interest expense	10	
	Cr	Liability		10
Dec 31, 02	Dr	Interest expense	11	
	Cr	Liability		11
Dec 31, 02	Dr	Liability	121	
	Cr	Cash		121

E's profit for 01 is CU 200. In 02, E generates the same profit. For simplification purposes it is assumed that these amounts do not include any items that are of a non-cash nature. However, it has not been investigated, yet, whether the interest expense from the bond is of a non-cash nature.

Required

Illustrate the effects of the bond on E's statement of cash flows for the years 01 and 02. E's reporting periods end on Dec 31. E presents its cash flows from operating activities according to the indirect method and classifies interest paid as:

(a) cash flows from operating activities
(b) cash flows from financing activities

Hints for solution

In particular Sections 2 and 3.1.

Solution

Year 01

The amount of CU 100 received for issuing the bond is presented as financing activities. E's profit for 01 has been reduced by the interest expense of CU 10. This deduction has to be reversed, since the amount of CU 10 represents a non-cash expense. As a result, E's cash flows from operating activities do not include interest expense.

In 01, the effects of the bond on the statement of cash flows are the same in both version (a) and (b), since no interest is paid in 01.

Profit for 01	200
Interest expense (reversal of the deduction)	10
Cash flows from operating activities	**210**
Bond issue	100
Cash flows from financing activities	**100**
Cash flows	**310**

Year 02

The difference between the amount received in connection with the bond issue in 01 (CU 100) and the redemption amount (CU 121) represents interest paid. Interest paid can be classified either as cash flows from operating activities (version a) or as cash flows from financing activities (version b) (IAS 7.12, 7.31, and 7.33):

Version (a)	
Profit for 02	200
Interest expense (reversal of the deduction)	11
Interest paid	−21
Cash flows from operating activities	**190**
Redemption of the bond	−100
Cash flows from financing activities	**−100**
Cash flows	**90**

Version (b)	
Profit for 02	200
Interest expense (reversal of the deduction)	11
Cash flows from operating activities	**211**
Redemption of the bond	−100
Interest paid	−21
Cash flows from financing activities	**−121**
Cash flows	**90**

Example 6

Acquisitions and disposals of subsidiaries[8]

On Dec 31, 01, entity E acquires 100% of the shares of entity S1 (which is free of debt) for CU 11. Payment is effected in cash on the same day. On the acquisition date, the fair values of S1's assets are as follows:

Machines	3
Buildings	2
Finished goods	3
Cash and cash equivalents	2
Goodwill	1
Purchase price	**11**

Moreover, on Dec 31, 01, E sells 100% of the shares of entity S2 (which is also free of debt) for CU 8. Payment is effected in cash on the same day. The carrying amounts of S2's assets before deconsolidation are as follows:

Buildings	4
Merchandise	3
Cash and cash equivalents	1
Selling price	**8**

[8] *For simplification purposes, it is assumed in this example that the subsidiaries only have a limited number of assets.*

Required

Illustrate the acquisition of S1 as well as the disposal of S2 in E's consolidated statement of cash flows. E's reporting period ends on Dec 31, 01.

Hints for solution

In particular Section 4.2.

Solution

Cash outflows arising from obtaining control of subsidiaries	−9
Cash inflows arising from losing control of subsidiaries	7
Cash flows from investing activities	**−2**

The amount of the cash paid by E as consideration for obtaining control of S1 (CU 11) is reported in E's statement of cash flows net of S1's cash and cash equivalents (CU 2). Similarly, the amount of the cash received by E as consideration for losing control of S2 (CU 8) is reported in E's statement of cash flows net of S2's cash and cash equivalents (CU 1). The cash outflows arising from obtaining control of subsidiaries and the cash inflows arising from losing control of subsidiaries have to be classified as investing activities and must not be offset (IAS 7.39 and 7.41–7.42).

IAS 8 ACCOUNTING POLICIES, CHANGES IN ACCOUNTING ESTIMATES, AND ERRORS

1 INTRODUCTION[1]

IAS 8 establishes rules with regard to (a) the selection and change of accounting policies, (b) changes in accounting estimates, and (c) corrections of prior period errors (IAS 8.1).

Accounting policies are the specific principles, bases, rules, conventions, and practices applied in preparing and presenting financial statements.

A **change in accounting estimate** is an adjustment of the carrying amount of an asset or a liability or the amount of the periodic consumption of an asset that results from new information or new developments.

Prior period errors are omissions from and misstatements in an entity's financial statements for one or more prior periods arising from a failure to use or the misuse of reliable information that was available or obtainable when financial statements for those periods were authorized for issue. Such errors include the effects of mistakes in applying accounting policies, oversights or misinterpretations of facts, mathematical mistakes, and fraud.

Changes in accounting policies and corrections of prior period errors are generally effected **retrospectively**, i.e. as if the new policy had always been applied or as if the prior period error had never occurred.

Accounting estimates are changed **prospectively**, i.e. by recognizing the effect of the change in the statements of comprehensive income of the current and future periods.

2 ACCOUNTING POLICIES

2.1 Selection and Application of Accounting Policies

When an IFRS applies specifically to a transaction, other event or condition, the accounting policy applied is determined according to the corresponding IFRS (IAS 8.7).

If the effect of applying an accounting policy of an IFRS is **immaterial**, the policy need not be applied. However, it is inappropriate to depart immaterially from an IFRS to achieve a particular presentation of the entity's situation (IAS 8.8).

---

[1] *The terms explained in this chapter are based on the definitions in IAS 8.5.*

In the **absence of an IFRS** that specifically applies to a transaction, other event or condition, management has to **develop an accounting policy** that results in relevant and reliable information (IAS 8.10). In doing so, the following sources are considered in descending order (IAS 8.11–8.12):

- **Primarily**, the **requirements in IFRSs** dealing with similar and related issues are taken into account (conclusion by analogy).
- **Secondarily**, the **Framework** criteria are considered.
- **In addition**, the following sources may also be considered to the extent that they do not conflict with the sources above:
  - **Pronouncements of other standard-setting bodies** that use a similar conceptual framework to develop accounting standards (e.g. FASB).
  - **Other accounting literature**.
  - **Accepted industry practices**.

In our opinion, the procedure described above not only applies to situations for which there is no rule in IFRSs, but also for situations in which the rules are imprecise and have to be interpreted.

2.2 The Principle of Consistency

Accounting policies have to be applied **consistently** for similar transactions, other events and conditions (IAS 8.13).

This rule applies to many situations in which IFRSs permit an entity to choose between different **accounting policies**, for example:

- Investment property is measured after recognition either according to the fair value model or according to the cost model. Generally, the same model has to be applied to all of the entity's investment property (IAS 40.30).[2]
- Application of the FIFO or weighted average cost formula for all inventories having a similar nature and use to the entity (IAS 2.25).[3]

An important **exception** applies to **business combinations**: The **non-controlling interest** in the acquiree is generally measured on the acquisition date either at its fair value or at its proportionate share in the recognized amounts of the acquiree's identifiable net assets. This option may be exercised differently for each business combination (IFRS 3.19 and 3.32).[4]

The principle of consistency also applies to the **interpretation of rules and terms** that are imprecise (e.g. interpretation of the term "major part" in IAS 17.10c as a margin of 75% when distinguishing between finance leases and operating leases[5]) and generally to the selection between different **methods used to make estimates** with regard to an item **in the case of uncertainty** (e.g. if the entity decides to apply the straight-line method instead of the diminishing balance method as depreciation method for a new machine).

---

[2] *See the chapter on IAS 40, Section 4.*

[3] *See the chapter on IAS 2, Section 2.1.*

[4] *See the chapter on IFRS 3, Sections 6.1 and 6.3.*

[5] *See the chapter on IAS 17, Section 3.2.*

However, the principle of consistency **does not apply to individual estimates**, i.e. to the choice of specific assumptions for estimates in an individual case. For example, if the estimate of useful life of an item of property, plant, and equipment changes in a subsequent period from 15 to 12 years because repairs are necessary more often than previously expected, this has to be taken into account in the financial statements.

2.3 When an Accounting Policy Has to be Changed

An entity shall change an accounting policy only if the change is **required by an IFRS** (IAS 8.14a) or results in the financial statements providing **reliable and more relevant information** (IAS 8.14b).

Assessing whether a change in accounting policy results in reliable and more relevant information involves **discretion**. Due to the examples in IAS 8.IE in which such changes are **justified** by more or less superficial arguments, the following conclusion can be drawn: Pointing out reliability, relevance, industry practices, the fact that the new procedure is down to the last detail, etc., is often sufficient to justify a change.

2.4 Consequences of a Change in Accounting Policy

A change in accounting policy resulting from the initial application of an IFRS is accounted for in accordance with the **specific transitional provisions in that IFRS** (IAS 8.19a). When an entity changes an accounting policy upon initial application of an IFRS that does not include specific transitional provisions in this respect or changes an accounting policy voluntarily, the change is accounted for retrospectively (**retrospective application**) (IAS 8.19b).

If a change in accounting policy requires **retrospective adjustment**, the following **procedure** is generally necessary (IAS 8.22–8.26):

- **Recognition** of assets and liabilities has to be assessed and their **measurement** has to be determined as if the new accounting policy had always been applied.
- Resulting differences compared to the previous procedure relating to periods before those presented in the financial statements are directly recognized in the **opening balance of equity** (usually in **retained earnings**) of the earliest prior period presented.
- Any **comparative information** presented is adjusted.
- It is necessary to present the **adjusted statement of financial position as at the beginning of the preceding period** (IAS 1.10(f) and 1.40A–1.40D).

In the **absence of an IFRS** that specifically applies to a transaction, other event or condition, it is possible to fall back on the most recent pronouncements of other standard-setting bodies in certain cases (IAS 8.12). If, following an amendment of such a pronouncement, the entity chooses to change an accounting policy, the change is treated as a voluntary change in accounting policy (IAS 8.21).

3 CHANGES IN ACCOUNTING ESTIMATES

3.1 Introduction

The use of reasonable estimates is an essential part of the preparation of financial statements (e.g. determining fair value using option pricing models; determining useful life of an item of property, plant, and equipment; or calculating an impairment loss on a receivable measured at amortized cost) (IAS 8.32).

An estimate may need **revision** if changes occur in the circumstances on which the estimate was based or as a result of more experience or new information (IAS 8.34).

When it is difficult to distinguish a change in an accounting policy from a change in an estimate, the change is treated as a change in an estimate (IAS 8.35). In our opinion, the same principle should be applied to situations in which it is difficult to distinguish a correction of an error from a change in an estimate.

3.2 Accounting Treatment

Estimates are changed **prospectively**. This means that the effect of the change is recognized in the statement of comprehensive income of the current period and, to the extent affected (e.g. in the case of a change in depreciable amount), also in the statements of comprehensive income of future periods (IAS 8.5 and 8.36).

A change in estimate is **normally** recognized **in profit or loss**. However, in exceptional cases, it is recognized outside profit or loss. An example for the latter situation is an increase in the estimated amount which is necessary to settle a provision recognized for a decommissioning liability. Such a change would result in the entry "Dr Property, plant, and equipment Cr Provision" (IFRIC 1).

In the case of property, plant, and equipment (IAS 16) and intangible assets (IAS 38), a change in the estimate of their **useful lives** affects depreciation or amortization expense in the current period (IAS 8.38).

4 CORRECTION OF PRIOR PERIOD ERRORS

Errors can arise in applying the recognition, measurement, presentation or disclosure requirements. Financial statements do not comply with IFRSs if they contain either material errors or immaterial errors made intentionally to achieve a particular presentation of an entity's situation. Normally, errors relating to the current reporting period are discovered and corrected before the financial statements are authorized for issue. However, material errors are sometimes not discovered until a subsequent period. These prior period errors are corrected in the comparative information presented in the financial statements for that subsequent period. If the error occurred before the earliest prior period presented, the opening balances of assets, liabilities, and equity for the earliest prior period presented have to be restated. Such **retrospective restatement** is generally necessary. Normally, retrospective restatement means that the correction of the accounting treatment is effected as if the error had never occurred. The **procedure** is the same as in the case of a change in accounting policy accounted for retrospectively (see Section 2.4).

Corrections of errors differ from changes in accounting estimates. Estimates are approximations that may need revision as additional information becomes known (IAS 8.48).

When it is difficult to distinguish a change in an accounting policy from a change in estimate, the change is treated as a change in estimate (IAS 8.35). In our opinion, the same principle should be applied to situations in which it is difficult to distinguish a correction of an error from a change in an estimate.

5 EXAMPLES WITH SOLUTIONS

Example 1

Scope of the principle of consistency

(a) Useful life of a wind-driven power station of entity E was initially estimated to be 16 years. When preparing the financial statements for a later period, it turns out that repairs are necessary more often than originally expected and that there are more down times than previously expected.

(b) Contingent liabilities are disclosed in the notes unless the possibility of an outflow of resources embodying economic benefits is remote (IAS 37.28 and 37.86).[6] In its previous financial statements, E interpreted the term "remote" as a probability of 5%. E's chief financial officer would like to interpret the term "remote" as a probability of 10% in E's financial statements for the current period. He has no specific arguments to do so.

(c) E acquired a machine. Both the straight-line method and the diminishing balance method were considered acceptable as depreciation methods.[7] E decided to apply the diminishing balance method in its previous financial statements. E's chief financial officer would like to change to the straight-line method in the financial statements for the current period. The pattern in which the machine's future economic benefits are expected to be consumed did not change. The change of the depreciation method was not planned from the beginning.

Required

Assess whether the principle of consistency applies in the above situations in E's financial statements. If the principle does not apply, describe the accounting treatment in E's financial statements.

Hints for solution

In particular Section 2.2.

Solution

(a) The original estimate of useful life has to be revised because the principle of consistency does not apply to individual estimates. The reduction in useful life is accounted for prospectively because it is a change in an estimate (IAS 8.36). Since there is a change in useful life of an item of property, plant, and equipment (IAS 16), depreciation of the current period is affected (IAS 8.38).

---

[6] *See the chapter on IAS 37, Section 3.*

[7] *See the chapter on IAS 16, Section 4.2.3.*

(b) The principle of consistency applies to the interpretation of terms that are imprecise (e.g. "remote"). Accordingly, it is not possible to change the interpretation of the term "remote" from 5% to 10% without specific justifications.
(c) The principle of consistency generally applies to the choice between different methods used to make estimates in the case of uncertainty. The depreciation method selected for the machine has to be applied consistently from period to period unless there is a change in the expected pattern of consumption of the future economic benefits (IAS 16.62). Therefore, the change from the diminishing balance method to the straight-line method is not possible. The situation would have been different if the depreciation schedule had provided for that change from the beginning. In this case, the question whether the principle of consistency applies would not have arisen. Instead, the procedure to change from the diminishing balance method to the straight-line method after a certain time would have been a specific depreciation method.

Example 2

Changes in accounting estimates

(a) On Jan 01, 01, entity E acquired a machine (property, plant, and equipment) for CU 100 that was available for use on the same date. The machine's useful life was originally estimated to be 10 years. At the end of 05 it becomes clear that the entire useful life of the machine is eight years instead of 10 years due to changed circumstances.

Posting status:

Depreciation expense of CU 10 was recognized in each of the years 01–04.

(b) On Dec 31, 04, E recognized a provision in the amount of CU 8. On Dec 31, 05, the best estimate of the expenditure required to settle the obligation is CU 12 due to changed circumstances.

Required

Prepare any necessary entries in E's financial statements as at Dec 31, 05. E has to present only one comparative period (i.e. the year 04) in its financial statements.

Hints for solution

In particular Section 3.2.

Solution (a)

The change in the machine's useful life is a change in accounting estimate. Since that change in estimate affects depreciation expense for the year 05 (IAS 8.38), the new depreciation expense is calculated by dividing the carrying amount as at Jan 01, 05 (CU 60) by the new remaining useful life as at the same date (four years). In other words, the change is accounted for prospectively as from Jan 01, 05. In contrast to a retrospective adjustment, the comparative period 04 is not affected and the opening statement of financial position as at Jan 01, 04 is neither adjusted nor does it have to be presented.

Dec 31, 05	Dr	Depreciation expense	15	
	Cr	Machine		15

Solution (b)

The carrying amount of a provision has to reflect the best estimate of the expenditure required to settle the obligation at the end of the reporting period (IAS 37.36). That estimate may need revision in a later period if changes occur in the circumstances on which the estimate was based or as a result of more experience or new information. This represents a change in an accounting estimate and not the correction of an error (IAS 8.34 and 8.48). The change in the carrying amount of the provision from CU 8 to CU 12 is accounted for prospectively and recognized in profit or loss (IAS 8.36–8.37).

Dec 31, 05	Dr	Profit or loss	4	
	Cr	Provision		4

Example 3

Retrospective restatement

On Jan 01, 01, entity E acquired software for CU 5 that was available for use on the same date. The useful life of the software is 5 years. On Jan 01, 01, the cost of the software was capitalized ("Dr Software Cr Cash CU 5") (IAS 38.24). Mistakenly, no amortization expense was recognized for the software in E's financial statements as at Dec 31, 01 and Dec 31, 02. This error is discovered when preparing the financial statements as at Dec 31, 03.

Posting status:

Jan 01, 01	Dr	Software	5	
	Cr	Cash		5

Required

(a) Prepare any necessary entries in E's financial statements as at Dec 31, 03.
(b) Illustrate the effects of the entries (including the effects of the posting status) on E's statement of financial position, separate income statement, and statement of changes in equity in simplified presentations of these statements.

E has to present only one comparative period (i.e. the year 02) in its financial statements.

Hints for solution

In particular Sections 2.4 and 4.

Solution (a)

The prior period error has to be corrected retrospectively.

The year 01 is not presented as a comparative period in the financial statements as at Dec 31, 03. Instead, the separate income statement is only presented for 02 and 03. Hence, amortization for 01 cannot be included in amortization expense in the separate income statement. However, it has to be recognized as a reduction in retained earnings in the opening statement of financial position as at Jan 01, 02 in order to present the correct carrying amount of retained earnings.

Jan 01, 02	Dr	Retained earnings	1	
	Cr	Software		1
Dec 31, 02	Dr	Amortization expense	1	
	Cr	Software		1
Dec 31, 03	Dr	Amortization expense	1	
	Cr	Software		1

Solution (b)

*Effects on the **separate income statement***

	03	*02*
Amortization expense	−1	−1
Profit for the year	**−1**	**−1**

*Effects on the **statement of changes in equity***

	Retained earnings
Balance as at Jan 01, 02	0
Correction of a prior period error	−1
Adjusted balance as at Jan 01, 02	**−1**
Total comprehensive income	−1
Balance as at Dec 31, 02	**−2**
Total comprehensive income	−1
Balance as at Dec 31, 03	**−3**

*Effects on the **statement of financial position***

It is important to note that the adjusted opening statement of financial position as at Jan 01, 02 also has to be presented (IAS 1.10(f) and 1.39).

Assets	*Dec 31, 03*	*Dec 31, 02*	*Jan 01, 02*	*Equity and liabilities*	*Dec 31, 03*	*Dec 31, 02*	*Jan 01, 02*
Software	2	3	4	Retained earnings	−3	−2	−1
Cash	−5	−5	−5				
Total	**−3**	**−2**	**−1**	**Total**	**−3**	**−2**	**−1**

Example 4

Retrospective restatement

On Jan 01, 03, entity E entered into an interest rate swap for CU 0. E decided to measure the swap at cost. At the end of 05, it is noticed that it would have been necessary to measure the derivative at fair value through profit or loss since its acquisition (IFRS 9.B4.1.9).[8] Fair value of the swap developed as follows:

Jan 01, 03	0
Dec 31, 03	4
Dec 31, 04	12
Dec 31, 05	52

Required

(a) Prepare any necessary entries in E's financial statements as at Dec 31, 05.
(b) Illustrate the effects of the entries on E's statement of financial position, separate income statement, and statement of changes in equity in simplified presentations of these statements.

E has to present only one comparative period (i.e. the year 04) in its financial statements.

Hints for solution

In particular Sections 2.4 and 4.

Solution (a)

E did not measure the derivative at fair value through profit or loss. This represents a prior period error that has to be corrected retrospectively. Consequently, retained earnings have to be adjusted in the opening statement of financial position as at Jan 01, 04, by the fair value increase of the year 03. This means that the corresponding entry as at Jan 01, 04 is "Dr Financial asset Cr Retained earnings" (instead of "Dr Financial asset Cr Fair value gain").

Jan 01, 04	Dr	Financial asset	4	
	Cr	Retained earnings		4
Dec 31, 04	Dr	Financial asset	8	
	Cr	Fair value gain		8
Dec 31, 05	Dr	Financial asset	40	
	Cr	Fair value gain		40

Solution (b)

Effects on the ***separate income statement***

[8] *See the chapter on IFRS 9/IAS 39, Section 2.3.3.*

	05	04
Fair value gain	40	8
Profit for the year	**40**	**8**

*Effects on the **statement of changes in equity***

	Retained earnings
Balance as at Jan 01, 04	0
Correction of a prior period error	4
Adjusted balance as at Jan 01, 04	**4**
Total comprehensive income	8
Balance as at Dec 31, 04	**12**
Total comprehensive income	40
Balance as at Dec 31, 05	**52**

*Effects on the **statement of financial position***

It is important to note that the adjusted opening statement of financial position as at Jan 01, 04 also has to be presented (IAS 1.10(f) and 1.39).

Assets	*Dec 31, 05*	*Dec 31, 04*	*Jan 01, 04*	*Equity and liabilities*	*Dec 31, 05*	*Dec 31, 04*	*Jan 01, 04*
Financial asset (derivative)	52	12	4	Retained earnings	52	12	4
Total	**52**	**12**	**4**	**Total**	**52**	**12**	**4**

Example 5

Retrospective application of an accounting policy

On Jan 01, 03, entity E acquired a building for CU 40 that was available for use on the same date. The building meets the criteria for classification as investment property (IAS 40). The building was measured according to the cost model, i.e. taking into account depreciation (IAS 40.56). The useful life of the building is 40 years. At the end of 05, E decides to account for its investment properties according to the fair value model. In applying the fair value model, no depreciation is recognized. Instead, all changes in fair value are recognized in profit or loss (IAS 40.33–40.55). Fair value of the building developed as follows:

Jan 01, 03	40
Dec 31, 03	43
Dec 31, 04	50
Dec 31, 05	61

Posting status:

Jan 01, 03	Dr	Building	40	
	Cr	Cash		40

Moreover, depreciation expense has been recognized as follows, in each of the years of 03–05:

Dr	Depreciation expense	1	
Cr	Building		1

Required

(a) Prepare any necessary entries in E's financial statements as at Dec 31, 05.
(b) Illustrate the effects of the entries (including the effects of the posting status) on E's statement of financial position, separate income statement, and statement of changes in equity in simplified presentations of these statements.

E has to present only one comparative period (i.e. the year 04) in its financial statements.

Hints for solution

In particular Section 2.4.

Solution (a)

After recognition, investment property is measured either according to the cost model (i.e. at cost less any accumulated depreciation and accumulated impairment losses) or according to the fair value model (i.e. at fair value through profit or loss) (IAS 40.30).[9] Initially, E decided to apply the cost model. The change to the fair value model is a voluntary change in an accounting policy (IAS 40.31) that has to be accounted for retrospectively (IAS 8.19 and 8.22).

Depreciation expense recognized in 03 has to be reversed in the opening statement of financial position as at Jan 01, 04, by adjusting retained earnings. This means that the corresponding entry as at Jan 01, 04 is "Dr Building Cr Retained earnings" (instead of "Dr Building Cr Depreciation expense"):

Jan 01, 04	Dr	Building	1	
	Cr	Retained earnings		1

The fair value change that arose in 03 is also recognized in the opening statement of financial position as at Jan 01, 04:

Jan 01, 04	Dr	Building	3	
	Cr	Retained earnings		3

Reversal of depreciation expense recognized in 04:

Dec 31, 04	Dr	Building	1	
	Cr	Depreciation expense		1

[9] *See the chapter on IAS 40, Section 4.*

Recognition of the fair value change that arose in 04:

Dec 31, 04	Dr	Building	7	
	Cr	Fair value gain		7

Reversal of depreciation expense recognized in 05:

Dec 31, 05	Dr	Building	1	
	Cr	Depreciation expense		1

Recognition of the fair value change that arose in 05:

Dec 31, 05	Dr	Building	11	
	Cr	Fair value gain		11

Solution (b)

Effects on the ***separate income statement***

	05	*04*
Fair value gain	11	7
Profit for the year	**11**	**7**

Effects on the ***statement of changes in equity***

Retained earnings		
Balance as at Jan 01, 04	−1	*Depreciation for 03*
Change in an accounting policy	4	*Change in retained earnings as at Jan 01, 04*
Adjusted balance as at Jan 01, 04	**3**	
Total comprehensive income	7	
Balance as at Dec 31, 04	**10**	
Total comprehensive income	11	
Balance as at Dec 31, 05	**21**	

Effects on the ***statement of financial position***

It is important to note that the adjusted opening statement of financial position as at Jan 01, 04 also has to be presented (IAS 1.10(f) and 1.39).

Assets	*Dec 31, 05*	*Dec 31, 04*	*Jan 01, 04*	*Equity and liabilities*	*Dec 31, 05*	*Dec 31, 04*	*Jan 01, 04*
Building	61	50	43	Retained earnings	21	10	3
Cash	−40	−40	−40				
Total	**21**	**10**	**3**	**Total**	**21**	**10**	**3**

Example 6

Retrospective application including deferred tax[10]

The situation is the same as in Example 5. However, deferred tax has to be taken into account. The applicable tax rate is 25%. According to the applicable tax law, only the cost model can be applied with regard to the building. Assume that the building's useful life according to IFRS is identical with its useful life for tax purposes and that unused tax losses of E do not meet the recognition criteria according to IAS 12.

Hints for solution

In particular Section 2.4.

Solution (a)

Jan 01, 04	Dr	Building	1	
	Cr	Retained earnings		1
Jan 01, 04	Dr	Building	3	
	Cr	Retained earnings		3

Carrying amount according to IFRS (as at Jan 01, 04)	43	
Carrying amount according to E's tax law (as at Jan 01, 04)	39	*= CU 40 – depreciation for 03 of CU 1*
Taxable temporary difference	**4**	
Tax rate	25%	
Deferred tax liability (as at Jan 01, 04)	**1**	

Jan 01, 04	Dr	Retained earnings	1	
	Cr	Deferred tax liability		1
Dec 31, 04	Dr	Building	1	
	Cr	Depreciation expense		1
Dec 31, 04	Dr	Building	7	
	Cr	Fair value gain		7

Change in deferred tax in 04:

Carrying amount under IFRS (as at Dec 31, 04)	50	
Carrying amount under E's tax law (as at Dec 31, 04)	38	*= CU 40 – depreciation for 03 and 04 of CU 2*
Taxable temporary difference	**12**	
Tax rate	25%	
Deferred tax liability (as at Dec 31, 04)	**3**	
Deferred tax liability (as at Jan 01, 04)	1	
Deferred tax expense 04	**2**	

[10] *See the chapter on IAS 12 regarding deferred tax.*

Dec 31, 04	Dr	Deferred tax expense	2	
	Cr	Deferred tax liability		2
Dec 31, 05	Dr	Building	1	
	Cr	Depreciation expense		1
Dec 31, 05	Dr	Building	11	
	Cr	Fair value gain		11

Change in deferred tax in 05:

Carrying amount under IFRS (as at Dec 31, 05)	61	
Carrying amount under E's tax law (as at Dec 31, 05)	37	*= CU 40 – depreciation for 03–05 of CU 3*
Taxable temporary difference	**24**	
Tax rate	25%	
Deferred tax liability (as at Dec 31, 05)	**6**	
Deferred tax liability (as at Dec 31, 04)	3	
Deferred tax expense 05	**3**	

Dec 31, 05	Dr	Deferred tax expense	3	
	Cr	Deferred tax liability		3

Solution (b)

Effects on the ***separate income statement***

	05	*04*
Fair value gain	11	7
Deferred tax expense	–3	–2
Profit for the year	**8**	**5**

Effects on the ***statement of changes in equity***[11]

Retained earnings		
Balance as at Jan 01, 04	–1	*Depreciation for 03 Change in retained earnings as at Jan 01, 04*[44]
Change in an accounting policy	3	
Adjusted balance as at Jan 01, 04	**2**	
Total comprehensive income	5	
Balance as at Dec 31, 04	**7**	
Total comprehensive income	8	
Balance as at Dec 31, 05	**15**	

[11] *Increase in the carrying amount of the building of CU 4 less deferred tax of CU 1.*

Effects on the ***statement of financial position***

It is important to note that the adjusted opening statement of financial position as at Jan 01, 04 also has to be presented (IAS 1.10(f) and 1.39).

Assets	*Dec 31, 05*	*Dec 31, 04*	*Jan 01, 04*	*Equity and liabilities*	*Dec 31, 05*	*Dec 31, 04*	*Jan 01, 04*
Building	61	50	43	Retained earnings	15	7	2
Cash	−40	−40	−40	Deferred tax liability	6	3	1
Total	**21**	**10**	**3**	**Total**	**21**	**10**	**3**

IAS 10 EVENTS AFTER THE REPORTING PERIOD

1 OVERVIEW

IAS 10 deals with the effects of events after the reporting period on an entity's financial statements (IAS 10.1–10.2). IAS 10 defines events after the reporting period as events that occur after an entity's reporting period, but before the date when the financial statements are authorized for issue. The **date that the financial statements are authorized for issue** is generally the date at which the financial statements are authorized and issued by management, either to the shareholders or to a supervisory board (made up solely of non-executives), if given. Even if the shareholders or a supervisory board are required to approve the financial statements, the date of authorization for issue is the date of authorization by management (IAS 10.5–10.6).[1] **Financial statements do not reflect events after the date when the financial statements were authorized for issue** (IAS 10.18).

It can be deduced from the information above that not all events after the reporting period are within the scope of IAS 10:[2]

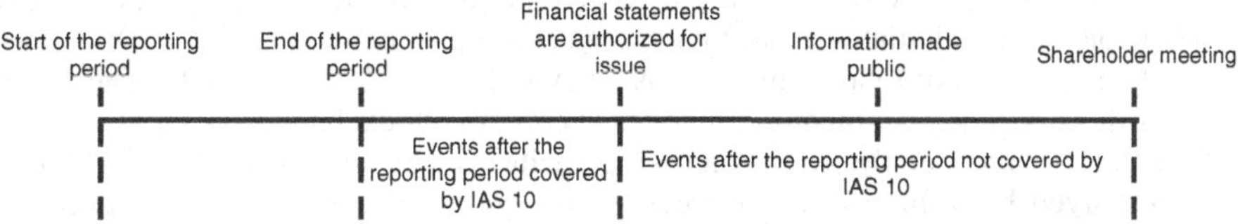

Events after the reporting period within the scope of IAS 10 can be subclassified as follows (IAS 10.3):

- **Adjusting events**: These events provide evidence of conditions that existed at the end of the reporting period (i.e. at the balance sheet date). Amounts recognized in the financial statements are adjusted in order to reflect adjusting events. It may also be necessary to recognize items that were not previously recognized or to update disclosures in the notes due to adjusting events (IAS 10.8–10.9 and 10.19–10.20).
- **Non-adjusting events**: These events are indicative of conditions that arose after the reporting period. Amounts recognized in the financial statements are not adjusted for such events (IAS 10.10). However, it is necessary to disclose the following for each material category of non-adjusting events after the reporting period (IAS 10.21):
  - The nature of the event.
  - An estimate of its financial effect or a statement that such an estimate cannot be made.

---

[1] *See KPMG,* Insights into IFRS, *5th edition, 2.9.15.20.*

[2] *See KPMG,* Insights into IFRS, *5th edition, 2.9.10.10.*

Examples of non-adjusting events after the reporting period that would generally result in disclosure are a major business combination, a disposal of a major subsidiary, and an announcement of a plan to discontinue an operation (IAS 10.22).

If an entity declares **dividends** after the reporting period (non-adjusting event), the entity must not recognize those dividends as a liability at the end of the reporting period because no obligation exists at that time (IAS 10.12–10.13).

The financial statements must not be prepared on a **going concern basis** if management determines in or after the reporting period either that it intends to liquidate the entity or to cease trading, or that it has no realistic alternative but to do so (IAS 10.14–10.15). This rule constitutes a departure from the general principles of IAS 10.

2 EXAMPLES WITH SOLUTIONS

Examples

1. Entity A was sued in 01. On Dec 31, 01, it is not clear whether the probability of conviction in the ongoing **trial** is more than 50%. Shortly after Dec 31, 01, A is convicted.
2. Entity B holds a **receivable** which is measured at amortized cost according to IFRS 9. Shortly after the reporting period, the debtor files for bankruptcy.[3]
3. In 01 and 02, Entity C carries out a **construction contract**. By Dec 31, 01, contract costs of CU 12 have been incurred. Total contract revenue is CU 30. The stage of completion is calculated according to the cost-to-cost method (IAS 11.30a). In Jan 02, the estimate of total contract costs is revised from CU 20 to CU 24. The reason for this revision is an increase in prices at commodity exchanges in Jan 02.
4. In Jan 02, **part of the manufacturing facilities and inventories** of entity D is **destroyed by a flood**. The damages are not covered by insurance. However, D's management expects that it will be possible to continue the business activities.
5. In Jan 02, the **entire manufacturing facilities and inventories** of entity E are **destroyed by a flood.** Because the damages are not covered by insurance, there is no realistic alternative for E but to cease its business activities.

Required

Illustrate the effects of the events after the reporting period (IAS 10.3) described above on the recognition and measurement in the financial statements of entities A–E as at Dec 31, 01.

[3] *If IFRS 9 and its consequential amendments were not applied early and if it is assumed that the receivable is classified into the category "loans and receivables" (IAS 39.9), the receivable would also be measured at amortized cost. In this case, the solution of the example is the same. This is because at the moment IFRS 9 still refers to the impairment requirements of IAS 39 (IFRS 9.5.2.2). Hence, financial assets measured at amortized cost according to IFRS 9 are subject to the same impairment rules as financial assets measured at amortized cost according to the old version of IAS 39 (i.e. according to the version of IAS 39 before any consequential amendments caused by IFRS 9).*

Solutions

1. The conviction after the reporting period sheds light on the fact that a present obligation existed as of Dec 31, 01. Hence, the conviction is an adjusting event. This means that A has to recognize a provision instead of merely disclosing a contingent liability (IAS 10.9(a) and IAS 37.15–37.16).
2. The fact that the debtor filed for bankruptcy shortly after the end of the reporting period indicates that he already had financial difficulties on Dec 31, 01. This means that B has received information about conditions (financial difficulties within the meaning of IAS 39.59) that existed at the end of the reporting period (adjusting event), indicating that recognition of an impairment loss is appropriate on Dec 31, 01. The amount of the loss is measured as the difference between the asset's carrying amount and the present value of the estimated future cash flows discounted at the financial asset's original effective interest rate (IAS 10.9(b)(i), IFRS 9.5.2.2, IAS 39.59 and 39.63).
3. The question is whether the stage of completion is (a) 60% (= CU 12 : CU 20) or (b) 50% (= CU 12 : CU 24). The reason for the adjustment to the estimate of the amount of total contract costs is an increase in prices at the commodities exchanges in Jan 02 (non-adjusting event). Therefore, the stage of completion in C's financial statements as at Dec 31, 01, is 60% (based on total contract costs of CU 20) and revenue of CU 18 (= CU 30 · 60%) has to be recognized in 01.
4. Since the flood occurred after Dec 31, 01, this represents a non-adjusting event. Thus, the amounts recognized in D's financial statements as at Dec 31, 01 are not adjusted for this event.
5. It is not entirely clear, whether IAS 10.14 and 10.15:
   (a) only refer to processes that began in the reporting period and continued after the reporting period (such as the deterioration in operating results and financial position mentioned in IAS 10.15), or
   (b) if they also refer to isolated events such as a flood which occurred after the reporting period all of a sudden.

   If opinion (b) is implemented, it is not entirely clear whether measurement should be based on the liquidation values of the destroyed assets or on those of the undamaged assets.

IAS 11 CONSTRUCTION CONTRACTS

1 INTRODUCTION

IAS 11 specifies the **accounting for construction contracts from the contractor's perspective** (IAS 11.1). A construction contract may be specifically negotiated for the construction of a **single asset** such as a bridge, building, dam, pipeline, road, ship or tunnel. However, a construction contract may also be specifically negotiated for the construction of a **number of assets** that are closely interrelated or interdependent in terms of their design, technology, and function or their ultimate purpose or use (e.g. the construction of a refinery) (IAS 11.3–11.4). The scope of IAS 11 also includes **construction contracts with a short duration** that are started in the reporting period and are completed after the reporting period.

Contracts for the construction of **real estate** meet the definition of a construction contract if the buyer is able to specify the major structural elements of the design of the real estate before construction begins and/or specify major structural changes once construction is in progress. If the definition of a construction contract is not met, IAS 18 applies instead of IAS 11 (IFRIC 15).

IAS 11 does not apply to **service contracts** (e.g. the specifically negotiated programming of software and the preparation of a tax return or of a legal opinion). However, the concept of IAS 18 for recognizing revenue and the associated expenses for transactions involving the rendering of services is generally consistent with the requirements of IAS 11 (IAS 18.21).

IAS 11 distinguishes between fixed price contracts and cost plus contracts (IAS 11.3):

- In the case of a **fixed price contract**, the contractor agrees to a fixed contract price or a fixed rate per unit of output (which in some cases is subject to cost escalation clauses).
- In the case of a **cost plus contract**, the contractor is reimbursed for allowable or otherwise defined costs, plus a percentage of these costs or a fixed fee.

According to IAS 11, contract revenue and the profit margin are generally recognized by reference to the **stage of completion** of the contract activity at the end of the reporting period. This means that profit is recognized on a continuing basis and is not deferred until the date of completion of the contract. This method is referred to as "**percentage of completion method**" or "PoC-method." This method is described in more detail in Section 4. In Sections 2 and 3, the concepts "contract revenue" and "contract costs" are defined.

2 CONTRACT REVENUE

Contract revenue comprises not only the **initial amount of revenue agreed** in the contract, but also (IAS 11.11–11.15):

- **variations in contract work** (i.e. a change in the scope of the work to be performed under the contract)
- **claims** (arising for example from a customer caused delay), and
- **incentive payments** (e.g. for early completion of the contract)

to the extent that it is probable that they will result in revenue and they are capable of being measured reliably.

Since the measurement of contract revenue is often affected by estimates, it may be necessary to revise these estimates from one period to the next. Such a change is accounted for as a **change in accounting estimate** according to IAS 8 (IAS 11.12 and 11.38).

3 CONTRACT COSTS

One component of contract costs comprises the costs that **relate directly to the contract**. Examples are site labor costs, costs of materials used in construction, and depreciation of plant and equipment used on the contract. Moreover, contract costs include costs that are **attributable to contract activity in general and can be allocated to the contract** (e.g. construction overheads) (IAS 11.16–11.18).

Abnormally high costs (e.g. abnormal amounts of wasted materials) and depreciation of **idle plant and equipment** that is not used on a particular contract are treated as part of the contract costs only if they relate directly to the contract (IAS 11.16a and 11.20d).

Contract costs also comprise such **other costs that are specifically chargeable to the customer** under the terms of the contract. These costs may include some general administration costs and development costs for which reimbursement is specified under the contract (IAS 11.16c and 11.19).

Selling costs do not constitute contract costs (IAS 11.20b).

Contract costs comprise the costs attributable to a contract **from the date of securing the contract to its final completion**. However, costs that relate directly to a contract and are incurred in **securing the contract** also constitute contract costs if they can be separately identified and measured reliably, and it is probable that the contract will be obtained. When costs incurred in securing a contract are recognized as an expense in the period in which they are incurred without the offsetting effect of revenues recognized, they must not be included in contract costs when the contract is obtained in a subsequent period (IAS 11.21).

A change in the estimate of contract costs is accounted for **in accordance with IAS 8** (IAS 11.38).

4 PERCENTAGE OF COMPLETION METHOD

4.1 Introduction

When the outcome of a construction contract can be **estimated reliably**, the **percentage of completion method** (PoC-method) is applied. When using this method, at first, the **stage of completion** is determined that reflects the completion progress of the contract at the end of the reporting period (IAS 11.22). For example, if an entity starts fulfilling a contract in the year 01 and performs one third of the contract in 01 (i.e. the stage of completion is 33.33% at the end of 01), one third of contract revenue, one third of the contract costs, and hence also one third of the profit margin are recognized in that period. Consequently, profit is recognized on a continuing basis and is not deferred until the date of completion of the contract.

4.2 Reliable Estimate of the Outcome of a Contract

The percentage of completion method is only applied if the outcome of the contract can be estimated reliably. This is the case if it is probable that the economic benefits associated with the contract will flow to the entity. Moreover, it is necessary that the contract costs attributable to the contract can be clearly identified and measured reliably. In the case of fixed price contracts it is necessary in addition that total contract revenue can be measured reliably and that both the contract costs to complete the contract and the stage of completion at the end of the reporting period can be measured reliably (IAS 11.22–11.24).

4.3 Determining the Stage of Completion

No specific method is prescribed for determining the stage of completion. An entity may use the more appropriate of **input measures** (consideration of the efforts devoted to a contract) or **output measures** (consideration of the results achieved) (IAS 11.30).[1]

The following methods are based on **input measures**:

- **Cost-to-cost method**: According to this method the stage of completion is calculated by dividing the contract costs incurred for work performed until the end of the reporting period by the estimated total contract costs (IAS 11.30a). Consequently (IAS 11.31):
  - Costs of materials or components that have been made specifically for the contract by the entity are included in the costs incurred until the end of the reporting period.
  - Standardized materials or components made by the entity (these have not been made specifically for the contract) are excluded when determining the costs incurred until the end of the reporting period. The same applies to purchased materials or components, irrespective of whether they are standardized. These materials or components are only included once they have been installed, used or applied during contract performance.
  - Payments made to subcontractors in advance of work performed under the subcontract are excluded when determining the costs incurred until the end of the reporting period.
- **Efforts-expended method**: According to this method the efforts incurred until the end of the reporting period are divided by the total efforts for performing the whole contract, whereby the efforts are not expressed in monetary units. Working hours may be used as a measure of other efforts expended (which makes sense in the case of labor-intensive activities) as well as machine hours (which makes sense in the case of capital-intensive activities).

[1] *See KPMG,* Insights into IFRS, *7th edition, 4.2.290.10.*

The following methods are based on **output measures**:

- **Physical proportions** of an entire object (e.g. whether, for instance, the bridge supports have already been constructed when building a bridge).
- **Stipulated milestones** of an entire object.
- **Units already produced** in the case of a sum of similar objects that are produced consecutively (e.g. 20 similar one-family houses).

The method applied by the entity has to result in a reliable measurement of the work already performed (IAS 11.30). The application of **methods other than the cost-to-cost method** is only appropriate if there is **approximately a linear relation** between the costs and the physical measure or if such a relation can be established via weighting factors. If the stage of completion is not determined according to the cost-to-cost method, the expenses recognized are adjusted to the stage of completion (IAS 11.22).

4.4 Recognition of Expected Losses

When it is probable that total contract costs will exceed total contract revenue, the **expected loss** has to be **recognized as an expense immediately** (IAS 11.22 and 11.36). In this case, at first, the contract costs and the contract revenue are recognized according to the stage of completion at the end of the reporting period. This leads to the recognition of that part of the loss that corresponds to the stage of completion. However, in addition, it is necessary to recognize the loss attributable to future periods (future loss) as an expense at the current balance sheet date. The amount of the loss is determined irrespective of whether work has commenced on the contract (IAS 11.37a).

4.5 Uncertainties in Collectibility

The outcome of a construction contract can only be estimated reliably when it is probable that the entity will receive the economic benefits associated with the contract. When uncertainty arises about the collectibility of an amount already recognized as revenue, the uncollectible amount or the amount that will probably not be recovered is recognized **as an expense rather than as an adjustment of contract revenue** (IAS 11.23b, 11.24a, and 11.28). Impairment losses and reversals of impairment losses with regard to **progress billings** (IAS 11.41) that have not yet been paid are treated according to IAS 39.[2]

4.6 Presentation and Disclosure

It is necessary to distinguish between advances and progress billings (IAS 11.41):

- **Advances** are amounts received by the contractor before the related work is performed.
- **Progress billings** are amounts billed for work performed on a contract whether or not they have been paid by the customer.

---

[2] *IFRS 9 did not yet replace the impairment requirements of IAS 39. Consequently, the same procedure applies with regard to impairment losses and reversals of impairment losses whether or not IFRS 9 and its consequential amendments are applied early (IFRS 9.5.2.2).*

The following amounts are compared for each contract (IAS 11.42–11.44):

(a) The costs incurred plus recognized profits less recognized losses.
(b) The total of the progress billings.

If (a) exceeds (b), the net amount is included in the "**gross amount due *from* customers** for contract work." If (b) exceeds (a), the net amount is included in the "**gross amount due *to* customers** for contract work." The amounts due from customers **must not be offset** with the amounts due to customers. Advances are not taken into account in the previous calculation. Instead, they are recognized as liabilities.

Gross amounts due from customers are generally presented as receivables and not as inventories. Gross amounts due to customers and advances represent liabilities.

Contract costs that relate to future activity on the contract are recognized as an asset, if it is probable that they will be recovered (IAS 11.27). Such costs are included in determining the gross amount due from or due to customers (IAS 11IE). However, they are not taken into account in determining the stage of completion. Gross amounts due from customers that result from such costs represent inventories and not receivables (IAS 11.27, 11.31a, and 11.IE). This procedure applies when the stage of completion is calculated according to the cost-to-cost method.

In the statement of comprehensive income, the expenses are generally presented as **cost of sales** when the **function of expense method** (= **cost of sales method**) (IAS 1.99 and 1.103) is applied.

5 WHEN THE OUTCOME OF A CONTRACT CANNOT BE ESTIMATED RELIABLY

If it is not possible to estimate the outcome of a construction contract reliably (IAS 11.32–11.34):

- the contract costs are recognized as an expense in the period in which they are incurred,
- revenue is recognized only to the extent of contract costs incurred for which recovery is probable, and
- no profit is recognized.

When it is probable that total contract costs will exceed total contract revenue, the expected loss has to be recognized as an expense immediately irrespective of whether work has commenced on the contract (IAS 11.32, 11.36, and 11.37a). This means that also the loss attributable to future periods (future loss) has to be recognized as an expense at the current balance sheet date.

6 EXAMPLES WITH SOLUTIONS

Example 1

Contract with progress billings and an advance

On Jan 01, 01, entity E concludes a fixed price contract. Total contract revenue is CU 120. The total contract costs of CU 90 will be incurred in thirds in each of the years 01–03. At the end of 01, E bills an amount of CU 35 to its customer, which is paid on Jan 15, 02. In 02, an amount of CU 45 is billed to the customer, which is paid promptly. Moreover, on Dec 31, 02, the customer pays an advance of CU 20 for work, which is performed in 03. The billing for the remaining amount of CU 20 that is still outstanding on Dec 31, 03 is effected at the beginning of 04.

Required

Prepare any necessary entries in E's financial statements as at Dec 31 for the years 01–03. The stage of completion is determined according to the cost-to-cost method (IAS 11.30a). E prepares its separate income statement in accordance with the function of expense method (= cost of sales method).

Hints for solution

In particular Sections 4.3 and 4.6.

Solution

Year 01

Year 01	Dr	Cost of sales	30	
	Cr	Cash		30
Dec 31, 01	Dr	Receivables arising from progress billings	35	
	Dr	Gross amounts due from customers	5	
	Cr	Revenue		40

The gross amount due from the customer is calculated by adding the recognized profit of CU 10 (= revenue of CU 40 – expenses of CU 30) to the costs incurred (CU 30) and deducting the billing of CU 35 (IAS 11.43).

Year 02

Jan 15, 02	Dr	Cash	35	
	Cr	Receivables arising from progress billings		35
Year 02	Dr	Cost of sales	30	
	Cr	Cash		30
Dec 31, 02	Dr	Cash	45	
	Cr	Revenue		40
	Cr	Gross amounts due from customers		5
Dec 31, 02	Dr	Cash	20	
	Cr	Liabilities arising from advances		20

In 02 revenue of CU 40 is recognized. This amount reflects the change in the stage of completion (CU 40 = CU 120 · 1/3).

The gross amount due from the customer as at Dec 31, 02 is calculated as follows (IAS 11.43):

Costs incurred in 01 and 02	60
Profits recognized in 01 and 02	20
Progress billings in 01 and 02 (CU 35 + CU 45)	−80
= Gross amount due from the customer	**0**

Hence, the gross amount due from the customer has to be reduced from CU 5 (carrying amount as at Dec 31, 01) to zero. The advance is recognized as a liability and is not taken into account in determining the gross amount due from the customer (IAS 11.43).

Year 03

Year 03	Dr	Cost of sales	30	
	Cr	Cash		30
Dec 31, 03	Dr	Gross amounts due from customers	20	
	Dr	Liabilities arising from advances	20	
	Cr	Revenue		40

On Dec 31, 03, the liability arising from the advance is derecognized because the work for this payment has already been performed in 03.

Example 2

Expected loss on a contract with progress billings

On Jan 01, 01, entity E concludes a fixed price contract. Total contract revenue is CU 180. When E prepares its financial statements as at Dec 31, 01, the estimate of total contract costs is CU 160 which are estimated to be incurred in fourths in each of the years 01–04.

However, in 02 contract costs of CU 70 are ultimately incurred. On the basis of a new estimate, E expects that contract costs of CU 50 will be incurred in 03 and that contract costs of CU 40 will be incurred in 04. Consequently, total contracts will be CU 200.

At the end of 02 there is a progress billing in the amount of CU 80. This amount is paid by the customer on Jan 15, 03.

The billing for the remaining amount of CU 100, which is still outstanding on Dec 31, 04, is effected at the beginning of 05.

Required

Prepare any necessary entries in E's financial statements as at Dec 31 for the years 01–04. The stage of completion is determined according to the cost-to-cost method (IAS 11.30a). E prepares its separate income statement in accordance with the function of expense method (= cost of sales method).

Hints for solution

In particular Sections 4.3, 4.4, and 4.6.

Solution

Year 01

Year 01	Dr	Cost of sales	40	
	Cr	Cash		40
Dec 31, 01	Dr	Gross amounts due from customers	45	
	Cr	Revenue		45

Year 02

Year 02	Dr	Cost of sales	70	
	Cr	Cash		70

Revenue to be recognized in 02:

On Dec 31, 02, the stage of completion is 55% (= contract costs incurred in 01 and 02 of CU 110 : total contract costs of CU 200). Hence, cumulative contract revenue to be recognized in 01 and 02 is CU 99 (= 55% · CU 180). Because contract revenue of CU 45 was recognized in 01, contract revenue of CU 54 has to be recognized in 02.

Loss to be recognized in 02:

In 01 and 02, contract revenue of CU 99 and contract costs of CU 110 are recognized. Hence, a cumulative loss of CU 11 is automatically recognized in 01 and 02, which can also be calculated as follows:

Total contract revenue	180
Total contract costs	–200
Total loss on the contract	**–20**
Stage of completion as at Dec 31, 02	55%
Loss for the years 01 and 02 determined according to the stage of completion (= –20 · 55%)	**–11**

The loss of CU 11 consists of the profit of CU 5 recognized in 01 (= CU 45 – CU 40) and of the loss of CU 16 that is recognized in 02 (= CU 54 – CU 70). The amount of CU 16 represents:

- a loss of CU 11 that has to be recognized in 02 according to the stage of completion, and in addition
- the reversal of the profit of CU 5 recognized in 01.

The total loss on the contract is CU 20 (= total contract revenue of CU 180 – total contract costs of CU 200). By Dec 31, 02, only a loss of CU 11 would be recognized according to the stage of completion. However, the standard requires the total loss on the contract to be recognized immediately *as an expense* (IAS 11.22 and 11.36). Hence, in 02 also the future loss on the contract of CU 9 [= CU 20 – CU 11 *or* CU 20 · (100% – 55%)] has to be recognized.

Gross amount due from the customer (IAS 11.43):

Costs incurred in 01 and 02	110
Total loss to be recognized in 01 and 02 (see above)	–20
Progress billing in 02	–80
Gross amount due from the customer as at Dec 31, 02	**10**
Gross amount due from the customer as at Dec 31, 01	45
Reduction	**35**

Dec 31, 02	Dr	Other expenses (future loss)	9	
	Dr	Receivables from progress billings	80	
	Cr	Gross amounts due from customers		35
	Cr	Revenue		54

Years 03 and 04

Revenue to be recognized:

On Dec 31, 03, the stage of completion is 80% (= CU 160 : CU 200). Hence, cumulative contract revenue for the years 01–03 is CU 144 (= 80% · CU 180). Cumulative contract revenue for 01 and 02 is CU 99. This means that contract revenue of CU 45 has to be recognized in 03 (= CU 144 – CU 99) and contract revenue of CU 36 has to be recognized in 04 (= CU 180 – CU 144).

Reversing the future loss of CU 9 recognized as an expense in 02:

The total loss on the contract of CU 20 (which includes the loss of CU 9 attributable to the years 03 and 04) has already been recognized in 01 and 02. Consequently, no further loss is recognized in 03 and 04. However, in 03, recognition of the contract costs of CU 50 and of the contract revenue of CU 45 would result in the recognition of an additional loss of CU 5 [= (80% – 55%) · CU 20]. Similarly, in 04 recognition of the contract costs of CU 40 and of the contract revenue of CU 36 would result in the recognition of an additional loss of CU 4 [= (100% – 80%) · CU 20]. According to that procedure, the loss of CU 9 that has already been recognized as other expense in 02 would be recognized once again. In order to avoid this effect the amounts of CU 5 and CU 4 are recognized as other income in 03 and 04, respectively.

Gross amounts due from the customer (IAS 11.43):

Costs incurred in the years 01–03	160
Total loss recognized in the years 01–03 (see above)	–20
Progress billing in 02	–80
Gross amount due from the customer as at Dec 31, 03	**60**
Gross amount due from the customer as at Dec 31, 02	10
Increase	**50**

Costs incurred in the years 01–04	200
Total loss recognized in the years 01–04 (see above)	–20
Progress billing in 02	–80
Gross amount due from the customer as at Dec 31, 04	**100**
Gross amount due from the customer as at Dec 31, 03	60
Increase	**40**

The gross amount due from the customer as at Dec 31, 04 corresponds with the contract revenue which has not been billed until Dec 31, 04 (CU 180 less the billing in 02 of CU 80).

Jan 15, 03	Dr	Cash	80	
	Cr	Receivables from progress billings		80
Year 03	Dr	Cost of sales	50	
	Cr	Cash		50
Dec 31, 03	Dr	Gross amounts due from customers	50	
	Cr	Other income		5
	Cr	Revenue		45

Year 04	Dr	Cost of sales	40	
	Cr	Cash		40
Dec 31, 04	Dr	Gross amounts due from customers	40	
	Cr	Other income		4
	Cr	Revenue		36

Example 3

Uncertainties about collectibility

Year 01

On Jan 01, 01, entity E concludes a fixed price contract. Under this contract, E constructs a special-purpose machine for customer C according to C's specifications. Total contract revenue is CU 39. The total contract costs of CU 30 will be incurred in thirds in each of the years 01–03. It is agreed that the billing for the whole price will be effected at the beginning of 04. When E prepares its financial statements as at Dec 31, 01, C has a high degree of creditworthiness.

Years 02 and 03

In 02, C's creditworthiness declines dramatically. At the end of Dec 02, E expects that it will not receive any part of the agreed price. Since E is entitled to stop performing the contract in such cases, construction of the machine is stopped. However, E negotiates with C about continuing construction because two thirds of the contract costs have already been incurred and there are no other customers who would need the machine.

Finally, it is agreed that construction will be continued. However, the price is reduced from CU 39 to CU 30. C provides a top bank guarantee for this payment. This agreement is achieved after E has authorized its financial statements as at Dec 31, 02 for issue.

Required

(a) Prepare any necessary entries in E's financial statements as at Dec 31 for the years 01–03. The stage of completion is determined according to the cost-to-cost method (IAS 11.30a). E prepares its separate income statement in accordance with the function of expense method (= cost of sales method).
(b) Presume alternatively to (a) that the agreement to continue construction is achieved before E's financial statements as at Dec 31, 02 are authorized for issue. Describe how the solution of (b) differs from the solution of (a).
(c) Presume alternatively to (a) that on May 01, 02 an amount of CU 13 is billed for work performed in 01, as stipulated. Due to the problems relating to C's creditworthiness, payment of this amount is deferred until the beginning of 04.

Hints for solution

In particular Sections 4.3, 4.5, 4.6, and 5.

Solution (a)

Year 01

Year 01	Dr	Cost of sales	10	
	Cr	Cash		10

On Dec 31, 01, it is probable that the economic benefits associated with the contract will flow to E (IAS 11.23b) because there are no uncertainties about collectibility. Consequently, all the criteria for the application of the PoC-method are met in this example (IAS 11.23). Consequently, revenue of CU 13 (= CU 39 · 1/3), costs of CU 10 (= CU 30 · 1/3), and a profit of CU 3 are recognized. The gross amount due from the customer is CU 13 (= costs incurred of CU 10 + recognized profit of CU 3) (IAS 11.43).

Dec 31, 01	Dr	Gross amounts due from customers	13	
	Cr	Revenue		13

Year 02

E expects that it will not receive any part of the agreed price. Consequently, it is *not* probable any more that the economic benefits associated with the contract will flow to E, which means that the PoC-method cannot be applied (IAS 11.22–11.23). Hence, revenue is recognized only to the extent of contract costs incurred for which recovery is probable (IAS 11.32). Since no costs are expected to be recoverable, only the costs are recognized, but no revenue.

Year 02	Dr	Cost of sales	10	
	Cr	Cash		10

The amount of CU 13 already recognized as contract revenue in 01 for which recovery has ceased to be probable is recognized as an expense rather than as an adjustment of the amount of contract revenue (IAS 11.28):

Dec 31, 02	Dr	Other expenses	13	
	Cr	Gross amounts due from customers		13

In summary, in 02 a loss of CU 23 is recognized (= cost of sales of CU 10 + other expenses of CU 13). This means that in 02, also the profit of CU 3 (= CU 13 – CU 10) recognized in 01 is reversed.

Year 03

Year 03	Dr	Cost of sales	10	
	Cr	Cash		10

Due to the agreement to continue construction under which C provides the top bank guarantee, the outcome of the contract can be estimated reliably again meaning the PoC-method is applied (IAS 11.22–11.23).

Total contract revenue is CU 30. This means that in the years 01–03, revenue of CU 30 has to be recognized in total. Up to now, only revenue of CU 13 has been recognized (CU 13 in 01 and zero in 02). Hence, the remaining amount of CU 17 is recognized in 03:

Dec 31, 03	Dr	Gross amounts due from customers	17	
	Cr	Revenue		17

Also, the effect of the other expenses of CU 13, recognized in 02, is reversed:

Dec 31, 03	Dr	Gross amounts due from customers	13	
	Cr	Other income		13

After these entries, the gross amount due from the customer is correctly CU 30:

Costs incurred in the years 01–03	30
Total loss/total profit	0
Gross amount due from the customer as at Dec 31, 03	**30**

Separate income statements[3]

	01	*02*	*03*
Revenue	13	0	17
Cost of sales	−10	−10	−10
Gross profit	**3**	**−10**	**7**
Other expenses		−13	
Other income			13
Profit or loss	**3**	**−23**	**20**

Solution (b)

In this case, it is presumed alternatively to (a) that the continuation of construction (including the provision of the top bank guarantee) is agreed before E's financial statements as at Dec 31, 02 are authorized for issue. Consequently, it has to be assessed whether this constitutes an adjusting or a non-adjusting event after the reporting period.[4] Regarding the distinction it is crucial whether an event provides evidence of conditions that existed at the end of the reporting period or whether it is indicative of conditions that arose after the reporting period (IAS 10.3). The bank guarantee is obtained after Dec 31, 02. Thus, the receipt of the guarantee is a non-adjusting event. Consequently, the solutions of (a) and (b) are the same.

Solution (c)

Year 01

Year 01	Dr	Cost of sales	10	
	Cr	Cash		10
Dec 31, 01	Dr	Gross amounts due from customers	13	
	Cr	Revenue		13

[3] *For simplification purposes, the exact presentation requirements of IAS 1 are ignored in this example.*
[4] *See the chapter on IAS 10.*

Year 02

As in version (a), in 02, only the costs are recognized but no revenue.

Year 02	Dr	Cost of sales	10	
	Cr	Cash		10

On May 01, 02, there is a progress billing in the amount of CU 13. Therefore, this amount does not represent a gross amount due from the customer, any more (IAS 11.43).

May 01, 02	Dr	Receivables arising from progress billings	13	
	Cr	Gross amounts due from customers		13

In contrast to gross amounts due from customers, receivables arising from progress billings are subject to the impairment rules of IAS 39 (IFRS 9.5.2.2):[5]

Dec 31, 02	Dr	Impairment loss (IAS 39)	13	
	Cr	Receivables arising from progress billings		13

Year 03

Year 03	Dr	Cost of sales	10	
	Cr	Cash		10
Dec 31, 03	Dr	Gross amounts due from customers	17	
	Cr	Revenue		17

The impairment loss recognized in 02 relating to the receivable from the progress billing is reversed (IAS 39.65):

Dec 31, 03	Dr	Receivables arising from progress billings	13	
	Cr	Reversals of impairment losses (IAS 39)		13

Example 4[6]

Cost-to-cost method: specific topics

Entity E constructs both standard and customized solar panels. The latter are constructed specifically for a particular contract. The solar panels are used as part of the façade of buildings and are installed at the building site of the customer, ready-to-use.

[5] *IFRS 9 did not yet replace the impairment requirements of IAS 39. Consequently, the same procedure applies with regard to impairment losses and reversals of impairment losses whether or not IFRS 9 and its consequential amendments are applied early (IFRS 9.5.2.2).*

[6] *See Lüdenbach, PiR 2005, p. 111–112 with regard to this example. PiR (= Praxis der internationalen Rechnungslegung) is a practice-oriented IFRS journal, which is published in the German language.*

In 01, E receives orders A and B (among others). Contract A requires customized solar panels, whereas standard solar panels are needed in respect of contract B. Both contracts are fixed price contracts with contract revenue of CU 1,100 and contract costs of CU 1,000 for each contract. In the case of both contracts, all of the solar panels have been delivered to the respective contract site by Dec 31, 01. However, only 20% of them have been installed by Dec 31, 01.

In the case of contract A (B), the costs of constructing the solar panels are CU 800 (CU 600) and the costs of the installation of the solar panels are CU 200 (CU 400).
The remaining solar panels are installed in 02. After the completion of both contracts in June 02, the billing is effected.

Posting status (contract A):

Year 01	Dr	Cost of sales	840	
	Cr	Cash		840
Year 02	Dr	Cost of sales	160	
	Cr	Cash		160

Posting status (contract B):

Year 01	Dr	Cost of sales	680	
	Cr	Cash		680
Year 02	Dr	Cost of sales	320	
	Cr	Cash		320

Required

Prepare any necessary entries in E's financial statements as at Dec 31 for the years 01 and 02. The stage of completion is determined according to the cost-to-cost method (IAS 11.30a). E prepares its separate income statement in accordance with the function of expense method (= cost of sales method).

Hints for solution

In particular Sections 4.3 and 4.6.

Solution – contract A

When determining the stage of completion, the costs of the customized solar panels are included in the costs incurred until the end of 01, irrespective of whether they have been installed. This is because these solar panels have been made by E specifically for the contract (IAS 11.31a).

Costs of the construction of the solar panels	800
Costs of the installation of the solar panels (= 20% of CU 200)	40
Contract costs incurred until Dec 31, 01	**840**
Total contract costs	1,000
Stage of completion	**84%**
Total contract revenue	1,100
Contract revenue in 01	**924**

Dec 31, 01	Dr	Gross amounts due from customers	924	
	Cr	Revenue		924
Jun 02	Dr	Receivables from progress billings	1,100	
	Cr	Gross amounts due from customers		924
	Cr	Revenue		176

Solution – contract B

The standard solar panels constructed by E are only taken into account in determining the stage of completion to the point that they have already been installed (IAS 11.31a).[7]

Costs of the construction of the solar panels (= 20% of CU 600)	120
Costs of the installation of the solar panels (= 20% of CU 400)	80
Contract costs incurred until Dec 31, 01	**200**
Total contract costs	1,000
Stage of completion	**20%**
Total contract revenue	1,100
Contract revenue in 01	**220**

Dec 31, 01	Dr	Gross amounts due from customers	220	
	Cr	Revenue		220

The standard solar panels that have been delivered to the contract site but have not yet been installed (80% of CU 600 = CU 480) are recognized as an asset (under the presumption that it is probable that they will be recovered) (IAS 11.27). The costs of the standard solar panels are included in determining the gross amount due from the customer (IAS 11.27 and 11.IE), but are presented as inventories and not as a receivable in E's statement of financial position. They are not included in determining the stage of completion. Since they are recognized as an asset, the costs of sales are reduced by the same amount:

Dec 31, 01	Dr	Gross amounts due from customers	480	
	Cr	Cost of sales		480
Jun 02	Dr	Receivables from progress billings	1,100	
	Cr	Gross amounts due from customers		220
	Cr	Revenue		880
Jun 02	Dr	Cost of sales	480	
	Cr	Gross amounts due from customers		480

[7] *If E had purchased solar panels from a third party they would have to be treated in the same way irrespective of the degree of their standardization (IAS 11.31a).*

Example 5

Output measures

(a) In 01, entity E agrees on a fixed price contract to program customized software. The contract defines 100 features of the software. By the end of 01, 80% of these features have been programmed. Thus, E intends to recognize 80% of the contract revenue in its separate income statement and only recognize the costs (primarily salaries for the year 01) actually incurred. Programming for the remaining 20% of the features will take approximately as many hours as were necessary for the 80% already completed. It is presumed that the same hourly rate applies to the employees involved in programming.
(b) In 01, entity F concludes a fixed price contract to construct 10 miles of a highway. For these 10 miles of the highway no bridges or tunnels are necessary. Consequently, the same costs will be incurred approximately for constructing each of the 10 miles. By the end of 01, three miles of the highway have been built.
(c) In 01, entity G closes a fixed price contract to build a railroad tunnel that will have a length of five miles. By the end of 01, two miles of the tunnel have been built. G wants to recognize contract revenue on the basis of a stage of completion of 40% in its separate income statement (= two miles : five miles). The first two miles represent the part of the tunnel for which the construction requires the lowest amount of time per mile.

Required

Assess whether determining the stage of completion by means of output measures is possible according to IAS 11 in the situations described above.

Hints for solution

In particular Section 4.3.

Solution

(a) IAS 11 does not apply to service contracts like the specifically negotiated programming of software. However, in this case, the same considerations apply according to IAS 18. It is not possible to use a stage of completion of 80% based on the output measure (features) because there is no approximate linear relation between the costs and the output measure. Instead, the stage of completion is 50%.
(b) Since there is an approximately linear relation between the costs and the output measure (miles), it is possible to use a stage of completion of 30% based on the output measure (= three miles : 10 miles).
(c) Since there is no approximately linear relation between costs and the output measure (miles) it is not possible to use a stage of completion of 40% based on the output measure (= two miles : five miles).

IAS 12 INCOME TAXES

1 INTRODUCTION

The objective of IAS 12 is to prescribe the accounting treatment for income taxes. Income taxes include all domestic and foreign taxes which are based on taxable profits and also include taxes, such as withholding taxes, which are payable by a subsidiary, joint venture or associate on distributions to the reporting entity (IAS 12.2).

This chapter consists of two main areas:

- Accounting treatment of **current tax**, which is the amount of income taxes payable with respect to the taxable profit for the current period (see Section 2).
- Accounting treatment of **deferred tax**, i.e. of future tax advantages and disadvantages (see Section 3).

2 CURRENT TAX

The entity calculates the amount of current tax payable on the basis of taxable profit for the period (taxable profit · tax rate = current tax payable). Current tax for current and prior periods is, to the extent unpaid, recognized as a liability. If the amount already paid relating to current and prior periods exceeds the amount due for those periods, the excess is recognized as an asset (IAS 12.12).

Current tax liabilities (current tax assets) are measured at the amount expected to be paid to (recovered from) the taxation authorities on the basis of the tax rates (and tax laws) that have been enacted or substantively enacted by the end of the reporting period (IAS 12.46).

Current tax is **normally** recognized in **profit or loss**. However, to the extent that the tax arises from a transaction or event that is recognized outside profit or loss, i.e. either in **other comprehensive income** or **directly in equity**, the relating tax is recognized in the same way. Moreover, if the tax arises from a **business combination**, it is neither recognized in profit or loss, nor in other comprehensive income (IAS 12.58 and 12.61A).[1]

Current tax assets and current tax liabilities have to be **offset** if the entity has a legally enforceable right to set off the recognized amounts and intends either to settle on a net basis or to realize the asset and settle the liability simultaneously (IAS 12.71–12.73).

3 DEFERRED TAX

3.1 The Logic Behind Recognizing Deferred Tax

The recognition of deferred tax in the statement of financial position may be necessary with respect to temporary differences, the carryforward of unused tax losses, and the carryforward of unused tax credits.

---

[1] *See the chapter on IFRS 3 regarding business combinations.*

Temporary differences are differences between the carrying amount of an item for tax purposes (its tax base) and its carrying amount according to IFRS which will result in future tax advantages or disadvantages for the entity. Temporary differences resulting in future tax advantages are referred to as "**deductible temporary differences**," whereas those resulting in future tax disadvantages are called "**taxable temporary differences**" (IAS 12.5). Temporary differences that meet the recognition criteria[2] are multiplied by the tax rate and recognized as a deferred tax asset (if the difference represents a future tax advantage) or as a deferred tax liability (if the difference represents a future tax disadvantage).

Conceptionally, there is the presumption that the carrying amount for tax purposes will increase or decrease to the carrying amount according to IFRS in the future. It is assumed that the difference between these carrying amounts will affect taxable profit when the carrying amount of the asset or liability is recovered or settled. Assume that the carrying amount of a piece of land is CU 10 according to IFRS and CU 8 for tax purposes. A fictitious sale of the land for CU 10 (i.e. at the carrying amount according to IFRS) would result in a gain of CU 2 under the applicable tax law. Hence, the entity's taxable profit would increase by CU 2 and (assuming that the tax rate is 25%) current tax payable would increase by CU 0.5. This means that a sale in a future period would result in a tax disadvantage of CU 0.5 for the entity. Consequently, the entity recognizes this disadvantage of CU 0.5 as a deferred tax liability.

In practice, it would be time-consuming to perform a detailed analysis for each asset or liability as in the example above. Instead, application of a simplified rule is recommendable. An example is the "**poorer-richer-rule**" (poorer in the statement of financial position according to IFRS = asset; richer in the statement of financial position according to IFRS = liability), which is illustrated in the table below:

	Carrying amount according to IFRS	*Carrying amount for tax purposes*	*Assessment*
Asset A	10	8	In its financial statements according to IFRS, the entity is **richer** than according to the applicable tax law (because the asset's carrying amount is higher under IFRS). This means that the entity recognizes a deferred tax **liability**.
Asset B	8	10	In its financial statements according to IFRS, the entity is **poorer** than according to the applicable tax law (because the asset's carrying amount is lower under IFRS). This means that the entity recognizes a deferred tax **asset**.
Liability C	10	8	In its financial statements according to IFRS, the entity is **poorer** than according to the applicable tax law (because the liability's carrying amount is higher under IFRS). This means that the entity recognizes a deferred tax **asset**.
Liability D	8	10	In its financial statements according to IFRS, the entity is **richer** than according to the applicable tax law (because the liability's carrying amount is lower under IFRS). This means that the entity recognizes a deferred tax **liability**.

[2] *See Section 3.2.*

In the table previously the differences between the carrying amounts have to be multiplied by the tax rate. This results in the carrying amount of the deferred tax liability or deferred tax asset. It is important to note that recognition of deferred tax assets and deferred tax liabilities in the statement of financial position requires that the recognition criteria (see below) are met.

3.2 Recognition Criteria

3.2.1 Taxable Temporary Differences Taxable temporary differences give rise to the recognition of a deferred tax liability. An important exception to this rule relates to goodwill. Deferred tax liabilities arising from the **initial recognition of goodwill** must not be recognized in the statement of financial position (IAS 12.15 and 12.21–12.21B).

3.2.2 Deductible Temporary Differences A future tax advantage in the form of reductions in tax payments will flow to the entity only if it earns sufficient taxable profits against which the deductions can be offset (IAS 12.27). Hence, the Standard requires (with some exceptions) recognition of a deferred tax asset for all deductible temporary differences to the extent that it is **probable** that **taxable profit will be available** against which the deductible temporary difference can be utilized (IAS 12.24).

This criterion is met when there are **sufficient taxable temporary differences** relating to the same taxation authority and the same taxable entity which are expected to reverse (IAS 12.28)

- in the same period as the expected reversal of the deductible temporary difference, **or**
- in periods into which a tax loss arising from the deferred tax asset can be carried forward or back.

When there are **insufficient taxable temporary differences**, the deferred tax asset is recognized to the extent that (IAS 12.29):

- it is probable that the entity will have sufficient taxable profit relating to the same taxation authority and the same taxable entity in the same period as the reversal of the deductible temporary difference (or in the periods into which a tax loss arising from the deferred tax asset can be carried forward or back),[3] **or**
- tax planning opportunities are available to the entity that will create taxable profit in appropriate periods (e.g. generating disposal gains on assets for tax purposes in a particular jurisdiction by sale and leaseback).

The existence of a **history of recent losses** is strong evidence that future taxable profit may not be available (IAS 12.31 and 12.35–12.36).

If the carrying amount of **goodwill** arising in a business combination is less than the amount that will be deductible for tax purposes with respect to goodwill, the difference gives rise to a deferred tax asset. The deferred tax asset arising from the initial recognition of goodwill is

[3] *Within the frame of this evaluation, taxable amounts arising from deductible temporary differences that are expected to originate in future periods are ignored because the deferred tax asset arising from these deductible temporary differences will itself require future taxable profit in order to be utilized (IAS 12.29).*

recognized as part of the accounting for a business combination to the extent that it is probable that taxable profit will be available against which the deductible temporary difference could be utilized (IAS 12.32A).

3.2.3 Unused Tax Losses and Unused Tax Credits The recognition criteria for deferred tax assets arising from the carryforward of unused tax losses and tax credits **are the same** as those for deferred tax assets arising from deductible temporary differences (IAS 12.35).

3.2.4 Reassessment of Unrecognized Deferred Tax Assets At the end of each reporting period, it is reassessed whether previously unrecognized deferred tax assets currently meet the recognition criteria. They are recognized to the extent that the recognition criteria are met, at the current balance sheet date. Examples of events that may result in such recognition in hindsight are a business combination or an improvement in trading conditions (IAS 12.37).

3.2.5 Outside Basis Differences vs. Inside Basis Differences When a subsidiary, a jointly controlled entity or an associate is consolidated, proportionately consolidated or accounted for using the equity method, deferred tax is systematized as follows:

- **Inside basis differences I**: Differences between the carrying amounts of the investee's assets and liabilities according to IFRS and for tax purposes in the investee's statement of financial position.
- **Inside basis differences II**: Fair value adjustments initially arising on consolidation, proportionate consolidation or application of the equity method, which are not recognized according to the applicable tax law.
- **Outside basis difference**: A difference between the investment's carrying amount determined according to the equity method, consolidation or proportionate consolidation and its carrying amount for tax purposes.

A deferred tax liability is recognized for all **taxable temporary outside basis differences** except to the extent that both of the following criteria are met (IAS 12.39):

(a) The parent, venturer or investor is able to control the timing of the reversal of the temporary difference.
(b) It is probable that the temporary difference will not reverse in the foreseeable future.

A deferred tax asset is recognized for all **deductible temporary outside basis differences** to the extent that it is probable that both of the following criteria are met (IAS 12.44):

(a) The temporary difference will reverse in the foreseeable future.
(b) Taxable profit will be available against which the temporary difference can be utilized.

3.3 Measurement

3.3.1 Applicable Tax Rates and Tax Laws The measurement of deferred tax assets and liabilities is usually based on the tax rates and tax laws that have been enacted or substantively enacted by the end of the reporting period (IAS 12.47).

3.3.2 Manner of Recovery or Settlement of the Carrying Amount of an Asset or a Liability In some jurisdictions, the manner in which an entity recovers (settles) the carrying amount of an asset (liability) may affect either or both of the following (IAS 12.51A):

- Tax rate applicable on recovery (settlement).
- Carrying amount of the asset (liability) for tax purposes.

In such cases, the deferred tax liabilities and deferred tax assets are measured using the tax rate and the tax base that are consistent with the expected manner of recovery or settlement (IAS 12.51–12.51A).

3.3.3 Prohibition of Discounting The Standard prohibits discounting of deferred tax liabilities and assets (IAS 12.53).

3.3.4 Impairment and Reversal of Impairment The carrying amount of a deferred tax asset has to be reviewed at the end of each reporting period. The carrying amount of a deferred tax asset is reduced to the extent that it is no longer probable that sufficient taxable profit will be available to allow the benefit of part or all of that deferred tax asset to be utilized (**"impairment"**). Any such reduction is reversed to the extent that it becomes probable that sufficient taxable profit will be available (**reversal of "impairment"**) (IAS 12.56).

3.4 Presentation

Deferred tax is recognized in **profit or loss**. However, there are exceptions to this rule (IAS 12.58 and 12.61A):

- Deferred tax is recognized in **other comprehensive income** if it relates to an item recognized in other comprehensive income.
- Deferred tax is recognized **directly in equity**, if it relates to an item recognized directly in equity.
- Moreover, if the deferred tax arises as part of the initial accounting of a **business combination** at acquisition date, it is neither recognized in profit or loss, nor in other comprehensive income.[4]

Deferred tax assets and deferred tax liabilities have to be **offset**, if both of the following criteria are met (IAS 12.74):

(a) The entity has a legally enforceable right to set off current tax assets against current tax liabilities.
(b) The deferred tax liabilities and the deferred tax assets relate to income taxes levied by the same taxation authority on either:
  - the same taxable entity, ***or***
  - different taxable entities which intend (in each future period in which significant amounts of deferred tax assets or liabilities are expected to be settled or recovered) either to settle current tax liabilities and assets on a net basis, or to realize the assets and settle the liabilities simultaneously.

---

[4] *See the chapter on IFRS 3, regarding business combinations.*

3.5 Specific Issues

3.5.1 Change in the Tax Rate In the case of a change in the tax rate, the carrying amount of the deferred tax assets and liabilities changes even though there is no change in the amount of the related temporary differences. The adjustment of the carrying amount is recognized in profit or loss or outside profit or loss, depending on the manner of previous recognition (IAS 12.60).

3.5.2 Business Combinations The accounting treatment of deferred tax relating to goodwill and fair value adjustments arising as part of the initial accounting of a business combination at acquisition date has been dealt with in the previous sections.

As a result of a business combination, the following situations may occur with respect to the **acquirer's deferred tax assets** (IAS 12.67):

- A previously unrecognized deferred tax asset of the acquirer **has to be recognized**.
- A previously recognized deferred tax asset of the acquirer **does not meet the recognition criteria anymore**.

In these cases, the acquirer recognizes a change in the deferred tax asset in the period of the business combination but does not include it as part of the accounting for the business combination. Therefore, the acquirer does **not take it into account in determining goodwill** (IAS 12.67).

An **acquiree's** income tax loss carryforwards or other **deferred tax assets** might not satisfy the criteria for separate recognition on initial accounting of a business combination. If the recognition criteria are met, subsequently, the following applies (IAS 12.68):

- Acquired deferred tax benefits recognized **within the measurement period**[5] (IFRS 3.45) that result from new information about **facts and circumstances** that existed **at the acquisition date** reduce the carrying amount of any goodwill related to that acquisition ("Dr Deferred tax asset Cr Goodwill"). If the carrying amount of that goodwill is zero, any remaining deferred tax benefits are recognized in profit or loss ("Dr Deferred tax asset Cr Income").
- **All other** acquired deferred tax benefits realized subsequently are recognized in profit or loss ("Dr Deferred tax asset Cr Income"), or, if IAS 12 so requires, outside profit or loss.

4 TAX (OR TAX RATE) RECONCILIATION

A tax (or tax rate) reconciliation has to be disclosed in the notes. Thereby, the product of profit before tax according to IFRS multiplied by the applicable tax rate is reconciled to the total of current and deferred tax expense (income). This reconciliation is presented either on an absolute number basis and/or percentage-wise. Percentage-wise means that the numbers are expressed as percentages of profit before tax according to IFRS (IAS 12.81c). The following example of a tax (rate) reconciliation takes only basic issues into account. The profit before

---

[5] *See the chapter on IFRS 3, Section 6.7.*

tax according to IFRS and the applicable tax rate, as well as the expenses not deductible for tax purposes, are based on random numbers.

Tax reconciliation in absolute numbers	
Profit before tax according to IFRS	40
Applicable tax rate	25%
Fictitious tax (at the applicable tax rate)	10
Expenses not deductible for tax purposes	2
(Current and deferred) tax expense	**12**
Tax rate reconciliation	
Applicable tax rate	25%
Expenses not deductible for tax purposes	5%
Average effective tax rate	**30%**

5 EXAMPLES WITH SOLUTIONS

References to other chapters

Deferred tax arising in **business combinations** is also dealt with in the chapter on IFRS 3 (Examples 5 and 6b). Deferred tax arising in the case of **revaluations** of property, plant, and equipment is dealt with in the chapter on IAS 16 (Example 7). The effects of a **retrospective adjustment** on deferred tax are illustrated in the chapter on IAS 8 (Example 6).

Example 1

Current tax

Entity E has to pay income tax of CU 5 for the year 01. This amount only relates to transactions recognized in profit or loss according to IFRS. In E's jurisdiction, entities have to make prepayments during the year (e.g. during 01) on their payable income tax for the year (e.g. for 01). These prepayments are based on taxable profit for the previous year (e.g. for 00).

Version (aa)

In 01, E has made prepayments of CU 4. E recognizes such prepayments in profit or loss during the year.

Version (ab)

In 01, E has made prepayments of CU 4. During the year, E recognizes such prepayments on a separate account which comprises the amounts already paid to the taxation authorities as receivables (clearing account with taxation authorities).

Version (ba)

In 01, E has made prepayments of CU 6. E recognizes such prepayments in profit or loss during the year.

Version (bb)

In 01, E has made prepayments of CU 6. During the year, E recognizes such prepayments on the clearing account with taxation authorities as receivables.

Required

Prepare any necessary entries in E's financial statements as at Dec 31, 01.

Hints for solution

In particular Section 2.

Solution (aa)

Year 01	Dr	Current tax expense	4	
	Cr	Cash		4

E's financial statements have to include current tax expense of CU 5. Current tax of CU 1 not yet settled has to be recognized as a liability:

Dec 31, 01	Dr	Current tax expense	1	
	Cr	Current tax liability		1

Solution (ab)

Year 01	Dr	Clearing account with taxation authorities	4	
	Cr	Cash		4

E's financial statements have to include current tax expense of CU 5. Current tax of CU 1 not yet settled has to be recognized as a liability. The clearing account with taxation authorities is an interim account that is not included in the financial statements.

Dec 31, 01	Dr	Current tax expense	5	
	Cr	Clearing account with taxation authorities		4
	Cr	Current tax liability		1

Solution (ba)

Year 01	Dr	Current tax expense	6	
	Cr	Cash		6

E's financial statements have to include current tax expense of CU 5. The prepayments were CU 6. Hence, E is able to reclaim an amount of CU 1 from the taxation authorities. That amount is recognized as a receivable:

Dec 31, 01	Dr	Current tax asset	1	
	Cr	Current tax expense		1

Solution (bb)

Year 01	Dr	Clearing account with taxation authorities	6	
	Cr	Cash		6

E's financial statements have to include current tax expense of CU 5. The amount of CU 1 prepaid in excess is reclaimed from the taxation authorities, by E. Hence, it is recognized as a receivable. The clearing account with taxation authorities is an interim account that is not included in the financial statements.

Dec 31, 01	Dr	Current tax asset	1	
	Dr	Current tax expense	5	
	Cr	Clearing account with taxation authorities		6

Example 2

Deferred tax – introductory example

Version (a)

On Jan 01, 01, entity E acquires software for CU 12, which is available for use on the same day. The software's **useful life** is **three years according to IFRS** and **four years under E's tax law**.

Version (b)

On Jan 01, 01, entity E acquires software for CU 12, which is available for use on the same day. The software's **useful life** is **four years according to IFRS** and **three years under E's tax law**.

Required

Prepare any necessary entries relating to deferred tax in E's financial statements as at Dec 31, 01. The tax rate is 25%. Assume for simplification purposes that deferred tax assets (if any) meet the recognition criteria of IAS 12.[6]

Hints for solution

In particular Section 3.1.

Solution (a)

Amortization for 01 is CU 4 according to IFRS and CU 3 for tax purposes. Thus, the carrying amount of the software as at Dec 31, 01 is CU 8 (= CU 12 – CU 4) according to IFRS and CU 9 (= CU 12 – CU 3) for tax purposes.

The carrying amount of the software is lower according to IFRS than for tax purposes, meaning that E is poorer in its financial statements according to IFRS. Hence, E recognizes a deferred tax asset according to the "poorer-richer-rule" (poorer in the statement of financial position according to IFRS = asset; richer in the statement of financial position according to IFRS = liability).[7]

The logic of recognizing the deferred tax asset can also be explained as follows: the determination of deferred tax is based on the presumption that the carrying amount for tax purposes (CU 9) will adjust to the carrying amount according to IFRS (CU 8) in the future.

[6] *See Section 3.2.2.*

[7] *See Section 3.1.*

This means that it is assumed that the entry "Dr Expense Cr Asset CU 1" will be made in the future, for tax purposes. As a result of this entry, taxable profit will decrease by CU 1 in the future. Assuming that the tax rate is 25%, this will lead to a reduction of the current tax liability by CU 0.25. In other words, a tax advantage of CU 0.25 will arise in the future. That future tax advantage is already recognized as an asset (deferred tax asset) on Dec 31, 01 (since it is presumed in this example that the recognition criteria for deferred tax assets are met):

Dec 31, 01	Dr	Deferred tax asset	0.25	
	Cr	Deferred tax income		0.25

Solution (b)

Amortization for 01 is CU 3 according to IFRS and CU 4 for tax purposes. Thus, the carrying amount of the software as at Dec 31, 01 is CU 9 (= CU 12 – CU 3) according to IFRS and CU 8 (= CU 12 – CU 4) for tax purposes.

The carrying amount of the software is higher under IFRS than for tax purposes, which means that E is richer in its financial statements according to IFRS. Hence, E recognizes a deferred tax liability according to the "poorer-richer-rule" (poorer in the statement of financial position according to IFRS = asset; richer in the statement of financial position according to IFRS = liability).[8]

The logic of recognizing the deferred tax liability can also be explained as follows: the determination of deferred tax is based on the presumption that the carrying amount for tax purposes (CU 8) will adjust to the carrying amount according to IFRS (CU 9) in the future. This means that it is assumed that the entry "Dr Asset Cr Income CU 1" will be made in the future, for tax purposes. As a result of this entry, taxable profit will increase by CU 1 in the future. Assuming that the tax rate is 25%, this will lead to an increase of the current tax liability by CU 0.25. In other words, a tax disadvantage of CU 0.25 will arise in the future. That future tax disadvantage is already recognized as a liability (deferred tax liability) on Dec 31, 01:

Dec 31, 01	Dr	Deferred tax expense	0.25	
	Cr	Deferred tax liability		0.25

Example 3
Expenses not deductible for tax purposes

In 01, entity E incurs expenses of CU 10. These expenses are not deductible for tax purposes, i.e. they do not decrease taxable profit.

Posting status:

The expenses of CU 10 have already been recognized correctly.

[8] *See Section 3.1.*

Required

Prepare any necessary entries in respect of deferred tax in E's financial statements as at Dec 31, 01. The tax rate is 25%.

Hints for solution

In particular Section 3.1.

Solution

In the following years (i.e. from 02 onwards) these expenses will result in neither a tax advantage nor a tax disadvantage. There are no temporary differences with respect to these expenses. Hence, no deferred tax asset and no deferred tax liability is recognized with respect to them.

Example 4

Deferred tax and tax (rate) reconciliation

Entity E was founded on Jan 01, 01. E's profit before tax according to IFRS for 01 is CU 100. E's taxable profit for 01 is CU 104. The difference between these amounts arose as follows:

- On Nov 01, 01, E acquired a machine for CU 120. The machine was available for use on the same day. E depreciates the machine on a monthly basis. However, under E's tax law, the machine has to be depreciated for six months in 01 because depreciation starts at the beginning of the half-year in which the machine is available for use. The machine's useful life is 10 years according to IFRS as well as for tax purposes.
- In 01, expenses of CU 8 were incurred for charitable donations. These are not deductible for tax purposes.

Required

(a) Prepare any necessary entries in E's financial statements as at Dec 31, 01, taking current and deferred tax into account. The tax rate is 25%. Assume that no tax prepayments (see Example 1) are necessary.

(b) Prepare (a) the tax reconciliation in absolute numbers (IAS 12.81(c)(i)) as well as (b) the tax rate reconciliation (IAS 12.81(c)(ii)) for 01.

Hints for solution

In particular Sections 3.1 and 4.

Solution (a)

Current tax for 01 is CU 26 (= taxable profit of CU 104 · 25%).

Dec 31, 01	Dr	Current tax expense	26	
	Cr	Current tax liability		26

Donation:

Year 01	Dr	Donation expense	8	
	Cr	Cash		8

Expenses not deductible for tax purposes do not result in deferred tax.

Machine:

Nov 01, 01	Dr	Machine	120	
	Cr	Cash		120

Depreciation for November and December 01 is CU 2 (= CU 120 : 10 years : 12 months · 2 months).

Dec 31, 01	Dr	Depreciation expense	2	
	Cr	Machine		2

Deferred tax:

On Dec 31, 01, the machine's carrying amount according to IFRS is CU 118 (= CU 120 – CU 2). By contrast, for tax purposes, depreciation for 01 is calculated on a six month basis, which results in depreciation of CU 6 (= CU 120 : 10 years : 12 months · 6 months). Thus, the carrying amount for tax purposes on Dec 31, 01 is CU 114 (= CU 120 – CU 6).

	Carrying amount according to IFRS as at Dec 31, 01	*Carrying amount for tax purposes as at Dec 31, 01*	*Deductible temporary differences*	*Taxable temporary differences*	*Deductible temporary differences multiplied by 25%*	*Taxable temporary differences multiplied by 25%*	*Presentation*
Machine	118	114		4		1	Profit or loss
Deferred tax liability						**1**	

Dec 31, 01	Dr	Deferred tax expense	1	
	Cr	Deferred tax liability		1

Solution (b)

Tax reconciliation in absolute numbers (IAS 12.81 (c)(i)):

Profit before tax according to IFRS	100	
Applicable tax rate	25%	
Fictitious tax (at the applicable tax rate)	**25**	
Expenses not deductible for tax purposes	2	*= 8 · 25%*
(Current and deferred) tax expense	**27**	*= 26 + 1 or 25 + 2*

The following table shows the *tax rate reconciliation* (IAS 12.81(c)(ii)). In this reconciliation, the percentages are derived by dividing the respective numbers from the table previously by profit before tax according to IFRS.

Applicable tax rate	**25%**
Expenses not deductible for tax purposes	2%
Average effective tax rate	**27%**

Example 5

Continuation of Example 4 in the following year

In the following year 02, entity E's profit before tax according to IFRS is CU 100. E's taxable profit for 02 is CU 140. The difference between these amounts arose as follows:

1. On Sep 01, 01, E acquired shares for CU 200 which are accounted for at fair value through other comprehensive income (IFRS 9.5.7.1b and 9.5.7.5). Fair value of the shares is CU 208 as at Dec 31, 02. On Dec 31, 01, fair value was CU 200. In 02, E received a dividend of CU 4 for the period Sept 01, 01 to Dec 31, 01. The dividend is outside the scope of taxation under E's tax law. According to E's tax law, the shares are measured at cost.
2. Regarding a lawsuit, E has recognized a provision of CU 100 according to IFRS. The carrying amount of that provision for tax purposes is CU 80.
3. In 02, an amount of CU 16 was paid to E's non-executive directors. According to E's tax law, only half of that amount is deductible for tax purposes.
4. On Jan 01, 02, E acquired a building for CU 2,000. The building is available for use on the same day. Under E's tax law depreciation is 3% p.a. The building's useful life according to IFRS is 25 years.
5. The carrying amount of a provision of E for tax purposes is CU 4. That provision does not meet the recognition criteria according to IFRS.

Posting status:

Apart from current tax and deferred tax for 02, all necessary entries have already been correctly effected. The current tax liability recognized for the year 01 has already been settled and this has already been entered correctly. The fair value change of the shares has been recognized as follows:[9]

Dec 31, 02	Dr	Shares	8	
	Cr	Other comprehensive income (fair value reserve)		8

The dividend of CU 4 has been recognized in profit or loss (IFRS 9.5.7.6).

[9] *If IFRS 9 were not yet applied, the same entry would be necessary if the shares were classified as "available for sale" (IAS 39.9).*

Required

(a) Prepare any necessary entries in E's financial statements as at Dec 31, 02, with respect to current and deferred tax. The tax rate is 25%. Assume that no tax prepayments (see Example 1) are necessary. Assume for simplification purposes that deferred tax assets (if any) meet the recognition criteria of IAS 12[10] and that the criteria for offsetting deferred tax assets and deferred tax liabilities in the statement of financial position[11] are met.

(b) Prepare (a) the tax reconciliation in absolute numbers (IAS 12.81(c)(i)) as well as (b) the tax rate reconciliation (IAS 12.81(c)(ii)) for 02.

Hints for solution

In particular Sections 3.1 and 4.

Solution (a)[12]

Current tax for 02 is CU 35 (= taxable profit of CU 140 · 25%).

Dec 31, 02	Dr	Current tax expense	35	
	Cr	Current tax liability		35

Deferred tax:

		Carrying amount according to IFRS as at Dec 31, 02	*Carrying amount for tax purposes as at Dec 31, 02*	*Deductible temporary differences*	*Taxable temporary differences*	*Deductible temporary differences multiplied by 25%*	*Taxable temporary differences multiplied by 25%*	*Presentation*
Example 1	Machine	106	102		4		1	Year 01
(1)	Shares	208	200		8		2	OCI
(2)	Provision	100	80	20		5		Profit or loss
(4)	Building	1,920	1,940	20		5		Profit or loss
(5)	Provision	0	4		4		1	Profit or loss
	Total					**10**	**4**	
	Deferred tax asset (Dec 31, 02)					**6**		
	To be recognized in profit or loss					9	(Deferred tax income)	
	To be recognized in other comprehensive income					2		
	Derecognition of the deferred tax liability recognized in 01					1		

[10] *See Section 3.2.2.*

[11] *See Section 3.4.*

[12] *The solution of this example would not change if IFRS 9 and its consequential amendments were not applied early and if the shares were classified as "available for sale" according to the "old" version of IAS 39 (IAS 39.9 and 39.55b).*

Dec 31, 02	Dr	Deferred tax asset	6	
	Dr	Deferred tax liability	1	
	Dr	Other comprehensive income (fair value reserve)	2	
	Cr	Deferred tax income		9

Solution (b)

Tax reconciliation in absolute numbers (IAS 12.81(c)(i)):

Profit before tax according to IFRS	100	
Applicable tax rate	25%	
Fictitious tax (at the applicable tax rate)	**25**	
Expenses not deductible for tax purposes	2	*= 8 · 25% (half of the compensation for non-executive directors)*
Income outside the scope of taxation	−1	*= −4 · 25% (dividend)*
(Current and deferred) tax expense	**26**	*= 25 + 2 − 1 or current tax expense (35) less deferred tax income (9)*

Tax rate reconciliation (IAS 12.81(c)(ii)):

Applicable tax rate	**25%**
Expenses not deductible for tax purposes	2%
Income outside the scope of taxation	-1%
Average effective tax rate	**26%**

Example 6

Deferred tax – different tax rates

On Dec 31, 01, a building of entity E has a carrying amount of CU 100 according to IFRS and a carrying amount of CU 80 for tax purposes. A tax rate of 25% would apply if the asset were sold. Otherwise, the applicable tax rate would be 30%.

Required

Determine the carrying amount of the deferred tax liability in E's financial statements as at Dec 31, 01.

Hints for solution

In particular Section 3.3.2.

Solution

The carrying amount of the deferred tax liability is CU 5 (= CU 20 · 25%) if E expects to sell the building without further use. The carrying amount of the deferred tax liability is CU 6 (= CU 20 · 30%) if E expects to retain the building and recover its carrying amount through use (IAS 12.52, Example A).

Example 7

Deferred tax – change in the tax rate[13]

Entity E holds the following shares which were each acquired for CU 900:

Shares of entity A: These shares meet the definition of "held for trading" (IFRS 9, Appendix A). Therefore, they are accounted for at fair value through profit or loss (IFRS 9.4.1.1–9.4.1.4, 9.5.7.1b, and 9.5.7.5). On Dec 31, 01, the carrying amount of these shares is CU 1,000 according to IFRS and CU 900 for tax purposes.

Shares of entity B: These shares are accounted for at fair value through other comprehensive income (IFRS 9.4.1.1–9.4.1.4, IFRS 9.5.7.1b, and 9.5.7.5). On Dec 31, 01, the carrying amount of these shares is CU 1,000 according to IFRS and CU 900 for tax purposes. The fair value reserve is CU 100.

On Dec 31, 01, the tax rate is changed from 30% to 25%.

Posting status:

All necessary entries have already been effected correctly. However, the change in the tax rate has not yet been taken into account.

Required

Prepare any necessary entries in E's financial statements as at Dec 31, 01.

Hints for solution

In particular Section 3.5.1.

Solution

The deferred tax liabilities relating to the shares of A and B change as follows:

Carrying amount according to IFRS as at Dec 31, 01	1,000
Carrying amount for tax purposes as at Dec 31, 01	900
Taxable temporary difference	**100**
Deferred tax liability as at Dec 31, 01 (on the basis of a tax rate of 30%)	30
Deferred tax liability as at Dec 31, 01 (on the basis of a tax rate of 25%)	25
Adjustment	**–5**

A change in a deferred tax liability is recognized in profit or loss except to the extent that it relates to items previously recognized outside profit or loss (IAS 12.60, 12.58, and 12.61A). Hence, the change in the deferred tax liability for the shares of A is recognized in profit or loss, while the change in the deferred tax liability for the shares of B is recognized in other comprehensive income. In the latter case, the fair value reserve increases by the reduction in the deferred tax liability of CU 5.

[13] *The solution of this example would be the same if IFRS 9 (and its consequential amendments) were not applied early and if the shares of B were classified as "available for sale" (IAS 39.9 and 39.55b).*

Shares of A:

Dec 31, 01	Dr	Deferred tax liability	5	
	Cr	Deferred tax expense		5

Shares of B:

Dec 31, 01	Dr	Deferred tax liability	5	
	Cr	Other comprehensive income (fair value reserve)		5

Example 8

Business combinations[14] and income tax loss carryforwards of the acquiree

On Dec 31, 01, entity E acquires 100% of the shares of entity S for CU 100. S is free of debt.

A simplified illustration of S's statement of financial position as at Dec 31, 01 is presented below. For simplification purposes it is assumed that it is identical with S's statement of financial position II as at the same date.

Various assets	90	Share capital	70
		Retained earnings	20
Total	**90**	**Total**	**90**

The value of the assets of S on acquisition date determined according to IFRS 3 is CU 95. Moreover, S owns income tax loss carryforwards amounting to CU 40 that do not meet the recognition criteria when the business combination is initially accounted for as at Dec 31, 01.

Version (a)

On Dec 31, 02, new information about facts and circumstances that existed at the acquisition date indicates that the recognition criteria for the income tax loss carryforwards were met on the acquisition date.

Version (b)

On Dec 31, 02, the recognition criteria are met due to a significant improvement in S's performance after acquisition date.

In its separate financial statements E accounts for its investment in S (shares) at cost (IAS 27.38a).

Posting status (in E's separate financial statements):

Dec 31, 01	Dr	Investment of E in S (shares)	100	
	Cr	Cash		100

[14] *See the chapter on IFRS 3 with regard to the basics of business combinations.*

Posting status (capital consolidation in E's consolidated financial statements):

Dec 31, 01	Dr	Goodwill	5	
	Dr	Various assets of S	5	
	Dr	Share capital	70	
	Dr	Retained earnings	20	
	Cr	Investment of E in S (shares)		100

Required

Prepare any necessary entries in E's consolidated financial statements as at Dec 31, 02 regarding deferred tax. The tax rate is 25%.

Hints for solution

In particular Section 3.5.2.

Solution (a)

Acquired deferred tax benefits recognized **within the measurement period** (IFRS 3.45) that result from new information about **facts and circumstances** that existed **at the acquisition date** reduce the carrying amount of any goodwill related to that acquisition. If the carrying amount of that goodwill is zero, any remaining deferred tax benefits are recognized in profit or loss (IAS 12.68a). In this example, the deferred tax benefit is CU 10 (= CU 40 · 25%).

Dec 31, 02	Dr	Deferred tax asset	10	
	Cr	Goodwill		5
	Cr	Income		5

Solution (b)

In contrast to version (a), the recognition criteria are met on Dec 31, 02, because of events arising after the acquisition date. This means that meeting the recognition criteria at that date is *not* the result of new information about facts and circumstances that existed at the acquisition date. Therefore, recognition of the deferred tax asset of CU 10 (= CU 40 · 25%) results in the recognition of income in the same amount and goodwill is not changed (IAS 12.68b).

Dec 31, 02	Dr	Deferred tax asset	10	
	Cr	Income		10

Example 9

Recognition of deferred tax with respect to goodwill

On Jan 01, 01, entity E acquires all of the shares of entity F. This business combination results in:

(a) Goodwill of CU 80 according to IFRS. The carrying amount of goodwill for tax purposes is zero.

(b) Goodwill of CU 80 according to IFRS. The carrying amount of goodwill for tax purposes is zero. On Dec 31, 01, an impairment loss of CU 10 is recognized with respect to goodwill according to IFRS.
(c) Goodwill of CU 80 according to IFRS. The carrying amount of goodwill for tax purposes is CU 60. According to the applicable tax law, goodwill has to be amortized over 15 years on a straight-line basis.

Required

Prepare the necessary entries (if any) in E's consolidated financial statements as at Dec 31, 01 for deferred tax relating to goodwill. The tax rate is 25%.

Hints for solution

In particular Section 3.2.1.

Solution

Case (a)

The taxable temporary difference of CU 80 results from the initial recognition of goodwill. A corresponding deferred tax liability must not be recognized because this is prohibited by the Standard (IAS 12.15a).

Case (b)

The taxable temporary difference of CU 80 results from the initial recognition of goodwill. A corresponding deferred tax liability must not be recognized (IAS 12.15a). This procedure is not affected by the impairment loss of CU 10 recognized on Dec 31, 01, according to IFRS (IAS 12.21A).

Case (c)

A taxable temporary difference of CU 20 results from the initial recognition of goodwill. A corresponding deferred tax liability must not be recognized (IAS 12.15a).

On Dec 31, 01, amortization expense of CU 4 (= CU 60 : 15 years) is recognized with respect to goodwill for tax purposes, which decreases the goodwill's carrying amount for tax purposes to CU 56. Since the pro rata carrying amount of goodwill according to IFRS (excluding the amount of CU 20 discussed above) is still CU 60, a taxable temporary difference of CU 4 arises. This difference has not been caused by the initial recognition of goodwill. Thus, a deferred tax liability is recognized (IAS 12.21B).

Pro rata carrying amount of goodwill according to IFRS as at Dec 31, 01	60
Carrying amount for tax purposes as at Dec 31, 01	56
Taxable temporary difference	**4**
Tax rate	25%
Deferred tax liability	**1**

Dec 31, 01	Dr	Deferred tax expense	1	
	Cr	Deferred tax liability		1

IAS 16 PROPERTY, PLANT, AND EQUIPMENT

1 INTRODUCTION

Property, plant, and equipment are tangible items that meet both of the following criteria (IAS 16.6):

- They are held for use in the production or supply of goods or services, for rental to others, or for administrative purposes.
- They are expected to be used during more than one period.

Typical examples of property, plant, and equipment are buildings used in the production of goods or for administrative purposes.

IAS 16 does not apply, for example, to property, plant, and equipment classified as "**held for sale**" in accordance with IFRS 5 (IAS 16.3), and IAS 40 contains specific requirements for **investment property**.

2 RECOGNITION

The cost of an item of property, plant, and equipment is **recognized as an asset** if both of the following conditions are met (**recognition principle**) (IAS 16.7):

- It is probable that future economic benefits associated with the item will flow to the entity.
- The cost of the item can be measured reliably.

Whether these criteria are met for the initial and subsequent costs of a particular item of property, plant, and equipment is a **question of recognition**. All property, plant, and equipment costs are assessed according to the **recognition principle** at the time they are incurred (IAS 16.7 and 16.10).

Subsequent costs incurred in order to add to, replace part of, or service an item of property, plant, and equipment are generally recognized in the carrying amount of the item if they increase the economic benefits of the item (e.g. by an extension of the remaining useful life or by an increase in capacity). **Parts** of some items of property, plant, and equipment may have to be **replaced**. For example, aircraft interiors such as seats and galleys may require replacement several times during the life of the airframe (IAS 16.13). The costs of replacing parts are recognized in the carrying amount of the item of property, plant, and equipment if the recognition criteria (IAS 16.7) are met. The carrying amounts of replaced parts are derecognized according to the derecognition provisions of IAS 16 (IAS 16.67–16.72)[1] (IAS 16.13). In the case of **regular major inspections** of items of property, plant, and equipment for faults, the cost of the inspection is recognized in the carrying amount of the item of property, plant, and equipment as a replacement if the recognition criteria are met. Any remaining carrying amount of the cost of the previous inspection is derecognized (IAS 16.14).

IAS 16 does not prescribe **what constitutes an item** of property, plant, and equipment. Consequently, judgment is required to determine the unit of measure for recognition. It may be appropriate to aggregate items that are individually insignificant such as molds, tools, and ties and to apply the recognition criteria to the aggregate value (IAS 16.9). In another example, a railroad company could regard an entire engine as a single item of property, plant, and equipment. Alternatively, each of the individual components of the engine (i.e. pivot mounting with wheel sets, the engine box, the transformer, the electric power converter, the control units, and the auxiliary converter) could be regarded as separate items of property, plant, and equipment. However, if the entire locomotive were defined as a single item of property, plant, and equipment, it would be necessary to depreciate the individually **significant** components separately (**component accounting** – see Section 4.2.4).

3 MEASUREMENT AT RECOGNITION

An item of property, plant, and equipment that qualifies for recognition as an asset is initially measured at its costs of purchase or conversion (IAS 16.15).

The **costs of purchase** comprise the following elements (IAS 16.16–16.21):

- The **purchase price** after deducting **trade discounts and rebates**. Import duties and nonrefundable purchase taxes are included, whereas **refundable purchase taxes** are excluded.
- **Acquisition-related costs**, i.e. any costs directly attributable to bringing the asset to the location and condition necessary for it to be capable of operating in the manner intended by the buyer.
- The **initial estimate of the costs of dismantling and removing the item and restoring the site on which it is located** to the extent that the entity incurs the obligation for them either when the item is acquired or as a consequence of having used the item during a particular period for purposes other than to produce inventories. By contrast, costs of these obligations that are incurred as a consequence of having used the item during a particular period to produce inventories are included in the costs of conversion of the inventories according to IAS 2 (IAS 16.16c, 16.18, and 16.BC15). These costs are normally included on the basis of their **present value** (IAS 16.18 and IAS 37.45).

The **costs of conversion** of an item of property, plant, and equipment are calculated according to the same principles that apply to property, plant, and equipment that was purchased. With regard to the determination of the costs of conversion of property, plant, and equipment, the Standard refers to the rules that apply for the calculation of the costs of conversion of inventories (IAS 16.22).

[1] *See Section 5.*

Criteria for the capitalization of **borrowing costs** are established in IAS 23. The initial measurement of items of property, plant, and equipment **leased under a finance lease** is dealt with in IAS 17 (IAS 16.27 and IAS 17.20). **Government grants** are dealt with in IAS 20 (IAS 16.28 and IAS 20.24).

4 MEASUREMENT AFTER RECOGNITION

4.1 Cost Model and Revaluation Model

After recognition, items of property, plant, and equipment have to be measured according to the cost model or according to the revaluation model. A choice between these models can be made **for each entire class** of property, plant, and equipment (IAS 16.29 and 16.36).

When the **cost model** is applied, the items of property, plant, and equipment are measured at their costs of purchase or conversion less any accumulated depreciation and accumulated impairment losses (IAS 16.30).

When the **revaluation model** is applied, the items of property, plant, and equipment are measured at their fair values at the time of the revaluation, less subsequent accumulated depreciation and impairment losses (IAS 16.31). Fair value is the amount for which an asset could be exchanged between knowledgeable, willing parties in an arm's length transaction (IAS 16.6).

In many countries, revaluations of property, plant, and equipment are rare and if and when they do occur, they are often revaluations of land.[2] Thus, only the revaluation of **land**, which is not depreciated, is described. In this case the changes in value are recognized in other comprehensive income to the extent that the changes in value take place above cost. For example, if the value increases from CU 100 to CU 140 and cost is CU 110, CU 30 are recognized in other comprehensive income (ignoring deferred tax in this example). The amounts recognized in other comprehensive income are accumulated in revaluation surplus. However, the changes in value are recognized in profit or loss to the extent that they take place below cost (IAS 1.7, 1.106d, 1.108, IAS 16.39–16.40, IAS 36.60–36.61, and 36.118–36.120). When a revaluation above cost is not permitted for tax purposes, an increase in fair value above cost leads to the recognition of a deferred tax liability (Dr Revaluation surplus, Cr Deferred tax liability) (IAS 12.61A–12.62). Upon derecognition of the land, the revaluation surplus may be transferred directly to retained earnings (i.e. not through profit or loss). However, it is also possible not to make any transfer at all (IAS 1.96 and IAS 16.41).

4.2 Depreciation

4.2.1 Depreciable Amount The **depreciable amount** is the costs of purchase or conversion of an asset (or other amount substituted for cost) less its residual value (IAS 16.6). The "other amount substituted for cost" can be, for instance, the new carrying amount of the asset after a revaluation.

---

[2] *See Christensen/Nikolaev, Does fair value accounting for non-financial assets pass the market test?, working paper no. 09–12; ICAEW, EU implementation of IFRS and the fair value directive, a report for the European Commission, 2007, p. 119–120; KPMG/von Keitz,* The Application of IFRS: Choices in Practice, 2006, *p. 11.*

The **residual value** is the estimated amount that an entity would currently obtain from disposal of the asset after deduction of the estimated costs of disposal if the asset were already of the age and in the condition expected at the end of its useful life (IAS 16.6). In practice, the residual value of an asset is **often insignificant**. Consequently it is often possible not to deduct it in determining depreciable amount due to materiality reasons (IAS 16.53 and IAS 8.8). However, it is important to deduct residual value, especially when assets are replaced far ahead of the end of their physical life (e.g. for economic reasons or due to technological progress). This may be the case with aircrafts, ships or trucks. The residual value may increase to an amount equal to or greater than the asset's carrying amount. In this case, depreciation is zero unless and until the residual value subsequently decreases to an amount below the carrying amount of the asset (IAS 16.54). The residual value of an asset has to be reviewed at least at the end of each financial year. If expectations differ from previous estimates, the change has to be treated as a **change in accounting estimates according to IAS 8** (IAS 16.51).

4.2.2 Depreciation Period The depreciable amount has to be allocated on a systematic basis over the **useful life** of the asset (IAS 16.50). An asset's useful life is (IAS 16.6):

- the period over which the asset is expected to be available for use by an entity, or
- the number of production or similar units expected to be obtained from the asset by an entity.

Useful life is defined in terms of the asset's expected utility to the entity. Under the entity's asset management policy, assets may be disposed of after a specified time or after consumption of a specified proportion of the future economic benefits embodied in the asset. Thus, the useful life of an asset may be shorter than its economic life (IAS 16.57).

Depreciation starts when the asset is **available for use,** i.e. when it is in the location and condition necessary for it to be capable of operating in the manner intended by management (IAS 16.55). In many cases applying the concept of materiality (IAS 8.8) will justify calculating depreciation on a monthly and not on a daily basis.

Depreciation ceases at the earlier of the following dates (IAS 16.55):

- Date at which the asset is classified as **held for sale** (or included in a disposal group that is classified as held for sale) according to **IFRS 5**.
- Date of **derecognition** of the asset.

Consequently, depreciation continues to be recognized when the asset becomes idle or is retired from active use. However, under usage methods of depreciation, the depreciation charge can be zero while there is no production (IAS 16.55).

The useful life of an asset has to be reviewed at least at the end of each financial year. If expectations differ from previous estimates, the change has to be treated as a **change in accounting estimates according to IAS 8** (IAS 16.51).

4.2.3 Depreciation Method The **depreciation method** has to reflect the pattern in which the asset's future economic benefits are expected to be consumed by the entity (IAS 16.60).

Examples of depreciation methods are the **straight-line method** and the **units of production method**. In the former case, depreciation is calculated by dividing the depreciable amount by the asset's useful life. In the latter case, depreciation expense depends on the expected use or output of the asset (IAS 16.62).

It is necessary to select the depreciation method that most closely reflects the expected pattern of consumption of the future economic benefits embodied in the asset (IAS 16.62).

The depreciation method has to be reviewed at least at the end of each financial year. If there has been a significant change in the expected pattern of consumption of the future economic benefits embodied in the asset, the depreciation method has to be changed in order to reflect the changed pattern. Such a change has to be treated as a **change in an accounting estimate according to IAS 8** (IAS 16.51).

4.2.4 Component Accounting Each part, i.e. each component of an item of property, plant, and equipment, with a cost that is **significant** in relation to the total cost of the item has to be **depreciated separately** unless the useful lives are at least approximately identical (component accounting). Component accounting is also necessary for **regular major inspections** for faults (IAS 16.14 and 16.43–16.47).

Although individual components are depreciated separately as described above, the statement of financial position continues to disclose a single asset. Moreover, component accounting does not necessitate the splitting of depreciation expense in the statement of comprehensive income. The issue of derecognition of components is dealt with in Section 5.

4.3 Impairment

The issue of impairment is dealt with in the chapter on IAS 36 in this book (IAS 16.63).

4.4 Changes in Existing Decommissioning, Restoration, and Similar Liabilities

Changes in existing decommissioning, restoration, and similar liabilities for items of property, plant, and equipment accounted for according to the **cost model** are treated as follows (IFRIC 1):

- If the change in measurement is due to a change in the estimated **timing or amount** of the outflow of resources embodying economic benefits required to settle the obligation or due to a change in the **discount rate**, the following applies: Changes in the liability are **added to or deducted from the carrying amount of the related asset** ("Dr Asset Cr Liability" respectively "Dr Liability Cr Asset"). When this procedure leads to a reduction in the asset's carrying amount to zero, each further reduction in the liability is recognized in profit or loss. If the adjustment results in an increase in the carrying amount of the asset, it has to be considered whether this is an indication that the new carrying amount of the asset is impaired (see IAS 36). The adjusted depreciable amount of the asset is depreciated over the asset's remaining useful life. Once the asset has reached the end of its useful life, all subsequent changes in the liability are recognized in profit or loss.
- The **periodic unwinding** of the discount is recognized in **profit or loss** as a **finance cost**.

5 DERECOGNITION

An item of property, plant, and equipment is derecognized **on disposal** (e.g. by sale or by entering into a finance lease) or when **no future economic benefits** are expected from its use or disposal (IAS 16.67). The gain or loss arising from the derecognition of an asset is the difference between the net disposal proceeds (if any) and the asset's carrying amount (IAS 16.71).

If, under the recognition principle (IAS 16.7), the cost of a replacement for part of an item of property, plant, and equipment is recognized in the carrying amount of the item, then the carrying amount of the **replaced part** is derecognized. This applies regardless of whether the replaced part had been depreciated separately (IAS 16.70). The procedure described also applies to a **major inspection** that was recognized in the carrying amount of the item (see Sections 2 and 4.2.4) and has not been fully depreciated at the time of the next major inspection (IAS 16.14).

The **intended sale of a single item** of property, plant, and equipment does not lead to a transfer of the item to inventories because the intended sale of the item is not in the ordinary course of business. Therefore, a gain is recognized when the item is derecognized that must not be classified as revenue (IAS 2.6 and IAS 16.68). This gain is presented by deducting the carrying amount of the asset and related selling expenses from the disposal proceeds (IAS 1.34a and IAS 16.71). When the criteria in IFRS 5.6–5.12 are met, the item is classified as "held for sale" in accordance with IFRS 5. In this case the item is presented separately in the statement of financial position (balance sheet) and measured at the lower of its carrying amount and fair value less costs to sell (IFRS 5.15 and 5.37–5.38).

However, if an entity **routinely sells items** of property, plant, and equipment in the course of its **ordinary activities** that it **has held for rental to others**, it has to transfer these assets to inventories at their carrying amount when they cease to be rented and become held for sale. IFRS 5 is not applied. The proceeds from the sale of such assets is recognized as revenue in accordance with IAS 18 (IAS 16.68A).

6 EXAMPLES WITH SOLUTIONS

Reference to another section

With regard to the illustration of the effects of a revaluation of land in the statement of comprehensive income and in the statement of changes in equity we refer to the chapter on IAS 1 (Example 7).

Example 1

Component accounting – engine

On Jan 01, 01, entity E, a railroad company, acquires a railway locomotive for CU 108 that is available for use on the same day. Payment is effected in cash on the same day. It is planned to use the engine for 24 years. After every six years a major inspection of the engine is necessary. On Jan 01, 01, the cost of this inspection would be CU 24. The engine consists of the following components:

	Costs of purchase
Pivot mounting with wheel sets	16
Engine box	19
Transformer	24
Electric power converter	13
Control units	18
Auxiliary converter	18
Total	**108**

The transformer is replaced after 12 years and is not serviced during the major inspection. The other parts each have a useful life of 24 years and are serviced during each major inspection.

Required

Prepare any necessary entries in E's financial statements as on Dec 31, 01. E regards the entire engine as a single item of property, plant, and equipment.

Hints for solution

In particular Sections 2 and 4.2.4.

Solution

Jan 01, 01	Dr	Engine	108	
	Cr	Cash		108

The transformer has to be depreciated separately because its useful life is different from that of the other parts and its cost is significant in relation to the cost of the entire item (IAS 16.43 and 16.45). The major inspection is a separate part of the cost of the asset (IAS 16.14), which has to be deducted from the cost of the parts that are serviced. The other parts can be grouped in determining the depreciation charge because they have identical useful lives (IAS 16.45).

Components	*Cost (as on Jan 01, 01)*	*Useful life (in years)*	*Depreciation*
Transformer	24.0	12	2.0
Major inspection	24.0	6	4.0
Other components	60.0	24	2.5
Total	**108.0**		**8.5**

Dec 31, 01	Dr	Depreciation expense	8.5	
	Cr	Engine		8.5

Example 2

Component accounting – engine (continuation of Example 1)

The first major inspection takes place on Dec 31, 06, as planned. The actual cost of the inspection is CU 30. Replacement of the transformer is already effected on Dec 31, 10 because E wants to take advantage of a new, technically advanced transformer. The cost of the new transformer is CU 28. It has a useful life of 14 years. For simplicity reasons it is assumed that the loss on derecognition of the old transformer corresponds to its carrying amount immediately before derecognition.

Required

Prepare any necessary entries in E's financial statements as on Dec 31, for the years 06, 10, and 11.

Hints for solution

In particular Sections 2, 4.2.4, and 5.

Solution

Year 06

Dec 31, 06	Dr	Depreciation expense	8.5	
	Cr	Engine		8.5

On Dec 31, 06, the carrying amount of the "old" component for major inspection is zero and the "new" component for major inspection is recognized in the carrying amount of the engine:

Dec 31, 06	Dr	Engine	30	
	Cr	Cash		30

Year 10

Depreciation of the component "major inspection" is CU 5 p.a. (= CU 30 : 6 years) from 07 onwards and no longer CU 4. Consequently, depreciation of the engine is CU 9.5 and no longer CU 8.5.

Dec 31, 10	Dr	Depreciation expense	9.5	
	Cr	Engine		9.5

On Dec 31, 10, a component (the transformer) is replaced. Therefore, the carrying amount of the old transformer is derecognized before the new transformer is recognized in the carrying amount of the engine. The carrying amount of the old transformer on Dec 31, 10 is CU 4 (CU 24–CU 2 · 10 years).

Dec 31, 10	Dr	Loss on derecognition	4	
	Cr	Engine		4
Dec 31, 10	Dr	Engine	28	
	Cr	Cash		28

Year 11

Dec 31, 11	Dr	Depreciation expense	9.5	
	Cr	Engine		9.5

Example 3

Depreciation methods and depreciable amount

On Jan 31, 01, entity E acquires a machine for CU 15 that is available for use on the same day. Payment is effected in cash on the same day. The residual value of the machine is CU 3.

Required

Determine the depreciation expense in E's financial statements as on Dec 31 for the years 01–03. Depreciation is calculated (a) according to the straight-line method and (b) according to the units of production method. The entries only have to be illustrated for version (a).

Assume for version (a) that the machine's useful life is three years and for version (b) that the expected and actual use of the machine in the years 01–03 is 12,000 hours (= 3,000 hours in 01 + 5,000 hours in 02 + 4,000 hours in 03).

Hints for solution

In particular Sections 4.2.1 and 4.2.3.

Solution (a) – straight-line method

Costs of purchase	15
Residual value	3
Depreciable amount	**12**
Useful life (in years)	3
Depreciation p.a.	**4**

Year	*Carrying amount (as on Jan 01)*	*Depreciation*	*Carrying amount (as on Dec 31, before derecognition)*
01	15	−4	11
02	11	−4	7
03	7	−4	3

Jan 01, 01	Dr	Machine	15	
	Cr	Cash		15

On Dec 31 of each of the years 01–03, the following entry is made:

Dec 31	Dr	Depreciation expense	4	
	Cr	Machine		4
Dec 31, 03	Dr	Cash	3	
	Cr	Machine		3

Solution (b) – units of production method

Depreciation 01 =	12 · 3,000 : 12,000 =	3
Depreciation 02 =	12 · 5,000 : 12,000 =	5
Depreciation 03 =	12 · 4,000 : 12,000 =	4
Total		**12**

Year	*Carrying amount (as on Jan 01)*	*Depreciation*	*Carrying amount (as on Dec 31, before derecognition)*
01	15	–3	12
02	12	–5	7
03	7	–4	3

Example 4

Decommissioning, restoration, and similar liabilities

On Jan 01, 01, entity E acquires a machine for CU 220 that is available for use on the same day. Payment is effected in cash on the same day. The useful life of the machine is three years. The machine consists of some materials that are ecologically harmful. Consequently, E is legally obliged to dispose of the machine appropriately at the end of its useful life. This obligation arises as a result of the acquisition of the machine by E, according to the relevant legal requirements. E estimates that costs of CU 92.61 will be incurred on Dec 31, 03 for disposing of the machine. The discount rate is 5% p.a.

On Dec 31, 02, E expects that the costs for disposing of the machine will be CU 63. This estimate corresponds with the amount that is ultimately paid on Dec 31, 03.

Required

Prepare any necessary entries in E's financial statements as on Dec 31 for the years 01–03.

Hints for solution

In particular Sections 3 and 4.4.

Solution

Year 01

Purchase price	**220**
Costs for disposing of the machine appropriately	92.61
Maturity (in years)	3
Discount rate (p.a.)	5%
Present value of the obligation	**80**
Costs of purchase	**300**

Jan 01, 01	Dr	Machine	300	
	Cr	Cash		220
	Cr	Provision		80

Dec 31, 01	Dr	Depreciation expense	100	
	Cr	Machine		100

The unwinding of the discount is recognized in profit or loss as interest expense (CU 4 = CU 80 · 5%) (IFRIC 1.8):

Dec 31, 01	Dr	Interest expense	4	
	Cr	Provision		4

Year 02

Dec 31, 02	Dr	Depreciation expense	100	
	Cr	Machine		100

The unwinding of the discount is CU 4.2 [(CU 80 + CU 4) · 5%].

Dec 31, 02	Dr	Interest expense	4.2	
	Cr	Provision		4.2

Provision as on Dec 31, 02 (CU 92.61)	88.20	*= CU 80 + CU 4 + CU 4.2 or CU 80 ·1.05² or CU 92.61 : 1.05*
Provision as on Dec 31, 02 (CU 63)	60.00	*= CU 63 : 1.05*
Reduction of the provision	**28.20**	

The reduction of the provision (CU 28.2) reduces the carrying amount of the machine from CU 100 (CU 300 – 2 · CU 100) to CU 71.80 (IFRIC 1.5):

Dec 31, 02	Dr	Provision	28.2	
	Cr	Machine		28.2

Year 03

Depreciation for 03 is CU 71.8 (= carrying amount of CU 71.8 as on Dec 31, 02 : remaining useful life of one year as on Dec 31, 02) (IFRIC 1.7):

Dec 31, 03	Dr	Depreciation expense	71.8	
	Cr	Machine		71.8

The unwinding of the discount is CU 3 (CU 60 · 5%).

Dec 31, 03	Dr	Interest expense	3	
	Cr	Provision		3
Dec 31, 03	Dr	Provision	63	
	Cr	Cash		63

Example 5

Accounting treatment of property, plant, and equipment (including a sale)

On Jan 01, 01, entity E acquires an automobile for CU 24 that represents an item of property, plant, and equipment in E's operations. Depreciation is calculated according to the straight-line method. Unexpectedly, the automobile is already sold on Jun 30, 02 for CU 20.

Version (a)

E is a car rental agency. Each year, E acquires a large number of new automobiles because it is E's policy to offer the newest automobiles to its customers via operating leases. After one or two years, the automobiles are usually sold profitably. Also, the automobile mentioned above is leased to E's customers via operating leases. Until its sale, a useful life of two years is assumed for the automobile (according to IAS 16.57) as well as a residual value of CU 16.

Posting status for (a):

The lease income arising from the operating leases has already been recognized correctly.

Version (b)

In contrast to (a), E does not sell the automobile in the course of its ordinary activities. Until its sale, a useful life of six years and a residual value of CU 6 are assumed for the automobile.

Required

Prepare any necessary entries in E's financial statements as on Dec 31 for the years 01 and 02.

Hints for solution

In particular Section 5.

Solution (a)

E leases the automobile to its customers through operating leases. Hence, E recognizes the automobile in its statement of financial position (balance sheet) (IAS 17.49):

Jan 01, 01	Dr	Automobile (property, plant, and equipment)	24	
	Cr	Cash		24

The depreciable amount of the automobile of CU 8 (i.e. the costs of purchase of CU 24 less the residual value of CU 16) (IAS 16.6) is allocated over the automobile's useful life of two years (IAS 17.53 and IAS 16.50):

Dec 31, 01	Dr	Depreciation expense	4	
	Cr	Automobile (property, plant and equipment)		4
Jun 30, 02	Dr	Depreciation expense	2	
	Cr	Automobile (property, plant, and equipment)		2

E routinely sells items of property, plant, and equipment (automobiles) that it has held for rental in the course of its ordinary activities. Thus, the automobile is transferred to inventories at its carrying amount of CU 18 (IAS 16.68A):

Jun 30, 02	Dr	Automobile (inventories)	18	
	Cr	Automobile (property, plant, and equipment)		18

The proceeds from the sale of the automobile (i.e. of an item of inventory) are recognized as revenue (IAS 16.68A). The carrying amount of the automobile is recognized as cost of sales[3] in the same period in which the revenue is recognized (IAS 2.34).

Jun 30, 02	Dr	Cash	20	
	Cr	Revenue		20
Jun 30, 02	Dr	Cost of sales	18	
	Cr	Automobile (inventories)		18

Solution (b)

Jan 01, 01	Dr	Automobile (property, plant, and equipment)	24	
	Cr	Cash		24
Dec 31, 01	Dr	Depreciation expense	3	
	Cr	Automobile (property, plant, and equipment)		3
Jun 30, 02	Dr	Depreciation expense	1.5	
	Cr	Automobile (property, plant, and equipment)		1.5

Derecognition of the automobile (i.e. of an item of property, plant, and equipment) results in a gain of CU 0.50 (proceeds of CU 20 less the carrying amount of the automobile of CU 19.5) (IAS 1.34a, IAS 16.68, and 16.71):

Jun 30, 02	Dr	Cash	20	
	Cr	Automobile (property, plant, and equipment)		19.5
	Cr	Gain on derecognition		0.5

[3] *See the chapter on IAS 2, Section 3.*

Example 6

Revaluation of land – without taking deferred tax into account

On Jan 01, 01, entity E acquires land for CU 40. Payment is effected in cash on the same day. The piece of land is measured according to the revaluation model after recognition. Revaluations are carried out on an annual basis. Fair value of the land changes as follows:

Dec 31, 01	44
Dec 31, 02	36
Dec 31, 03	48

Required

Prepare any necessary entries in E's financial statements as on Dec 31 for the years 01–03. Ignore deferred tax.

Hints for solution

In particular Section 4.1.

Solution

Jan 01, 01	Dr	Land	40	
	Cr	Cash		40

Changes in value of the land are recognized in revaluation surplus to the extent that they take place below cost and in profit or loss to the extent that they take place below cost:

Dec 31, 01	Dr	Land	4	
	Cr	Revaluation surplus (OCI)		4
Dec 31, 02	Dr	Revaluation surplus (OCI)	4	
	Dr	Profit or loss	4	
	Cr	Land		8
Dec 31, 03	Dr	Land	12	
	Cr	Profit or loss		4
	Cr	Revaluation surplus (OCI)		8

Example 7

Revaluation of land – taking deferred tax[4] into account

Required

The situation and the task are the same as in Example 6. However, deferred tax has to be taken into account. The tax rate is 25%. According to the applicable tax law an increase in the carrying amount of land above its cost is not possible. However, under the applicable tax law, a decrease in fair value of land below cost has to be recognized immediately.

[4] *See the chapter on IAS 12 regarding deferred tax.*

Hints for solution

In particular Section 4.1.

Solution

Jan 01, 01	Dr	Land	40	
	Cr	Cash		40

After recognition, the increase in value above cost (which is not possible according to the applicable tax law) leads to the recognition of a deferred tax liability that has to be recognized outside profit or loss (as a reduction in revaluation surplus) (IAS 12.61A–12.62).

Carrying amount according to IFRS (as on Dec 31, 01)	44
Carrying amount according to the applicable tax law (as on Dec 31, 01)	40
Taxable temporary difference	**4**
Tax rate	25%
Deferred tax liability	**1**

Dec 31, 01	Dr	Land	4	
	Cr	Deferred tax liability		1
	Cr	Revaluation surplus (OCI)		3

On Dec 31, 02, the carrying amounts according to IFRS and according to the applicable tax law are identical. Therefore, no deferred tax asset or liability relating to the land is included in the statement of financial position at that date. Consequently the deferred tax liability of CU 1, recognized on Dec 31, 01, is derecognized.

Dec 31, 02	Dr	Revaluation surplus (OCI)	3	
	Dr	Deferred tax liability	1	
	Dr	Profit or loss	4	
	Cr	Land		8

Carrying amount according to IFRS (as on Dec 31, 03)	48
Carrying amount according to the applicable tax law (as on Dec 31, 03)	40
Taxable temporary difference	**8**
Tax rate	25%
Deferred tax liability	**2**

Dec 31, 03	Dr	Land	12	
	Cr	Profit or loss		4
	Cr	Deferred tax liability		2
	Cr	Revaluation surplus (OCI)		6

IAS 17 LEASES

1 INTRODUCTION AND SCOPE

IAS 17 specifies the accounting treatment of leases from the perspective of both lessees and lessors (IAS 17.1). A **lease** is an agreement in which the lessor conveys the right to use an asset for an agreed period of time to the lessee in return for a payment or series of payments (IAS 17.4).

The following are excluded from the scope of the standard (IAS 17.2):

- Leases to explore for or use minerals, oil, natural gas, and similar non-regenerative resources.
- Licensing agreements for motion picture films, video recordings, plays, manuscripts, patents, copyrights, and similar items.

Specific issues that arise when manufacturers or dealers act as lessors of their products (e.g. in the automotive industry) are not dealt with in this section of the book.

2 DEFINITIONS RELATING TO TIME

The **inception of the lease** is the earlier of the following (IAS 17.4):

- Date of the lease agreement.
- Date of commitment by the parties to the principal provisions of the lease.

By contrast, the **commencement of the lease term** is the date from which the lessee is entitled to exercise its right to use the leased asset (IAS 17.4).

The **lease term** comprises (IAS 17.4):

- the **non-cancellable period** for which the lessee has contracted to lease the asset, as well as
- any further terms for which the lessee has the **option** to continue to lease the asset (with or without further payment) when at the inception of the lease it is **reasonably certain** that the lessee will exercise the option.

3 CLASSIFICATION OF LEASES AS FINANCE LEASES OR OPERATING LEASES

3.1 Introduction

Whether the leased asset has to be included in the statement of financial position of the lessee or of the lessor depends on whether the lease represents a finance lease or an operating lease. In the former case, the leased asset is included in the lessee's statement of financial position and in the latter case it is not.

A **finance lease** is a lease in which substantially all the risks and rewards incidental to ownership of an asset are transferred. Title may or may not be transferred. An **operating lease** is a lease other than a finance lease (IAS 17.4 and 17.8).

It is important to note that the criteria listed in IAS 17.10[1] and 17.11[2] are only examples of criteria relevant with respect to lease classification.

3.2 Primary Lease Classification Criteria

The following are indicators that usually would lead to a lease being classified as a **finance lease** (IAS 17.10) and generally the presence of any one of these indicators would point to classification as a finance lease. Ultimately, the lease classification is based on an overall assessment of whether substantially all of the risks and rewards incidental to ownership of the asset have been transferred from the lessor to the lessee.[3]

(a) **Transfer of ownership**: By the end of the lease term ownership of the asset is transferred to the lessee.
(b) **Favorable purchase option**: The lessee has an option to purchase the leased asset at a price that is expected to be sufficiently lower than the fair value of the asset at the date the option becomes exercisable. Thus, it is reasonably certain at the inception of the lease that the option will be exercised. **Fair value** is the amount for which the leased asset could be exchanged between knowledgeable, willing parties in an arm's length transaction (IAS 17.4). The Standard does not specify how the term "sufficiently lower" has to be interpreted. Consequently, discretion is exercised in this respect.
(c) **Lease term test**: The **lease term is for the major part of the economic life** of the leased asset. The Standard does not define what is meant by the term "major part." Practice has been to apply the lease accounting guidance in US GAAP similarly. Hence, the term "major part" is usually interpreted as "75% or more" under IFRS.[4] It is also important to note that the economic life of the leased asset differs from its useful life (IAS 17.4):
  - **Economic life** is either the period over which the leased asset is expected to be economically usable by one or more users, or the number of production or similar units expected to be obtained from the leased asset by one or more users.
  - By contrast, **useful life** is the estimated remaining period from the commencement of the lease term without limitation by the lease term over which the economic benefits embodied in the leased asset are expected to be consumed by the entity.

(d) **Present value test**: The **present value** of the minimum lease payments **amounts to at least substantially all of the fair value** of the leased asset at the inception of the lease. With regard to this assessment the following steps are necessary:
  1. **Determining the minimum lease payments** (IAS 17.4): These are the payments over the lease term that the lessee is or can be required to make. They exclude contingent rent, costs for services, and taxes to be paid by and reimbursed to the lessor. **Contingent rent** is the portion of the lease payments that is not fixed in

[1] *See Section 3.2.*
[2] *See Section 3.3.*
[3] *See KPMG,* Insights into IFRS, *7th edition, 5.1.120.10.*
[4] *See KPMG,* Insights into IFRS, *7th edition, 5.1.150.20.*

amount but is based on the future amount of a factor that changes other than with the passage of time (e.g. percentage of future sales, amount of future use, future price indices, future market rates of interest) (IAS 17.4). Minimum lease payments also comprise:

- for a lessee, any amounts guaranteed by the lessee or by a party related to the lessee.
- for a lessor, any residual value guaranteed to the lessor by:
  - the lessee,
  - a party related to the lessee, or
  - a third party unrelated to the lessor that is financially capable of discharging the obligations under the guarantee.

However, if the lessee has a **favorable purchase option** (as defined previously), the minimum lease payments comprise the minimum payments payable over the lease term to the expected date of exercise of the option and the payment required to exercise it.

2. **Determining the present value of the minimum lease payments**:
   - The **lessor** determines the present value on the basis of the **interest rate implicit in the lease**. This interest rate is the discount rate which, at the inception of the lease, causes the aggregate present value of (a) the minimum lease payments and (b) the unguaranteed residual value to be equal to the sum of (i) the fair value of the leased asset and (ii) any initial direct costs of the lessor. The **initial direct costs** are incremental costs that are directly attributable to negotiating and arranging a lease (IAS 17.4).
   - The **lessee** uses the **same discount rate as the lessor** if it is **practicable** to determine. If this is not the case the **lessee's incremental borrowing rate** is used (IAS 17.20), which is the interest rate (IAS 17.4):
     - the lessee would have to pay on a similar lease or, if that is not determinable,
     - the rate that, at the inception of the lease, the lessee would incur to borrow over a similar term and with a similar security, the funds necessary to purchase the asset.
3. **Comparing the present value of the minimum lease payments with fair value**: As described earlier, if (at the inception of the lease) the present value of the minimum lease payments amounts to substantially all of the fair value of the leased asset, then the lease is normally classified as a finance lease. The Standard does not define what is meant by the term "substantially all." Practice has been to apply the lease accounting guidance in US GAAP similarly. Hence, the term "substantially all" is usually interpreted as "90% or more" under IFRS.[5]

(e) **Specialized nature**: The leased assets are of such a specialized nature that only the lessee can use them without major modifications.

3.3 Supplemental Indicators of a Finance Lease

There are several additional **indicators** that a lease may be a finance lease (IAS 17.11):

(a) **Losses associated with the cancellation of the lease**: If the lessee can cancel the lease, the losses of the lessor associated with the cancellation are borne by the lessee.

[5] *See KPMG,* Insights into IFRS, *7th edition, 5.1.160.10 and 5.1.160.20.*

(b) **Gains or losses from the fluctuation in the fair value of the residual** accrue to the lessee.
(c) **Favorable option to continue the lease**: The lessee has the ability to continue the lease for a secondary period at a rent that is substantially lower than market rent.

4 ACCOUNTING OF LEASES BY LESSEES

4.1 Finance Leases

At the commencement of the lease term, the lessee recognizes the **leased asset** as well as a **lease liability** in its statement of financial position at the **lower of** the following amounts (which are both determined at the inception of the lease) (IAS 17.20):

- **Fair value** of the leased asset.
- **Present value of the minimum lease payments**. The **discount rate** to be used is the same as the discount rate used when calculating the present value of the minimum lease payments when performing the present value test (see Section 3.2).

Any **initial direct costs** (i.e. incremental costs that are directly attributable to negotiating and arranging a lease – IAS 17.4) of the lessee are added to the amount recognized as an asset (IAS 17.20).

The minimum lease payments have to be apportioned between the **finance charge** and the **reduction of the outstanding liability**. The finance charge is allocated to each period during the lease term so as to produce a constant periodic interest rate on the remaining balance of the liability. **Contingent rents** have to be charged as expenses in the periods in which they are incurred (IAS 17.25–17.26).

A finance lease gives rise to **depreciation** expense for depreciable assets. If there is no reasonable certainty that the lessee will obtain ownership by the end of the lease term, the asset has to be fully depreciated over the shorter of the lease term and its useful life. However, if there is such reasonable certainty, the asset is depreciated over its useful life (IAS 17.27–17.28).

4.2 Operating Leases

In contrast to finance leases, under an operating lease the lessee recognizes neither the leased asset nor the corresponding lease liability in its statement of financial position. **Lease payments** (excluding costs for services such as insurance and maintenance) under an operating lease are recognized as an expense **on a straight-line basis** over the lease term, unless **another systematic basis** is more representative of the time pattern of the user's benefit (IAS 17.33–17.34).

In negotiating a lease, the lessor may provide **incentives** for the lessee to enter into the agreement. For example, initial periods of the lease term may be agreed to be rent-free or at a reduced rent. The lessee recognizes the aggregate benefit of incentives as a reduction of rental expense over the lease term on a straight-line basis unless another systematic basis is more representative of the time pattern of the lessee's benefit from the use of the leased asset (SIC 15.1 and 15.5).

5 ACCOUNTING OF LEASES BY LESSORS

5.1 Finance Leases

Under a finance lease, the lessor recognizes a **receivable** in its statement of financial position instead of the leased asset. At **initial recognition**, the receivable is measured at an amount equal to the **net investment in the lease** (IAS 17.36):

	Minimum lease payments (which include any guaranteed residual value[6])
+	Estimated unguaranteed residual value
=	**Gross investment in the lease**
–	Unearned finance income
=	**Net investment in the lease**

Thereby, the **unguaranteed residual value** is the portion of the residual value of the leased asset, the realization of which by the lessor is not assured or is guaranteed solely by a party related to the lessor. The **net investment in the lease** is calculated by discounting the gross investment in the lease by the interest rate implicit in the lease (IAS 17.4).

When the receivable is measured subsequently, the **payments** are **separated into interest and redemption**. The recognition of finance income is based on a pattern reflecting a constant periodic rate of return on the lessor's net investment in the finance lease (IAS 17.39).

Estimated **unguaranteed residual values** used in determining the lessor's gross investment in the lease are reviewed regularly. If there has been a reduction in the estimated unguaranteed residual value, the lessor has to revise the income allocation over the lease term and to recognize any reduction in respect of amounts accrued immediately (IAS 17.41).

5.2 Operating Leases

Under an operating lease, the lessor presents the **leased asset** in its statement of financial position and not a lease receivable (IAS 17.49). **Depreciation** for depreciable leased assets is calculated according to IAS 16 and IAS 38 (IAS 17.53).

Lease income (excluding receipts for services provided such as insurance and maintenance) is recognized on a **straight-line basis** over the lease term unless **another systematic basis** is more appropriate (IAS 17.50–17.51).

In negotiating a lease, the lessor may provide **incentives** for the lessee to enter into the agreement. For example, initial periods of the lease term may be agreed to be rent-free or at a reduced rent. The lessor recognizes the aggregate cost of incentives as a reduction of rental income over the lease term on a straight-line basis unless another systematic basis is more appropriate (SIC 15.1 and 15.4).

Initial direct costs incurred by lessors in negotiating and arranging an operating lease are added to the carrying amount of the leased asset. They are recognized as an expense over the lease term on the same basis as the lease income (IAS 17.52).

---

[6] *See Section 3.2.*

6 SALE AND LEASEBACK TRANSACTIONS

Sale and leaseback transactions have two components:[7]

- The sale of the asset from the seller to the lessor.
- The leaseback of the asset from the buyer/lessor to the seller/lessee.

The accounting treatment depends on whether the lease is a finance lease or an operating lease (IAS 17.58).

If a sale and leaseback transaction results in a finance lease, the asset remains in the seller-lessee's statement of financial position. Hence, any excess of sales proceeds over the carrying amount must not be immediately recognized as income by the seller-lessee. Instead, it is deferred and amortized through profit or loss over the lease term (IAS 17.59 and IAS 1.34a).

7 EXAMPLES WITH SOLUTIONS

Example 1

Finance lease or operating lease?

As from Jan 01, 01 entity E leases a machine. The lease term is four years. The economic life (IAS 17.4) and the useful life (IAS 17.4) of the machine are six years. At the end of each year, a minimum lease payment of CU 1 has to be made. There is no purchase option and no transfer of ownership by the end of the lease term. The machine is a standardized product that is also used by E's competitors. It is not practicable for E to determine the interest rate implicit in the lease. E's incremental borrowing rate is 9% p.a. The fair value of the machine as at Jan 01, 01 is CU 3.

Required

Assess whether each of the criteria in IAS 17.10 indicates that the lease has to be treated as a finance lease in E's financial statements. Assume that apart from IAS 17.10, no further criteria are relevant for the assessment in this example.

Hints for solution

In particular Section 3.

Solution

Applying the criteria in IAS 17.10 leads to the following result:

Transfer of ownership (IAS 17.10a): By the end of the lease term there is no transfer of ownership of the machine to the lessee. Therefore, this criterion does not indicate that the lease is a finance lease.

Favorable purchase option (IAS 17.10b): There is no purchase option. Consequently, this criterion does not indicate that the lease is a finance lease.

[7] *See KPMG,* Insights into IFRS, *6th edition, 5.1.470.10.*

Lease term test (IAS 17.10c): The lease term (four years) is 66.67% (= 4 : 6) of the economic life of the leased machine (six years), which is clearly below 75%. Consequently, this criterion does not indicate that the lease is a finance lease.

Present value test (IAS 17.10d): Since it is not practicable for E to determine the interest rate implicit in the lease, E uses its incremental borrowing rate in order to determine the present value of the minimum lease payments (IAS 17.20):

	Payment	*Present value*
1st minimum lease payment (Dec 31, 01)	1	0.92
2nd minimum lease payment (Dec 31, 02)	1	0.84
3rd minimum lease payment (Dec 31, 03)	1	0.77
4th minimum lease payment (Dec 31, 04)	1	0.71
Present value as at Jan 01, 01		**3.24**
Fair value as at Jan 01, 01		**3.00**
Present value as a percentage of fair value		**107.99%**

107.99% is above 90%. Hence, the present value test indicates that the lease is a finance lease.

Specialized nature (IAS 17.10e): The machine is a standardized product. Thus, this criterion does not indicate that the lease is a finance lease.

One of the criteria in IAS 17.10 (namely the present value test) indicates that the lease is a finance lease. In this example, it is assumed that apart from IAS 17.10 no other criteria are relevant with regard to lease classification. Consequently, the lease is classified as a **finance lease**, which means that the machine is included in E's statement of financial position.

Example 2

Finance leases in the lessee's financial statements

Required

Prepare any necessary entries in E's financial statements as at Dec 31 for the years 01 and 02 relating to the lease described in Example 1.

Hints for solution

In particular Section 4.1.

Solution

On Jan 01, 01, E recognizes the leased asset as well as a liability in its statement of financial position at the lower of the fair value of the leased machine and the present value of the minimum lease payments (IAS 17.20):

Jan 01, 01	Dr	Machine	3	
	Cr	Lease liability		3

In this example there is no favorable purchase option and no transfer of ownership and there are no other criteria that indicate that the lessee will receive ownership of the leased machine by the end of the lease term with reasonable certainty. Hence, the machine is depreciated over the shorter of the lease term and its useful life (IAS 17.27–17.28) (CU 3 : four years):

Dec 31, 01	Dr	Depreciation expense	0.75	
	Cr	Machine		0.75

The minimum lease payments have to be apportioned into the **finance charge** and the **reduction of the outstanding liability**. The finance charge is allocated to each period during the lease term so as to produce a constant periodic interest rate on the remaining balance of the liability (IAS 17.25). For this purpose, the internal rate of return is determined:

Carrying amount of the liability as at Jan 01, 01	3.00	
1st minimum lease payment (Dec 31, 01)	−1.00	
2nd minimum lease payment (Dec 31, 02)	−1.00	
3rd minimum lease payment (Dec 31, 03)	−1.00	
4th minimum lease payment (Dec 31, 04)	−1.00	
Internal rate of return	**12.59%**	*Formula "IRR" in Excel*

The following table is prepared on the basis of the internal rate of return determined above. Interest expense for the year is calculated by using the formula "carrying amount of the liability as at Jan 01 of the year · internal rate of return." The reduction of the carrying amount of the liability is determined by using the formula "minimum lease payment less interest expense."[8]

Year	*Carrying amount of the liability as at Jan 01*	*Minimum lease payment*	*Interest expense*	*Reduction of the carrying amount of the liability*	*Carrying amount of the liability as at Dec 31*
01	3.00	1.00	0.38	0.62	2.38
02	2.38	1.00	0.30	0.70	1.68
03	1.68	1.00	0.21	0.79	0.89
04	0.89	1.00	0.11	0.89	0.00
Total		**4.00**	**1.00**	**3.00**	

Dec 31, 01	Dr	Lease liability	0.62	
	Dr	Interest expense	0.38	
	Cr	Cash		1.00
Dec 31, 02	Dr	Depreciation expense	0.75	
	Cr	Machine		0.75
Dec 31, 02	Dr	Lease liability	0.70	
	Dr	Interest expense	0.30	
	Cr	Cash		1.00

[8] *The amounts in the table have been calculated with the exact internal rate of return and not with a rounded rate.*

Example 3

Operating leases in the lessee's financial statements

Entity E leases a machine under an operating lease from lessor F. The lease term, which begins on Jan 01, 01, is three years. F provides an incentive for E to enter into the lease by granting three rent-free months at the beginning of the lease term. After the rent-free period of time, the monthly lease payments, which are payable at the end of each month, are CU 1 per month.

Required

Prepare any necessary entries in E's financial statements as at Dec 31 for the years 01–03. Assume that it is appropriate to recognize the aggregate benefit of the incentives on a straight-line basis (SIC 15.5).

Hints for solution

In particular Section 4.2.

Solution

Each year the actual payments reduce cash in the statement of financial position. The aggregate expense of CU 33 (33 payments of CU 1) is allocated to the three years of the lease term on a straight-line basis, i.e. each year, an expense of CU 11 is recognized. The difference is recognized as a liability or as a reduction of that liability.

For example, in 01 a liability of CU 2 is recognized because CU 9 have been paid, as compared with a recognized expense of CU 11. In 02, the liability has to be reduced by CU 1 because CU 12 have been paid, as compared with a recognized expense of CU 11. Hence, on Dec 31, 02 the carrying amount of the liability is CU 1. The carrying amount of CU 1 represents the difference between accumulated expenses in 01 and 02 (CU 22) and the accumulated payments in 01 and 02 (CU 21): Expenses of CU 1 have not been paid yet.

Year	*Lease payments*	*Expense*	*Carrying amount of the liability as at Dec 31*
01	9	11	2
02	12	11	1
03	12	11	0
Total	**33**	**33**	

Dec 31, 01	Dr	Lease expense	11	
	Cr	Cash		9
	Cr	Liability		2
Dec 31, 02	Dr	Lease expense	11	
	Dr	Liability	1	
	Cr	Cash		12

Dec 31, 03	Dr	Lease expense	11	
	Dr	Liability	1	
	Cr	Cash		12

Example 4

Finance leases in the lessor's financial statements

On Jan 01, 01 entity E acquires a machine which it leases to entity F starting the same date. The lease term, the economic life (IAS 17.4), and the useful life (IAS 17.4) of the machine are three years. At the end of each year, E receives a minimum lease payment of CU 1. On Jan 01, 01, the fair value of the machine and the lessor's costs of purchase are identical and amount to CU 2.4.

Required

Prepare any necessary entries in E's financial statements as at Dec 31 for the years 01 and 02.

Hints for solution

In particular Sections 3 and 5.1.

Solution

The interest rate implicit in the lease (IAS 17.4) (i.e. the lessor's internal rate of return) is determined as follows:

Fair value of the machine as at Jan 01, 01	2.40	
1st minimum lease payment (Dec 31, 01)	−1.00	
2nd minimum lease payment (Dec 31, 02)	−1.00	
3rd minimum lease payment (Dec 31, 03)	−1.00	
Internal rate of return	**12.04%**	*Formula "IRR" in Excel*

The lease term test and the present value test lead to classification of the lease as a finance lease (IAS 17.10).

The following table is prepared on the basis of the internal rate of return determined above:

Year	*Carrying amount of the receivable as at Jan 01*	*Minimum lease payment*	*Interest income*	*Reduction of the carrying amount of the receivable*	*Carrying amount of the receivable as at Dec 31*
01	2.40	1.00	0.29	0.71	1.69
02	1.69	1.00	0.20	0.80	0.89
03	0.89	1.00	0.11	0.89	0.00
Total		**3.00**	**0.60**	**2.40**	

Jan 01, 01	Dr	Machine	2.4	
	Cr	Cash		2.4

On Jan 01, 01, the lessor recognizes a **receivable** in the amount of the net investment in the lease (IAS 17.36 and 17.4) and derecognizes the machine:

Jan 01, 01	Dr	Lease receivable	2.4	
	Cr	Machine		2.4

The minimum lease payments are apportioned between the finance charge and the reduction of the outstanding liability (see table previously).

Dec 31, 01	Dr	Cash	1.00	
	Cr	Interest income		0.29
	Cr	Lease receivable		0.71
Dec 31, 02	Dr	Cash	1.0	
	Cr	Interest income		0.2
	Cr	Lease receivable		0.8

Example 5

Finance leases with residual values in the lessor's financial statements

Required

Prepare any necessary entries with respect to the lease described in Example 4 in E's financial statements as at Dec 31 for the years 01 and 02. However, in contrast to Example 4, assume that there is an unguaranteed residual value of CU 0.1 as at Dec 31, 03.

Hints for solution

In particular Sections 3 and 5.1.

Solution

The unguaranteed residual value is not part of the minimum lease payments (IAS 17.4). The interest rate implicit in the lease (i.e. the lessor's internal rate of return) is determined as follows (IAS 17.4):

Fair value of the machine as at Jan 01, 01	2.40	
1st minimum lease payment (Dec 31, 01)	−1.00	
2nd minimum lease payment (Dec 31, 02)	−1.00	
3rd minimum lease payment and unguaranteed residual value (Dec 31, 03)	−1.10	
Internal rate of return	**13.73%**	*Formula "IRR" in Excel*

When performing the present value test, present value is calculated on the basis of the minimum lease payments (i.e. excluding the unguaranteed residual value). The lease term test and the present value test lead to the classification of the lease as a finance lease (IAS 17.10).

The following table is prepared on the basis of the internal rate of return determined previously:

Year	*Carrying amount of the receivable as at Jan 01*	*Minimum lease payment*	*Interest income*	*Reduction of the carrying amount of the receivable*	*Carrying amount of the receivable as at Dec 31*
01	2.40	1.00	0.33	0.67	1.73
02	1.73	1.00	0.24	0.76	0.97
03	0.97	1.00	0.13	0.87	0.10
Total		**3.00**	**0.70**	**2.30**	

Jan 01, 01	Dr	Machine	2.4	
	Cr	Cash		2.4

On Jan 01, 01, the lessor recognizes a **receivable** in the amount of the net investment in the lease (which is the present value of the minimum lease payments and the unguaranteed residual value) (IAS 17.36 and 17.4) and derecognizes the machine:

Jan 01, 01	Dr	Lease receivable	2.4	
	Cr	Machine		2.4

The minimum lease payments are apportioned into the finance charge and the reduction of the outstanding liability (see the table above).

Dec 31, 01	Dr	Cash	1.00	
	Cr	Interest income		0.33
	Cr	Lease receivable		0.67
Dec 31, 02	Dr	Cash	1.00	
	Cr	Interest income		0.24
	Cr	Lease receivable		0.76

Example 6

Operating leases in the lessor's financial statements

Required

Prepare any necessary entries with respect to the lease described in Example 3 in the financial statements of the lessor (i.e. of entity F) as at Dec 31. Assume that the machine has been acquired on Jan 01, 01 (costs of purchase: CU 90, economic life and useful life: 10 years). Assume that it is appropriate to recognize the aggregate cost of the incentives on a straight-line basis (SIC 15.4).

Hints for solution

In particular Section 5.2.

Solution

The aggregate cost of the incentives is recognized as a reduction of income over the lease term (SIC 15.4). The set-up of the entries is similar to Example 3. In 01, a receivable in the amount of CU 2 has to be recognized. This is because lease income of CU 11 is recognized in 01 and only payments of CU 9 are received.

Year	*Lease payments*	*Income*	*Carrying amount of the receivable as at Dec 31*
01	9	11	2
02	12	11	1
03	12	11	0
Total	**33**	**33**	

Dec 31, 01	Dr	Cash	9	
	Dr	Receivable	2	
	Cr	Lease income		11

Moreover, the machine is recognized in F's statement of financial position and depreciated over its useful life (IAS 17.53 and IAS 16.50).

Jan 01, 01	Dr	Machine	90	
	Cr	Cash		90
Dec 31, 01	Dr	Depreciation expense	9	
	Cr	Machine		9
Dec 31, 02	Dr	Depreciation expense	9	
	Cr	Machine		9
Dec 31, 02	Dr	Cash	12	
	Cr	Receivable		1
	Cr	Lease income		11
Dec 31, 03	Dr	Depreciation expense	9	
	Cr	Machine		9
Dec 31, 03	Dr	Cash	12	
	Cr	Receivable		1
	Cr	Lease income		11

Example 7

Sale and leaseback transactions

Entity E owns a machine with a carrying amount of CU 10 and a fair value of CU 12.8 as at Jan 01, 01. On Jan 01, 01, E sells the machine for CU 12.8 to entity F and leases the machine back starting the same date for a minimum lease payment of CU 4 p.a., payable at the end of each year. The lease term is four years. The economic life (IAS 17.4) and the useful life (IAS 17.4) of the machine are six years. There is no purchase option and no transfer of ownership by the end of the lease term. The machine is a standardized product that is also used by E's competitors. It is not practicable for E to determine the interest rate implicit in the lease. E's incremental borrowing rate of interest is 8% p.a.

Required

Prepare any necessary entries in E's financial statements as at Dec 31 for the year 01. Assume that in this example, apart from IAS 17.10, no further criteria are relevant for the classification as a finance lease or as an operating lease.

Hints for solution

In particular Sections 3 and 6.

Solution

Since it is not practicable for E to determine the interest rate implicit in the lease, E uses its incremental borrowing rate in order to determine the present value of the minimum lease payments when performing the present value test (IAS 17.20):

	Payment	*Present value*
1st minimum lease payment (Dec 31, 01)	4	3.70
2nd minimum lease payment (Dec 31, 02)	4	3.43
3rd minimum lease payment (Dec 31, 03)	4	3.18
4th minimum lease payment (Dec 31, 04)	4	2.94
Present value as at Jan 01, 01		**13.25**
Fair value as at Jan 01, 01		**12.80**
Present value as a percentage of fair value		**103.52%**

One of the criteria in IAS 17.10 (namely the present value test) indicates that the lease is a finance lease. In this example, it is assumed that apart from IAS 17.10 no other criteria are relevant with regard to lease classification. Consequently, the lease is classified as a **finance lease**.

The machine continues to be included in E's statement of financial position, because the lease is classified as a finance lease. E increases the carrying amount of the machine of CU 10 to the lower amount of fair value and present value of the minimum lease payments, i.e. to CU 12.8 (IAS 17.20). In addition, a lease liability is recognized at the lower amount of the fair value of the machine and the present value of the minimum lease payments (IAS 17.20). The excess of the sales proceeds (CU 12.8) over the previous carrying amount of the machine (CU 10) is recognized as deferred income (IAS 17.59 and IAS 1.34a).

Jan 01, 01	Dr	Machine	2.8	
	Dr	Cash	12.8	
	Cr	Deferred income		2.8
	Cr	Lease liability		12.8

The deferred income is amortized over the lease term through profit or loss (IAS 17.59 and IAS 1.34a):

Dec 31, 01	Dr	Deferred income	0.7	
	Cr	Income		0.7

In this example there is no favorable purchase option and no transfer of ownership and there are no other criteria which indicate that the lessee will receive ownership of the leased machine by the end of the lease term with reasonable certainty. Hence, the machine is depreciated over the shorter of the lease term and its useful life (IAS 17.27–17.28) (CU 12.8 : four years):

Dec 31, 01	Dr	Depreciation expense	3.2	
	Cr	Machine		3.2

The internal rate of return is determined as follows:

Carrying amount of the liability as at Jan 01, 01	12.80	
1st minimum lease payment (Dec 31, 01)	−4.00	
2nd minimum lease payment (Dec 31, 02)	−4.00	
3rd minimum lease payment (Dec 31, 03)	−4.00	
4th minimum lease payment (Dec 31, 04)	−4.00	
Internal rate of return	**9.56%**	*Formula "IRR" in Excel*

The following table is prepared on the basis of the internal rate of return determined above. Interest expense for the year is calculated by using the formula "carrying amount of the liability as at Jan 01 of the year · internal rate of return." The reduction of the carrying amount of the liability is determined by using the formula "minimum lease payment less interest expense":[9]

Year	*Carrying amount of the liability as at Jan 01*	*Minimum lease payment*	*Interest expense*	*Reduction of the carrying amount of the liability*	*Carrying amount of the liability as at Dec 31*
01	12.80	4.00	1.22	2.78	10.02
02	10.02	4.00	0.96	3.04	6.98
03	6.98	4.00	0.67	3.33	3.65
04	3.65	4.00	0.35	3.65	0.00
Total		**16.00**	**3.20**	**12.80**	

Dec 31, 01	Dr	Lease liability	2.78	
	Dr	Interest expense	1.22	
	Cr	Cash		4.00

[9] *The amounts in the table have been calculated with the exact internal rate of return and not with a rounded rate.*

IAS 18 REVENUE

1 INTRODUCTION AND SCOPE

IAS 18 prescribes the accounting treatment of revenue. In particular, the issue regarding **when to recognize revenue** is dealt with. On the basis of the definitions in the Conceptual Framework,[1] IAS 18 defines **revenue** as the gross inflow of economic benefits during the accounting period arising in the course of the ordinary activities of an entity. These inflows have to result in increases in equity other than increases relating to contributions from equity participants. **Revenue** is a particular form of **income** and differs from **gains** that arise, for example, due to fair value changes or on disposal of property, plant, and equipment (Objective of IAS 18, IAS 18.6(a), 18.7, F.70(a), and F.74).

IAS 18 applies to the accounting for revenue arising from the following transactions and events (IAS 18.1):

- The sale of **goods** (Section 3)
- The rendering of **services** (Section 4)
- The use by others of entity assets yielding **interest**, **royalties**, and **dividends** (Section 5)

However, in particular revenue arising from the following transactions and events falls **outside the scope of IAS 18** (IAS 18.6):

- Lease agreements (IAS 17)
- Dividends arising from investments accounted for under the equity method (IAS 28)
- Insurance contracts within the scope of IFRS 4
- Changes in the fair value of financial assets and financial liabilities or their disposal (IFRS 9)
- Changes in the value of other current assets

Moreover, revenue recognition for **construction contracts** is subject to the specific requirements of IAS 11 and not to those of IAS 18. However, the concept of IAS 18 for recognizing revenue and the associated expenses for transactions involving the **rendering of services** is generally consistent with the requirements of IAS 11 (IAS 18.21).

2 MEASUREMENT OF REVENUE

Revenue is measured at the **fair value of the consideration** received or receivable. Revenue is reduced by **trade discounts** and **volume rebates** allowed by the entity (IAS 18.9–18.10).[2]

---

[1] *See the chapter on Conceptual Framework, Section 6.1.*

[2] *Discounting of the consideration that may be necessary in certain situations is dealt with in Section 6.2.1.*

Fair value is the amount for which an asset could be exchanged, or a liability settled, between knowledgeable, willing parties in an arm's length transaction (IAS 18.7).

Revenue comprises only the gross inflows of economic benefits received and receivable by the entity on its own account. **Amounts collected on behalf of third parties** (e.g. sales taxes, goods and services taxes, and value added taxes) are not economic benefits that flow to the entity and do not increase equity. Thus, they **do not represent revenue**. For this reason, a commission agent only recognizes its commission as revenue, instead of the selling price of the goods sold (IAS 18.8).[3]

3 SALE OF GOODS

The term "goods" includes goods produced by the entity for the purpose of sale (i.e. finished goods) and merchandise (IAS 18.3).

Revenue from the sale of goods is **recognized** when all of the following criteria are met (IAS 18.14):

- The **significant risks and rewards** of ownership of the goods have been transferred to the buyer.
- The seller retains neither effective **control** over the goods sold, nor continuing managerial involvement to the degree usually associated with ownership.
- The amount of revenue and the costs relating to the transaction can be **measured reliably**.
- It is probable that the **economic benefits** associated with the transaction will flow to the entity.

The assessment of when to recognize revenue is based on the concept of **beneficial ownership**. In many cases, the transfer of beneficial ownership coincides with the transfer of legal title or the passing of possession. This is the case for most retail sales (IAS 18.15). However, in some situations the transfer of beneficial ownership may occur at a different time from the transfer of legal title or the passing of possession (e.g. when goods are sold under **retention of title**).[4]

Revenue is only recognized when it is probable that the economic benefits associated with the transaction will flow to the seller. If goods are supplied to an already defaulting customer, it is not possible to make the entries on a gross basis, i.e. to recognize both revenue and an expense relating to the impairment. Instead, no revenue is recognized. However, when an uncertainty arises about the collectibility of an amount already correctly included in revenue, the uncollectible amount or the amount for which recovery has ceased to be probable is recognized as an expense rather than as an adjustment of revenue (IAS 18.18).

Revenue and expenses that relate to the same transaction or other event are recognized simultaneously. This is referred to as the **matching of revenues and expenses**. Revenue is not

---

[3] *Sales commissions from the perspective of the commission agent are dealt with in more detail in the chapter on Conceptual Framework (Section 4.2.2 and Example 3).*

[4] *Transactions involving retention of title are dealt with in more detail in the chapter on Conceptual Framework (Section 4.2.2 and Example 2).*

recognized when the expenses cannot be measured reliably; in such cases, any consideration already received for the sale of the goods is recognized as a liability (IAS 18.19).

4 RENDERING OF SERVICES

The rendering of services typically involves the performance of a contractually agreed task by the entity over an agreed period of time (IAS 18.4). In this context, it is important to note that revenue arising from **construction contracts** is dealt with in IAS 11 and not in IAS 18. Some contracts for the rendering of services are directly related to construction contracts (e.g. the services of an architect). These contracts are also accounted for according to IAS 11 (IAS 18.4).

IAS 18 requires for service contracts (e.g. contracts to create software (intangible assets) or to render expert opinions) whose outcome can be estimated reliably that revenue is recognized according to the **stage of completion** (**"percentage of completion method"** or "PoC-method"). For example, if an entity starts executing a contract in the year 01 and performs one third of the contract in 01 (i.e. the stage of completion is 33.33% at the end of 01), one third of contract revenue, one third of the contract costs, and hence also one third of the profit margin are recognized in that period. This corresponds with the requirements of IAS 11 for construction contracts. The concept of IAS 18 for recognizing revenue and the associated expenses for transactions involving the rendering of services is generally consistent with the requirements of IAS 11 (IAS 18.20–18.24).

For practical purposes, when services are performed by an **indeterminate number of acts over a specified period of time**, revenue is recognized on a **straight-line basis** over the specified period unless some other method better represents the stage of completion. When a specific act is much more significant than any other acts, revenue recognition is postponed until the significant act is executed (IAS 18.25).

5 INTEREST, ROYALTIES, AND DIVIDENDS

The use of the reporting entity's assets by others gives rise to revenue in the form of (IAS 18.5):

- **Interest**: Charges for the use of cash or cash equivalents or amounts due to the entity.
- **Royalties**: Charges for the use of long-term intangible assets of the entity (e.g. patents and copyrights).
- **Dividends**: Distributions of profits to holders of equity investments in proportion to their holdings of a particular class of capital.

The following requirements apply with respect to the recognition of the types of revenue described above (IAS 18.29):

- It is probable that the **economic benefits** associated with the transaction will flow to the entity.
- The amount of the revenue can be **measured reliably**.

Revenue is recognized as follows (IAS 18.30–18.33):

- **Interest** is recognized according to the **effective interest method**[5] (IAS 39.9 and 39.AG5–39.AG8).
- **Royalties**:
  - The accounting treatment of royalties arising from **leases** is dealt with in IAS 17.
  - **License fees**: When property rights are licensed for more than one period, revenue is generally recognized on a straight-line basis. However, it is necessary to take into account the substance of the agreement:
    - When rights are licensed without limitation of time and without further obligations of the licensor, revenue is recognized immediately and not on a straight-line basis (IAS 18.IE20).
    - When the receipt of the license fee is contingent on the occurrence of uncertain future events or if the amount of the license fee depends on the licensee's quantity produced or on the licensee's sales, revenue is generally not recognized until these specifications occur (IAS 18.IE20 and 18.16c).
- **Dividends** are recognized when the **shareholder's right** to receive payment is **established**. Dividends arising from investments that are accounted for under the equity method are not within the scope of IAS 18 (IAS 18.6b).[6]

According to the above criteria, revenue recognition requires that it is probable that the economic benefits associated with the transaction will flow to the entity. However, when uncertainty arises about the collectibility of an amount already correctly included in revenue, the uncollectible amount or the amount for which recovery has ceased to be probable is recognized as an expense rather than as an adjustment of revenue (IAS 18.34).

6 MULTIPLE ELEMENT TRANSACTIONS AND LINKED TRANSACTIONS

6.1 Introduction

Normally, the recognition criteria of IAS 18 are applied separately to each transaction. However, in certain circumstances, this does not reflect the substance of the transaction(s) meaning that it is necessary (IAS 18.13):

- to apply the recognition criteria to the separately identifiable components of a single transaction (**multiple element transactions**) (see Section 6.2) or conversely,
- to apply the recognition criteria to two or more transactions together (**linked transactions**) (see Section 6.3).

6.2 Multiple Element Transactions

6.2.1 Sale on Credit When payment for goods sold or services provided is deferred beyond normal credit terms and the entity does not charge a market interest rate, the transaction effectively includes a financing arrangement and interest has to be imputed unless the impact is immaterial.[7] This means that the consideration is discounted in such cases. Hence, the

[5] *See the chapter on IFRS 9/IAS 39, Section 2.3.5.*

[6] *See the chapter on IAS 28 (Section 2.2.1) and the chapter on IAS 31/IFRS 11 (Section 2.2.3.2).*

[7] *See KPMG,* Insights into IFRS, *7th edition, 4.2.20.20.*

entry "Dr Receivable Cr Sales revenue" is effected in the amount of the present value of the consideration. Subsequently, the carrying amount of the receivable is increased (Dr Receivable Cr Interest income) (IAS 18.11). This reflects the substance of the transaction because the consideration is divided into sales revenue (e.g. for the sale of merchandise) (main transaction) and interest income (financing transaction).

6.2.2 Servicing Component When the selling price of a product includes an identifiable amount for subsequent servicing by the seller, that amount is deferred and recognized as revenue over the period during which the service is performed (IAS 18.13).

6.2.3 Customer Loyalty Programs This chapter only discusses the accounting treatment of customer loyalty programs from the **perspective of the granting entity**. From the granting entity perspective, customer loyalty programs are within the **scope of IFRIC 13**, if (IFRIC 13.3):

- the award credits (often described as "points") are granted to the entity's customers as part of a sales transaction (e.g. a sale of goods or rendering of services), and
- the customers can redeem the award credits in the future for free or discounted goods or services (subject to meeting further conditions).

Hence, cash bonuses are not within the scope of IFRIC 13. Customer loyalty programs through which the customer receives the bonus at the same time as the main transaction takes place (e.g. the customer may receive an additional bar of chocolate for free, if he buys two bars of chocolate) are not within the scope of IFRIC 13 either.

This section concentrates only on such customer loyalty programs in which no further parties are involved apart from the granting entity and its customers.

Contracts involving customer loyalty programs (award credits) are multiple element contracts, i.e. the fair value of the consideration has to be apportioned between the main transaction and the award credits. Thereby, the revenue attributable to the **main transaction** is often realized immediately. By contrast, the amount attributable to the **award credits** is at first recognized as deferred revenue. This results in the entry "Dr Cash Cr Revenue (main transaction) Cr Deferred revenue (award credits)." At the end of the reporting period in which this entry has been made, the amount of deferred revenue that is transferred to revenue is calculated by dividing the number of award credits redeemed by the end of the reporting period by the number of award credits that are expected to be redeemed in total. For example, entity E started granting award credits to its customers on Jan 01, 01. Assume that deferred revenue of CU 10 has been recognized in 01, 40 award credits have been redeemed in 01 and that it is expected that 100 of the award credits granted in 01 will be redeemed in total. In this case, an amount of CU 4 (= 40% of CU 10) is transferred from deferred revenue to revenue in 01 ("Dr Deferred revenue Cr Revenue CU 4").

According to IFRIC 13, two different methods of allocating the consideration between the main transaction and the award credits are possible (IFRIC 13.BC14):

- **Residual value method**: The amount allocated to the award credits is equal to their fair value (irrespective of the fair value of the main transaction). The revenue attributable to the main transaction is the remainder of the consideration.

- **Relative fair value method**: The amount allocated to the award credits is a proportion of the total consideration based on the fair value of the award credits relative to the fair value of the main transaction.

A change in estimate on subsequent balance sheet dates regarding the number of award credits expected to be redeemed affects the amount of revenue to be recognized in the corresponding period.

6.3 Linked Transactions

In certain circumstances it is necessary to apply the recognition criteria to two or more transactions together in order to reflect the substance of the transactions. For example, an entity may sell goods and, at the same time, enter into a separate agreement to repurchase the same goods at a later date, thus negating the substantive effect of the sale. In such a case, the two transactions are dealt with together, i.e. they are regarded as one transaction for accounting purposes (IAS 18.13).

7 EXAMPLES WITH SOLUTIONS

References to Other Chapters

Examples illustrating revenue recognition relating to **sales commissions** and sales of goods under **retention of title** are included in the chapter on Conceptual Framework (Examples 2 and 3). Examples illustrating the **effective interest method** are included in the chapter on IFRS 9/IAS 39 (Examples 7–9). Examples with regard to revenue recognition according to the **stage of completion (percentage of completion method)** are included in the chapter on IAS 11.

Example 1

Realized and unrealized consideration – introductory example

Entity E sells merchandise to entity F. E receives the consideration of CU 5 on Dec 23, 01. Delivery (= transfer of risks) takes place on (a) Dec 29, 01 and (b) Jan 02, 02.

Required

Prepare any necessary entries in E's financial statements as at Dec 31 for the years 01 and 02 with respect to revenue recognition.

Hints for solution

In particular Section 3.

Solution (a)

E receives the consideration on Dec 23, 01. However, at that date E has not yet delivered the merchandise. Hence, E has to recognize a liability that represents E's obligation to deliver the merchandise:

Dec 23, 01	Dr	Cash	5	
	Cr	Liability		5

Delivery is effected on Dec 29, 01. Consequently, E recognizes revenue of CU 5:

Dec 29, 01	Dr	Liability	5	
	Cr	Revenue		5

Solution (b)

Dec 23, 01	Dr	Cash	5	
	Cr	Liability		5

In contrast to version (a), no revenue is recognized in E's financial statements as at Dec 31, 01. Instead, these financial statements include a liability of CU 5 and revenue is presented in the financial statements for 02:

Jan 02, 02	Dr	Liability	5	
	Cr	Revenue		5

Example 2

Sale on credit

On Jan 01, 01 entity E delivers merchandise to entity F. The consideration of CU 121 is payable on Dec 31, 02 and is paid on that date. The interest rate is 10% p.a.

Required

Prepare any necessary entries in E's financial statements as at Dec 31 for the years 01 and 02 with respect to revenue recognition.

Hints for solution

In particular Section 6.2.1.

Solution

Revenue and the receivable are recognized on Jan 01, 01 at fair value (= present value) (IAS 18.9–18.11). Fair value is CU 100 (= CU 121 : 1.1^2).

Jan 01, 01	Dr	Receivable	100	
	Cr	Sales revenue		100

In 01 and 02, the carrying amount of the receivable increases (year 01: CU 100 · 1.1 = CU 110; year 02: CU 110 · 1.1 = CU 121) and interest is recognized (IAS 18.11).

Dec 31, 01	Dr	Receivable	10	
	Cr	Interest income		10
Dec 31, 02	Dr	Receivable	11	
	Cr	Interest income		11
Dec 31, 02	Dr	Cash	121	
	Cr	Receivable		121

Example 3

Servicing component

On Jan 01, 01 entity E sells a copy machine for CU 13. The selling price contains consideration for the subsequent servicing of the copy machine by E for the years 01–03. The selling price for that copy machine would have been CU 10 without subsequent servicing by E.

Required

Prepare any necessary entries in E's financial statements as at Dec 31 for the years 01–03 with respect to revenue recognition.

Hints for solution

In particular Section 6.2.2.

Solution

The consideration of CU 10 that is attributable to the main transaction (sale of the copy machine) is realized and therefore also recognized on Jan 01, 01 (IAS 18.14). The servicing component of CU 3 is deferred and recognized as revenue in the years 01–03 (IAS 18.13).

Jan 01, 01	Dr	Cash	13	
	Cr	Revenue		10
	Cr	Deferred revenue		3
Dec 31, 01	Dr	Deferred revenue	1	
	Cr	Revenue		1
Dec 31, 02	Dr	Deferred revenue	1	
	Cr	Revenue		1
Dec 31, 03	Dr	Deferred revenue	1	
	Cr	Revenue		1

Example 4

Customer loyalty program – allocation of the consideration

Entity E operates a restaurant chain. If a guest consumes dishes and/or beverages worth at least CU 10, he is granted a coupon that entitles him to consume a free piece of Sacher torte (fair value = CU 1).

On Dec, 29, 01, Mr X consumes dishes and beverages worth CU 19. Thus, he is granted a coupon. He redeems the coupon on Jan 10, 02.

Required

Prepare any necessary entries in E's financial statements as at Dec 31, 01. E applies (a) the residual value method and (b) the relative fair value method in order to allocate the consideration between the main transaction and the coupon.

Hints for solution

In particular Section 6.2.3.

Solution (a)

An amount of CU 1 is allocated to the coupon and the remainder of CU 18 (= CU 19 – CU 1) is allocated to the main transaction:

Dec 29, 01	Dr	Cash	19	
	Cr	Revenue		18
	Cr	Deferred revenue		1

Solution (b)

The consideration to be allocated is CU 19. Fair value of the coupon is CU 1. Fair value of the main transaction is CU 19. Hence the total of the fair values is CU 20. According to the relative fair value method, the consideration is apportioned as follows:

Main transaction	18.05	*(CU 19 : CU 20) · CU 19*
Coupon	0.95	*(CU 1 : CU 20) · CU 19*
Total	**19.00**	

Dec 29, 01	Dr	Cash	19.00	
	Cr	Revenue		18.05
	Cr	Deferred revenue		0.95

Example 5

Customer loyalty program – realization of the consideration attributable to the award credits

In 01, entity E generated sales revenue amounting to CU 1,000. According to IFRIC 13, CU 900 thereof was allocated to the main transactions and the remaining amount of CU 100 was allocated to the 100 award credits granted in 01 within the scope of a customer loyalty program. The award credits granted in 01 can be redeemed until the end of the year 03.

At the respective balance sheet dates, the following information is available in respect of the number of award credits redeemed until the end of the year, and with regard to the number of award credits that are expected to be redeemed in the future:

Redemption in	*Dec 31, 01*	*Dec 31, 02*	*Dec 31, 03*
01	20	20	20
02	40	52	52
03	20	18	21
Total	**80**	**90**	**93**

It is presumed that the amount of CU 900 attributable to the main transaction has to be recognized as revenue in 01 in its entirety according to the rules of IAS 18.

Required

Prepare any necessary entries in E's financial statements as at Dec 31 for the years 01–03.

Hints for solution

In particular Section 6.2.3.

Solution

Jan 01, 01	Dr	Cash	1,000	
	Cr	Revenue		900
	Cr	Deferred revenue		100

Consideration attributable to the award credits	**100**	
Number of award credits redeemed by Dec 31, 01	20	
Number of award credits expected to be redeemed in total	80	
Award credits redeemed by Dec 31, 01 (in %)	**25%**	
Revenue (attributable to the award credits) for 01	**25**	

Dec 31, 01	Dr	Deferred revenue	25	
	Cr	Revenue		25

Consideration attributable to the award credits	**100**	
Number of award credits redeemed by Dec 31, 02	72	*= 20 + 52*
Number of award credits expected to be redeemed in total	90	
Award credits redeemed by Dec 31, 02 (in %)	**80%**	
Accumulated revenue (award credits) for 01 and 02	**80**	
Revenue (award credits) for 01	25	
Revenue (award credits) for 02	**55**	

Dec 31, 02	Dr	Deferred revenue	55	
	Cr	Revenue		55

Consideration attributable to the award credits	**100**	
Number of award credits redeemed by Dec 31, 03	93	*= 20 + 52 + 21*
Number of award credits redeemed in total	93	
Award credits redeemed by Dec 31, 03 (in %)	**100%**	
Accumulated revenue (award credits) for 01–03	**100**	
Revenue (award credits) for 01 and 02	80	
Revenue (award credits) for 03	**20**	

Dec 31, 03	Dr	Deferred revenue	20	
	Cr	Revenue		20

Example 6

License fees

In 01, entity E developed new software. The software was not developed for E's own use. Instead, it is licensed to E's customers. The software's useful life is three years.

On Jan 01, 02 (which is identical with the date on which amortization begins), a non-exclusive license agreement is signed with a major customer. The term of that agreement is three years. On Jan 01, 02, E receives a one-time payment of CU 30 from the major customer.

Version (a)

E is obliged to train the major customer's employees and to perform other important services for the major customer in the years 02–04 relating to the software. This will result in costs of CU 4 p.a.

Version (b)

E has no obligations aside from licensing. If new versions of the software (updates) are released before the end of the licensing arrangement, the major customer only receives this update for the same price as new customers.

Required

Prepare any necessary entries relating to revenue recognition in E's financial statements as at Dec 31 for the years 01 and 02.

Hints for solution

In particular Section 5.

Solution (a)

Software licensing agreements are outside the scope of IAS 17 (IAS 17.2b).

E licenses the software to its major customer for a period of three years. E is obliged to perform several services for the customer relating to the software. Hence, it is appropriate to recognize revenue on a straight-line basis over three years. This results in the recognition of revenue in the accounting periods in which the costs for providing these services are incurred, which is in line with the matching principle (F.4.50–F.4.51).[8]

Jan 01, 02	Dr	Cash	30	
	Cr	Deferred revenue		30
Dec 31, 02	Dr	Deferred revenue	10	
	Cr	Revenue		10

Solution (b)

Jan 01, 02	Dr	Cash	30	
	Cr	Revenue		30

[8] *The matching principle is dealt with in the chapter on Conceptual Framework, Section 6.2 and Example 4.*

IAS 19 EMPLOYEE BENEFITS AND IAS 26 ACCOUNTING AND REPORTING BY RETIREMENT BENEFIT PLANS

1 INTRODUCTION

IAS 19 prescribes the accounting treatment of **employee benefits**. In **June 2011**, the **IASB amended IAS 19**. The new version of the Standard has to be applied in the financial statements as at **Dec 31, 2013** (if the entity's reporting periods are identical with the calendar years). **Earlier application** is **permitted** (IAS 19.172). In the **European Union**, new IFRSs have to be endorsed by the European Union before they can be applied. The new version of IAS 19 has already been endorsed by the EU. The amended standard has to be applied **retrospectively** with two exceptions (IAS 19.173).

This chapter of the book is structured as follows:

- Section 2 discusses the rules applicable if the entity decides not to apply the new version of IAS 19 early.
- Section 3 discusses the main differences between the "old" and the "new" version of IAS 19.

2 FINANCIAL REPORTING WITHOUT EARLY APPLICATION OF THE AMENDMENTS TO IAS 19 ISSUED IN JUNE 2011

2.1 Introduction and Scope

IAS 19 prescribes the accounting treatment of **employee benefits**. Employee benefits comprise all forms of consideration given by an entity in exchange for service rendered by employees (IAS 19.7). Employees include directors and other management personnel (IAS 19.6). IAS 19 is applied to all employee benefits except those to which IFRS 2 (**share-based payment**) applies (IAS 19.1). In IAS 19 and in the remainder of this chapter of the book, employee benefits are classified as follows:

- Short-term employee benefits (Section 2.2)
- Post-employment benefits (Section 2.3)
- Other long-term employee benefits (Section 2.4)
- Termination benefits (Section 2.5)

IAS 19 is generally based on the following principles (objective of IAS 19):

- A **liability** is recognized when an employee has provided service in exchange for employee benefits to be paid in the future.
- An **expense** is recognized when the entity consumes the economic benefit arising from service provided by an employee in exchange for employee benefits.

The **reporting by employee benefit plans** is not within the scope of IAS 19 because it is dealt with by IAS 26 (IAS 19.2). In some countries (e.g. Germany), the practical significance of the rules of IAS 26 is low because national laws and frequently also the articles of association require reports according to national GAAP. Consequently, the significance of IAS 26 has to be assessed from country to country.

2.2 Short-term Employee Benefits

This category comprises employee benefits that are due to be settled within 12 months after the end of the period in which the employees render the related service (and which do not represent termination benefits) (IAS 19.7). **Examples** are the following (IAS 19.4 and 19.8):

- Wages, salaries, and social security contributions.
- Compensated absences (where the compensation for the absences is due to be settled within 12 months after the end of the period in which the employees render the related employee service).
- Profit-sharing and bonuses (which are payable within 12 months after the end of the period in which the employees render the related service).
- Non-monetary benefits for current employees (such as medical care, housing, cars, and free or subsidized goods or services).

The accounting treatment of short-term employee benefits is generally straightforward. This is because **no actuarial assumptions** are required and measurement of short-term employee benefit obligations is effected on an **undiscounted** basis (IAS 19.9).

When an employee has rendered service to an entity during an accounting period, the undiscounted amount of short-term employee benefits expected to be paid in exchange for that service is generally recognized by the entry "Dr Expense Cr Liability."

2.3 Post-employment Benefits

2.3.1 Introduction Post-employment benefits are employee benefits which are payable after the completion of employment (and which do not represent termination benefits) (IAS 19.7). Examples are pensions, post-employment life insurance, and post-employment medical care (IAS 19.4 and 19.24). IAS 19 applies to all such plans whether or not they involve the establishment of a separate entity to receive contributions and to pay benefits (IAS 19.24).

Post-employment benefit plans are classified on the basis of the economic substance of the plan as follows (IAS 19.7 and 19.25–19.27):

- Under a **defined contribution plan**, the entity pays fixed contributions into a separate entity (i.e. into a fund) and will have no (legal or constructive) obligation to pay further contributions if the fund does not hold sufficient assets to pay all employee benefits (relating to employee service in the current and prior periods). Under defined benefit plans, actuarial risk (that benefits will be less than expected) and investment risk (that assets invested will be insufficient to meet expected benefits) fall on the employee.

- **Defined benefit plans** are defined as post-employment benefit plans which do not represent defined contribution plans. Under such a plan, the entity's obligation is to provide the agreed benefits to current and former employees. Actuarial risk (that benefits will cost more than expected) and investment risk fall, in substance, on the entity.

2.3.2 Defined Contribution Plans Defined contribution plans are generally accounted for like short-term employee benefits (IAS 19.43–19.44 and 19.9–19.10).[1] Where contributions to a defined contribution plan do not fall due wholly within 12 months after the end of the period in which the employees render the related service, discounting is necessary (IAS 19.43 and 19.45).

2.3.3 Defined Benefit Plans

2.3.3.1 Measurement of the obligation The post-employment benefit obligation is measured on a **discounted** basis (IAS 19.48). The **interest rate** is generally determined by reference to market yields at the end of the reporting period on high quality corporate bonds. The currency and term of these corporate bonds has to be consistent with the currency and estimated term of the obligation (IAS 19.78).

The **present value of the defined benefit obligation** is the present value (without deducting any plan assets) of the expected future payments required to settle the obligation (IAS 19.7). Present value is determined according to the "**projected unit credit method**." According to this method, each period of service gives rise to an additional unit of benefit entitlement and each unit is measured separately in order to build up the final obligation.[2] The whole of a post-employment benefit obligation is discounted, even if part of the obligation falls due within 12 months after the reporting period (IAS 19.64–19.66).

Current service cost is the increase in the present value of the defined benefit obligation resulting from employee service in the current period. **Interest cost** is the increase during a period in the present value of the obligation which arises because the benefits are one period closer to settlement (IAS 19.7).

2.3.3.2 Plan assets Sometimes **plan assets** exist relating to defined benefit plans. Plan assets comprise the following types of assets (IAS 19.7):

- **Assets held by long-term employee benefit funds**: These are assets (other than non-transferable financial instruments issued by the reporting entity) that meet both of the following conditions:
  - They are held by an entity (a fund) that is legally separate from the reporting entity and that exists solely to pay or fund employee benefits.
  - They are available to be used only to pay or fund employee benefits, are not available to the reporting entity's own creditors (even in the case of bankruptcy), and cannot be returned to the reporting entity unless either:

---

[1] *See Section 2.2.*

[2] *See Example 1.*

  - the remaining assets of the fund are sufficient to meet all the related employee benefit obligations of the plan or the reporting entity, or
  - the assets are returned to the reporting entity to reimburse it for employee benefits that were already paid.
- **Qualifying insurance policies**[3]: A qualifying insurance policy is an insurance policy issued by an insurer that is not a related party (as defined in IAS 24) of the reporting entity. Both of the following conditions must be met:
  - The proceeds of the policy can be used only to pay or fund employee benefits under a defined benefit plan.
  - The proceeds of the policy are not available to the reporting entity's own creditors (even in the case of bankruptcy) and cannot be paid to the reporting entity unless either:
    - the proceeds represent surplus assets that are not needed for the policy to meet all the related employee benefit obligations, or
    - the proceeds are returned to the reporting entity in order to reimburse it for employee benefits already paid.

In the **statement of financial position**, the defined benefit liability is **reduced** by the fair value of the related plan assets. Fair value is the amount for which an asset could be exchanged or a liability settled between knowledgeable, willing parties in an arm's length transaction (IAS 19.7, 19.54, and 19.102–19.104).

2.3.3.3 Actuarial gains and losses **Actuarial assumptions** are assumptions which are necessary when measuring the defined benefit obligation. They comprise assumptions relating to the following parameters (IAS 19.73):

- **Demographic parameters** (e.g. mortality, rates of employee turnover, and retirement age).
- **Financial parameters** (e.g. discount rate, future salary levels including career trends, and the expected rate of return on plan assets (such as interest and gains or losses on the plan assets – IAS 19.7)).

At the beginning of the reporting period, the development of the actuarial parameters (i.e. the rate of fluctuation, future salary levels, etc.) until the end of the reporting period is estimated. On the basis of these assumptions, an expected amount of the obligation and of the plan assets as at the balance sheet date is determined. At the end of the reporting period, the actual values of the obligation and of the plan assets are compared with the expected amounts. Differences result in actuarial gains or losses.

If the obligation is higher (lower) than initially expected, this is disadvantageous (advantageous) for the entity. This means that there is an actuarial loss (gain). If the value of plan assets is finally higher (lower) than initially expected, this is advantageous (disadvantageous) for the entity. This means that there is an actuarial gain (loss).

---

[3] *A qualifying insurance policy within the meaning of IAS 19 is not necessarily an insurance contract as defined in IFRS 4 (IAS 19.7, Footnote 1).*

The following table illustrates these considerations:[4]

Defined benefit obligation

	Actual obligation as at Dec 31, 00 (based on the actuarial calculation as at Dec 31, 00)
+	Current service cost 01 (based on the actuarial calculation as at Jan 01, 01)
+	Interest cost 01 (based on the interest rates and on the obligation as at Jan 01, 01)
−	Employee benefits (actually) paid in 01
=	**Expected obligation as at Dec 31, 01**
−	Actual obligation as at Dec 31, 01 (based on the actuarial calculation as at Dec 31, 01)
=	**Actuarial loss (if the total is negative)**
=	**Actuarial gain (if the total is positive)**

Plan assets

	Fair value of the plan assets as at Dec 31, 00 (actual value as at Dec 31, 00)
+	Expected return 01 (based on the actuarial calculation as at Jan 01, 01)
+	Contributions 01 (actual amounts received by the fund)
−	Employee benefits (actually) paid by the fund in 01
=	**Expected fair value of the plan assets as at Dec 31, 01**
−	Actual fair value of the plan assets as at Dec 31, 01
=	**Actuarial gain (if the total is negative)**
=	**Actuarial loss (if the total is positive)**

Actuarial gains or losses are accounted for in one of the following ways:

- **Corridor method** (IAS 19.92–19.93):[5] According to this method, actuarial gains or losses are not recognized until they exceed a certain level. This means that the previously unrecognized actuarial gains and losses (offset against each other) as at the end of the prior period 00 have to be compared with a limit (called the corridor). The amount in excess of the corridor divided by the expected average remaining working lives of the employees participating in the plan is recognized in the current period (i.e. in 01). Such a pro rata actuarial loss (gain) that has to be recognized in the current period (01) increases (decreases) the expense of the current period (01). The corridor (which has to be determined separately for each defined benefit plan as at the end of the prior period) is the greater of the following amounts:
  - 10% of the present value of the defined benefit obligation (before deducting plan assets).
  - 10% of the fair value of any plan assets.

  Regarding the comparison of the previously unrecognized actuarial gains or losses with the corridor (as described above), the actuarial gains or losses arising on the plan assets are offset with those arising on the defined benefit obligation (IAS 19.105).

- **Faster recognition in profit or loss than under the corridor method** (IAS 19.93 and 19.95): It is possible to apply any systematic method that results in faster recognition of actuarial gains and losses than under the corridor method, provided that the same basis is applied to both gains and losses and the basis is applied consistently from period to period. An example is the immediate recognition of all actuarial gains and losses in profit or loss in the period in which they occur.

---

4 *See KPMG,* Insights into IFRS, *5th edition, 4.4.500.30.*

5 *In the following text it is assumed that IAS 19.58A does not apply (IAS 19.92).*

- **Recognition in other comprehensive income** (IAS 19.93A–19.93D): If all actuarial gains and losses are recognized in the period in which they occur, they may be recognized in other comprehensive income. This requires that the entity does so for all of its defined benefit plans and for all of its actuarial gains and losses.

2.3.3.4 Presentation In determining the defined benefit liability presented in the **statement of financial position**, the defined benefit obligation is reduced by the fair value of the related plan assets or vice versa. This means that only a net asset or a net liability is presented (IAS 19.54 and 19.102). However, a net asset cannot always be recognized in full (IAS 19.58–19.60 and IFRIC 14). An asset relating to one plan is only offset against a liability relating to another plan if certain criteria are met (IAS 19.116–19.117).

In the **statement of comprehensive income**, interest costs arising on defined benefit obligations and the expected return on plan assets can be presented either within the results of operating activities or within the results of financing activities (IAS 19.119).

If actuarial gains and losses are recognized in other comprehensive income, they have to be recognized immediately in retained earnings (IAS 19.93D). In the **statement of changes in equity**, retained earnings arising from actuarial gains and losses recognized in other comprehensive income are presented as a separate column in addition to other retained earnings. This is to ensure that profit or loss relating to other retained earnings is presented at the crossing of the column "other retained earnings" and the line "total comprehensive income" (as required by IAS 1.106(d)(i)).

2.4 Other Long-term Employee Benefits

Other long-term employee benefits are employee benefits that are not due to be settled within 12 months after the end of the period in which the employees render the related services and which are neither post-employment benefits, nor termination benefits (IAS 19.7). Examples are long-service leave, jubilee benefits, and profit-sharing arrangements, if they are not payable wholly within 12 months after the end of the period (IAS 19.4 and 19.126).

In the case of other long-term employee benefits, all **actuarial gains and losses** are recognized immediately in profit or loss. Neither application of the corridor method, nor recognition in other comprehensive income is possible (IAS 19.127).[6] The amount recognized as a **liability** is calculated by reducing the present value of the defined benefit obligation by the fair value of the related plan assets (IAS 19.128).

2.5 Termination Benefits

Termination benefits are employee benefits payable as a result of either (IAS 19.7):

- the entity's decision to terminate an employee's employment before the normal retirement date *or*
- an employee's decision to accept voluntary redundancy in exchange for those benefits.

---

[6] *See KPMG,* Insights into IFRS, *5th edition, 4.4.990.10.*

Consequently, in the case of termination benefits the event that gives rise to an obligation is the **termination rather than employee service** (IAS 19.132).

Termination benefits are recognized as an **expense** and as a **liability** when the entity is demonstrably committed to either (IAS 19.133):

- terminate the employment of an employee or of a group of employees before the normal retirement date, *or*
- provide termination benefits as a result of an offer made in order to encourage voluntary redundancy.

The entity is demonstrably committed to a termination when the entity has a detailed formal plan (which has to comply with certain minimum requirements) for the termination and is without realistic possibility of withdrawal (IAS 19.134).

With regard to recognition, it is not necessary that the specific employees who will be made redundant have been informed that they are being made redundant (i.e. communication of a restructuring or termination plan to an employee group that includes the affected employees is sufficient to raise a valid expectation).[7]

In the case of voluntary redundancies, a liability is recognized only if it is probable that the offer will be accepted and if it is possible to estimate the number of acceptances reliably.[8]

When termination benefits fall due more than 12 months after the reporting period, they are **discounted** (using the discount rate specified in IAS 19.78 with regard to defined benefit plans that represent post-employment benefits[9]). In the case of an offer made to encourage voluntary redundancy, the measurement of termination benefits is based on the number of employees expected to accept the offer (IAS 19.139–19.140).

2.6 Examples with Solutions

Example 1

Illustrating the projected unit credit method

On Jan 01, 01, entity E hires Mr X. Upon termination of service, a lump sum is payable to Mr X equaling 1% of final annual salary for each year of service. Mr X's salary in 01 is CU 100, which is assumed to increase at 8% (compound) p.a. The discount rate is 10% p.a. It is expected that Mr X will leave entity E on Dec 31, 04. For simplification purposes it is assumed that there are no changes in actuarial assumptions. Moreover, the additional adjustment needed to reflect the probability that Mr X may leave entity E at an earlier or later date is ignored in this example.

Required

Determine (a) the carrying amount of the liability as at Dec 31 and (b) the current service cost and interest cost in E's financial statements as at Dec 31 for the years 01–04.

[7] *See KPMG,* Insights into IFRS, *7th edition, 4.4.1060.50.*

[8] *See KPMG,* Insights into IFRS, *7th edition, 4.4.1070.20.*

[9] *See Section 2.3.3.1.*

Hints for solution

In particular Section 2.3.3.1.

Solution

Salary 01	100.00	
Salary 02	108.00	*(= 100 · 1.08)*
Salary 03	116.64	*(= $100 \cdot 1.08^2$)*
Salary 04	125.97	*(= $100 \cdot 1.08^3$)*
Mr X's claim p.a. on termination on Dec 31, 04	**1.26**	*(= 125 · 97.1%)*

	00	*01*	*02*	*03*	*04*
Benefit entitlement as at Dec 31	0.00	1.26	2.52	3.78	5.04
Liability as at Dec 31 (e.g. 01: 1.26 : $1{,}1^3$)	0.00	0.95	2.08	3.44	5.04
Total expense (e.g. 02: 2.08 – 0.95)	0.00	0.95	1.13	1.36	1.60
thereof interest (e.g. 03: 2.08 · 10%)	0.00	0.00	0.10	0.21	0.34
thereof current service cost (e.g. 03: 1.36 – 0.21)	0.00	0.95	1.03	1.15	1.26

Example 2

Defined benefit plan without plan assets

Entity E stipulated a defined benefit plan with its employees:

	01	*02*
Actual obligation as at Jan 01	100	130
Current service cost	14	20
Interest cost	10	13
Benefits paid	8	11
Actual obligation as at Dec 31	130	140

Posting status:

There have not yet been any entries.

Required

Prepare any necessary entries in E's financial statements as at Dec 31 for the years 01 and 02. E recognizes actuarial gains and losses:

(a) **according to the corridor method** (IAS 19.92–19.93) and under the assumption that the cumulative unrecognized actuarial losses as at Jan 01, 01 are CU 20. The expected average remaining working life of the employees is 10 years.
(b) **entirely immediately in profit or loss** (IAS 19.93 and 19.95).
(c) **entirely immediately in other comprehensive income** (IAS 19.93A–19.93D).

Also determine the carrying amount of the liability for each of these versions as at Jan 01, 01, Dec 31, 01, and Dec 31, 02.

Hints for solution

In particular Sections 2.3.3.3 and 2.3.3.4.

Solution (general explanations)

Actuarial gains (–)/losses (+) arising in 01 and 02

	01	*02*
Actual obligation as at Jan 01	100	130
Current service cost	14	20
Interest cost	10	13
Benefits paid	−8	−11
Expected obligation as at Dec 31	**116**	**152**
Actual obligation as at Dec 31	130	140
Actuarial gains/losses	**14**	**–12**

Solution (a)

Actuarial gains (–)/losses (+) to be recognized in 01 and 02

	01	*02*
Actual obligation as at Jan 01	100	130
Corridor (10% according to IAS 19.92)	10	13
Cumulative unrecognized actuarial gains/losses as at Jan 01	20	33
Actuarial gains/losses in excess of the corridor	10	20
Average remaining working lives of the employees (in years)	10	10
Actuarial gains/losses to be recognized	**1**	**2**

Development of the cumulative unrecognized actuarial gains (–)/losses (+)

	01	*02*
Balance as at Jan 01	20	33
Actuarial gains/losses for the year	14	−12
Removal (actuarial gains/losses to be recognized)	1	2
Balance as at Dec 31	**33**	**19**

Expense to be recognized and change in the carrying amount of the liability

	01	*02*
Current service cost	14	20
Interest cost	10	13
Actuarial gains (–)/losses (+)	1	2
Expense to be recognized	**25**	**35**
Benefits paid	−8	−11
Change in the carrying amount of the liability	**17**	**24**

Dec 31, 01	Dr	Profit or loss	25	
	Cr	Cash		8
	Cr	Defined benefit liability		17
Dec 31, 02	Dr	Profit or loss	35	
	Cr	Cash		11
	Cr	Defined benefit liability		24

When there are unrecognized actuarial losses (gains) at a particular balance sheet date, this means that the carrying amount of the liability is smaller (larger) than the actual obligation.

Thus, the carrying amount of the liability is calculated according to the following formula: Actual obligation + cumulative unrecognized actuarial gains – cumulative unrecognized actuarial losses.

Carrying amount of the liability

	Jan 01, 01	*Dec 31, 01*	*Dec 31, 02*
Actual obligation	100	130	140
Cumulative unrecognized actuarial losses	20	33	19
Carrying amount of the liability	**80**	**97**	**121**
Verification of the results			
Carrying amount of the liability as at Jan 01, 01	80		
Expense recognized	25		
Benefits paid	–8		
Carrying amount of the liability as at Dec 31, 01	**97**		
Expense recognized	35		
Benefits paid	–11		
Carrying amount of the liability as at Dec 31, 02	**121**		

Solution (b)

Expense to be recognized

	01	*02*
Current service cost	14	20
Actuarial gains (–)/losses (+)	14	–12
Interest cost	10	13
Expense to be recognized	**38**	**21**
Verification of the results		
Carrying amount of the liability (= actual obligation) as at Jan 01, 01	100	
Expense to be recognized	38	
Benefits paid	–8	
Carrying amount of the liability (= actual obligation) as at Dec 31, 01	**130**	
Expense to be recognized	21	
Benefits paid	–11	
Carrying amount of the liability (= actual obligation) as at Dec 31, 02	**140**	

Dec 31, 01	Dr	Profit or loss	38	
	Cr	Cash		8
	Cr	Defined benefit liability		30
Dec 31, 02	Dr	Profit or loss	21	
	Cr	Cash		11
	Cr	Defined benefit liability		10

Solution (c)

In this version, actuarial gains and losses are recognized entirely immediately in other comprehensive income.

Expense to be recognized in profit or loss and change in the carrying amount of the liability

	01	*02*
Current service cost	14	20
Interest cost	10	13
Expense to be recognized in profit or loss	**24**	**33**
Actuarial gains (–)/losses (+) (other comprehensive income)	14	–12
Benefits paid	–8	–11
Change in the carrying amount of the liability	**30**	**10**
Verification of the results		
Carrying amount of the liability (= actual obligation) as at Jan 01, 01	100	
Expense to be recognized in profit or loss	24	
Actuarial gains (–)/losses (+) (other comprehensive income)	14	
Benefits paid	–8	
Carrying amount of the liability (= actual obligation) as at Dec 31, 01	**130**	
Expense to be recognized in profit or loss	33	
Actuarial gains (–)/losses (+) (other comprehensive income)	–12	
Benefits paid	–11	
Carrying amount of the liability (= actual obligation) as at Dec 31, 02	**140**	

Dec 31, 01	Dr	Profit or loss	24	
	Dr	Other comprehensive income	14	
	Cr	Cash		8
	Cr	Defined benefit liability		30
Dec 31, 02	Dr	Profit or loss	33	
	Cr	Other comprehensive income		12
	Cr	Cash		11
	Cr	Defined benefit liability		10

Example 3

Defined benefit plan with plan assets

Entity E stipulated a defined benefit plan with its employees. This plan is the same as the plan described in Example 2. However, there are also plan assets.

	01	*02*
Actual obligation as at Jan 01	100	130
Current service cost	14	20
Interest cost	10	13
Benefits paid	8	11
Actual obligation as at Dec 31	130	140
Actual fair value of the plan assets as at Jan 01	70	90
Contributions	6	10
Expected return on plan assets	12	10
Actual fair value of the plan assets as at Dec 31	90	100

Posting status:

There have not yet been any entries.

Required

Prepare any necessary entries in E's financial statements as at Dec 31 for the years 01 and 02. E recognizes actuarial gains and losses **entirely and immediately in other comprehensive income** (IAS 19.93A–19.93D). Also determine the carrying amount of the liability as at Jan 01, 01, Dec 31, 01, and Dec 31, 02.

Hints for solution

In particular Sections 2.3.3.2–2.3.3.4.

Solution

Actuarial gains (–)/losses (+) arising in 01 and 02

	01	*02*
Actual obligation as at Jan 01	100	130
Current service cost	14	20
Interest cost	10	13
Benefits paid	–8	–11
Expected obligation as at Dec 31	**116**	**152**
Actual obligation as at Dec 31	130	140
Actuarial gains/losses arising on the obligation	**14**	**–12**
Actual fair value of the plan assets as at Jan 01	70	90
Expected return on plan assets	12	10
Contributions	6	10
Benefits paid	–8	–11
Expected fair value of the plan assets as at Dec 31	**80**	**99**
Actual fair value of the plan assets as at Dec 31	90	100
Actuarial gains/losses arising on the plan assets	**–10**	**–1**
Total actuarial gains/losses	**4**	**–13**

If the actuarial gains and losses are recognized immediately, the carrying amount of the liability is the difference between the actual obligation and the actual fair value of the plan assets.

Expense to be recognized in profit or loss and change in the carrying amount of the liability

	01	*02*
Current service cost	14	20
Expected return on plan assets	–12	–10
Interest cost	10	13
Expense to be recognized in profit or loss	**12**	**23**
Actuarial gains (–)/losses (+) (other comprehensive income)	4	–13
Benefits paid	–6	–10
Change in the carrying amount of the liability	**10**	**0**
Verification of the results		
Carrying amount of the liability as at Jan 01, 01	30 = *100 – 70*	
Expense to be recognized in profit or loss	12	
Actuarial gains (–)/losses (+) (other comprehensive income)	4	
Contributions	–6	
Carrying amount of the liability as at Dec 31, 01	**40** = *130 – 90*	
Expense to be recognized in profit or loss	23	
Actuarial gains (–)/losses (+) (other comprehensive income)	–13	
Contributions	–10	
Carrying amount of the liability as at Dec 31, 02	**40** = *140 – 100*	

Dec 31, 01	Dr	Profit or loss	12	
	Dr	Other comprehensive income	4	
	Cr	Cash		6
	Cr	Defined benefit liability		10
Dec 31, 02	Dr	Profit or loss	23	
	Cr	Other comprehensive income		13
	Cr	Cash		10

Example 4

Statement of comprehensive income and statement of changes in equity – actuarial losses[10]

In 02, entity E decides on a retirement plan for its employees that constitutes a defined benefit plan. In 02, actuarial losses of CU 3 are incurred on the plan and the remaining employee benefits expense (including interest costs) is CU 7.

Required

(a) Prepare any necessary **entries** in E's financial statements as at Dec 31, 02.
(b) Illustrate the effects of the entries on E's **single statements of comprehensive income** for the years 01 and 02.
(c) Illustrate the effects of the entries on E's **statement of changes in equity** as at Dec 31, 02.

E presents interest costs in employee benefits expense, i.e. within the results of operating activities and recognizes actuarial gains and losses in other comprehensive income.

In 01 and 02, the carrying amount of E's issued capital is CU 100 and the carrying amount of E's capital reserve is CU 20.

Hints for solution

In particular Section 2.3.3.4.

Solution

Dec 31, 02	Dr	Employee benefits expense	7	
	Dr	Other comprehensive income – actuarial loss	3	
	Cr	Defined benefit liability		10

The actuarial loss is presented within other comprehensive income in the statement of comprehensive income and as a separate category of retained earnings in the statement of changes in equity (IAS 19.93D, IAS 1.96, and 1.IG). Actuarial gains and losses are part of other comprehensive income I. Thus, they are never reclassified to profit or loss (IAS 1.96 and 1.7).

---

[10] *See the chapter on IAS 1, Section 6.3 with regard to the presentation of the statement of changes in equity.*

The defined benefit plan has the following effects on the **statement of comprehensive income**:

	02	*01*
PROFIT OR LOSS SECTION		
Employee benefits expense	–7	0
Results of operating activities	**–7**	**0**
LOSS FOR THE YEAR	**–7**	**0**
OCI SECTION		
Items that will not be reclassified to profit or loss (OCI I):		
Actuarial loss on the defined benefit plan	–3	0
Subtotal	**–3**	**0**
OTHER COMPREHENSIVE INCOME	**–3**	**0**
TOTAL COMPREHENSIVE INCOME	**–10**	**0**

The defined benefit plan has the following effects on the **statement of changes in equity**:

	Issued capital	*Capital reserve*	*Retained earnings (arising from) (actuarial losses)*	*Other retained earnings*	*Total equity*
Balance as at Jan 01, 01	**100**	**20**	**0**	**0**	**120**
Total comprehensive income	–	–	0	0	0
Balance as at Dec 31, 01	**100**	**20**	**0**	**0**	**120**
Total comprehensive income	–	–	–3	–7	–10
Balance as at Dec 31, 02	**100**	**20**	**–3**	**–7**	**110**

In the statement of changes in equity, the retained earnings arising from actuarial losses are disclosed in a separate column, which is presented in addition to other retained earnings (IAS 19.93D, IAS 1.96, and 1.IG). In 02, an amount of CU –7 is presented at the crossing of the column "other retained earnings" and the line "total comprehensive income." This corresponds with the loss for the year 02 presented in the statement of comprehensive income.

Example 5

Termination benefits or post-employment benefits?

Entity E hires its employees by way of short-term employment contracts. After the contract period, the employees are entitled to receive a lump sum payment. In the case of early termination (irrespective of the reason for termination), the employees are entitled to receive the lump sum pro rata temporis.

Required

Assess whether these employee benefits are termination benefits or post-employment benefits according to IAS 19 in E's financial statements.

Hints for solution

In particular Sections 2.3.1 and 2.5.

Solution

These employee benefits represent post-employment benefits. This is because the obligation does not arise because of the decision to terminate an employment contract. Instead, payment of the (*pro rata temporis*) lump sum represents consideration for the work performance of the employees.

Example 6

Redundancy payments

Version (a)

In Dec, 01, entity E has prepared a detailed formal plan under which employees may request voluntary redundancy. The plan corresponds with the requirements of IAS 19.134.

On Jan 02, 02, the plan is communicated to the representatives of E's employees. It is planned to start implementing the plan in May 02.

Version (b)

The situation is the same as in version (a). However, the plan is communicated to the representatives of E's employees on Dec 30, 01.

Required

Assess whether the circumstances described above necessitate recognition of a liability in E's financial statements as at Dec 31, 01.

Hints for solution

In particular Section 2.5.

Solution (a)

No liability is recognized because the plan has not been communicated to the representatives of E's employees by the end of 01.

Solution (b)

A liability is recognized because the plan has been communicated to the representatives of E's employees by the end of 01.

3 THE AMENDMENTS TO IAS 19 ISSUED IN JUNE 2011

This section describes the **most important changes from the previous version of IAS 19**.

Only changes that relate to topics discussed in Section 2 are explained.

3.1 Post-employment Benefits

To begin with, **different terms** are used in the new version of the standard, although this does not change the accounting treatment of defined benefit plans:

- According to the new version of IAS 19, the **net defined benefit liability (asset)** represents the deficit or surplus, adjusted for any effect of limiting a net defined benefit asset to the asset ceiling (IAS 19.8 and 19.64). The **deficit or surplus** is the present value of the defined benefit obligation less the fair value of any plan assets. The **asset ceiling** represents the present value of any economic benefits available in the form of refunds from the plan or reductions in future contributions to the plan (IAS 19.8).

Moreover, some of the **definitions** used in the standard have been **changed** (e.g. the definitions relating to defined benefit cost explained later), which has consequences for financial reporting (IAS 19.8):

- **Net interest on the net defined benefit liability (asset)** represents the change during the period in the net defined benefit liability (asset) that arises from the passage of time. Net interest is determined by **multiplying the net defined benefit liability (asset) by the discount rate** specified by IAS 19, both as determined at the beginning of the annual reporting period (taking into account any changes in the net defined benefit liability or asset during the period as a result of contribution and benefit payments). Net interest consists of interest income on plan assets, interest cost on the defined benefit obligation, and interest on the effect of the asset ceiling (IAS 19.83 and 19.123–19.124).
- The amended standard introduces the term "**remeasurements** of the net defined benefit liability (asset)", which represent the period-to-period fluctuations in the amounts of defined benefit obligations and plan assets (IAS 19.BC65c). To state this more precisely, remeasurements consist of the following **three components** (IAS 19.8, 19.57d, and 19.127):
    - **Actuarial gains and losses.** According to the amended standard, these gains and losses only comprise changes in the present value of the **defined benefit obligation** resulting from (a) experience adjustments (which are the effects of differences between the previous actuarial assumptions and what has actually occurred) and (b) the effects of changes in actuarial assumptions.
    - The **return on plan assets** (e.g. interest, dividends, and realized and unrealized gains or losses on plan assets) excluding amounts included in net interest on the net defined benefit liability or asset. This means in effect that the difference between the interest income on plan assets and the return on plan assets is included in the remeasurement (IAS 19.125).
    - Any change in the effect of the **asset ceiling** excluding amounts included in net interest on the net defined benefit liability or asset (IAS 19.126).

According to the **"old" version of the standard**, entities are allowed to choose between different methods of recognizing and presenting actuarial gains or losses (IAS 19.BC66):[11]

- **Corridor method**
- **Faster recognition** in profit or loss than under the corridor method
- Recognition in **other comprehensive income.**

---

[11] *See Section 2.3.3.3.*

These options are not available according to the **amended version of IAS 19**, under which **remeasurements** of the net defined benefit liability (asset) have to be recognized and presented in **other comprehensive income** (IAS 19.120). Remeasurements are never reclassified from other comprehensive income to profit or loss. However, it is possible to transfer the amounts recognized in other comprehensive income from one category of equity to another one (IAS 19.122). The prohibition of reclassification corresponds with the "old" version of the standard.

The 2010 ED proposed to carry forward the requirement to transfer amounts recognized in other comprehensive income directly to retained earnings. However, the amendments made in June 2011 **permit transferring the cumulative remeasurements within equity**, and **do not impose specific requirements on that transfer** (see IAS 19.BC100 and the amendment of IAS 1.96 due to the amendment of IAS 19 in June 2011).

3.2 Termination Benefits

The IASB **changed the recognition and measurement rules** for termination benefits. In this section, the new rules are presented.

3.2.1 Recognition A liability for termination benefits has to be **recognized at the earlier of** the following dates (IAS 19.165):

- When the entity can no longer withdraw the offer of those benefits.
- When the entity recognizes costs for a restructuring that is within the scope of IAS 37 and involves the payment of termination benefits.

For termination benefits which are payable as a result of an **employee's decision to accept an offer** of benefits in exchange for the termination of employment, the time when an entity can no longer withdraw the offer of termination benefits is the **earlier of** the following (IAS 19.166):

- When the employee accepts the offer.
- When a restriction (e.g. a legal, regulatory or contractual requirement) on the entity's ability to withdraw the offer takes effect. This would be when the offer is made if the restriction existed at the time of the offer.

For termination benefits payable as a result of an **entity's decision to terminate an employee's employment**, the entity can no longer withdraw the offer of termination benefits when it has **communicated a plan** of termination meeting all of the following criteria to the affected employees (IAS 19.167):

- Actions required to complete the plan indicate that it is **unlikely that there will be significant changes** to the plan.
- The plan identifies the **number of employees** whose employment is to be terminated, their **job classifications or functions**, and their **locations** (but the plan need not identify each individual employee) as well as the expected **completion date**.
- The plan **establishes the termination benefits** that employees will receive **in sufficient detail** so that employees can determine the type and amount of benefits they will receive when their employment is terminated.

3.2.2 Measurement **Before the amendments** were made in June 2011, IAS 19 required termination benefits that became due more than 12 months after the reporting date to be discounted, but **provided no further measurement guidance**. The IASB amended IAS 19 to state explicitly that the measurement of termination benefits should be consistent with the measurement requirements for the nature of the underlying benefits (IAS 19.BC261).

According to the amended standard, it is necessary to measure termination benefits on initial recognition, and to measure and recognize subsequent changes **in accordance with the nature of the employee benefit**, provided that if the termination benefits are an enhancement to post-employment benefits, the entity has to apply the requirements for **post-employment benefits**. Otherwise (IAS 19.169):

- if the termination benefits are expected to be settled wholly before 12 months after the end of the annual reporting period in which the termination benefit is recognized, the requirements for **short-term employee benefits** have to be applied.
- if the termination benefits are not expected to be settled wholly before 12 months after the end of the annual reporting period, the requirements for **other long-term employee benefits** have to be applied.

Since termination benefits are not provided in exchange for services, IAS 19.70–19.74 relating to the attribution of the benefit to periods of service are not relevant (IAS 19.170).

IAS 20 GOVERNMENT GRANTS

1 INTRODUCTION AND SCOPE

IAS 20 deals primarily with government grants. The term **government** refers to state authorities and similar bodies whether local, national or international, irrespective of their legal form (IAS 20.3).

Government grants are assistance from the government in the form of transfers of resources to an entity in return for past or future compliance with certain conditions relating to operating activities of the entity (IAS 20.3). Government assistance also meets the definition of government grants if there are no conditions specifically relating to operating activities of the entity other than the requirement to operate in certain regions or industry sectors (SIC 10). Government grants exclude those forms of government assistance that cannot be measured reasonably (e.g. free technical advice), as well as transactions with the government that cannot be distinguished from the normal trading transactions of the entity (IAS 20.3 and 20.34–20.35). **Government grants for biological assets measured at fair value less costs to sell**[1] are within the scope of **IAS 41** and are therefore excluded from the scope of IAS 20 (IAS 20.2d, IAS 41.1c, and 41.34–41.38).

Grants related to assets are government grants whose primary condition is that the entity acquires or constructs long-term assets. Subsidiary conditions may also be attached (e.g. with regard to the type or location of the assets or the periods during which they are to be acquired or held). **Grants related to income** are defined as government grants other than those related to assets (IAS 20.3).

2 RECOGNITION AND MEASUREMENT

Government grants (including non-monetary grants at fair value) are recognized when there is **reasonable assurance** that the entity will **comply with the conditions** attaching to them and that the grants **will be received** (IAS 20.7). Receipt of a grant itself does not provide evidence that the conditions attaching to the grant have been or will be fulfilled (IAS 20.8). Any contingent liability or contingent asset relating to a government grant has to be treated according to IAS 37 (IAS 20.11).

The accounting treatment of a grant does not depend on the manner in which a grant is received (e.g. whether the grant is received in cash or as a reduction of a liability to the government) (IAS 20.9).

A lender may give a loan that will be forgiven if certain conditions are met (**forgivable loan**) (IAS 20.3). A forgivable loan from the government is treated as a government grant only when there is reasonable assurance that the entity will meet the terms of forgiveness of the loan (IAS 20.10).

---

[1] *See the chapter on IAS 41, Section 4.*

The benefit of a **government loan** at a **below-market interest rate** is treated as a government grant. The loan is recognized and measured according to IFRS 9. The benefit of the below-market interest rate is the difference between the initial carrying amount of the loan determined according to IFRS 9, and the proceeds received. The benefit is accounted for in accordance with IAS 20. When identifying the costs for which the benefit of the loan is intended to compensate, it is necessary to consider the conditions and obligations that have been, or must be, met (IAS 20.10A).

A government grant is **recognized in profit or loss on a systematic basis** over the periods in which the expenses are recognized, for which the grant is intended to compensate (IAS 20.12). In the case of a grant being related to a depreciable asset, the grant is usually recognized in profit or loss over the periods and in the proportions in which depreciation expense on the asset is recognized (IAS 20.17). If a grant related to a non-depreciable asset requires the fulfillment of certain obligations, it is recognized in profit or loss over the periods that bear the cost of meeting the obligations (IAS 20.18).

A government grant may become receivable as compensation for expenses already incurred or for the purpose of giving immediate financial support to an entity with no future related costs. Such a grant is recognized in profit or loss of the period in which it becomes receivable (IAS 20.20).

A government grant may take the form of a transfer of a **non-monetary asset** (e.g. land). In such cases, the entity proceeds in one of the following ways at **initial recognition** (IAS 20.23):

- The asset and the grant are measured at the asset's **fair value**. Fair value is the amount for which an asset could be exchanged between a knowledgeable, willing buyer and a knowledgeable, willing seller in an arm's length transaction (IAS 20.3).
- The asset and the grant are measured at a **nominal amount**.

3 PRESENTATION

3.1 Grants Related to Assets

A government grant related to an asset (including a non-monetary grant at fair value) is presented in the **statement of financial position** in one of the following ways (IAS 20.24–20.27):

- **Gross method**: The grant is recognized as **deferred income**, which is recognized in profit or loss (other operating income) on a systematic basis over the asset's useful life.
- **Net method**: The grant is recognized as a **reduction of the asset's carrying amount**, which subsequently leads to a reduction of depreciation expense.

3.2 Grants Related to Income

A grant related to income is presented in the **statement of comprehensive income** in one of the following ways (IAS 20.29):

- **Gross method**: The grant is presented as a **credit** (either under a general heading such as "Other income" or separately).
- **Net method**: The grant is presented as a deduction from the related expense.

Grants related to income affect profit or loss and not other comprehensive income (IAS 20.29A and 20.12). In the case of a government grant that becomes receivable for the purpose of giving immediate financial support to an entity, the grant has to be presented according to the gross method.

4 REPAYMENT OF GOVERNMENT GRANTS

If a government grant **becomes repayable**, this is accounted for as a **change in accounting estimate** (IAS 20.32 and IAS 8.32–8.38).

Repayment of a **grant related to income** results in the derecognition of any unamortized deferred income recognized relating to the grant and in the recognition of a liability relating to the repayment of the grant. The difference between these amounts is recognized in profit or loss (IAS 20.32).

In the case of the repayment of a **grant related to an asset**, it is necessary to distinguish between the gross method and the net method (IAS 20.24).[2] If the **gross method** is applied, the deferred income is derecognized and a liability relating to the repayment of the grant is recognized. The difference between these amounts is recognized in profit or loss. If the **net method** is applied, the carrying amount of the asset is increased to the carrying amount that would exist had no government grant ever been received. A liability is recognized relating to the repayment of the grant. Moreover, the cumulative additional depreciation that would have been recognized in profit or loss to date in the absence of the grant is recognized immediately in profit or loss (IAS 20.32). If a government grant related to an asset becomes repayable, this may result in the recognition of an impairment loss (IAS 20.33).

5 EXAMPLES WITH SOLUTIONS

Reference to another chapter

Government grants related to **biological assets measured at fair value less costs to sell** are dealt with in the chapter on IAS 41 (Example 3).

Example 1

Grant related to income

On Jan 01, 01, entity E receives a government grant of CU 4 for its research activities that will be performed in 01 and 02. Starting on this date, there is reasonable assurance that E will comply with the conditions attaching to the grant. In both 01 and 02 research costs of CU 10 are incurred.

Required

Prepare any necessary entries in E's financial statements as at Dec 31 for the years 01 and 02. The grant is presented in E's statement of comprehensive income according to the:

(a) gross method,
(b) net method.

[2] *See Section 3.1.*

Hints for solution

In particular Section 3.2.

Solution (a)

The recognition criteria (reasonable assurance that E will comply with the conditions attaching to the grant and that the grant will be received) (IAS 20.7) are fulfilled from Jan 01, 01 onwards. Half of the grant is recognized in 01 and half in 02 because half of the research expenses are recognized in each of these years (IAS 20.12).

Jan 01, 01	Dr	Cash	4	
	Cr	Deferred income		4
Year 01	Dr	Research expense	10	
	Cr	Cash		10
Dec 31, 01	Dr	Deferred income	2	
	Cr	Other operating income		2
Year 02	Dr	Research expense	10	
	Cr	Cash		10
Dec 31, 02	Dr	Deferred income	2	
	Cr	Other operating income		2

Solution (b)

Jan 01, 01	Dr	Cash	4	
	Cr	Deferred income		4
Year 01	Dr	Research expense	10	
	Cr	Cash		10
Dec 31, 01	Dr	Deferred income	2	
	Cr	Research expense		2
Year 02	Dr	Research expense	10	
	Cr	Cash		10
Dec 31, 02	Dr	Deferred income	2	
	Cr	Research expense		2

Example 2

Repayment of a grant related to income

Required

The situation is the same as in Example 1. However, on Jun 30, 02, E surprisingly violates a condition attaching to the grant. For this reason the whole grant of CU 4 becomes repayable on the same date. For simplification purposes it is assumed that repayment is effected on the same date.

Hints for solution

In particular Sections 3.2 and 4.

Solution (a)

At first, deferred income of CU 1 (= CU 2 · 6 : 12) is derecognized and other operating income is recognized in the same amount:

Jun 30, 02	Dr	Deferred income	1	
	Cr	Other operating income		1

Afterwards, the remaining carrying amount of deferred income is derecognized, the payment is recognized, and the difference between these amounts is recognized in profit or loss:

Jun 30, 02	Dr	Deferred income	1	
	Dr	Other operating expenses	3	
	Cr	Cash		4

Solution (b)

Jun 30, 02	Dr	Deferred income	1	
	Cr	Research expense		1
Jun 30, 02	Dr	Deferred income	1	
	Dr	Research expense	3	
	Cr	Cash		4

Example 3

Grant related to an asset

On Apr 01, 01, entity E acquires a new building for CU 600 to be used for administrative purposes. It has a useful life of 30 years. The building is available for use on the same date.

Since the building is located in a development area, E receives a government grant of CU 120 on Apr 01, 01. Starting on this date there is reasonable assurance that E will comply with the conditions attaching to the grant.

Required

Prepare any necessary entries in E's financial statements as at Dec 31 for the years 01 and 02. The grant is presented in E's statement of financial position according to the

(a) gross method,
(b) net method.

Hints for solution

In particular Section 3.1.

Solution (a)

Apr 01, 01	Dr	Building	600	
	Cr	Cash		600
Apr 01, 01	Dr	Cash	120	
	Cr	Deferred income		120

Recognition of the building's depreciation for 01 (CU 600 : 30 years : 12 months · nine months = CU 15):

Dec 31, 01	Dr	Depreciation expense	15	
	Cr	Building		15

Deferred income is derecognized to the same extent that the asset is depreciated (CU 120 : 30 : 12 · 9 = CU 3):

Dec 31, 01	Dr	Deferred income	3	
	Cr	Other operating income		3

Recognition of the building's depreciation for 02 (CU 600 : 30 = CU 20):

Dec 31, 02	Dr	Depreciation expense	20	
	Cr	Building		20

Deferred income is derecognized to the same extent that the asset is depreciated (CU 120 : 30 = CU 4):

Dec 31, 02	Dr	Deferred income	4	
	Cr	Other operating income		4

Solution (b)

Apr 01, 01	Dr	Building	600	
	Cr	Cash		600
Apr 01, 01	Dr	Cash	120	
	Cr	Building		120

The grant reduces the building's costs of purchase from CU 600 to CU 480. Accordingly, the building's depreciation for 01 is CU 12 (= CU 480 : 30 years : 12 months · 9 months):

Dec 31, 01	Dr	Depreciation expense	12	
	Cr	Building		12

Recognition of the building's depreciation for 02 (CU 480 : 30 = CU 16):

Dec 31, 02	Dr	Depreciation expense	16	
	Cr	Building		16

Example 4

Repayment of a grant related to an asset

On Jan 01, 01, entity E acquires a machine with a useful life of 10 years for CU 100. The machine is available for use on the same date.

On Jan 01, 01, E receives a government grant of CU 20 for the machine. Hereon out there is reasonable assurance that E will comply with the conditions attaching to the grant.

However, on Dec 31, 02, E violates a condition attaching to the grant. For this reason the entire grant of CU 20 becomes repayable on the same date. Repayment is effected by E on Jan 20, 03.

Required

Prepare any necessary entries in E's financial statements as at Dec 31 for the years 01–03.

Version (a)

The grant is presented according to the **gross method**. Depreciation is recognized directly, i.e. no allowance account is used.

Version (b)

The grant is presented according to the **net method**. Depreciation is recognized

(ba) directly, i.e. no allowance account is used.
(bb) through the use of an allowance account.

Assume that the fact that the government grant becomes repayable does not result in an impairment of the machine (IAS 20.33).

Hints for solution

In particular Sections 3.1 and 4.

Solution (a)

Jan 01, 01	Dr	Machine	100	
	Cr	Cash		100
Jan 01, 01	Dr	Cash	20	
	Cr	Deferred income		20
Dec 31, 01	Dr	Depreciation expense	10	
	Cr	Machine		10
Dec 31, 01	Dr	Deferred income	2	
	Cr	Other operating income		2
Dec 31, 02	Dr	Depreciation expense	10	
	Cr	Machine		10
Dec 31, 02	Dr	Deferred income	2	
	Cr	Other operating income		2

On Dec 31, 02, the deferred income of CU 16 (= CU 20 – CU 2 · 2) is derecognized and a liability of CU 20 relating to the repayment of the grant is recognized. The difference between these amounts is recognized in profit or loss. The depreciation of the machine is not adjusted because under the gross method, depreciation is always calculated on the basis of the costs of purchase of CU 100.

Dec 31, 02	Dr	Deferred income	16	
	Dr	Other operating expenses	4	
	Cr	Other liabilities		20
Jan 20, 03	Dr	Other liabilities	20	
	Cr	Cash		20
Dec 31, 03	Dr	Depreciation expense	10	
	Cr	Machine		10

Solution (ba)

Jan 01, 01	Dr	Machine	100	
	Cr	Cash		100
Jan 01, 01	Dr	Cash	20	
	Cr	Machine		20
Dec 31, 01	Dr	Depreciation expense	8	
	Cr	Machine		8
Dec 31, 02	Dr	Depreciation expense	8	
	Cr	Machine		8

The machine's carrying amount of CU 64 as at Dec 31, 02 (= CU 80 – CU 8 · 2) is increased to the carrying amount that would exist at the same date had no government grant ever been received. The latter amount is CU 80 (= CU 100 – CU 10 · 2). A liability of CU 20 is recognized relating to the repayment of the grant. Moreover, the cumulative additional depreciation that would have been recognized in profit or loss to date in the absence of the grant is recognized immediately in profit or loss. This amount is CU 4 [= (CU 10 – CU 8) · 2].

Dec 31, 02	Dr	Machine	16	
	Dr	Depreciation expense	4	
	Cr	Other liabilities		20
Jan 20, 03	Dr	Other liabilities	20	
	Cr	Cash		20

The machine's depreciation for 03 is determined by dividing the machine's carrying amount as at Dec 31, 02 (CU 80) by the machine's remaining useful life (eight years):

Dec 31, 03	Dr	Depreciation expense	10	
	Cr	Machine		10

Solution (bb)

Apart from the fact that depreciation is recognized through an allowance account ("Dr Depreciation expense Cr Allowance account"), the entry presented next is effected on Dec 31, 02. By means of this entry, the balance of the account "machine" is increased from CU 80 (= costs of purchase reduced by the grant) to CU 100 (= costs of purchase without deduction of the grant).

Dec 31, 02	Dr	Machine	20	
	Dr	Depreciation expense	4	
	Cr	Allowance account		4
	Cr	Other liabilities		20

IAS 21 THE EFFECTS OF CHANGES IN FOREIGN EXCHANGE RATES

1 SCOPE

IAS 21 specifies (IAS 21.3)

- the **translation of foreign currency transactions** (e.g. revenue billed in foreign currency, the acquisition of goods or services billed in foreign currency, and the taking up and granting of loans in foreign currency) (see Section 3) as well as
- the **translation of financial statements of foreign operations to another currency** when preparing the consolidated financial statements (see Section 4). Foreign operations are subsidiaries, joint ventures, associates or branches of the reporting entity, the activities of which are based or conducted in a country or currency other than those of the reporting entity (IAS 21.8).

IAS 21 does not apply to foreign currency derivatives that are within the scope of **IFRS 9**. In such cases, IAS 21 applies only with regard to the translation of the corresponding amounts from the functional currency (= currency of the primary economic environment in which the entity operates) to the presentation currency (= currency in which the financial statements are presented) (IAS 21.4). Moreover, IAS 21 does not apply to hedge accounting for foreign currency items (including the hedging of a net investment in a foreign operation) because hedge accounting is dealt with in IAS 39 (IAS 21.5).

IAS 21 does not apply to the presentation in a statement of cash flows of the cash flows arising from transactions in a foreign currency or to the translation of cash flows of a foreign operation (see IAS 7.25–7.28) (IAS 21.7).

2 MONETARY VS. NON-MONETARY ITEMS

Certain rules of IAS 21 use the terms "monetary" and "non-monetary." Consequently, it is necessary to understand the criteria for classifying assets and liabilities as monetary items or as non-monetary items. **Monetary items** are units of currency held as well as assets and liabilities that represent a right to receive or an obligation to deliver a fixed or determinable number of units of currency. Examples of monetary items are trade receivables and provisions that are to be settled in cash. Examples of **non-monetary items** are property, plant, and equipment, intangible assets (including goodwill), provisions that are to be settled by the delivery of non-monetary assets (e.g. provisions for warranties), and inventories. Inventories are non-monetary items because they do not represent a right to receive cash. However, the trade receivable resulting from the sale of an inventory item represents a right to receive cash, which means that it is monetary (IAS 21.8 and 21.16). Not all financial assets are monetary items. For example, an investment in an equity instrument does not represent a monetary item – there is no right to receive a fixed or determinable amount of cash.[1]

3 TRANSLATION OF FOREIGN CURRENCY TRANSACTIONS

3.1 Initial Recognition

Upon initial recognition, a foreign currency transaction is recorded in the functional currency (= currency of the primary economic environment in which the entity operates) by applying the **spot exchange rate at the date of the transaction** to the foreign currency amount. The date of the transaction is the date on which the transaction first qualifies for recognition. It is possible to use, for example, an **average rate for a week or a month** as an approximation for the transactions occurring during that period if exchange rates do not fluctuate significantly (IAS 21.21–21.22 and 21.8). If fluctuations are not significant, it is also possible to use the rate from the end of the previous period for the entries of the current period (week or month).

3.2 Subsequent Reporting – Monetary Items

Foreign currency monetary items are translated at each balance sheet date using the **closing rate** (spot exchange rate) (IAS 21.23a and 21.8). Exchange differences are generally recognized in **profit or loss** (IAS 21.28).[2]

3.3 Subsequent Reporting – Non-monetary Items

When translating non-monetary items, the following distinction is necessary. A non-monetary item measured:

- on the basis of **historical cost** in a foreign currency is translated using the (historical) exchange rate at the date of the transaction (IAS 21.23b),
- at **fair value** in a foreign currency is translated using the exchange rate at the date when fair value was determined (IAS 21.23c).

When non-monetary items are **tested for impairment** according to IAS 36 (e.g. property, plant, and equipment) or according to IAS 2 (inventories), the following procedure applies (IAS 21.25):

- The cost (after deduction of depreciation or amortization, if any) is translated using the (historical) exchange rate at the date of the transaction.
- The recoverable amount (IAS 36) or net realizable value (IAS 2) is translated at the exchange rate at the date when that value was determined (e.g. the closing rate at the end of the reporting period).
- The lower of these amounts is the asset's new carrying amount.

---

[1] *See PwC,* Manual of Accounting, *IFRS 2011, 7.61.*

[2] *Under the "old" version of IAS 39 (i.e. the version before IFRS 9 and its consequential amendments), exchange differences were partly recognized in profit or loss and partly in other comprehensive income in the case of debt instruments classified as "available for sale" (IAS 39.AG83 and 39.9). In IFRS 9, the category "available for sale" no longer exists. According to IFRS 9, certain equity instruments may be accounted for at fair value through other comprehensive income (IFRS 9.5.7.1b and 9.5.7.5). However, in IFRS 9 this option is not available for debt instruments.*

This rule only makes sense when income or other expected benefits to be derived from the asset will arise in foreign currency. If, for example, the net realizable value of an inventory item will arise in the entity's functional currency and not in foreign currency, no translation of net realizable value is necessary.

The exchange differences are presented in the statement of comprehensive income in the same way as the underlying item. This means that when a gain or loss on a non-monetary item is recognized in other comprehensive income (e.g. as a result of a revaluation of property, plant, and equipment according to IAS 16), any exchange component of that gain or loss is also recognized in other comprehensive income. Conversely, when a gain or loss on a non-monetary item is recognized in profit or loss, any exchange component of that gain or loss is also recognized in profit or loss (IAS 21.30–21.31).

4 TRANSLATION OF FINANCIAL STATEMENTS OF FOREIGN OPERATIONS WHEN PREPARING THE CONSOLIDATED FINANCIAL STATEMENTS

4.1 Determining the Functional Currency and the Method of Foreign Currency Translation

When foreign currency financial statements of subsidiaries, etc. are translated, the **functional currency** of the foreign operation has to be **determined**. The functional currency is the currency that mainly determines:

- the sales prices for goods and services (IAS 21.9a), and
- labor, material, and other costs of providing goods or services (IAS 21.9b).

The factors above are the **primary indicators** of the foreign operation's functional currency. IAS 21.10 and 21.11 contain **additional indicators** that are applied when the primary indicators (IAS 21.9) do not clearly indicate the foreign operation's functional currency. In many cases, the determination of the functional currency involves **exercising discretion**. However, the aim of exercising discretion has to be to determine the currency that best represents the economic effects of the underlying transactions, events, and conditions (IAS 21.12.).

The **method of translation** of the foreign operation's financial statements depends on the foreign operation's functional currency:

(a) The investor's presentation currency (e.g. euro) may differ from the foreign operation's functional currency (e.g. Swiss franc). In this case, the financial statements of the foreign operation prepared in its functional currency are translated into the investor's presentation currency according to the **current rate method** (also referred to as the **closing rate method**) (see Section 4.2).
(b) It may also be the case that a foreign operation keeps its books and records in a currency (e.g. Swiss franc) that is not identical with its functional currency (e.g. USD). In this case, the translation into the foreign operation's functional currency (in the example from Swiss franc into USD) is effected on the basis of the **monetary/non-monetary method** (see Section 4.3).

The following diagram represents an example of a European group that has a Japanese subsidiary:

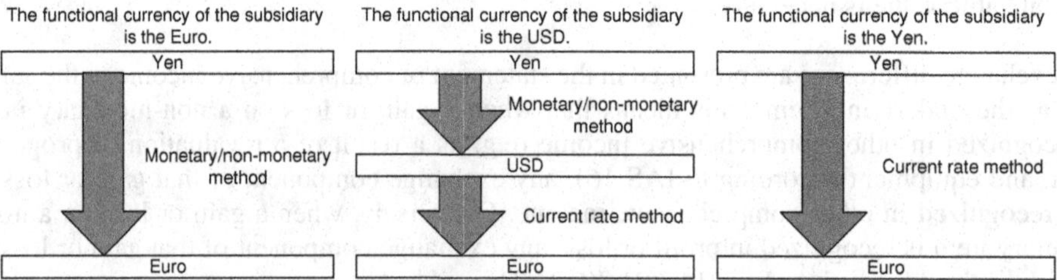

Once determined, the **functional currency** is only **changed** if there is a change in the underlying transactions, events, and conditions (IAS 21.13).

4.2 Current Rate (or Closing Rate) Method

In practice, the current rate (or closing rate) method is applied in most cases. Despite its name, not all items in the financial statements are translated at the (spot) exchange rate at the end of the reporting period. In particular, equity is generally translated using the historical exchange rate (i.e. the exchange rate at the date of acquisition of the acquiree) and the items included in profit or loss are translated using the exchange rates at the dates of the transactions. If fluctuations in exchange rates are low, average exchange rates may be used for translating the items included in profit or loss (sometimes even an average rate for the year). Using an average rate for the whole year means that the total amount of profit or loss is translated by that average rate. Since profit or loss is a component of equity, the principle that equity has to be translated using the historical rate is breached at this point. Consequently, the value of equity as at the end of the previous reporting period is used as the opening balance for the current period. The classification of the items of the statement of financial position as monetary or non-monetary does not affect foreign currency translation.

Under the current rate method, exchange differences are recognized in **other comprehensive income** (IAS 21.39c) and accumulated in the **foreign currency reserve**.

Any **goodwill** and any **fair value adjustments** to the carrying amounts of assets and liabilities arising on the acquisition of a foreign operation are treated as **assets and liabilities of the foreign operation**. Thus, they are expressed in the functional currency of the foreign operation and are translated at the closing rate (IAS 21.47).

Upon **disposal of a foreign operation**, the foreign currency reserve is reclassified to profit or loss. A disposal may be effected by sale, liquidation, repayment of share capital or abandonment of the foreign operation (IAS 21.48–21.49). In addition to the disposal of the entire interest in a foreign operation, the following are accounted for as disposals (and not as partial disposals) even if the entity retains an interest in the former subsidiary, jointly controlled entity or associate (IAS 21.48A):

- The loss of control of a subsidiary that includes a foreign operation.
- The loss of joint control over a jointly controlled entity that includes a foreign operation.
- The loss of significant influence over an associate that includes a foreign operation.

Upon disposal of a subsidiary that includes a foreign operation, the cumulative amount of the exchange differences relating to that foreign operation that have been attributed to the **non-controlling interests** are derecognized, but must not be reclassified to profit or loss (IAS 21.48B).

Upon the **partial disposal** of a subsidiary that includes a foreign operation, the proportionate share of the foreign currency reserve is re-attributed to the non-controlling interests in that foreign operation. In any other partial disposal of a foreign operation, only the proportionate share of the foreign currency reserve is reclassified to profit or loss (IAS 21.48C).

A partial disposal of the entity's interest in its foreign operation is any reduction in the entity's ownership interest in its foreign operation, except those reductions that are accounted for as disposals. A write-down of the carrying amount of a foreign operation either because of its own losses or because of an impairment recognized by the investor does not represent a partial disposal (IAS 21.48D–21.49).

4.3 Monetary/Non-monetary Method

When translating the **statement of financial position** of a foreign operation, it is assumed that the transactions of the foreign operation represent foreign currency transactions of the group. Consequently, the normal rules for translating foreign currency transactions are applied. This means that monetary items are translated using the closing rate (= spot exchange rate at the end of the reporting period). Non-monetary items measured on the basis of historical cost are translated using the (historical) exchange rate at the date of the transaction, while non-monetary items measured at fair value are translated using the exchange rate at the date when fair value was determined (which is usually the closing rate at the end of the reporting period). However, when non-monetary items are tested for impairment, the procedure described in Section 3.3 applies. Dividends paid are translated using the exchange rate at the date of the distribution.

The items included in **profit or loss** are translated using the exchange rates at the dates of the transactions. If fluctuations in exchange rates are low, average exchange rates may be used for translating these items (sometimes even an average rate for the year). When depreciable assets are translated using historical rates, it is appropriate to also translate depreciation or amortization expense of these assets at historical rates. Otherwise, there would be no conformity between the costs, accumulated depreciation or amortization, and carrying amounts of these assets. The line item "cost of raw material and consumables used" (IAS 1.IG) is translated using historical rates, which corresponds with the usual translation of inventories at historical rates. Dividend income is translated using the exchange rate at the date of the distribution.

Under the monetary/non-monetary method, the **exchange difference**, which is recognized in **profit or loss**, is determined as follows:

- At first, the final profit or loss for the year is derived from the statement of financial position by comparing the carrying amount of equity as at the beginning of the year with the carrying amount of equity as at the end of the year and then adjusting by transactions with owners.

- Then, preliminary profit or loss is derived from the translated separate income statement, which does not yet take the exchange difference into account.
- Finally, the final profit or loss is compared with preliminary profit or loss. The exchange difference is the difference between these amounts.

5 EXAMPLES WITH SOLUTIONS

The effects of the recognition and derecognition of a **foreign currency reserve** in the **statement of changes in equity** and in the **statement of comprehensive income** are illustrated in Example 8 of the chapter on IAS 1.

Example 1

Monetary vs. non-monetary items

(a) In Dec 01, entity E delivers merchandise to entity F. Hence, E recognizes a **trade receivable**.
(b) On Dec 31, 01, **merchandise** is stored in E's warehouse.
(c) On Dec 01, 01, E pays the rent for a machine rented under an operating lease for the period Dec 01, 01 to Feb 28, 02 in advance. The rent is CU 1 per month. Correctly, E makes the following entry:

Dec 01, 01	Dr	**Deferred expense**	2	
	Dr	Expense	1	
	Cr	Cash		3

(d) E holds 3% of the **shares** of entity G.
(e) E has recognized a **deferred tax liability** in its statement of financial position.

Required

Determine whether the bold items are monetary or non-monetary items in E's financial statements as at Dec 31, 01.

Hints for solution

In particular Section 2.

Solution

(a) After fulfillment of its obligations (delivery of the merchandise), E has a right to receive cash. Consequently, the **trade receivable** is a monetary item.
(b) The possession of **merchandise** does not entitle E to claim cash from a third party. Therefore, merchandise is a non-monetary item.
(c) On Dec 01, 01, E has paid the rent for Jan 02 and Feb 02 in advance. Thus, the **deferred expense** represents E's right to use the machine in January and February 02. In other words, the deferred expense will not be settled in cash. Consequently, it is a non-monetary item.

(d) The **shares** are non-monetary – there is no right to receive a fixed or determinable amount of cash.
(e) Most deferred tax items represent cash that will have to be paid to or received from the tax authorities in the future. Thus, we prefer the approach that an entity's **deferred tax liability** is classified as monetary in its entirety.[3]

Example 2

Foreign currency transactions – monetary items

On Dec 31, 01, entity E has trade receivables from the foreign customers A and B. E's functional currency is the yen. The following quotes are direct (1 foreign currency unit = x yen):[4]

	Date of the transaction	*Foreign currency units*	*Exchange rate on the date of the transaction*	*Exchange rate on Dec 31, 01*
Customer A	Nov 01, 01	20 m	3	4
Customer B	Dec 01, 01	50 m	10	8

Required

Prepare any necessary entries in E's financial statements as at Dec 31, 01.

Hints for solution

In particular Sections 3.1 and 3.2.

Solution

Upon initial recognition, a foreign currency transaction is recorded in the functional currency by applying the spot exchange rate at the date of the transaction (IAS 21.21–21.22). Trade receivables are monetary items because they represent a right to receive cash (IAS 21.8 and 21.16). Hence, they are translated using the closing rate at each balance sheet date (IAS 21.23a) and exchange differences are recognized in profit or loss (IAS 21.28).

Customer A:

Nov 01, 01	Dr	Trade receivable	60 m	
	Cr	Sales revenue		60 m
Dec 31, 01	Dr	Trade receivable	20 m	
	Cr	Foreign exchange gains		20 m

[3] *See also KPMG,* Insights into IFRS, *5th edition, 2.7.120.30.*

[4] *Example (Dec 31, 01, customer A): 20 m foreign currency units = 80 m JPY.*

Customer B:

Dec 01, 01	Dr	Trade receivable	500 m	
	Cr	Sales revenue		500 m
Dec 31, 01	Dr	Foreign exchange losses	100 m	
	Cr	Trade receivable		100 m

Example 3

Foreign currency transactions – testing for impairment

On Dec 31, 01, merchandise is stored in entity E's warehouse. This merchandise was acquired from a foreign supplier located in country C for 10 m foreign currency units and delivered on Nov 15, 01. E's functional currency is the yen. The exchange rate was 10 at the date of the transaction and is 8 on Dec 31, 01. The quotes are direct (1 foreign currency unit = x yen).[5]

Required

Prepare any necessary entries in E's financial statements as at Dec 31, 01. E intends to sell the merchandise after the reporting period:

(a) In country C for 11 m foreign currency units.
(b) Domestically for 95 m yen.

For simplification purposes it is assumed that no costs will be incurred with respect to the sale of the inventories after the reporting period.

Hints for solution

In particular Sections 3.1 and 3.3.

Solution

Upon initial recognition, E records the foreign currency transaction in its functional currency (i.e. in yen) by applying the spot exchange rate at the date of the transaction (IAS 21.21–21.22):

Nov 15, 01	Dr	Merchandise	100 m	
	Cr	Cash		100 m

At the end of the reporting period, the merchandise has to be measured at the lower of costs of purchase and net realizable value (IAS 2.9).

[5] *Example (Dec 31, 01): 10 m foreign currency units = 80 m yen.*

Version (a)

The net realizable value is 88 m yen (= 11 m · 8). Hence, the carrying amount of the merchandise decreases:

Dec 31, 01	Dr	Cost of sales	12 m	
	Cr	Merchandise		12 m

Version (b)

Since net realizable value will arise in yen (i.e. in E's functional currency) and not in foreign currency, no translation is necessary. Net realizable value is 95 m yen. Thus, the carrying amount of the merchandise decreases:

Dec 31, 01	Dr	Cost of sales	5 m	
	Cr	Merchandise		5 m

Example 4

Translation of foreign currency financial statements – current rate method

On Jan 01, 01, entity E (a Chinese entity) acquires 100% of the shares of a foreign operation. E's consolidated financial statements are presented in CNY (presentation currency). The financial statements of the foreign operation are presented in foreign currency F. Assume that currency F is the foreign operation's functional currency. Consequently, translation is effected according to the current rate method. The following quotes are direct (1 unit of currency F = x CNY):[6]

Exchange rate on Jan 01, 01	4
Exchange rate on Dec 31, 01	6
Average exchange rate for 01	5

The following tables are simplified presentations of the foreign operation's statement of financial position II as at Dec 31, 01 and its separate income statement II for the year 01 (in currency F):

Statement of financial position II	*Dec 31, 01*
Land	50 m
Buildings	50 m
Inventories	20 m
Cash	30 m
Total assets	**150 m**
Share capital	80 m
Retained earnings	10 m
Liabilities	60 m
Total equity and liabilities	**150 m**

6 *Example (Jan 01, 01): 1 unit of currency F = 4 CNY.*

Separate income statement II	*Year 01*
Revenue	80 m
Raw material and consumables used	–50 m
Depreciation expense	–10 m
Other expenses	–10 m
Profit for the year	**10 m**

Required

E prepares its consolidated financial statements as at Dec 31, 01. Perform the necessary foreign currency translation of the financial statements of the foreign operation. Assume for simplification purposes that it is acceptable to use an average exchange rate for the year for the appropriate items.

Hints for solution

In particular Sections 4.1 and 4.2.

Solution

Since the current rate method has to be applied, share capital is translated using the historical exchange rate (i.e. the exchange rate at the date of the acquisition of the acquiree which was effected on Jan 01, 01) and the assets and liabilities are translated using the closing rate as at Dec 31, 01. Translation of the separate income statement is effected on the basis of the average exchange rate for 01.

	Foreign currency F	*Exchange rate*	*Presentation currency CNY*
Land	50 m	6	300 m
Buildings	50 m	6	300 m
Inventories	20 m	6	120 m
Cash	30 m	6	180 m
Total assets	**150 m**		**900 m**
Share capital	80 m	4	320 m
Retained earnings	10 m		50 m
Foreign currency reserve (exchange difference)			170 m
Liabilities	60 m	6	360 m
Total equity and liabilities	**150 m**		**900 m**
Revenue	80 m	5	400 m
Raw material and consumables used	–50 m	5	–250 m
Depreciation expense	–10 m	5	–50 m
Other expenses	–10 m	5	–50 m
Profit for the year	**10 m**		**50 m**

Comparing the translated assets of 900 m CNY with the translated share capital, retained earnings, and liabilities of CU 730 m CNY results in an exchange difference of CU 170 m CNY, which is recognized in **other comprehensive income** (IAS 21.39c) and accumulated in the **foreign currency reserve**.

Example 5

Disposals or partial disposals of foreign operations

On Dec 31, 01, entity E holds 80% of the shares of entity F (which is a foreign subsidiary). F's financial statements are translated according to the current rate method. Exchange differences of CU +10 have been recognized in other comprehensive income from the acquisition date until Dec 31, 01. Thereof, CU 8 have been attributed to the foreign currency reserve and CU 2 to the non-controlling interests.

Version (a)

On Jan 01, 02, E sells its entire interest in F.

Version (b)

On Apr 01, 02, a dividend of CU 5 is declared. 80% of that amount is paid to E on the same date.

Version (c)

On Jan 01, 02, E sells a part of its interest in F. The sale leads to a reduction of E's interest in F to 60%. However, E does not lose control of F.

Version (d)

On Jan 01, 02, E sells a part of its interest in F. The sale leads to a reduction of E's interest in F to 40%, which means that E loses control over F.

Required

Describe the accounting treatment of the foreign currency reserve (CU 8) and the exchange differences attributed to the non-controlling interests (CU 2) in E's consolidated financial statements as at Dec 31, 02.

Hints for solution

In particular Section 4.2.

Solution (a)

Since the foreign operation has been disposed of, the foreign currency reserve of CU 8 is reclassified to profit or loss (IAS 21.48). The exchange differences attributed to the non-controlling interests of CU 2 are derecognized, but must not be reclassified to profit or loss (IAS 21.48B).

Solution (b)

Dividends do not represent partial disposals. Consequently, neither the foreign currency reserve (IAS 21.49 and 21.BC35) nor the exchange differences attributed to the non-controlling interests are affected.

Solution (c)

E sold one fourth of its interest in F. Since E did not lose control of F, the sale constitutes a partial disposal. Hence, one fourth of the foreign currency reserve is re-attributed to the non-controlling interests (IAS 21.48C):

Jan 01, 02	Dr	Foreign currency reserve	2	
	Cr	Non-controlling interests		2

Solution (d)

E lost control of F. Consequently, the sale represents a disposal and not a partial disposal even though E retains an interest of 40% in F (IAS 21.48A(a) and 21.48D). The procedure is the same as in version (a).

Example 6

Translation of foreign currency financial statements – monetary/non-monetary method

Required

The situation is the same as in Example 4. However, CNY is the functional currency of the foreign operation. Consequently, translation is effected according to the monetary/non-monetary method. Moreover, the liabilities of the foreign operation only consist of bank loans. Thus, they represent monetary items. The land, buildings, and inventories are measured at (amortized) cost. The equity (= share capital) of the foreign operation as at Jan 01, 01 is 80 m units of currency F. Assume for simplification purposes that it is acceptable to use an average exchange rate for the year for the appropriate items.

Hints for solution

In particular Sections 4.1 and 4.3.

Solution

	Foreign currency F	*Exchange rate*	*Presentation currency CNY*
Land	50 m	4	200 m
Buildings	50 m	4	200 m
Inventories	20 m	4	80 m
Cash	30 m	6	180 m
Total assets	**150 m**		**660 m**
Share capital	80 m	4	320 m
Retained earnings	10 m		−20 m
Liabilities	60 m	6	360 m
Total equity and liabilities	**150 m**		**660 m**
Revenue	80 m	5	400 m

	Foreign currency F	*Exchange rate*	*Presentation currency CNY*
Raw material and consumables used	−50 m	4	−200 m
Depreciation expense	−10 m	4	−40 m
Other expenses	−10 m	5	−50 m
Exchange differences			−130 m
Profit or loss for the year	**10 m**		**−20 m**

Supplementary calculation:

	CNY	
Assets as at Dec 31, 01	660 m	
Liabilities as at Dec 31, 01	−360 m	
Equity as at Dec 31, 01	300 m	
Equity as at Jan 01, 01	**320 m**	*(= 80 · 4)*
Final loss	−20 m	
Preliminary profit (before exchange differences)	110 m	*(= 400 – 200 – 40 – 50)*
Exchange differences	**−130 m**	

IAS 23 BORROWING COSTS

1 INTRODUCTION

IAS 23 is applied to the accounting for borrowing costs (IAS 23.2–23.3). **Borrowing costs** are interest costs and other costs that the entity incurs in connection with the borrowing of funds (IAS 23.5). Borrowing costs may include the following (IAS 23.6):

- Interest expense calculated according to the effective interest method (IFRS 9, Appendix A and IAS 39.9).
- Finance charges relating to finance leases recognized according to IAS 17 (IAS 17.25–17.26).

Borrowing costs, which are **directly attributable to the acquisition, construction or production of a qualifying asset**, form part of the cost of that asset, i.e. they are **capitalized** (IAS 23.1 and 23.8–23.9). A **qualifying asset** is an asset that necessarily takes a substantial period of time to get ready for its intended use or sale (IAS 23.5). The term "substantial period of time" is not quantified in the standard. In our opinion, this term can be interpreted as a period of at least 12 months. Assets that are ready for their intended use or sale when they are acquired are not qualifying assets (IAS 23.7).

Among others, an entity is **not required** to apply IAS 23 to the borrowing costs for **inventories** that are **produced in large quantities on a repetitive basis** (e.g. whiskey in the financial statements of the producer) (IAS 23.4b).

2 SPECIFIC AND GENERAL BORROWINGS

When calculating the amount of borrowing costs to capitalize, two categories are to be distinguished (IAS 23.10–23.15):

- **Specific borrowings** (i.e. funds specifically borrowed for the purpose of acquiring, constructing or producing a qualifying asset).
- **General borrowings** (i.e. other borrowings that could have been repaid if the expenditure on the asset had not been incurred[1]).

In the case of **specific borrowings**, the amount to be capitalized is represented by the actual borrowing costs incurred on these borrowings during the period. Investment income on the temporary investment of those borrowings is deducted from the amount to be capitalized (IAS 23.12).

---

[1] *See KPMG,* Insights into IFRS, *6th edition, 4.6.390.20.*

In the case of **general borrowings**, the amount to be capitalized is calculated by (IAS 23.14):

- applying the weighted average rate for the borrowing costs of general borrowings outstanding during the period,
- to the expenditures on the qualifying asset that are not financed by specific borrowings.

The borrowing costs to be capitalized are those borrowing costs that **would have been avoided** if the expenditure on the qualifying asset had not been made (IAS 23.10).

The amount of the borrowing costs capitalized during a period must not exceed the amount of borrowing costs incurred during that period (IAS 23.14).

Expenditures on a qualifying asset include only those expenditures that have resulted in payments of cash, transfers of other assets or the assumption of interest-bearing liabilities. Expenditures are reduced by any progress payments received and grants received in connection with the qualifying asset (see IAS 20). The average carrying amount of the qualifying asset during a period, including borrowing costs previously capitalized, is usually a reasonable approximation of the expenditures to which the capitalization rate is applied (IAS 23.18).

3 PERIOD OF CAPITALIZATION

Capitalization of borrowing costs as part of the cost of a qualifying asset begins when the entity first meets all of the following conditions (**commencement of capitalization**) (IAS 23.17 and 23.19):

- Expenditures for the asset are incurred.
- Borrowing costs are incurred.
- Activities have started that are necessary to prepare the asset for its intended use or sale.

Capitalization of borrowing costs is suspended during extended periods in which the entity suspends active development of a qualifying asset (**suspension of capitalization**) (IAS 23.20–23.21). During this period of time the borrowing costs are recognized as an expense.

Capitalization of borrowing costs ceases when substantially all activities necessary to prepare the qualifying asset for its intended use or sale are complete (**cessation of capitalization**) (IAS 23.22–23.23). It may be the case that an entity completes the construction of a qualifying asset in parts and each part is capable of being used while construction continues on other parts (e.g. the construction of a business park consisting of several buildings). In this case, the capitalization of borrowing costs ceases when the entity completes substantially all the activities necessary to prepare that part for its intended use or sale (IAS 23.24–23.25).

4 EXAMPLES WITH SOLUTIONS

Example 1

Are these assets qualifying assets?

Case (a): A particular **item of inventory** is produced by entity E in large quantities on a repetitive basis. Production takes (aa) 15 months, (ab) one week.

Case (b): At the beginning of 01, E starts constructing a **building**. Construction will take three years. Once completed, the building will be used for administrative purposes.

Case (c): E acquires a **warehouse** from entity F. F has used this warehouse for a long period of time. The warehouse is changed neither by E, nor by F. It is ready for its intended use at the time of acquisition by E.

Required

Determine whether the assets of entity E described above are qualifying assets according to IAS 23.

Hints for solution

In particular Section 1.

Solution

Case (a): Borrowing costs directly attributable to the production of inventories that are produced in large quantities on a repetitive basis may be accounted for according to IAS 23 (IAS 23.4b). When E decides to apply IAS 23 to these inventories, the question arises whether these inventories are qualifying assets:

(aa) In our opinion, when production takes 15 months the inventories are qualifying assets because the criterion "substantial period of time", interpreted as "at least 12 months", is met.

(ab) Inventories produced over such a short time as one week are not qualifying assets because the criterion "substantial period of time" is not met (IAS 23.7).

Case (b): Construction of the building will take three years. Consequently, the building is a qualifying asset because a substantial period of time is necessary for the building to get ready for its intended use (IAS 23.5).

Case (c): The warehouse is ready for its intended use when acquired by E. Consequently, it is not a qualifying asset (IAS 23.7).

Example 2

Borrowing costs to be capitalized

In Oct, 00, entity E decides to construct a building and immediately begins with preliminary activities (planning, obtaining a permit for the construction, etc.). The amounts attributable to these preliminary activities are not material. The physical construction of the building begins on Jan 01, 01. Once completed, E will use this building for administrative purposes. Construction ends on Dec 31, 01. Since the period of time necessary for construction is more than 12 months, the building is a qualifying asset. The period of capitalization is 12 months. Expenditures amount to CU 400. They are paid in 01. These payments are effected in equal amounts and at regular intervals in 01.

The following borrowings of E are outstanding during the entire year 01. Only the funds of loan A have been borrowed specifically for the construction of the building. In this example there is no difference between effective interest and contractually stipulated interest.

	Par value	*Interest rate*	*Interest*	
Loan A	100	6.5%	6.5	
Loan B	100	5.0%	5.0	
	Credit limit	***Average drawdown in 01***	***Interest rate***	***Interest***
Overdraft	120	100	Variable	7

Posting status:

The borrowing costs were recognized in profit or loss.

Required

Prepare any necessary entries with regard to the borrowing costs in E's financial statements as at Dec 31, 01. E prepares its separate income statement according to the function of expense method (= cost of sales method) (IAS 1.103 and IAS 1.IG).

Hints for solution

In particular Section 2.

Solution

Loan B	100	
Overdraft	100	
General borrowings (I)	**200**	
Borrowing costs (loan B)	5	
Borrowing costs (overdraft)	7	
General borrowing costs in total (II)	**12**	
Weighted average rate for general borrowing costs (III) = (II : I)	**6%**	
Average expenditures in 01	200	*CU 400 : 2*
Less specific borrowings (loan A)	100	
Expenditures financed by general borrowings (IV)	**100**	
Borrowing costs for general borrowings attributable to the construction of the qualifying asset (= III · IV)	**6**	

Remarks to the table above:

Since it is presumed that the expenditures of CU 400 are paid in equal amounts and at regular intervals in 01, the average of these expenditures has to be calculated "(Accumulated expenditures on Jan 01, 01 of CU 0 + accumulated payments effected by Dec 31, 01 of CU 400) : 2."

An amount of CU 100 of the average expenditures of CU 200 is financed by a specific borrowing (loan A), and the remainder of CU 100 is financed by general borrowings (i.e.

by loan B and the overdraft). For the borrowing costs relating to loan B and the overdraft, a weighted average rate of 6% is calculated. This rate is then multiplied by the expenditures financed by general borrowings of CU 100, which results in borrowing costs for general borrowings attributable to the construction of the qualifying asset of CU 6.

The total amount of borrowing costs to be capitalized for the qualifying asset is CU 12.5, i.e. CU 6 for the general borrowings and CU 6.5 for the specific borrowing (loan A),

Dec 31, 01	Dr	Building	12.5	
	Cr	Interest expense		12.5

IAS 24 RELATED PARTY DISCLOSURES

1 INTRODUCTION

The purpose of the disclosures required by IAS 24 is to draw attention to the possibility that the entity's financial statements may have been affected by the existence of related parties and by transactions and outstanding balances with such parties. For example, an entity may grant a loan to its associate on favorable terms (IAS 24.1 and 24.5–24.8).

2 RELATED PARTIES AND RELATIONSHIPS WITH THEM

Before defining the concept "related party," the following terms have to be explained (IAS 24.9):

- **Close members of the family** of a person are those family members who may be expected to influence, or be influenced by, that person in their dealings with the entity. They include:
  - that person's children and spouse or domestic partner as well as the children of that spouse or domestic partner, and
  - dependants of that person or that person's spouse or domestic partner.
- The term **key management personnel** refers to those persons having authority and responsibility for planning, directing, and controlling the activities of the entity, directly or indirectly, including any director (whether executive or otherwise) of that entity.

A **related party** is a **person or entity** that is related to the reporting entity. The reporting entity is the entity that is preparing its financial statements (IAS 24.9).

(a) A **person** or a **close member of that person's family** is related to a reporting entity if one of the following criteria is met with regard to that person (IAS 24.9):
   (i) He/she has control or joint control over the reporting entity.
   (ii) He/she has significant influence over the reporting entity.
   (iii) He/she is a member of the key management personnel of the reporting entity or of a parent of the reporting entity.

(b) An **entity** is related to a reporting entity especially if any of the following conditions apply (IAS 24.9):
   (i) The entity and the reporting entity are members of the same group (which means that each parent, subsidiary, and fellow subsidiary is related to the others).
   (ii) One entity is an associate or joint venture of the other entity (or an associate or joint venture of a member of a group of which the other entity is a member).
   (iii) Both entities are joint ventures of the same third party.
   (iv) One entity is a joint venture of a third entity and the other entity is an associate of the third entity.

(v) The entity is controlled or jointly controlled by a person identified in (a).
(vi) A person identified in (a)(i) has significant influence over the entity or is a member of the key management personnel of the entity (or of a parent of the entity).

In the definition of the concept "related party," an **associate** includes subsidiaries of the associate and a **joint venture** includes subsidiaries of the joint venture. Hence, for example, an associate's subsidiary and the investor that has significant influence over the associate are related to each other (IAS 24.12).

A **customer** and a **supplier** with whom an entity transacts a significant volume of business are not related parties simply by virtue of the resulting economic dependence (IAS 24.11d).

A **related party transaction** represents a transfer of resources, services or obligations between a reporting entity and a related party, regardless of whether a price is charged (IAS 24.9).

In considering each possible related party relationship, attention is directed to the **substance of the relationship** and not merely the legal form (IAS 24.10).

3 DISCLOSURES

Relationships between a parent and its subsidiaries have to be disclosed irrespective of whether there have been transactions between them (IAS 24.13).

Compensation includes all employee benefits (as defined in IAS 19) including employee benefits to which IFRS 2 applies (IAS 24.9). **Key management personnel compensation** has to be disclosed in total and for each of the following categories (IAS 24.17):

- Short-term employee benefits (see IAS 19)
- Post-employment benefits (see IAS 19)
- Other long-term benefits (see IAS 19)
- Termination benefits (see IAS 19)
- Share-based payment (see IFRS 2)

If there have been related party **transactions**, the entity has to disclose the **nature of the** related party **relationship** as well as **information about the transactions and outstanding balances**, necessary for users to understand the potential effect of the relationship on the financial statements. These disclosure requirements are in addition to those in IAS 24.17 for key management personnel compensation. At a minimum, disclosures have to include the following (IAS 24.18):

- The amount of the transactions.
- The amount of outstanding balances, and
  - their terms and conditions, including whether they are secured, and the nature of the consideration that has to be provided in settlement, as well as
  - details of any guarantees given or received.

- Provisions for doubtful debts related to the amount of outstanding balances.
- The expense recognized during the period with regard to bad or doubtful debts due from related parties.

The disclosures required by IAS 24.18 (see previously) have to be made **separately for each of the following categories** (IAS 24.19):

- The parent
- Entities with joint control or significant influence over the entity
- Subsidiaries
- Associates
- Joint ventures in which the entity is a venturer
- Key management personnel of the entity or its parent
- Other related parties

Disclosures that related party transactions were made on terms **equivalent to those that prevail in arm's length transactions** shall only be made if such terms can be substantiated (IAS 24.23).

Items of a similar nature may be disclosed in aggregate except when separate disclosure is necessary for an understanding of the effects of related party transactions on the entity's financial statements (IAS 24.24).

Certain reliefs from the disclosure requirements apply in the case of transactions in which **governments, government agencies, etc.** are related parties (IAS 24.9 and 24.25–24.27).

4 APPLICATION OF IAS 24 IN THE CONSOLIDATED FINANCIAL STATEMENTS

Intragroup transactions and intragroup outstanding balances with related parties are eliminated when preparing the consolidated financial statements (IAS 24.4).

5 EXAMPLES WITH SOLUTIONS

Example 1

Close members of a person's family

It is discussed whether the CEO of entity E is a related party of E. Moreover, it is discussed whether the following members of the CEO's family are close members of the CEO's family as defined in IAS 24.9 and related parties of E:

- His wife
- His adult daughter
- His wife's adult son of her first marriage

Required

Assess which of the persons mentioned previously are close members of the CEO's family and which are related parties of E.

Hints for solution

In particular Section 2.

Solution

E's CEO is a member of E's key management personnel. Therefore, he is a related party of E (IAS 24.9(a)(iii)).

There is a presumption that the CEO's adult daughter and his wife's adult son of her first marriage are close members of the CEO's family as defined in IAS 24.9. However, this presumption can be rebutted, for example, if it is proven that the persons are completely independent (economically) from the CEO. There is also a rebuttable presumption that the CEO's wife is a close member of the CEO's family as defined in IAS 24.9. However, rebutting the presumption for the CEO's wife will be more difficult than for the adult children mentioned above.

If the opinion is that the CEO's adult daughter is a close member of his family as defined in IAS 24.9, she is also a related party of E. The same applies to the CEO's wife and to her adult son of her first marriage (IAS 24.9(a)(iii)).

Example 2

Are these entities related parties?

Entity A holds shares of entities B and C:

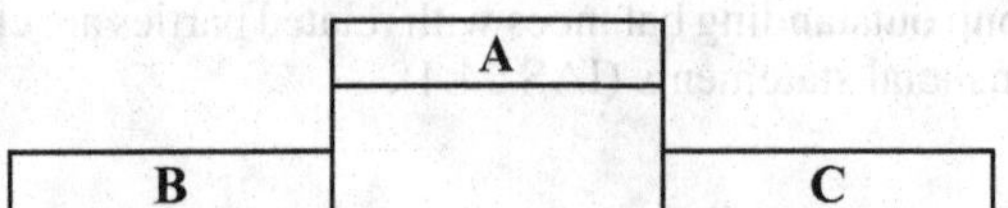

Version (a): B and C are both joint ventures of A.

Version (b): B is a joint venture of A and C is an associate of A.

Version (c): B and C are both associates of A.

Required

Assess whether C is a related party in B's financial statements and whether B is a related party in C's financial statements.

Hints for solution

In particular Section 2.

Solution (a)

For B's financial statements C is a related party. Similarly, for C's financial statements B is a related party (IAS 24.9(b)(iii) and 24.IE24–IE26).

Solution (b)

For B's financial statements C is a related party. Similarly, for C's financial statements B is a related party (IAS 24.9(b)(iv) and 24.IE24–IE26).

Solution (c)

For B's financial statements, C is not a related party. Similarly, for C's financial statements B is **not** a related party (IAS 24.9 and 24.IE7).

Example 3

Disclosures – does an "arm's length criterion" exist?

In 01, construction company B builds a luxury villa for its CFO. The price paid by the CFO is:

(a) equivalent to the price that would have been paid in an arm's length transaction,
(b) equivalent to the costs of conversion incurred by B for building the luxury villa.

Required

Assess whether the construction of the luxury villa for B's CFO has to be disclosed in the notes to B's financial statements as at Dec 31, 01.

Hints for solution

In particular Sections 2 and 3.

Solution

B's CFO is a related party of B (IAS 24.9(a)(iii)). Therefore, the construction of the luxury villa has to be disclosed in B's notes. This applies irrespective of whether the price paid by the CFO represents arm's length terms (IAS 24.23).

Example 4

Major customer

Entity E sells 40% of its products to its major customer, entity C.

Version (a): C does not belong to E's group.
Version (b): C holds 35% of the shares of E and exercises significant influence over E.

Required

Assess whether C is a related party in E's financial statements.

Hints for solution

In particular Section 2.

Solution

A customer with whom an entity transacts a significant volume of business is not a related party simply by virtue of the resulting economic dependence (IAS 24.11d). Thus, C is not a related party in *version (a)*.

In *version (b)*, C exercises significant influence over E. This means that E is an associate of C. Therefore, C is a related party of E (IAS 24.9(b)(ii) and 24.IE7).

IAS 26 ACCOUNTING AND REPORTING BY RETIREMENT BENEFIT PLANS

See the chapter on IAS 19/IAS 26

IAS 27 (2008) CONSOLIDATED AND SEPARATE FINANCIAL STATEMENTS, IAS 27 (2011) SEPARATE FINANCIAL STATEMENTS, AND IFRS 10 (2011) CONSOLIDATED FINANCIAL STATEMENTS

1 INTRODUCTION

Consolidated financial statements are the financial statements of a group presented as if the individual subsidiaries of the group and the parent were a single entity. Consolidated financial statements present the individual assets (e.g. buildings, machines, and inventories) and liabilities of the subsidiaries rather than the direct equity interests in the subsidiaries. A subsidiary is an entity that is controlled by another entity (known as the parent). In **separate financial statements** of a parent, the investments in subsidiaries are accounted for on the basis of the direct equity interest. They do not present the individual assets and liabilities of the subsidiaries (IAS 27.4). The term "separate financial statements" does not comprise the financial statements of an entity that does not have a subsidiary, associate or venturer's interest in a jointly controlled entity (IAS 27.7).

The effects of changes in foreign exchange rates (IAS 21) as well as the aspects with respect to business combinations covered by IFRS 3 (e.g. the acquisition method) are not described in this chapter of the book.

In **May 2011**, the **IASB issued IFRS 10** "Consolidated Financial Statements" as well as a **new version of IAS 27** named "Separate Financial Statements." The new standards have to be applied in the financial statements as at **Dec 31, 2013** (if the entity's reporting periods start on Jan 01 and end on Dec 31). **Earlier application** is **permitted** by the IASB (IFRS 10.C1 and IAS 27.18). However, in the **European Union**, new IFRSs have to be endorsed by the European Union before they can be applied. There has been no endorsement with regard to IFRS 10 and the new version of IAS 27 as yet.

The remainder of this chapter is structured as follows:

- Section 2 discusses the rules applicable if the entity decides not to apply the new standards early.
- Section 3 presents the rules of IFRS 10.
- Section 4 introduces the new version of IAS 27.

2 FINANCIAL REPORTING WITHOUT EARLY APPLICATION OF IFRS 10 AND IAS 27 (2011)

2.1 The Concept of "Control"

A **subsidiary** is an entity that is **controlled** by another entity (known as the parent). Consolidated financial statements have to include all subsidiaries of the parent (IAS 27.4 and 27.12).

Control is the power to govern the financial and operating policies of an entity so as to obtain benefits from its activities (IAS 27.4). Control is **presumed to exist** when the parent owns **more than half of the voting power** of an entity directly or indirectly through subsidiaries. However, in exceptional circumstances it may be clearly demonstrated that such ownership does not constitute control (IAS 27.13).

Control also exists when the parent owns **half or less of the voting power** when one of the following criteria is met (IAS 27.13):

- The investor has power over more than half of the voting rights by virtue of an agreement with other investors.
- The investor has the power to govern the financial and operating policies of the entity under a statute or an agreement.
- The investor has the power to appoint or remove the majority of the members of the board of directors or equivalent governing body and control of the entity is by that board or body.
- The investor has the power to cast the majority of votes at meetings of the board of directors or equivalent governing body and control of the entity is by that board or body.

Control is not only assessed on the basis of existing voting rights. **Potential voting rights** (e.g. share call options or convertible bonds that give the investor additional voting power when they are exercised or converted) also have to be taken into account if they are currently exercisable or convertible. Potential voting rights are not currently exercisable or convertible when, for example, they cannot be exercised or converted until the occurrence of a future event or until a future date. All facts and circumstances that affect potential voting rights have to be examined except the intention of management and the financial ability to exercise or convert (IAS 28.8–28.9). The rules for the consideration of **potential voting rights** when determining if there is control correspond to those when determining if there is significant influence and hence, an associate (IAS 27.14–27.15 and IAS 28.8–28.9).[1]

The Interpretation SIC 12 deals with the question under which circumstances **special purpose entities (SPEs)** have to be consolidated. SPEs are created to accomplish a narrow and well-defined objective to the benefit of another entity (= sponsor). Examples of such an objective are to effect a lease, research and development activities or securitization of financial assets (SIC 12.1).

---

[1] *See the chapter on IAS 28, Section 2.1.*

If the sponsor owns more than 50% of the shares of the SPE there is a rebuttable presumption (IAS 27.13) that this constitutes control. Hence, it is not necessary to apply SIC 12. However, in many cases the sponsor owns less than 50% of the shares of an SPE because it is intended to relieve the sponsor's consolidated financial statements, for example, by avoiding presenting doubtful receivables or liabilities and making related disclosures. In such cases SIC 12 is of particular importance.

SIC 12 contains criteria that may indicate that an entity controls an SPE and consequently has to consolidate the SPE. However, some of these criteria are too vague to use them to determine whether consolidation is necessary. Thus, the question of whether there is control is regularly determined on the basis of the risks and benefits. This means that the SPE is consolidated when the entity is exposed to a majority of the risks and benefits of the SPE (under the presumption that the risks and benefits are allocated symmetrically) (SIC 12.10).

2.2 Balance Sheet Date of the Consolidated Financial Statements and Diverging Balance Sheet Dates of Subsidiaries

The balance sheet date of the consolidated financial statements is the balance sheet date of the parent. Subsidiaries can be consolidated on the basis of financial statements with a different balance sheet date provided that the difference between the balance sheet dates is no more than three months, and that it is impracticable to prepare additional financial statements for the subsidiary. When the financial statements of a subsidiary are prepared at a date different from that of the parent's financial statements, adjustments have to be made for the effects of significant transactions or events (IAS 27.22–27.23).

2.3 Preparing the Consolidated Financial Statements

2.3.1 Overview The following steps are necessary in preparing the consolidated financial statements (IAS 27.18–27.21 and 27.24–27.29):[2]

1. Preparation of the **statement of financial position II** (also called the **balance sheet II**) and of the **statement of comprehensive income II** of the parent and of each subsidiary:
   (a) If the separate financial statements are not prepared according to IFRS, they have to be adjusted so that they comply with IFRS.
   (b) The separate financial statements of all subsidiaries have to be adjusted so that they correspond to uniform accounting policies for like transactions and other events in similar circumstances. For example, it is generally not possible that the investment properties of one subsidiary are measured according to the fair value model and that the investment properties of another subsidiary are measured according to the cost model.[3]
2. Preparation of the **aggregated statement of financial position** (also called **aggregated balance sheet**) and of the **aggregated statement of comprehensive income**: This means that the statements of financial position II and the statements of comprehensive income II are combined line by line by adding together like items of assets, liabilities,

[2] *The rules for the translation of the financial statements of foreign subsidiaries into the presentation currency of the consolidated financial statements are described in the chapter on IAS 21 (Section 4).*

[3] *See the chapter on IAS 40, Section 4.1.*

equity, income, and expenses (e.g. calculating the total of all inventories of the parent and its subsidiaries or calculating the total of all short-term provisions of the parent and its subsidiaries).

3. **Capital consolidation**[4]
   (a) Elimination of the carrying amount of the parent's investment in its subsidiary and of the parent's portion of equity of the subsidiary as at the acquisition date. Moreover, the non-controlling interests are recognized, which represent the equity in a subsidiary not attributable, directly or indirectly, to the parent (IAS 27.4).
   (b) Recognition of the assets and liabilities of subsidiaries that have not been recognized in the statements of financial position II of the subsidiaries but have to be recognized according to IFRS 3 in the consolidated statement of financial position.
   (c) Adjustment of the carrying amounts of the assets and liabilities of the subsidiaries to the amounts determined according to IFRS 3 (which are generally fair values) on acquisition date. Moreover, the change in the fair value adjustments since the date the subsidiary was consolidated for the first time has to be taken into account. For example, a building's acquisition-date fair value has to be depreciated, subsequently.
   (d) Recognition of goodwill.
4. **Intragroup balances, transactions, income, and expenses** have to be **eliminated in full** Profits and losses resulting from intragroup transactions that are recognized in the carrying amounts of assets (such as inventories and property, plant, and equipment), are also eliminated in full.

Step (4) is explained in more detail in the following sections of this chapter. With regard to step (3) we refer to the chapter on IFRS 3. Different aspects of non-controlling interests are described in this chapter and in the chapter on IFRS 3.

2.3.2 Elimination of Intragroup Receivables and Liabilities A group can have neither liabilities to nor receivables from itself. Hence, **intragroup receivables and liabilities have to be eliminated** (elimination entry on consolidation: "Dr Liability Cr Receivable").

The **accounting treatment of assets and liabilities may differ** under IFRS. This situation exists in the following examples:

- At the beginning of 01, subsidiary A grants a loan to subsidiary B. Consequently, A recognizes a receivable whereas B recognizes a liability. It is assumed that B encounters significant financial difficulty, at the end of 01. Thus, A recognizes an impairment loss for its receivable. However, the measurement of the liability in B's financial statements is normally not affected. For this reason, the carrying amount of the receivable differs from the carrying amount of the liability on Dec 31, 01. Therefore, in 01, the elimination entry on consolidation is "Dr Liability Cr Receivable Cr Impairment loss."[5]
- An obligation might require recognition as a provision in the debtor's financial statements, but the corresponding claim does not qualify for recognition in the financial statements of the creditor.

---

[4] *The capital consolidation is discussed in more detail in the chapter on IFRS 3.*

[5] *See Example 2.*

Furthermore, differences between the carrying amounts of receivables and the corresponding liabilities may result from different balance sheet dates.

2.3.3 Elimination of Intragroup Income and Expenses The consolidated statement of comprehensive income presents only the income and expenses of the group. Consequently, intragroup income and expenses have to be eliminated. For example, subsidiary A may lease a machine to subsidiary B under an operating lease. A recognizes lease income and B recognizes lease expenses. These items have to be eliminated because the group (which is regarded as a single entity for consolidation purposes) cannot lease a machine to itself. Therefore, the elimination entry on consolidation is "Dr Lease income Cr Lease expense."

2.3.4 Elimination of Intragroup Profits and Losses that are Recognized in the Carrying Amounts of Assets Profits and losses resulting from intragroup transactions that are recognized in the carrying amounts of assets in the separate financial statements are eliminated in full. For example, in 01 subsidiary A purchases merchandise from a supplier for CU 10 which is an unrelated entity from the group's perspective. A sells the merchandise to subsidiary B for CU 12. B does not resell the merchandise in 01. Hence, the consolidated statement of comprehensive income neither includes cost of sales, nor sales revenue with respect to the merchandise since it has not yet been sold from a group perspective. The cost of purchase of the merchandise is CU 10 because this represents the amount paid by the group in order to acquire the merchandise.[6]

Intragroup losses may indicate an impairment that requires recognition in the consolidated financial statements (IAS 27.20–27.21).

2.3.5 Non-controlling Interests IAS 27 and IFRS 3[7] both contain rules regarding non-controlling interests. **Non-controlling interests** represent the equity in a subsidiary not attributable, directly or indirectly, to a parent (IAS 27.4).

Non-controlling interests are presented **within equity** in the **consolidated statement of financial position**. However, they are presented separately from the equity of the owners of the parent (IAS 27.27 and IAS 1.54q).

Profit or loss and each component of other comprehensive income are attributed to the owners of the parent and to the non-controlling interests, even if this results in the non-controlling interests having a deficit balance (IAS 27.28).

When **potential voting rights** exist, the proportions of profit or loss and changes in equity allocated to the non-controlling interests and to the parent are determined on the basis of present ownership interests. They do not reflect the possible exercise or conversion of potential voting rights (IAS 27.19).

---

[6] *Example 4 illustrates the entries necessary in a similar situation.*

[7] *See the chapter on IFRS 3, Section 6.3.*

2.4 Acquisition and Disposal of Shares

IFRS 3 deals with the situation in which an acquirer obtains control of an acquiree in which it held an equity interest immediately before the acquisition date (**business combination achieved in stages** or **step acquisition**) (IFRS 3.41–3.42 and 3.32). Consequently, we refer to the chapter on **IFRS 3** in this regard.[8]

By contrast, the following situations are dealt with in IAS 27:

(a) **Increase in a parent's ownership interest in an existing subsidiary**: The parent acquires additional interest of an entity that it already controls, i.e. of an existing subsidiary.
(b) **Decrease in a parent's ownership interest that does not result in a loss of control**: The parent disposes of shares of an entity that it controls, i.e. of an existing subsidiary and this disposal does not result in a loss of control.
(c) **Loss of control**: The parent disposes of shares of a subsidiary and this disposal results in a loss of control.

Both **(a) and (b)** are accounted for as **equity transactions**, i.e. as transactions with owners in their capacity as owners, which means that the following procedure is necessary (IAS 27.30–27.31):

- The carrying amount of the non-controlling interests is adjusted.
- Any difference to the fair value of the consideration paid or received is recognized directly in equity (e.g. in retained earnings) and attributed to the owners of the parent.

The accounting treatment of **(c)** is described in the remainder of this section. In the consolidated financial statements, the disposal of the shares, which results in a loss of control, is regarded as a disposal of the individual assets (including goodwill) and liabilities of the subsidiary.

Assume that parent P holds 90% of the shares of entity E. P sells 60% of the shares. This means that P holds only 30% of the shares of E afterwards, resulting in a loss of control of P over E. The gain or loss on deconsolidation (which has to be recognized in profit or loss attributable to the parent) is calculated as follows:

	Fair value of the consideration received (i.e. for the 60% sold)
+	Carrying amount of the non-controlling interest (10%)
+	Fair value of the investment retained in E (30%)
=	**Value of E (100%)**
–	Carrying amount of E's net assets (including goodwill) (100%)
=	**Gain or loss on deconsolidation**

As can be seen from the table above, the parent derecognizes the carrying amount of any **non-controlling interests** in the former subsidiary at the date when control is lost. If the carrying amount of the non-controlling interests is positive, derecognition increases a gain on deconsolidation or decreases a loss on deconsolidation (IAS 27.34).

[8] *See the chapter on IFRS 3, Sections 6.1, 6.5, and 6.6, as well as Example 6.*

If a parent loses control of a subsidiary, the parent has to account for all amounts recognized in **other comprehensive income** in relation to that subsidiary on the same basis as would be required if the parent had directly disposed of the related assets or liabilities (IAS 27.34e and 27.35).

The treatment of **goodwill** on **deconsolidation** has to be described more precisely. It may be the case that an entity sells an operation that was part of a cash-generating unit to which goodwill has been allocated. Upon disposal, the goodwill attributable to the operation disposed of is generally calculated on the basis of the relative values of the operation disposed of and the portion of the CGU retained. The goodwill attributable with the operation disposed of is included in the carrying amount of the operation when determining the gain or loss on disposal (IAS 36.86).

The fair value of any investment retained in the former subsidiary represents the **carrying amount on initial recognition** of a financial asset according to IFRS 9, or the carrying amount on initial recognition when applying the equity method according to IAS 28 or IAS 31 (IAS 27.36–27.37).

If the loss of control is the result of two or more arrangements (transactions), it may be necessary under certain circumstances to treat them as a single transaction for accounting purposes (IAS 27.33). This means that the principle of substance over form[9] applies.

A parent may **lose control** of a subsidiary (which requires deconsolidation) **without disposing of shares**. This could occur when the quorum for making decisions is changed from 51% to 67% or when the subsidiary becomes subject to the control of a government, court, administrator or regulator (IAS 27.32).

2.5 Investments in Subsidiaries, Jointly Controlled Entities, and Associates in Separate Financial Statements

In the entity's separate financial statements (IAS 27.4 and 27.7), investments in subsidiaries, jointly controlled entities, and associates are accounted for **either** (IAS 27.38):

(a) **at cost, or**
(b) in accordance with **IFRS 9** (i.e. measurement at **fair value**). According to IFRS 9, fair value is always presumed to be reliably determinable. In certain circumstances, cost may be an appropriate estimate of fair value (IFRS 9.B5.4.14–9.B5.4.17).[10]

If investments in jointly controlled entities and associates are accounted for in accordance with IFRS 9 in the consolidated financial statements, they have to be accounted for in the same way in the investor's separate financial statements (IAS 27.40). A **dividend** from a subsidiary, jointly controlled entity or associate is recognized in profit or loss when the right to receive the dividend is established (IAS 27.38A).

---

[9] *See the chapter on Conceptual Framework, Section 4.2.2.*

[10] *If IFRS 9 were not applied early, the investments would normally be measured at fair value. However, the equity instruments would be measured at cost if fair value were not determinable, reliably (IAS 39.AG80–39.AG81).*

2.6 Examples with Solutions

Example 1

Potential voting rights

Required

Determine, relating to the situations described in Example 7, which of the entities controls the investee according to IAS 27 (as amended in 2008).

Hints for solution

In particular Section 2.1.

Solution (a)

In the situation described, the purchase option is deeply out of the money (and is expected to remain so for the two-year period). In our opinion, this means that the potential voting rights are not taken into account when assessing control, although the purchase option is currently exercisable. Consequently, A controls the investee.

Solution (b)

The conversion rights, which are currently exercisable, are out of the money, but not deeply out of the money. This means that they have to be taken into account when assessing control. Thus, A controls the investee.

Example 2

Elimination of intragroup receivables and liabilities

On Jan 01, 01, parent P grants a loan in the amount of CU 5 to its subsidiary S, which has to be repaid on Dec 31, 03. P and S measure the loan at amortized cost in their balance sheets II. However, in this example the accounting treatment of interest is not illustrated. On Dec 31, 01, P recognizes an impairment loss of CU 3 on the receivable. On Dec 31, 03, S settles the liability.

Posting status (in S's separate financial statements):

Jan 01, 01	Dr	Cash	5	
	Cr	Liability		5
Dec 31, 03	Dr	Liability	5	
	Cr	Cash		5

Posting status (in P's separate financial statements):

Jan 01, 01	Dr	Receivable	5	
	Cr	Cash		5
Dec 31, 01	Dr	Impairment loss	3	
	Cr	Receivable		3

Dec 31, 03	Dr	Receivable	3	
	Cr	Reversals of impairment losses		3
Dec 31, 03	Dr	Cash	5	
	Cr	Receivable		5

Required

Prepare any necessary entries in P's consolidated financial statements as at Dec 31 for the years 01–03. The aggregated financial statements have already been prepared.

Hints for solution

In particular Section 2.3.2.

Solution

Year 01

The intragroup receivable has to be eliminated with the intragroup liability. However their carrying amounts differ. Hence, the impairment loss on the intragroup receivable has to be eliminated too. This is because the group cannot have a receivable against itself and consequently there can be no impairment loss in the consolidated statement of comprehensive income on a non-existing receivable.

Dec 31, 01	Dr	Liability	5	
	Cr	Receivable		2
	Cr	Impairment loss		3

Year 02

The aggregated financial statements for 02 are the starting point for the preparation of the consolidated financial statements for 02. Hence, it is first necessary to repeat the consolidation entry of 01 in order to achieve the correct posting status. However, in 02, a credit entry on the account "retained earnings" is necessary in order to repeat the derecognition of the impairment loss recognized in 01. This is because in P's separate financial statements for 02, the impairment loss recognized in 01 is part of P's retained earnings as at Dec 31, 02 and is not presented in P's statement of comprehensive income for the year 02.[11]

Dec 31, 02	Dr	Liability	5	
	Cr	Receivable		2
	Cr	Retained earnings		3

Year 03

The carrying amounts of the receivable and of the liability have already been derecognized in P's and S's separate financial statements. Consequently, there is no elimination entry on consolidation in this respect. However, the reversal of the impairment loss recognized

[11] *See the chapter on IFRS 3, Section 9 with regard to the repetition of consolidation entries of previous periods.*

by P has to be eliminated. Moreover, a credit entry on the account "retained earnings" is necessary for the same reason as in 02.

Dec 31, 03	Dr	Reversals of impairment losses	3	
	Cr	Retained earnings		3

Example 3

Elimination of intragroup income and expenses

S1 and S2 are subsidiaries of parent P. On Jan 01, 01, S1 leases a machine to S2 under an operating lease for an annual charge of CU 2.

Posting status (in S1's separate financial statements):

Dec 31, 01	Dr	Cash	2	
	Cr	Lease income		2

Posting status (in S2's separate financial statements):

Dec 31, 01	Dr	Lease expense	2	
	Cr	Cash		2

Required

Prepare any necessary entries in P's consolidated financial statements as at Dec 31, 01. The aggregated financial statements have already been prepared.

Hints for solution

In particular Section 2.3.3.

Solution

Intragroup lease income and expenses have to be eliminated:

Dec 31, 01	Dr	Lease income	2	
	Cr	Lease expense		2

Example 4

Elimination of intragroup profits and losses that are recognized in the carrying amounts of assets

S1 and S2 are subsidiaries of parent P. On Dec 15, 01, S1 purchases merchandise for CU 4 from a supplier, which is an unrelated entity from the group's perspective. On the same day, S1 sells the merchandise to S2 for CU 5. S2 does not resell the merchandise in 01.

Posting status (in S1's separate financial statements):

Dec 15, 01	Dr	Merchandise	4	
	Cr	Cash		4
Dec 15, 01	Dr	Cash	5	
	Cr	Revenue		5
Dec 15, 01	Dr	Cost of sales	4	
	Cr	Merchandise		4

Posting status (in S2's separate financial statements):

Dec 15, 01	Dr	Merchandise	5	
	Cr	Cash		5

Required

Prepare any necessary entries in P's consolidated financial statements as at Dec 31, 01. The aggregated financial statements have already been prepared.

Hints for solution

In particular Section 2.3.4.

Solution

The aggregated financial statements include revenue of CU 5 (sale by S1 to S2), cost of sales of CU 4 (derecognition of the merchandise by S1), and merchandise of CU 5 (recognition of the merchandise by S2).

However, the group actually purchased the merchandise for CU 4 from the supplier. Moreover, from a group perspective there has neither been any revenue nor any cost of sales because the group did not resell the merchandise in 01. Hence the carrying amount of the merchandise has to be adjusted from CU 5 to CU 4, and the revenue and the cost of sales have to be eliminated:

Dec 31, 01	Dr	Revenue	5	
	Cr	Cost of sales		4
	Cr	Merchandise		1

The consolidation entry above eliminated the intragroup profit of CU 1 (revenue of CU 5 – cost of sales of CU 4), which has been recognized in the separate financial statements of S1.

Example 5

Elimination of intragroup profits and losses that are recognized in the carrying amounts of assets

Subsidiary S is included in P's consolidated financial statements as at Dec 31, 01.

Case 1

On Jan 01, 01, subsidiary S purchases a machine for CU 10 from a supplier that is an unrelated entity from the group's perspective. On the same day, S sells the machine to P for CU 15. From P's perspective the machine is an item of property, plant, and equipment (IAS 16). The machine's useful life is five years.

Posting status (in S's separate financial statements):

Jan 01, 01	Dr	Merchandise	10	
	Cr	Cash		10
Jan 01, 01	Dr	Cash	15	
	Cr	Revenue		15
Jan 01, 01	Dr	Cost of sales	10	
	Cr	Merchandise		10

Posting status (in P's separate financial statements):

Jan 01, 01	Dr	Machine (property, plant and equipment)	15	
	Cr	Cash		15
Dec 31, 01	Dr	Depreciation expense	3	
	Cr	Machine		3

Case 2

On Dec 15, 01, P sells finished goods to S for CU 8 that have been produced by P in 01. P's costs of conversion are CU 6. S is responsible for selling these products; thus, they are merchandise from S's perspective. S did not sell any of these products in 01.

Posting status (in S's separate financial statements):

Dec 15, 01	Dr	Merchandise	8	
	Cr	Cash		8

Posting status (in P's separate financial statements):

Year 01	Dr	Cost of sales	6	
	Cr	Cash		6
Dec 15, 01	Dr	Cash	8	
	Cr	Revenue		8

Case 3

On Jan 01, 01, S grants a loan of CU 9 to P. In 01, S receives interest of CU 1 from P for this loan. P capitalizes this interest expense because it represents borrowing costs for the construction of a building, which meets the definition of a qualifying asset according to IAS 23.

Posting status (in S's separate financial statements):

Jan 01, 01	Dr	Receivable	9	
	Cr	Cash		9
Dec 31, 01	Dr	Cash	1	
	Cr	Interest income		1

Posting status (in P's separate financial statements):

Jan 01, 01	Dr	Cash	9	
	Cr	Liability		9
Dec 31, 01	Dr	Interest expense	1	
	Cr	Cash		1
Dec 31, 01	Dr	Building under construction	1	
	Cr	Interest expense		1

Posting status (elimination of intragroup receivables and liabilities):

Dec 31, 01	Dr	Liability	9	
	Cr	Receivable		9

Required

Prepare any necessary entries in P's consolidated financial statements as at Dec 31, 01. The aggregated financial statements have already been prepared.

Hints for solution

In particular Section 2.3.4.

Solution (Case 1)

The revenue and the cost of sales included in the aggregated statement of comprehensive income have to be eliminated. This is due to the fact that the group acquired an item of property, plant, and equipment and neither bought nor resold merchandise. The machine's costs of purchase are CU 10, which represent the amount paid by the group. Therefore, depreciation on the machine in 01 is CU 2 and the machine's carrying amount as at Dec 31, 01 is CU 8.

The following entry leads to the adjustment of the machine's costs of purchase from CU 15 to CU 10 and to the elimination of revenue and the cost of sales:

Dec 31, 01	Dr	Revenue	15	
	Cr	Cost of sales		10
	Cr	Machine		5

The following entry leads to the adjustment of the machine's depreciation:

Dec 31, 01	Dr	Machine	1	
	Cr	Depreciation expense		1

Solution (Case 2)

From a group perspective, the products are finished goods (instead of merchandise) because the group itself has produced the products.

Dec 31, 01	Dr	Finished goods	8	
	Cr	Merchandise		8

From a group perspective there is no revenue because there has not been a sale to a third party. The costs of conversion of 01 (CU 6) are recognized as a reduction of cost of sales because finished goods were recognized. The carrying amount of the finished goods has to be adjusted from CU 8 to the costs of conversion of CU 6:

Dec 31, 01	Dr	Revenue	8	
	Cr	Cost of sales		6
	Cr	Finished goods		2

Solution (Case 3)

The carrying amount of the building under construction must not be increased by intragroup interest costs. It must only include those costs that are payable to third parties. Moreover, the intragroup interest income recognized by S has to be eliminated:

Dec 31, 01	Dr	Interest income	1	
	Cr	Building under construction		1

Example 6

Acquisition and disposal of shares[12]

On Dec 31, 01, entity P acquires 80% of the shares of entity S for CU 8. The value of S's identifiable net assets determined according to IFRS 3 as at Dec 31, 01, is CU 5. For simplification purposes, it is assumed that this amount corresponds with the carrying amount of S's net assets in S's separate financial statements.

The non-controlling interest is measured at its proportionate share of S's net assets. Therefore, goodwill is CU 4 [= consideration of CU 8 + non-controlling interest of CU 1 (= 20% of CU 5) – net assets of CU 5] (IFRS 3.32 and 3.19).[13] In its separate financial statements, P accounts for its investment in S at cost (IAS 27.38a).

The following table provides a (simplified) presentation of P's aggregated statement of financial position, of capital consolidation, and of P's consolidated statement of financial position as at Dec 31, 01:[14]

---

12 *We refer to the chapter on IFRS 3 with regard to the basics of capital consolidation.*

13 *See the chapter on IFRS 3, Section 6.1 with regard to the computation of goodwill.*

14 *In this table debit entries and assets are shown with a plus sign whereas credit entries, liabilities, and items of equity are shown with a minus sign.*

	P	*S*	*Aggregated balance sheet*	*Capital consolidation*	*Consolidated balance sheet*
Goodwill				4	4
Investment of P in S (shares)	8		8	−8	0
Other assets	50	15	65		65
Total assets	**58**	**15**	**73**	**−4**	**69**
Share capital	−18	−3	−21	3	−18
Retained earnings	−10	−2	−12	2	−10
Non-controlling interest				−1	−1
Liabilities	−30	−10	−40		−40
Total equity and liabilities	**−58**	**−15**	**−73**	**4**	**−69**

It is presumed that S is a cash-generating unit in P's consolidated financial statements to which all goodwill of CU 4 is allocated for impairment testing according to IAS 36 (IAS 36.80).[15]

For simplification purposes, it is presumed that P and S did not effect any transaction in 02, apart from the following transaction:

Version (a)

On Dec 31, 02, P acquires an additional 10% of the shares of S for CU 1.

Posting status (in P's separate financial statements):

Dec 31, 02	Dr	Investment of P in S (shares)	1	
	Cr	Cash		1

Version (b)

On Dec 31, 02, P sells 10% of the shares of S for CU 1.[16]

Posting status (in P's separate financial statements):

Dec 31, 02	Dr	Cash	1	
	Cr	Investment of P in S (shares)		1

[15] *See the chapter on IAS 36, Section 7.1.*

[16] *This does not result in a gain on disposal in P's separate financial statements because the proceeds on disposal and the carrying amount of the investment derecognized (CU 8 were paid for 80% of the shares and consequently the carrying amount of 10% of the shares is CU 1 if it is presumed that there was no control premium) are both CU 1.*

Version (c)

On Dec 31, 02, P sells 40% of the shares of S for CU 5. This results in a loss of control of P over S.[17] The remaining investment of P in S (40%) represents an investment in an associate, which is accounted for using the equity method. Fair value of the remaining 40% of the shares is CU 5.

Posting status (in P's separate financial statements):

Dec 31, 02	Dr	Cash	5
	Cr	Gain on disposal	1
	Cr	Investment of P in S (shares)	4

*Posting status (**for all versions**):*

The capital consolidation as conducted during the preparation of the consolidated financial statements as at Dec 31, 01 has already been repeated during the preparation of the consolidated financial statements as at Dec 31, 02.

Required

Prepare any necessary entries in P's consolidated financial statements as at Dec 31, 02.

Hints for solution

In particular Section 2.4.

Solution for versions (a) and (b)

The purchase of an additional 10% of the shares of S and the sale of 10% of the shares of S results neither in losing control nor in obtaining control. Consequently, they are accounted for as equity transactions.

At first the carrying amount of the non-controlling interest is adjusted (IAS 27.30–27.31):

Previous carrying amount of the non-controlling interest	1.0	*20% of CU 5*
Version (a)		
S's net assets	5.0	
New percentage of the non-controlling interest	10%	*100%–90%*
New carrying amount of the non-controlling interest	0.5	
Reduction of the non-controlling interest's carrying amount	**0.5**	
Version (b)		
S's net assets	5.0	
New percentage of the non-controlling interest	30%	*100%–70%*
New carrying amount of the non-controlling interest	1.5	
Increase of the non-controlling interest's carrying amount	**0.5**	

***

[17] *This results in a gain on disposal of CU 1 in P's separate financial statements which is presented on a net basis (IAS 1.34a). The gain is calculated by deducting the carrying amount of 40% of the shares of CU 4 (CU 8 were paid for 80% of the shares and consequently the carrying amount of 40% of the*

Any difference between the amount by which the non-controlling interests are adjusted and the consideration paid or received is recognized directly in equity and attributed to the owners of the parent (retained earnings) (IAS 27.31):

Version (a)

Dec 31, 02	Dr	Non-controlling interest	0.5	
	Dr	Retained earnings	0.5	
	Cr	Investment of P in S (shares)		1.0

If this entry and the entry "Dr Investment of P in S (shares) Cr Cash CU 1.0" (see posting status for version (a)) are aggregated, the result is the entry "Dr Non-controlling interest CU 0.5 Dr Retained earnings CU 0.5 Cr Cash CU 1.0."

Version (b)

Dec 31, 02	Dr	Investment of P in S (shares)	1.0	
	Cr	Retained earnings		0.5
	Cr	Non-controlling interest		0.5

If this entry and the entry "Dr Cash Cr Investment of P in S (shares) CU 1.0" (see posting status for version (b)) are aggregated, the result is the entry "Dr Cash CU 1.0 Cr Retained earnings CU 0.5 Cr Non-controlling interest CU 0.5."

Conclusion

The treatment of the acquisition and disposal of 10% of S as equity transactions as required by IAS 27 is only conclusive if the non-controlling interest is measured at its fair value, because in that case, the entire goodwill (100%) is recognized (IFRS 3.32 and 3.19). However, in this example the non-controlling interest is measured at its proportionate share of S's identifiable net assets. This means goodwill continues to be recognized in P's consolidated statement of financial position on the basis of an interest of 80% in S, although P's interest in S changes to 90% in version (a) and to 70% in version (b).

Solution for version (c)

Fair value of the consideration received (i.e. for the 40% sold)	5	
Carrying amount of the non-controlling interest (20%)	1	
Fair value of the investment retained in S (40%)	5	
Value of S (100%)	**11**	
Carrying amount of S's net assets (including goodwill) (100%)	9	*CU 5 + CU 4*
Gain on deconsolidation	**2**	

shares is CU 4 if it is presumed that there was no control premium) from the proceeds on disposal of CU 5.

Dec 31, 02	Dr	Investment of P in S (shares)[18]	4	
	Dr	Liabilities[19]	10	
	Dr	Non-controlling interest	1	
	Dr	Investments in associates (shares)	5	
	Dr	Gain on disposal[20]	1	
	Cr	Gain on deconsolidation		2
	Cr	Goodwill		4
	Cr	Other assets[21]		15

The fair value of the investment retained in S represents the carrying amount on initial recognition when applying the equity method according to IAS 28 (IAS 27.36–27.37).

3 IFRS 10 (ISSUED IN MAY 2011)

3.1 Introduction

In May 2011, the IASB issued IFRS 10 as well as a new version of IAS 27. Together, the two new standards supersede IAS 27 (as amended in 2008) and the Interpretation SIC 12 "Consolidation – Special Purpose Entities" (IAS 27.20 and IFRS 10.C8–10.C9).

IFRS 10 contains requirements for **consolidated financial statements**. The new **explanations and rules** of IFRS 10 relevant when **assessing control** are **much more detailed** than those of the "old" version of IAS 27. They are dealt with in Section 3.2. By contrast, the **remaining rules** of the "old" version of IAS 27 relating to consolidated financial statements were carried forward **nearly unchanged** to IFRS 10 in most areas.

IFRS 10 has to be applied in the financial statements as at **Dec 31, 2013** (if the entity's reporting periods are identical with the calendar years). **Earlier application** is **permitted** by the IASB (IFRS 10.C1). IFRS 10 has to be applied **retrospectively**. However there are several exceptions to this principle (IFRS 10.C2–10.C6). In the European Union, there has been no endorsement as yet.[22]

3.2 Assessing Control

3.2.1 Overview According to IFRS 10, an investor **controls** an investee if the investor has all of the following (IFRS 10.6–10.7 and 10.B2):

- **Power** over the investee (i.e. that the investor has existing rights that give it the current ability to direct the relevant activities of the investee). The **relevant activities** are the activities of the investee that significantly affect the investee's returns (IFRS 10.10

In P's separate financial statements, the account "Investment of P in S (shares)" was credited with CU 4 (see posting status for version (c)). This credit entry has to be reversed in the consolidated financial statements.

S's liabilities have to be derecognized since S is no longer a subsidiary of P.

The gain on disposal recognized in P's separate financial statements has to be derecognized.

S's other assets have to be derecognized since S is no longer a subsidiary of P.

[22] *See Section 1.*

and 10, Appendix A). The following are examples of activities that may be relevant activities of a particular investee (IFRS 10.B11):
  - The purchase and sale of goods or services.
  - Researching and developing new products or processes.
  - Determining a funding structure or obtaining funding.
  - Selecting, acquiring or disposing of assets.
- Exposure or rights to **variable returns** from its involvement with the investee (i.e. the investor's returns from its involvement have the potential to vary as a result of the investee's performance) (IFRS 10.15 and 10.B55).
- The ability to use its power over the investee to affect the amount of the investor's returns from its involvement with the investee (**link between power and returns**). Hence, an investor that is an **agent** does not control an investee when it exercises decision-making rights delegated to it (IFRS 10.17–10.18).

When assessing control of an investee, it is necessary to consider the investee's **purpose and design** (IFRS 10.B5).

According to IFRS 10, it may also be necessary to consolidate only a **portion of an investee** in certain circumstances (IFRS 10.B76–10.B79).

It is necessary to **reassess** whether an investor controls an investee if facts and circumstances indicate that there are changes to one or more of the three elements of control listed in IFRS 10.7 (see above) (IFRS 10.B80–10.B85).

3.2.2 Power Assessing **power** may be straightforward. This is the case when power of the investee is obtained directly and solely from the voting rights granted by equity instruments such as shares. In this situation, power is assessed by considering the voting rights from these shares. In other situations, the assessment will be more complex (IFRS 10.11).

The following are **examples of rights** that either individually or in combination may give the investor power over the investee (IFRS 10.B15):

- Rights in the form of voting rights (or potential voting rights) of an investee.
- Rights to appoint, remove or reassign members of the investee's key management personnel who are able to direct the relevant activities of the investee.
- Rights to appoint or remove another entity that directs the relevant activities of the investee.
- Rights to direct the investee to enter into, or veto any changes to, transactions for the benefit of the investor.
- Other rights (e.g. decision-making rights specified in a management contract) that enable the holder to direct the relevant activities of the investee.

For the purpose of assessing power, only **substantive rights** relating to the investee (held by the investor and others) and rights that are **not protective** are considered (IFRS 10.B9 and 10.B22):

- **Protective rights** represent rights designed in order to protect the interest of the party holding those rights without giving that party power over the entity to which those rights relate (IFRS 10, Appendix A). An example is the right of a party holding a non-controlling interest in an investee to approve the issue of equity or debt instruments (IFRS 10.B28b).

- For a right to be **substantive**, the holder must have the practical ability to exercise the right. The determination whether a right is substantive requires judgment, taking into account all facts and circumstances. The following are examples of factors to consider in making that determination (IFRS 10.B23):
  - Whether there are any barriers that prevent the holder from exercising the rights (e.g. financial penalties and incentives that would prevent or deter the holder from exercising the rights).
  - Whether the party that holds the rights (e.g. potential voting rights) would benefit from exercising them.

Usually, in order to be substantive, the rights have to be currently exercisable (IFRS 10. B24). Substantive rights exercisable by other parties may prevent an investor from controlling the investee (IFRS 10.B25).

In many cases, voting rights will indicate that the investee is controlled. However, in other situations voting rights are not the main criterion for determining whether there is control (e.g. when voting rights relate to administrative tasks only and contractual arrangements determine the direction of the relevant activities) (IFRS 10.B16–10.B17). Hence, the investor has to consider whether the **relevant activities** of the investee are **directed through voting rights** (IFRS 10.B34). If this is the case, the investor usually has power in each of the following situations if it holds **more than half of the voting rights** of the investee (IFRS 10. B35):

- The relevant activities of the investee are directed by a vote of the holder of the majority of the voting rights.
- A majority of the members of the governing body that directs the relevant activities of the investee are appointed by a vote of the holder of the majority of the voting rights.

An investor can have power even if it holds **less than a majority of the voting rights** of the investee, for example, through the following (IFRS 10.B38):

- A contractual arrangement between the investor and other vote holders.
- Rights arising from other contractual arrangements.
- Potential voting rights.

Subsequently, the treatment of **potential voting rights** when assessing control according to IFRS 10 is discussed in more detail. Potential voting rights represent rights to obtain voting rights of the investee, such as those arising from convertible instruments or options, including forward contracts (IFRS 10.B47).

When determining whether it has power, the investor has to consider its potential voting rights as well as the potential voting rights held by other parties. Potential voting rights are considered only if the rights are **substantive** (IFRS 10.B47).[23] This means that the holder of potential voting rights has to consider, among others, the exercise or conversion price of the instrument. The terms and conditions of potential voting rights are more likely to be substantive when the

[23] *See the explanations above with regard to the term "substantive."*

instrument is in the money or the investor would benefit for other reasons (e.g. by realizing synergies between the investor and the investee) from exercising or converting the instrument (IFRS 10.B23c). Hence, when considering potential voting rights the investor has to consider the purpose and design of the instrument and the purpose and design of any other involvement the investor has with the investee. This includes an assessment of the terms and conditions of the instrument and of the investor's apparent expectations, motives, and reasons for agreeing to them (IFRS 10.B48).

3.2.3 Exposure or Rights to Variable Returns Variable returns represent returns that are not fixed and have the potential to vary as a result of the performance of an investee. When assessing whether returns from an investee are variable and how variable they are, the principle "**substance over form**"[24] applies. This means that the assessment is made on the basis of the substance of the arrangement and regardless of the legal form of the returns. For example, an entity may hold a bond with fixed interest payments. The fixed interest payments represent variable returns within the meaning of IFRS 10 because they are subject to default risk and they expose the entity to the credit risk of the issuer of the bond. The amount of variability (i.e. how variable those returns are) depends on the credit risk of the bond (IFRS 10.B56).

The following are **examples of returns** (IFRS 10.B57):

- **Dividends** and **changes in the value of the** investor's **investment** in the investee.
- **Returns not available to other interest holders**. For example, the investor might use its assets in combination with the assets of the investee, such as combining operating functions in order to achieve economies of scale, cost savings, sourcing scarce products, gaining access to proprietary knowledge or limiting some operations or assets to enhance the value of the investor's other assets.

3.2.4 Link Between Power and Returns A **decision maker** (i.e. an entity with decision-making rights) has to determine whether it is a **principal or an agent** for the purpose of determining whether it controls an investee. An investor also has to assess whether another entity with decision-making rights is acting as an agent for the investor (IFRS 10.B58).

An agent is a party primarily engaged to act on behalf of and for the benefit of another party (the principal). The principal's power is held and exercisable by the agent, but on behalf of the principal. Therefore, the agent does not control the investee when it exercises its decision-making rights. The investor has to treat the decision-making rights delegated to its agent as held by itself directly for the purpose of determining whether it controls the investee (IFRS 10.B58–10.B59).

In particular, the following factors have to be considered in determining whether a decision maker is an agent (IFRS 10.B60):

- The scope of its decision-making authority over the investee.
- The rights held by other parties.
- The remuneration to which it is entitled according to the remuneration agreements.
- Its exposure to variability of returns resulting from other interests that it holds in the investee.

[24] *See the chapter on Conceptual Framework, Section 4.2.2.*

3.2.5 Conclusion The explanations and rules of IFRS 10 relevant when assessing control are set out in a large number of paragraphs and address many aspects and situations. They are much more detailed than those of the "old" version of IAS 27. Nevertheless, it is unclear in some respects **how the new rules for assessing control will be interpreted** when applying them in practice. Moreover, application of the new rules also requires **judgment** in many cases (which can hardly be avoided in this area of accounting). It will be seen in the future whether they will lead to an improvement in financial reporting compared with the "old" rules of IAS 27 (as amended in 2008).

3.3 Example with Solution

Example 7[25]

Potential voting rights

(a) Entity A holds 80% of the voting rights of entity X. Entity B has 20% of the voting rights of X as well as an option to acquire half of A's voting rights. The option is exercisable for the next two years at a fixed price, which is deeply out of the money (and is expected to remain so for the two-year period). A has been exercising its votes and is actively directing the relevant activities of X.

(b) Entities A, B, C, and D each hold one fourth of the voting rights of entity X. The business activity of X is closely related to entity A. Moreover, A holds convertible bonds. These are convertible into ordinary shares of X at any time for a fixed price that is out of the money (but not deeply out of the money). If the bonds were converted, A would hold 55% of the voting rights of X. A would benefit from realizing synergies if the bonds were converted.

Required

Determine which of the entities mentioned above has power over the investee (power criterion according to IFRS 10.7a), which is a prerequisite for the existence of control.

Hints for solution

In particular Section 3.2.2.

Solution (a)

In the situation described, it is likely that A meets the power criterion because it appears to have the current ability to direct the relevant activities of X. Although B has currently exercisable purchase options (which if exercised, would give it a majority of the voting rights in the investee), the terms and conditions associated with those options are such that the options are not considered substantive (IFRS 10.B50).

Solution (b)

A has power over X because it holds voting rights of X together with substantive potential voting rights, which give it the current ability to direct the relevant activities of X (IFRS 10.B23(c) and 10.B50).

---

[25] *The examples are based on IFRS 10.B50.*

4 THE NEW VERSION OF IAS 27 (ISSUED IN MAY 2011)

In May 2011, the IASB issued IFRS 10 as well as a new version of IAS 27. Together the two new standards supersede IAS 27 (as amended in 2008) and the Interpretation SIC 12 "Consolidation – Special Purpose Entities" (IAS 27.20 and IFRS 10.C8–10.C9).

The **new version of IAS 27** only contains accounting and disclosure requirements for **investments in subsidiaries, joint ventures, and associates** in the investor's **separate financial statements**. These requirements were carried forward nearly unchanged from the "old" version of IAS 27. The issues relating to consolidated financial statements that were part of the "old version" of IAS 27 have been deleted because these are now within the scope of IFRS 10.

The new standard has to be applied in the financial statements as at **Dec 31, 2013** (if the entity's reporting periods are identical with the calendar years). **Earlier application** is **permitted** by the IASB (IAS 27.18). In the **European Union**, there has been no endorsement as yet.[26]

[26] *See Section 1.*

IAS 28 INVESTMENTS IN ASSOCIATES AND IAS 28 (2011) INVESTMENTS IN ASSOCIATES AND JOINT VENTURES

1 INTRODUCTION

IAS 28 prescribes the accounting treatment of **investments in associates**. Associates are generally accounted for according to the equity method in the investor's consolidated financial statements.

In **May 2011**, the **IASB amended IAS 28**. The new version of the standard has to be applied in the financial statements as at **Dec 31, 2013** (if the entity's reporting periods start on Jan 01 and end on Dec 31). **Earlier application** is **permitted** by the IASB (IAS 28.45). However, in the **European Union**, new IFRSs have to be endorsed by the European Union before they can be applied. There has been no endorsement with regard to the new version of IAS 28 as yet.

This chapter of the book is structured as follows:

- Section 2 discusses the rules applicable if the entity decides not to apply the new version of IAS 28 early.
- Section 3 discusses the main differences between the "old" and the "new" version of IAS 28.

2 FINANCIAL REPORTING WITHOUT EARLY APPLICATION OF THE AMENDMENTS TO IAS 28 ISSUED IN MAY 2011

2.1 The Term "Associate" and Scope of IAS 28

IAS 28 is applied in accounting for investments in associates (IAS 28.1). An **associate** is an entity (IAS 28.2).

- over which the investor has **significant influence**, and
- that is **neither a subsidiary nor a joint venture**.

Significant influence is the *power* to participate in the financial and operating policy decisions of the investee. However, if there is control or joint control, this rules out the existence of significant influence within the meaning of IAS 28 (IAS 28.2).

If an investor holds – directly or indirectly (e.g. through subsidiaries) – (IAS 28.6):

- 20% or more of the voting power of the investee, it is presumed that this results in significant influence over the investee unless it can be clearly demonstrated that this is not the case (**refutable presumption of significant influence**).

- Less than 20% of the voting power of the investee, it is presumed that this does not result in significant influence over the investee unless such influence can be clearly demonstrated (**refutable presumption that there is no significant influence**).

A substantial or majority ownership by another investor does not necessarily eliminate the possibility of the investor having significant influence (IAS 28.6). However, together with other facts this may indicate that there is no significant influence.

The presumptions above may be refuted by assessing **qualitative criteria**, which may involve discretion. Significant influence generally exists when one or more of the following criteria are met (IAS 28.7):

- Representation on the board of directors or equivalent governing body of the investee.
- Participation in policy-making processes, including participation in decisions about dividends of the investee.
- Material transactions between the investor and the investee.
- Interchange of managerial personnel between the investor and the investee.
- Provision of essential technical information.

Assessing whether there is significant influence is not only made on the basis of existing voting rights. **Potential voting rights** (e.g. share call options or convertible bonds that give the investor additional voting power when they are exercised or converted) also have to be taken into account if they are currently exercisable or convertible. Potential voting rights are not currently exercisable or convertible when, for example, they cannot be exercised or converted until the occurrence of a future event or until a future date. All facts and circumstances that affect potential voting rights have to be examined except the intention of management and the financial ability to exercise or convert (IAS 28.8–28.9). The rules regarding potential voting rights in IAS 28.8–28.9 correspond with those for subsidiaries in IAS 27.14–27.15.[1]

IAS 28 does not apply to investments in associates held by venture capital organizations and mutual funds, unit trusts and similar entities (including investment-linked insurance funds) that are measured at fair value through profit or loss in accordance with IFRS 9 (IAS 28.1).

2.2 The Equity Method

2.2.1 Overview In the investor's consolidated financial statements, investments in associates are **usually** accounted for using the **equity method** (IAS 28.13–28.14). According to this method, the shares are initially recognized at cost and adjusted thereafter for the post-acquisition **change in the investor's share of net assets of the investee** (IAS 28.2).

More precisely, the carrying amount of an investment in an associate is at first increased or decreased by the investor's share of the **profit or loss** of the investee after the acquisition date. This means that the investor's entry is "Dr Share of the profit or loss of associates Cr Investment" (if the associate has suffered a loss) or "Dr Investment Cr Share of the profit or loss of associates" (if the associate has generated a profit). **Distributions** received from an

[1] *See the chapter on IAS 27/IFRS 10, Section 2.1.*

investee reduce the carrying amount of the investment, meaning that the entry in the investor's statement of financial position is "Dr Cash Cr Investment" (IAS 28.11). The carrying amount of the investment in the associate also changes, for example, if the associate **issues shares against cash**. In this case, the investor's entry is "Dr Investment Cr Cash".

On the acquisition date it is necessary to determine the difference between the fair values of the investee's identifiable assets and liabilities and their carrying amounts in the investee's financial statements (**fair value differences**). A positive difference between the cost of the investment and the investor's share of the net fair value of the associate's identifiable assets and liabilities represents **goodwill**. In the investor's consolidated statement of financial position, such goodwill is **not recognized as a separate asset**. Instead, it is included in the carrying amount of the investment in the associate (IAS 28.23). This applies similarly regarding the investor's share of the fair value differences.

After the acquisition date, goodwill must not be amortized. Moreover, after the acquisition date, the investor's share of the change in the fair value differences (see above) of the associate has to be taken into account. For example, it might be the case that the fair value of a building of the associate exceeded the building's carrying amount on acquisition date. The resulting fair value difference has to be depreciated after the acquisition date. The investor's share of that depreciation affects the carrying amount of the investment in the associate as well as the investor's share of the profit or loss of the associate (IAS 28.23).

If the cost of the investment is below the investor's share of the net fair value of the associate's identifiable assets and liabilities, the difference (**negative goodwill**) is included as income when determining the investor's share of the associate's profit or loss in the period in which the investment is acquired (IAS 28.23b). As a result of the corresponding entry "Dr Investment Cr Share of the profit or loss of associates", the carrying amount of the investment increases above cost.

The investor's share of the investee's **other comprehensive income** (e.g. arising from revaluations according to IAS 16) has to be taken into account when applying the equity method. This affects the investor's other comprehensive income (IAS 28.11). If an investor loses significant influence over an associate, the investor shall account for all amounts recognized in other comprehensive income related to that associate on the same basis as would be required if the associate had directly disposed of the related assets or liabilities. For example, if an associate has cumulative exchange differences relating to a foreign operation and the investor loses significant influence over the associate, the investor reclassifies the amounts previously recognized in other comprehensive income in relation to the foreign operation to profit or loss (IAS 28.19A).

The following applies when determining the **share of the investor in the associate** (expressed as a percentage) for the purpose of applying the **equity method**:

- The investor's share reflects present ownership interests, which means that it does not include potential voting rights. This differs from the assessment of whether there is significant influence (IAS 28.12).
- The group's share in an associate is the aggregate of the holdings in that associate by the parent and its subsidiaries. The holdings of the group's other associates or joint ventures are ignored for this purpose (IAS 28.21).

An important exception from applying the equity method to associates in the investor's consolidated financial statements are those investments that meet the definition of "**held for sale**" and are therefore accounted for in accordance with IFRS 5 (IAS 28.13–28.14). When the definition of "held for sale" is no longer met, the investment has to be accounted for according to the equity method as from the date of its classification as "held for sale." This means that it is also necessary to adjust comparative information for prior periods (IAS 28.15).

2.2.2 Impairment Losses and Reversals of Impairment Losses Investments in associates are tested for impairment as follows (IAS 28.31–28.33):

- The requirements of IAS 39 are applied when assessing whether the investment is impaired.
- If this is the case, the amount of the impairment loss is determined according to IAS 36 by comparing the investment's carrying amount with its recoverable amount. The recoverable amount of an investment is the higher of its value in use and its fair value less costs to sell.

Value in use is determined by estimating either of the following amounts (IAS 28.33):

- The investor's share of the present value of the estimated future cash flows expected to be generated by the associate.
- The present value of the estimated future cash flows expected to arise from dividends to be received from the associate and from its ultimate disposal. In our opinion it is necessary to assume that the entire profits are distributed even if this is not expected to take place in reality.

An **impairment loss is not allocated** to any asset that is included in the carrying amount of the investment in the associate. Therefore, the components goodwill and fair value adjustments that form part of the investment's carrying amount are not affected by the impairment loss. Instead, the impairment loss is treated as a separate component of the investment's carrying amount, which has a negative amount. Any reversal of the impairment loss is recognized according to IAS 36 to the extent that the recoverable amount of the investment subsequently increases (IAS 28.33).

The recoverable amount of an investment in an associate is determined for each associate, unless the associate does not generate cash inflows from continuing use that are largely independent of those from other assets of the entity (IAS 28.34).

2.2.3 Uniform Accounting Policies When applying the equity method, the financial statements of the associate have to be adjusted to the accounting policies that are applied in the investor's consolidated financial statements (IAS 28.26–28.27).

When an associate has subsidiaries, joint ventures or associates, the profits or losses and net assets taken into account in applying the equity method are those recognized in the associate's financial statements (including the associate's share of the profits or losses and net assets of its joint ventures and associates), after any adjustments to uniform accounting policies (IAS 28.21).

2.2.4 Elimination of Intragroup Profits and Losses Many of the procedures appropriate for the application of the equity method are similar to the consolidation procedures of IAS 27 for subsidiaries (IAS 28.20). An example is the elimination of intragroup profits or losses, required by IAS 27 (IAS 27.21).[2] Profits and losses resulting from transactions between the investor (including its consolidated subsidiaries) and an associate are recognized by the investor only to the extent of unrelated investors' interests in the associate. For example, if the interest in an associate is 25%, this means that 25% of such profits and losses are eliminated while 75% of such profits or losses are presented in the investor's consolidated financial statements. Moreover, the following distinction is necessary (IAS 28.22):

- **Upstream transactions** (e.g. sales of assets from the associate to the investor): In such cases, the asset acquired is recognized in the investor's consolidated financial statements whereas the profit arising from the sale of the asset is included in the associate's financial statements. Therefore, the investor's elimination entry is "Dr Share of the profit or loss of associates Cr Asset acquired." However, some authors believe that the entry "Dr Share of the profit or loss of associates Cr Investment" is acceptable, or even more appropriate.
- **Downstream transactions** (e.g. sales of assets from the investor to the associate): In such cases, the asset has already been derecognized in the investor's consolidated financial statements. Therefore, the investor's elimination entry is "Dr Profit (from the sale of the asset) Cr Investment."

2.2.5 Continuing Losses According to the equity method, losses of the associate reduce the carrying amount of the investment in the associate. Hence, in the case of continuing losses, the carrying amount of the investment would decrease to below zero after a certain period of time. However, according to IAS 28, the investor discontinues recognizing its share of further losses in such cases. This means that the carrying amount of the investment cannot become negative. If the associate subsequently reports profits, the investor resumes recognizing its share of those profits (by increasing the carrying amount of the investment) only after its share of the profits equals the share of losses that have not been recognized. There are some exceptions to these procedures (e.g. when the investor has incurred legal or constructive obligations or made payments on behalf of the associate) (IAS 28.29–28.30).

2.2.6 Balance Sheet Date of the Financial Statements of the Associate When the associate's reporting period ends before the investor's balance sheet date, the difference between the balance sheet dates must not be more than three months. Otherwise, the associate has to prepare (for the use of the investor) financial statements as of the same date as the financial statements of the investor. In the case of differing balance sheet dates, adjustments have to be made for the effects of significant transactions or events that occur between these dates (IAS 28.24–28.25).

2.2.7 Application of the Concept of Materiality In the case of associates, application of the concept of materiality (IAS 8.8) is often of particular importance. IFRSs, and consequently also the rules of IAS 28, relating to the equity method need not be applied when the effect of applying them is immaterial. Consequently, simplified procedures may be possible when applying the equity method in some cases.

---

[2] *See the chapter on IAS 27/IFRS 10, Section 2.3.4.*

2.3 Presentation

Investments accounted for using the equity method have to be presented as a separate line item in the statement of financial position (IAS 1.54e). The share of the **profit or loss** of these investments has to be presented as a separate line item in the statement of comprehensive income (IAS 1.82c). Also, the share of the **other comprehensive income I** and of the **other comprehensive income II** of investments accounted for using the equity method have to be presented as separate line items in the statement of comprehensive income. They must not be allocated to the other items of other comprehensive income (IAS 1.82A and 1.BC106c).

It is questionable whether **impairment losses and reversals of impairment losses** relating to investments in associates have to be included in the line item "share of the profit or loss of investments accounted for using the equity method" or not. In our opinion both approaches are acceptable.

2.4 Separate Financial Statements of the Investor

In separate financial statements it is not possible to account for investments in associates using the equity method. Instead, investments in associates are accounted for **either** (IAS 28.35 and IAS 27.38):

(a) **at cost, or**
(b) in accordance with **IFRS 9**, which means that they are measured **at fair value**. According to IFRS 9, it is always presumed that fair value can be determined reliably. However, in certain circumstances, cost may be an appropriate estimate of fair value (IFRS 9.B5.4.14–9.B5.4.17).[3]

If investments in associates are accounted for in accordance with IFRS 9 in the consolidated financial statements they have to be accounted for in the same way in the investor's separate financial statements (IAS 27.40).

2.5 Preparation of the Consolidated Financial Statements

The starting point for the application of the equity method is the aggregated financial statements of the investor and its subsidiaries. The aggregated financial statements result from adding together like items of assets, liabilities, equity, income, and expenses included in the statements of financial position II and in the statements of comprehensive income II of the investor and its subsidiaries.[4] In the aggregated statement of financial position, the investment is included on the basis of its carrying amount determined according to the rules described in Section 2.4. Thus, at each balance sheet date of the investor's consolidated financial statements, that carrying amount has to be adjusted to the carrying amount determined according to the equity

[3] *If IFRS 9 was not applied early, the investments would normally be measured at fair value. However, the equity instruments would be measured at cost if fair value could not be determined reliably (IAS 39.AG80–39.AG81).*

[4] *See the chapter on IAS 27/IFRS 10, Section 2.3.1.*

method. Thereby, amounts having affected profit or loss of previous periods are recognized directly in retained earnings, in the current period.[5]

2.6 Examples with Solutions[6]

Example 1

Indirect voting power

Parent P and its subsidiary S hold shares of entity A:

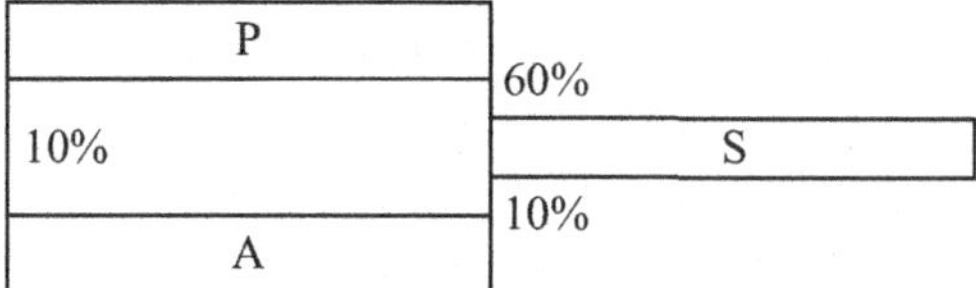

Required

(a) Determine whether it can be refutably presumed that A is an associate in P's consolidated financial statements.
(b) If this is the case, assume that A is an associate and determine the interest in A (expressed as a percentage) that is used when applying the equity method.

Hints for solution

In particular Sections 2.1 and 2.2.1.

Solution

(a) When determining whether there is significant influence over A, the shares held by S also have to be taken into account in full. Together P and S hold 20% of the voting power of A. This means that it is refutably presumed that there is significant influence over A and that A is therefore an associate (IAS 28.6).
(b) The equity method is applied on the basis of 20%, which means that 20% of the associate's profit or loss is recognized in P's consolidated financial statements. For example, 20% of a loss of A would have to be recognized as a reduction of the carrying amount of the investment in A (IAS 28.21). Part of the associate's profit or loss is attributed to the non-controlling interest in S.

[5] *In this respect we also refer to the considerations in the chapter on IFRS 3, Section 9, regarding the repetition of consolidation entries of prior periods.*

[6] *Deferred tax is ignored in these examples. Moreover, it is presumed that there are no differences between the associate's separate financial statements and its statement of financial position II and statement of comprehensive income II.*

Example 2

Application of the equity method – introductory example

On Jan 01, 01, entity E gains significant influence over entity A by acquiring 25% of the shares of A for CU 100. Thus, A becomes an associate of E. The carrying amount of A's equity as at Jan 01, 01, is CU 280. On Jan 01, 01, fair value of A's buildings exceeds their carrying amount in A's separate financial statements by CU 40. On that date, the remaining useful life of these buildings is 10 years. On Dec 31, 03, A pays a dividend of CU 20 to its owners. E's share of this dividend is CU 5 (= CU 20 · 25%).

A generates the following amounts of profit or loss:

Year	*A's profit or loss for the year*
01	40
02	–72
03	76

E accounts for its investment in A at cost in its separate financial statements (IAS 28.35 and IAS 27.38).

Posting status (in E's separate financial statements):

Jan 01, 01	Dr	Investment of E in A	100	
	Cr	Cash		100
Dec 31, 03	Dr	Cash	5	
	Cr	Dividend income		5

Required

Prepare any necessary entries in E's consolidated financial statements for the years 01–03 and determine the amount of goodwill that is part of the carrying amount of E's investment in A. The reporting periods of both E and A end on Dec 31.

Hints for solution

In particular Sections 2.2.1 and 2.5.

Solution

Goodwill, which is part of the carrying amount of the investment in A, is the excess of the cost of the investment over the investor's share of the net fair value of the associate's identifiable assets and liabilities (IAS 28.23a):

	100%	*25%*
Carrying amount of A's equity	280	70
Fair value adjustment (buildings)	40	10
Fair value of A's equity	**320**	**80**
Cost		100
Goodwill		**20**

Jan 01, 01

In E's consolidated financial statements the shares are initially measured at their cost of CU 100 (IAS 28.11). This is the same accounting treatment as in E's separate financial statements. Hence, no further entry is necessary on Jan 01, 01.

Dec 31, 01

In E's separate financial statements as at Dec 31, 01, no entry is necessary with regard to the investment, which is accounted for at cost. This means that the investment's carrying amount remains CU 100.

By contrast, in E's consolidated financial statements the equity method has to be applied. Consequently, the carrying amount of the investment is adjusted for E's share of A's profit and for E's share of the depreciation of the fair value adjustment in respect of the buildings:

	100%	*25%*
Carrying amount of the investment as at Jan 01, 01		**100**
Profit for 01	40	10
Depreciation of the fair value adjustment	−4	−1
Change in the carrying amount in 01		**9**
Carrying amount of the investment as at Dec 31, 01		**109**

Dec 31, 01	Dr	Investment of E in A	9	
	Cr	Share of the profit or loss of associates		9

Dec 31, 02

In 02, the carrying amount of the investment changes as follows in E's consolidated financial statements according to the equity method:

	100%	**25%**
Carrying amount of the investment as at Jan 01, 02		**109**
Loss for 02	−72	−18
Depreciation of the fair value adjustment	−4	−1
Change in the carrying amount in 02		**−19**
Carrying amount of the investment as at Dec 31, 02		**90**

The starting point for the entries necessary when applying the equity method is E's aggregated financial statements for the current reporting period in which the carrying amount of the investment in A is included on the basis of its cost of CU 100. Thus, the carrying amount of the investment of CU 100 has to be reduced to CU 90. E's share of A's loss and of the depreciation of the fair value adjustment relating to the buildings result in a loss of CU −19, which has to be recognized by E in 02 according to the equity method. The amount of CU +9 recognized in profit or loss in 01 is recognized in retained earnings in 02.[7]

Dec 31, 02	Dr	Share of the profit or loss of associates	19	
	Cr	Retained earnings		9
	Cr	Investment of E in A		10

[7] *See Section 2.5.*

Dec 31, 03

In 03, the carrying amount of the investment changes as follows in E's consolidated financial statements according to the equity method:

	100%	*25%*
Carrying amount of the investment as at Jan 01, 03		**90**
Profit for 03	76	19
Distribution	–20	–5
Depreciation of the fair value adjustment	–4	–1
Change in the carrying amount in 03		**13**
Carrying amount of the investment as at Dec 31, 03		**103**

The starting point for the entries necessary when applying the equity method is E's aggregated financial statements for the current reporting period in which the carrying amount of the investment in A is included on the basis of its cost of CU 100. Thus, the carrying amount of the investment of CU 100 has to be increased to CU 103. The dividend income that is included in E's aggregated statement of comprehensive income has to be eliminated because, according to the equity method, dividends reduce the carrying amount of the investment. E's share of A's profit and of the depreciation of the fair value adjustment result in income of CU +18, which has to be recognized by E in 03 according to the equity method. The amount of CU –19 recognized in profit or loss in 02 as well as the amount of CU +9 recognized in retained earnings in 02 are recognized in retained earnings in 03 (CU –19 + CU 9 = CU –10).[8]

Dec 31, 03	Dr	Investment of E in A	3	
	Dr	Dividend income	5	
	Dr	Retained earnings	10	
	Cr	Share of the profit or loss of associates		18

Example 3

Impairment loss and reversal of the impairment loss

The situation is the same as in Example 2. However, it is assumed that A's profit or loss in each of the years 01–03 is zero and that there is no dividend. Recoverable amount of the investment in A is CU 75 on Dec 31, 01, CU 74 on Dec 31, 02, and CU 105 on Dec 31, 03. Assume that no impairment loss for the investment in A is recognized in E's separate financial statements.

Required

Prepare any necessary entries in E's consolidated financial statements for the years 01–03. The reporting periods of both E and A end on Dec 31.

E does not include impairment losses relating to associates in the line item "share of the profit or loss of investments accounted for using the equity method" in its statement of comprehensive income.

---

[8] *See Section 2.5.*

Hints for solution

In particular Sections 2.2.1, 2.2.2, and 2.5.

Solution

Year 01

In E's consolidated financial statements the shares are initially measured at their cost of CU 100 (IAS 28.11). This is the same accounting treatment as in E's separate financial statements. Hence, no further entry is necessary on Jan 01, 01.

In E's separate financial statements as at Dec 31, 01 no entry is made with regard to the investment which is accounted for at cost. This means that the investment's carrying amount remains CU 100.

By contrast, in E's consolidated financial statements the **equity method** has to be applied, which is illustrated below.

On Jan 01, 01, the carrying amount of the investment consists of the following components (see Example 2):

Goodwill	20
Fair value adjustment (buildings)	10
Remaining part of the investment	70
Carrying amount of the investment as at Jan 01, 01	**100**

In 01, the carrying amount of the investment changes as follows:

Carrying amount as at Jan 01, 01	100
Depreciation of the fair value adjustment	−1
Carrying amount as at Dec 31, 01 (before testing for impairment)	**99**
Recoverable amount	75
Impairment loss	**−24**

It is important to note that the impairment loss must not be allocated to any asset that is included in the carrying amount of the investment in the associate. Consequently, goodwill and the fair value adjustment are not changed by the impairment. Instead, the impairment loss is a separate component of the investment's carrying amount, which has a negative amount (IAS 28.33). Hence, the investment consists of the following components as at Dec 31, 01:

Goodwill	20
Fair value adjustment (buildings)	9
Impairment	−24
Remaining part of the investment	70
Carrying amount of the investment as at Dec 31, 01	**75**

E does not include impairment losses relating to associates in the line item "share of the profit or loss of investments accounted for using the equity method" in its statement of comprehensive income. Consequently, the following entry is made:

Dec 31, 01	Dr	Share of the profit or loss of associates	1	
	Dr	Impairment loss	24	
	Cr	Investment of E in A		25

Year 02

Dec 31, 02	Dr	Retained earnings	25	
	Cr	Investment of E in A		25

In 02, only the fair value adjustment relating to the buildings is depreciated, which has the following effect on the carrying amount of the investment and its components:

Goodwill	20
Fair value adjustment (buildings)	8
Impairment	–24
Remaining part of the investment	70
Carrying amount of the investment as at Dec 31, 02	**74**

Dec 31, 02	Dr	Share of the profit or loss of associates	1	
	Cr	Investment of E in A		1

Year 03

Dec 31, 03	Dr	Retained earnings	26	
	Cr	Investment of E in A		26

In 03, the fair value adjustment relating to the buildings is depreciated, which reduces the carrying amount of the investment to CU 73:

Dec 31, 03	Dr	Share of the profit or loss of associates	1	
	Cr	Investment of E in A		1

Reversing the impairment loss of CU 24 recognized in 01 would increase the carrying amount of the investment from CU 73 to CU 97. Since the recoverable amount is CU 105 on Dec 31, 03, the reversal of the impairment loss is recognized in full:

Dec 31, 03	Dr	Investment of E in A	24	
	Cr	Reversals of impairment losses		24

Accordingly, the investment consists of the following components, on Dec 31, 03:

Goodwill	20
Fair value adjustment (buildings)	7
Remaining part of the investment	70
Carrying amount of the investment as at Dec 31, 03	**97**

Example 4

Negative goodwill

On Dec 31, 01, entity E gains significant influence over entity A, by acquiring 25% of the shares of A for CU 8. This means that A becomes an associate of E. Fair value of A's equity as at Dec 31, 01, is CU 40. E accounts for the investment in A at cost in its separate financial statements (IAS 28.35 and IAS 27.38).

Posting status (in E's separate financial statements):

Dec 31, 01	Dr	Investment of E in A	8	
	Cr	Cash		8

Required

Assess whether negative goodwill arises in E's consolidated financial statements in connection with the acquisition of A. If this is the case, prepare the appropriate entry. The reporting periods of both E and A end on Dec 31, 01.

Hints for solution

In particular Section 2.2.1.

Solution

Since the cost of the investment of CU 8 is below E's share of the fair value of A's equity of CU 10 (= CU 40 · 25%), negative goodwill of CU 2 arises, which has to be recognized as income (IAS 28.23b). In E's separate financial statements the carrying amount of the investment is CU 8. Consequently, the carrying amount of the investment has to be increased by CU 2 (i.e. from CU 8 to CU 10) in E's consolidated financial statements.

Dec 31, 01	Dr	Investment of E in A	2	
	Cr	Share of the profit or loss of associates		2

Example 5

Continuing losses

On Jan 01, 01, entity E makes a contribution in cash of CU 10 during the incorporation of entity A, for which E receives 25% of the shares of A. After that, A is an associate of E.

A generates the following amounts of profit or loss:

Year	*A's profit or loss for the year*
01	−24
02	−28
03	+20

E accounts for its investment in A at cost, in its separate financial statements (IAS 28.35 and IAS 27.38).

Posting status (in E's separate financial statements):

Jan 01, 01	Dr	Investment of E in A	10	
	Cr	Cash		10

Required

Prepare any necessary entries in E's consolidated financial statements for the years 01–03. The reporting periods of both E and A end on Dec 31. Presume that E has neither incurred legal or constructive obligations nor made payments on behalf of the associate (IAS 28.30).

Hints for solution

In particular Section 2.2.5.

Solution

In E's consolidated financial statements the shares are initially recognized at their cost of CU 10 (IAS 28.11). This is the same accounting treatment as in E's separate financial statements. Hence, no further entry is necessary on Jan 01, 01.

On Dec 31, 01, E recognizes its share of A's loss of CU 6 (= CU 24 · 25%):

Dec 31, 01	Dr	Share of the profit or loss of associates	6	
	Cr	Investment of E in A		6

E's share of A's loss for 02 of CU 7 (= CU 28 · 25%) is only recognized to the extent of CU 4 because the carrying amount of the investment would otherwise become negative (IAS 28.29–28.30).

Dec 31, 02	Dr	Share of the profit or loss of associates	4	
	Cr	Investment of E in A		4

In 03, E resumes recognizing its share of A's profits of CU 5 (= CU 20 · 25%) only after its share of the profits equals the share of losses that have not been recognized in 02. The latter amount is CU 3. Therefore, E only recognizes income in the amount of CU 2 (IAS 28.30).

Dec 31, 03	Dr	Investment of E in A	2	
	Cr	Share of the profit or loss of associates		2

Example 6A

Other comprehensive income arising from equity instruments held by the associate – early application of IFRS 9 (as issued in Oct 2010)[9]

The situation is the same as in Example 5. However, A's profit or loss for 01 is zero. Moreover, on Jan 01, 01, A acquires shares of entity X for CU 8, which are measured by A

[9] *See the chapter on IFRS 9/IAS 39, Section 2.3.7 with regard to equity instruments designated as "at fair value through other comprehensive income."*

at fair value through other comprehensive income (IFRS 9.5.7.1b and 9.5.7.5). On Dec 31, 01, fair value of these shares is CU 12. On Aug 03, 02, A sells the shares for CU 12. With respect to equity instruments measured at fair value through other comprehensive income, no transfers of the fair value reserve to retained earnings are made (IFRS 9.B5.7.1).

Required

Prepare any necessary entries in E's consolidated financial statements from Jan 01, 01 until Aug 03, 02. The reporting periods of both E and A end on Dec 31.

Hints for solution

In particular Section 2.2.1.

Solution

In E's consolidated financial statements, the shares are initially recognized at their cost of CU 10 (IAS 28.11). This is the same accounting treatment as in E's separate financial statements. Hence, no further entry is necessary on Jan 01, 01.

On Dec 31, 01, A makes the following entry in its financial statements relating to the shares: "Dr Shares Cr Other comprehensive income I (fair value reserve) CU 4." Accordingly, E recognizes its share of the associate's other comprehensive income I (OCI I) of CU 1 (= CU 4 · 25%) in a separate item of OCI in its consolidated financial statements (IAS 1.82A and 1.BC106c):

Dec 31, 01	Dr	Investment of E in A	1	
	Cr	Share of the OCI I of associates		1

On Aug 03, 02, A derecognizes the shares ("Dr Cash Cr Shares"). No further entry is made by A. According to the equity method, E does not make any entry in this regard.

Example 6B

Other comprehensive income arising from equity instruments held by the associate – application of the "old" version of IAS 39[10]

The situation is the same as in Example 5. However, A's profit or loss for 01 is zero. Moreover, on Jan 01, 01, A acquires shares of entity X for CU 8, which are classified as "available for sale" (IAS 39.9) by A. On Dec 31, 01, fair value of these shares is CU 12. On Aug 03, 02 A sells the shares for CU 12.

Required

Prepare any necessary entries in E's consolidated financial statements from Jan 01, 01 until Aug 03, 02. The reporting periods of both E and A end on Dec 31.

[10] *The "old" version of IAS 39 refers to the version of IAS 39 before IFRS 9 and its consequential amendments. See the chapter on IFRS 9/IAS 39, Section 3.2 with regard to equity instruments classified as "available for sale."*

Hints for solution

In particular Section 2.2.1.

Solution

In E's consolidated financial statements, the shares are initially recognized at their cost of CU 10 (IAS 28.11). This is the same accounting treatment as in E's separate financial statements. Hence, no further entry is necessary on Jan 01, 01.

On Dec 31, 01, A makes the following entry in its financial statements relating to the shares classified as "available for sale" (IAS 39.55b): "Dr Shares Cr Other comprehensive income II (fair value reserve) CU 4." Accordingly, E recognizes its share of the associate's other comprehensive income II (OCI II) of CU 1 (= CU 4 · 25%) in a separate item of OCI in its consolidated financial statements (IAS 1.82A and 1.BC106c):

Dec 31, 01	Dr	Investment of E in A	1	
	Cr	Share of the OCI II of associates		1

On Aug 03, 02, A derecognizes the shares and consequently also the fair value reserve in its financial statements (IAS 39.55b): "Dr OCI II (fair value reserve) Cr Profit or loss CU 4." E makes a corresponding entry in its consolidated financial statements:

Aug 03, 02	Dr	Share of the OCI II of associates	1	
	Cr	Share of the profit or loss of associates		1

Example 7

Elimination of intragroup profits and losses

Entity E holds 25% of the shares of its associate A.

Version (a)

In 01, A purchases merchandise for CU 16, which it sells (and delivers) to E for CU 20, i.e. A's profit margin is CU 4 (ignoring other costs). In 02, E sells (and delivers) that merchandise to its customers.

Version (b)

In 01, E purchases merchandise for CU 16, which it sells (and delivers) to A for CU 20, i.e. E's profit margin is CU 4 (ignoring other costs). In 02, A sells (and delivers) that merchandise to its customers.

Required

Prepare any necessary entries in E's consolidated financial statements for the years 01 and 02. The reporting periods of both E and A end on Dec 31.

Hints for solution

In particular Sections 2.2.4 and 2.5.

Solution (a)

Year 01

The sale of the merchandise to E represents an upstream transaction. A has generated an intragroup profit of CU 4 (= CU 20 – CU 16) by selling the merchandise to E. The intragroup profit has to be eliminated to the extent of E's interest in A, i.e. to the extent of 25% (CU 4 · 25% = CU 1). The elimination is effected by reducing the carrying amount of the merchandise (or alternatively, the carrying amount of the investment in A) by CU 1:

Dec 31, 01	Dr	Share of the profit or loss of associates	1	
	Cr	Merchandise (or: Investment of E in A)		1

Year 02

At first the profit or loss recognized in 01 has to be recognized in retained earnings. Since E already sold the merchandise the profit of CU 1 has to be recognized:

Dec 31, 02	Dr	Retained earnings	1	
	Cr	Share of the profit or loss of associates		1

Solution (b)

Year 01

The sale of the merchandise to A represents a downstream transaction. In E's consolidated financial statements, revenue and cost of sales are only included to the extent of 75%. This means that 25% of E's revenue (CU 5) and 25% of E's cost of sales (CU 4) are eliminated. The difference of CU 1 reduces the carrying amount of E's investment in A because the merchandise sold has already been derecognized in E's consolidated financial statements:

Dec 31, 01	Dr	Revenue	5	
	Cr	Cost of sales		4
	Cr	Investment of E in A		1

Year 02

The entry presented above resulted in a total reduction of profit or loss of CU 1. This amount has to be recognized in retained earnings, in 02. Since A already sold the merchandise, the revenue and cost of sales eliminated in 01 have to be recognized.

Dec 31, 02	Dr	Retained earnings	1	
	Dr	Cost of sales	4	
	Cr	Revenue		5

3 THE AMENDMENTS TO IAS 28 ISSUED IN MAY 2011

The most important changes from the previous version of IAS 28 are as follows (IAS 28.BC56):

- The **accounting for joint ventures** has been **incorporated** into IAS 28. IFRS 11 is applied in order to determine the type of joint arrangement in which the investor is involved. Once it has determined that it has an interest in a joint venture, the investor recognizes an investment and accounts for it using the **equity method** according to IAS 28 (unless the investor is exempted from applying the equity method) (IAS 28.IN6). However, it is important to note that the "old" requirements for jointly controlled entities specified in IAS 31 also referred to IAS 28 with regard to the rules for applying the equity method (if the entity elected to measure jointly controlled entities according to the equity method and not using proportionate consolidation) (IAS 31.40). Hence, this change (excluding the new rules of IFRS 11,[11] which among others prohibit proportionate consolidation) will not affect the accounting treatment of interests in joint ventures, in most cases.
- The **scope exceptions** for venture capital organizations and mutual funds, unit trusts and similar entities, including investment-linked insurance funds[12] have been **eliminated** and **characterized as measurement exemptions** from the requirement to measure investments in joint ventures and associates according to the equity method.
- The new version of IAS 28 also requires a **portion of an investment** in a joint venture or an associate to be classified as **"held for sale"** if the disposal of that portion would fulfill the criteria to be so classified according to IFRS 5. Any retained portion in the investment not classified as "held for sale" has to be accounted for according to the equity method until disposal of the portion classified as "held for sale" takes place (even if the disposal will have the effect that neither significant influence nor joint control will exist in the future). After the disposal has effectively taken place, the entity has to assess whether (IAS 28.20 and 28.15):
  - the retained interest is still an interest in an associate or joint venture that has to be accounted for according to the equity method, or
  - the retained interest neither represents a joint venture nor an associate, which means that it has to be accounted for according to IFRS 9.
- The consensus of **SIC 13** has been incorporated into IAS 28.
- The **disclosure requirements** have been placed in IFRS 12.

[11] *See the chapter on IAS 31/IFRS 11, Section 3.*
[12] *See Section 2.1.*

IAS 29 FINANCIAL REPORTING IN HYPERINFLATIONARY ECONOMIES[1]

1 INTRODUCTION

IAS 29 comprises rules relating to financial reporting in hyperinflationary countries. In such countries money loses purchasing power at such a rate that comparison of amounts from transactions and other events that have occurred at different times even within the same accounting period would be misleading (IAS 29.2). For most entities, the rules of IAS 29 are only relevant to their foreign operations (subsidiaries, associates or jointly controlled entities) whose functional currency is hyperinflationary. In such cases, the investee's financial statements should be adjusted before being translated and included in the investor's consolidated financial statements.

2 APPLICATION OF IAS 29 RELATING TO FOREIGN OPERATIONS: THE "7-STEP-APPROACH"

Step 1: Does hyperinflation exist?

The application of IAS 29 presupposes that there is hyperinflation. A **cumulative inflation** rate over **three years** that is approaching or exceeds **100%** is the strongest indicator of hyperinflation (IAS 29.3e). An inflation rate of over 50% that is increasing massively can also be an indicator of hyperinflation.

Step 2: Determining the appropriate price index

A general price index is used with regard to the inflation adjustment. If there is more than one price index (e.g. a consumer price index (CPI) and a producer or wholesale price index (PPI or WPI)), determining the appropriate index is a matter of proper judgment (IAS 29.11 and 29.17).

Step 3: Adjustment of non-monetary items

With regard to the distinction between monetary items and non-monetary items, we refer to the chapter on IAS 21 (Section 2). Non-monetary items (e.g. inventories, property, plant, and equipment, and intangible assets including goodwill) measured on the basis of historical cost are adjusted by applying the price index to the costs of purchase or conversion (and to cumulative depreciation, amortization, and impairment losses). It is important to note that the change in the price index from the date of acquisition to the end of the reporting period is

[1] *See Lüdenbach/Hoffmann,* IFRS Commentary, *9th edition, 2011, Section 27, Chapter 4 with regard to the explanations and the example in this chapter of the book. The commentary cited is published in the German language.*

relevant and not the change in the index within the reporting period (IAS 29.15). By contrast, monetary items (e.g. cash and trade payables) are not adjusted.

Step 4: Adjustment of the statement of comprehensive income

All items in the statement of comprehensive income are expressed in terms of the **purchasing power at the end of the reporting period** (IAS 29.26). In the case of income and expenses that occur on a relatively regular basis during the period (this may be the case if there is no seasonal business), and an inflation rate that develops rather consistently during the period, the adjustment from the transaction date to the end of the reporting period might be possible by applying half of the inflation rate for the year.

Step 5: Gain or loss on the net monetary position

In a period of inflation, an entity holding an excess of monetary assets over monetary liabilities loses purchasing power, whereas an entity with an excess of monetary liabilities over monetary assets gains purchasing power to the extent the assets and liabilities are not linked to a price level. The gain or loss on the net monetary position is recognized in profit or loss (IAS 29.27–29.28).

In the system of double-entry book-keeping, the gain or loss on the net monetary position can be determined via a so-called **"purchasing power account**." That account comprises the adjustment of all initial balances of and additions to non-monetary items and of certain items of the statement of comprehensive income (e.g. sales revenue). The account balance is the gain or loss on the net monetary position that becomes part of the statement of comprehensive income and therefore also of the statement of financial position. The balance of the purchasing power account should equal approximately the gain or loss on the net monetary position calculated by dividing the change in the net monetary position during the period by two.

Step 6: Determining the comparative figures

When the results and financial position of an entity whose functional currency is hyperinflationary are translated into a non-hyperinflationary presentation currency, comparative amounts are those that were presented as current year amounts in the relevant prior year financial statements (i.e. not adjusted for subsequent changes in exchange rates or subsequent changes in the price level) (IAS 29.34 and IAS 21.42–21.43).

Step 7: Translation into the presentation currency

After inflation adjustment, translation into the presentation currency of the group is effected according to the normal rules for foreign currency translation (IAS 29.35).

3 REPORTING PERIOD IN WHICH AN ENTITY IDENTIFIES HYPERINFLATION WHEN THE CURRENCY WAS NOT HYPERINFLATIONARY IN THE PRIOR PERIOD

In the reporting period during which an entity identifies the existence of hyperinflation in the country of its functional currency that was not hyperinflationary in the prior period, IAS 29 is applied as if the economy had always been hyperinflationary. Therefore, in relation to non-monetary items measured on the basis of historical cost, the opening statement of financial position at the beginning of the earliest period presented is restated to reflect the effect of inflation from the date the assets were acquired and the liabilities were incurred or assumed until the end of the reporting period (IFRIC 7.3).

4 EXAMPLE WITH SOLUTION[2]

Example

Illustration of steps 3–5

E prepares its consolidated financial statements as at Dec 31, 02. This requires, among others, adjusting the financial statements of the hyperinflationary subsidiary H (balance sheet date: Dec 31, 02) for changes in purchasing power.

In 01, an appropriate index adjustment has been made, which resulted in the following statement of financial position as at Dec 31, 01:

Statement of financial position as at Dec 31, 01 *(index as at Dec 31, 01)*

Building (old)	6	Share capital	20
Merchandise (old)	30	Retained earnings	10
Trade receivables and cash	20	Loan payable	26
Total	**56**	**Total**	**56**

In 02, the inflation rate is 100%. Among others, the following business activities take place in 02:

- The old building (remaining useful life: three years) is depreciated by the amount of CU 2 (on the basis of the amount indexed as at Dec 31, 01).[3]
- A new building (useful life: 20 years) is acquired on Jul 01, 02 for CU 80. Depreciation of CU 2 is recognized for that building.
- All of the old merchandise is sold in 02.
- On Jul 01, 02, new merchandise is acquired for CU 80. Half of the new merchandise is sold in 02.

An assumed profit for the year 02 of CU 20 and the business activities described above result in the statement of financial position as at Dec 31, 02 presented below. The old building, share capital, and retained earnings (excluding profit for 02) are included in that statement on the basis of values indexed as at Jan 01, 02.

Statement of financial position as at Dec 31, 02 *(index as at Jan 01, 02)*

Building (old)	4	Share capital	20
Building (new)	78	Retained earnings (excluding the profit for 02)	10
Merchandise (old)	0	Profit for 02	20
Merchandise (new)	40	Loan payable	76
Trade receivables and cash	4		
Total	**126**	**Total**	**126**

[2] *In this example, the presentation specifications of IAS 1 are ignored.*

[3] *In this example, the term CU is used to denote the currency units of the hyperinflationary currency.*

The separate income statement for 02 has not yet been indexed:

Separate income statement for 02

Sales revenue	110
Old merchandise sold	–30
New merchandise sold	–40
Depreciation expense (old building)	–2
Depreciation expense (new building)	–2
Other expenses	–16
Profit for 02	**20**

In 02, sales revenue and other expenses occur on a regular basis and the inflation rate also develops consistently.

Posting status:

There have not yet been any entries with respect to the inflation adjustment for 02. All other entries have already been made.

Required

Perform steps 3–5 of the 7-step-approach. Prepare any necessary entries relating to inflation adjustments.

Hints for solution

In particular Section 2.

Solution

The statement of financial position as at Dec 31, 02 has to be adjusted for inflation as follows:

- The monetary items (i.e. H's trade receivables, H's cash, and H's loan payable) are not adjusted.
- The share capital and the retained earnings as at Dec 31, 01 are multiplied by 2.
- The adjustment of the merchandise and of the buildings is explained below.

Adjustment of the merchandise for inflation

By Dec 31, 02, all of the old inventories have been sold, whereas half of the new inventories have not yet been sold. Thus, the costs of purchase of the new inventories that have not yet been sold are CU 40 (= CU 80 : 2). Since the new inventories were acquired in the middle of the year (on Jul 01, 02) they are indexed with half of the inflation rate (i.e. with 50%, instead of 100%). The indexed carrying amount as at Dec 31, 02, is therefore CU 60 (= 40 · 150%). For determining the cost of the merchandise sold in 02, the carrying amount of the old merchandise as at Dec 31, 01 is indexed with 100% and the new merchandise acquired in the middle of 02 (on Jul 01, 02) is indexed with 50%:

	Historical values/old index	*Index as at Dec 31, 02*
Balance as at Jan 01, 02	30	60
+ Acquisition on Jul 01, 02	80	120
– Balance as at Dec 31, 02	40	60
= Cost of the merchandise sold in 02	**70**	**120**

The account "merchandise" is presented below (with historical values and values based on the old index on the left and values after inflation adjustment on the right):[4]

Merchandise (Dec 31, 02)

Balance as at Jan 01, 02	30	30	Cost of merchandise sold	70	70
Adjustment		30	Adjustment		50
Acquisition on Jul 01, 02	80	80	Balance as at Dec 31, 02	40	60
Adjustment		40			
Total	**110**	**180**	**Total**	**110**	**180**

Dec 31, 02	Dr	Merchandise[4]	70	
	Cr	Purchasing power account		70

The increase in the cost of the merchandise sold of CU 50 (see above) is caused by the old merchandise in the amount of CU 30 (= CU 30 · 100%) and by the new merchandise in the amount of CU 20 (= CU 40 · 50%). According to the posting status, the cost of the merchandise sold has already been recognized in the amount of CU 70. However, the corresponding inflation adjustment has not yet been recognized.

Dec 31, 02	Dr	Cost of merchandise sold	50	
	Cr	Merchandise		50

Adjustment of the buildings for inflation

The old building and corresponding depreciation are indexed at 100%, whereas the new building (which was acquired on Jul 01, 02) and corresponding depreciation are indexed at half of the inflation rate (50%). The account "buildings" is shown below (with historical values and values based on the old index on the left and values after inflation adjustment on the right). The carrying amount of the buildings as at Dec 31, 02, is the remainder.

Buildings (Dec 31, 02)

Balance as at Jan 01, 02	6	6	Depreciation (old)	2	2
Adjustment		6	Adjustment		2
Acquisition as at Jul 01, 02	80	80	Depreciation (new)	2	2
Adjustment		40	Adjustment		1
			Balance as at Dec 31, 02	82	125
Total	**86**	**132**	**Total**	**86**	**132**

Dec 31, 02	Dr	Building (old)	6	
	Cr	Purchasing power account		6

According to the posting status, the depreciation for the old building of CU 2 has already been recognized. However, the corresponding inflation adjustment has not yet been recognized.

[4] *CU 70 = CU 30 (balance as at Jan 01, 02) + CU 40 (acquisition on Jul 01, 02).*

Dec 31, 02	Dr	Depreciation expense	2	
	Cr	Building (old)		2
Dec 31, 02	Dr	Building (new)	40	
	Cr	Purchasing power account		40
Dec 31, 02	Dr	Depreciation expense	1	
	Cr	Building (new)		1

Further inflation adjustments

Share capital and retained earnings as at Dec 31, 01 are adjusted by 100%:

Dec 31, 02	Dr	Purchasing power account	20	
	Cr	Share capital		20
Dec 31, 02	Dr	Purchasing power account	10	
	Cr	Retained earnings		10

In this example it is assumed that sales revenue and other expenses occur on a regular basis in 02. Hence, they are adjusted by half of the inflation rate (i.e. 50%):

Dec 31, 02	Dr	Purchasing power account	55	
	Cr	Sales revenue		55
Dec 31, 02	Dr	Other expenses	8	
	Cr	Purchasing power account		8

Determining the gain on the net monetary position

The gain on the net monetary position is the balance of the purchasing power account:

Purchasing power account

Share capital	20	Merchandise	70
Retained earnings as at Dec 31, 01	10	Buildings	46
Sales revenue	55	Other expenses	8
Balance	**39**		
Total	**124**	**Total**	**124**

The net monetary position (which represents a liability, in this example) is calculated by deducting the trade receivables and cash from the loan payable. Thus, the net monetary position is CU 6 (= CU 26 – CU 20) as at Jan 01, 02 and CU 72 (= CU 76 – CU 4) as at Dec 31, 02. This means that there is a change of CU 66 in 02. The average of the change for the year 02 is CU 33 (= CU 66 : 2). The balance of the purchasing power account (CU 39) equals approximately the gain on the net monetary position calculated by dividing the change in the net monetary position during the period by two (CU 33).

Preparation of the inflation-adjusted statement of financial position and separate income statement

The gain on the net monetary position is inserted in the separate income statement. The profit for 02 is the balance.[5]

Separate income statement for 02

Old merchandise sold	30	**60**	Sales revenue	110	**165**
New merchandise sold	40	**60**	Gain on the net monetary position		**39**
Depreciation expense (old)	2	**4**			
Depreciation expense (new)	2	**3**			
Other expenses	16	**24**			
Profit for 02	20	**53**			
Total	**110**	**204**	**Total**	**110**	**204**

Statement of financial position as at Dec 31, 02 (*index as at Dec 31, 02*)

Building (old)	8	Share capital	40
Building (new)	117	Retained earnings (excluding the profit for 02)	20
Merchandise (old)	0	Profit for 02	53
Merchandise (new)	60	Loan payable	76
Trade receivables and cash	4		
Total	**189**	**Total**	**189**

These amounts (expressed in units of the hyperinflationary currency) are translated into the presentation currency of the group according to the normal rules for foreign currency translation.

[5] *The unadjusted values are shown on the left.*

IAS 31 INTERESTS IN JOINT VENTURES AND IFRS 11 JOINT ARRANGEMENTS

1 INTRODUCTION

In **May 2011**, the **IASB issued IFRS 11** "Joint Arrangements." The new standard has to be applied in the financial statements as at **Dec 31, 2013** (if the entity's reporting periods start on Jan 01 and end on Dec 31). **Earlier application** is **permitted** by the IASB (IFRS 11.C1). However, in the European Union, new IFRSs have to be endorsed by the European Union before they can be applied. There has been no endorsement with regard to IFRS 11 as yet.

If an entity decides not to apply IFRS 11 early, the rules of IAS 31 "Interests in Joint Ventures" have to be applied. Consequently, the remainder of this chapter of the book discusses both standards:

- Section 2 gives an overview over the rules of IAS 31.
- Section 3 introduces the rules of IFRS 11.

2 IAS 31 "INTERESTS IN JOINT VENTURES"

2.1 The Term "Joint Venture" and Forms of Joint Ventures

The following characteristics are common to all **joint ventures** (IAS 31.3 and 31.7):

- Two or more venturers are bound by a **contractual arrangement**.
- The contractual arrangement establishes **joint control**.

Joint control is the contractually agreed sharing of control over an economic activity, and exists only when the strategic financial and operating decisions relating to the activity require the unanimous consent of the parties sharing control (the venturers). A venturer is a party to a joint venture which has joint control over that joint venture (IAS 31.3).

IAS 31 sets out the accounting treatment of interests in joint ventures and differentiates between the following **types of joint ventures**:

- **Jointly controlled operations** are carried on by each venturer using its own assets in pursuit of the joint operation. The agreement usually provides a means by which the revenue from the sale of the joint product and any expenses incurred in common are shared among the venturers. For example, three construction companies may agree to act as a consortium to construct a hotel for a customer. One contract is signed between the members of the consortium and the customer. All three companies are party to the contract as the consortium is not a legal entity.[1]

---

[1] *See KPMG,* Insights into IFRS, *7th edition, 3.5.150.20.*

- **Jointly controlled assets** arise from an arrangement that is a joint venture carried on with assets that are controlled jointly, whether or not owned jointly, but not through a separate entity. In addition, one's own assets can be used. An example is two oil producers sharing the use of a pipeline to transport oil. Both parties bear an agreed proportion of the operating expenses.[2]
- **Jointly controlled entities** are joint venture activities carried on through separate entities (e.g. corporations or partnerships) (IAS 31.24). Jointly controlled entities are the most common form of joint ventures. An example is the founding of a sales company in Japan by a German producer together with a Japanese chain.

2.2 Accounting Treatment in the Financial Statements of the Venturer

2.2.1 Jointly Controlled Operations in Consolidated and Separate Financial Statements

With respect to its interests in jointly controlled operations, a venturer recognizes (IAS 31.15):

- the assets that it controls and the liabilities that it incurs, as well as
- the expenses that it incurs and its share of the income that it earns from the sale of goods or services by the joint venture.

Jointly controlled assets do not exist in jointly controlled operations.

2.2.2 Jointly Controlled Assets in Consolidated and Separate Financial Statements In the case of jointly controlled assets, the venturer recognizes its share of the jointly controlled assets and its share of any liabilities incurred jointly with the other venturers in relation to the joint venture, in addition to its own assets and liabilities. Moreover, the venturer recognizes the expenses it has incurred in respect of its interest in the joint venture, its share of any expenses incurred by the joint venture, and any income from the sale or use of its share of the output of the joint venture (IAS 31.21).

2.2.3 Jointly Controlled Entities

2.2.3.1 Separate financial statements In the venturer's separate financial statements, interests in jointly controlled entities are accounted for **either** (IAS 31.46 and IAS 27.38):

(a) **at cost, or**
(b) in accordance with **IFRS 9**. This means measurement **at fair value**. IFRS 9 is based on the irrefutable presumption that fair value can always be determined reliably. In certain circumstances, cost may be an appropriate estimate of fair value (IFRS 9.B5.4.14–9. B5.4.17).[3]

If investments in jointly controlled entities are accounted for in accordance with IFRS 9 in the consolidated financial statements, they have to be accounted for in the same way in the venturer's separate financial statements (IAS 27.40).

---

[2] *See KPMG,* Insights into IFRS, *7th edition, 3.5.150.10.*

[3] *If IFRS 9 were not applied early, the investments would normally be measured at fair value. However, the equity instruments would be measured at cost if it were not possible to determine fair value reliably (IAS 39.AG80–39.AG81).*

2.2.3.2 Consolidated financial statements In the venturer's consolidated financial statements, interests in jointly controlled entities are accounted for in one of the following ways (IAS 31.30 and 31.38):

- **Proportionate consolidation**: According to this method, the venturer recognizes its share of the assets that it controls jointly and of the liabilities for which it is jointly responsible. Moreover, the venturer recognizes its share of the income and expenses of the jointly controlled entity.
- **Equity method**: This method is not described in IAS 31 but rather in IAS 28. Therefore, we refer to the chapter on IAS 28.[4]

When applying **proportionate consolidation**, it is possible to choose between one of the two reporting formats described later (IAS 31.34):

- **Combined presentation**: The venturer combines its share of each of the assets, liabilities, income, and expenses of the jointly controlled entity with the similar items, line by line, in its financial statements. For example, the venturer combines its share of the jointly controlled entity's inventory with its inventory.
- **Separate presentation**: The venturer includes separate line items for its share of the assets, liabilities, income, and expenses of the jointly controlled entity in its financial statements.

When applying **proportionate consolidation**, the procedures for the consolidation of subsidiaries are applied correspondingly (IAS 31.33):[5]

- If the **balance sheet date** of the jointly controlled entity **differs** from the balance sheet date of the consolidated financial statements, it might be necessary to prepare additional financial statements.
- **Adjustment to uniform accounting policies**.
- When **capital consolidation** is carried out**, fair value adjustments**, and **goodwill** are recognized. Subsequently, goodwill is not amortized. Instead, it has to be tested for impairment. Fair value adjustments of depreciable assets have to be depreciated.
- **Negative goodwill** is immediately recognized in profit or loss.
- **Elimination of intragroup receivables and liabilities**.
- **Elimination of intragroup income and expenses**.
- **Elimination of intragroup profits and losses that are recognized in the carrying amounts of assets**.

The **consolidation entries** are only effected **to the extent of the venturer's interest** in the jointly controlled entity.

2.3 Example with solution

Examples relating to the **equity method** are included in the chapter on IAS 28.

---

[4] *See the chapter on IAS 28, Section 2.2.*

[5] *See the chapter on IAS 27/IFRS 10, Section 2.3 and the chapter on IFRS 3, Section 6.*

Example 1

Proportionate consolidation of a jointly controlled entity

Entity A and entity B each own 50% of the jointly controlled entity J. On Dec 31, 01, B sells its shares for CU 45 to entity E. The following table includes simplified illustrations of the statements of financial position II of E and J as at Dec 31, 01:[6]

	E	*J (100%)*
Buildings	90	40
Merchandise	50	20
Cash	15	
Investment of E in J (shares)	45	
Total assets	**200**	**60**
Issued capital	−130	−30
Retained earnings	−70	−30
Total equity and liabilities	**−200**	**−60**

The fair value of J's buildings as at Dec 31, 01 is CU 60.

In its separate financial statements as at Dec 31, 01, E accounts for its investment in J (shares) at cost (IAS 31.46 and IAS 27.38a).

Posting status (in E's separate financial statements):

Dec 31, 01	Dr	Investment of E in J (shares)	45	
	Cr	Cash		45

Required

Prepare any necessary entries in E's consolidated financial statements as at Dec 31, 01 and present E's consolidated statement of financial position as at Dec 31, 01. E applies proportionate consolidation with respect to its interests in jointly controlled entities.

Hints for solution

In particular Section 2.2.3.2.

Solution[7]

The aggregated statement of financial position is prepared first, which also incorporates 50% of J's statement of financial position. Afterwards, proportionate consolidation is

[6] *In this table, debit entries and assets are shown with a plus sign, whereas credit entries, liabilities, and items of equity are shown with a minus sign. For simplification purposes, the exact presentation requirements of IAS 1 are ignored in this example.*

[7] *For more information on the aggregated statement of financial position and capital consolidation, we refer to the chapter on IAS 27/IFRS 10, Section 2.3 and the chapter on IFRS 3, Sections 6 and 9.*

carried out (including the recognition of the pro rata fair value adjustment for the building). This results in E's consolidated statement of financial position:[8]

Dec 31, 01	*E*	*J (50%)*	*Aggregated balance sheet*	*Capital consolidation*	*Consolidated balance sheet*
Goodwill				5	5
Buildings	90	20	110	10	120
Merchandise	50	10	60		60
Cash	15		15		15
Investment of E in J (shares)	45		45	−45	0
Total assets	**200**	**30**	**230**	**−30**	**200**
Issued capital	−130	−15	−145	15	−130
Retained earnings	−70	−15	−85	15	−70
Total equity and liabilities	**−200**	**−30**	**−230**	**30**	**−200**

The goodwill presented in the table above is the positive difference between the acquisition cost of CU 45 and the fair value of the net assets on acquisition date:

Acquisition cost		**45**
Proportionate issued capital	15	
Proportionate retained earnings	15	
Proportionate fair value adjustment	10	
Proportionate net assets (measured at fair value)		**40**
Goodwill		**5**

In order to improve the illustration, the entry for capital consolidation is given again:

Dec 31, 01	Dr	Goodwill	5	
	Dr	Building	10	
	Dr	Issued capital	15	
	Dr	Retained earnings	15	
	Cr	Investment of E in J (shares)		45

3 IFRS 11 "JOINT ARRANGEMENTS" (ISSUED IN MAY 2011)

3.1 Introduction

In May 2011, the IASB issued IFRS 11, which **supersedes IAS 31** "Interests in Joint Ventures" as well as the Interpretation SIC 13 "Jointly Controlled Entities – Non-Monetary Contributions by Venturers" (IFRS 11.C15). IFRS 11 applies to **all entities that are a party to joint arrangement** (IFRS 11.3).

The **main changes** to financial reporting **caused by IFRS 11** are the following:

- The **terminology** and the **definitions** of different types of arrangements that are jointly controlled have changed.

[8] *In this table, debit entries and assets are shown with a plus sign, whereas credit entries, liabilities, and items of equity are shown with a minus sign.*

- **IFRS 11 prohibits proportionate consolidation** for including jointly controlled entities (which are referred to as joint ventures by IFRS 11) in the venturer's consolidated financial statements.[9]

IFRS 11 has to be applied in the financial statements as at **Dec 31, 2013** (if the entity's reporting periods are identical with the calendar years). **Earlier application** is **permitted** (IFRS 11.C1). In the **European Union**, there has been no endorsement of IFRS 11 as yet.[10]

A **joint arrangement** represents an arrangement of which two or more parties have joint control (IFRS 11.4 and 11.Appendix A). A joint arrangement has both of the following characteristics (IFRS 11.5):

- The parties are bound by a **contractual arrangement**. The contractual arrangement specifies the terms upon which the parties participate in the activity that is the subject of the arrangement (IFRS 11.B4).
- The contractual arrangement gives two or more of those parties **joint control** of the arrangement.

Joint arrangements are established for a variety of purposes. For instance, they may be established in order to enable the parties to share costs and risks, or as a way to provide the parties with access to new markets or new technology (IFRS 11.B12).

3.2 Assessing Joint Control

Joint control is the **contractually agreed sharing of control** of an arrangement. It exists only when decisions about the relevant activities (i.e. activities that significantly affect the returns of the arrangement) require the **unanimous consent** of the parties sharing control (IFRS 11.7, 11.9, and 11.Appendix A).

Hence, assessing whether a party has joint control of an arrangement as a result of a contract involves the following **steps** (IFRS 11.4, 11.8–11.11, 11.Appendix A, 11.B5-11.B6, and 11.B9–11.B10):

- **It first** has to be determined **whether all the parties or a group of the parties control the arrangement collectively**. The Standard **IFRS 10** defines control and has to be used in order to determine whether all the parties or a group of the parties are exposed or have rights to variable returns from their involvement with the arrangement and have the ability to affect those returns through their power over the arrangement.[11] When all the parties or a group of the parties considered collectively are able to direct the relevant activities, these parties control the arrangement collectively.
- After concluding that the arrangement is controlled collectively (see above), it has to be determined whether the **decisions about the relevant activities** require the **unanimous consent** of the parties that collectively control the arrangement. If this is the case, the arrangement is jointly controlled and represents a joint arrangement. The requirement

[9] *See Section 2.2.3.2.*

[10] *See Section 1.*

[11] *See the chapter on IAS 27/IFRS 10, Section 3.2.*

for unanimous consent means that any party with joint control of the arrangement is able to prevent any of the other parties or a group of the parties from making unilateral decisions about the relevant activities without its consent.

When the **minimum required proportion** of the voting rights necessary to make decisions about the relevant activities can be achieved by **more than one combination of the parties** agreeing together, the arrangement does not represent a joint arrangement (unless the contractual arrangement specifies which parties or combination of parties are required to agree unanimously to decisions about the relevant activities of the arrangement) (IFRS 11. B8).

3.3 Types of Joint Arrangement

3.3.1 Introduction A joint arrangement is either a joint operation or a joint venture (IFRS 11.6). In assessing in which type of joint arrangement a party is involved, the party has to consider its rights and obligations arising from the arrangement in the normal course of business (IFRS 11.15–11.17, 11.Appendix A, and 11.B14):

- In the case of a **joint operation**, the parties that have joint control of the arrangement have **rights to the assets**, and **obligations for the liabilities**, relating to the arrangement. Those parties are called joint operators.
- In the case of a **joint venture**, the parties that have joint control of the arrangement have **rights to the net assets** of the arrangement. Those parties are called joint venturers.

Joint arrangements can be established using **different structures and legal forms**. In some cases, the activity that is the subject of the arrangement is undertaken in a **separate vehicle**. In other cases, no separate vehicle is established (IFRS 11.B12–11.B13). A separate vehicle is a separately identifiable financial structure, including separate legal entities or entities recognized by statute, regardless of whether those entities have a legal personality (IFRS 11.Appendix A).

As described above, a party to an arrangement has to consider its **rights and obligations arising from the arrangement** in the normal course of business. When making that assessment the party has to consider the following (IFRS 11.17, 11.B14, 11.B15, and 11.B21):

- The structure of the joint arrangement.
- When the joint arrangement is structured through a separate vehicle:
  - The legal form of the separate vehicle.
  - The terms agreed by the parties in the contractual arrangement.
  - When relevant, other facts and circumstances.

3.3.2 Structure of the Joint Arrangement

3.3.2.1 Joint arrangements not structured through a separate vehicle A joint arrangement not structured through a separate vehicle **is a joint operation**. In such cases, the contractual arrangement establishes the parties' rights to the assets and obligations for the liabilities relating to the arrangement as well as the parties' rights to the corresponding revenues and their obligations for the corresponding expenses (IFRS 11.B16). In these cases, the parties agree to **undertake activities together** (for instance to manufacture a product together with each party responsible for a specific task and each party using its own assets and incurring its own liabilities) or to **share and operate an asset together** (IFRS 11.B17–11. B18).

3.3.2.2 Joint arrangements structured through a separate vehicle A joint arrangement in which the assets and liabilities relating to the arrangement are held in a separate vehicle can represent **either a joint venture or a joint operation** (IFRS 11. B19).

The following chart gives a rough overview of the rules specified in IFRS 11.B22–11.B33 for assessing whether a joint arrangement structured through a separate vehicle represents a joint operation or a joint venture:[12]

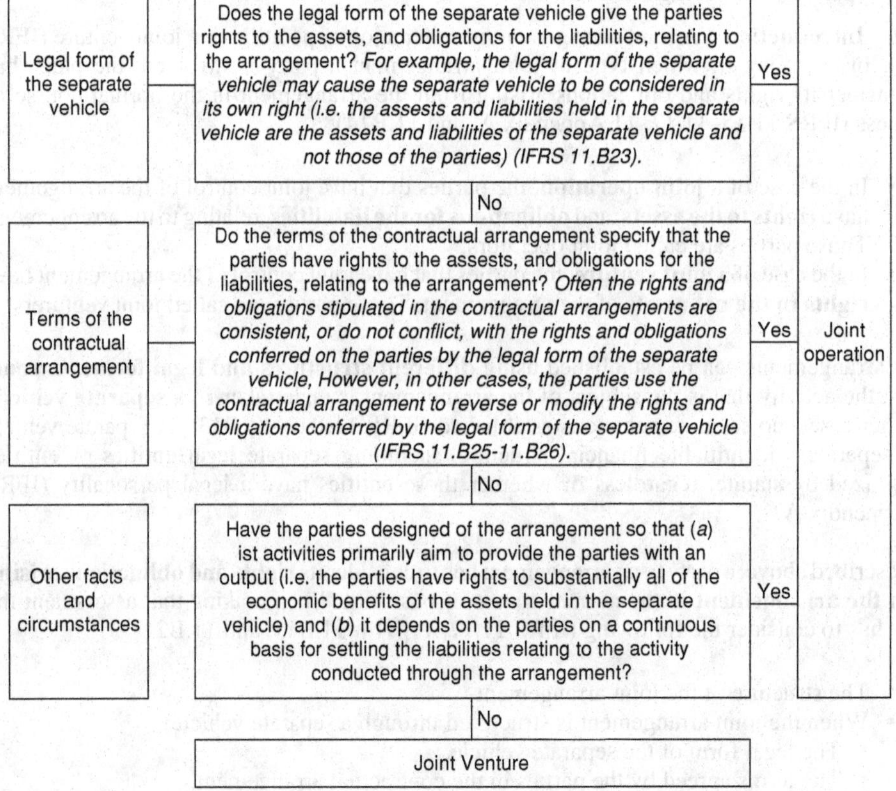

3.4 Consolidated Financial Statements of Parties to a Joint Arrangement

IFRS 11 distinguishes between (IFRS 11.11 and 11.Appendix A):

- **parties that have joint control** of a joint arrangement (joint operators or joint venturers), and
- **parties that participate** in but **do not have joint control** of a joint arrangement.

[12] *This chart is based on IFRS 11.B33.*

3.4.1 Joint Operations

3.4.1.1 Joint operators A joint operator recognizes the following in relation to its interest in a joint operation (IFRS 11.20):

- Its assets, including its share of any assets held jointly.
- Its liabilities, including its share of any liabilities incurred jointly.
- Its revenue from the sale of its share of the output arising from the joint operation.
- Its share of the revenue from the sale of the output by the joint operation.
- Its expenses, including its share of any expenses incurred jointly.

The assets, liabilities, revenues, and expenses relating to a joint operator's interest in a joint operation are accounted for in accordance with the **IFRSs applicable** to them (IFRS 11.21).

When the joint operator **sells or contributes assets to the joint operation**, it is conducting the transaction with the other parties to the joint operation. Hence, the joint operator recognizes gains and losses resulting from such a transaction only to the extent of the other parties' interests in the joint operation. When the joint operator **purchases assets from the joint operation**, it must not recognize its share of the gains and losses until it resells those assets to a third party (IFRS 11.22, 11.B34, and 11.B36).

3.4.1.2 Participants in a joint operation that do not have joint control If a party participates in but does not have joint control of a joint operation, two situations have to be distinguished (IFRS 11.23):

- If such a party has **rights to the assets** and **obligations for the liabilities** relating to the joint operation, it accounts for its interest in the joint operation **in the same way as a joint operator**.
- If such a party **does not have rights to the assets and obligations for the liabilities** relating to the joint operation, it accounts for its interest in the joint operation according to the **IFRSs applicable to that interest**.

3.4.2 Joint Ventures

3.4.2.1 Joint venturers A joint venturer has to recognize its interest in a joint venture as an investment and account for that investment using the **equity method according to IAS 28**[13] (unless the entity is exempted from applying the equity method as specified in IAS 28) (IFRS 11.24).

3.4.2.2 Participants in a joint venture that do not have joint control A party that participates in but does not have joint control of a joint venture has to account for its interest in the arrangement according to **IFRS 9, unless** it has **significant influence** over the joint venture in which case it has to account for it according to **IAS 28** (IFRS 11.25).

3.5 Separate Financial Statements of Parties to a Joint Arrangement

IFRS 11 distinguishes between (IFRS 11.11 and 11.Appendix A):

- **parties that have joint control** of a joint arrangement (joint operators or joint venturers), and
- **parties that participate** in but **do not have joint control** of a joint arrangement.

---

[13] *See the chapter on IAS 28 with regard to the equity method.*

3.5.1 Joint Operations

3.5.1.1 Joint operators In its separate financial statements, a joint operator has to account for its interest in a joint operation **in the same way as in its consolidated financial statements** (IFRS 11.26a).

3.5.1.2 Participants in a joint operation that do not have joint control In its separate financial statements, a party that participates in but does not have joint control of a joint operation has to account for its interest in the joint operation **in the same way as in its consolidated financial statements** (IFRS 11.27a).

3.5.2 Joint Ventures

3.5.2.1 Joint Venturers In its separate financial statements, a joint venturer has to account for its interest in a joint venture according to **IAS 27.10 (as amended in 2011)** (IFRS 11.26b). Consequently, we refer to the chapter on IAS 27/IFRS 10 (Sections 2.5 and 4) in this regard.

3.5.2.2 Participants in a joint venture that do not have joint control In its separate financial statements, a party that participates in but does not have joint control of a joint venture has to account for its interest according to **IFRS 9** unless it has significant influence over the joint venture, in which case **IAS 27.10 (as amended in 2011)**[14] has to be applied (IFRS 11.27b).

3.6 Example with solution

With regard to examples illustrating the application of the **equity method**, we refer to the chapter on **IAS 28**.

Example 2

Assessing whether arrangements represent joint arrangements

(a) Entities A and B establish an arrangement in which each of them holds 50% of the voting rights. The contractual arrangement between them specifies that at least 51% of the voting rights are required in order to make decisions about the relevant activities.
(b) Entities A, B, and C establish an arrangement. A and B each hold 40% of the voting rights in the arrangement, and C holds the remaining 20%. According to the contractual arrangement between the three parties, at least 75% of the voting rights are required in order to make decisions about the relevant activities of the arrangement.
(c) Entities A, B, and C establish an arrangement. A holds 40% of the voting rights in the arrangement, whereas B and C each hold 30%. According to the contractual arrangement between the three parties, at least 70% per cent of the voting rights are required in order to make decisions about the relevant activities of the arrangement.

Required

Determine whether the arrangements described above represent joint arrangements.

---

[14] *See the chapter on IAS 27/IFRS 10, Sections 2.5 and 4.*

Hints for solution

In particular Sections 3.1 and 3.2.

Solution (a)

A and B have implicitly agreed by contract that they have joint control of the arrangement because decisions about the relevant activities cannot be made without both A and B agreeing (IFRS 11.B7). Hence, the arrangement represents a joint arrangement.

Solution (b)

At least 75% of the voting rights are necessary in order to make decisions about the relevant activities of the arrangement. This quorum cannot be achieved by any party on its own. This means that, although A and B can each block any decision, none of them controls the arrangement.

However, the quorum can be achieved by the combined voting rights of A and B. Decisions about the relevant activities cannot be made without both A and B agreeing. This means that as a result of the contractual arrangement, A and B have joint control of the arrangement (IFRS 11.B8). Thus, the arrangement represents a joint arrangement.

Solution (c)

At least 70% of the voting rights are necessary in order to make decisions about the relevant activities of the arrangement. This quorum cannot be achieved by any party on its own. This means that although A can block any decision, it does not control the arrangement.

However, the quorum can be achieved by the combined voting rights of A and B or of A and C. This means that there is more than one combination of parties that can agree to reach 70% of the voting rights. In such a situation, the contractual arrangement between the parties would need to specify which combination of the parties is required to agree unanimously to decisions about the relevant activities for it to be a joint arrangement (IFRS 11.B8).

IAS 32 FINANCIAL INSTRUMENTS: PRESENTATION

1 THE TERM "FINANCIAL INSTRUMENT"

The term "financial instrument" used in IAS 32 as well as in other standards is defined in IAS 32. According to this definition, a financial instrument is any contract that gives rise to a financial asset of one entity and a financial liability or an equity instrument of another entity (IAS 32.11). The terms used in this definition are defined as follows:

- The term "**entity**" includes individuals, partnerships, incorporated bodies, government agencies, and trusts (IAS 32.14).
- An **equity instrument** (e.g. a share) is a contract that demonstrates a residual interest in the assets of an entity after deducting all of its liabilities (IAS 32.11).
- **Financial assets** include (among others) (IAS 32.11):
  - Cash.
  - Equity instruments of other entities held by the entity.
  - A contractual right to receive cash or another financial asset from another entity (i.e. certain receivables).
  - A contractual right to exchange financial assets or financial liabilities with another entity under conditions that are potentially favorable to the entity (this definition comprises financial derivatives with a positive fair value).
- **Financial liabilities** include (among others) (IAS 32.11):
  - A contractual obligation to deliver cash or another financial asset to another entity.
  - A contractual obligation to exchange financial assets or financial liabilities with another entity under conditions that are potentially unfavorable to the entity (this definition comprises financial derivatives with a negative fair value).
- **Contracts** within the scope of IAS 32 need not be in writing (IAS 32.13). Tax assets and tax liabilities are not contractual because they are created as a result of statutory requirements imposed by governments. Thus, they are not financial liabilities or financial assets. Income taxes are dealt with in IAS 12 (IAS 32.AG12).

The following examples illustrate the definitions above (IAS 32AG3–32.AG12):

- Examples of financial assets and financial liabilities:
  - Trade receivables and trade payables
  - Bonds from the holder's perspective (financial asset) as well as from the issuer's perspective (financial liability)
  - Loans from the holder's perspective (financial asset) as well as from the debtor's perspective (financial liability)
  - Financial guarantees from both the holder's and the issuer's perspective
  - Finance lease receivables and finance lease liabilities
  - Equity instruments of other entities, held by the entity

- Examples of non-financial assets and non-financial liabilities:
  - Inventories
  - Intangible assets
  - Property, plant, and equipment
  - Tax assets and tax liabilities
  - Constructive obligations within the meaning of IAS 37

2 SCOPE

The scope of IAS 32 does not include all financial instruments. For example, interests in subsidiaries, associates or joint ventures that are accounted for in accordance with IAS 27, IAS 28 or IAS 31 are outside the scope of IAS 32 (IAS 32.4–32.10).

3 DIFFERENTIATION BETWEEN EQUITY AND LIABILITIES

The issuer of a financial instrument has to classify the instrument or its component parts on initial recognition as a financial liability, a financial asset or an equity instrument (IAS 32.15).

Problems may occur in differentiating between equity and liabilities, in particular, in the case of **mezzanine financing** (e.g. contributions of capital that have equity characteristics in substance, but are debt from a legal perspective). Financing is generally regarded as equity if there is neither a conditional or unconditional contractual obligation to deliver cash or another financial asset, nor a contractual obligation to exchange financial assets or financial liabilities with another entity under conditions that are potentially unfavorable to the entity (IAS 32.16–32.20).

An example of an **unconditional obligation** to deliver cash is a preference share that provides for mandatory redemption by the issuer for a fixed or determinable amount at a fixed or determinable future date. An example of a **conditional obligation** to deliver cash is a preference share that gives the holder the right to require the issuer to redeem the instrument at or after a particular date for a fixed or determinable amount (IAS 32.18a). In both cases the obligation to deliver cash leads to classification as a liability.

A **compound financial instrument** is a non-derivative financial instrument that contains both a liability and an equity component. Such components have to be classified separately as financial liabilities, financial assets or equity instruments according to IAS 32.15 (IAS 32.28). An important example of compound financial instruments comprises **convertible bonds**. The holder of a convertible bond has the right to convert the bond (liability) into shares (equity). This means that the holder can choose between redemption of the bond and receiving shares of the debtor.

The issuer of a compound financial instrument has to measure the equity component and the liability component based on the **residual value method**. According to this method the issuer of a convertible bond first determines the carrying amount of the liability component by discounting the future interest and redemption payments of the bond with the market interest rate for similar bonds having no conversion rights. The carrying amount of the equity component (conversion right) is then determined by deducting the carrying amount of the liability component from the proceeds of the bond issue (IAS 32.31–32.32) (under the presumption that there are no transaction costs).

The application of the classification rules of IAS 32, which are generally based on the existence of a (conditional or unconditional) contractual obligation to deliver cash or another financial asset, sometimes leads to **inadequate results**. For example, the capital contribution of a member in a partnership has to be classified as a liability if the member has the right to withdraw the investment and to receive cash from the entity as compensation for the investment in the case of withdrawal.

Thus, the IASB has introduced **exceptional rules** in order to solve this problem. However, these exceptional rules are not applicable when classifying non-controlling interests in the consolidated financial statements. Therefore, instruments classified as equity instruments in accordance with these special rules in the separate financial statements that are non-controlling interests are classified as liabilities in the consolidated financial statements of the group (IAS 32.AG29A and 32.BC68).

Another problematic topic comprises **perpetual bonds**. In many cases, the issuer of a perpetual bond has the right to redeem the bond at any time, whereas the holder of the perpetual bond cannot demand redemption. After several years the issuer may have no other economically rational choice than redeeming the bond due to accelerating interest payments. Consequently, it is clear that the bond will be redeemed in the future. Nevertheless, such contracts may be prepared in a way that leads to classification as equity under IAS 32 because the holder of the bond does not have the contractual right to demand redemption of the bond.[1] This classification is more form-based than substance-based.

4 ACCOUNTING FOR A CONVERTIBLE BOND AFTER RECOGNITION BY THE ISSUER

After recognition, the liability component of a convertible bond is accounted for either at amortized cost (i.e. according to the effective interest method) or at fair value through profit or loss, depending on the circumstances.[2] However, the carrying amount of the equity component is not affected by changes in fair value of the conversion feature after recognition (IAS 32.36 last sentence and IAS 39.2d). If the holder of a convertible bond chooses to receive shares of the debtor, he is waiving his receivable. The waiving of the receivable constitutes a contribution in kind in the issuer's statement of financial position (the entry is "Dr Liability Cr Share capital Cr Premium (equity)"). At the end of the term of the convertible bond, the original equity component remains as equity, although it may be transferred from one line item within equity to another (without affecting profit or loss or other comprehensive income), irrespective of whether the conversion right is exercised (IAS 32.AG32 and IAS 1.7).

5 TREASURY SHARES

If an entity reacquires its own equity instruments, these instruments (treasury shares) are deducted from equity. No financial asset is recognized for these instruments. This procedure corresponds with the view that a reacquisition of own equity instruments has the same effects

[1] *See* IASB Update, *June 2006, p. 4.*

[2] *See the chapter on IFRS 9/IAS 39.*

as a reduction in capital. A purchase, sale, issue or cancellation of an entity's own equity instruments neither affects profit or loss, nor other comprehensive income (IAS 32.33, 32.AG36, and IAS 1.7).

With regard to presentation, the following procedures are generally regarded as being acceptable when an entity reacquires and subsequently sells its own equity instruments:[3]

- The consideration paid is presented as a **one-line adjustment of equity** (i.e. as a separate item of equity with a negative amount). When the treasury shares are sold at a later date, a credit entry is made for that item. If the consideration paid for acquiring the instruments differs from the consideration received when selling the instruments, the separate item of equity remains in the entity's financial statements with a positive or negative amount.
- The par value of the entity's own equity instruments reduces share capital, whereas the difference between par value and the higher consideration paid for the instruments reduces share premium (**par value method**). When the treasury shares are sold at a later date, the par value of the instruments increases share capital and the difference between par value and the higher consideration received for the instruments increases share premium. A positive or negative difference between the consideration paid for acquiring the instruments and the consideration received for selling them remains within the share premium.

6 COSTS OF AN EQUITY TRANSACTION

An example of an equity transaction is an increase in capital due to a contribution in cash. The par value of the shares issued increases share capital and the difference between par value and the higher consideration received for the shares increases share premium.

Costs of an equity transaction are **deducted from equity**, net of any related income tax benefit. This affects neither profit or loss nor other comprehensive income (IAS 32.35, 32.35A, and 32.BC33B). Assuming the costs of an equity transaction, which are deductible for tax purposes, are CU 100 and that the tax rate is 25%, equity is reduced by CU 75. The costs reduce cash by CU 100. The remaining amount of CU 25 represents a tax advantage. This is because the costs reduce taxable profit by CU 100, which leads to a reduction in income taxes payable by CU 25. Consequently, the tax advantage of CU 25 increases the current tax asset or reduces the current tax liability.

The procedure described above is implemented only to the extent that the costs are **incremental costs directly attributable** to the equity transaction that otherwise would have been avoided (IAS 32.37). By contrast, the costs that would have been incurred anyway are recognized in profit or loss. In practice this means that external costs (e.g. registration and other regulatory fees as well as amounts paid to legal advisers) are incremental costs. On the other hand, internal costs would have generally been incurred regardless and are therefore recognized in profit or loss. An exception is overtime, which is incurred due to the equity transaction and

---

[3] *SIC 16, which contained examples with regard to the question of which item(s) of equity may be affected, has been withdrawn.*

which is reimbursed separately. These are incremental costs and are therefore treated in the same way as external costs.

7 OFFSETTING

A **financial asset and a financial liability** have to be **offset** and the net amount presented in the statement of financial position when both of the following conditions are met (IAS 32.42):

- The entity currently has a legally enforceable right to set off the recognized amounts.
- The entity intends either to settle on a net basis, or to realize the asset and settle the liability simultaneously.

8 EXAMPLES WITH SOLUTIONS

Example 1

Existence of a financial asset or of a financial liability

(a) Entity E owns cash in the amount of CU 100.
(b) E owns a demand deposit in the amount of CU 100.
(c) E's statement of financial position includes shares of entity G.
(d) E owns merchandise.
(e) In December 01, E delivers merchandise to F. The invoice is not paid in 01. Therefore, on Dec 31, 01, the amount outstanding represents a trade receivable from E's perspective and a trade payable from F's perspective.
(f) In December 01, F orders merchandise from E and pays the invoice amount in advance. The merchandise is delivered in January 02. E makes the following entry: "Dr Cash Cr Advance payments from customers." F makes the following entry: "Dr Advance payments to suppliers Cr Cash."
(g) E's statement of financial position includes a current tax liability as well as a deferred tax liability.

Required

Determine whether the items above are financial assets or financial liabilities in the financial statements of E and F as at Dec 31, 01.

Hints for solution

In particular Section 1.

Solution

(a) Currency (cash) is a financial asset because it represents the medium of exchange and is therefore the basis on which all transactions are measured and recognized in an entity's financial statements (IAS 32.AG3).
(b) The demand deposit is a financial asset because it represents the contractual right of the depositor to obtain cash from the institution.
(c) The shares of G held by E are equity instruments. Thus, they are financial assets of E (IAS 32.11).

(d) The sale of merchandise leads to cash inflows. However, ownership of merchandise alone does not give rise to a present right to receive cash or another financial asset. Therefore, merchandise itself does not represent financial assets (IAS 32.AG10).
(e) E's trade receivable represents a financial asset because E already delivered the merchandise and therefore has a right to receive cash from F. F's trade payable represents a financial liability because F already received the merchandise and therefore has an obligation to deliver cash to E (IAS 32.11 and 32.AG4).
(f) F's account "advance payments to suppliers" represents F's right to receive the merchandise for which F already paid but not a right to receive cash from E. Therefore this asset is not a financial asset. E's account "advance payments from customers" represents E's obligation to deliver the merchandise for which E already received the invoice amount, and not an obligation to deliver cash to F. Therefore, this liability is not a financial liability.
(g) Current tax liabilities and deferred tax liabilities are not financial liabilities. This is due to the fact that they are created as a result of statutory requirements imposed by governments and do not represent contractual obligations (IAS 32.AG12).

Example 2

Treasury shares

On Dec 31, 01, entity E acquires some of its own shares for CU 6 in order to offer its executive directors the possibility to purchase them the next year. The par value of these shares is CU 2. On Feb 14, 02, the shares are sold to the executive directors for (a) CU 7 and (b) CU 5.

Required

Prepare any necessary entries in E's financial statements as at Dec 31 for the years 01 and 02. Regarding the treasury shares, E (a) makes a one-line adjustment of equity and (b) applies the par value method.

Hints for solution

In particular Section 5.

Solution (a): One-line adjustment

Dec 31, 01	Dr	Treasury shares (equity)	6	
	Cr	Cash		6

Version (a)

Feb 14, 02	Dr	Cash	7	
	Cr	Treasury shares (equity)		7

Version (b)

Feb 14, 02	Dr	Cash	5	
	Cr	Treasury shares (equity)		5

The amounts (a) CU +1 and (b) CU –1 remain separate items of equity even though E does not hold these shares anymore.

Solution (b): Par value method

Dec 31, 01	Dr	Share capital (equity)	2	
	Dr	Share premium (equity)	4	
	Cr	Cash		6

Version (a)

Feb 14, 02	Dr	Cash	7	
	Cr	Share capital (equity)		2
	Cr	Share premium (equity)		5

Version (b)

Feb 14, 02	Dr	Cash	5	
	Cr	Share capital (equity)		2
	Cr	Share premium (equity)		3

The amounts (a) CU +1 and (b) CU –1 remain in share premium even though E does not hold these shares anymore.

Example 3

Costs of an equity transaction

In 01, entity E issues shares with a par value of CU 100 for CU 400.

In 01, an amount of CU 16 is paid regarding the issue to external advisers, banks, etc. This amount is deductible for tax purposes. Moreover, internal departments of E (e.g. accounting and finance) are involved with the issue:

- Further costs of CU 4 are incurred in 01 for overtime relating to the issue, which is reimbursed separately. These costs are deductible for tax purposes.
- Further costs of CU 10 are attributable to the equity transaction. However, these costs would have been incurred without the equity transaction. For simplicity reasons, it is presumed that these costs are not deductible for tax purposes.

Required

Prepare any necessary entries in E's financial statements as at Dec 31, 01. The tax rate is 25%.

Hints for solution

In particular Section 6.

Solution

Year 01	Dr	Various expenses	30	
	Cr	Cash		30
Dec 31, 01	Dr	Cash	400	
	Cr	Share capital		100
	Cr	Share premium		300

The costs incurred for overtime relating to the issue which is reimbursed separately as well as the external costs (CU 4 + CU 16 = CU 20) are deducted from equity net of the related income tax benefit. The related income tax benefit is CU 5 (= CU 20 · 25%). The costs of CU 20 reduce taxable profit, which leads to a reduction in income taxes payable by CU 5. Thus, the tax advantage of CU 5 increases the current tax asset or reduces the current tax liability.

Dec 31, 01	Dr	Share premium	15	
	Dr	Current tax asset/current tax liability	5	
	Cr	Various expenses		20

The entries above lead to the recognition of the economic benefit arising from the issue of shares of CU 385 (= CU 100 + CU 300 – CU 15) in share capital and share premium. This is correct because E receives CU 400 as a consideration for issuing the shares. Incremental costs directly attributable to the equity transaction of CU 20 are incurred and these costs give rise to a tax advantage of CU 5.

Example 4

Convertible bond – separation on initial recognition

On Jan 01, 01, entity E issues a convertible bond (maturity: Jan 01, 01 until Dec 31, 01). The bond is issued at par with a face value of CU 100. Interest of 6% p.a. is payable on Dec 31, 01. The bond can be converted into five ordinary shares of E on Dec 31, 01. When the bond is issued, the prevailing market interest rate for similar debt without conversion rights is 9% p.a.

Required

Prepare any necessary entries in E's financial statements on initial recognition of the convertible bond.

Hints for solution

In particular Section 3.

Solution

	Jan 01, 01	*Dec 31, 01*
Cash flows (interest and principal)		–106
Discount rate	9%	
Liability component (= present value as at Jan 01, 01)	97.25	
Equity component (= 100 – 97.25)	2.75	

Jan 01, 01	Dr	Cash	100.00	
	Cr	Liability		97.25
	Cr	Premium (equity)		2.75

Example 5

Convertible bond – accounting treatment after recognition

Required

The facts are the same as in Example 4. Prepare the remaining entries that are necessary in E's financial statements as at Dec 31, 01. Assume that the liability component is measured at amortized cost (i.e. according to the effective interest method).[4] Assume further that the creditor of the bond makes the following decision on Dec 31, 01:

(a) The creditor does not exercise his conversion right. Consequently, the bond is redeemed.
(b) The creditor exercises his conversion right. Thus, E issues shares. Par value of one of the five shares issued is CU 12.

Hints for solution

In particular Section 4.

Solution[5]

The recognition of the proceeds of the bond issue on initial recognition has already been illustrated in Example 4.

The carrying amount of the equity component is not affected by changes in fair value of the conversion feature after recognition (IAS 32.36 last sentence and IAS 39.2d).

According to the effective interest method, the carrying amount of the liability of CU 97.25 is increased to the redemption amount by applying the effective interest rate to the carrying amount as at Jan 01, 01 while taking into account the interest payment of 6%. The effective interest rate is 9% p.a. (see Example 4).

Carrying amount of the liability as at Jan 01, 01	97.25
Effective interest rate	9%
Effective interest for 01	**8.75**
Interest payment	–6.00
Carrying amount of the liability as at Dec 31, 01 (before redemption or conversion)	**100.00**

Dec 31, 01	Dr	Interest expense	8.75	
	Cr	Liability		2.75
	Cr	Cash		6.00

[4] *See the chapter on IFRS 9/IAS 39 (Section 2.3.5) regarding the effective interest method.*

[5] *The solution would be the same if IFRS 9 and its consequential amendments were not applied early.*

Version (a)

Since there is no conversion, the liability is redeemed on Dec 31, 01 at its par value:

Dec 31, 01	Dr	Liability	100	
	Cr	Cash		100

The original equity component remains as equity although it may be transferred from one line item within equity to another (without affecting profit or loss or other comprehensive income) (IAS 32.AG32):

Dec 31, 01	Dr	Premium (equity)	2.75	
	Cr	Retained earnings		2.75

Version (b)

The holder of the convertible bond chooses to receive shares of E. This means that he waives his receivable. The waiving of the receivable constitutes a contribution in kind in E's statement of financial position.

Dec 31, 01	Dr	Liability	100	
	Cr	Share capital		60
	Cr	Share premium		40

The original equity component remains as equity, although it may be transferred from one line item within equity to another (without affecting profit or loss or other comprehensive income) (IAS 32.AG32):

Dec 31, 01	Dr	Premium (equity)	2.75	
	Cr	Retained earnings		2.75

IAS 33 EARNINGS PER SHARE

1 INTRODUCTION AND SCOPE

Earnings per share are calculated by dividing a **measure of profit or loss (numerator)** by a **number of shares (denominator)**. IAS 33 contains specific rules for this calculation, which are dealt with in this chapter. The objective of earnings per share information is to provide a measure of the interest of each ordinary share in the performance of an entity (IAS 33.11 and 33.32).

The determination and presentation of earnings per share is only **necessary for** (IAS 33.2):

- entities whose equity instruments are already traded in a public market (e.g. a domestic or foreign stock exchange), and
- for entities that file, or are in the process of filing, their financial statements with a securities commission (or other regulatory organization) for the purpose of issuing ordinary shares in a public market.

2 ORDINARY SHARES AND POTENTIAL ORDINARY SHARES

IAS 33 defines an **ordinary share** as an equity instrument that is subordinate to all other classes of equity instruments with regard to the participation in profit for the period (IAS 33.5–33.6).

A **potential ordinary share** is a financial instrument or other contract that may entitle its holder to ordinary shares (IAS 33.5), e.g. a convertible bond or an option.

3 BASIC EARNINGS PER SHARE

Basic earnings per share are calculated as follows (IAS 33.9–33.10):

$$\frac{\text{Profit or loss attributable to ordinary equity holders of the parent entity}}{\text{Weighted average number of ordinary shares outstanding during the period}}$$

The **numerator** comprises all items that are recognized in profit or loss for the period (IAS 33.13). Dividends paid to ordinary equity holders in respect of the current period or previous periods do not affect the numerator.

The **denominator** is affected (among others) when shares are issued for consideration during the period or when treasury shares are purchased or sold. IAS 33 requires that the denominator is calculated on a daily basis. However, a reasonable approximation (e.g. calculation on a weekly or on a monthly basis) is often adequate (IAS 33.20).

By contrast to the cases described above, the number of shares may also change although the **resources** of the entity **do not change**. This is for instance the case if the entity makes the entry "Dr Reserves Cr Share capital" and issues bonus shares at the same time (e.g. each shareholder receives one additional share for each share previously held). In these situations, the calculation of basic (and diluted) earnings per share for all periods presented has to be adjusted **retrospectively**. Moreover, basic (and diluted) earnings per share of all periods presented have to be adjusted for the effects of errors and changes in accounting policies accounted for retrospectively (IAS 33.64 and IAS 8).

4 DILUTED EARNINGS PER SHARE

In calculating diluted earnings per share, the effects of **dilutive potential ordinary shares** are taken into account (IAS 33.31). **Dilution** is a reduction in profit per share or an increase in loss per share resulting from the presumption that potential ordinary shares are exercised (e.g. that a convertible bond is converted or that an option is exercised) (IAS 33.5). The purpose of calculating diluted earnings per share is to determine what earnings per share would be if the dilutive potential ordinary shares were actually exercised. When potential shares exist, diluted earnings per share are a better indication of the interest of a shareholder in the performance of an entity than basic earnings per share.

Profit or loss from continuing operations attributable to the parent entity is used as the **control number** in order to establish whether potential ordinary shares are dilutive. This means that the control number does not include items relating to discontinued operations. In particular cases (preference shares) adjustments may be necessary in order to determine the control number (IAS 33.41–33.43, 33.12, 33.A3, and IFRS 5.Appendix A).

IAS 33 prescribes two different methods for determining diluted earnings per share. Which method has to be applied depends on the nature of the dilutive potential ordinary shares:

- **If-converted method**: This method is applied in the case of **convertible bonds**, among others (IAS 33.49–33.50). Under the presumption of conversion the entity would save paying interest expense for the convertible bond, on the one hand. However, interest is generally deductible for tax purposes. Thus, if there was no interest expense, tax payable would increase. This means that the entity would lose the benefit resulting from the tax deductibility of interest expense, on the other hand. These effects have to be taken into account when determining the **numerator** of diluted earnings per share. Consequently, the numerator increases by the after-tax effect of any interest recognized in the period related to dilutive convertible bonds (because the entity would receive an advantage in this amount in the case of conversion). Due to the presumption of conversion the number of shares (i.e. the **denominator**) also increases. Conversion is only presumed if its effect is **dilutive**. This is the case if the change in the numerator (increase by the after-tax effect of interest recognized) divided by the change in the denominator (additional ordinary shares in the case of conversion) is less than basic profit per share from continuing operations (control number) (IAS 33.41–33.44, 33.49–33.50, and 33.A3).
- **Treasury stock method**: This method is applied, among others, in the case of options to purchase shares of the reporting entity under which the reporting entity is the option writer (**written call options**). Written call options have a dilutive effect only when the average market price of ordinary shares during the period exceeds the exercise price of the options (i.e. they are "in the money") (IAS 33.47). Otherwise no exercise of the options shall be assumed. If an option is "in the money" according to IAS 33,

exercise of the option would result in a disadvantage for the existing shareholders because the option holders would receive shares of the entity against a payment below market price. Hence, this disadvantage is the difference between the average market price of ordinary shares that can be purchased by the option holder and the purchase price (exercise price). Dividing the disadvantage by the average market price of one share results in the number of shares that would have to be issued by the entity for no consideration (bonus shares) to receive the same disadvantage. When determining diluted earnings per share, the denominator has to be increased by this fictitious number of bonus shares while the numerator does not change. Consequently, profit per share from continuing operations (i.e. the control number) decreases. However, if there were a loss per share from continuing operations (control number), the options would not be taken into account in determining diluted earnings per share. This is because the inclusion of additional shares in the denominator would result in a decrease in loss per share, i.e. there would not be dilution (IAS 33.41–33.43 and 33.A3).

If **different issues or series of potential ordinary shares** exist, the sequence in which these issues or series are considered may affect whether they are dilutive. In order to maximize dilution of basic earnings per share, each issue or series of potential ordinary shares is taken into account in sequence from the most dilutive to the least dilutive. The degree of dilution is measured by the figure "earnings per incremental share" (which result from conversion or from exercising options). The lower this figure is, the higher is the degree of potential dilution (IAS 33.44).

5 PRESENTATION AND DISCLOSURE

If the entity presents a single statement of comprehensive income (IAS 1.81a), this statement has to comprise basic and diluted earnings per share for profit or loss from continuing operations attributable to the ordinary equity holders of the parent entity, as well as basic and diluted earnings per share for profit or loss attributable to the ordinary equity holders of the parent entity (IAS 33.66). Basic and diluted earnings per share from discontinued operations are disclosed either in the single statement of comprehensive income or in the notes (IAS 33.68).

If the entity presents a separate income statement and a separate statement of comprehensive income (IAS 1.81b), the amounts mentioned above are presented in the separate income statement (IAS 33.67A). However, basic and diluted earnings per share from discontinued operations are disclosed either in the separate income statement or in the notes (IAS 33.68A).

6 EXAMPLES WITH SOLUTIONS

Example 1

Basic earnings per share

In 01, the number of entity E's ordinary shares outstanding develops as follows:

Balance as at Jan 01, 01	**100**
Purchase of treasury shares for cash (Jul 01, 01)	–10
Issue of shares for cash (Oct 01, 01)	20
Balance as at Dec 31, 01	**110**

E's profit for 01 is CU 500.

Required

Calculate basic earnings per share for entity E for 01.

Hints for solution

In particular Section 3.

Solution

The denominator represents the weighted average number of ordinary shares outstanding during 01. In order to calculate this weighted average, it is first necessary to determine the number of shares outstanding for each month. The sum of these balances is then divided by 12:[1]

Sum of the balances of the months Jan, Feb, Mar, Apr, May, and Jun	600	*6 · 100*
Sum of the balances of the months Jul, Aug, and Sep	270	*3 · (100 – 10)*
Sum of the balances of the months Oct, Nov, and Dec	330	*3 · (100 – 10 + 20)*
Sum of the balances of the year 01	**1,200**	
Months per year	12	
Weighted average	**100**	

Consequently, basic earnings per share amounts to CU 5 (= CU 500 : 100 ordinary shares).

Example 2

Basic earnings per share – share split

In 01, the number of entity E's ordinary shares outstanding develops as follows:

Balance as at Jan 01, 01	**100**
Purchase of treasury shares for cash (Jul 01, 01)	–10
Balance as at Jul 01, 01	**90**
Share split on Aug 01, 01 (1:4)	**360**
Issue of shares for cash (Oct 01, 01)	80
Balance as at Dec 31, 01	**440**

As a result of the share split, each shareholder receives three additional shares for each share previously held. Share capital is increased by the entry "Dr Reserves Cr Share capital." Consequently, E's share price decreases to one fourth of its previous value. However, each shareholder owns four times the number of shares previously held.

In 00, 100 shares of E were outstanding. This number did not change in 00. E's profit is CU 400 for 00 and CU 800 for 01.

Required

Calculate basic earnings per share of entity E in its financial statements as at Dec 31, 01 for the year 01 as well as for the comparative period 00.

[1] *In practice, it may be necessary to calculate the weighted average on a weekly or even on a daily basis (IAS 33.20) (see Section 3).*

Hints for solution

In particular Section 3.

Solution

In the financial statements as at Dec 31, 01 the calculation of basic earnings per share for all periods presented has to be adjusted retrospectively (IAS 33.64). Thus, the weighted average number of shares for 00 is 400 (= 100 · 4) instead of 100, which means that basic earnings per share for 00 is CU 1 (= CU 400 : 400 ordinary shares).

When determining the weighted average number of shares for 01, the balance as at Jan 01, 01 as well as the number of treasury shares purchased have to be adjusted (IAS 33.64). Consequently, these numbers of shares have to be multiplied by 4. However, the number of shares issued on Oct 01, 01 is not adjusted because the issue was effected after the share split.

Sum of the balances of the months Jan, Feb, Mar, Apr, May, and Jun	2,400	*6 · 100 · 4*
Sum of the balances of the months Jul, Aug, and Sep	1,080	*3 · (4 · 100 – 4 · 10)*
Sum of the balances of the months Oct, Nov, and Dec	1,320	*3 · (4 · 100 – 4 · 10 + 80)*
Sum of the balances of the year 01	**4,800**	
Months per year	12	
Weighted average	**400**	

Consequently, basic earnings per share for 01 amounts to CU 2 (= CU 800 : 400 ordinary shares).

Example 3

Discontinued operation

Entity E's profit from continuing operations for 01 is CU 200. There is also a loss from a discontinued operation in the amount of CU –600. 100 ordinary shares are outstanding. Moreover, E has written call options for shares of E which are "in the money" according to IAS 33. In this example, it is assumed that exercise of these options would be equivalent to the issue of 100 shares by E for no consideration (bonus shares) according to the treasury stock method.

Required

Calculate the different figures for basic and diluted earnings per share that have to be disclosed by E for the year 01.

Hints for solution

In particular Sections 3–5.

Solution

Profit from continuing operations is E's control number to establish whether potential ordinary shares are dilutive (IAS 33.41–33.43 and 33.A3).

The 100 bonus shares (determined according to the treasury stock method) are included in the diluted earnings per share calculation because the resulting CU 1.00 earnings per share for continuing operations is dilutive. Because profit from continuing operations is the control number, the 100 bonus shares are also included in the calculation of the other diluted earnings per share amounts, even though the resulting earnings per share amounts are antidilutive to their comparable basic earnings per share amounts.

	Profit or loss	*Earnings per share*	
		Basic	*Diluted*
Continuing operations	200	2	1
Discontinued operation	–600	–6	–3
Loss for 01	–400	–4	–2

Example 4

Diluted earnings per share – if-converted method

Entity E's profit (after tax) for 01 is CU 400. In 01, 200 ordinary shares are outstanding. Hence, basic earnings per share of E is CU 2 (= CU 400 : 200 shares).

Some years ago E issued 10 convertible bonds.[2] Interest expense for 01 relating to the liability component of the convertible bond is CU 8. Current and deferred tax relating to that interest expense is CU 2. Each bond is convertible into two ordinary shares. Until Dec 31, 01, no bond has been converted.

Required

Calculate diluted earnings per share of entity E for 01.

Hints for solution

In particular Section 4.

Solution

The numerator and the denominator have to be calculated under the presumption that the bonds are converted if the effect of conversion is dilutive.

Change in profit before tax	8	
Change in profit after tax	6	*CU 8 – CU 2*
Change in the number of ordinary shares	20	*10 · 2*
Change in earnings per share (in CU) under the presumption of conversion	**0.3**	*0.3 < 2.0, i.e. the effect is dilutive*

The effect of conversion is dilutive, because profit per share would decrease as a result of conversion. Consequently, the convertible bonds are taken into account in determining diluted earnings per share. This procedure results in diluted earnings per share of CU 1.85 [= (CU 400 + CU 6) : (200 + 20)].

2 *See the chapter on IAS 32, Sections 3–4 and Examples 4–5 with regard to the accounting treatment of convertible bonds from the issuer's perspective.*

Example 5

Diluted earnings per share – treasury stock method

Entity E's profit (after tax) for 01 is CU 400. In 01, there are 200 ordinary shares outstanding. Hence, basic earnings per share of E is CU 2 (= CU 400 : 200 shares).

In 01, the average market price of one ordinary share of E is CU 5. In 01, there are employee share options that enable their holders to acquire 50 ordinary shares of E. The exercise price is CU 2 per share. In addition, there are further employee share options that enable their holders to acquire 30 ordinary shares of E. The exercise price is CU 6 per share. E has written all of these options. Exercise of the options is only possible after the end of the vesting period (Dec 31, 02).

Required

Calculate diluted earnings per share of entity E for 01.

Hints for solution

In particular Section 4.

Solution

Only options that are "in the money" (i.e. for which exercise is favorable) are taken into account (IAS 33.47). It is not relevant whether the vesting period is already over because exercise has to be presumed fictitiously. Application of the treasury stock method (IAS 33.45) only results in a change of the denominator: The issue of ordinary shares for a price of CU 2 per share, i.e. below the average market price of CU 5 per ordinary share, would result in a disadvantage for the existing shareholders. This disadvantage is divided by the average market price of one ordinary share, which results in the number of shares that would have to be issued by E for no consideration (bonus shares) to effect the same disadvantage. This number of bonus shares increases the denominator. Since the numerator does not change, E's profit per share decreases (dilution).

Shares that can be purchased under the options	50	
Market price of these shares	250	*50 · CU 5*
Exercise price of the options (= purchase price for these shares)	100	*50 · CU 2*
Disadvantage (in CU)	**150**	*CU 250 – CU 100*
Disadvantage (in bonus shares)	**30**	*CU 150 : 5*

Diluted earnings per share is CU 1.74 [= CU 400 : (200 + 30)].

Example 6

Diluted earnings per share – different issues or series of potential ordinary shares

In 01, the following potential ordinary shares of entity E are outstanding:

(a) E has written 100 options. For each option, the holder can buy one share. The exercise price is CU 4 per ordinary share and the average market price in 01 is CU 5 per ordinary share.

(b) 100 convertible bonds, each of which can be converted into one ordinary share of E. Interest expense for 01 relating to the liability component of these convertible bonds is CU 100. Current and deferred tax relating to that interest expense is CU 40.[3]
(c) 100 convertible bonds, each of which can be converted into three ordinary shares of E. Interest expense for 01 relating to the liability component of these convertible bonds is CU 50. Current and deferred tax relating to that interest expense is CU 20.

E's profit (after tax) for 01 is CU 600. In 01, there are 800 ordinary shares outstanding. Hence, basic earnings per share of E is CU 0.75 (= CU 600 : 800 shares).

Required

Calculate diluted earnings per share of entity E for 01.

Hints for solution

In particular Sections 2 and 4.

Solution

First, the figure "earnings per incremental share" is calculated for each issue or series of potential ordinary shares:

(a) With regard to the **options**, the treasury stock method is applied. According to this method, the number of shares (i.e. the denominator) increases by 20 = [(CU 5 – CU 4) · 100] : CU 5. However, profit is not affected, i.e. the effect on the numerator is zero. Thus, earnings per incremental share are **zero**.
(b) In the case of the **convertible bonds, described in (b) above**, the numerator increases by CU 60 (CU 100 – CU 40). The denominator increases by 100 shares (100 bonds · 1). Therefore, earnings per incremental share is **CU 0.6** (CU 60 : 100 shares).
(c) In the case of the **convertible bonds, described in (c) above**, the numerator increases by CU 30 (CU 50 – CU 20). The denominator increases by 300 shares (100 bonds · 3). Thus, earnings per incremental share is **CU 0.1** (CU 30 : 300 shares).

Comparing "earnings per incremental share" (which measure the degree of dilution) of the different issues or series of potential ordinary shares results in the following sequence of including the potential ordinary shares when calculating diluted earnings per share (starting with the most dilutive and ending with the least dilutive issue or series of potential ordinary shares in order to maximize dilution) (IAS 33.44):

[3] *See the chapter on IAS 32, Sections 3–4 and Examples 4–5 regarding the accounting treatment of convertible bonds from the issuer's perspective.*

1. Inclusion of the **options** would lead to a decrease in earnings per share from CU 0.75 (basic earnings per share) to CU 0.73 [= (profit after tax of CU 600 + CU 0) : (800 shares + 20 shares)], which means that the effect of the options is dilutive. Hence, they are taken into account in determining diluted earnings per share.
2. Inclusion of the **convertible bonds described in (c)** would lead to a decline in earnings per share from CU 0.73 (diluted earnings per share after inclusion of the options) to CU 0.56 [= (CU 600 + CU 0 + CU 30) : (800 shares + 20 shares + 300 shares)], which means that the effect of the convertible bonds described in (c) is dilutive. Hence, they are taken into account in determining diluted earnings per share.
3. Inclusion of the **convertible bonds described in (b)** would lead to an increase in earnings per share from CU 0.56 (diluted earnings per share after inclusion of the options and of the convertible bonds described in (c)) to CU 0.57 [(CU 600 + CU 0 + CU 30 + CU 60) : (800 shares + 20 shares + 300 shares + 100 shares)], which means that the effect of the convertible bonds described in (b) is *not* dilutive. Hence, they are *not* taken into account when determining diluted earnings per share.

According to the considerations above, diluted earnings per share is CU 0.56

IAS 34 INTERIM FINANCIAL REPORTING

1 INTRODUCTION

The objective of IAS 34 is to prescribe the minimum content of an **interim financial report** (i.e. of **interim financial statements**) and to prescribe the principles for recognition and measurement in such a report. An interim financial report is presented for an **interim period**, i.e. for a financial reporting period that is shorter than a full financial year (IAS 34.1 and 34.4). For example, an entity may prepare quarterly financial statements.

While all entities that apply IFRSs are required to present financial statements at least annually (IAS 1.36), IAS 34 does not contain a commitment to prepare interim reports. Moreover, IAS 34 does not prescribe the length of interim periods. These issues are left to be decided by governments, securities regulators, stock exchanges, and accountancy bodies. However, if an entity is required or elects to publish an interim financial report in accordance with IFRSs, IAS 34 has to be applied (IAS 34.1).

If the entity's most recent annual financial statements were consolidated statements, the entity's interim financial reports also have to be prepared on a consolidated basis (IAS 34.14).

2 CONTENT OF AN INTERIM FINANCIAL REPORT

2.1 Components

IAS 34 defines the minimum content of an interim report as including condensed financial statements (condensed interim report). However, an entity may also prepare a complete set of financial statements as described in IAS 1[1] (comprehensive interim report) (IAS 34.4. and 34.6).

A **condensed interim report** consists of the following components (IAS 34.8):

- A condensed statement of financial position
- Either:
    - a condensed single statement of comprehensive income (one statement approach) or
    - a condensed separate income statement and a condensed separate statement of comprehensive income (two statement approach)
- A condensed statement of changes in equity
- A condensed statement of cash flows
- Selected explanatory notes

If the components of profit and loss are presented in a separate income statement as described in IAS 1.10A, interim condensed information is presented from that separate statement (IAS 34.8A).

---

[1] *See the chapter on IAS 1, Section 5.*

A condensed interim report has to include, at a minimum, each of the headings and subtotals that were included in its most recent annual financial statements as well as the selected explanatory notes as required by IAS 34. Additional line items or notes have to be included if their omission would make the condensed interim report misleading (IAS 34.10).

If an entity publishes a complete set of financial statements in its interim report (**comprehensive interim report**), the form and content of those statements have to conform to the requirements of IAS 1 for a complete set of financial statements (IAS 34.4–34.5 and 34.9).

2.2 Periods and dates to be presented in interim reports

The **statement of financial position** has to be presented as at the end of the current interim period and as at the end of the immediately preceding financial year (IAS 34.20a). In some cases, it may be necessary to present a third statement of financial position (IAS 34.5f).

The **single statement of comprehensive income** (one statement approach) or the **separate income statement and the separate statement of comprehensive income** (two statement approach) have to be presented for the following periods (IAS 34.20b):

- Current interim period
- Cumulatively for the current financial year to date
- Comparable periods (current and year-to-date) of the immediately preceding financial year

The **statement of changes in equity** and the **statement of cash flows** are presented cumulatively for the current financial year to date with a comparative statement for the comparable year-to-date period of the immediately preceding financial year (IAS 34.20(c) and (d)).

3 MATERIALITY

In deciding how to recognize, measure, classify or disclose an item for interim financial reporting purposes, materiality has to be assessed in relation to the interim period financial data. In making assessments of materiality, it has to be recognized that interim measurements may rely on estimates to a greater extent than measurements of annual financial data (IAS 34.23).

4 RECOGNITION AND MEASUREMENT

The recognition and measurement guidance of IAS 34 also applies to complete financial statements for an interim period (i.e. to a comprehensive interim report) (IAS 34.7).

4.1 Discrete approach vs. integral approach

The same accounting policies are applied in an entity's interim financial statements as are applied in its annual financial statements. Departures from these accounting policies are subject to the general rules of IFRS (IAS 34.28–34.29). For example, initial application of a new Standard or of an amended version of an existing Standard may lead to the application of a different measurement method in the entity's first quarterly financial statements of the year (as at Mar 31, 02) than in its last annual financial statements (as at Dec 31, 01).

Interim financial reporting according to IAS 34 is primarily based on a discrete view. By contrast, interim financial reporting according to US GAAP (see among others: APB 28) is more based on an integral view:

- Under the **discrete approach (IAS 34)** interim period profit or loss is measured by viewing each interim period separately and not by anticipation of the annual financial statements. For assets, the same tests of future economic benefits apply at interim dates as at the end of the financial year. Costs that by their nature would not qualify as assets at the financial year-end would not qualify at interim dates either. Similarly, a liability at the end of an interim period has to represent an existing obligation at that date, just as it must at the end of an annual reporting period (IAS 34.32).
- Under the **integral approach**, interim period profit or loss is measured by viewing each interim period as an integral part of the corresponding annual period. The interim report is intended to enable forecasts of the annual financial statements. For example, it may be the case that an entity performs the day-to-day servicing for its machines during its off-season, which is the first quarter of the year. The expenditures for this work do not qualify for capitalization in the entity's annual financial statements as at Dec 31. Under the discrete approach, the total of these expenditures would be recognized in profit or loss in the entity's first quarterly financial statements as at Mar 31 (IAS 34.B2). However, under the integral approach, an appropriate portion of these expenditures is allocated to each interim period of the year.

4.2 Independence of the annual result from the frequency of reporting

The frequency of an entity's reporting (annual, half-yearly or quarterly) must not affect its annual results (IAS 34.28).

This principle is breached in the case of reversals of impairment losses relating to goodwill. Reversing goodwill impairment losses is prohibited in the annual financial statements (IAS 36.124–36.125). IFRIC 10 extends the scope of that prohibition. It also prohibits, for example, reversing an impairment loss relating to goodwill recognized in the first quarterly financial statements of the year in the annual financial statements.

4.3 Quantity component and price component

Revenues and expenses regularly have a quantity component as well as a price component:

- **Quantity component**: Under the discrete approach, the actual quantity structure of the quarter is relevant. This means that it is prohibited to recognize an appropriate portion of revenues and expenses that arise in subsequent quarters according to IFRSs in the current quarterly financial statements. Vice versa, it is prohibited to recognize an appropriate portion of revenues and expenses that arise in the current quarter according to IFRSs in the interim reports of the next quarters.
- With regard to the **price component**, the illustrations in IAS 34 Appendix B are rather based on an integral view than on a discrete view. If the price component depends on

whether certain limits will be exceeded for the whole year, the price that is recognized in the first quarters depends on an estimate of whether those limits will be exceeded by the end of the year. An example is a contractually agreed volume rebate, the percentage of which depends on the quantity purchased during the year (IAS 34.B23).

These considerations also apply when **measuring interim income tax expense** (IAS 34.30c and 34.B12–34.B16):

- The tax base is the taxable profit for the interim period (quantity component in a broader sense).
- In the case of a progressive tax system, the tax rate (price component) is determined on the basis of the estimated amount of taxable profit for the year (estimated weighted average tax rate for the year).
- Finally, the tax rate is multiplied with taxable profit for the interim period.

The estimate of the tax rate for the year may have to be adjusted as a result of the taxable profit for the following interim period (IAS 34.B13).

5 EXAMPLES WITH SOLUTIONS

Example 1

Periods and dates to be presented in interim reports

Entity E prepares quarterly financial statements as at Jun 30, 01. E's financial year ends on Dec 31, 01.

Required

Assess at which dates or for which periods the statement of financial position, the single statement of comprehensive income (or the separate income statement and the separate statement of comprehensive income), the statement of changes in equity, and the statement of cash flows have to be presented in E's quarterly financial statements as at Jun 30, 01. Also make these assessments for the comparative information. E has to present comparative information for the previous year in its annual financial statements.

Hints for solution

In particular Section 2.2.

Solution

E's **statement of financial position** has to be presented as at Jun 30, 01. The comparative figures for this statement are presented as at Dec 31, 00 (i.e. as at the end of the previous financial year).

The single statement of comprehensive income (or the separate income statement, as well as the separate statement of comprehensive income) of E are presented for the following periods:

Jan 01, 01 – Jun 30, 01	Jan 01, 00 – Jun 30, 00	Apr 01, 01 – Jun 30, 01	Apr 01, 00 – Jun 30, 00

The **statement of changes in equity** and the **statement of cash flows** have to be presented for the following periods:

Jan 01, 01 – Jun 30, 01	Jan 01, 00 – Jun 30, 00

Example 2

Discrete approach vs. integral approach

Entity E performs the day-to-day servicing of its production machines during its off-season, which is the first quarter of the year. The corresponding expenditures of CU 4 are paid on Mar 31, 01. They do not qualify for capitalization in E's annual financial statements as at Dec 31.

Required

Prepare any necessary entries in E's quarterly financial statements as at Mar 31, 01. E's financial year ends on Dec 31, 01. Illustrate the procedure under the:

(a) discrete approach (IFRS),
(b) integral approach.

Hints for solution

In particular Section 4.1.

Solution (a) – discrete approach (IFRS)

Under the discrete approach, the expenses of CU 4 are recognized in profit or loss in the entity's first quarterly financial statements as at Mar 31, 01 (IAS 34.B2):

Mar 31, 01	Dr	Maintenance expense	4	
	Cr	Cash		4

Solution (b) – integral approach

An amount of CU 1 (i.e. one fourth of the expenses) is attributed to each quarter. Therefore, expenses of CU 1 are recognized in the first quarter of 01. Because the total amount of CU 4 has already been paid in the first quarter, E recognizes deferred expenses of CU 3 in its statement of financial position.

Mar 31, 01	Dr	Maintenance expense	1	
	Dr	Deferred expenses	3	
	Cr	Cash		4

In each of the subsequent quarters, the following entry is made:

Dr	Maintenance expense	1	
Cr	Deferred expenses		1

Example 3

Independence of the annual result from the frequency of reporting

In the first quarter of 01, entity E has been sued for damages. Hence, E recognizes a provision for damages in the amount of CU 10 in its quarterly financial statements as at Mar 31, 01. On Jun 30, 01, E loses the case and pays damages in the amount of CU 9.

Required

Prepare any necessary entries in E's quarterly financial statements as well as in E's annual financial statements. E's financial year ends on Dec 31, 01.

Hints for solution

In particular Section 4.2.

Solution

1st quarterly financial statements:

Mar 31, 01	Dr	Expense	10	
	Cr	Provision		10

2nd quarterly financial statements:

The following entry affects E's separate income statement for the second quarter of 01 as well as E's separate income statement presented cumulatively for the year 01 to date:

Jun 30, 01	Dr	Provision	10	
	Cr	Income		1
	Cr	Cash		9

In the *annual financial statements* it is not appropriate to present an expense of CU 10 as well as income of CU 1. Instead, an expense of CU 9 and no income is presented. This applies even though IAS 34.28 only refers to the measurement of the annual results and not to its presentation. The offsetting prohibition (IAS 1.32) does not apply in this situation.

Dec 31, 01	Dr	Income	1	
	Cr	Expense		1

Example 4

Quantity component and price component

Entity E sells merchandise M to entity F. E and F contractually agree on a rebate of 5% if F's annual purchases of merchandise M exceed CU 100. In the first quarter of 01, F buys 400 units of M at a price of CU 0.1, which results in a total purchase price of CU 40. After consideration of seasonality, it is expected that F's purchases in the entire year 01 will amount to CU 140.

Required

Prepare any necessary entries in E's and F's quarterly financial statements as at Mar 31, 01. E's and F's financial year end on Dec 31, 01.

Hints for solution

In particular Section 4.3.

Solution

Volume rebates are anticipated in interim periods by both the buyer and the seller if it is probable that they have been earned or will take effect (IAS 34.B23).

In this example it is estimated that F's purchase in the entire year 01 will amount to CU 140. Consequently, it is expected that F will be able to deduct the rebate from the purchase price.

The 400 units bought by F in the first quarter of 01 represent the **quantity component**. The **price component** is taken into account by reducing the unit price of CU 0.1 by the rebate of 5%. Hence, the carrying amount of the merchandise in F's statement of financial position and E's sales revenue amount to CU 38 (= 400 units · 0.1 · 95% = CU 38).

Entries in *E's quarterly financial statements* as at Mar 31, 01:

Jan – Mar 01	Dr	Cash	40	
	Cr	Sales revenue		40
Mar 31, 01	Dr	Sales revenue	2	
	Cr	Liability		2

Entries in *F's quarterly financial statements* as at Mar 31, 01:

Jan – Mar 01	Dr	Merchandise	40	
	Cr	Cash		40
Mar 31, 01	Dr	Receivable	2	
	Cr	Merchandise		2

Example 5

Various cases

Case (a)

According to entity E's local tax law, the first CU 20 of E's taxable profit are taxed at a rate of 20% and E's taxable profit in excess of CU 20 is taxed at a rate of 40%. E's taxable profit for the first quarter of 01 is CU 10. E expects to generate the same taxable profit in each of the three remaining quarters of 01.

Case (b)

Entity E holds shares of entity F which are measured at fair value through other comprehensive income (IFRS 9.5.7.1b and 9.5.7.5). On Mar 25, 01, E becomes legally entitled to receive a dividend from F in the amount of CU 4. The dividend is paid to E on Mar 30, 01.

Required

Prepare any necessary entries in E's quarterly financial statements as at Mar 31, 01. E's financial year ends on Dec 31, 01.

Hints for solution

In particular Sections 4.1 and 4.3.

Solution (a)

	1st quarter	*2nd quarter*	*3rd quarter*	*4th quarter*	*Year 01*	
(Estimated) taxable profit	10	10	10	10	40	
Taxation at 20%					4	*= CU 20 · 20%*
Taxation at 40%					8	*= CU 20 · 40%*
Current tax payable					12	
Estimated weighted average tax rate for 01					30%	*= CU 12 : CU 40*
Current tax for the 1st quarter	3		*= CU 10 · 30%*			

Mar 31, 01	Dr	Current tax expense	3	
	Cr	Current tax liability		3

Solution (b)

The dividend is recognized in profit or loss when E's right to receive payment of the dividend is established (IFRS 9.5.7.6, 9.B5.7.1, and IAS 18.30c). Allocation over the interim periods of 01 is not possible.[2]

Mar 25, 01	Dr	Receivable	4	
	Cr	Income		4
Mar 30, 01	Dr	Cash	4	
	Cr	Receivable		4

[2] *If E did not apply IFRS 9 early, and if the shares were classified as "available for sale" (IAS 39.9), the solution of this example would be the same (IAS 39.55b and IAS 18.30c).*

IAS 36 IMPAIRMENT OF ASSETS

1 INTRODUCTION AND SCOPE OF IAS 36

IAS 36 contains rules with regard to the **impairment** and the **reversal of impairment losses** of specific assets. For the purpose of consolidated financial statements, the **scope** of IAS 36 mainly comprises items of property, plant, and equipment (IAS 16), intangible assets including any goodwill resulting from a business combination (IAS 38 and IFRS 3), and investment property measured according to the cost model (IAS 40) (IAS 36.2–36.5). The rules of IAS 36 relating to the quantitative impairment test also apply to investments in associates and jointly controlled entities accounted for using the equity method. However, in these cases, a simplified calculation is possible (IAS 28.31–28.34, IAS 31.38, and 31.40).[1]

An impairment loss is recognized if the carrying amount of an asset (after deduction of depreciation or amortization for the period) exceeds its **recoverable amount**. The recoverable amount of an asset is the higher of its **value in use** (present value of the future cash flows expected to be derived by the entity from the asset) and its **fair value less costs to sell** (amount obtainable from the sale of an asset in an arm's length transaction between knowledgeable, willing parties, less the costs of disposal).

In practice, it is often not possible to determine the future cash inflows generated by an individual asset on a rational basis, which would be necessary for calculating its value in use. For example, entity E produces (among others) product P. The machines and the factory building are employed in the production of P, as well as in the production of other products. It is therefore not possible to state to which extent the cash inflows from the sale of P are generated by each machine, by the factory building, by E's administrative building, etc. However, it is possible to allocate the cash inflows from the sale of P (and of other products) to the group of assets (which consists of the different machines, the buildings, etc.) as a whole. Such a group of assets to which cash inflows can be allocated and for which value in use can consequently be determined is referred to as a **cash-generating unit (CGU)**. According to the Standard, a CGU is the smallest identifiable group of assets that generates cash inflows that are largely independent of the cash inflows from other assets or groups of assets (IAS 36.6. 36.59, 36.66–36.67, and 36.104).

2 WHEN TO TEST FOR IMPAIRMENT

The recoverable amount has to be calculated if there is an indication that an asset or a CGU is impaired (**triggering event**) (IAS 36.8). Whether such an indication exists is assessed at the end of each reporting period (IAS 36.9). The following are examples of such indications (IAS 36.12–36.16):

- The asset's market value has decreased significantly more than would be expected as a result of the passage of time or normal use.

[1] *See the chapter on IAS 28, Section 2.2.2.*

- Evidence is available of physical damage or obsolescence of an asset.
- Evidence is available from internal reporting which indicates that the economic performance of an asset is, or will be, worse than expected.

The concept of **materiality** may be helpful in identifying whether the recoverable amount needs to be estimated. For example, if previous calculations show that an asset's or CGU's recoverable amount was significantly greater than its carrying amount, it is not necessary to re-estimate the recoverable amount if no events have occurred that could have eliminated that difference (IAS 36.15–36.16).

Irrespective of whether there is an indication of impairment (i.e. irrespective of whether there are **triggering events**), the recoverable amount always has to be calculated annually for the following assets or CGUs (IAS 36.10 and 36.90):

- Intangible assets with indefinite useful lives.[2]
- Intangible assets not yet available for use.
- A CGU to which goodwill (acquired in a business combination)[3] has been allocated.

The calculation of the recoverable amount for an intangible asset or for CGUs just described may be performed **at any time during an annual period**, provided that the test is performed at the **same time every year**. Different intangible assets or CGUs may be tested for impairment at different times. However, if some or all of the goodwill allocated to a CGU was acquired in a business combination during the current annual period, or if such an intangible asset was initially recognized during the current annual period, the recoverable amount has to be calculated for that CGU or intangible asset before the end of the current annual period (IAS 36.10, 36.90, and 36.96).

3 WHEN TO REVERSE AN IMPAIRMENT LOSS

At the end of each reporting period it is necessary to assess whether there is any indication that an impairment loss recognized in prior periods for an asset (other than goodwill) no longer exists or has decreased. This applies equally to a CGU. If there is such an indication, the recoverable amount has to be calculated (IAS 36.110). The examples of indications in the standard of a possible decrease of an impairment loss (IAS 36.111) mainly mirror the indications of a possible impairment loss in IAS 36.12 (IAS 36.112).

4 DETERMINING THE RECOVERABLE AMOUNT FOR AN INDIVIDUAL ASSET OR FOR AN ASSET'S CGU?

The **recoverable amount** has to be calculated **for an individual asset**, if possible. The recoverable amount **cannot be determined for the individual asset** if both of the following criteria are met (IAS 36.22 and 36.66–67):

- The asset's value in use cannot be estimated to be close to its fair value less costs to sell.

[2] *See the chapter on IAS 38, Section 5.3.*
[3] *See the chapter on IFRS 3, Section 6.1.*

- The asset does not generate cash inflows that are largely independent of those from other assets.[4]

In such cases, value in use and thus the recoverable amount, can be determined only for the asset's CGU, unless the asset's fair value less costs to sell exceeds its carrying amount (IAS 36.22 and 36.66–67). In the latter case, the asset is not impaired (IAS 36.19).

In most cases, an asset is only able to generate cash inflows together with other assets.[5] Consequently, impairment tests are **normally** conducted **on the level of CGUs** and not on the level of individual assets. In the case of assets rented to others, impairment tests are possible for the individual assets.

A CGU is the smallest identifiable group of assets that generates **cash inflows** that are **largely independent** of the cash inflows from other assets or groups of assets (IAS 36.6). Cash inflows are inflows of cash and cash equivalents received from parties external to the reporting entity. In determining whether cash inflows from an asset (or group of assets) are largely independent of the cash inflows from other assets (or groups of assets), various factors are considered, including the following (IAS 36.69):

- How management monitors the entity's operations (such as by product lines or geographic criteria).
- How management makes decisions about continuing or disposing of the entity's assets and operations.

A CGU may be a product line, a plant, a business operation, a geographical area, or a reportable segment as defined in IFRS 8 (IAS 36.130d).

If an **active market** exists for the output produced by an asset or by a group of assets, it is likely that that asset or group is a CGU. This applies even if some or all of the output (e.g. products at an intermediate stage of a production process) is used internally. Consequently, what is critical is regularly the existence of an active market for the output, irrespective of whether this output is actually sold there (IAS 36.70–36.71, 36.IE6, and 36.IE12). An active market is a market that meets all the following criteria (IAS 36.6):

- The items traded within the market are homogeneous.
- Willing sellers and buyers can normally be found at any time.
- Prices are available to the public.

5 DETERMINING THE RECOVERABLE AMOUNT

5.1 General Aspects

It is not always necessary to determine both an asset's or CGU's fair value less costs to sell and its value in use. If either of these amounts exceeds the asset's or CGU's carrying amount,

[4] *See Section 1.*

[5] *See Section 1.*

the asset or CGU is not impaired and it is not necessary to estimate the other amount (IAS 36.19).

If it is not possible to determine fair value less costs to sell, value in use may be used as the recoverable amount (IAS 36.20). However, fair value less costs to sell can only be used as the recoverable amount if it is appropriate to assume that value in use does not significantly exceed fair value less costs to sell (IAS 36.21–36.22 and 36.67).

In some cases, estimates, averages, and computational short cuts may provide reasonable approximations of the detailed computations illustrated in IAS 36 for determining value in use or fair value less costs to sell (IAS 36.23).

5.2 Fair Value Less Costs to Sell

Fair value less costs to sell is the amount obtainable from the sale of an asset or of a CGU in an arm's length transaction between knowledgeable, willing parties, less the costs of disposal. The **costs of disposal** are incremental costs directly attributable to the disposal of an asset or of a CGU, excluding income tax expense and finance costs. However, costs of disposal recognized as a liability are not deducted in determining fair value less costs to sell (IAS 36.6 and 36.28).

IAS 36 specifies a **measurement hierarchy** for determining fair value less costs to sell (IAS 36.25–36.27):

- The best evidence of fair value less costs to sell is a price in a **binding sale agreement** in an arm's length transaction.
- If there is no binding sale agreement but an asset is traded in an **active market**, fair value is the asset's market price on that market. When current bid prices are unavailable, the price of the most recent transaction may provide a basis from which to estimate fair value.
- If there is no binding sale agreement or active market, fair value less costs to sell is based on the **best information available.** In determining fair value in such situations, the outcome of **recent transactions for similar assets within the same industry** is considered. Fair value less costs to sell does not reflect a forced sale unless the entity is compelled to sell immediately (IAS 36.27). If fair value less costs to sell is determined using **discounted cash flow projections**, additional disclosures are necessary under certain circumstances (IAS 36.134e). It is important to note that fair value reflects the market's expectation and not the entity's expectation of the present value of the future cash flows (IAS 36.BCZ11).
- **Replacement cost techniques** must not be applied when measuring fair value less costs to sell according to IAS 36 (IAS 36.BCZ29).

5.3 Value in Use

5.3.1 Introduction Value in use of an asset or of a CGU is calculated by discounting the future cash inflows and outflows from continuing use and from the ultimate disposal with the appropriate discount rate (IAS 36.31). The **following elements** are reflected in the calculation of value in use (IAS 36.30 and 36.A1):

(a) An estimate of the future cash flows expected to be derived from the asset or CGU.
(b) Expectations about possible variations in the amount or timing of those future cash flows.
(c) Time value of money (represented by the current market risk-free interest rate).
(d) The price for bearing the uncertainty inherent in the asset or CGU.
(e) Other factors that would be taken into account by market participants (e.g. illiquidity).

There are two approaches to computing value in use (IAS 36.A2):

- **Traditional approach**: Adjustments for factors (b) to (e) are embedded in the discount rate.
- **Expected cash flow approach**: Factors (b), (d), and (e) cause adjustments in arriving at risk-adjusted expected cash flows.

It is important to note that **interest rates** used to discount **cash flows** have to reflect **assumptions that are consistent** with those inherent in the estimated cash flows. This means that interest rates must not reflect risks for which the cash flows have been adjusted. Otherwise, the effect of some presumptions would be double-counted (IAS 36.56, 36.A3, and 36.A15).

5.3.2 Estimating the Future Cash Flows Cash flow projections have to be based on **reasonable and supportable presumptions**, whereby greater weight has to be given to external evidence (IAS 36.33a and 36.34). Moreover, cash flow projections have to be based on the **most recent financial budgets/forecasts approved by management**. Projections based on these budgets/forecasts have to cover a maximum period of **five years**, unless a longer period can be justified (IAS 36.33b and 36.35). Cash flows beyond the period covered by the most recent budgets/forecasts have to be determined by **extrapolating** the projections based on the budgets/forecasts. In doing so, a **steady or declining growth rate** is used unless an increasing rate can be justified (IAS 36.33c, 36.36, and 36.37).

The future **cash flows** include (IAS 36.39, 36.41, 36.51, and 36.52):

- cash inflows from continuing use of the asset or CGU,
- cash outflows necessary to generate these cash inflows (including overheads that can be directly attributed, or allocated on a reasonable and consistent basis, to the use of the asset or CGU), and
- net cash flows, if any, to be received (or paid) for the disposal of the asset or CGU at the end of its useful life.

To avoid double-counting, cash flows do not include cash outflows that relate to obligations that have been recognized as liabilities (e.g. pensions) (IAS 36.43b).

Cash outflows include those for the **day-to-day servicing** of the asset or CGU that are necessary to maintain the level of economic benefits expected to arise from the asset or CGU in its current condition from continuing use (IAS 36.39b, 36.41, and 36.49).

The cash flows are estimated for the asset or CGU in its current condition. Hence, they do not include estimated future cash flows from **future restructuring** (to which the entity is not yet committed according to IAS 37) or **improving or enhancing the performance** of the asset or CGU. However, when the cash outflows that improve or enhance performance have already been incurred, the resulting future cash inflows are included in the cash flows. Once the entity is committed to a restructuring, the cash flows for the purpose of determining value in use (IAS 36.33b, IAS 36.44-36.48, and 36.IE44-36.IE61):

- reflect the cost savings and other benefits from the restructuring, but
- do not include the future cash outflows for the restructuring because these are already included in a restructuring provision according to IAS 37.

When a **single asset** consists of components with different useful lives, the replacement of components with shorter lives is part of the day-to-day servicing of the asset when estimating the future cash flows (IAS 36.49).

When a **CGU** consists of assets with different useful lives, all of which are essential to the ongoing operation of the CGU, the replacement of assets with shorter lives is part of the day-to-day servicing of the unit when estimating the future cash flows (IAS 36.49).

When the carrying amount of an asset does not yet include all the cash outflows to be incurred before it is ready for use (e.g. a **building under construction**), any further cash outflow that is expected to be incurred before the asset is ready for use is included when determining value in use (IAS 36.39b and 36.42).

Estimates of future cash flows must not include cash inflows or outflows from **financing activities** and **income tax** receipts or payments (IAS 36.50).

In estimating cash flows the effects of **internal transfer prices** that do not correspond to future prices that could be achieved in arm's length transactions have to be eliminated (IAS 36.70–36.71).

5.3.3 Determining the Discount Rate When an asset-specific rate is not directly available from the market, surrogates are used in order to estimate the discount rate (IAS 36.57 and 36.A16). The following rates might be taken into account as a starting point in making such an estimate (IAS 36A17):

- The entity's weighted average cost of capital (WACC) determined using techniques such as the capital asset pricing model (CAPM).
- The entity's incremental borrowing rate.
- Other market borrowing rates.

The discount rate has to reflect current market assessments of the time value of money (represented by the risk-free rate of interest) and the risks specific to the asset or CGU for which the future cash flows have not been adjusted (IAS 36.55, 36.A1, 36.A16, and 36.A18).

The discount rate is independent of the entity's capital structure and of the way the entity financed the acquisition of the asset or CGU (IAS 36.A19). The discount rate used has to be a pre-tax rate (IAS 36.55 and 36.A20). Normally, a single discount rate is used. However, separate discount rates have to be used for different future periods where value in use is sensitive to a difference in risks for different periods or to the term structure of interest rates (IAS 36.A21).

6 DETERMINING THE CARRYING AMOUNT OF A CGU

The carrying amount of a CGU has to be determined on a basis **consistent with** the way the **recoverable amount** of the CGU is determined (IAS 36.75). The carrying amount of a CGU includes the carrying amount of the assets that can be attributed directly, or allocated on a reasonable and consistent basis to the CGU and will generate the future cash inflows used in determining the CGU's value in use. The carrying amount of a CGU does not include the carrying amount of any recognized liability unless the recoverable amount of the CGU cannot be determined without consideration of this liability. The latter situation may occur if the disposal of a CGU would require the buyer to assume the liability (IAS 36.76–36.78).

For practical reasons, the recoverable amount of a CGU is sometimes determined after consideration of **assets that are not part of the CGU** (e.g. financial assets) or **liabilities that have been recognized**. In such cases, the CGU's carrying amount is increased by the carrying amount of those assets and decreased by the carrying amount of those liabilities (IAS 36.79). However, to begin with, the assets and liabilities outside the scope of IAS 36 are measured according to the applicable standards. For example, at first inventories are written down to their net realizable value (if net realizable value is below cost) before they are added to the carrying amount of the CGU (IAS 2.9).

7 GOODWILL

7.1 Allocating Goodwill to CGUs

For the purpose of impairment testing, goodwill acquired in a business combination[6] has to be allocated to each of the acquirer's **CGUs** or **groups of CGUs** that is expected to **benefit from the synergies of the business combination** (IAS 36.80). Consequently, the quantified synergies are used as the basis for allocating goodwill. Goodwill may also be allocated on the basis of fair values, EBIT, EBITDA, etc., if they reflect synergies approximately.

Each CGU or group of CGUs to which the goodwill is allocated as described above (IAS 36.80–36.83):

- has to represent the lowest level within the entity at which the goodwill is monitored for internal management purposes, and
- must not be larger than an operating segment (as defined by IFRS 8.5 before aggregation).

7.2 Multi-level Impairment Test

In some cases, a multi-level impairment test is necessary (IAS 36.97–36.98):

- If the assets of a CGU to which goodwill has been allocated are tested for impairment at the same time as that CGU, they have to be tested for impairment first and any impairment loss is recognized. Afterwards, the CGU to which goodwill has been allocated is tested for impairment.

[6] *See the chapter on IFRS 3, Section 6.1.*

- Similarly, if the CGUs constituting a group of CGUs to which goodwill has been allocated are tested for impairment at the same time as that group of CGUs, the individual CGUs have to be tested for impairment first and any impairment loss is recognized. Afterwards, the group of CGUs containing the goodwill is tested for impairment.

8 CORPORATE ASSETS

Corporate assets are assets **other than goodwill** that **contribute to the future cash flows of at least two CGUs** (IAS 36.6). Whether an asset meets the definition of a corporate asset depends on the structure of the entity. Typical examples of corporate assets are the building of a headquarters or of a division, EDP equipment or a research center (IAS 36.100). Normally, the recoverable amount of an individual corporate asset cannot be determined (IAS 36.101).

When testing a CGU for impairment, all the corporate assets that relate to the CGU have to be identified. If **allocation** of a portion of the carrying amount of a corporate asset to the CGU **on a reasonable and consistent basis** (IAS 36.102):

- Is **possible**, the carrying amount of the CGU (including the pro rata carrying amount of the corporate asset) is compared with its recoverable amount. Any impairment loss is recognized.
- Is **not possible**, at first, the carrying amount of the CGU (excluding the corporate asset) is compared with its recoverable amount. Afterwards, the smallest group of CGUs, which includes the CGU under review and to which a portion of the carrying amount of the corporate asset can be allocated on a reasonable and consistent basis, is identified. Finally, the carrying amount of the group of CGUs (including the pro rata carrying amount of the corporate asset) is compared with its recoverable amount. Any impairment loss is recognized.

9 RECOGNIZING AND REVERSING AN IMPAIRMENT LOSS[7]

In the case of a **reversal of an impairment loss** of an **individual asset**, the carrying amount of the asset **must not be increased above the fictitious carrying amount** (which is the carrying amount that would have been determined had no impairment loss been recognized for the asset in prior years) (IAS 36.117).

An **impairment loss recognized for goodwill must not be reversed** in a subsequent period (IAS 36.124–36.125). Even if the impairment loss was recognized in respect of goodwill in an interim financial statement, the recognition of a reversal of the impairment loss is prohibited in the following interim financial statements as well as in the annual financial statements (IFRIC 10.8).

An **impairment loss** determined for a **CGU** or **group of CGUs** has to be allocated to reduce the carrying amount of the assets of the unit (group of units). **At first**, the carrying amount of **goodwill** allocated to the unit (group of units) is reduced. Afterwards, the remaining impairment

---

[7] *This section does not deal with the rules that are effective when the revaluation model of IAS 16 or IAS 38 is applied. This is due to the fact that the revaluation model is seldom applied in practice (see the chapter on IAS 16, Section 4.1 and the chapter on IAS 38, Section 5.1).*

loss is allocated to the **other assets** of the unit (group of units) **pro rata** on the basis of the carrying amount of each asset in the unit (group of units) (IAS 36.104). Thereby, the carrying amount of an asset must not be reduced below the highest of the following amounts (**floor**) (IAS 36.105):

- Its fair value less costs to sell (if determinable).
- Its value in use (if determinable).
- Zero.

The amount of the **impairment loss** that would have been **recognized** as described above **in the absence of the floor** has to be **allocated pro rata** to the other assets of the unit (group of units) on the basis of their carrying amounts (IAS 36.105).

These reductions in carrying amounts are treated and recognized as impairment losses on individual assets (IAS 36.104). After the requirements described above (IAS 36.104 and 36.105) have been applied, a liability is recognized for any remaining amount of an impairment loss for a CGU only if this is required by another standard (IAS 36.108).

A **reversal of an impairment loss** for a **CGU** has to be **allocated to the assets** of the unit, **except for goodwill, pro rata** with the carrying amounts of those assets. These increases in carrying amounts are treated and recognized as reversals of impairment losses for individual assets (IAS 36.122). In allocating a reversal of an impairment loss for a CGU, the carrying amount of an asset must not be increased above the lower of the following amounts (**cap**) (IAS 36.123):

- Its recoverable amount (if determinable).
- The **fictitious carrying amount**, i.e. the carrying amount that would have been determined had no impairment loss been recognized for the asset in prior periods.

The amount of the reversal of the impairment loss that **would have been allocated** to one or more assets **in the absence of the cap** has to be allocated **pro rata** to the **other assets** of the CGU, **except for goodwill** (IAS 36.123).

10 NON-CONTROLLING INTERESTS

For each business combination, the acquirer generally measures any **non-controlling interest** in the acquiree on acquisition date either (a) at its **fair value** or (b) at the non-controlling interest's proportionate **share** in the recognized amounts of the acquiree's identifiable **net assets** (IFRS 3.19), which also affects goodwill (**goodwill option**).[8]

If a subsidiary with a non-controlling interest is itself a CGU, the impairment loss is allocated between the parent and the non-controlling interest on the same basis as that on which profit or loss is allocated (IAS 36.C6).

If a non-controlling interest is measured at its **proportionate share of the acquiree's identifiable net assets** (see above), goodwill attributable to the non-controlling interest is not recognized in the parent's consolidated financial statements. However, it is included in the

[8] *See the chapter on IFRS 3, Section 6.3.*

recoverable amount of the related CGU. Consequently, the carrying amount of the CGU is increased (only for the purpose of impairment testing) by the goodwill attributable to the non-controlling interest. This adjusted carrying amount is then compared with the recoverable amount of the CGU (IAS 36.C4 and 36.IE65). If an impairment loss attributable to a non-controlling interest relates to goodwill that is not recognized in the parent's consolidated financial statements, that impairment loss is not recognized (IAS 36.C8).

11 EXAMPLES WITH SOLUTIONS

Example 1

Identification of CGUs

Case (a):[9] Entity E owns and operates a large waste recycling plant and a private railway which transports the processed waste in containers from the plant to the main public rail network. The private railway could be sold only for scrap value and it does not generate cash inflows from continuing use which are largely independent of the cash inflows of the plant as a whole.

Case (b): Soccer club S, whose shares are quoted on a stock exchange, has to prepare financial statements according to IFRS. According to IFRS, the individual soccer players are intangible assets. S generates significant income in the following areas: income from spectators (i.e. from the sale of admission tickets to the stadium and of food and drinks in the stadium), TV rights, advertising income (i.e. offering advertising space to other entities), and the sale of memorabilia.

Case (c)[10]***:*** A railroad company transports passengers on five different routes. In order to be allowed to perform these services, it received a license from the state that requires minimum service on each of the five routes. Assets devoted to each route and the cash flows from each route can be identified separately.

Required

Determine which asset or group of assets represents a CGU.

Hints for solution

In particular Sections 1 and 4.

Solution

Case (a): It is not possible to estimate the recoverable amount of the private railway because its value in use cannot be determined and is probably different from scrap value. The scrap value of the railway is below its carrying amount. E therefore estimates the recoverable amount of the CGU (which includes both the plant and the private railway).

[9] *Case (a) is based on IAS 36.67 and PwC, Manual of Accounting, IFRS 2011, 18.99.*

[10] *Case (c) is based on IAS 36.68.*

Case (b): Generally, it is not possible to allocate the cash inflows generated by the soccer club to the individual soccer players even if the performance of individual players is exceptionally good or bad. For example, it is not possible to assess which part of the cash inflows from spectators is due to the good performance of player X and which part is due to the performance and sympathy of player Y. The same problem occurs in the area "sale of memorabilia." For example, it is not possible to determine which part of the cash inflows from the sale of balls, bedding or scarves with logos is due to player Z. The situation could be different with regard to the sale of jerseys on which the name of a particular player is printed. However, in general the success of the whole business of S depends on the success of the entire soccer team, which means that it is generally not possible to allocate cash inflows to a particular player. Consequently, the whole soccer club is the CGU.

Case (c): The railroad company does not have the option to curtail any of the five routes (e.g. when a particular route operates at a significant loss) because, in this case, it would lose its license for all five routes. Thus, the lowest level of identifiable cash inflows that are largely independent of the cash inflows from other assets or groups of assets is the cash inflows generated by the five routes together. Consequently, the railroad company as a whole is the CGU instead of each route being a separate CGU.

Example 2

Individual asset – determining value in use, recognizing and reversing an impairment loss

Entity E leases a machine to entity L under an operating lease. On Dec 31, 00, the machine's remaining useful life is four years and its carrying amount is CU 60.

On Dec 31, 01, it is planned to modify the machine in order to enhance its performance (i.e. to increase the machine's annual output). This work is performed by entity F on Dec 28, 02. The amount of CU 10 charged by F for this work is paid by E on Dec 28, 02.

It is presumed that there is an indication that the machine is impaired on Dec 31, 01. Consequently, the recoverable amount of the machine has to be determined. In addition, it is presumed that the machine's value in use always exceeds fair value less costs to sell and that the discount rate (which is a pre-tax rate according to IAS 36.55) is 10% p.a. The future cash flows (estimated on a pre-tax basis according to IAS 36.50 and 36.51) are presented in the table below. The second column does not include cash inflows and cash outflows that are due to the modification of the machine and also excludes cash outflows for the day-to-day servicing of the machine:

Year	*Future cash flows*	*Cash outflows for the day-to-day servicing*	*Cash outflows for the modification of the machine*	*Additional cash inflows due to the modification of the machine*
02	16	−1	−10	0
03	17	−1	0	9
04	17	−1	0	9

Required

Prepare any necessary entries in E's financial statements as at Dec 31 for the years 01 and 02.

Hints for solution

In particular Sections 5.3.2 and 9.

Solution

Year 01

Dec 31, 01	Dr	Depreciation expense	15	
	Cr	Machine		15

On Dec 31, 01, value in use is calculated by discounting the future cash flows (after deduction of the cash outflows for the day-to-day servicing, but without taking into account the cash inflows and outflows that are due to the modification of the machine) (IAS 36.33b, 36.44–36.45, and 36.48):

Year	*Future cash flows*	*Cash outflows for the day-to-day servicing*	*Total*	*Present value*
02	16	−1	15	13.64
03	17	−1	16	13.22
04	17	−1	16	12.02
Value in use (rounded)				**39**

In this example, it is presumed that the machine's value in use always exceeds fair value less costs to sell. Consequently, the machine's recoverable amount is also CU 39. Comparing the recoverable amount of the machine with its carrying amount results in an impairment loss:

Carrying amount as at Dec 31, 00	60
Depreciation for 01	−15
Carrying amount as at Dec 31, 01	**45**
Recoverable amount as at Dec 31, 01	39
Impairment loss	**−6**

Dec 31, 01	Dr	Impairment loss	6	
	Cr	Machine		6

Year 02

At first the depreciation for 02 is recognized (= carrying amount of CU 39 as at Dec 31, 01 : remaining useful life as at Dec 31, 01 of three years):

Dec 31, 02	Dr	Depreciation expense	13	
	Cr	Machine		13
Dec 28, 02	Dr	Machine	10	
	Cr	Cash		10

After these entries, the carrying amount is CU 36:

Carrying amount as at Dec 31, 01	39
Depreciation for 02	−13
Modification of the machine (Dec 28, 02)	10
(Preliminary) carrying amount as at Dec 31, 02	**36**

The modification of the machine was effected at the end of 02. This represents an indication that the impairment loss recognized in 01 may no longer exist or may have decreased (IAS 36.111d). Thus, value in use has to be calculated including the future cash inflows that are due to the modification of the machine (IAS 36.110):

Year	*Future cash flows before modification of the machine*	*Cash outflows for the day-to-day servicing*	*Additional cash inflows due to the modification of the machine*	*Total*	*Present value*
03	17	−1	9	25	22.73
04	17	−1	9	25	20.66
Value in use (rounded)					**43**

In this example it is presumed that the machine's value in use always exceeds fair value less costs to sell. Therefore, the machine's recoverable amount is also CU 43. However, the machine's carrying amount must not be increased to CU 43 because the carrying amount must not be increased above the **fictitious carrying amount** (= carrying amount that would have been determined had no impairment loss been recognized in prior years) (IAS 36.117):

Carrying amount as at Dec 31, 00	60
Depreciation for 01	−15
Depreciation for 02 (fictitious)	−15
Modification of the machine in 02	10
Fictitious carrying amount as at Dec 31, 02	**40**

Consequently, the machine's carrying amount is only increased from CU 36 to CU 40:

Dec 31, 02	Dr	Machine	4	
	Cr	Reversal of impairment losses		4

Example 3

Impairment loss on a CGU

On Jul 01, 01, entity E acquires all the shares of entity F. In the consolidated financial statements of E, F is a CGU. The following table shows the carrying amounts as at

Dec 31, 01 of the assets of F, as well as of goodwill attributable to F in the preliminary consolidated financial statements of E:[11]

	Carrying amount	*Fair value less costs to sell (IAS 36.6)*	*Value in use (IAS 36.6)*	*Net realizable value (IAS 2.6)*
A. Non-current assets				
Land (IAS 16)	70	74	*Not determinable*	
Building (IAS 16)	300	250	*Not determinable*	
Machine (IAS 16)	150	*Not determinable*	*Not determinable*	
Software (IAS 38)	150	*Not determinable*	*Not determinable*	
Goodwill	50	*Not determinable*	*Not determinable*	
B. Current assets				
Cash	100			
Trade receivable	70			
Merchandise	110			100
TOTAL ASSETS	**1,000**			

In E's preliminary consolidated financial statements as at Dec 31, 01, F's provisions amount to CU 100 and F's other liabilities amount to CU 300.

It is presumed that the trade receivable, which is measured at amortized cost, is not impaired (IFRS 9.5.2.2, IAS 39.58, and 39.59). The position "cash" comprises cash on hand and demand deposits, and the position "merchandise" only consists of homogeneous items (which have the same carrying amount and the same net realizable value).

For practical purposes, E also includes assets that are not within the scope of IAS 36, as well as liabilities that have been recognized in determining the recoverable amount and the carrying amount of the CGU (IAS 36.79). On Dec 31, 01, the CGU's value in use is CU 340 and its fair value less costs to sell is CU 270.

Required

Prepare any necessary entries in E's consolidated financial statements as at Dec 31, 01. For simplification purposes taxes are ignored in this example.

Hints for solution

In particular Sections 6 and 9.

Solution

Normally the recoverable amount would have to be determined only for the assets that are within the scope of IAS 36 (IAS 36.2–36.5). Only F's property, plant, and equipment, and intangible assets (including goodwill) are in the scope of IAS 36. However, as described above, E includes assets that are not within the scope of IAS 36, as well as liabilities recognized in the statement of financial position in determining the recoverable amount of the CGU. Consequently, these assets and liabilities are also taken into account in the calculation of the carrying amount of the CGU (IAS 36.79). When determining the CGU's

[11] *For simplification purposes this example only includes a small number of assets.*

carrying amount, first, the items that are not in the scope of IAS 36 are measured according to the applicable standards:

- Cash is not written down because of its nature.
- In this example it is assumed that the trade receivable is not impaired (IFRS 9.5.2.2, IAS 39.58, and 39.59) (see previous).
- The inventories are written down to net realizable value (IAS 2.9, 2.34, and IAS 1.103):

Dec 31, 01	Dr	Cost of sales	10	
	Cr	Merchandise		10

Comparing the CGU's recoverable amount with the carrying amount of its net assets results in an impairment loss on the CGU:

Total assets	**1,000**
Provisions	−100
Other liabilities	−300
Net assets (preliminary)	**600**
Write–down of inventories	−10
Net assets	**590**
Recoverable amount	340
Impairment loss on the CGU	**250**

This impairment loss of CU 250 has to be allocated to reduce the carrying amounts of the individual assets that are within the scope of IAS 36:

- At first, the carrying amount of goodwill is reduced from CU 50 to zero (IAS 36.104a).
- The remaining part of the impairment loss on the CGU of CU 200 (= CU 250 – CU 50) is allocated to the other assets that are within the scope of IAS 36 pro rata on the basis of their carrying amounts (IAS 36.104b). However, no impairment loss is allocated to the land because its fair value less costs to sell exceeds its carrying amount (IAS 36.19, 36.22, and 36.105).

	Carrying amount in CU	*Carrying amount in %*	*Pro rata impairment loss*
Building	300	50%	100
Machine	150	25%	50
Software	150	25%	50
Total	**600**	**100%**	**200**

However, by allocating the impairment loss as illustrated in the table above, the carrying amount of an asset must not be reduced below the highest of the following amounts (**floor**) (IAS 36.105):

- Its fair value less costs to sell (if determinable).
- Its value in use (if determinable).
- Zero.

The floor for the machine and for the software is zero while the floor for the building is CU 250 (fair value less costs to sell of the building). Consequently, the carrying amount of the building cannot be decreased by CU 100 (i.e. from CU 300 to CU 200). It can only be decreased from CU 300 to CU 250, i.e. by CU 50. The remaining impairment loss of CU 50 has to be allocated to the machine and to the software pro rata on the basis of their carrying amounts (IAS 36.105):[12]

	Carrying amount in CU	*Carrying amount in %*	*Pro rata impairment loss*
Machine	150	50%	25
Software	150	50%	25
Total	**300**	**100%**	**50**

In summary, allocation of the impairment loss on the CGU to the individual assets leads to the following result:

	Preliminary carrying amount (Dec 31, 01)	*1st allocation of the impairment loss*	*2nd allocation of the impairment loss*	*Total of impairment losses*	*Carrying amount (Dec 31, 01)*
Land	70	0	0	0	70
Building	300	–50	0	–50	250
Machine	150	–50	–25	–75	75
Software	150	–50	–25	–75	75
Goodwill	50	–50	0	–50	0
Total	**720**	**–200**	**–50**	**–250**	**470**
Not attributable		***–50***	***0***	***0***	

Dec 31, 01	Dr	Impairment loss	250	
	Cr	Building		50
	Cr	Machine		75
	Cr	Software		75
	Cr	Goodwill		50

Example 4

Reversing an impairment loss on a CGU – continuation of Example 3 in 02

Entity E (from Example 3) prepares its consolidated financial statements for the year 02. For simplification purposes it is presumed that there were no transactions and events in 02. In this example, only depreciation and amortization are illustrated in addition to the application

[12] *Allocation on the basis of the original carrying amounts of the machine and of the software (CU 150 each) leads to the same result as allocation on the basis of the reduced carrying amounts (CU 100 each).*

of the requirements of IAS 36 with regard to the reversing of an impairment loss on a CGU.

	*Remaining useful life as at Dec 31, **01** (in years)*	*Value in use as at Dec 31, **02***	*Fair value less costs to sell as at Dec 31, **02***
Land	*Not applicable*	*Not determinable*	74
Building	25	*Not determinable*	285
Machine	5	*Not determinable*	*Not determinable*
Software	5	*Not determinable*	*Not determinable*
Goodwill	*Not applicable*	*Not determinable*	*Not determinable*

The CGU's recoverable amount as at Dec 31, 02 is CU 480.

For practical purposes, E also includes assets that are not within the scope of IAS 36, as well as liabilities that have been recognized in determining the recoverable amount and the carrying amount of the CGU (IAS 36.79).

Required

Prepare any necessary entries in E's consolidated financial statements as at Dec 31, 02. For simplification purposes taxes are ignored in this example.

Hints for solution

In particular Sections 6 and 9.

Solution

The carrying amounts as at Dec 31, 01 (see Example 3) have to be allocated over their remaining useful lives in 02 (i.e. carrying amount as at Dec 31, 01 : remaining useful life as at Dec 31, 01 = depreciation or amortization for 02) (IAS 36.104 and 36.63):

	Carrying amount as at Dec 31, 01	*Remaining useful life as at Dec 31, 01 (in years)*	*Depreciation and amortization for 02*	*Preliminary carrying amount as at Dec 31, 02*
Land	70	*Not applicable*	*Not applicable*	70
Building	250	25	−10	240
Machine	75	5	−15	60
Software	75	5	−15	60
Goodwill	0	*Not applicable*	*Not applicable*	0
Total	**470**		**−40**	**430**

Dec 31, 02	Dr	Depreciation expense	25	
	Cr	Building		10
	Cr	Machine		15
Dec 31, 02	Dr	Amortization expense	15	
	Cr	Software		15

Comparing the CGU's recoverable amount with the carrying amount of the CGU's net assets results in a reduction in the impairment loss recognized in 01:

Total of the carrying amounts from the table above	430
Cash	100
Trade receivable	70
Merchandise (after the write-down in 01)	100
Total assets	**700**
Provisions	−100
Other liabilities	−300
Net assets	**300**
Recoverable amount	480
Reduction in the impairment loss on the CGU	**180**

This reduction in the impairment loss on the CGU of CU 180 has to be allocated to the individual assets of the CGU that are within the scope of IAS 36 (except for goodwill) pro rata with the carrying amounts of those assets (IAS 36.122 and 36.124).
By allocating the reduction in the impairment loss, the carrying amount of an asset must not be increased above the lower of the following amounts (**cap**) (IAS 36.123):

- The recoverable amount of the asset (if determinable).
- The fictitious carrying amount, i.e. the carrying amount that would have been determined had no impairment loss been recognized for the asset in prior periods.

In this example, it is not possible to determine the recoverable amount of an individual asset. The fair values less costs to sell of the land and of the building do not constitute recoverable amounts (IAS 36.67). Hence, the cap of an asset is identical with its fictitious carrying amount.

Apart from goodwill, land is also excluded from the allocation of the reduction in the impairment loss because its carrying amount already corresponds with its cap since no impairment loss was allocated to the land in 01.

	Carrying amount in CU	*Carrying amount in %*	*Pro rata reduction in the impairment loss*
Building	240	66.66%	120
Machine	60	16.67%	30
Software	60	16.67%	30
Total	**360**	**100%**	**180**

	Carrying amount as at Dec 31, 01 before allocation of the impairment loss	*Fictitious depreciation and amortization for 02*	*Fictitious carrying amount as at Dec 31, 02*
Building	300	12	288
Machine	150	30	120
Software	150	30	120

The carrying amounts of the machine and software as at Dec 31, 02 (CU 60 each) are increased by CU 30 each (pro rata reductions in the impairment loss), because this does not result in exceeding the caps (fictitious carrying amounts) of CU 120 each. However, the carrying amount of the building as at Dec 31, 02 (CU 240) can not be increased by CU 120 (pro rata reduction in the impairment loss) because this would result in exceeding the cap of CU 288. Thus, the carrying amount of the building is only increased by CU 48, i.e. from CU 240 to CU 288. The remaining reduction in the impairment loss of CU 72 (= CU 120 – CU 48) is allocated to the machine and to the software (IAS 36.123):[13]

	Carrying amount in CU	*Carrying amount in %*	*Pro rata reduction in the impairment loss*
Machine	60	50%	36
Software	60	50%	36
Total	**120**	**100%**	**72**

The following table illustrates the allocation of the reduction in the impairment loss. It turns out that the pro rata reversals of the impairment loss for the machine and for the software of CU 36 each (see above) cannot be allocated in full (due to the caps). Therefore, a part of the reduction in the CGU's impairment loss (CU 12) cannot be recognized:

	Preliminary carrying amount (Dec 31, 02)	*Cap (IAS 36.123 and 36.124)*	*1st allocation of the reduction in the impairment loss*	*Carrying amount after the 1st allocation*	*2nd allocation of the reduction in the impairment loss*	*Carrying amount after the 2nd allocation*	*Total of the reductions in impairment losses*
Land	70	70	0	70	0	70	0
Building	240	288	48	288	0	288	48
Machine	60	120	30	90	30	120	60
Software	60	120	30	90	30	120	60
Goodwill	0	0	0	0	0	0	0
Total	**430**		**108**		**60**		**168**
Not attributable:			***72***		***12***		***12***

Dec 31, 02	Dr	Building	48	
	Dr	Machine	60	
	Dr	Software	60	
	Cr	Reduction in impairment losses		168

[13] *Allocation on the basis of the original carrying amounts of the machine and of the software (CU 60 each) leads to the same result as allocation on the basis of the increased carrying amounts (CU 90 each).*

Example 5

Goodwill – multi-level impairment test

On Jan 01, 01, entity E acquires all the shares of entity F. F consists of CGU 1 and CGU 2. The carrying amount of the goodwill attributable to F for the purpose of impairment testing according to IAS 36 is CU 10. It is presumed that this amount cannot be allocated to the individual CGUs of F (i.e. to CGU 1 and CGU 2), but only to F (group of CGUs) as a whole (IAS 36.80–36.81).

As at Dec 31, 01, the following information is available:

	CGU 1	*CGU 2*
Carrying amount	40	38
Recoverable amount	42	33

The recoverable amount of F (including the goodwill) is CU 80.

Required

Prepare any necessary entries in E's consolidated financial statements as at Dec 31, 01.

Hints for solution

In particular Sections 7 and 9.

Solution

In this example, a multi-level impairment test is necessary. At first, the CGUs are tested for impairment individually, and any impairment loss is recognized. Subsequently, the sum of the carrying amounts of CGU 1, CGU 2, and of the goodwill is compared with the recoverable amount of CU 80 (IAS 36.97–36.98).

	CGU 1	*CGU 2*	*Goodwill*
Carrying amount	40	38	
Recoverable amount	42	33	
Impairment loss on the first level	**0**	**−5**	
Carrying amounts after impairment loss on the first level	40	33	10
Total of the carrying amount	**83**		
Recoverable amount	80		
Impairment loss on the second level	**−3**		

Dec 31, 01	Dr	Impairment loss	8	
	Cr	Various assets (CGU 2)		5
	Cr	Goodwill		3

The second impairment loss (i.e. the loss for the group of CGUs containing the goodwill) has to be recognized as a reduction of goodwill because the standard requires allocation to goodwill first (IAS 36.104).

Example 6

Corporate assets

Entity E consists of the CGUs A and B. There is no goodwill. E determines the recoverable amounts for these CGUs because there are indications of impairment. On Dec 31, 01, the carrying amounts of A and B are CU 20 and CU 40 (before allocation of corporate assets), respectively. The recoverable amounts for A and B are CU 18 and CU 50 and the remaining useful lives are 20 and 15 years. The recoverable amount of E is CU 80.

The operations of E are conducted from its headquarters. The headquarters consists of a headquarters building (carrying amount as at Dec 31, 01: CU 10) and a research center (carrying amount as at Dec 31, 01: CU 12). The carrying amounts of the CGUs, weighted based on their remaining useful lives, are a reasonable basis for the allocation of the carrying amount of the headquarters building to the individual CGUs. However, it is not possible to allocate the carrying amount of the research center to the individual CGUs on a reasonable basis.

Required

Prepare any necessary entries in E's consolidated financial statements as at Dec 31, 01.

Hints for solution

In particular Sections 8 and 9.

Solution

In this example, it is presumed that the carrying amounts of the CGUs, weighted based on their remaining useful lives, are a reasonable basis for the allocation of the carrying amount of the headquarters building to the CGUs A and B. However, it is presumed that it is not possible to allocate the carrying amount of the research center to the CGUs A and B on a reasonable basis. Hence, at first, CGUs A and B are tested for impairment, including the portion of the carrying amount of the headquarters building allocated to the respective CGU (IAS 36.102a):

	CGU A	*CGU B*	*Total*
Carrying amount	20	40	60
Remaining useful life (weighting factor)	20	15	
Weighted carrying amount in CU	**400**	**600**	**1,000**
Weighted carrying amount in %	40%	60%	
Allocation of the carrying amount of the headquarters building	4	6	10
Carrying amount of the CGU after allocation	**24**	**46**	**70**
Recoverable amount	18	50	
Impairment loss	**–6**	**0**	

The impairment loss on CGU A is allocated to the headquarters building in the amount of CU 1 (= CU 6 · CU 4 : CU 24) and to the other assets of CGU A in the amount of CU 5 (= CU 6 · CU 20 : CU 24) (IAS 36.102a and 36.104).

The smallest group of CGUs to which (a portion of) the carrying amount of the research center can be allocated is entity E itself. Hence, the carrying amount of E (including the corporate assets) is compared with the recoverable amount of E (IAS 36.102b):

	CGU A	*CGU B*	*Headquarters building*	*Research center*	*Total*
Carrying amount	20	40	10	12	82
Impairment loss on the first level	–5	0	–1	Not applicable	–6
Carrying amount after impairment loss on the first level	**15**	**40**	**9**	**12**	**76**
Recoverable amount					**80**
Impairment loss on the second level					**0**

Dec 31, 01	Dr	Impairment loss	6	
	Cr	Headquarters building		1
	Cr	Various assets (CGU A)		5

Example 7

Non-controlling interest[14]

On Oct 01, 01, entity E acquires 80% of the shares of entity S for CU 90. At that time, the value of the net assets of S, determined according to IFRS 3, is CU 100 and the fair value of the non-controlling interest is CU 22. In E's group, profit or loss is always allocated on the basis of ownership interests.

S represents a CGU. It is presumed that half of the difference between the purchase price and E's share of S's net assets (determined according to IFRS 3) is allocated to S, and that the other half is allocated to the other CGUs of E (on the basis of the synergies of the business combination).

The recoverable amount of CGU S (including the goodwill attributable to the non-controlling interest) is CU 101, as at Dec 31, 01. For simplification purposes, assume that the carrying amount of S's net assets (determined according to IFRS 3) did not change until Dec 31, 01.

Required

Conduct the impairment test for CGU S in E's consolidated financial statements as at Dec 31, 01 and prepare any entries that are necessary in this regard. The non-controlling interest is measured (IFRS 3.19):

(a) At its proportionate share in the recognized amounts of S's identifiable net assets.
(b) At its fair value.

[14] *See the chapter on IFRS 3 (Sections 6.1 and 6.3) with regard to non-controlling interests.*

Hints for solution

In particular Section 10.

Solution – general remarks

Since the subsidiary (entity S) (where a non-controlling interest exists) is a CGU, the impairment loss is allocated between the parent (entity E) and the non-controlling interest on the same basis as that on which profit or loss is allocated. Thus, 80% of the impairment loss is allocated to E and 20% to the non-controlling interest (IAS 36.C6).

Solution (a)

Consideration transferred	90
Non-controlling interest (measured at the NCI's proportionate share of S's net assets) (20% of CU 100)	20
Value of the acquiree	**110**
Net assets of S (measured according to IFRS 3)	100
Goodwill recognized in the statement of financial position	**10**
Part of this goodwill allocated to CGU S (50%)	**5**

The goodwill attributable to the non-controlling interest has not been recognized in the statement of financial position. However, goodwill attributable to the non-controlling interest is included in the recoverable amount. As a consequence, the goodwill attributable to the non-controlling interest has to be included in the carrying amount of CGU S for the purpose of impairment testing (i.e. the carrying amount is adjusted) (IAS 36.C4 and 36.IE62–36.IE68). The carrying amount of the goodwill adjusted for the purpose of impairment testing can be computed as follows: CU 5 : 0.8 = CU 6.25.

	Goodwill	*Net assets*	*Total*
Carrying amount	5.00	100.00	105.00
Adjusted carrying amount	6.25	100.00	106.25
Recoverable amount			101.00
Impairment loss			**5.25**
Impairment loss allocated to E (80%)			**4.20**
Impairment loss allocated to the non-controlling interest (20%)			**1.05**

Since goodwill attributable to the non-controlling interest has not been recognized in the statement of financial position, only the impairment loss allocated to E is recognized:

Dec 31, 01	Dr	Impairment loss	4.20	
	Cr	Goodwill		4.20

Solution (b)

Consideration transferred	90
Non-controlling interest (fair value)	22
Value of the acquiree	**112**
Net assets of S (measured according to IFRS 3)	100
Goodwill	**12**
Goodwill allocated to CGU S	**7**
Goodwill allocated to other CGUs	5

	Goodwill	*Net assets*	*Total*
Carrying amount	7.0	100.0	107.0
Recoverable amount			101.0
Impairment loss			**6.0**
Impairment loss allocated to E (80%)			**4.8**
Impairment loss allocated to the non-controlling interest (20%)			**1.2**

The impairment loss is allocated to goodwill (IAS 36.104). Since the entire goodwill (which includes the goodwill attributable to the non-controlling interest) has been recognized in the statement of financial position, the whole impairment loss is recognized:

Dec 31, 01	Dr	Impairment loss	6	
	Cr	Goodwill		6
Dec 31, 01	Dr	Non-controlling interest	1.2	
	Cr	Profit or loss attributable to the non-controlling interest		1.2

IAS 37 PROVISIONS, CONTINGENT LIABILITIES, AND CONTINGENT ASSETS

1 SCOPE

IAS 37 specifies the accounting treatment of **provisions, contingent liabilities and contingent assets** in the financial statements.

Executory contracts only fall under IAS 37 if they are **onerous**,[1] i.e. if losses are expected. Executory contracts represent contracts under which neither party has performed any of its obligations or both parties have partially performed their obligations to an equal extent (IAS 37.1 and 37.3).

Furthermore, IAS 37 does not apply to provisions, contingent liabilities, and contingent assets covered by **another Standard**. Examples are financial instruments (including guarantees) that are within the scope of IFRS 9, current and deferred tax liabilities (IAS 12), as well as provisions relating to employee benefits (IAS 37.1c, 37.2, and 37.5).

IAS 37 applies to **provisions for restructurings** (including discontinued operations). When a restructuring meets the definition of a **discontinued operation** (IFRS 5Appendix A), additional disclosures may be required by IFRS 5 (IAS 37.9).

2 DEFINITION AND RECOGNITION OF PROVISIONS

2.1 Overview

Provisions are liabilities of uncertain timing or amount. A **liability** represents a **present obligation** of the entity that arises from **past events**, the settlement of which is expected to result in an outflow from the entity of resources embodying economic benefits. A liability is created by a **legal** or **constructive** obligation[2] that results in the entity having **no realistic alternative** to settling the obligation. A provision is only **recognized** if an outflow of resources is **probable**, which means that the outflow is more likely than not, or in other words, the probability of the outflow is more than 50%. If a **reliable estimate** of the amount of the obligation cannot be made, a provision must not be recognized (IAS 37.10, 37.14, 37.19, and 37.23).

2.2 Existence of a Present Obligation

Recognition of a provision requires that the entity has a present obligation that may be on a legal or constructive basis (IAS 37.14a).

A **legal obligation** is an obligation that derives from a contract (through its explicit or implicit terms), legislation or other operation of law (IAS 37.10).

---

[1] *See Section 8.1.*

[2] *See Section 2.2.*

A **constructive obligation** derives from an entity's actions where (IAS 37.10):

- the entity has indicated to other parties that it will accept certain responsibilities by an established pattern of past practice, published policies or a sufficiently specific current statement and
- as a result the entity has created a valid expectation on the part of those other parties that it will discharge those responsibilities.

2.3 Past Event

A provision only exists when the **present** (legal or constructive) **obligation** results from a **past event** (IAS 37.10, 37.14a, and 37.17). **Expected future operating losses** must not be recognized as provisions unless they result from an onerous contract (IAS 37.18 and 37.63–37.65).[3]

It is only those obligations that arise from past events which exist **independent of the entity's future actions** that are recognized as provisions. An intention or a future law does not result in an **unavoidable obligation**. For example, it may be necessary to fit smoke filters in a certain type of factory in the future or to retrain employees in order to comply with new laws so that the entity can continue its activities in the respective country in the future. In such cases, the expenditures can be avoided by the entity's future actions (e.g. by relocating production to another country or by employing new employees who already have the necessary knowledge), even if the entity does not intend to do so. Hence, no obligating event exists in such situations (IAS 37.19 and 37.C6).

Pursuant to laws, a manufacturer may become liable for **waste management costs on historical electrical and electronic household equipment** based on its share of the market during a measurement period and not as a result of the production or sale of the equipment. In this case, it is the participation of the entity in the market during the measurement period that is the obligating event and not the sale or production of the household equipment (IFRIC 6).[4]

An obligation always involves **another party** to whom it is owed. However, it is not necessary to know the identity of the party to whom the obligation is owed. Indeed, it is possible that the obligation is to the **public at large** (IAS 37.20).

Where details of a **proposed new law** have yet to be finalized, an obligation arises only when the legislation is virtually certain to be enacted as drafted. In many cases it will be impossible to be virtually certain of the enactment of a law until it is enacted (IAS 37.22).

2.4 Probability of an Outflow of Resources

Recognition of a provision requires (among others) that it is **probable** that an **outflow of resources** embodying economic benefits will be required to settle the obligation. The term "probable" has to be interpreted as a likelihood of more than 50% (*more likely than not*) (IAS 37.14b and 37.23).

In the case of a **number of similar obligations** (e.g. product warranties), the probability that an outflow will be required in settlement is determined by considering the class of obligations as a

---

[3] *See Section 8.1 with regard to onerous contracts.*

[4] *See KPMG,* Insights into IFRS, *7th edition, 3.12.90.30.*

whole. Although the likelihood of outflow for any one item may be small, it might be probable that some outflow of resources will be needed to settle the class of obligations as a whole. If this is the case and if the other recognition criteria are met, a provision is recognized (IAS 37.24).

2.5 Reliable Estimate of the Amount of the Obligation

Except in extremely rare cases, it is possible to determine the amount of the obligation reliably. Therefore, the criterion "reliable estimate" is almost always met (IAS 37.25–37.26).

2.6 Distinction from Other Liabilities

Contingent liabilities are discussed in Section 3. Provisions are distinguished from **other liabilities** (e.g. trade payables and amounts relating to accrued vacation pay) in that the uncertainty about the timing or amount of the future expenditure is generally much less in the case of other liabilities than for provisions (IAS 37.11).

3 CONTINGENT LIABILITIES

The term "contingent liability" encompasses different types of obligations (IAS 37.10):

- The first type is a **possible obligation** that arises from past events and whose existence will be confirmed only by the occurrence or non-occurrence of one or more uncertain future events not wholly within the control of the entity.
- The second type is a **present obligation** that arises from past events but is **not recognized** because:
  - it is **not probable** that an **outflow of resources** embodying economic benefits will be required to settle the obligation or
  - the amount of the obligation **cannot be determined with sufficient reliability**. Such a situation is, however, extremely rare (IAS 37.25–37.26).

A contingent liability also exists when it is not probable that the entity has a present obligation (IAS 37.16b and 37.23).

Contingent liabilities must **not be recognized in the statement of financial position**. However, disclosures relating to contingent liabilities have to be made in the **notes** unless the possibility of an outflow of resources embodying economic benefits is **remote** (IAS 37.27–37.28 and 37.86).

4 CONTINGENT ASSETS

A contingent asset represents a **possible asset** that arises from past events and whose existence will be confirmed only by the occurrence or non-occurrence of one or more uncertain future events not wholly within the control of the entity (IAS 37.10). An example of a contingent asset is a claim that an entity is pursuing through legal processes for which the outcome is uncertain (IAS 37.32).

Contingent assets **must not be recognized in the statement of financial position** (IAS 37.31). However, disclosures relating to contingent assets have to be made in the **notes** if an inflow of economic benefits is probable (IAS 37.34 and 37.89–37.90). Again, the term "probable" has to be interpreted as a likelihood of more than 50% (*more likely than not*) (IAS 37.23).

When the realization of income is **virtually certain**, the related asset **does not represent a contingent asset** and its **recognition** in the statement of financial position is appropriate (IAS 37.33).

5 MEASUREMENT

The amount recognized as a provision is the **best estimate** of the expenditure that the entity would rationally pay to settle the obligation or to transfer it to a third party at the end of the reporting period. Deliberate overstatement or understatement of provisions is prohibited (IAS 37.36–37.37 and 37.42–37.43).

IAS 37 is based on the following distinction with regard to the measurement of provisions:

- When the provision being measured involves a **large population of items**, the provision is measured at **expected value**. Expected value is **estimated** by weighting all possible outcomes by their associated probabilities. When there is a continuous range of possible outcomes and each point in that range is as likely as any other, the **mid-point of the range** is used (IAS 37.39).
- When a **single obligation** is being measured, the individual **most likely outcome** may be the best estimate of the liability. However, even in such a case, **other possible outcomes** are considered. Where other possible outcomes are either mostly lower or mostly higher than the most likely outcome, the best estimate will be a higher or lower amount (IAS 37.40).

Provisions are measured **before tax** as the tax consequences of provisions are dealt with under IAS 12 (IAS 37.41).

If the effect of the time value of money is **material**, **discounting** of the expected expenditure is necessary. The discount rate is a pre-tax rate that reflects current market assessments of the time value of money and the risks specific to the liability. The discount rate must not reflect risks for which future cash flow estimates have been adjusted (IAS 37.45–37.47). The **periodic unwinding of the discount** in subsequent periods represents a component of **interest expense** (IAS 37.60).

Future events that may affect the amount required to settle an obligation have to be reflected in the amount of the provision where there is sufficient objective evidence that they will occur. For example, it is appropriate to take expected cost reductions associated with increased experience in applying existing technology into account (IAS 37.48–37.49).

Gains from the expected **disposal of assets** must not be taken into account when measuring a provision (IAS 37.51–37.52).

6 REIMBURSEMENTS

Where some or all of the expenditure necessary to settle a provision is expected to be reimbursed by another party (e.g. by an insurance company), the **reimbursement** has to be **recognized** when it is **virtually certain** that reimbursement will be received if the entity settles the obligation. The reimbursement represents a **separate asset**. The amount recognized for the reimbursement must not exceed the amount of the provision. In the **statement of comprehensive income**, the expense relating to a provision **may be netted** against the amount recognized for the reimbursement (IAS 37.53–37.54 and IAS 1.34b).

7 CHANGES IN PROVISIONS

Provisions have to be adjusted to reflect the current best estimate at the end of each reporting period (IAS 37.59).

A change in a provision may be the result of the following:

- **Reversal** of a provision or of part of it: If it is no longer probable that an outflow of resources embodying economic benefits will be required to settle the obligation, the provision has to be reversed (IAS 37.59). Also, part of a provision may be reversed.
- Where discounting is used when measuring a provision,[5] the carrying amount of a provision **increases** in each subsequent period to reflect the passage of time (**unwinding of the discount**). This increase represents a component of **interest expense** (IAS 37.60).
- **Use** of a provision: A provision is only used for expenditures for which the provision was originally recognized (IAS 37.61–37.62).

8 SPECIFIC ISSUES

8.1 Onerous Contracts

An **onerous contract** is a contract in which the unavoidable costs of meeting the obligations under the contract exceed the economic benefits expected to be received under it. The **unavoidable costs** reflect the least net cost of exiting from the contract, which is the lower of the cost of fulfilling it and any compensation or penalties arising from failure to fulfill it. If an entity has a contract that is onerous, the present obligation under the contract has to be recognized and measured as a **provision** (IAS 37.10, 37.66, 37.68, and 37.C8).

Contracts that can be cancelled without paying compensation to the other party do not constitute an obligation. Other contracts establish both rights and obligations for each of the parties to the contract. Where events make such a contract onerous, the contract falls within the scope of IAS 37 and a liability exists which is recognized (IAS 37.67).

Before a separate provision for an onerous contract is established, the entity recognizes any **impairment loss** that has occurred on assets dedicated to that contract (IAS 37.69 and IAS 36).

8.2 Provisions for Decommissioning, Restoration, and Similar Obligations

Provisions for decommissioning, restoration, and similar obligations relating to property, plant, and equipment are dealt with in the chapter on IAS 16,[6] and those relating to investment properties are dealt with in the chapter on IAS 40.[7]

---

[5] *See Section 5.*

[6] *See the chapter on IAS 16, Sections 3 and 4.4.*

[7] *See the chapter on IAS 40, Sections 3, 4.2, and 4.3.*

8.3 Restructurings

A restructuring is a program that is planned and controlled by management and materially changes either the scope of a business undertaken by an entity or the manner in which that business is conducted (IAS 37.10). The definition of restructuring may be met in the following cases (IAS 37.70):

- The termination or sale of a line of business.
- The closure of business locations in a region or country or the relocation of business activities from one region or country to another.
- Changes in management structure (e.g. eliminating a layer of management).
- Fundamental reorganizations that have a material effect on the nature and focus of the entity's operations.

Recognition of a restructuring provision requires that the **general recognition criteria for provisions** (IAS 37.14) are met. IAS 37.72–37.83 set out how the general recognition criteria apply to restructurings (IAS 37.71).

A **constructive obligation to restructure** arises only when both of the following criteria are met (IAS 37.72):

- The entity has a **detailed formal restructuring plan** identifying at least;
  - the business or part of a business concerned,
  - the principal locations affected,
  - the function, location, and approximate number of employees who will be compensated for terminating their services,
  - the expenditures that will be undertaken, and
  - when the plan will be implemented, and
- the entity has raised a valid expectation in those affected that it will carry out the restructuring by starting to implement that plan or announcing its main features to those affected by it.

For a plan to be sufficient to give rise to a constructive obligation when communicated to those affected by it, the implementation of the plan needs to be **planned to begin as soon as possible** and to be completed **in a timeframe that makes significant changes** to the plan **unlikely**. Should it be expected that there will be a long delay before the restructuring begins or that the restructuring will take an unreasonably long time, it is unlikely that the plan will raise a valid expectation on the part of others that the entity is presently committed to restructuring because the timeframe allows opportunities for the entity to change its plans (IAS 37.74).

No obligation arises for the **sale of an operation** until the entity is committed to the sale (i.e. there is a binding sale agreement). When a sale is only part of a restructuring, a constructive obligation may arise for the other parts of the restructuring before existence of a binding sale agreement (IAS 37.78–37.79).

A restructuring provision only includes the **direct expenditures arising from the restructuring**. These are expenditures that are both (IAS 37.80):

- necessarily entailed by the restructuring, and
- not associated with the ongoing activities of the entity.

A restructuring provision does not include costs such as (IAS 37.81):

- relocating or retraining of continuing staff,
- marketing, or
- investment in new systems and distribution networks.

These expenditures relate to the future conduct of the business and do not represent liabilities for restructuring at the end of the reporting period. Such expenditures have to be recognized on the same basis as if they arose independently of a restructuring (IAS 37.81).

8.4 Decommissioning Funds

The contributor must recognize its obligation to pay decommissioning costs as a **liability** and recognize its interest in the fund separately unless the contributor is not liable to pay decommissioning costs even if the fund fails to pay (IFRIC 5.7).

The contributor must determine whether it has **control, joint control or significant influence** over the fund. For this assessment and its consequences, IAS 27, SIC 12, IAS 28, and IAS 31 are relevant (IFRIC 5.8).[8] If the contributor does not have control, joint control or significant influence over the fund, the contributor has to recognize the right to receive reimbursement from the fund as a **reimbursement** according to IAS 37. This reimbursement is measured at the lower of the following amounts (IFRIC 5.9):

- The amount of the decommissioning obligation recognized.
- The contributor's share of the fair value of the fund's net assets attributable to contributors.

In some cases, there may be **contingent liabilities** (IFRIC 5.10).

9 EXAMPLES WITH SOLUTIONS

References to other chapters

Provisions for decommissioning, restoration, and similar obligations relating to property, plant, and equipment are dealt with in the chapter on IAS 16 (Example 4). Such provisions relating to investment properties:

- Accounted for according to the **fair value model** are dealt with in the chapter on IAS 40 (Example 4).
- Accounted for according to the **cost model** are dealt with in the chapter on IAS 16 (Example 4).

Example 1

Is recognition of a provision appropriate?[9]

(a) Under new legislation, entity E is required to fit smoke filters to its factories by Sep 30, 02. However, E has not fitted the smoke filters in 01 and 02.

[8] *We refer to the corresponding chapters and sections of this book.*

[9] *This example is based on IAS 37. Appendix C.*

(b) E (which is a producer) gives warranties to purchasers of its product at the time of sale. In this way, E is required to make good manufacturing defects that become apparent within two years from the date of sale by repair or replacement. Based on past experience, it is probable (i.e. the likelihood is greater than 50%) that there will be some claims under the warranties.

(c) E offers its customers high-quality products and is therefore interested in creating and maintaining an elite brand image. Thus, among others, E pursues the policy to repair certain product defects free of charge, even if there is no obligation for E to do so under the customers' warranty claims. This accommodating policy of E is well known.

(d) The government of country C introduces a number of changes to the income tax system. As a result of these changes, a part of E's employees has to be retrained. By Dec 31, 01 no retraining has taken place. At the end of 02, a part of E's employees is retrained by a specialized entity. That entity charges an hourly rate plus a relatively small amount of other costs related to the seminars (e.g. traveling expenses of the lecturers). E receives the invoice after its financial statements are authorized for issue. Consequently, the amount of the "other costs" is not known by E when preparing its financial statements for 02.

(e) In 01, five people died possibly as a result of food poisoning from products sold by E (retailer). Hence, legal proceedings are started in 01 with E being sued for damages. E disputes its liability. For the financial statements as at Dec 31, 01, E's lawyers advise that the probability that E will be found liable is 30%. However, for the financial statements as at Dec 31, 02, E's lawyers estimate that that probability has increased to 70% (due to developments in the case).

Required

Assess whether E has to recognize a provision in its financial statements as at Dec 31, 01 and Dec 31, 02 with respect to each of the situations described above.

Hints for solution

In particular Sections 2 and 3.

Solution (a)

Smoke filters (financial statements as at Dec 31, 01): Expenditures for the fitting of smoke filters can be avoided by E's future actions (e.g. by relocating production to another country). Whether E intends to do so or not is irrelevant. Therefore, there is no past event that results in a present obligation. Consequently, no provision is recognized.

Smoke filters (financial statements as at Dec 31, 02): Regarding the expenditures for the fitting of smoke filters, there has also been no past event which results in a present obligation as at Dec 31, 02. Therefore, no provision is recognized. The reason is the same as for the financial statements as at Dec 31, 01.

Penalties: The non-compliant operation of the factories from Oct 02 until Dec 02 (i.e. without the necessary smoke filters) represents an obligating event, which gives rise to a present obligation for E as at Dec 31, 02. This means that E recognizes a provision in its financial statements as at Dec 31, 02 if it is probable (i.e. the likelihood is greater than 50%) that an outflow of resources embodying economic benefits will be required to settle the obligation and the amount of the obligation can be measured reliably. The latter condition is normally met. Since there has been no non-compliant operation of the factories in 01, E does not recognize a provision in its financial statements as at Dec 31, 01.

Solution (b)

The sale of a product with a warranty (past event) results in a legal obligation. Although an outflow of resources with respect to the sale of a single item might not be probable (i.e. the likelihood might not be more than 50%), an outflow of resources is probable (i.e. the likelihood is more than 50%) for the class of obligations as a whole. It is possible to measure the amount of the obligation reliably. Hence, E recognizes a provision.

Solution (c)

The sale of products with a warranty (past event) results in a **legal obligation**. E recognizes a provision for this obligation because an outflow of resources is probable for the class of obligations as a whole (i.e. the likelihood is more than 50%) and it is possible to measure that obligation reliably.

Furthermore, there is a **constructive obligation** for the additional free repairs for which E is not legally obliged. This is because, E has created a valid expectation on the part of its customers that it will do such repairs in the future due to the well-known practice of free repairs for which E is not legally obliged. It is probable (i.e. the likelihood is more than 50%) that some of the products have defects that will require the repairs that E conducts on a voluntary basis. Consequently, a corresponding outflow of resources is probable (IAS 37.24). It is possible to measure the amount of the obligation reliably. Therefore, a provision is recognized.

Solution (d)

In 01, no retraining has taken place. Therefore, at the end of 01 there is no past event that results in a present obligation. Instead, the expenditures can be avoided by E's future actions (e.g. by employing new employees who already have the necessary knowledge). Whether E intends to do so is not relevant. Hence, E does not recognize a provision in its financial statements as at Dec 31, 01.

However, at the end of 02, a part of E's employees was retrained by a specialized entity. Therefore, on Dec 31, 02 E is legally obliged to pay the training costs to the specialized entity. The uncertainty (amount of "other costs" like traveling expenses) relating to that obligation is very low. Hence, the liability recognized represents an accrual and not a provision (IAS 37.11).

Solution (e)

Financial statements as at Dec 31, 01: The probability that a present obligation exists is 30%, which means that it is not greater than 50%. Hence, no provision is recognized because there is no present obligation. However, there is a contingent liability that requires certain disclosures in the notes (IAS 37.15–37.16 and 37.86).

Financial statements as at Dec 31, 02: Since the probability that E will be found liable is 70% (i.e. since it is greater than 50%), E recognizes a provision (under the presumption that the amount of the obligation can be measured reliably, which is normally the case).

Example 2

Is recognition of a restructuring provision appropriate?[10]

(a) On Dec 01, 01, E's board decided to close down a division. By Dec 31, 01, the decision was not communicated to any of those affected and no other steps were taken in order to implement the decision.

(b) On Dec 01, 01, E's board decided to close down a division. On Dec 05, 01 a detailed plan for the closing of the division was agreed by E's board. On Dec 10, 01, letters were sent to customers warning them to seek an alternative source of supply and written notice was given to the staff of the division.

Required

Assess whether E has to recognize a restructuring provision in its financial statements as at Dec 31, 01.

Hints for solution

In particular Section 8.3.

Solution (a)

There is no constructive obligation. Consequently, no provision is recognized (IAS 37.10, 37.14, and 37.72).

Solution (b)

The past obligating event is the communication of the decision to the customers and employees. This results in a constructive obligation at that time because it creates a valid expectation that the division will be closed. An outflow of resources embodying economic benefits is probable. Therefore, E recognizes a provision in its financial statements as at Dec 31, 01 for the costs of closing the division (IAS 37.14 and 37.72).

Example 3

Measurement of a provision at the most likely outcome

Mr Miller sued entity E for damages in 01 because he was injured while visiting an exhibition organized by E. E estimates that the probability that it will have to pay damages of CU 100 is 60% and that the probability that it will win the case is 40%.

Required

Prepare the necessary entry (if any) in E's financial statements as at Dec 31, 01. If recognition of a provision is appropriate, assume that E does not discount the future payments, because the effect of discounting is immaterial.

[10] *This example is based on IAS 37.C5A–37.C5B.*

Hints for solution

In particular Section 5.

Solution

Since the probability that E will have to pay damages is 60% (i.e. it is greater than 50%), E recognizes a provision. The provision is measured at the most likely outcome, which is CU 100.

Dec 31, 01	Dr	Expense	100	
	Cr	Provision		100

Example 4

Measurement of a provision at expected value

Entity E started the sale of a new product in Feb 01. In 01, E sold 1,000 units of that product with a warranty under which E has to repair defective products free of charge if the defect becomes apparent within the first 12 months after purchase. E expects that of the products sold in 01, 10% will have minor defects (repair costs: CU 1 per unit) and 5% will have major defects (repair costs: CU 5 per unit). For the remaining 85% of the products sold, no defects are expected.

Required

Prepare the necessary entry (if any) in E's financial statements as at Dec 31, 01. If recognition of a provision is appropriate, assume that E does not discount the future payments, because the effect of discounting is immaterial.

Hints for solution

In particular Section 5.

Solution

E has to recognize a provision (see Example 1(b) for the rationale). Since the provision being measured involves a large population of items, it is measured at expected value. Consequently, all possible outcomes are weighted by their associated probabilities. This results in a provision in the amount of CU 350:

	In %	*In units*	*Repair costs per unit*	*Repair costs total*
No defect	85%	850	0	0
Minor defects	10%	100	1	100
Major defects	5%	50	5	250
Total	**100%**	**1,000**		**350**

Dec 31,01	Dr	Expense	350	
	Cr	Provision		350

IAS 38 INTANGIBLE ASSETS

1 SCOPE OF IAS 38

IAS 38 prescribes the accounting treatment for intangible assets. Intangible assets subject to the scope of another standard are **excluded from the scope** of IAS 38, e.g. (IAS 38.2–8.3):

- Intangible assets that are held by an entity for sale in the ordinary course of business (IAS 2 and IAS 11).
- Intangible assets subject to leases within the scope of IAS 17.
- Goodwill acquired in a business combination (IFRS 3).
- Non-current intangible assets classified as "held for sale" in accordance with IFRS 5.

In determining whether an asset that **incorporates both intangible and tangible elements** should be treated as property, plant, and equipment according to IAS 16 or as an intangible asset according to IAS 38, it is necessary to assess which element is more significant. For example, **software** for a computer-controlled machine tool that cannot operate without that specific software is considered an integral part of the related machine. The software is treated as part of the machine tool (i.e. as property, plant, and equipment) if the physical and not the intangible component is more significant. By contrast, when a physical and an intangible asset do not constitute an integral unit (e.g. application software for a computer) they are treated as two different assets (IAS 38.4).

Rights under licensing agreements for items such as motion picture films, video recordings, plays, manuscripts, patents, and copyrights are excluded from the scope of IAS 17 and are included within the scope of IAS 38 (IAS 38.6 and IAS 17.2).

2 THE TERM "INTANGIBLE ASSET"

An **asset** is a resource controlled by the entity as a result of past events and from which future economic benefits are expected to flow to the entity (IAS 38.8 and F49a). An **intangible asset** is an identifiable non-monetary asset of the entity without physical substance. **Monetary assets** comprise money held and assets to be received in fixed or determinable amounts of money (IAS 38.8).

In practice, a large number of intangible *items* exists (e.g. software, patents, and customer loyalty). However, not all of them are intangible *assets*. According to the definitions above, an intangible item meets the definition of an intangible asset only if all of the following three criteria are met (IAS 38.8–38.17):

- **Future economic benefits**: It is expected that future economic benefits will flow to the entity from the item (IAS 38.8). The future economic benefits may include revenue from the sale of products or services or other benefits (e.g. cost savings) resulting from the use of the item by the entity (IAS 38.17).

- **Control**: This criterion is met if the entity has the power to obtain the future economic benefits flowing from the underlying item and to restrict the access of others to these benefits. Normally, control stems from legally enforceable rights, although such rights are not always a prerequisite (IAS 38.13–38.16).
- **Identifiability**: This criterion, which refers to the discriminability from goodwill, is – along the lines of IFRS 3 (IFRS 3.Appendix A) – met if one of the following conditions is met (IAS 38.11–38.12):
  - The item is separable, i.e. it is capable of being separated or divided from the entity and sold, transferred, licensed, rented or exchanged either individually or together with a related contract, identifiable asset or liability, regardless of whether the entity intends to do so (**criterion "separability"**).
  - The item arises from contractual or other legal rights regardless of whether those rights are transferable or separable from the entity or from other rights and obligations (**contractual-legal criterion**).

3 RECOGNITION AND INITIAL MEASUREMENT

3.1 Introduction

The question of whether an intangible item is **recognized as an intangible asset in the statement of financial position** is answered in two steps (IAS 38.18):

1. The item must meet the **definition of an intangible asset**, i.e. it must meet the criteria described in Section 2 (IAS 38.8–38.17).
2. If the item has met the definition of an intangible asset, the intangible asset must additionally meet the **recognition criteria**, i.e. the inflow of future economic benefits has to be probable and it must be possible to measure the cost of the intangible asset reliably (IAS 38.21–38.23).

This procedure not only applies to the costs incurred initially to acquire or internally generate an intangible item, but also to those incurred subsequently to add to, replace part of, or service an intangible asset (IAS 38.18). However, in practice most subsequent expenditures for intangible assets will not meet the criteria for recognition in the statement of financial position (IAS 38.20).

An intangible asset is **measured initially at cost** (IAS 38.24).

3.2 Separate Acquisition of Intangible Assets

For separately acquired intangible assets, it is always presumed that the probability recognition criteria (IAS 38.21a) are met (IAS 38.25). Moreover, the cost of a separately acquired intangible asset can usually be measured reliably (IAS 38.26). The costs also include any directly attributable cost of preparing the asset for its intended use (IAS 38.27–38.32).

3.3 Acquisition of Intangible Assets as Part of a Business Combination

IAS 38.33–38.43 contain rules with respect to the acquisition of intangible assets as part of a business combination in addition to IFRS 3. These rules are in line with those of IFRS 3.[1]

---

[1] *See the chapter on IFRS 3, Section 6.2.*

3.4 Internally Generated Intangible Assets

In addition to the general requirements for the recognition and initial measurement of an intangible item, IAS 38 contains further requirements and guidance for internally generated intangible items (IAS 38.51).

First it is necessary to distinguish between research and development (IAS 38.8):

- **Research** is the original and planned investigation undertaken with the prospect of gaining new scientific or technical knowledge and understanding.
- **Development** is the application of research findings or other knowledge to a plan or design for the production of new or substantially improved materials, devices, processes, products, systems or services before the start of commercial production or use.

The following are examples of research activities (IAS 38.56):

- Activities aimed at obtaining new knowledge.
- The search for alternatives for materials, devices, processes, products, systems or services.

The following are examples of development activities (IAS 38.59):

- The design, construction, and testing of pre-use or pre-production prototypes and models.
- The design of tools and dies involving new technology.
- The design, construction, and operation of a pilot plant that is not of a scale economically feasible for commercial production.

The internal generation of intangible assets is divided into two phases (IAS 38.8 and 38.52):

- Research phase
- Development phase

Although the terms "research" and "development" are defined in the standard, the terms "research phase" and "development phase" have a **broader meaning** (IAS 38.52). They are not restricted to the generation of new technology. Instead, these terms are used in a broader context, whereby the research phase is the early, conceptual phase of the generation of an intangible asset, and the development phase is the advanced phase, near to realization. Consequently, even the creation of a **website** consists of a research phase and a development phase (SIC 32) as well as the generation of **human capital** (e.g. competitive athletes and artists).

Sometimes an entity **cannot distinguish** between the research phase and the development phase of an internal project to create an intangible asset. In this case, the **expenditure** on that project is **treated as if it were only incurred in the research phase** (IAS 38.53).

Expenditure on **research** (or on the **research phase** of an internal project) is recognized as an **expense** when it is incurred (IAS 38.54).

An intangible asset arising from **development** (or from the development phase of an internal project) is **recognized in the statement of financial position**, if the entity can **demonstrate** all of the following (IAS 38.57):

- The **technical feasibility** of completing the asset so that it will be available for sale or use.
- Its **intention** to complete the asset and sell or use it.
- Its **ability** to sell or use the asset.
- How the asset will generate probable future **economic benefits**. Among others, the entity must be able to demonstrate the existence of a market for the output of the asset or the asset itself or, if it is to be used internally, the usefulness of the asset. The economic benefits are assessed according to the principles in IAS 36. If the intangible asset will generate economic benefits only in combination with other assets, the entity applies the concept of cash-generating units in IAS 36 (IAS 38.60).
- The **availability** of adequate technical, financial, and other resources to complete the development and to use or sell the asset (demonstrated for example by a business plan or a lender's indication of willingness to fund the plan – IAS 38.61).
- Its ability to **reliably measure** the expenditure attributable to the asset during its development.

The capitalization of development costs, i.e. the interpretation and application of the criteria above, is an area in which **discretion** is exercised. How the discretion is exercised depends on the profit situation of the entity and of the industry in which it operates. Huge differences in interpreting the criteria can be observed internationally between the pharmaceutical industry and the automotive industry.

An intangible asset is **measured initially at cost** (IAS 38.24). For this purpose, cost is the sum of expenditure incurred from the date when the intangible asset first meets the recognition criteria in IAS 38.21–38.22 and 38.57 (see above). The standard **prohibits capitalization of expenditure initially recognized as an expense** (IAS 38.65 and 38.71).

The cost of an internally generated intangible asset comprises all directly attributable costs that are necessary to create, produce, and prepare the asset to be capable of operating in the manner intended by management (IAS 38.66).

Goodwill resulting from a business combination has to be recognized in the consolidated statement of financial position.[2] However, **internally generated goodwill** must not be recognized in the statement of financial position. Internally generated goodwill results from expenditures incurred to generate future economic benefits that do not result in the creation of an intangible asset that meets the recognition criteria of IAS 38 (IAS 38.48–38.50).

Irrespective of the criteria described in this chapter, **recognition** of the following internally generated items as intangible assets in the statement of financial position is always **prohibited** (IAS 38.63–38.64):

- Brands
- Mastheads

---

[2] *See the chapter on IFRS 3, Sections 6.1 and 6.4.*

- Publishing titles
- Customer lists
- Items similar in substance

Criteria for the recognition of **borrowing costs** as an element of the cost of an internally generated intangible asset are specified in IAS 23 (IAS 38.66).

4 FURTHER PROHIBITIONS OF CAPITALIZATION

Further examples of expenditure that is recognized as an expense when it is incurred include (IAS 38.69):

- Expenditure on start-up activities (i.e. **start-up costs**), unless this expenditure is included in the cost of property, plant, and equipment (IAS 16). Start-up costs may consist of:
  - establishment costs such as secretarial and legal costs incurred in establishing a legal entity,
  - expenditure to open a new facility or business (i.e. pre-opening costs), or
  - expenditures for starting new operations or launching new products or processes (i.e. pre-operating costs).
- Expenditure on training activities.
- Expenditure on advertising and promotional activities.
- Expenditure on relocating or reorganizing all or part of an entity.

Expenditure on an intangible item that was **initially recognized as an expense must not be capitalized** (i.e. must not be recognized as part of the cost of an intangible asset) **at a later date** (IAS 38.71).

5 MEASUREMENT AFTER RECOGNITION

5.1 Cost Model and Revaluation Model

After recognition, intangible assets are measured either according to the cost model or according to the revaluation model (IAS 38.72).

If an intangible asset is accounted for using the **cost model**, it is measured at its cost less any accumulated amortization and less accumulated impairment losses (IAS 38.74).

The main features of the **revaluation model** for intangible assets (IAS 38.75–38.87) are generally consistent with those of property, plant, and equipment (IAS 16.31–16.42).[3]

In contrast to IAS 16 for the purpose of revaluations according to IAS 38, **fair value** has to be determined by reference to an **active market** (IAS 38.75). An active market is a market that meets all the following criteria (IAS 38.8):

- The items traded in the market are homogeneous.
- Willing sellers and buyers can normally be found at any time.
- Prices are available to the public.

[3] *See the chapter on IAS 16, Section 4.1.*

It is uncommon for an active market to exist for an intangible asset, although this may happen. For example, in some countries, an active market may exist for freely transferable taxi licenses, fishing licenses or production quotas. However, an active market cannot exist for brands, music and film publishing rights, newspaper mastheads, patents or trademarks because each of such intangible assets is unique (IAS 38.78).

If the revaluation model is applied to an intangible asset, all the other assets in its class also have to be accounted for according to the revaluation model, unless there is no active market for those assets. However, it is possible to apply the revaluation model to a particular class of intangible assets while other classes are accounted for using the cost model (IAS 38.72 and 38.81). A class is a grouping of intangible assets of a similar nature and use in an entity's operations (IAS 38.73 and 38.119).

In many countries, revaluations of intangible assets are rare or do not occur at all.[4]

5.2 Intangible Assets With Finite Useful Lives

Intangible assets with finite useful lives[5] are **amortized** (IAS 38.89). In determining the useful life of an intangible asset, many factors are considered and the entity exercises discretion (IAS 38.90). Software and many other intangible assets are susceptible to technological obsolescence. Thus, it is likely that their useful lives are short. Uncertainty justifies estimating useful lives on a prudent basis, but does not justify choosing useful lives that are unrealistically short (IAS 38.92–38.93).

The useful life of an intangible asset that arises from **contractual or other legal rights** must not exceed the period of these rights, but may be shorter depending on the period over which the entity expects to use the asset. If these rights are conveyed for a limited term that can be renewed, the useful life includes the renewal period(s) only if there is evidence to support renewal by the entity without significant cost. The useful life of a **reacquired right** recognized as an intangible asset in a business combination is the remaining contractual period of the contract in which the right was granted and does not include renewal periods (IAS 38.94–38.96, IFRS 3.55, and 3.B35).

The **depreciable amount** (i.e. the cost or other amount substituted for cost less residual value – IAS 38.8) of an intangible asset with a finite useful life is allocated on a systematic basis over its useful life (IAS 38.97). In the case of an intangible asset with a finite useful life, **residual value is normally zero** (IAS 38.100–38.101).

Amortization of an intangible asset **begins** when it is available for use, i.e. when the asset is in the location and condition necessary for it to be capable of operating in the manner intended by management (IAS 38.97).

---

[4] *See Christensen/Nikolaev, Does fair value accounting for non-financial assets pass the market test?, working paper no. 09-12; ICAEW, EU implementation of IFRS and the fair value directive, a report for the European Commission, 2007, p. 122–123; and KPMG/von Keitz,* The Application of IFRS: Choices in Practice, *2006, p. 11.*

[5] *See Section 5.3 with regard to the distinction from an indefinite useful life.*

Amortization of an intangible asset **ceases** at the earlier of the following dates (IAS 38.97):

- Date at which the asset is classified as "**held for sale**" (or included in a disposal group that is classified as "held for sale") according to **IFRS 5**.
- Date at which the asset is **derecognized**.

The **amortization method** used has to reflect the pattern in which the future economic benefits of the intangible asset are expected to be consumed by the entity. The amortization method is applied consistently from period to period, unless there is a change in the expected pattern. If the pattern cannot be determined reliably, the straight-line method has to be applied (IAS 38.97–38.98).

Amortization is recognized in **profit or loss** unless IAS 38 or another Standard permits or requires it to be included in the carrying amount of another asset (IAS 38.97 and 38.99).

At least at the end of each financial year, the amortization period and the amortization method for an intangible asset with a finite useful life have to be **reviewed**. If the expected useful life is different from previous estimates, the amortization period has to be changed accordingly. If there has been a change in the expected pattern of consumption of the future economic benefits embodied in the intangible asset, the amortization method has to be changed to reflect the changed pattern. These changes are treated as changes in accounting estimates according to IAS 8 (IAS 38.104–38.106).

5.3 Intangible Assets With Indefinite Useful Lives

The useful life of an intangible asset is indefinite when there is no foreseeable limit to the period over which the asset is expected to generate net cash inflows for the entity (IAS 38.88). The term "indefinite" does not mean "infinite" (IAS 38.91).

Rights which are obtained only for a limited term but can be renewed at a low cost may have an indefinite life. A typical example is a brand protected by law only for 10 years but with an option to renew the protection several times for another 10 years without significant cost.

An intangible asset with an indefinite useful life is **not amortized** (IAS 38.89 and 38.107). However, it is necessary to test such an asset for **impairment** by comparing its recoverable amount with its carrying amount annually, i.e. even if there is no indication of impairment. The same applies to intangible assets **not yet available for use** (IAS 38.108 and IAS 36.9–36.10).

In the case of an intangible asset that is not being amortized, its useful life has to be **reviewed** each period to determine whether it is still appropriate to assume that the useful life of the asset is indefinite. Reassessing the useful life as finite rather than indefinite is an indicator of impairment. Therefore, the asset is tested for impairment by comparing its recoverable amount with its carrying amount (IAS 38.109–38.110).

5.4 Impairment

The issue of impairment is dealt with in the chapter on IAS 36 in this book (IAS 38.111).

6 DERECOGNITION

An intangible asset is derecognized on **disposal** (e.g. by sale or by entering into a finance lease) or when **no future economic benefits** are expected from its use or disposal. The **gain or loss** arising from derecognition (i.e. the difference between the net disposal proceeds, if any, and the carrying amount of the asset) is recognized in profit or loss when the asset is derecognized (unless IAS 17 requires otherwise on a sale and leaseback[6]). Gains must not be classified as revenue (IAS 38.112–38.114).

According to the recognition principle (IAS 38.21)[7] if an entity recognizes the **cost of a replacement for part of an intangible asset** in the carrying amount of the asset, then it derecognizes the carrying amount of the replaced part (IAS 38.115).

7 EXAMPLES WITH SOLUTIONS

Reference to another chapter

With regard to the **revaluation model**, we refer to the chapter on IAS 16 (Examples 6 and 7).

Example 1

Scope of IAS 38

Case (a): Entity E acquired a computer-controlled machine for production purposes together with software. Without the software the machine would not be able to operate. The tangible element (i.e. the machine) is more significant than the intangible element (i.e. the software).

Case (b): E has produced a new computer game. E sells this game to its customers in the ordinary course of business.

Case (c): E created a software program that is used by E's employees for handling E's accounting.

Required

Assess which standard has to be applied by E to the items described above.

Hints for solution

In particular Section 1.

Solution

Case (a): The software is an integral part of the machine because the machine would not be able to operate without the software. Since the tangible element is more significant than the intangible element, the machine (including the software) is treated as property, plant, and equipment according to IAS 16 (IAS 38.4).

---

6 *See the chapter on IAS 17, Section 6.*

7 *See Section 3.1.*

Case (b): The computer game is held for sale in the ordinary course of business. Consequently IAS 2 is applicable instead of IAS 38 (IAS 38.3a and IAS 2.6).

Case (c): The software is not excluded from the scope of IAS 38. Therefore the rules of IAS 38 for internally generated intangible assets are applied in order to determine which costs have to be capitalized.

Example 2

Is capitalization of the following expenses appropriate?

In 01 entity E incurred the following expenses:

- Implementation of an advertising campaign
- Testing of a preproduction prototype
- Internal generation of a brand
- Search for alternatives for a production process

Required

Assess if these expenses have to be capitalized.

Hints for solution

In particular Sections 3.4 and 4.

Solution

Implementation of an advertising campaign	These costs are not capitalized, because IAS 38 prohibits the capitalization of expenditure on advertising and promotional activities (IAS 38.69c).
Testing of a pre-production prototype	These activities are development activities (IAS 38.59a). The expenses are capitalized as part of the cost of the internally generated asset (IAS 38.24 and 38.65–38.67) if the entity can demonstrate that all of the criteria in IAS 38.57 are met.
Internal generation of a brand	IAS 38.63–38.64 prohibit the recognition of internally generated brands as intangible assets.
Search for alternatives for a production process	These activities are research activities (IAS 38.56c). Consequently, the expenditures are not capitalized (IAS 38.54–38.55).

Example 3

Human capital

Entity E, which produces musicals, discovers an exceptionally talented promising singer. E engages her for six years and gives her lessons in singing and acting, free of charge.

Required

Assess the treatment of the singer according to IAS 38.

Hints for solution

In particular Section 3.4.

Solution

Although the terms "research" and "development" are defined in the standard, the terms "research phase" and "development phase" have a **broader meaning** (IAS 38.52). They are not restricted to the generation of new technology. Instead, these terms are used in a broader context, whereby the research phase is the early, conceptual phase of the generation of an intangible asset and the development phase is the advanced phase, near to realization.

With regard to the promising singer, capitalization of costs starts as soon as the recognition criteria in IAS 38.57 for development costs are met.

Example 4

Research and development costs – pharmaceutical industry

Entity E operates in the pharmaceutical industry. From Jan 01, 01 until May 31, 01, research costs (within the meaning of IAS 38) of CU 15 are incurred for a new research project.

On the basis of the research results, E starts the development (within the meaning of IAS 38) of a new medicine on Jun 01, 01. On Nov 30, 01, E receives market approval for the new medicine. E regards the recognition criteria for development costs (IAS 38.57) as being fulfilled on this date, but not earlier. However, the development phase ends on this date. On Dec 01, 01, commercial production of the medicine begins. From Jun 01, 01 until Nov 30, 01, development costs of CU 27 were incurred. This amount does not include the following costs because E was not sure how to treat them:

	Jun 01, 01 until Nov 30, 01	*Dec, 01*
Administrative costs for the project management	3	
Allocation of general administrative costs of E to the project	3	
Costs of an advertising campaign for the new medicine		7

Posting status:
All of the expenditure mentioned above was recognized as an expense in 01.

Required

Assess which costs have to be capitalized in E's financial statements as at Dec 31, 01.

Hints for solution

In particular Sections 3.4 and 4.

Solution

The research costs of CU 15 were not capitalized, which is correct (IAS 38.54). The development costs of CU 30 (CU 27 + the administrative costs for the project management of CU 3) are not capitalized because the criteria in IAS 38.57 are met on Nov 30, 01 (i.e. at the end of the development phase) and it is prohibited to capitalize expenditure previously recognized as expense (IAS 38.71). It is also prohibited to capitalize the general administrative costs of E of CU 3 allocated to the project and the costs of the advertising campaign of CU 7 (IAS 38.67a and 38.69c).

Example 5

Research and development costs – software

Programmers of entity E have created new software in 01, which will be used by E for administrative purposes. During the generation of the software there were creative phases of generating new ideas, as well as phases of programming these ideas. There were a large number of such phases that alternated permanently (i.e. generating ideas was followed by programming and programming was followed by a new phase of generating ideas and so on). In 01 research and development costs for the software were CU 20. Due to the characteristics of the process of generating the software described above, it was not possible to separate the research phase from the development phase.

Posting status:
The expenditures of CU 20 were recognized in profit or loss in 01.

Required

Assess how the generation of the software has to be accounted for in E's financial statements as at Dec 31, 01, according to IAS 38.

Hints for solution

In particular Section 3.4.

Solution

E cannot distinguish the research phase from the development phase. This is because there were a large number of research and development phases that alternated permanently (i.e. generating ideas was followed by programming and programming was followed by a new phase of generating ideas and so on). There was not a process that started with the research phase followed by the development phase once the whole research phase was completed.

Therefore, the expenditures of CU 20 are treated as if they were incurred in the research phase in total (IAS 38.53), i.e. they must not be capitalized (IAS 38.54). Consequently, there is no further entry in this example.

Example 6

TV rights

On Nov 10, 01, entity E acquires the TV rights for the coming soccer world championship that will take place in 02 for CU 10. Advertising income associated with the tournament begins to flow in, during Feb, 01. The soccer world championship starts on Jun 01, 02 and ends on Jun 30, 02.

Required

Describe how the TV rights are treated in E's financial statements as at Dec 31 for the years 01 and 02 and prepare any necessary entries.

Hints for solution

In particular Section 5.2.

Solution

The TV rights represent current intangible assets (provided that the acquisition of the TV rights is not regarded as a prepayment). They are treated according to IAS 38, which is not restricted to non-current intangible assets.

Nov 10, 01	Dr	TV rights	10	
	Cr	Cash		10

Although advertising income associated with the soccer world championship begins to flow in before the tournament, the TV rights are amortized over the period of time in which the tournament takes place. This procedure is justified by the fact that the main part of the income arises during the tournament.

The TV rights are not yet amortized in the financial statements as at Dec 31, 01. However, an intangible asset not yet available for use has to be tested for impairment annually by comparing its carrying amount with its recoverable amount (irrespective of whether there is any indication of impairment). Since the TV rights were initially recognized in 01, they have to be tested for impairment before the end of 01 (IAS 36.10a). In this example it is assumed that the recoverable amount of the TV rights is not below their carrying amount.

During the soccer world championship (June 02), the TV rights are amortized (see above):

June 02	Dr	Amortization expense	10	
	Cr	TV rights		10

Example 7

Customer relationships

Entity E acquires 100% of the shares of entity F. F owns a radio station. F negotiates airtimes directly with advertisers, which are mostly large entities. The advertising contracts are renegotiated every six months. F presumes that the relationships with the advertisers (customer relationships) are long term, and that their length can be estimated approximately.

E recognizes the customer relationships of F in its consolidated statement of financial position.

Required

Describe the measurement after recognition of the customer relationships recognized in E's consolidated statement of financial position.

Hints for solution

In particular Sections 5.2 and 5.3.

Solution

According to IAS 38, the useful life of an intangible asset is indefinite when there is no foreseeable limit to the period over which the asset is expected to generate net cash inflows for the entity (IAS 38.88). The term "indefinite" does not mean "infinite" (IAS 38.91).

Given the definition of the term "indefinite," it is unlikely that customer relationships have indefinite useful lives. The reason for this is that the customers may be lost to another entity or that the corporate strategy may change.[8]

In this example, the customer relationships do not have indefinite useful lives. Consequently, amortization has to be calculated. In determining the useful lives, E exercises discretion (IAS 38.89–38.93).

[8] *See PwC,* IFRS Manual of Accounting 2008, *15.208.*

IAS 39 FINANCIAL INSTRUMENTS: RECOGNITION AND MEASUREMENT

See the chapter on IFRS 9/IAS 39

IAS 40 INVESTMENT PROPERTY

1 THE CONCEPT OF "INVESTMENT PROPERTY"

Investment property is property (i.e. land or a building – or part of a building – or both) held (by its owner or by the lessee under a finance lease) to earn rentals or for capital appreciation or both (IAS 40.5).

Properties held for sale in the ordinary course of business are **inventories** and not investment property (IAS 40.5 and IAS 2.6). The business model of an entity (i.e. the entity's intentions regarding that property) is the primary criterion for classifying a property as inventory or as investment property.[1]

Investment property also has to be distinguished from **owner-occupied property**. Owner-occupied property is held (by the owner or by the lessee under a finance lease) for use in the production or supply of goods or services or for administrative purposes. If owner-occupied property is expected to be used during more than one period, it meets the definition of property, plant, and equipment (IAS 40.5 and IAS 16.6).

Property being **constructed or developed on behalf of third parties** does not represent investment property. Instead, revenue is recognized according to IAS 11 if the buyer is able to specify the major structural elements of the design of the real estate, and otherwise according to IAS 18 (IAS 40.9b, IAS 11.3, and IFRIC 15).

A building owned by the entity or held by the entity under a finance lease and **leased out** under one or more **operating leases** is an example of investment property (IAS 40.8c). However, if the building is **leased out under a finance lease** it is not investment property because, in this case, the building is no longer recognized in the lessor's statement of financial position (IAS 40.9e).

Property that is being **constructed or developed for future use as investment property** represents investment property (IAS 40.8e).

In the case of **dual-use property**, part of the property is owner-occupied property and the other part is used as an investment property. If these parts could be sold separately (or leased out separately under a finance lease) they are accounted for separately. Otherwise, the entire property represents investment property only if an insignificant portion is owner-occupied (IAS 40.10).

An entity may provide **ancillary services** to the occupants of a property it holds. Such a property is treated as investment property if the services are insignificant to the arrangement as a whole (IAS 40.11–40.13).

---

[1] *See also KPMG,* Insights into IFRS, *6th edition, 3.4.60.30.*

In certain cases an entity owns property that is leased to, and occupied by, its **parent** or another **subsidiary**. In the individual financial statements of the lessor the property is investment property if the criteria for investment property are met. However, the property does not qualify as investment property in the consolidated financial statements since it is owner-occupied from the group perspective (IAS 40.15).

2 RECOGNITION

The recognition criteria for the initial and subsequent cost of investment property correspond with the criteria for property, plant, and equipment in IAS 16.[2]

3 MEASUREMENT AT RECOGNITION

An investment property is initially measured **at its cost**. The cost of a **purchased investment property** includes its purchase price and any directly attributable expenditure (IAS 40.20–40.21).

Similar to IAS 16, the costs of purchase of investment property also include the **initial estimate of the costs of dismantling and removing the item and restoring the site** on which it is located, the obligation for which the entity incurs when the item is acquired (IAS 16.16c, 16.18, and 16.BC15). These costs are normally included on the basis of their **present value** (IAS 16.18 and IAS 37.45).

The costs of purchase of a **property leased under a finance lease** which is an investment property are recognized as an asset at the lower of the following amounts (IAS 40.25 and IAS 17.20):

- Fair value of the property.
- Present value of the minimum lease payments.

4 MEASUREMENT AFTER RECOGNITION

4.1 Introduction

An entity has to choose either the **fair value model**[3] or the **cost model**[4] as its accounting policy and the entity generally has to apply that policy to all of its investment property (IAS 40.30 and IAS 40.32A–40.32C).

The standard states that it is highly unlikely that a **change** from the fair value model to the cost model will result in the financial statements providing more relevant information (IAS 40.31). Therefore, normally, it is not possible to change from the fair value model to the cost model. However, a change from the cost model to the fair value model is generally possible.

---

[2] *See the chapter on IAS 16, Section 2.*

[3] *See Section 4.2.*

[4] *See Section 4.3.*

4.2 Fair Value Model

An entity that chooses the fair value model generally has to measure all of its investment property at **fair value** after initial recognition (IAS 40.32A, 40.33, and 40.53–40.55). Fair value is the amount for which an asset could be exchanged between knowledgeable, willing parties in an arm's length transaction (IAS 40.5).

A gain or loss arising from a change in fair value is recognized in **profit or loss** (IAS 40.35). According to the fair value model **no depreciation** is recognized.

The procedure just described **distinguishes** the **fair value model** as set out in IAS 40 from the **revaluation model** according to IAS 16 (property, plant, and equipment)[5] and IAS 38 (intangible assets).[6] That is to say, according to the revaluation model, fair value changes are recognized in other comprehensive income in some situations and in profit or loss in other situations. Moreover, depreciation or amortization is generally recognized according to the revaluation model.

Fair value of an investment property is the amount for which a property could be exchanged between knowledgeable, willing parties in an arm's length transaction (IAS 40.5). Fair value is determined without any deduction for transaction costs the entity may incur on sale or other disposal (IAS 40.37).

The standard contains a **hierarchy for the methods to determine fair value** of an investment property.

(a) The best evidence of fair value is given by **current prices in an active market** for similar property in the same condition and location and subject to similar lease and other contracts (IAS 40.45). The term "active market" is not defined in IAS 40. Hence, in our opinion, it is appropriate to use the definition in IAS 36.6 for the term "active market:" "An active market is a market in which all of the following conditions exist:
   - the items traded within the market are homogeneous;
   - willing buyers and sellers can normally be found at any time; and
   - prices are available to the public."

(b) In many cases there is no active market. Consequently, the determination of the fair value of an investment property described in (a) is often not possible. In these situations, **alternative methods** to determine fair value have to be applied, which include **discounting** future **cash flows** (IAS 40.46).

It is recommended but not required to determine fair value on the basis of the valuation by an **independent appraiser** (IAS 40.32).

If an entity that applies the fair value model has previously measured an investment property at fair value, it has to continue to measure this property at fair value until disposal (or until the property becomes owner-occupied property or the entity begins to develop the property for subsequent sale as inventory) (IAS 40.55).

---

[5] *See the chapter on IAS 16, Section 4.1.*

[6] *See the chapter on IAS 38, Section 5.1.*

When the fair value model is applied, **investment property under construction** is also measured at fair value unless its fair value cannot be determined reliably. In the latter case, investment property under construction is measured at cost according to the cost model of IAS 16 (IAS 40.8e and 40.53).

The entity's statement of financial position may include a **decommissioning, restoration, or similar provision** for a particular investment property. If the amount of the provision were deducted from the fair value of the investment property, the obligation would be taken into account twice in the statement of financial position. Consequently, the obligation must not be taken into account, when determining fair value of the investment property. **Changes** in such provisions are treated in the following way when applying the fair value model:

- The periodic unwinding of the discount is recognized in profit or loss as a finance cost.
- If the change in measurement is due to a change in the discount rate, it is recognized as a finance expense or as finance income. If the change of the provision is due to a change in the estimated timing or amount of the outflow of resources, it is presented in the line item other operating expenses or other operating income.

4.3 Cost Model

If the entity measures its investment properties after recognition according to the **cost model**, the rules of **IAS 16** apply (IAS 40.56) and consequently also the rules of **IAS 36** for **impairment testing** (IAS 16.63). However, investment properties that are classified as **held for sale** (or are included in a disposal group that is classified as held for sale) in accordance with **IFRS 5** have to be measured according to that standard (IAS 40.56).

Changes in existing decommissioning, restoration, and similar liabilities in respect of an investment property measured according to the cost model are treated in the same way as in the case of property, plant, and equipment measured according to the cost model.[7]

According to the **cost model** it is necessary to determine **fair values** in order to comply with the **disclosure requirements** of IAS 40. If it is not possible to determine fair values reliably, other disclosures are required (IAS 40.32, 40.53, and 40.79e).

5 DERECOGNITION

An investment property has to be derecognized on disposal. Disposal may be achieved through sale or by entering into a finance lease. An investment property is also derecognized when the investment property is permanently withdrawn from use and no future economic benefits are expected from its disposal (IAS 40.66–40.67). The difference between the net disposal proceeds and the carrying amount of the asset is recognized in profit or loss unless IAS 17 requires otherwise on a sale and leaseback[8] (IAS 40.69).

---

[7] *See the chapter on IAS 16, Section 4.4.*

[8] *See the chapter on IAS 17, Section 6.*

6 PRESENTATION

Gains and losses on disposal are presented on a net basis in the statement of comprehensive income, which means that the net disposal proceeds and the carrying amount of the asset are offset (IAS 1.34a and IAS 40.69).

When the fair value model is applied, gains from fair value adjustments (**fair value gains**) are not offset with **fair value losses** in the statement of comprehensive income if these gains and losses are material. In a similar way, **gains on disposal** are not offset with **losses on disposal** (IAS 1.35).

7 EXAMPLES WITH SOLUTIONS

References to Other Chapters

Examples relating to the **cost model** and to **impairment when the cost model is applied** are illustrated in the chapters on IAS 16 and IAS 36. Regarding the accounting treatment of **decommissioning, restoration, and similar liabilities under the cost model**, we refer to the chapter on IAS 16 (Sections 3 and 4.4, as well as Example 4).

Example 1

Classification of property

Case (a): Entity E acquires a building ground. However, the future use has not yet been determined. The acquisition took place because of the low purchase price.

Case (b): According to E's business model, properties are acquired and sold within E's normal operating cycle.

Case (c): E owns an office building. E leases out the office building under operating leases. E is obliged to provide maintenance and security services to the lessees who occupy the building.

Case (d): E owns and manages a hotel.

Case (e): At the moment, E is constructing a building on behalf of entity F. The building will be delivered to F on completion of construction. F is able to specify the major structural elements of the design of the building.

Case (f): At the moment, E is constructing a building. After completion of construction, it is planned to lease out the building under an operating lease for some time. Moreover, it is planned to hold the building for long-term capital appreciation.

Case (g): E leases land to entity F under a finance lease.

Case (h): E owns 100% of the shares of entity S. E leases out a building to S under an operating lease. This building is used solely for administrative purposes, by S.

Required

Determine which IFRSs apply to E's property.

Hints for solution

In particular Section 1.

Solution

Case (a): Since the future use of the building ground has not yet been determined it represents investment property (IAS 40.8b), which means that IAS 40 is applied.

Case (b): Since properties are acquired and sold within E's normal operating cycle pursuant to E's business model, they are treated as inventories. Consequently, IAS 2 applies. The reason is that the business model of an entity, i.e. the entity's intentions regarding a property, is the primary criterion for classifying the property as inventory or as investment property.[9]

Case (c): The operating lease of the office building does not result in derecognition of the building, i.e. it continues to be recognized in E's (i.e. in the lessor's) statement of financial position. Maintenance and security services provided to the lessees of a building are not significant. Thus, the office building is an investment property (IAS 40.8c and 40.11), which means that IAS 40 is applied.

Case (d): In the case of a hotel, the services provided to guests are significant. Therefore, the owner-managed hotel represents owner-occupied property rather than investment property (IAS 40.12). If the hotel (owner-occupied property) is expected to be used during more than one period it meets the definition of property, plant, and equipment (IAS 40.5 and IAS 16.6). In this case IAS 16 applies.

Case (e): Property being constructed or developed on behalf of third parties is not investment property. Since F is able to specify the major structural elements of the design of the building, revenue is recognized according to IAS 11 (IAS 40.9b, IAS 11.3, and IFRIC 15).

Case (f): The future operating lease will not lead to derecognition of the building in E's (i.e. the lessor's) statement of financial position. The future operating lease and the objective to hold the building for long-term capital appreciation will lead to the classification of the building as investment property in the future (IAS 40.5, 40.8a, and 40.8c). Since the building is being constructed for future use as investment property, it is investment property (IAS 40.8e). Consequently, IAS 40 applies.

Case (g): The land is not an investment property of E because it is no longer recognized in E's statement of financial position due to the finance lease (IAS 40.9e).

Case (h) – E's separate financial statements: The operating lease of the building does not result in derecognition of the building, i.e. it continues to be recognized in E's (i.e. in the lessor's) statement of financial position. Due to the operating lease, the building represents investment property (IAS 40.8c and 40.15), which means that IAS 40 is applied.

Case (h) – E's consolidated financial statements: The building does not qualify as investment property in E's consolidated financial statements since it is owner-occupied from the

[9] *See KPMG,* Insights into IFRS, *7th edition, 3.4.60.30.*

group perspective (i.e. it is a building held for administrative purposes from the perspective of the group) (IAS 40.15). If the building (owner-occupied property) is expected to be used during more than one period, it meets the definition of property, plant, and equipment (IAS 40.5 and IAS 16.6). In this case IAS 16 applies.

Example 2

Fair value model

On Jan 01, 01, entity E acquires a building (investment property) for CU 100. E measures its investment properties after recognition according to the fair value model.

The following table shows the fair values of the building at different balance sheet dates:

Dec 31, 01	112
Dec 31, 02	112
Dec 31, 03	96

Required

Prepare any necessary entries in E's financial statements as at Dec 31 for the years 01–03.

Deferred tax[10] is (a) ignored and (b) taken into account. In version (b) assume that the building's useful life for tax purposes is 25 years and that the tax rate is 25%.

Hints for solution

In particular Section 4.2.

Solution (a)

Jan 01, 01	Dr	Building	100	
	Cr	Cash		100

Gains and losses from fair value adjustments are recognized in profit or loss (IAS 40.35). According to the fair value model no depreciation is recognized.

Dec 31, 01	Dr	Building	12	
	Cr	Fair value gain		12
Dec 31, 03	Dr	Fair value loss	16	
	Cr	Building		16

Solution (b)

Jan 01, 01	Dr	Building	100	
	Cr	Cash		100
Dec 31, 01	Dr	Building	12	
	Cr	Fair value gain		12

[10] *See the chapter on IAS 12 regarding deferred tax.*

On Dec 31, 01, the difference between the building's carrying amount according to IFRS and its carrying amount for tax purposes results in a deferred tax liability:[11]

Carrying amount according to IFRS	112	
Carrying amount for tax purposes	96	*= CU 100 – CU 100 : 25*
Taxable temporary difference	**16**	
Tax rate	25%	
Deferred tax liability	**4**	

Dec 31, 01	Dr	Deferred tax expense	4	
	Cr	Deferred tax liability		4

In 02, the building's fair value does not change. However, the difference between the building's carrying amount according to IFRS and its carrying amount for tax purposes changes.

Carrying amount according to IFRS	112	
Carrying amount for tax purposes	92	*= CU 100 – CU 4 · 2*
Taxable temporary difference	**20**	
Tax rate	25%	
Deferred tax liability (as at Dec 31, 02)	**5**	
Deferred tax liability (as at Dec 31, 01)	4	
Deferred tax expense 02	**1**	

Dec 31, 02	Dr	Deferred tax expense	1	
	Cr	Deferred tax liability		1
Dec 31, 03	Dr	Fair value loss	16	
	Cr	Building		16

In 03, the carrying amount of the deferred tax liability changes again:

Carrying amount according to IFRS	96	
Carrying amount for tax purposes	88	*= CU 100 – CU 4 · 3*
Taxable temporary difference	**8**	
Tax rate	25%	
Deferred tax liability (as at Dec 31, 03)	**2**	
Deferred tax liability (as at Dec 31, 02)	5	
Deferred tax income 03	**3**	

Dec 31, 03	Dr	Deferred tax liability	3	
	Cr	Deferred tax income		3

[11] *See the chapter on IAS 12, Section 3.1.*

Example 3

Dual-use property

On Jul 05, 01, entity E acquires land for CU 10. It is expected that the land will be used by E during more than one period. The land consists of two pieces that could be sold separately (or leased out separately under a finance lease). One piece is held for long-term capital appreciation and the other piece for constructing a new head office building for E. Fair value of each half is CU 4 on Dec 31, 01 and CU 6 on Dec 31, 02.

Required

(a) Assess whether the two pieces of the land have to be treated separately for accounting purposes and which standard(s) is/are applicable.
(b) If one half constitutes investment property, prepare any necessary entries in E's financial statements as at Dec 31 with respect to that half for the years 01 and 02. E applies the fair value model to its investment properties.

Hints for solution

In particular Sections 1 and 4.2.

Solution (a)

The piece of land is a **dual-use property** because one half represents investment property, while the other half is held as owner-occupied property. Since these two pieces could be sold separately (or leased out separately under a finance lease), they are accounted for separately (IAS 40.10). IAS 40 applies to the half that represents investment property. The other half that is owner-occupied constitutes property, plant, and equipment, to which IAS 16 applies, because it is expected that it will be used during more than one period.

Solution (b)

Gains or losses from fair value adjustments are recognized in **profit or loss** (IAS 40.35).

Jul 05, 01	Dr	Land	5	
	Cr	Cash		5
Dec 31, 01	Dr	Fair value loss	1	
	Cr	Land		1
Dec 31, 02	Dr	Land	2	
	Cr	Fair value gain		2

Example 4

Decommissioning, restoration, and similar liabilities

Entity E is the lessee of a piece of land. The lease represents an operating lease and will end on Dec 31, 04. At the beginning of Jan 01, another entity builds a warehouse for E on that land for CU 300. At the beginning of Jan 01, E leases out the warehouse to entity F under an operating lease until Dec 31, 04. Due to the acquisition of the building,

E is legally obliged to demolish the building at the end of Dec 04 at its own expense. E expects that the costs for removing the building at the end of Dec 04 will be CU 146.41. The discount rate is 10% p.a.

The fair values of the building at E's balance sheet dates are presented in the table below. The obligation to demolish the building has not been taken into account in determining these fair values.

Dec 31, 01	450
Dec 31, 02	300
Dec 31, 03	150
Dec 31, 04	0

On Dec 31, 03, E expects that at the end of December 04 the costs for demolishing the building will amount to only CU 121. This amount is finally paid on Dec 31, 04.

Required

Prepare any necessary entries regarding the **warehouse** in E's financial statements as at Dec 31 for the years 01–04. E applies the **fair value model** for its investment properties. Ignore the entries regarding the lease income.

Hints for solution

In particular Sections 3 and 4.2.

Solution

Year 01

Investment properties are initially measured at cost (IAS 40.20), which includes the present value of the expenses for demolishing the building (IAS 37.45).

Purchase price	**300**
Costs for demolishing the building	146.41
Maturity (in years)	4
Discount rate (p.a.)	10%
Present value of the obligation	**100**
Costs of purchase	**400**

Jan 01	Dr	Building	400	
	Cr	Cash		300
	Cr	Provision		100

The unwinding of the discount is recognized in profit or loss as interest expense (CU 10 = CU 100 · 10%):

Dec 31, 01	Dr	Interest expense	10	
	Cr	Provision		10

It is important to highlight that the provision has already been recognized in E's statement of financial position. If the amount of the provision were deducted from the fair value of the investment property, the obligation would be taken into account twice in the statement of financial position. Consequently, the obligation must not be taken into account when determining fair value of the investment property, which means that the investment property's carrying amount as at Dec 31, 01 is CU 450.

Dec 31, 01	Dr	Building	50	
	Cr	Fair value gain		50

Year 02

Provision as at Jan 01, 02	110	*CU 100 · 1.1 or CU 146.41 : 1.1³*
Interest rate	10%	
Interest expense 02	**11**	

Dec 31, 02	Dr	Interest expense	11	
	Cr	Provision		11
Dec 31, 02	Dr	Fair value loss	150	
	Cr	Building		150

Year 03

Provision as at Jan 01, 03	121	*CU 110 · 1.1 or CU 146.41 : 1.1²*
Interest rate	10%	
Interest expense 03	**12.1**	

Dec 31, 03	Dr	Interest expense	12.1	
	Cr	Provision		12.1
Dec 31, 03	Dr	Fair value loss	150	
	Cr	Building		150

On Dec 31, 03, the carrying amount of the provision changes, due to a change in the estimate of the costs for demolishing the building:

Provision as at Dec 31, 03 (CU 146.41)	133.1	*CU 100 · 1.1³ or CU 146.41 : 1.1*
Provision as at Dec 31, 03 (CU 121)	110.0	*CU 121 : 1.1*
Reduction in the provision	**23.1**	

Since the reduction in the provision results from a change in estimate of the amount payable at the end of Dec 04, it is recognized as other operating income:

Dec 31, 03	Dr	Provision	23.1	
	Cr	Other operating income		23.1

Year 04

Provision as at Jan 01, 04	110
Interest rate	10%
Interest expense 04	**11**

Dec 31, 04	Dr	Interest expense	11	
	Cr	Provision		11
Dec 31, 04	Dr	Fair value loss	150	
	Cr	Building		150
Dec 31, 04	Dr	Provision	121	
	Cr	Cash		121

IAS 41 AGRICULTURE

1 INTRODUCTION AND SCOPE

IAS 41 applies to biological assets, agricultural produce at the point of harvest, and government grants covered by IAS 41.34–41.35 when they relate to agricultural activity (IAS 41.1).

A **biological asset** is a living animal (e.g. a sheep) or plant. **Agricultural produce** is the harvested product (e.g. wool) of the entity's biological assets. **Harvest** is the detachment of produce from a biological asset or the cessation of the life processes of a biological asset (IAS 41.4–41.5).

Agricultural activity is the management by an entity of the biological transformation and harvest of biological assets for sale or for conversion into additional biological assets or into agricultural produce. **Biological transformation** comprises the processes of growth, degeneration, production, and procreation that cause quantitative or qualitative changes in a biological asset (IAS 41.5–41.7).

IAS 41 neither applies to land related to agricultural activity (see IAS 16 and IAS 40) nor to intangible assets related to agricultural activity (see IAS 38) (IAS 41.2).

IAS 41 applies to **agricultural produce** only at the **point of harvest**. Thereafter, IAS 2 or another applicable Standard is applied. Accordingly, IAS 41 does not deal with the processing of agricultural produce after harvest because such processing is not included within the definition of agricultural activity (IAS 41.3).

2 RECOGNITION

A biological asset or agricultural produce is **recognized** when all of the following criteria are met (IAS 41.10–41.11):

- The asset is controlled by the entity as a result of past events.
- It is probable that future economic benefits associated with the asset will flow to the entity.
- The fair value or the cost of the asset can be measured reliably.

These recognition criteria correspond with the general recognition criteria set out in the Conceptual Framework (F.49a and F.83).

3 MEASUREMENT

A **biological asset** is measured on initial recognition and at the end of each reporting period at **fair value less costs to sell**, unless fair value cannot be measured reliably (IAS 41.12). **Fair value** is the amount for which an asset could be exchanged, or a liability settled, between knowledgeable, willing parties in an arm's length transaction (IAS 41.8). **Costs to sell** are the incremental costs directly attributable to the disposal of an asset, excluding income taxes and finance costs (IAS 41.5). **Gains or losses** arising on initial and subsequent measurement of a biological asset at fair value less costs to sell are recognized in **profit or loss** (IAS 41.26–41.27).

Agricultural produce harvested from an entity's biological assets is measured at **fair value less costs to sell** at the **point of harvest**. After harvest, IAS 2 or another applicable Standard is applied instead of IAS 41. Fair value less costs to sell is the cost at the point of harvest for the application of IAS 2 or another applicable Standard (IAS 41.3 and 41.13). A **gain or loss** arising on initial measurement at fair value less costs to sell is recognized in **profit or loss** (IAS 41.28–41.29).

The **fair value** of an asset is based on its present location and condition. Thus, for example, the fair value of cattle at a farm is the price for the cattle in the relevant market less the transport and other costs of getting the cattle to that market (IAS 41.8–41.9). IAS 41 specifies a **fair value hierarchy**. If an active market exists for a biological asset or agricultural produce in its present location and condition, the quoted price in that market is used for determining the fair value (IAS 41.17). An **active market** is a market that meets all of the following conditions (IAS 41.8):

- The items traded within the market are homogeneous.
- Willing sellers and buyers can normally be found at any time.
- Prices are available to the public.

For **biological assets** there is a **rebuttable presumption that fair value can be measured reliably**. However, rebutting is only possible on initial recognition if specified criteria are met. If the presumption is rebutted, the biological asset is measured at its cost less any accumulated depreciation and any accumulated impairment losses. If the fair value of such a biological asset becomes reliably measurable at a later date, it is measured at fair value less costs to sell. There is an **irrefutable presumption** that the fair value of **agricultural produce** at the point of harvest can be measured reliably (IAS 41.30–41.33).

4 GOVERNMENT GRANTS

IAS 20 is applied to a government grant related to a biological asset measured at **cost** less any accumulated depreciation and any accumulated impairment losses (IAS 41.37–41.38). However, IAS 41 requires the following treatment for a government grant related to a biological asset measured at **fair value less costs to sell** (or when a government grant requires an entity not to engage in specified agricultural activity) that **differs from IAS 20** (IAS 41.34–41.36):

- If the grant is **unconditional**, it is recognized in profit or loss when the grant becomes receivable.
- If the grant is **conditional**, it is recognized in profit or loss when the conditions attaching to the grant are met. If a government grant is paid to the entity before all of the conditions are met, a liability is recognized at an equal amount until all of the conditions are met.

5 EXAMPLES WITH SOLUTIONS

Example 1

Terminology

Required

Assign the following terms to the categories "biological assets," "agricultural produce," and "products that are the result of processing after harvest:" clothing, thread, dairy cattle, harvested cane, wool, yarn, milk, cotton, sugar, cheese, plants, sheep, and carpets.

Hints for solution

In particular Section 1.

Solution

The terms are categorized as follows (IAS 41.4–41.5):

Biological assets	*Agricultural produce*	*Products that are the result of processing after harvest*
Sheep	Wool	Yarn, carpets
Dairy cattle	Milk	Cheese
Plants	Cotton	Thread, clothing
	Harvested cane	Sugar

Example 2

Terminology, scope, and measurement

Entity E owns **vineyards** that include a large number of **vines**. These vineyards are held only for production purposes. The **grapes** are harvested by E and processed to make **wine** afterwards with E's **technical equipment**. Finally, E sells the wine to its customers.

Required

Assess **which standard** applies to the accounting of the bold terms in E's financial statements and explain their **measurement** by E.

Hints for solution

In particular Sections 1 and 3.

Solution

The **vineyards** (land) are held for production purposes. Therefore, they are treated as property, plant, and equipment according to IAS 16 (IAS 41.2). The same applies to the **technical equipment**. Consequently, the vineyards as well as the technical equipment are measured at cost at initial recognition (IAS 16.15) and according to the cost model or the revaluation model after recognition (IAS 16.31–16.42).

The **vines** are biological assets because they are living plants (IAS 41.4–41.5). According to IAS 41 they are measured at fair value less costs to sell on initial recognition and at the end of each reporting period (IAS 41.12). Gains or losses arising on initial and subsequent measurement at fair value less costs to sell are recognized in profit or loss (IAS 41.26–41.27). For biological assets the presumption that fair value can be measured reliably can be rebutted in certain circumstances.

The **grapes** represent agricultural produce. Consequently, they are within the scope of IAS 41 at the point of harvest. At that date, they are measured at fair value less costs to sell. After harvest, the processing of the grapes is subject to IAS 2 instead of IAS 41. Fair value less costs to sell is the cost at the point of harvest for the application of IAS 2. The **wine** is treated as an inventory item according to IAS 2 (IAS 41.3, 41.13, and IAS 2.6).

Example 3

Government grant

Entity E owns olive plantations, which contain a large number of olive trees. The olive trees are biological assets (IAS 41.5) and are measured at fair value less costs to sell (IAS 41.12).

On Jan 01, 01, a government grant of CU 2 for the olive trees becomes receivable. The grant is paid to E on the same date.

Version (a): The government grant is unconditional.

Version (b): Payment of the government grant is subject to the condition that E operates the olive plantations at least until Dec 31, 02. If this condition is not met, the **whole** grant of CU 2 has to be paid back. Assume that E finally meets this condition.

Version (c): Payment of the government grant is subject to the condition that E operates the olive plantations at least until Dec 31, 02. If this condition is not met, the terms of the grant allow **part of it to be retained** according to the time that has elapsed. Assume that E finally meets this condition.

Required

Prepare any necessary entries in E's financial statements as at Dec 31 for the years 01 and 02 regarding the government grant.

Hints for solution

In particular Section 4.

Solution (a)

An unconditional government grant is recognized in profit or loss when it becomes receivable (IAS 41.34):

Jan 01, 01	Dr	Cash	2	
	Cr	Income		2

Solution (b)

A conditional government grant is recognized in profit or loss when the conditions attaching to it are met. In this example the grant is paid to E on Jan 01, 01. At this date the condition is not met. Consequently, a liability is recognized at an equal amount, on Jan 01, 01 (IAS 41.35–41.36):

Jan 01, 01	Dr	Cash	2	
	Cr	Liability		2

On Dec 31, 02, the condition is met. Therefore, the grant is recognized in profit or loss (IAS 41.35–41.36):

Dec 31, 02	Dr	Liability	2	
	Cr	Income		2

Solution (c)

In contrast to (b), income is recognized in profit or loss over time. This is because the grant only has to be repaid on a pro rata basis (according to the time that has elapsed) when E stops operating the olive plantations (IAS 41.35–41.36). Hence, on Dec 31, 01, 50% of the grant is recognized in profit or loss, because one of the two years has elapsed.

Jan 01, 01	Dr	Cash	2	
	Cr	Liability		2
Dec 31, 01	Dr	Liability	1	
	Cr	Income		1
Dec 31, 02	Dr	Liability	1	
	Cr	Income		1

IFRS 1 FIRST-TIME ADOPTION OF INTERNATIONAL FINANCIAL REPORTING STANDARDS

1 INTRODUCTION AND SCOPE

IFRS 1 contains rules relating to the first-time adoption of IFRSs. IFRS 1 has to be applied in an entity's first annual financial statements according to IFRSs as well as in interim financial reports (prepared in accordance with IAS 34) that are presented for part of the period covered by the entity's first annual financial statements according to IFRSs (IFRS 1.2).

The **first IFRS financial statements** are the **first annual financial statements** in which an entity adopts IFRS through an explicit and unreserved statement that the financial statements comply with IFRSs (i.e. with all standards (IASs and IFRSs) and interpretations of the SIC and IFRIC) (**statement of compliance**).[1] An entity that presents its first IFRS financial statements is referred to as a first-time adopter. A first-time adopter has to apply IFRS 1 (IFRS 1.2–1.3, IFRS 1.Appendix A, and IAS 1.16).

Financial statements in accordance with IFRSs are the entity's first IFRS financial statements if, for example, the entity (IFRS 1.3):

- presented its most recent previous financial statements;
  - in conformity with national requirements that are not consistent with IFRSs in all respects,
  - in accordance with IFRSs in all respects, except that the financial statements did not contain an explicit and unreserved statement of compliance, or
  - in conformity with national requirements, with a reconciliation of some amounts to the amounts determined in accordance with IFRSs,
- prepared a reporting package according to IFRSs for consolidation purposes without preparing a complete set of financial statements as defined in IAS 1, or
- prepared financial statements according to IFRSs for internal use only without making them available to the entity's owners or any other external users.

There is no first-time adoption when, for example, the entity did not apply IFRSs correctly in its most recent previous financial statements, but falsely disclosed a statement of compliance in the notes.

Notwithstanding the above requirements, an entity that has applied IFRSs in a previous reporting period, but whose most recent previous annual financial statements did not contain a statement of compliance, must either apply IFRS 1 (**repeated application of IFRS 1**) or

[1] *See the chapter on IAS 1, Section 3.*

otherwise apply IFRSs retrospectively in accordance with IAS 8 as if it had never stopped applying IFRSs (IFRS 1.4A).

The **date of transition to IFRSs** is the beginning of the earliest period for which the entity presents full comparative information under IFRSs in its first IFRS financial statements. The entity's statement of financial position at the date of transition to IFRS is referred to as the **opening IFRS statement of financial position** (IFRS 1.Appendix A). That statement already has to correspond with the recognition and measurement requirements of IFRSs and has to be presented in the entity's financial statements (IFRS 1.6, 1.10, and 1.21). If an entity that is required to present one comparative period in its financial statements prepares its first IFRS financial statements as at Dec 31, 02, the year 02 is the **first IFRS reporting period**, the year 01 is the **comparative period**, and Jan 01, 01 is the date of transition to IFRSs (i.e. the balance sheet date of the opening IFRS statement of financial position).

2 RECOGNITION AND MEASUREMENT

2.1 Accounting Policies

An entity has to use **the same accounting policies** in its opening IFRS statement of financial position and throughout all periods presented in its first IFRS financial statements. These policies have to comply with each IFRS that is effective at the end of the entity's first IFRS reporting period.[2] However, there are a number of exceptions to this rule (IFRS 1.7).

IFRS 1 does not apply to **changes in accounting policies** made by an entity that already applies IFRSs. Such changes are the subject of IAS 8 and of specific transitional requirements in other IFRSs (IFRS 1.5). On the other hand, IAS 8 does not apply to changes in accounting policies that are made when an entity adopts the standards of the IASB for the first time (IFRS 1.27). The transitional provisions in other IFRSs do not apply to a first-time adopter's transition to IFRSs, although there are exceptions to this rule (IFRS 1.9).

The accounting policies that an entity uses in its opening IFRS statement of financial position may differ from those that the entity used for the same date according to its previous GAAP. Therefore, as at the date of the entity's opening IFRS statement of financial position, **entries** are necessary in order to **adjust the statement of financial position from the entity's previous GAAP to IFRSs**. These adjustments arise from events and transactions before the date of transition to IFRSs. Thus, the adjustments relating to recognition or measurement of items are recognized **directly in retained earnings** or, if appropriate, **another category of equity** (e.g. in the foreign currency reserve) (IFRS 1.11). In the case of adjustments that relate only to presentation (e.g. if an adjustment is necessary because current and non-current liabilities were not presented separately in the entity's statement of financial position according to its previous GAAP), there is generally no effect on the amount of equity presented.

A first-time adopter has to apply IFRSs **retrospectively**, i.e. as if the entity had always applied them. However, IFRS 1 specifies **exceptions** from this principle. Some important exceptions are discussed in Sections 2.2 and 2.3.

---

[2] *See Section 1.*

2.2 Exceptions to Retrospective Application of Other IFRSs (Mandatory)

IFRS 1 **prohibits retrospective application of some aspects of other IFRSs**. These exemptions are set out in IFRS 1.14–1.17 and IFRS 1.Appendix B (IFRS 1.12–1.13). One of these exemptions is described below.

An entity's **estimates** according to IFRSs that are necessary when preparing its **opening IFRS statement of financial position** have to be consistent with estimates made for the same date with regard to its statement of financial position according to previous GAAP. For example, an entity may prepare its opening IFRS statement of financial position as at Jan 01, 04. Its statement of financial position according to previous GAAP has been prepared as at Dec 31, 03. The estimates with regard to that IFRS statement have to be consistent with the estimates made for the statement under previous GAAP. This means that information received by the entity in hindsight about estimates made under previous GAAP must not be reflected in its opening IFRS statement of financial position. Exceptions are the need for an adjustment of estimates to reflect any difference in accounting policies and objective evidence that the estimates were in error (IFRS 1.14–1.15).

It may be necessary to make estimates in accordance with IFRSs at the date of transition to IFRSs that were not required at that date under previous GAAP. Those estimates have to reflect conditions that existed at the date of transition to IFRSs. In particular, estimates at the date of transition to IFRSs of market prices, interest rates or foreign exchange rates have to reflect market conditions at that date (IFRS 1.16).

The above considerations with regard to estimates (IFRS 1.14–1.16) also apply to the **statement of financial position as at the end of a comparative period** presented in the entity's first IFRS financial statements (IFRS 1.17).

2.3 Exemptions from Other IFRSs (Optional)

2.3.1 Overview An entity may **elect to use** one or more of the exemptions contained in Appendices C–E of IFRS 1. However, they must not be applied by analogy to other items (IFRS 1.18). Some of these exemptions refer to fair value. Fair values have to reflect conditions that existed at the date for which they were determined (IFRS 1.19). Subsequently, selected exemptions are described.

2.3.2 Measurement of Property, Plant, and Equipment In the opening IFRS statement of financial position several options are available for measuring property, plant, and equipment. In addition to measuring property, plant, and equipment in the opening IFRS statement of financial position on the basis of **depreciated cost**, the measurement may also be based on **deemed cost**. Deemed cost represents an amount used as a surrogate for cost or depreciated cost at a given date. Subsequent depreciation assumes that the entity had initially recognized the item of property, plant, and equipment at the given date and that its cost was equal to the deemed cost (IFRS 1.Appendix A, IFRS 1.D5–1.D6, and 1.D8).

If the entity opts for **deemed cost**, there are several further **options** for the opening IFRS statement of financial position that can be exercised differently for each item of property, plant, and equipment (IFRS 1.BC45):

- Measurement at fair value at the date of transition to IFRSs (IFRS 1.D5).
- Use of a previous GAAP revaluation (at or before the date of transition to IFRSs) as deemed cost at the date of the revaluation. This requires that the revaluation was, at the date of the revaluation, broadly comparable to (IFRS 1.D6):

  (a) fair value, or
  (b) cost or depreciated cost according to IFRSs (adjusted to reflect, for example, changes in a general or specific price index).

- A first-time adopter may have established a deemed cost according to previous GAAP for some or all of its assets and liabilities by measuring them at their fair value at one particular date because of an event such as a privatization or initial public offering. If the measurement date is at or before the date of transition to IFRSs, such event-driven fair value measurements may be used as deemed cost for IFRSs at the date of that measurement (IFRS 1.D8a).

2.3.3 Foreign Currency Reserve When foreign currency financial statements are translated according to the **current rate method**, exchange differences are recognized in **other comprehensive income** and accumulated in the **foreign currency reserve**. On **disposal** of the foreign operation, the foreign currency reserve for that foreign operation is **reclassified to profit or loss** as part of the gain or loss on disposal (IFRS 1.D12).[3]

However, a **first-time adopter** need not comply with these requirements for cumulative translation differences that existed at the date of transition to IFRSs. If a first-time adopter uses this exemption, the following applies (IFRS 1.D13):

- The cumulative translation differences for all foreign operations are **deemed to be zero at the date of transition to IFRSs**, i.e. the previous differences are recognized in retained earnings.
- The gain or loss on a subsequent disposal of any foreign operation excludes translation differences that arose before the date of transition to IFRSs and includes later translation differences.

2.3.4 Business Combinations IFRS 1 contains a large number of possibilities for first-time adopters with regard to the recognition of business combination effects in the financial statements (IFRS 1.Appendix C).

2.4 Deferred Tax

IFRS 1 does not contain special rules with regard to deferred tax. A change in the carrying amount of an item in the **opening IFRS statement of financial position** also changes the difference to the item's carrying amount for tax purposes. The resulting change in the deferred tax asset or deferred tax liability is normally presented in retained earnings (e.g. the entry may be "Dr Retained earnings Cr Deferred tax liability").

---

[3] *See the chapter on IAS 21, Section 4.2.*

3 PRESENTATION AND DISCLOSURE

IFRS 1 does not provide exemptions from the presentation and disclosure requirements in other IFRSs (IFRS 1.20).

The entity's first IFRS financial statements have to include **at least the following components** (IFRS 1.21):

- Three statements of financial position. This means that it is also necessary to present the opening IFRS statement of financial position (IFRS 1.6 and 1.21).
- Either:
  - two single statements of comprehensive income (one statement approach), or
  - two separate income statements and two separate statements of comprehensive income (two statement approach).
- Two statements of cash flows.
- Two statements of changes in equity.
- Related notes, including comparative information for all statements presented.

Among others, the entity's first IFRS financial statements must include **reconciliations** (that give sufficient detail) of its **equity** reported according to previous GAAP to its equity according to IFRSs. Such reconciliations have to be disclosed for the date of transition to IFRSs and for the end of the latest period presented in the entity's most recent annual financial statements according to previous GAAP (IFRS 1.24–1.25).

If the entity did not present financial statements for previous periods, this fact has to be disclosed in its first IFRS financial statements (IFRS 1.28). A newly established company is also a first-time adopter, but in contrast to those entities changing from national GAAP to IFRSs, there are no comparative figures to be presented and no adjustment is recognized in equity.

4 EXAMPLES WITH SOLUTIONS

Example 1

Which entities are first-time adopters of IFRSs?

The most recent previous financial statements of entity **A** (as at Dec 31, 01) include an explicit and unreserved statement of compliance with IFRSs. However, A's auditors issued a qualified audit opinion because A did not apply all requirements of IFRSs correctly.

The most recent previous financial statements of entity **B** (as at Dec 31, 01) merely include an explicit and unreserved statement of compliance with some, but not all IFRSs.

Until now, the financial statements of entity **C** were prepared according to IFRSs and included explicit and unreserved statements of compliance. However, they were prepared for internal use only, without making them available to C's owners or to any other external users.

The (published) financial statements of entity **D** as at Dec 31, 00 include an explicit and unreserved statement of compliance with IFRSs. On Dec 31, 01, D did not prepare its financial statements according to IFRSs. On Dec 31, 02, D again prepares its financial statements in accordance with IFRSs.

Required

Assess whether the next financial statements of the entities as at Dec 31, 02 represent the entities' first IFRS financial statements according to IFRS 1.

Hints for solution

In particular Section 1.

Solution

The financial statements of **A** as at Dec 31, 02 do not represent A's first IFRS financial statements according to IFRS 1. This is because the financial statements as at Dec 31, 01 included an explicit and unreserved statement of compliance with IFRSs. Whether that statement of compliance was correct or false is not decisive. It is also not crucial that the auditors qualified their audit opinion (IFRS 1.4(c)).

The financial statements of **B** as at Dec 31, 02 represent B's first IFRS financial statements according to IFRS 1. This is because the financial statements as at Dec 31, 01 do not include an explicit and unreserved statement of compliance with all IFRSs (IFRS 1.3(a)(iii)).

The previous financial statements of **C** include explicit and unreserved statements of compliance. However, they were only used internally. Consequently, C's financial statements as at Dec 31, 02 represent C's first IFRS financial statements according to IFRS 1 (IFRS 1.3b).

The financial statements of **D** as at Dec 31, 02 represent D's first IFRS financial statements according to IFRS 1. This is because D's most recent previous financial statements (i.e. those as at Dec 31, 01) were prepared according to other rules than IFRSs (IFRS 1.3a).

Example 2

Estimates relating to provisions

At the end of the year 00, entity E was sued for damages. In E's statement of financial position as at Dec 31, 00, according to E's local GAAP, a provision in the amount of CU 40 was recognized because E expected that it would ultimately have to pay damages. However, contrary to expectations E won the lawsuit in Nov 01. It is presumed that E would also have had to recognize a provision in the amount of CU 40 if E had already applied IFRSs when preparing its financial statements as at Dec 31, 00.

Required

Assess the accounting treatment of the events described in E's first IFRS financial statements as at Dec 31, 02.

Hints for solution

In particular Section 2.2.

Solution

The court decision in Nov 01 represents an adjusting event. However, the court decision could not be taken into account because it took place after E's financial statements as at Dec 31, 00 were authorized for issue.

E's estimates according to IFRSs that are necessary when preparing its opening IFRS statement of financial position as at Jan 01, 01 have to be consistent with estimates made for the same date with regard to its statement of financial position according to its previous GAAP (Dec 31, 00). This means that the court decision that took place in Nov 01 must not be reflected in E's opening IFRS statement of financial position (IFRS 1.14–1.15). Hence, E's opening IFRS statement of financial position also includes the same provision in the amount of CU 40.

However, the provision has to be derecognized in 01. This affects the comparative period 01 as well as the statement of financial position as at Dec 31, 01, which have to be presented in E's financial statements as at Dec 31, 02.

Dec 31, 01	Dr	Provision	40	
	Cr	Other operating income		40

Example 3

Measurement of property, plant, and equipment in the opening IFRS statement of financial position

Entity E prepares its first IFRS financial statements as at Dec 31, 04. Hence, its opening IFRS statement of financial position is prepared as at Jan 01, 03.

E owns an administrative building that represents property, plant, and equipment. E elects to measure that building on Jan 01, 03 at its fair value of CU 80 and use that amount as the building's deemed cost at that date (IFRS 1.D5). Subsequently, the building is measured according to the cost model set out in IAS 16. According to E's previous GAAP and according to E's tax law, the carrying amount of the building as at Jan 01, 03 is CU 60.

Required

Prepare any necessary entries in E's opening IFRS statement of financial position. Deferred tax:

(a) Has to be ignored.
(b) Has to be taken into account. E's tax rate is 25%.

Hints for solution

In particular Sections 2.3.2 and 2.4.

Solution (a)

Jan 01, 03	Dr	Building	20	
	Cr	Retained earnings		20

Solution (b)

Jan 01, 03	Dr	Building	20	
	Cr	Retained earnings		20

The increase in the building's carrying amount in the opening IFRS statement of financial position (above the carrying amount for tax purposes) gives rise to a deferred tax liability of CU 5 (= CU 20 · 25%):[4]

Jan 01, 03	Dr	Retained earnings	5	
	Cr	Deferred tax liability		5

[4] *See the chapter on IAS 12, Section 3.1.*

IFRS 2 SHARE-BASED PAYMENT

1 A GENERAL INTRODUCTION TO EMPLOYEE SHARE OPTIONS[1]

IFRS 2 specifies the financial reporting of **share-based payment transactions**. In practice, the most important types of share-based payment transactions are:

- contributions in kind in which the entity acquires goods and settles the transaction by issuing equity instruments, and
- employee share options in which the entity receives employee services and gives the employees the right (or the virtual right) to acquire equity instruments below their market price.

A **share option** is a contract that gives its holder the right, but not the obligation, to subscribe to the entity's shares at a fixed or determinable price. The vast majority of options are either European or American (style) options. A **European option** can be exercised only at the expiry date of the option, i.e. at a single pre-defined date. By contrast, an **American option** may be exercised on any trading day on or before expiry.

When **measuring options**, **fair value** is of particular importance. Fair value is the amount for which an asset could be exchanged, a liability settled, or an equity instrument granted could be exchanged between knowledgeable, willing parties in an arm's length transaction. Fair value of a share option consists of the following components:

- **Intrinsic value**: Intrinsic value of an option to acquire one share is the positive difference between fair value of the share and the price that has to be paid to acquire this share under the option (exercise price). In this case, the option is "in the money." For example, if fair value of the share amounts to CU 3 and the exercise price is CU 2, intrinsic value of the option to purchase the share is CU 1. Intrinsic value of this option cannot be negative because the holder of the option would not exercise it if its exercise price exceeded fair value of the share.
- **Time value**: The time value of an option is the difference between its fair value and its intrinsic value. It reflects the probability that the intrinsic value of the option will increase or that the option will become profitable to exercise before it expires. Time value depends on the remaining maturity and on the expected volatility of the underlying (e.g. of the shares that can be acquired under the option).

The right to exercise an option may be subject to various **conditions**. The following chart shows the classification of such conditions:

<table>
<tr><td colspan="3">Vesting conditions</td><td rowspan="3">Non-vesting conditions</td></tr>
<tr><td rowspan="2">Service conditions</td><td colspan="2">Performance conditions</td></tr>
<tr><td>Non-market conditions</td><td>Market conditions</td></tr>
</table>

[1] *See IFRS 2.Appendix A with regard to the definitions of the technical terms.*

In the case of employee share options, different forms of **vesting conditions** may be stipulated:

- **Service conditions** require the employee to complete a specified period of service in order to be able to exercise the option.
- **Performance conditions** require specified performance targets to be met by the entity or the employee (e.g. a specified increase in the entity's sales or profit).

A performance condition might include a **market condition**. In the case of a market condition, the performance target is related to the market price of the entity's equity instruments. Examples of such performance targets are attaining a specified share price or a specified amount of intrinsic value of a share option. However, if the right to exercise the option depends on a specified increase in sales or profit instead of the market price of the entity's equity instruments, this is not a market condition.

The **vesting period** is the period of time during which all the specified vesting conditions are to be satisfied. The **vesting date** is the date on which the vesting conditions are satisfied, whereby the employee effectively becomes the holder of the option. Also, the expression **"to vest"** has the same meaning. The **exercise date** is the date on which the share option is exercised by the employee.

The ability to exercise the option may not only depend on vesting conditions, but also on **non-vesting conditions**. The latter do not constitute service conditions or performance conditions. Meeting non-vesting conditions is in the discretion of:

- none of the contracting parties (e.g. if meeting the condition depends on the development of an index),
- the employee (e.g. paying in a specified amount during the vesting period), or
- the entity (e.g. if cessation of the share-based payment is possible at any time).

2 SCOPE OF IFRS 2

The separate acquisition of financial assets by issuing equity instruments is not within the scope of IFRS 2 because financial instruments are not goods within the meaning of the standard (IFRS 2.5). The acquisition of goods as part of the net assets acquired in a business combination, to which IFRS 3 applies, is excluded from the scope of IFRS 2 (IFRS 2.5). However, a business combination may involve aspects that are subject to IFRS 2.

In the absence of specifically identifiable goods or services, other circumstances may indicate that goods or services have been (or will be) received, in which case IFRS 2 applies (IFRS 2.2).

3 THE ACCOUNTING OF EMPLOYEE SHARE OPTIONS

3.1 Introduction

Section 3 only deals with **employee share options**, i.e. only with situations in which the entity receives **employee services** as consideration **for the granting of share options** to employees. The receipt of employee services for the granting of share options usually does not result in the receipt of an asset that is recognized in the statement of financial position. Consequently, the employee services are recognized in profit or loss as employee benefits expenses (IFRS 2.7–2.8). The credit entry and the subsequent accounting depend on whether the employee options are part of an equity-settled share-based payment transaction (see Section 3.2) or of a cash-settled share-based payment transaction (see Section 3.3) (IFRS 2. Appendix A):

- **Equity-settled transactions**: The entity receives employee services as consideration for options to purchase shares of the entity. Consequently, when the share options are exercised, the entity either issues new shares or reacquires its own shares (treasury shares).[2]
- **Cash-settled transactions**: The entity receives employee services by incurring a liability to transfer cash or other assets to the employee for amounts that are based on the price (or value) of the entity's shares. For example, entity E may incur a liability to make a payment to its CEO for an amount that depends upon the development of the value of the E's shares during a specified period of time. However, E will neither issue shares nor reacquire its own shares.

3.2 Equity-settled Transactions

In the case of equity-settled transactions, the employee services received by the entity are generally recognized by means of the entry **"Dr Employee benefits expense Cr Equity"** because usually the employee services do not result in the receipt of an asset that is recognized in the statement of financial position. IFRS 2 does not specify where in equity the credit entry should be made. In this regard, it may be necessary to take legal advice in order to comply with local legislation. In the examples in this section of the book, the credit entry is effected in a separate component of equity.

The fair value of the equity instruments granted represents the value of the employee services received by the entity. The fair value is measured at the **grant date** (IFRS 2.11–2.12). The grant date is the date on which the entity and the employee agree to a share-based payment arrangement. If the agreement is subject to an approval process (e.g. by shareholders), the grant date is the date when that approval is obtained (IFRS 2. Appendix A).

The fair value of the equity instruments granted is determined on the basis of market prices, if available. If market prices are not available, a valuation technique is applied. Such valuation techniques have to comply with certain requirements (IFRS 2.16–2.18 and IFRS 2. Appendix B). Normally, fair value can be estimated reliably (IFRS 2.24).

Two different cases have to be distinguished (IFRS 2.14–2.15):

- The equity instruments granted **vest immediately**: In this situation the entity presumes – in the absence of evidence to the contrary – that the employee services have already been received. In this case, the services received by the entity are recognized **in full on the grant date** ("Dr Employee benefits expense 100% Cr Equity 100%").
- The equity instruments granted **do not vest until the employee completes a specified period of service**: In this case, the entity presumes that it will receive the services to be rendered by the employee in the future, i.e. during the vesting period. The entity

---

[2] *See the chapter on IAS 32, Section 5 regarding treasury shares.*

accounts for those services as they are rendered by the employee **during the vesting period**. This means that the entry "Dr Employee benefits expense 50% Cr Equity 50%" is made in each year of the vesting period if the vesting period is two years.

Vesting conditions which are *not* market conditions are (IFRS 2.19–2.20):

- *not* taken into account when estimating the fair value at the measurement date;
- taken into account by adjusting the number of equity instruments that are expected to vest in the future. For example, it may be expected after the second year of the vesting period that in total 20 equity instruments will not vest because of employees who already left or will leave the entity early. In this case, no employee services are recognized for these 20 equity instruments. If expectations change in this regard, the number of equity instruments that are expected to vest is changed.

Vesting conditions that are market conditions (e.g. achieving a target share price) have to be taken into account in determining fair value of the equity instruments granted. The employee services received by the entity have to be recognized irrespective of whether a market condition is expected to be met if it is expected that all other vesting conditions, which do not represent market conditions, will be satisfied (IFRS 2.21).

After the vesting date the amount recognized for employee services is not reversed if employee share options are not exercised. However, this does not preclude the entity from recognizing a transfer within equity, i.e. a transfer from component of equity to another (IFRS 2.23).

When an employee exercises his options, he receives shares of the entity. Therefore, the entity has to **issue shares** or **reacquire its own shares (treasury shares)** (IAS 32.33 and 32.AG36).[3]

3.3 Cash-settled Transactions

In the case of cash-settled transactions, the employee services received and the liability incurred are measured at the **fair value of the liability.** Until the liability is settled, fair value is remeasured at the end of each reporting period and at the date of settlement. Changes in fair value are recognized in profit or loss (IFRS 2.30–2.31).

The employee services received and the liability to pay for these services are recognized **as the employees render service** (IFRS 2.32). For example, entity E grants share appreciation rights to its employees on Jan 01, 01. The vesting period is three years. On Dec 31, 01 fair value of the share appreciation rights is CU 3. Consequently, on Dec 31, 01, a liability of CU 1 is recognized.

The employee services received and the liability are recognized immediately if the share options are granted for employee services that have already been received by the entity (IFRS 2.32).

---

[3] *See the chapter on IAS 32, Section 5 regarding treasury shares.*

4 EXAMPLES WITH SOLUTIONS

Example 1

Equity-settled transaction – service condition

On Jan 01, 01, entity E grants share options to 10 of its employees. Each of these employees receives 10 share options. The share options vest after the employee has been employed by E for three more years (service condition). On Jan 01, 01, fair value per option is CU 3.

On Dec 31, 01, it is expected that during the whole vesting period of three years, 10% of the employees will leave E. On Dec 31, 02 this expectation is revised to 30%. Finally, by Dec 31, 03, 20% of the employees left E.

All the options of the employees who are entitled to exercise them are finally exercised on Jan 01, 04.

On Jan 01, 04, E issues shares for the employees who exercise their options. It is presumed that the exercise price of the options, received by E, is CU 250. The par value of the shares is CU 100.

Required

Prepare any necessary entries in E's financial statements as at Dec 31 for the years 01–04.

Hints for solution

In particular Sections 1 and 3.2.

Solution

E receives the employee services during the vesting period (IFRS 2.15). The vesting condition (i.e. the service condition that the employee has to be employed by E from Jan 01, 01 until Dec 31, 03) is not a market condition. Thus, the number of share options that are expected to vest has to be adjusted at the end of each reporting period (IFRS 2.19–2.20). The options are measured at fair value at the grant date (IFRS 2.11). The latter amount is not changed for accounting purposes, when measuring the share-based payment arrangement subsequently. The following table shows the carrying amount of the separate component of equity for the share-based payments at the end of each reporting period. The employee benefits expense represents the change in the separate component of equity.

Fair value of the options at grant date: *300*

Year	*Employees expected to leave E*	*Options expected to vest*	*Part of the vesting period that has passed*	*Separate component of equity = accumulated employee benefits expense (as at Dec 31)*	*Auxiliary calculation*	*Employee benefits expense for the year*
01	10%	90%	1/3	90	CU 300 · 90% · 1 : 3	90
02	30%	70%	2/3	140	CU 300 · 70% · 2 : 3	50
03	20%	80%	3/3	240	CU 300 · 80% · 3 : 3	100

Dec 31, 01	Dr	Employee benefits expense	90	
	Cr	Share-based payments (equity)		90

Dec 31, 02	Dr	Employee benefits expense	50	
	Cr	Share-based payments (equity)		50
Dec 31, 03	Dr	Employee benefits expense	100	
	Cr	Share-based payments (equity)		100

When the share options are exercised, the employees receive shares of E.

These **shares are issued** by E. The payment (i.e. the exercise price of the options) received by E is credited to "share premium" to the extent that it exceeds par value.

Jan 01, 04	Dr	Cash	250	
	Cr	Share capital (equity)		100
	Cr	Share premium (equity)		150

Example 2

Equity-settled transaction – service condition and performance condition

The situation is the same as in Example 1. However, there is also a performance condition in addition to the service condition. According to the performance condition, the options only vest if E's **sales revenue increases** by at least 20% by Dec 31, 03. On Dec 31, 01 and on Dec 31, 02 it is expected that this target will be met. However, the target is not met by Dec 31, 03. For this reason, E neither issues shares nor reacquires any of its own shares.

Required

Prepare any necessary entries in E's financial statements as at Dec 31 for the years 01–03.

Hints for solution

In particular Sections 1 and 3.2.

Solution

The performance condition is **not a market condition** since an increase in sales revenue is not (directly) related to the market price of E's equity instruments (IFRS 2. Appendix A). Consequently, the employee benefits expense is only recognized if it is expected that the performance condition will be met. In this example, an employee benefits expense is recognized in 01 and 02 because at the end of these periods it is expected that the performance condition will be met. However, the performance condition is not finally met until Dec 31, 03. Therefore, the employee benefits expenses recognized in 01 and 02 have to be reversed at the end of 03 (IFRS 2.19–2.20).

Dec 31, 01	Dr	Employee benefits expense	90	
	Cr	Share-based payments (equity)		90
Dec 31, 02	Dr	Employee benefits expense	50	
	Cr	Share-based payments (equity)		50
Dec 31, 03	Dr	Share-based payments (equity)	140	
	Cr	Employee benefits expense		140

Example 3

Equity-settled transaction – service condition and performance condition

The situation is the same as in Example 1. However, there is also a performance condition in addition to the service condition. According to the performance condition, the options only vest if E's **share price** on Dec 31, 03 exceeds E's share price on Jan 01, 01 by at least 20%. On Dec 31, 01 and on Dec 31, 02, it is expected that this target will be met. However, the target is not met on Dec 31, 03. For this reason, E neither issues shares nor reacquires any of its own shares.

For simplification purposes, the effect of the performance condition on fair value is neglected, i.e. it is assumed that fair value is the same as in Example 1.

Required

Prepare any necessary entries in the financial statements of E as at Dec 31 for the years 01–03.

Hints for solution

In particular Sections 1 and 3.2.

Solution

The performance condition is a **market condition** since an increase in E's share price has been stipulated (IFRS 2.Appendix A). Hence, the employee services received by E are recognized irrespective of whether the market condition is expected to be met if it is expected that all other vesting conditions that are not market conditions (i.e. the service condition in this example) will be satisfied.

On Dec 31, 01 and on Dec 31, 02 it is expected that the performance condition will be met. However, the performance condition is not met on Dec 31, 03. Nevertheless, an additional employee benefits expense is recognized in 03 (for the employees who meet the service condition – see Example 1) (IFRS 2.21).

Dec 31, 01	Dr	Employee benefits expense	90	
	Cr	Share-based payments (equity)		90
Dec 31, 02	Dr	Employee benefits expense	50	
	Cr	Share-based payments (equity)		50
Dec 31, 03	Dr	Employee benefits expense	100	
	Cr	Share-based payments (equity)		100

Example 4

Cash-settled transaction

On Jan 01, 01, entity E grants share appreciation rights (SARs) to 10 of its employees. Each of these employees receives 10 such rights. The SARs can be exercised at any time during the years 03 and 04 if the employee was employed by E from Jan 01, 01 until Dec 31, 02.

On Dec 31, 01, it is expected that a total of two employees will leave E during 01 and 02. However, by Dec 31, 02 only one employee leaves E.

On Dec 31, 03 three employees exercise their SARs and on Dec 31, 04, the remaining six employees exercise their rights.

The following data are available with regard to the SARs:

Date	*Fair value*	*Intrinsic value*
Dec 31, 01	7	5
Dec 31, 02	4	3
Dec 31, 03	8	6
Dec 31, 04	9	9

Required

Prepare any necessary entries in E's financial statements as at Dec 31 for the years 01–04.

Hints for solution

In particular Section 3.3.

Solution

E recognizes a liability that is measured at fair value of the *SARs* at the end of each reporting period. Changes in fair value are recognized in profit or loss (IFRS 2.30). However, the actual cash outflow when a SAR is exercised is equivalent to the intrinsic value of the SAR since the employee receives the difference between the exercise price of the option and the higher fair value *of the shares.*

Date	*Expense*	*Liability*	*Explanations*
Dec 31, 01	280	280	(10 – 2) employees · 10 SARs · CU 7 · 1/2 = CU 280
Dec 31, 02	80	360	**Liability** = (10 – 1) employees · 10 SARs · CU 4 · 2/2 = CU 360 **Expense** = CU 360 – CU 280 = CU 80
Dec 31, 03	300	480	While nine employees are entitled to exercise their SARs, three of them actually exercise them on Dec 31, 03. **Liability** = (9 – 3) employees · 10 SARs · CU 8 = CU 480 The **expense** consists of two components: •The liability increases by 120 (i.e. from CU 360 to CU 480). •There is a payment of CU 180 to the employees who exercise their SARs (= 3 employees · 10 SARs · CU 6). Consequently, the expense is CU 300 in total.
Dec 31, 04	60	0	All of the nine employees who were entitled to exercise their SARs exercised them until Dec 31, 04. Thus, the carrying amount of the liability decreases from CU 480 to CU 0. Moreover, there is a payment of CU 540 to the remaining six employees who exercised their SARs in 04 (= 6 employees · 10 SARs · CU 9). Since the payment is higher than the reduction of the liability, an additional expense of CU 60 (CU 540 – CU 480) is recognized.

Date		Account	Dr	Cr
Dec 31, 01	Dr	Employee benefits expense	280	
	Cr	Liability		280
Dec 31, 02	Dr	Employee benefits expense	80	
	Cr	Liability		80
Dec 31, 03	Dr	Employee benefits expense	300	
	Cr	Liability		120
	Cr	Cash		180
Dec 31, 04	Dr	Employee benefits expense	60	
	Dr	Liability	480	
	Cr	Cash		540

IFRS 3 BUSINESS COMBINATIONS

1 INTRODUCTION AND SCOPE

In a **business combination**, an acquirer obtains **control** of one or more businesses. A **business** is an integrated set of activities and assets that is capable of being conducted and managed for the purpose of providing economic benefits (e.g. dividends) directly to investors, members or participants. **Control** is the power to govern the financial and operating policies of an entity so as to obtain benefits from its activities (IFRS 3.Appendix A).

The **acquisition of a group of assets or net assets**, which do not constitute a business, is not a business combination (IFRS 3.3). In such a case, the cost of acquisition is allocated between the individual identifiable assets and liabilities on the basis of their relative fair values at the date of acquisition (IFRS 3.2b). **Fair value** is the amount for which an asset could be exchanged, or a liability settled, between knowledgeable, willing parties in an arm's length transaction (IFRS 3.Appendix A). The remaining part of this chapter on IFRS 3 only deals with business combinations.

IFRS 3 does not apply to a **combination** of entities or businesses **under common control** (IFRS 3.2c). This is a business combination in which all of the combining businesses or entities are ultimately controlled by the same party or parties both before and after the combination and the control is not transitory (IFRS 3.B1–3.B4). Such transactions often occur during the reorganization of groups.

Frequently, **equity interests** (i.e. in particular ownership interests of investor-owned entities) are acquired in a business combination. The term "**owners**" is defined along the same lines (IFRS 3.Appendix A).

2 ACQUISITION OF SHARES VS. ACQUISITION OF THE INDIVIDUAL ASSETS

In the case of an **acquisition of shares** in which the acquirer obtains control of the acquiree, the acquirer recognizes the shares in its **separate financial statements** and measures them either at cost or at fair value according to IFRS 9 in these statements (IAS 27.38). According to IFRS 9 there is an irrefutable presumption that fair value can always be determined reliably. However, in some situations cost may be an appropriate estimate of fair value (IFRS 9. B5.4.14–9.B5.4.17).[1] In the case of an acquisition of shares, the acquisition method, which requires presentation of the individual assets and liabilities of the acquiree instead of the shares (IFRS 3.5), is only applied in the acquirer's **consolidated financial statements**.

[1] *If IFRS 9 was not applied early, the shares would be measured either at cost or according to IAS 39 (IAS 27.38). In the latter case, the investments would normally be measured at fair value. However, the equity instruments would be measured at cost if it were not possible to determine fair value reliably (IAS 39.AG80–39.AG81).*

By contrast, it may also be the case that the acquirer **acquires the individual assets and assumes the individual liabilities** of the acquiree instead of purchasing shares. In this case, IFRS 3 applies to the consolidated financial statements of the acquirer as well as to its separate financial statements (i.e. in both financial statements, the individual assets and liabilities of the acquiree are recognized).

3 IDENTIFYING THE ACQUIRER

The **acquirer** is the entity that obtains control of the **acquiree** (IFRS 3.Appendix A). For each business combination, one of the combining entities has to be identified as the acquirer (IFRS 3.6). In many situations, identification of the acquirer is straightforward. However, in some cases the business combination is a **reverse acquisition**. This means that the legal acquirer is the acquiree for financial reporting purposes according to the principle of "substance over form"[2] (IFRS 3.B15 and 3.B19–B27).

4 ACQUISITION DATE

The acquisition date is the date on which the acquirer **obtains control** of the acquiree (IFRS 3.8). The acquisition date is determined according to the principle of "substance over form"[3] (IFRS 3.9).

5 ACQUISITION-RELATED COSTS

Acquisition-related costs (e.g. external legal and advisory costs and the costs of maintaining an internal acquisitions department) are costs the acquirer incurs to carry through a business combination. These costs are accounted for as expenses in the periods in which the costs are incurred and the services are received. However, the costs to issue debt or equity instruments are recognized according to IAS 32 and IFRS 9 (IFRS 3.53).[4]

6 ACCOUNTING FOR A BUSINESS COMBINATION ON THE ACQUISITION DATE

6.1 Overview

On the acquisition date, the acquirer generally recognizes the **assets** (e.g. buildings, machines, intangible assets, and inventories) and **liabilities** (e.g. issued bonds, trade payables, and provisions) of the **acquiree** and measures them at their **fair values**. In a simple situation, in which 100% of another entity is acquired, the acquired net assets (assets less liabilities) are compared with the consideration transferred in order to acquire the acquiree. If the consideration transferred with regard to the acquisition exceeds the acquiree's net assets, **goodwill is recognized in the statement of financial position.**

These deliberations have to be extended when they are applied to situations in which, e.g. **80%** (i.e. not 100%) of another entity (in which the acquirer previously did not hold any equity

[2] *See the chapter on Conceptual Framework, Section 4.2.2.*

[3] *See the chapter on Conceptual Framework, Section 4.2.2.*

[4] *Regarding costs to issue equity instruments, see the chapter on IAS 32, Section 6 and Example 3.*

instruments) is **acquired**. In this case, the consideration paid only reflects 80% of the acquiree. However, **100% of the individual assets and liabilities** of the acquiree have to be **recognized**. Consequently in the consolidated statement of financial position, a credit entry has to be made that reflects the interest in a subsidiary of the other shareholders (20%). This interest is called the **non-controlling interest**. It has to be presented as a component of **equity**, according to IFRS (IAS 27.27 and IAS 1.54q). More precisely, the non-controlling interest is the equity in a subsidiary not attributable, directly or indirectly, to a parent (IFRS 3.Appendix A).

When a non-controlling interest exists, the **calculation of goodwill has to be modified** because it would not be appropriate to compare the consideration for the acquisition of 80% of the acquiree with 100% of the acquiree's net assets. Therefore, IFRS 3 requires comparing the value of the entire acquiree (100%) determined according to IFRS 3 with the entire net assets of the acquiree (100%) measured according to IFRS 3. This results in the following formula: consideration transferred (for 80%) + carrying amount of the **non-controlling interest** determined in accordance with IFRS 3 (20%) – net assets (100%) = goodwill (if > 0). The non-controlling interest is generally measured either at its fair value or at its proportionate share in the recognized amounts of the acquiree's identifiable net assets (IFRS 3.19). In the former case, goodwill is recognized with respect to the non-controlling interest. In the latter case, no goodwill is recognized with regard to the non-controlling interest.

An acquirer may obtain control of an acquiree in which it held an equity interest immediately before the acquisition date. This is referred to as a **business combination achieved in stages** or as a **step acquisition** (IFRS 3.41).[5] In this case the above formula for calculating goodwill has to be extended so that goodwill is increased by the **previously held equity interest** in the acquiree measured at its **acquisition-date fair value**.

The table below summarizes important aspects of the accounting for a business combination, which are described in more detail in the following sections (IFRS 3.32 and 3.19):

	Consideration transferred	The consideration transferred is generally measured at acquisition-date fair value.
+	**Non-controlling interest**	The non-controlling interest is generally measured either at its fair value or at its proportionate share of the acquiree's identifiable net assets.
+	**Previously held equity interest**	The acquisition-date fair value of the acquirer's previously held equity interest in the acquiree.
=	**Value of the acquiree (100%)**	
–	**Net assets acquired (100%)**	The net of the acquisition-date amounts of the identifiable assets acquired and the liabilities assumed determined according to IFRS 3.
=	**Goodwill**	If > 0.

6.2 Identifiable Assets Acquired and Liabilities Assumed

6.2.1 Recognition in the Statement of Financial Position To qualify for recognition in a business combination, an item must meet the definition of an asset or a liability in the

[5] *See Section 6.5.*

Conceptual Framework at the acquisition date (IFRS 3.11).[6] There is an irrefutable assumption that the recognition criteria of the Conceptual Framework (i.e. reliability of measurement and probability of an inflow or outflow of benefits)[7] are always satisfied.[8] Hence, the probability of an inflow or outflow of future economic benefits is relevant only for determining fair value of the item (i.e. with regard to measurement).

An asset is **identifiable** if one of the following criteria is met. These criteria are particularly relevant for intangible assets (IFRS 3.Appendix A and 3.B31–3.B34).

- **Separability criterion**: The asset is separable, i.e. capable of being separated or divided from the entity and sold, transferred, rented, licensed or exchanged, either individually or together with a related contract, identifiable asset or liability, regardless of whether the entity intends to do so.
- **Contractual-legal criterion**: The asset arises from contractual or other legal rights, regardless of whether those rights are separable or transferable from the entity or from other rights and obligations.

In a business combination it may be necessary to recognize some assets and liabilities that the acquiree had not previously recognized as assets and liabilities in its financial statements (e.g. internally generated brands that could not be capitalized by the acquiree due to IAS 38.63) (IFRS 3.13).

The acquirer recognizes no assets or liabilities related to an **operating lease** in which the acquiree is the **lessee**. However, there are exceptions to this rule (IFRS 3.B28–3.B30):

- The acquirer recognizes an intangible asset if the terms of an operating lease are favorable relative to market terms and a liability if the terms are unfavorable relative to market terms.
- Other benefits may be associated with an operating lease, which may represent an identifiable intangible asset.

6.2.2 Classifications and Designations At the acquisition date the acquirer has to classify or designate the identifiable assets acquired and liabilities assumed as necessary in order to apply other IFRSs after the acquisition date. These classifications or designations are made on the basis of the conditions as they are at the acquisition date (IFRS 3.15). An example of such a classification is the assignment of financial assets and financial liabilities as measured at amortized cost or at fair value for the purpose of measurement after recognition. An example of a designation is the designation of a derivative as a hedging instrument (IFRS 3.16).[9]

6.2.3 Measurement The identifiable assets acquired and the liabilities assumed are measured by the acquirer at their **acquisition-date fair values** (IFRS 3.18). Fair value is the amount for which an asset could be exchanged or a liability settled between knowledgeable,

---

6 *See the chapter on Conceptual Framework, Section 6.1.*

7 *See the chapter on Conceptual Framework, Section 6.*

8 *See KPMG,* Insights into IFRS, *7th edition, 2.6.570.20*

9 *See the chapter on IFRS 9/IAS 39, Section 2.7. IFRS 9 has not yet changed the hedge accounting requirements of IAS 39. Instead, IFRS 9 refers to IAS 39 in this regard (IFRS 9.5.2.3 and 9.5.3.2).*

willing parties in an arm's length transaction (IFRS 3.Appendix A). Fair value is an **objective** and not a subjective value. This means that fair value is determined under the presumption that the item will be used by the entity in a way in which other market participants would use it. This also applies when the acquirer intends not to use an acquired asset or intends to use the asset in a way that is different from the way in which other market participants would use it (IFRS 3.B43).

The determination of the fair value of a **brand** acquired in a business combination according to the "**relief from royalty method**" as well as the **tax amortization benefit** are illustrated in the chapter on IFRS 13.[10]

6.2.4 Exception to the Recognition Rules The term "**contingent liability**" is defined in IAS 37.[11] The requirements in IAS 37 do not apply in determining which contingent liabilities are recognized on acquisition date. Instead, a contingent liability assumed in a business combination is recognized at the acquisition date if there is a present obligation that arises from past events and its fair value can be determined reliably. This means that, contrary to IAS 37, the acquirer recognizes a contingent liability although it is not probable (i.e. it is not more likely than not) that an outflow of resources will be required to settle the obligation (IFRS 3.22–3.23).

6.2.5 Exceptions to the Recognition and Measurement Rules **Deferred tax assets or liabilities** arising from the assets acquired and liabilities assumed in a business combination are recognized and measured by the acquirer in accordance with IAS 12 (IFRS 3.24). The potential tax effects of temporary differences and carryforwards of an acquiree that exist at the acquisition date or arise as a result of the acquisition are accounted for by the acquirer in accordance with IAS 12 (IFRS 3.25).[12]

As a result of the exception to the recognition and measurement rules with regard to IAS 12, deferred tax assets or liabilities recognized in a business combination are not measured at their acquisition-date fair values because IAS 12.53 **prohibits discounting**.

A liability (or asset, if any) related to the **acquiree's employee benefit arrangements** is recognized and measured by the acquirer in accordance with IAS 19 (IFRS 3.26).

6.2.6 Exception to the Measurement Rules The acquirer measures an acquired **non-current asset (or disposal group)** that is classified as **held for sale** at the acquisition date according to IFRS 5 at fair value less costs to sell (in accordance with IFRS 5.15–5.18) (IFRS 3.31).

6.3 Non-controlling Interest

The non-controlling interest in the acquiree is generally measured on the acquisition date either at its **fair value** or at its **proportionate share in the recognized amounts of the acquiree's identifiable net assets**. Since this choice also affects the amount of goodwill recognized, it

---

[10] *See the chapter on IFRS 13, Sections 4.3 and 4.4, as well as Example 3.*

[11] *See the chapter on IAS 37, Section 3.*

[12] *See the chapter on IAS 12, Sections 3.2.5 and 3.5.2.*

can be referred to as the **full goodwill option**. The full goodwill option may be exercised **differently for each business combination** (IFRS 3.19).

In the case of measurement of the non-controlling interest at its **fair value**, this value is determined on the basis of active market prices for the equity shares not held by the acquirer. When active market prices are not available, the acquirer uses other valuation techniques. The fair value of the acquirer's interest in the acquiree might differ from the fair value of the non-controlling interest on a per-share basis. The main reason is likely to be a **control premium**. This means that the acquirer might pay a significantly higher price for the acquisition of 51% of the shares (which allows him to exercise the majority of the voting rights) than for the acquisition of 49% of the shares (which does not allow him to exercise the majority of the voting rights) (IFRS 3.B44–3.B45).

6.4 Goodwill and Gain on a Bargain Purchase

Goodwill is the positive difference between the value of the acquiree and the net assets acquired, both determined according to IFRS 3.[13] The acquirer subsumes into goodwill any value attributed to items that do not qualify for recognition as assets or liabilities by the acquirer at the acquisition date (IFRS 3.B37–3.B38).

Sometimes the value of the acquiree (determined according to IFRS 3) may exceed the net assets acquired (also determined according to IFRS 3). In these situations, the acquirer has to assess whether it has correctly identified all of the assets acquired and all of the liabilities assumed and whether they have been measured correctly. Moreover, it has to be assessed whether the consideration transferred, the non-controlling interest, and any previously held equity interest have been measured correctly. If the excess remains afterwards, the acquirer recognizes the resulting **gain on the bargain purchase** in **profit or loss** on the acquisition date. The gain has to be **attributed to the acquirer** (IFRS 3.34–3.36).

6.5 Business Combination Achieved in Stages

An acquirer may obtain control of an acquiree in which it held an equity interest immediately before the acquisition date (**business combination achieved in stages** or **step acquisition**) (IFRS 3.41). In this case, the formula for calculating goodwill has to be extended so that the goodwill is increased by the **previously held equity interest** in the acquiree measured at its **acquisition-date fair value**.[14]

If the equity instruments held by the acquirer before the business combination were investments accounted for using the equity method or investments measured at fair value through profit or loss according to IFRS 9, a **gain or loss from the remeasurement** of these equity instruments to fair value is recognized in profit or loss. However, if the previously held equity interest was measured at fair value through other comprehensive income (IFRS 9.5.7.1b and 9.5.7.5), a gain or loss resulting from remeasurement to fair value at the acquisition date is also included in other comprehensive income. Amounts recognized in other comprehensive

[13] *See the table in Section 6.1.*

[14] *See the table in Section 6.1.*

income according to IFRS 9 are not transferred subsequently to profit or loss (IFRS 3.42 and IFRS 9.B5.7.1).[15]

6.6 Consideration Transferred (Including Contingent Consideration)

The consideration transferred in a business combination is generally measured at **acquisition-date fair value**, which is the sum of the fair values of (IFRS 3.37 and 3.32):

- the assets transferred by the acquirer,
- the liabilities incurred by the acquirer to former owners of the acquiree, and
- the equity interests issued by the acquirer.

When the consideration transferred includes assets or liabilities of the acquirer that have **carrying amounts that differ from their fair values** at the acquisition date, they are **remeasured** at their fair values as of the acquisition date. A gain or loss arising on remeasurement is recognized in **profit or loss**. However, sometimes the transferred assets or liabilities **remain within the combined entity** after the business combination (e.g. because the assets or liabilities were transferred to the acquiree rather than to its former owners), and consequently the acquirer retains control of them. In this situation the acquirer measures those assets and liabilities at their carrying amounts immediately before the acquisition date and **does not adjust** them to their fair values (IFRS 3.38).

Sometimes a business combination may be achieved without the transfer of consideration, e.g. in the following situations (IFRS 3.43):

- **Minority veto rights lapse** that previously kept the acquirer from controlling an acquiree in which the acquirer held the majority voting rights.[16]
- The acquirer previously held 49% of the voting rights of the acquiree that did not result in control. At a particular date, the acquiree **repurchases** some of its **own shares** from other shareholders. As a result, the acquirer now holds 51% of the voting rights, which means that it has obtained the majority of the voting rights and control.

In the examples described above, which also represent examples of business combinations achieved in stages, the value of the acquiree at the acquisition date (determined according to IFRS 3)[17] is the sum of the carrying amount of the non-controlling interest and the acquisition-date fair value of the acquirer's previously held equity interest in the acquiree (IFRS 3.19, 3.32–3.33, and 3.41–3.42).

The consideration transferred by the acquirer in exchange for the acquiree includes any asset or liability resulting from a **contingent consideration** arrangement (IFRS 3.39). Contingent

---

[15] *If IFRS 9 is not yet applied, a gain or loss from the remeasurement of the equity interest held by the acquirer before the business combination to fair value has to be recognized in profit or loss. Changes in the value of the equity interest that were recognized in other comprehensive income in prior reporting periods (available-for-sale financial assets) have to be transferred to profit or loss (presumption of a disposal of the equity interest).*

[16] *See Example 6 regarding minority veto rights that lapse.*

[17] *See the table in Section 6.1.*

consideration is usually an obligation of the acquirer to transfer additional assets or equity interests to the former owners of the acquiree if specified future events occur or conditions are met. However, contingent consideration may also entitle the acquirer to the return of previously transferred consideration if specified conditions are met (IFRS 3.Appendix A).

The **acquisition-date fair value** of contingent consideration has to be recognized by the acquirer as part of the consideration transferred in exchange for the acquiree (IFRS 3.39). An obligation to pay contingent consideration has to be classified by the acquirer as a **liability** or as **equity** on the basis of the definitions of an equity instrument and a financial liability in IAS 32.11, or other applicable IFRSs. For those contingent consideration arrangements where the agreement gives the acquirer the right to the return of previously transferred consideration if specified future events or conditions are met, such a right has to be classified as an **asset** (IFRS 3.40).[18]

6.7 Measurement Period

If the initial accounting for a business combination is incomplete by the end of the reporting period in which the combination occurs, the acquirer's consolidated financial statements include **provisional amounts** for the items for which the accounting is incomplete. During the measurement period, the acquirer **retrospectively** adjusts these provisional amounts to reflect new information obtained about **facts and circumstances that existed as of the acquisition date** and, if known, would have affected the measurement of the amounts recognized as of that date. In the same way, it may be necessary to retrospectively recognize additional assets or liabilities (IFRS 3.45).

The measurement period ends when the acquirer receives the information it was seeking about facts and circumstances that existed as of the acquisition date or learns that more information is not obtainable. However, the measurement period must not exceed **one year** from the acquisition date (IFRS 3.45).

The acquirer has to determine whether information obtained after the acquisition date should lead to a **retrospective adjustment** to the provisional amounts recognized or whether that information results from **events** that occurred **after the acquisition date** (IFRS 3.47).

A **retrospective adjustment** of provisional carrying amounts of assets or liabilities within the measurement period is recognized by means of a **decrease or increase in goodwill** (IFRS 3.48). Thus, adjustments of the provisional amounts during the measurement period are effected as if the accounting for the business combination had been completed at the acquisition date. Consequently, **comparative information** (e.g. depreciation expense) for prior periods presented in the financial statements is also **revised** as needed (IFRS 3.49).

After the measurement period ends the accounting for a business combination is **only revised** in order to **correct an error** in accordance with IAS 8 (IFRS 3.50).

---

[18] *See Ernst & Young,* International GAAP 2011, *536. See Section 7 of this chapter regarding the subsequent measurement and accounting of contingent consideration.*

7 SUBSEQUENT MEASUREMENT AND ACCOUNTING

Assets acquired, liabilities assumed or incurred, and equity instruments issued in a business combination are generally subsequently measured and accounted for by the acquirer according to other **applicable IFRSs** for those items, depending on their nature. However, IFRS 3 contains **specific guidance** for particular items (IFRS 3.54). Some of these items are discussed below.

A **contingent liability** recognized in a business combination is measured by the acquirer after initial recognition and until it is settled, cancelled or expires at the higher of the following (IFRS 3.56):

- The amount that would be recognized according to IAS 37.
- The amount initially recognized less, if appropriate, cumulative amortization recognized according to IAS 18.

This requirement does not apply to contracts accounted for according to IFRS 9 (IFRS 3.56).

A change in the fair value of **contingent consideration** within the **measurement period** as the result of additional information that the acquirer obtained after the acquisition date about **facts and circumstances that existed at the acquisition date** results in a **retrospective adjustment of goodwill**. In addition, comparative information for prior periods presented is revised (IFRS 3.58 and 3.45–3.49).

Changes in fair value resulting from **events after the acquisition date** (e.g. meeting an earnings target, reaching a specified share price or reaching a milestone on a research and development project) are **not measurement period adjustments**. These changes are accounted for by the acquirer as follows (IFRS 3.58):

- Contingent consideration that represents **equity** is **not remeasured** and its subsequent **settlement** is accounted for **within equity**.
- If contingent consideration is classified as an **asset** or a **liability**, subsequent measurement and accounting depend on whether there is a **financial instrument** within the scope of **IFRS 9**.
  - If this is the case, measurement is at **fair value** with any resulting gain or loss recognized either in **profit or loss** or in **other comprehensive income** in accordance with IFRS 9.
  - If this is not the case, **IAS 37** is applied or **other IFRSs** as appropriate.

After acquisition date, the carrying amount of the **non-controlling interest** is adjusted for the non-controlling interest's **share of changes in equity** since acquisition date (IAS 27.18c). Consequently, also changes in **deferred tax** that affect the acquiree's net assets have to be taken into account when measuring the non-controlling interest. Moreover, if the non-controlling interest has been measured at its **fair value at acquisition date**, its carrying amount has to be adjusted for the non-controlling interest's share of **goodwill impairment losses**.[19]

---

[19] *See the chapter on IAS 36, Section 10 and Example 7.*

8 DEFERRED TAX

Regarding deferred tax, we refer to the chapter on IAS 12 and to Examples 5 and 6(b) in Section 11 of this chapter.

9 ENTRIES NECESSARY IN ORDER TO PREPARE THE CONSOLIDATED FINANCIAL STATEMENTS

When preparing consolidated financial statements, it is first necessary to adjust the separate financial statements of the parent and of the subsidiaries so that uniform accounting policies for like transactions and other events in similar circumstances are used (IAS 27.24–27.25). The result is the **statement of financial position II** (also called **balance sheet II**) and the **statement of comprehensive income II** of each of these entities.[20]

Afterwards, the **aggregated statement of financial position** (also called **aggregated balance sheet**) and the **aggregated statement of comprehensive income** are prepared. This means that the balance sheets II and the statements of comprehensive income II of the parent and of the subsidiaries are combined line by line by adding together like items of assets, liabilities, equity, income, and expenses (e.g. machines, inventories, the parent's investments in its subsidiaries, and the amounts of share capital) (IAS 27.18).

After this addition, the aggregated balance sheet includes the carrying amounts of the parent's investments in its subsidiaries (from the parent's balance sheet II), which often equal cost (IAS 27.38a) (entry "Dr Investment Cr Cash"). Moreover, the aggregated balance sheet not only comprises the assets and liabilities of a particular subsidiary, but also its equity (from the subsidiary's balance sheet II) **(current posting status)**. However, in the consolidated financial statements it is presumed that the acquirer did not acquire the shares of its subsidiary. Instead, the business combination is accounted for as if the acquirer had acquired the individual assets and assumed the individual liabilities of the acquiree **(target posting status)**. Therefore, in order to arrive at the target posting status, the carrying amount of the parent's investment in its subsidiary and the subsidiary's equity (from its balance sheet II) as at the acquisition date have to be eliminated ("Dr Equity Cr Investment"), since they do not occur in the target posting status (IAS 27.18a). Moreover, any goodwill and/or any non-controlling interest are recognized.[21] This entry is referred to as **capital consolidation**.

When effecting the capital consolidation, **further adjustments** pertaining to the business combination are also made (e.g. increasing or decreasing the carrying amounts of the acquiree's assets and liabilities to the amount required by IFRS 3 – which is generally acquisition-date fair value – and recognition of additional assets or liabilities that have not been recognized in the acquiree's statement of financial position II).

The accounting treatment of a business combination at the acquisition date may necessitate further adjustments after the acquisition date. For example, if the carrying amount of a building has been increased to acquisition-date fair value (which means that the building's depreciable

---

[20] *See the chapter on IAS 27/IFRS 10, Section 2.3.1.*

[21] *The logic of recognizing goodwill and a non-controlling interest is explained in Section 6.1.*

amount has increased), it is also necessary to increase depreciation expense after the acquisition date.

When preparing the consolidated financial statements for **future periods**, the aggregated financial statements for these future periods are used as a basis. By nature, aggregated financial statements do not include consolidation entries. Thus, in order to reach the correct posting status, the **capital consolidation**, as it has been effected at the acquisition date, has to be **repeated**. Also, further adjustments made in previous periods in respect of a subsidiary (e.g. an increase in depreciation expense) have to be repeated. Amounts recognized in profit or loss on or after the acquisition date, but before the current reporting period, have to be recognized directly in **retained earnings** in the current period (e.g. a gain on a bargain purchase[22] or an increase in depreciation expense, which has to be recognized for the previous year) and not in the profit or loss for the current period.

Profit or loss for the period as well as **total comprehensive income** for the period have to be separated into the amounts attributable to the **owners of the parent** and to the **non-controlling interest**. These four amounts have to be **disclosed** in the statement of comprehensive income as **allocations for the period** (IAS 1.81B). Nevertheless, the entire amounts of profit for the year and total comprehensive income for the year have to be presented in a separate line item in the statement of comprehensive income (IAS 1.81A). If a subsidiary generates a profit for the year, the entry "Dr Profit attributable to the non-controlling interest Cr Non-controlling interest" is made. The former account is a subaccount of the account "profit for the year." This entry results in an increase in the carrying amount of the non-controlling interest by the pro rata amount of profit (IAS 27.18c).

10 DETERMINING WHAT IS PART OF THE BUSINESS COMBINATION TRANSACTION

The acquirer and the acquiree may have a **pre-existing relationship** or other arrangement **before negotiations** for the business combination began (IFRS 3.51). Such a relationship may be on a contractual basis (e.g. licensor and licensee) or on a non-contractual basis (e.g. plaintiff and defendant). Moreover, the acquirer and the acquiree may enter into an arrangement **during the negotiations** for the business combination that is separate from the business combination (IFRS 3.51).

The following are examples of **separate transactions** that are not included in applying the acquisition method (IFRS 3.52):

- A transaction that in effect settles pre-existing relationships between the acquiree and acquirer.
- A transaction that remunerates employees or former owners of the acquiree for future services.
- A transaction that reimburses the acquiree or its former owners for paying the acquirer's acquisition-related costs.[23]

[22] *See Section 6.4.*

[23] *See Section 5.*

Separate transactions are accounted for according to the **relevant IFRSs** (IFRS 3.12, 3.51, and 3.B51). If the business combination in effect settles a pre-existing relationship, the acquirer recognizes a gain or loss, measured in accordance with the requirements of IFRS 3.B52.

11 EXAMPLES WITH SOLUTIONS[24]

Changes in a parent's ownership interest in a subsidiary that do not result in a loss of control as well as such changes that result in a loss of control are dealt with in the chapter on **IAS 27/IFRS 10** (Section 2.4 and Example 6). Some of the following examples are first illustrated without deferred tax and afterwards by taking deferred tax into account. Pertaining to the basics of deferred tax, we refer to the chapter on **IAS 12**. The measurement of a brand acquired in a business combination according to the relief from royalty method (including the tax amortization benefit) is illustrated in the chapter on **IFRS 13** (Sections 4.3 and 4.4 and Example 3).

Example 1

Capital consolidation – introductory example

On Dec 31, 01, entity E acquires all of the shares (i.e. 100%) of entity S for CU 2. E's statement of financial position (in E's separate financial statements) as at Dec 31, 01 before this acquisition is presented as follows:

Statement of financial position of E (before acquisition of S)

Cash	3	Share capital	4
Building	3	Liabilities	4
Merchandise	2		
Total	**8**	**Total**	**8**

The statement of financial position of S as at Dec 31, 01, which is not affected by the business combination, is presented as follows:

Statement of financial position of S

Building	1	Share capital	2
Merchandise	1		
Total	**2**	**Total**	**2**

Required

Prepare any necessary entries in E's separate and consolidated financial statements as at Dec 31, 01 and present E's consolidated statement of financial position as at the same date. Presume for simplicity reasons that the balance sheets and the balance sheets II are identical.

[24] *The examples in this section are based on simplified illustrations of financial statements.*

Hints for solution

In particular Sections 2, 6.1, and 9.

Solution

E's separate financial statements

The acquisition of S is accounted for as follows:

Dec 31, 01	Dr	Investment of E in S (shares)	2	
	Cr	Cash		2

Statement of financial position of E (after acquisition of S)

Cash	1	Share capital	4
Investment of E in S (shares)	2	Liabilities	4
Building	3		
Merchandise	2		
Total	**8**	**Total**	**8**

Aggregated statement of financial position

The aggregated statement of financial position is prepared by adding together the line items of the statements of financial position of E (see above) and S:[25]

Dec 31, 01	*E*	*S*	*Total*
Cash	1		1
Investment of E in S (shares)	2		2
Buildings	3	1	4
Merchandise	2	1	3
Total assets	**8**	**2**	**10**
Share capital	−4	−2	−6
Liabilities	−4		−4
Total equity and liabilities	**−8**	**−2**	**−10**

Interim summary: current posting status

The acquisition of S affects the aggregated statement of financial position as follows:

(a) The individual assets of S (i.e. the building (CU 1) and merchandise (CU 1)) are included.
(b) Cash decreases by CU 2. This is because CU 2 are paid to the former owners of S.
(c) The investment of E in S (shares) of CU 2 is included.
(d) The share capital of S (CU 2) is included.

Target posting status

If E had acquired a building for CU 1 and merchandise for CU 1 instead of the shares in S, E would have made the following entry in its separate financial statements: "Dr Building CU 1 Dr Merchandise CU 1 Cr Cash CU 2." This corresponds to (a) and (b) above and

[25] *In this table, assets are shown with a plus sign whereas liabilities and items of equity are shown with a minus sign.*

represents the target posting status because in the consolidated financial statements the acquisition of S is not presented as an acquisition of shares, but as an acquisition of the individual assets of S.

Capital consolidation

In order to transition from the current posting status to the target posting status, it is necessary to eliminate the investment of E in S (shares) and the share capital of S. In other words, items (c) and (d) (see previously) are eliminated, which means that the effects of (a) and (b) (see previous) remain.

Dec 31, 01	Dr	Share capital	2	
	Cr	Investment of E in S (shares)		2

Summary[26]

Dec 31, 01	*E*	*S*	*Aggregated balance sheet*	*Capital consolidation*	*Consolidated balance sheet*
Cash	1		1		1
Investment of E in S (shares)	2		2	−2	0
Buildings	3	1	4		4
Merchandise	2	1	3		3
Total assets	**8**	**2**	**10**	**−2**	**8**
Share capital	−4	−2	−6	2	−4
Liabilities	−4		−4		−4
Total equity and liabilities	**−8**	**−2**	**−10**	**2**	**−8**

Example 2

Business combination – initial recognition and measurement without deferred tax

On Dec 31, 01, entity E acquires 60% of the shares of entity S for CU 110. The purchase price includes a control premium (IFRS 3.B45). Fair value of the remaining 40% of S's shares as at Dec 31, 01 is CU 68.

In its separate financial statements, E accounts for its investment in S (shares) at cost (IAS 27.38a).

Posting status (in E's separate financial statements):

Dec 31, 01	Dr	Investment of E in S (shares)	110	
	Cr	Cash		110

[26] *In this table, debit entries and assets are shown with a plus sign whereas credit entries, liabilities and items of equity are shown with a minus sign.*

E's and S's statements of financial position II as at Dec 31, 01 are presented below:[27]

Dec 31, 01	*E*	*S*
Buildings	250	60
Merchandise	90	30
Cash	40	10
Investment of E in S (shares)	110	
Total assets	**490**	**100**
Share capital	−250	−60
Retained earnings	−50	−10
Loans payable	−190	−30
Total equity and liabilities	**−490**	**−100**

In addition, the following information is available:

- Fair value of S's building is CU 80.
- S discloses a contingent liability (which can be measured reliably) of CU 4 arising from a present obligation in its notes to its separate financial statements. By nature, this amount has not been recognized in S's statement of financial position (IAS 37.27).[28]
- E identifies a brand, which has been generated internally by S. Its fair value is CU 24. That brand is not recognized in S's statement of financial position (IAS 38.63).[29] However, it qualifies for recognition in E's consolidated statement of financial position according to IFRS 3.

Required

Prepare any necessary entries in E's consolidated financial statements as at Dec 31, 01 and present E's consolidated statement of financial position as at the same date. The non-controlling interest is measured (a) at its fair value and (b) at the proportionate share of S's identifiable net assets (IFRS 3.19). Ignore deferred taxes in this example.

Hints for solution

In particular Sections 2, 6.1, 6.3, and 9.

Solution (a)

					Remark
Dec 31, 01	Dr	Building	20		**(1)**
	Dr	Brand	24		**(1)**
	Dr	Goodwill	68		**(4)**
	Dr	Share capital	60		**(3)**
	Dr	Retained earnings	10		**(3)**
	Cr	Contingent liability		4	**(1)**
	Cr	Investment of E in S (shares)		110	**(2)**
	Cr	Non-controlling interest		68	**(3)**

[27] *In this table, assets are shown with a plus sign whereas liabilities and items of equity are shown with a minus sign.*

[28] *See the chapter on IAS 37, Section 3.*

[29] *See the chapter on IAS 38, Section 3.4.*

Remarks on the previous entry:

1. S's assets and liabilities that are already included in S's balance sheet II (and which are therefore also part of the aggregated balance sheet) are not included in the above entry. The carrying amount of S's building in S's statement of financial position II as well as in the aggregated statement of financial position is CU 60. Consequently, the **building**'s carrying amount has to be increased to fair value of CU 80. Moreover, the **brand** identified and the **contingent liability** (which arises from a present obligation and can be measured reliably) have not been recognized as an asset and as a liability in S's statement of financial position II. However, they have to be recognized in E's consolidated statement of financial position.
2. The **investment of E in S** (shares) is derecognized because it is replaced by S's identifiable assets (e.g. S's building) and liabilities.
3. S's entire **equity as at the acquisition date** (Dec 31, 01) is **derecognized**. The equity to be derecognized also includes S's retained earnings (which comprise profit or loss) incurred before the acquisition date. In addition, the **non-controlling interest** (40%) is recognized in the consolidated statement of financial position as a separate category of equity (IAS 1.54q). The line item "non-controlling interest" is necessary because 100% of the identifiable assets and liabilities are recognized, although E only owns 60% of S.[30] In version (a) of this example, the non-controlling interest is measured at its fair value (CU 68) (IFRS 3.19).
4. **Goodwill** is calculated as follows (IFRS 3.32):

Consideration transferred (60%)	110	
Carrying amount of the non-controlling interest (40%)	68	
Value of S (determined according to IFRS 3) (100%)		**178**
Net assets (equity) of S (in S's balance sheet II) (100%)	70	
Increase in the carrying amount of S's building	20	
Brand	24	
Contingent liability	–4	
Net assets of S (according to IFRS 3)		**110**
Goodwill		**68**

Summary

The following table summarizes the steps described above, which result in the consolidated statement of financial position:[31]

Dec 31, 01	*E*	*S*	*Aggregated balance sheet*	*Capital consolidation*	*Consolidated balance sheet*
Goodwill				68	68
Brand				24	24
Buildings	250	60	310	20	330
Merchandise	90	30	120		120
Cash	40	10	50		50
Investment of E in S (shares)	110		110	–110	0
Total assets	**490**	**100**	**590**	**2**	**592**

[30] *See Section 6.1.*

[31] *In this table, debit entries and assets are shown with a plus sign whereas credit entries, liabilities, and items of equity are shown with a minus sign.*

Dec 31, 01	*E*	*S*	*Aggregated balance sheet*	*Capital consolidation*	*Consolidated balance sheet*
Share capital	−250	−60	−310	60	−250
Retained earnings	−50	−10	−60	10	−50
Non-controlling interest				−68	−68
Contingent liability				−4	−4
Loans payable	−190	−30	−220		−220
Total equity and liabilities	**−490**	**−100**	**−590**	**−2**	**−592**

Solution (b)

					Remark
Dec 31, 01	Dr	Building	20		
	Dr	Brand	24		
	Dr	Goodwill	44		**(2)**
	Dr	Share capital	60		
	Dr	Retained earnings	10		
	Cr	Contingent liability		4	
	Cr	Investment of E in S (shares)		110	
	Cr	Non-controlling interest		44	**(1)**

Remarks to the above entry:

1. The non-controlling interest is measured at its proportionate share of S's identifiable net assets (IFRS 3.19):

Net assets (equity) of S (in S's balance sheet II)	70	
Increase in the carrying amount of S's building	20	
Brand	24	
Contingent liability	−4	
Net assets of S (according to IFRS 3)		**110**
Non-controlling interest (40% thereof)		**44**

2. **Goodwill** is calculated as follows (IFRS 3.32):

Consideration transferred (60%)	110	
Carrying amount of the non-controlling interest (40%)	44	
Value of S (determined according to IFRS 3) (100%)		**154**
Net assets of S (according to IFRS 3) (100%) (see remark 1)		**110**
Goodwill		**44**

Summary

The following table summarizes the steps described above, which result in the consolidated statement of financial position:[32]

Dec 31, 01	*E*	*S*	*Aggregated balance sheet*	*Capital consolidation*	*Consolidated balance sheet*
Goodwill				44	44
Brand				24	24
Buildings	250	60	310	20	330
Merchandise	90	30	120		120
Cash	40	10	50		50
Investment of E in S (shares)	110		110	−110	0
Total assets	**490**	**100**	**590**	**−22**	**568**

[32] *In this table, debit entries and assets are shown with a plus sign whereas credit entries, liabilities, and items of equity are shown with a minus sign.*

Dec 31, 01	E	S	Aggregated balance sheet	Capital consolidation	Consolidated balance sheet
Share capital	−250	−60	−310	60	−250
Retained earnings	−50	−10	−60	10	−50
Non–controlling interest				−44	−44
Contingent liability				−4	−4
Loans payable	−190	−30	−220		−220
Total equity and liabilities	**−490**	**−100**	**−590**	**22**	**−568**

Example 3

Continuation of Example 2(b) in 02 (without deferred tax)

In addition to the information given in Example 2, the following information is available:

(a) The remaining useful life of S's **building** (according to IFRS and for tax purposes) as at Dec 31, 01 is 10 years. In May, 02, E receives an expert report with regard to the measurement of S's building, which states that fair value as at Dec 31, 01 is CU 100 (instead of CU 80).
(b) The **brand** is an intangible asset with an indefinite useful life. Hence, it is not amortized (IAS 38.107).
(c) S's **profit for the year 02** (before preparing the consolidation entries) is CU 100.

Required.

E already prepared its consolidated financial statements as at Dec 31, 01 (see Example 2b). Prepare any necessary entries in E's consolidated financial statements as at Dec 31, 02.

Hints for solution

In particular Sections 6.7, 7, and 9.

Solution

First, the capital consolidation has to be repeated on Dec 31, 02 as it has been effected on the acquisition date Dec 31, 01 (see the column "capital consolidation" in the table at the end of Example 2b). This is necessary in order to achieve the correct posting status.

Measurement period adjustments

During the measurement period, E obtains new information about facts and circumstances that existed as of the acquisition date. Consequently, the adjustments described subsequently have to be effected retrospectively, i.e. as at Dec 31, 01 (i.e. that an adjustment of comparative information presented in E's consolidated financial statements is also necessary). The carrying amount of the building has to be increased by CU 20 (i.e. from CU 80 to CU 100) as at Dec 31, 01. Goodwill is reduced by the same amount (IFRS 3.45–3.49 and 3.IE50–3.IE53).[33]

[33] *See Section 6.7.*

Dec 31, 01	Dr	Building	20	
	Cr	Goodwill		20

This entry retrospectively changes S's net assets (excluding goodwill) as at Dec 31, 01. Consequently, the carrying amount of the non-controlling interest as at Dec 31, 01 increases from CU 44 to CU 52:

Net assets (equity) of S (in S's balance sheet II)	70	
Increase in the carrying amount of S's building	40	
Brand	24	
Contingent liability	−4	
Net assets of S (according to IFRS 3)		**130**
Non-controlling interest (40% thereof)		**52**

This increase of CU 8 leads to an increase in goodwill since new information was obtained within the measurement period about facts and circumstances that existed as of the acquisition date:

Dec 31, 01	Dr	Goodwill	8	
	Cr	Non-controlling interest		8

The new carrying amount of goodwill as at Dec 31, 01 can be derived in one of the following ways:

Goodwill (in E's consolidated financial statements as at Dec 31, 01)	44
1st retrospective entry	−20
2nd retrospective entry	8
Retrospectively adjusted goodwill as at Dec 31, 01	**32**

Consideration transferred (60%)	110
Carrying amount of the non-controlling interest (40%)	52
Value of S (determined according to IFRS 3) (100%)	**162**
Net assets of S (according to IFRS 3) (100%)	130
Goodwill as at Dec 31, 01	**32**

Entries for the period 02

The depreciation expense recognized for the **building** in S's statement of comprehensive income II is CU 6 (= CU 60 : 10 years). However, the carrying amount of the building in E's consolidated financial statements as at Dec 31, 01 is CU 100. Thus, depreciation expense has to be increased to CU 10 (= CU 100 : 10 years):

Dec 31, 02	Dr	Depreciation expense	4	
	Cr	Building		4

S's profit for the year 02 (before preparing the consolidation entries) is CU 100. That amount is reduced by the additional depreciation expense of CU 4. These facts are important when determining the carrying amount of the non-controlling interest, which changes by the amount of profit or loss attributable to the non-controlling interest (IAS 27.18c):

Non-controlling interest as at Dec 31, 01		**52**
Pro rata profit (40% of CU 100)	40.0	
NCI's share of the additional depreciation expense (40% of CU -4)	−1.6	
Profit attributable to the non-controlling interest		**38.4**
Non-controlling interest as at Dec 31, 02		**90.4**

Since S generates a profit for the year 02, the entry "Dr Profit attributable to the non-controlling interest Cr Non-controlling interest" is made. The former account is a subaccount of the account "profit for the year." This entry results in an increase in the carrying amount of the non-controlling interest by the pro rata amount of profit determined above (IAS 27.18c):[34]

Dec 31, 02	Dr	Profit attributable to the NCI	38.4	
	Cr	Non-controlling interest		38.4

Example 4

Continuation of Example 3 in 03 (without deferred tax)

In addition to the information given in Examples 2 and 3, the following information is available:

(a) S's **loss for the year** 03 (before preparing the consolidation entries) is CU 20.
(b) In 03, S pays a **dividend** of CU 30 from the profit for the year 02. In S's separate financial statements, the entry "Dr Retained earnings Cr Cash CU 30" has been made with respect to the dividend.

Required

E already prepared its consolidated financial statements as at Dec 31, 01 and Dec 31, 02 (see Examples 2b and 3). Prepare any necessary entries in E's consolidated financial statements as at Dec 31, 03.

Hints for solution

In particular Sections 7 and 9.

Solution

First, the capital consolidation has to be repeated on Dec 31, 03 as it has been effected on the acquisition date Dec 31, 01 (see the column "capital consolidation" in the table at the end of Example 2b). Afterwards, the other consolidation entries effected when preparing the consolidated financial statements as at Dec 31, 02 (see Example 3) have to be repeated. This is necessary in order to achieve the correct posting status. Amounts recognized in profit or loss in 02 have to be recognized in retained earnings and not in profit or loss for 03.[35]

Dec 31, 01	Dr	Building	20	
	Cr	Goodwill		20

[34] *See Section 9.*
[35] *See Section 9.*

Dec 31, 01	Dr	Goodwill	8	
	Cr	Non-controlling interest		8
Dec 31, 03	Dr	Retained earnings	4	
	Cr	Building		4
Dec 31, 03	Dr	Retained earnings	38.4	
	Cr	Non-controlling interest		38.4

Entries for the period 03

Dec 31, 03	Dr	Depreciation expense	4	
	Cr	Building		4

In 03, the carrying amount of the non-controlling interest changes as follows:

Non-controlling interest as at Dec 31, 02			**90.4**
Pro rata loss (40% of CU –20)	−8.0		
NCI's share of the additional depreciation expense (40% of CU –4)	−1.6		
Loss attributable to the non-controlling interest		**−9.6**	
Pro rata dividend (40% of CU 30)		−12.0	
Change in the carrying amount of the non-controlling interest			**−21.6**
Non-controlling interest as at Dec 31, 03			**68.8**

Dec 31, 03	Dr	Non-controlling interest	9.6	
	Cr	Loss attributable to the NCI		9.6
Dec 31, 03	Dr	Non-controlling interest	12	
	Cr	Retained earnings		12

Example 5

Examples 2–4, taking deferred tax (inside basis differences II[36]) into account

In addition to the information given in Examples 2–4, the following information is available:

- The carrying amount of the building for tax purposes as at Dec 31, 01, is CU 60. The building's remaining useful life for tax purposes as at the same date is 10 years.
- The contingent liability and the brand are not recognized as an asset or as a liability for tax purposes.

Required

Illustrate the solutions of Examples 2(b)–4, taking into account deferred tax (inside basis differences II[37]). The tax rate is 25%. Assume that the criteria for offsetting deferred tax assets and deferred tax liabilities in the statement of financial position (IAS 12.74) are met.

Hints for solution

In particular Sections 2, 6.1, 6.3, 6.7, 7, and 9.

[36] *See the chapter on IAS 12, Section 3.2.5.*

[37] *See the chapter on IAS 12, Section 3.2.5.*

Solution for the consolidated financial statements as at Dec 31, 01

					Remark
Dec 31, 01	Dr	Building	20		
	Dr	Brand	24		
	Dr	Goodwill	50		(3)
	Dr	Share capital	60		
	Dr	Retained earnings	10		
	Cr	Contingent liability		4	
	Cr	Deferred tax liability		10	(1)
	Cr	Investment of E in S (shares)		110	
	Cr	Non-controlling interest		40	(2)

Remarks on the above entry:

(1) Deferred tax: According to IFRS, the carrying amount of S's building has to be increased to fair value (i.e. from CU 60 to CU 80). This results in a temporary difference, because the building's carrying amount for tax purposes is CU 60. Further temporary differences arise from the recognition of the brand and of the contingent liability according to IFRS, because they are not recognized as an asset or as a liability for tax purposes. The initial recognition of goodwill does not result in the recognition of a deferred tax liability (IAS 12.15a).

	Carrying amount as at Dec 31, 01 (IFRS)	*Carrying amount as at Dec 31, 01 (for tax purposes)*	*Deductible temporary differences*	*Taxable temporary differences*	*Deferred tax assets (25%)*	*Deferred tax liabilities (25%)*
Building (fair value adjustment)	20	0		20		5
Brand	24	0		24		6
Contingent liability	4	0	4		1	
Total					**1**	**11**
Deferred tax liability (after offsetting according to IAS 12.74)						**10**

(2) The **non-controlling interest** is measured at its proportionate share of S's identifiable net assets (IFRS 3.19):

Net assets (equity) of S (in S's balance sheet II)	70	
Increase in the carrying amount of S's building	20	
Brand	24	
Contingent liability	–4	
Deferred tax liability	–10	
Net assets of S (according to IFRS 3)		**100**
Non-controlling interest (40% thereof)		**40**

(3) Goodwill is calculated as follows (IFRS 3.32):

Consideration transferred (60%)	110	
Carrying amount of the non-controlling interest (40%)	40	
Value of S (determined according to IFRS 3) (100%)		**150**
Net assets of S (according to IFRS 3) (100%)		100
Goodwill		**50**

Summary

The following table summarizes the steps described previously, which result in the consolidated statement of financial position:[38]

Dec 31, 01	*E*	*S*	*Aggregated balance sheet*	*Capital consolidation*	*Consolidated balance sheet*
Goodwill				50	50
Brand				24	24
Buildings	250	60	310	20	330
Merchandise	90	30	120		120
Cash	40	10	50		50
Investment of E in S (shares)	110		110	−110	0
Total assets	**490**	**100**	**590**	**−16**	**574**
Share capital	−250	−60	−310	60	−250
Retained earnings	−50	−10	−60	10	−50
Non–controlling interest				−40	−40
Contingent liability				−4	−4
Deferred tax liability				−10	−10
Loans payable	−190	−30	−220		−220
Total equity and liabilities	**−490**	**−100**	**−590**	**16**	**−574**

Solution for the consolidated financial statements as at Dec 31, 02

First, the capital consolidation has to be repeated on Dec 31, 03 as it has been effected on the acquisition date Dec 31, 01 (see the column "capital consolidation" in the table above). This is necessary in order to achieve the correct posting status.

Measurement period adjustments

During the measurement period, E obtains new information about facts and circumstances that existed as of the acquisition date. Consequently, the adjustments described subsequently have to be effected retrospectively, i.e. as at Dec 31, 01 (i.e. also an adjustment of comparative information presented in E's consolidated financial statements is necessary). The carrying amount of the building has to be increased by CU 20 (i.e. from CU 80 to CU 100) as at Dec 31, 01. This leads to an increase in the deferred tax liability by CU 5 (= CU 20 · 25%) as at the same date. As a result, goodwill is reduced by CU 15, because measurement period adjustments also lead to an adjustment of goodwill (IFRS 3.45–3.49 and 3.IE50–IE53).

[38] *In this table, debit entries and assets are shown with a plus sign whereas credit entries, liabilities, and items of equity are shown with a minus sign.*

Dec 31, 01	Dr	Building	20	
	Cr	Deferred tax liability		5
	Cr	Goodwill		15

The above entry retrospectively changes S's net assets (excluding goodwill) as at Dec 31, 01. Consequently, the carrying amount of the non-controlling interest as at Dec 31, 01, increases by CU 6 (i.e. from CU 40 to CU 46):

Net assets (equity) of S (in S's balance sheet II)	70	
Increase in the carrying amount of S's building	40	
Brand	24	
Contingent liability	–4	
Deferred tax liability	–15 (= *10 + 5*)	
Net assets of S (according to IFRS 3)		**115**
Non-controlling interest (40% thereof)		**46**

This increase of CU 6 leads to an increase in goodwill, since new information was obtained within the measurement period about facts and circumstances that existed as of the acquisition date:

Dec 31, 01	Dr	Goodwill	6	
	Cr	Non-controlling interest		6

The new carrying amount of goodwill as at Dec 31, 01 can be derived in one of the following ways:

Goodwill (in E's consolidated financial statements as at Dec 31, 01)	50
1st retrospective entry	–15
2nd retrospective entry	6
Retrospectively adjusted goodwill as at Dec 31, 01	**41**

Consideration transferred (60%)	110	
Carrying amount of the non-controlling interest (40%)	46	
Value of S (determined according to IFRS 3) (100%)		**156**
Net assets of S (according to IFRS 3) (100%)		115
Goodwill		**41**

Entries for the period 02

Dec 31, 02	Dr	Depreciation expense	4	
	Cr	Building		4

On Dec 31, 01, the carrying amount of S's building is CU 100 according to IFRS and CU 60 for tax purposes. This gives rise to a taxable temporary difference of CU 40 and consequently, to a deferred tax liability of CU 10 (= CU 40 · 25%). On Dec 31, 02, the carrying amount of S's building is CU 90 (= CU 100 – CU 100 : 10) according to IFRS and CU 54 (= CU 60 – CU 60 : 10) for tax purposes. Hence, the taxable temporary difference is CU 36 (= CU 90 – CU 54 or CU 40 – CU 4) and the deferred tax liability is CU 9 (= CU 36 · 25%). Thus, the deferred tax liability decreases by CU 1:

Dec 31, 02	Dr	Deferred tax liability	1	
	Cr	Deferred tax income		1

The carrying amount of the non-controlling interest changes by the amount of profit or loss attributable to the non-controlling interest (IAS 27.18c):

Non-controlling interest as at Dec 31, 01		**46.0**
Pro rata profit (40% of CU 100)	40.0	
NCI's share of the additional depreciation expense (40% of CU –4)	−1.6	
NCI's share of deferred tax income (40% of CU 1)	0.4	
Profit attributable to the non-controlling interest		**38.8**
Non-controlling interest as at Dec 31, 02		**84.8**

Dec 31, 02	Dr	Profit attributable to the NCI	38.8	
	Cr	Non-controlling interest		38.8

Solution for the consolidated financial statements as at Dec 31, 03

First, the capital consolidation as it has been effected on the acquisition date Dec 31, 01 (see above) as well as the other consolidation entries effected when preparing the consolidated financial statements as at Dec 31, 02 (see above) have to be repeated on Dec 31, 03. This is necessary in order to achieve the correct posting status. Amounts recognized in profit or loss in 02 have to be recognized in retained earnings and not in profit or loss for 03.[39]

Dec 31, 01	Dr	Building	20	
	Cr	Deferred tax liability		5
	Cr	Goodwill		15
Dec 31, 01	Dr	Goodwill	6	
	Cr	Non-controlling interest		6
Dec 31, 03	Dr	Retained earnings	4	
	Cr	Building		4
Dec 31, 03	Dr	Deferred tax liability	1	
	Cr	Retained earnings		1
Dec 31, 03	Dr	Retained earnings	38.8	
	Cr	Non-controlling interest		38.8

Entries for the period 03

Dec 31, 03	Dr	Depreciation expense	4	
	Cr	Building		4
Dec 31, 03	Dr	Deferred tax liability	1	
	Cr	Deferred tax income		1

[39] *See Section 9.*

In 03, the carrying amount of the non-controlling interest changes as follows:

Non-controlling interest as at Dec 31, 02			**84.8**
Pro rata loss (40% of CU –20)	−8.0		
NCI's share of the additional depreciation expense (40% of CU –4)	−1.6		
NCI's share of deferred tax income (40% of CU 1)	0.4		
Loss attributable to the non-controlling interest		**−9.2**	
Pro rata dividend (40% of CU 30)		−12.0	
Change in the carrying amount of the non-controlling interest			**−21.2**
Non-controlling interest as at Dec 31, 03			**63.6**

Dec 31, 03	Dr	Non-controlling interest	9.20	
	Cr	Loss attributable to the NCI		9.20
Dec 31, 03	Dr	Non-controlling interest	12	
	Cr	Retained earnings		12

Example 6

Business combination achieved in stages and without the transfer of consideration[40]

On Dec 31, 00, entity E acquires 60% of the shares of entity S (which is free of debt) for CU 50. At that date, minority veto rights keep E from controlling S. Instead, S is an associate of E and is therefore accounted for using the equity method in E's consolidated financial statements. In E's separate financial statements the investment is measured at cost (IAS 28.35 and IAS 27.38a).

On Dec 31, 01, the minority veto rights lapse, which means that E obtains control of S. As at Dec 31, 01, fair value of the shares held by E (60%) is CU 60 and fair value of the remaining 40% of the shares is CU 40. A control premium is ignored for simplicity reasons. The statement of financial position II of S as at Dec 31, 01, is presented below:

Statement of financial position II of S

Building	40	Share capital	50
Merchandise	10	Retained earnings	10
Cash	10		
Total	**60**	**Total**	**60**

On Dec 31, 01, fair value of the building is CU 48. On Dec 31, 00, fair value of the building was identical with the building's carrying amount according to IFRS. The building's carrying amount for tax purposes as at Dec 31, 01 is CU 40.

[40] *The solution of this example does not change if IFRS 9 (and the consequential amendment of IFRS 3.42 caused by IFRS 9) is not applied early. This is because the previously held shares are an investment in an associate accounted for using the equity method and in that case there is no difference between the "old" and the "new" requirements under IFRS.*

S's profit for the year 01 is CU 10.

Posting status (in E's separate financial statements):

Dec 31, 00	Dr	Investment of E in S (shares)	50	
	Cr	Cash		50

Required

Prepare any necessary entries in E's consolidated financial statements as at Dec 31, 01. The non-controlling interest is measured at its fair value (IFRS 3.19).

(a) Ignore deferred tax.
(b) Take deferred tax (inside basis differences II[41]) into account. The tax rate is 25%.

Hints for solution

In particular Sections 6.1, 6.5, and 6.6.

Solution (a)

Until Dec 30, 01, S is an associate of E accounted for using the equity method in E's consolidated financial statements. Accordingly, E's share of S's profit for 01 increases the carrying amount of the investment of E in S:[42]

Dec 30, 01	Dr	Investment of E in S (shares)	6	
	Cr	Share of the profit or loss of associates		6

Thus, on Dec 30, 01 the carrying amount of the investment is CU 56 (= CU 50 + CU 6).

Since the minority veto rights lapse, E obtains control of S on Dec 31, 01 (IFRS 3.43b), which constitutes a business combination without the transfer of consideration (IFRS 3.33, 3.43, and 3.B46). At the same time, the business combination represents a business combination achieved in stages because E held an equity interest in S immediately before the acquisition date (IFRS 3.41–3.42).

E's equity interest is remeasured at its acquisition-date fair value. The gain arising from remeasurement is recognized in profit or loss (IFRS 3.42).

Carrying amount of the investment as at Dec 30, 01	56
Acquisition-date fair value of the investment	60
Gain	**4**

[41] *See the chapter on IAS 12, Section 3.2.5.*

[42] *See the chapter on IAS 28, Section 2.2.1.*

Goodwill is calculated as follows (IFRS 3.32):

Consideration transferred (0%)	0	
Acquisition-date fair value of the investment (60%)	60	
Carrying amount of the non-controlling interest (40%)	40	
Value of S (determined according to IFRS 3) (100%)		**100**
Net assets (equity) of S (in S's balance sheet II)	60	
Increase in the carrying amount of S's building	8	
Net assets of S (according to IFRS 3) (100%)		**68**
Goodwill		**32**

Dec 31, 01	Dr	Building	8
	Dr	Goodwill	32
	Dr	Share capital	50
	Dr	Retained earnings	10
	Cr	Gain (profit or loss)	4
	Cr	Investment of E in S (shares)	56
	Cr	Non-controlling interest	40

Solution (b)

The solution is similar to (a). However, deferred tax is taken into account.

Consideration transferred (0%)	0	
Acquisition-date fair value of the investment (60%)	60	
Carrying amount of the non-controlling interest (40%)	40	
Value of S (determined according to IFRS 3) (100%)		**100**
Net assets (equity) of S (in S's balance sheet II) (100%)	60	
Increase in the carrying amount of S's building	8	
Deferred tax liability hereto	–2	
Net assets of S (according to IFRS 3)		**66**
Goodwill		**34**

Dec 31, 01	Dr	Building	8
	Dr	Goodwill	34
	Dr	Share capital	50
	Dr	Retained earnings	10
	Cr	Gain (profit or loss)	4
	Cr	Investment of E in S (shares)	56
	Cr	Deferred tax liability	2
	Cr	Non-controlling interest	40

Example 7

Contingent consideration

On Dec 31, 01, entity E acquires all of the individual assets[43] of entity F, which is free of debt. E does not purchase shares. On Dec 31, 01, the carrying amount of the acquired assets is CU 40 in F's financial statements. On the same day, their value determined in accordance with IFRS 3 is CU 50.

---

[43] *See Section 2.*

During the negotiations it was difficult to fix the purchase price due to differing expectations regarding the future cash flows of F's business. Therefore, in addition to a fixed payment of CU 55 (which is effected on Dec 31, 01), E has to pay CU 5 if accumulated EBITDA[44] for the years 02–04 is at least CU 16, and pay CU 10 if it is at least CU 20.

On Dec 31, 01, E estimates the probabilities that it will have to pay the following amounts of contingent consideration as follows:

Accumulated EBITDA for the years 02–04	*Contingent consideration*	*Probability*
< CU 16	0	20%
≥ CU 16 and < CU 20	5	40%
≥ CU 20	10	40%

As a result of additional information obtained by E within the measurement period (year 02) about facts and circumstances that existed at the acquisition date, E concludes on Dec 31, 02 that fair value of the contingent consideration as at Dec 31, 01 has been CU 3. This amount corresponds with fair value on Dec 31, 02.

On Dec 31, 03, fair value is CU 7.

On Dec 31, 04, it turns out that the accumulated EBITDA for the years 02–04 is only CU 14.

Required

Prepare any necessary entries in E's separate financial statements as at Dec 31 for the timeframe Dec 31, 01 until Dec 31, 04. The contingent consideration arrangement results in a financial liability that is within the scope of IFRS 9, which is measured at fair value through profit or loss (IAS 3.58). For simplification purposes, ignore the effect of discounting.

Hints for solution

In particular Sections 2, 6.6, 6.7, and 7.

Solution

In this example, E acquires the individual assets of F (which is free of debt) instead of purchasing shares.[45] In this case IFRS 3 also applies to E's separate financial statements (i.e. that the individual assets of F have to be recognized in E's separate financial statements).

[44] *EBITDA = earnings before interest, taxes, depreciation, and amortization.*

[45] *See Section 2.*

Effects on E's separate financial statements as at Dec 31, 01

Fair value of contingent consideration as at Dec 31, 01, is determined as follows:

Accumulated EBITDA for the years 02-04	*Contingent consideration*	*Probability*	*Calculation of expected value*
< CU 16	0	20%	0
≥ CU 16 and < CU 20	5	40%	2
≥ CU 20	10	40%	4
	Fair value as at Dec 31, 01		**6**

The value of F's business determined according to IFRS 3 is CU 61, which consists of the fixed payment of CU 55 and the fair value of contingent consideration of CU 6. On Dec 31, 01, the value of the net assets acquired determined according to IFRS 3 is CU 50. Hence, goodwill is CU 11.

Dec 31, 01	Dr	Various assets	50	
	Dr	Goodwill	11	
	Cr	Cash		55
	Cr	Liability		6

Effects on E's separate financial statements as at Dec 31, 02

As a result of additional information obtained by E within the measurement period (year 02) about facts and circumstances that existed at the acquisition date, E concludes on Dec 31, 02 that fair value of the contingent consideration as at Dec 31, 01 has been CU 3. This amount corresponds with fair value on Dec 31, 02.

The adjustment of the liability's carrying amount also changes goodwill. This represents a retrospective adjustment, i.e. the prior period figures presented in the financial statements as at Dec 31, 02 are also adjusted.

Dec 31, 01	Dr	Liability	3	
	Cr	Goodwill		3

Effects on E's separate financial statements as at Dec 31, 03

Fair value of contingent consideration as at Dec 31, 03 is CU 7. Since the measurement period which must not exceed one year from the acquisition date has already lapsed, the change in fair value does not result in a measurement period adjustment (IFRS 3.45). The contingent consideration, which represents a financial liability within the scope of IFRS 9, is measured at fair value through profit or loss (IFRS 3.58):

Dec 31, 03	Dr	Profit or loss	4	
	Cr	Liability		4

Effects on E's separate financial statements as at Dec 31, 04

On Dec 31,04, no payment is made because the accumulated EBITDA for the years 02–04 is CU 14, which is less than CU 16.

Dec 31, 04	Dr	Liability	7	
	Cr	Profit or loss		7

IFRS 4 INSURANCE CONTRACTS

1 INTRODUCTION AND SCOPE

IFRS 4 is a **stepping stone standard** (IFRS 4.IN2) that is used to specify the financial reporting for insurance contracts by insurers (i.e. by entities that issue such contracts) until the IASB completes the second phase of its project on insurance contracts. Accordingly, IFRS 4 specifies only certain aspects of the accounting and specifies selected disclosures (IFRS 4.1).

2 INSURANCE CONTRACTS, INSURANCE RISK, AND THE SCOPE OF IFRS 4[1]

An insurance contract is a contract under which the insurer accepts significant insurance risk by agreeing to compensate the policyholder if a specified uncertain future event adversely affects the policyholder.

Insurance risk is risk, other than financial risk, transferred from the holder of a contract to the issuer. **Financial risk** is the risk of a possible future change in one or more of the following variables: interest rate, financial instrument price, commodity price, foreign exchange rate, index of prices or rates, credit rating, credit index or other variables. In the case of a non-financial variable, the variable must not be specific to a party to the contract, i.e. no contract party must be subject to an actual risk with regard to the variable.

The **scope** of IFRS 4 comprises all insurance contracts that the reporting entity issues as insurer as well as reinsurance contracts that it holds (IFRS 4.2a).

IFRS 4 also applies to financial instruments that the reporting entity issues with a **discretionary participation feature** (IFRS 4.2b).

Financial guarantee contracts issued by the entity are insurance contracts and would therefore principally be a matter of IFRS 4. However, they are scoped out by IFRS 4.4(d) unless the issuer has previously asserted explicitly that it regards such guarantees as insurance contracts and has used accounting applicable to insurance contracts. In the latter case, the issuer may elect to apply either IAS 32, IFRS 7, and IFRS 9[2] or IFRS 4 to such financial guarantee contracts. The issuer may make that election contract by contract, but the election for each contract is irrevocable (IFRS 4.4d).

3 FINANCIAL REPORTING FOR INSURANCE CONTRACTS

In certain cases it is necessary to separate a **derivative embedded in an insurance contract** from its host contract and measure the derivative at fair value and include changes in its fair value in profit or loss (IFRS 4.7–4.9). Fair value is the amount for which an asset could be

---

[1] *See IFRS 4.Appendix A regarding the definitions in this chapter.*

[2] *See the chapter on IFRS 9/IAS 39, Section 2.6 and Example 13.*

exchanged, or a liability settled, between knowledgeable, willing parties in an arm's length transaction (IFRS 4.Appendix A).

Some insurance contracts contain both an insurance component and a deposit component. A deposit component is a contractual component that is not accounted for as a derivative under IAS 39 and would be within the scope of IAS 39 if it were a separate instrument (IFRS 4.Appendix A). In certain cases, **unbundling of the insurance component and of the deposit component** of an insurance contract is required or permitted. To unbundle a contract, the insurer applies IFRS 4 to the insurance component and IAS 39 to the deposit component (IFRS 4.10–4.12).

IFRS 4 permits insurers to **continue with their existing accounting policies** for insurance contracts that they issue and reinsurance contracts that they hold if those policies meet certain minimum criteria. Thus, applying IFRS 4 may not have a large impact on recognizing and measuring insurance contracts.[3]

An insurer must comply with the following rules (IFRS 4.14–4.20):

- It is not possible to recognize provisions for risks arising under insurance contracts that do not exist at the end of the reporting period. Hence, **catastrophe provisions** and **equalization provisions** must not be recognized.
- An **adequacy test** has to be carried out for **insurance liabilities**. This means that it has to be assessed at the end of each reporting period whether the insurer's recognized insurance liabilities are adequate, using current estimates of future cash flows under the insurer's insurance contracts. If that assessment shows that the carrying amount of the insurance liabilities (less related deferred acquisition costs and related intangible assets) is inadequate in the light of the estimated future cash flows, the entire deficiency has to be recognized in profit or loss.
- An **insurance liability** (or a part of it) is **removed** from the statement of financial position only when it is extinguished (e.g. by payment).
- It is prohibited to offset reinsurance assets against the related insurance liabilities and to offset income or expense from reinsurance contracts against the expense or income from the related insurance contracts (**prohibition to offset reinsurance contracts**).
- It has to be considered whether **reinsurance assets** are **impaired**.

4 EXAMPLE WITH SOLUTION

Example

Scope of IFRS 4

Entity E sells only its own finished goods to wholesalers.

(a) E issues a product warranty for its own finished goods directly.
(b) E issues a product warranty for the finished goods produced by entity F. F is an unrelated third party of E.

[3] *See PwC,* Manual of Accounting, *IFRS 2011, 8.18.*

Required

Assess whether the product warranties are within the scope of IFRS 4 in E's financial statements.

Hints for solution

In particular Section 2.

Solution

(a) A product warranty issued directly by a manufacturer is outside the scope of IFRS 4 because it is within the scope of IAS 18 and IAS 37 (IFRS 4.4a and 4.B18h).

(b) E issues a product warranty for the finished goods produced by F (i.e. by an unrelated third party of E). The product warranty is an insurance contract provided that the insurance risk is significant (IFRS 4.B18h).

IFRS 5 NON-CURRENT ASSETS HELD FOR SALE AND DISCONTINUED OPERATIONS

1 INTRODUCTION AND OVERVIEW[1]

IFRS 5 includes rules with respect to the sale or abandonment of non-current assets. The differentiation between current and non-current assets according to IFRS 5 corresponds to the differentiation in IAS 1[2] (IFRS 5.Appendix A and IAS 1.66).

Non-current assets are sold individually in the simplest situation.

However, it may also be the case that a **disposal group** is sold. A disposal group is a group of assets to be disposed of as a group in a single transaction. A disposal group also includes liabilities directly associated with those assets that will be transferred in the transaction. The group also includes goodwill acquired in a business combination if the group is a cash-generating unit (CGU) according to IAS 36 to which goodwill has been allocated, or if it is an operation within such a CGU (IFRS 5.Appendix A and IAS 36.80–36.87).

A **component of an entity** comprises operations and cash flows that can be clearly distinguished from the rest of the entity both operationally and for financial reporting purposes. In other words, a component of an entity will have been a CGU or a group of CGUs, while being held for use (IFRS 5.31).

A **discontinued operation** is a component of an entity that is held for sale or has been disposed of. Furthermore, the component of the entity must meet one of the following criteria (IFRS 5.32):

- It represents a separate major line of business or geographical area of operations.
- It is part of a single coordinated plan to dispose of a separate major line of business or geographical area of operations.
- It is a subsidiary acquired exclusively with a view to resale.

Meeting the above definitions has the following consequences for **financial reporting**:

- **If non-current assets** held for sale are **to be sold individually**, they have to be presented separately in the statement of financial position. In some cases, they are also subject to the specific measurement provisions of IFRS 5.
- **Disposal groups** that are held for sale have to be presented separately in the statement of financial position. However, the specific measurement provisions of IFRS 5 are not effective for all types of assets that may be part of disposal groups.

---

[1] *With regard to the definitions in this section we refer to IFRS 5.Appendix A.*

[2] *See the chapter on IAS 1, Section 6.1.*

- In the case of **discontinued operations**, the following differentiation is necessary:
  - If the component of the entity **has already been sold**, i.e. if the assets and liabilities have already been derecognized, the issues of applying the specific measurement provisions of IFRS 5 and of separate presentation in the statement of financial position are obsolete. However, separate presentation in the statement of comprehensive income is necessary.
  - It may be the case that the assets and liabilities of a **disposal group held for sale**, which represents a discontinued operation, have **not been derecognized** until the end of the reporting period. In this case, in addition to separate presentation in the statement of comprehensive income, separate presentation in the statement of financial position and measurement according to IFRS 5 are also necessary.
  - If a business unit has been **abandoned**, separate presentation in the statement of comprehensive income is necessary. However, there is no separate presentation in the statement of financial position and the specific measurement provisions of IFRS 5 are not applied.

2 SCOPE

Regarding the **scope** of IFRS 5, the following distinction is necessary (IFRS 5.2):

- The requirements of IFRS 5 for **classification** as "held for sale"[3] apply to all recognized non-current assets and to all disposal groups of an entity. Classification as "held for sale" requires the application of the **presentation** requirements of IFRS 5. Moreover, the Standard includes specific presentation requirements with respect to discontinued operations.
- The **measurement** provisions of IFRS 5 do not apply to all non-current assets and to all assets included in disposal groups classified as held for sale. The following assets are excluded from the measurement requirements of IFRS 5 regardless of whether they are individual assets or part of a disposal group. Instead, the standards listed apply with respect to their measurement (IFRS 5.5):
  - Deferred tax assets (IAS 12).
  - Assets arising from employee benefits (IAS 19).
  - Financial assets within the scope of IFRS 9.
  - Non-current assets that are accounted for in accordance with the fair value model in IAS 40.
  - Non-current assets that are measured at fair value less costs to sell in accordance with IAS 41.
  - Contractual rights under insurance contracts as defined in IFRS 4.

3 NON-CURRENT ASSETS AND DISPOSAL GROUPS HELD FOR SALE

3.1 Classification as "Held for Sale"

A non-current asset or disposal group is classified as "**held for sale**," if its carrying amount will be recovered principally through a sale transaction rather than through continuing use (IFRS 5.6). For this to be the case, the asset or disposal group must be **available for immediate**

[3] *See Section 3.1.*

sale in its present condition, subject only to terms that are **usual and customary** for sales of such assets or disposal groups. In addition, the sale must be highly probable (IFRS 5.7).

The term "**highly probable**" is quantitatively defined as a probability of significantly more than 51% (IFRS 5.Appendix A). The standard does not leave preparers to interpret what this might mean. Instead, it sets out the criteria for a sale to be highly probable.[4] Accordingly, the criterion "highly probable" is met when the following criteria are cumulatively met (IFRS 5.8):

- The appropriate **level of management** is committed to a plan to sell the asset or disposal group.
- An **active program** to locate a buyer and complete the plan has been initiated.
- The asset or disposal group is **actively marketed** for sale at a **price** that is **reasonable** in relation to its current fair value.
- The sale should be expected to qualify for recognition as a completed sale within **12 months** from the date of classification. However, events or circumstances may extend this period of time (IFRS 5.9 and 5.B1).
- Actions required to complete the plan should indicate that it is **unlikely** that **significant changes** to the plan will be made or that the plan will be **withdrawn**.

The **probability of approval of the shareholders** (if required in the jurisdiction) should also be considered as part of the assessment as to whether the sale is highly probable (IFRS 5.8).

If the criteria of IFRS 5.7 and 5.8 (see above) are **not met until the end of the reporting period**, the non-current asset or disposal group in question must not be classified as "held for sale" (IFRS 5.12).

An entity that is committed to a sale plan involving **loss of control of a subsidiary** must classify all the assets and liabilities of that subsidiary as held for sale when the criteria above (IFRS 5.6–5.8) are met. This applies regardless of whether the entity will retain a non-controlling interest in its former subsidiary after the sale (IFRS 5.8A).

In the case of non-current assets or disposal groups that are **exclusively acquired with a view to their subsequent disposal**, the following applies: The non-current asset or disposal group is classified as held for sale at the acquisition date only if the 12 month requirement (see above) is met (under consideration of the corresponding exceptions). Furthermore, it must be highly probable that any other criteria mentioned above that are not met at that date will be met within a short period following the acquisition (usually within three months) (IFRS 5.11).

Non-current assets or disposal groups that are **to be abandoned** must not be classified as "held for sale." This is because the carrying amount will be recovered principally through continuing use. Non-current assets or disposal groups to be abandoned include non-current assets or disposal groups (IFRS 5.13):

- which are to be used to the end of their economic life,
- that are to be closed rather than sold.

---

[4] *See PwC,* Manual of Accounting, *IFRS 2011, 26.47.*

A **non-current asset** that has been **temporarily taken out of use** must not be accounted for as if it had been abandoned (IFRS 5.14). The entity may not, for example, stop depreciating the asset.[5]

3.2 Measurement of Non-current Assets and Disposal Groups Classified as "Held for Sale"

3.2.1 General Aspects The measurement requirements of IFRS 5 apply to all non-current assets and disposal groups classified as held for sale. However, certain assets are **excluded from the measurement provisions of IFRS 5** regardless of whether they are individual assets or part of a disposal group.[6]

A non-current asset or a disposal group classified as "held for sale" is measured at the **lower of its carrying amount and fair value less costs to sell** (IFRS 5.15). **Fair value** is the amount for which an asset could be exchanged, or a liability settled, between knowledgeable, willing parties in an arm's length transaction. **Costs to sell** are the incremental costs directly attributable to the disposal of an asset or of a disposal group, excluding finance costs and income tax expense (IFRS 5.Appendix A). Also, when a newly acquired asset (or disposal group) is classified as "held for sale," it is measured at the lower amount as described above. In this case, measurement at initial recognition is effected at the lower of the carrying amount that the asset (or disposal group) would have had without this classification (e.g. costs of purchase) and fair value less costs to sell (IFRS 5.16).

In the case of a **business combination**, the acquiree's assets and liabilities are generally measured at fair value. However, if a non-current asset (or disposal group) held for sale is received in a business combination, it is measured on the acquisition date at fair value less costs to sell and not at fair value, which differs from the general rules of IFRS 3 (IFRS 5.16 and IFRS 3.31). The difference is not recognized as an impairment loss.

Immediately before the initial classification of an asset or of a disposal group as "held for sale," the asset or all the assets and liabilities in the group have to be measured **in accordance with the applicable Standards** (IFRS 5.18). A disposal group continues to be consolidated while it is held for sale. Therefore, revenue (e.g. from the sale of inventory) and expenses (including interest) continue to be recognized. However, property, plant, and equipment (IAS 16), and intangible assets (IAS 38) that are classified as "held for sale" or are part of a disposal group classified as "held for sale" are **not depreciated or amortized** (IFRS 5.25).[7]

Impairment losses on initial classification of a non-current asset (or disposal group) as held for sale are included in profit or loss even if the asset is (or the disposal group includes assets that are) measured at a revalued amount. The same applies to gains and losses on subsequent remeasurement (IFRS 5.20).[8]

---

[5] *See PwC,* Manual of Accounting, *IFRS 2011, 26.74.*

[6] *See Section 2.*

[7] *See KPMG,* Insights into IFRS, *7th edition, 5.4.60.70.*

[8] *See KPMG,* Insights into IFRS, *6th edition, 5.4.60.40*

The application of the measurement requirements of IFRS 5 for **disposal groups** results in a complex interplay of measurement on an individual basis and on a group basis:

- Immediately before classification of the disposal group as "held for sale," the individual assets and liabilities in the group have to be measured in accordance with the applicable standards **(measurement on an individual basis)** (IFRS 5.18). In this way, items of property, plant, and equipment are depreciated until the date of classification as "held for sale." An impairment test which is normally effected only at the end of the reporting period according to the general accounting rules (e.g. IAS 2, IAS 36, or IAS 39) is also necessary at the date of classification as "held for sale."
- The resulting net carrying amount of the disposal group (assets less liabilities) has to be compared with the group's fair value less costs to sell **(measurement on a group basis)** (IFRS 5.4).
- If this results in an impairment loss with respect to the group, the loss has to be **allocated** to the non-current assets in the group that are within the scope of the measurement requirements of IFRS 5, in the order of allocation set out in IAS 36.104 (IFRS 5.23). Thus, the carrying amount of any goodwill is reduced first. The remaining impairment loss is allocated to the other assets defined above (e.g. items of property, plant, and equipment, and intangible assets) pro rata on the basis of the carrying amount of each asset. Examples of assets that are excluded from the allocation are inventories.

The measurement requirements of IFRS 5 are applied to a disposal group as a whole (i.e. its carrying amount is compared with its fair value less costs to sell), only if the disposal group contains at least one non-current asset that is subject to the measurement requirements of IFRS 5 (IFRS 5.4).

3.2.2 Changes to a Plan of Sale If an asset (or a disposal group) has been classified as "held for sale," but the criteria for such classification are no longer met at a later point in time, the classification of the asset (disposal group) as "held for sale" ceases (IFRS 5.26). A non-current asset that ceases to be classified as "held for sale" (or ceases to be included in a disposal group classified as held for sale) is measured **at the lower of** the following amounts (IFRS 5.27):

- Its carrying amount before classification of the asset (or disposal group) as "held for sale," adjusted for any depreciation, amortization or revaluations that would have been recognized had the asset (or disposal group) not been classified as "held for sale."
- Its recoverable amount (according to IAS 36) at the date of the decision not to sell. If the non-current asset is part of a CGU, its recoverable amount is the carrying amount that would have been recognized after the allocation of any impairment loss arising on that CGU according to IAS 36.

3.3 Presentation

A non-current asset classified as "held for sale" and the assets of a disposal group classified as "held for sale" have to be presented **separately from other assets** in the statement of financial position. The total of these amounts has to be presented as a **separate line item** in that statement (IFRS 5.38 and IAS 1.54(j)).

The liabilities of a disposal group classified as "held for sale" have to be presented **separately from other liabilities** in the statement of financial position. The total of these liabilities has to be presented as a **separate line item** in that statement (IFRS 5.38 and IAS 1.54(p)). However, the content of that line item has to be determined restrictively. Liabilities are only part of a disposal group if they are directly associated with the assets of the group and are also transferred on disposal of the assets (IFRS 5.Appendix A).

The assets and liabilities that have to be presented in the statement of financial position according to IFRS 5 (IAS 1.54(j) and 1.54(p)) **must not be offset**. The **major classes** of assets and liabilities classified as "held for sale" generally have to be separately disclosed either in the statement of financial position or in the notes. The **cumulative income or expense recognized in other comprehensive income** relating to a non-current asset or disposal group classified as held for sale shall be presented separately in the statement of financial position (e.g. the fair value reserve in respect of equity instruments measured at fair value through other comprehensive income according to IFRS 9.5.7.1b and 9.5.7.5[9]) (IFRS 5.38–5.39, 5.BC58, 5.IG Example 12, IAS 1.32, and 1.54).

Classification of non-current assets or of disposal groups as "**held for sale**" in the reporting period does **not** result in **reclassification or re-presentation** of the corresponding amounts in the **statements of financial position** for prior periods (IFRS 5.40).

Non-current assets (as well as assets of a class that the entity would normally regard as non-current that are acquired exclusively with a view to resale) must not be (re)classified as current unless they meet the criteria for classification as "held for sale" according to IFRS 5 (IFRS 5.3). The differentiation between **current and non-current assets** according to IFRS 5 corresponds to the differentiation in IAS 1 (IFRS 5.Appendix A and IAS 1.66).

According to the guidance on implementing IFRS 5 (IFRS 5.IG, Example 12), a subtotal is presented in the statement of financial position for current assets and current liabilities, without taking into account the amounts classified as "held for sale." After the subtotal, the latter amounts are presented as separate line items. Afterwards, the total for current assets or current liabilities is presented.

4 PRESENTATION OF DISCONTINUED OPERATIONS

4.1 General Aspects

Meeting the definition of a discontinued operation results in **additional disclosures**. Among others, a **single amount** has to be disclosed in the statement of comprehensive income which is the **total of the following amounts** (IFRS 5.33a and IAS 1.82a):

- Post-tax profit or loss of discontinued operations.
- Post-tax gain or loss recognized on the measurement to fair value less costs to sell or on the disposal of the assets or disposal group(s) constituting the discontinued operation.

---

[9] *Before the consequential amendments to IAS 39 caused by IFRS 9, equity instruments of the category "available for sale" (IAS 39.9) were generally also measured at fair value through other comprehensive income (IAS 39.55b).*

This total amount is determined and disclosed for the **entire reporting period** and not only for the period of time starting on discontinuation. It must also be determined and disclosed for **prior periods** presented in the financial statements (IFRS 5.34). This amount has to be disclosed separately from continuing operations. In the statement of comprehensive income, all line items from revenue down to profit or loss from continuing operations are presented **excluding the amounts attributable to discontinued operations**. Generally, among others, the revenue, expenses, and pre-tax profit or loss of discontinued operations included in the amount defined above (IFRS 5.33a) must also be presented in the statement of comprehensive income or in the notes (IFRS 5.33b).

Discontinued operations include operations that were already disposed of and operations classified as "held for sale." If the entire discontinued operation or a part thereof meets the definition of "**held for sale**," the **presentation requirements** described in Section 3.3 have to be met **in addition** to those of this chapter. The assets and liabilities that are part of discontinued operations need not be presented or disclosed separately from other assets or liabilities held for sale. If a disposal group becomes a discontinued operation in the reporting period and is classified as "held for sale" in the same period, the prior period information is not adjusted in the statement of financial position.

If a **disposal group to be abandoned** meets one of the criteria in IFRS 5.32(a)–(c), the results and cash flows of the disposal group are presented as discontinued operations according to IFRS 5.33–5.34 in the period in which the disposal takes place. The figures for prior periods have to be adjusted (IFRS 5.34). A disposal group to be abandoned does not meet the definition of "held for sale" (IFRS 5.13).

4.2 Selected Specifics in Consolidated Financial Statements

Generally, among others, the revenue, expenses, and pre-tax profit or loss of discontinued operations must be presented in the statement of comprehensive income or in the notes (IFRS 5.33b). If a subsidiary represents a discontinued operation and revenue and expenses arise between that subsidiary and another subsidiary or the parent of the group, in our view, the following procedure is necessary. In the statement of comprehensive income and in the notes, the marginal revenue and marginal expenses of the group, which are attributable to the discontinued operation, are presented as discontinued operations.

5 EXAMPLES WITH SOLUTIONS

Example 1

Individual asset classified as "held for sale"

On Jul 01, 01, a machine of entity E with a carrying amount of CU 10 and a remaining useful life of 5 years is classified as "held for sale." On Jun 30, 02, the machine is sold at its fair value. From Jul 01, 01 until Jun 30, 02, the machine's fair value is CU 8 and costs to sell are CU 1.

Required

Prepare any necessary entries in E's financial statements for the timeframe Jul 01, 01 until Jun 30, 02. E's reporting periods end on Dec 31.

Hints for solution

In particular Sections 3.2.1 and 3.3.

Solution

Jul 01, 01	Dr	Machine (held for sale)	10	
	Cr	Machine		10

Write-down to fair value less costs to sell of CU 7:

Jul 01, 01	Dr	Impairment loss	3	
	Cr	Machine (held for sale)		3

While the machine is classified as "held for sale" (i.e. from Jul 01, 01 onwards), the machine is not depreciated (IFRS 5.25).

Before taking costs to sell into account, a gain on the disposal of CU 1 is recognized (IAS 1.34a).

Jun 30, 02	Dr	Cash	8	
	Cr	Gain on disposal		1
	Cr	Machine (held for sale)		7

Finally, the costs to sell are recognized as a reduction of the gain on disposal, which means that the gain on disposal is reduced to zero (IAS 1.34a):

Jun 30, 02	Dr	Gain on disposal	1	
	Cr	Cash		1

Example 2

Cessation of the classification of an asset as "held for sale"

Required

The situation is the same as in Example 1. However, assume that the classification as "held for sale" ceases on Jul 01, 02 and that the machine will be used until the end of its original useful life. Assume that the value in use (according to IAS 36) is CU 9 on Jul 01, 02. Prepare any necessary entries in E's financial statements for the timeframe Jul 01, 01 until Dec 31, 02.

Hints for solution

In particular Section 3.2.2.

Solution

Jul 01, 01	Dr	Machine (held for sale)		10	
	Cr	Machine			10
Jul 01, 01	Dr	Impairment loss		3	
	Cr	Machine (held for sale)			3

Fair value less costs to sell (as at Jul 01, 02)	7		
Value in use (as at Jul 01, 02)	9		
Recoverable amount (as at Jul 01, 02) **(IFRS 5.27b)**		**9**	
Carrying amount before classification as "held for sale" (i.e. on Jun 30, 01)	10		
Depreciation (Jul 01, 01 to Jun 30, 02) in the absence of classification as "held for sale"	2		*= 10 : 5*
Carrying amount (as at Jul 01, 02) in the absence of classification as "held for sale" **(IFRS 5.27a)**		**8**	
Lower amount according to IFRS 5.27		**8**	
Carrying amount according to IFRS 5 as at Jun 30, 02		7	
Income		**1**	

Jul 01, 02	Dr	Machine	7	
	Cr	Machine (held for sale)		7
Jul 01, 02	Dr	Machine	1	
	Cr	Income		1

The depreciation for 02 (**Jul 01, 02 – Dec 31, 02**) is calculated as follows: carrying amount (as at Jul 01, 02) of CU 8 : remaining useful life (as at Jul 01, 02) of 4 years · 6 : 12:

Dec 31, 02	Dr	Depreciation expense	1	
	Cr	Machine		1

Example 3

Measurement of a disposal group classified as "held for sale"

On Jul 01, 01, entity E classifies a disposal group as "held for sale." The group comprises the following assets:[10]

	Carrying amount as at Dec 31, 00	*Additional information*
Machine	20	Remaining useful life as at Dec 31, 00: 5 years
Acquired patent	10	Remaining useful life as at Dec 31, 00: 5 years
Finished goods	8	The net realizable value (IAS 2.6) as at Jun 30, 01 is CU 7
Receivables	6	The receivables are measured at amortized cost. On Jun 30, the value of the receivables determined according to IAS 39.63 is CU 5 (IFRS 9.5.2.2)

For both the machine and the patent, which were accounted for according to the cost model of IAS 16 and IAS 38, there is no indication of impairment on Jun 30, 01. The receivables are current assets.

[10] *If IFRS 9 (and its consequential amendments to IAS 39) were not applied early, and if the receivables belonged to the category "loans and receivables" (IAS 39.9), the example and its solution would not change.*

On Jun 30, 01, fair value less costs to sell of the disposal group is CU 33.

Required

Prepare any necessary entries in E's financial statements for the timeframe Jan 01, 01 until Jul 01, 01. E's reporting periods end on Dec 31.

Hints for solution

In particular Section 3.2.1.

Solution

	Carrying amount as at Dec 31, 00	*Measurement on an individual basis on Jun 30, 01*	*Allocation of the impairment loss of the disposal group*	*Carrying amount on Jul 01, 01*
Machine	20	18	*–4 (= –6 · 18 : 27)*	*14*
Acquired patent	10	9	*–2 (= –6 · 9 : 27)*	*7*
Finished goods	8	7		7
Receivables	6	5		5
Total	**44**	**39**	**–6**	**33**
Fair value less costs to sell		33		
Impairment loss of the group		**–6**		

Comments:

Immediately before the initial classification as "held for sale," the individual assets of the disposal group are measured according to the applicable Standards (IFRS 5.18):

- The machine is depreciated and the patent is amortized.
- The finished goods are tested for impairment (i.e. they are measured at the lower of cost and net realizable value) (IAS 2.9).
- The carrying amount of the receivables is reduced to the amount determined according to IAS 39.63.

Jun 30, 01	Dr	Depreciation expense	2	
	Cr	Machine		2
Jun 30, 01	Dr	Amortization expense	1	
	Cr	Patent		1
Jun 30, 01	Dr	Cost of sales	1	
	Cr	Finished goods		1
Jun 30, 01	Dr	Impairment loss	1	
	Cr	Receivables		1

Jul 01, 01	Dr	Machine (held for sale)	18	
	Cr	Machine		18
Jul 01, 01	Dr	Patent (held for sale)	9	
	Cr	Patent		9
Jul 01, 01	Dr	Finished goods (held for sale)	7	
	Cr	Finished goods		7
Jul 01, 01	Dr	Receivables (held for sale)	5	
	Cr	Receivables		5
Jul 01, 01	Dr	Impairment loss	6	
	Cr	Machine (held for sale)		4
	Cr	Patent (held for sale)		2

Example 4

Content of the line item "liabilities included in disposal groups classified as held for sale"

Entity E owns several pieces of land that were accounted for according to IAS 16. These pieces of land constitute a disposal group that is classified as "held for sale." The pieces of land are burdened with mortgage loans. The bank will only issue the clearance necessary for sale after redemption of the loans.

Required

Assess whether the mortgage loans are part of the line item "liabilities included in disposal groups classified as held for sale" (IAS 1.54p) in the statement of financial position.

Hints for solution

In particular Section 3.3.

Solution

The mortgage loans are not included in the line item "liabilities included in disposal groups classified as held for sale," because they will not be transferred to the buyer.

Example 5

Presentation of a disposal group classified as "held for sale"

Entity E owns two disposal groups that are initially classified as "held for sale" on Dec 31, 01. However, they do not constitute discontinued operations. The disposal groups also include directly associated liabilities that will be transferred during the sale:

Carrying amounts as at Dec 31, 01 (after classification as "held for sale")

	Disposal group A	*Disposal group B*
Property, plant, and equipment	30	50
Shares	10	–
Liabilities	–20	–5
Net carrying amount	**20**	**45**

The shares are accounted for at fair value through other comprehensive income (IFRS 9.5.7.1b and 9.5.7.5). The fair value reserve (= cumulative amount recognized in other comprehensive income) is CU +2 on Dec 31, 01.[11]

Required

Illustrate the presentation of both disposal groups in E's consolidated statement of financial position as at Dec 31, 01.

Hints for solution

In particular Section 3.3.

Solution

Both of the disposal groups classified as "held for sale" are presented in E's consolidated statement of financial position as follows (IFRS 5.38). It is important to note that the classification as "held for sale" does not result in reclassification or re-presentation of the corresponding amounts in the statement of financial position for the prior period 00 (IFRS 5.40).

ASSETS	*Dec 31, 01*	*Dec 31, 00*	*EQUITY AND LIABILITIES*	*Dec 31, 01*	*Dec 31, 00*
Non-current assets			**Equity**		
AA	X	X	**Equity attributable to owners of the parent**		
BB	X	X			
	X	X	EE	X	X
			FF	X	X
Current assets			Accumulated OCI relating to a disposal group held for sale	2	–
CC	X	X			
DD	X	X			
	X	X		X	X
Assets included in disposal groups held for sale	90	–	**Non-controlling interests**	X	X
	X	X	Total equity	X	X
			Non-current liabilities		
			GG	X	X
			HH	X	X
				X	X
			Current liabilities		
			II	X	X
			JJ	X	X
				X	X
			Liabilities included in disposal groups held for sale	25	–
				X	X
			Total liabilities	X	X
Total assets	**X**	**X**	**Total equity and liabilities**	**X**	**X**

[11] *If IFRS 9 (and its consequential amendments to IAS 39) were not applied early, the solution to this example would not change if the shares belonged to the category "available for sale" (IAS 39.9).*

Example 6

Transactions between a discontinued subsidiary and its parent

Production Company P holds 100% of the shares of Trading Company T. T buys the products manufactured by P at arm's length prices and sells them at a markup of 20% to customers that are not related to the group.

In 01, **P** generates revenue of CU 10 from selling its products to T. P only has external costs of CU 9 and therefore generates a profit of CU 1.

In 01, **T** generates revenue of CU 12. T's external costs are CU 1 and its internal costs (cost of sales relating to the products bought from P) are CU 10. Thus, T generates a profit of CU 1.

T was sold on Dec 31, 01 and constitutes a discontinued operation in P's consolidated financial statements. It is expected that the acquirer of T will continue to operate with unchanged conditions for P.

Required

Present the revenue, expenses, and profit from continuing operations and from the discontinued operation in a simplified illustration of P's consolidated separate income statement for the year 01. Ignore taxes.

Hints for solution

In particular Section 4.2.

Solution

The transactions between P and T result in revenue and expenses between these entities. In our opinion, it is necessary to present T's marginal revenue and marginal expenses as discontinued operations. Hence, P's consolidated separate income statement for the year 01 is presented as follows:

Continuing operations	
Revenue	10
Expenses	–9
Profit from continuing operations	**1**
Discontinued operations	
Revenue	2
Expenses	–1
Profit from discontinued operations	**1**
Profit	**2**

This procedure reflects the fact that group revenue (external revenue) of CU 2 (= CU 12 – CU 10) is attributable to an operation that no longer belongs to the group as a result of the disposal on Dec 31, 01. Hence, in P's consolidated separate income statement, revenue of CU 2 is presented in the section for discontinued operations, whereas the remaining revenue of CU 10 is presented in the section for the continuing operations.

These considerations apply analogously with regard to the expenses. Group expenses of CU 1 (which represent T's external expenses) are attributable to an operation that will no longer belong to the group in the future. Hence, in P's consolidated separate income statement, expenses of CU 1 are presented in the section for discontinued operations, whereas the remaining expenses of CU 9 (P's external expenses) are presented in the section for the continuing operations.

Example 7

Presentation of a discontinued operation

(a) On Dec 31, 01, entity E classifies a disposal group as "held for sale." The disposal group also meets the definition of a discontinued operation starting on that date. The group's marginal revenue attributable to the discontinued operation is CU 40 in 01 and CU 36 in 00. The group's marginal expenses attributable to the discontinued operation are CU 32 in 01 and CU 34 in 00. In 01, an expense of CU 1 is recognized as a result of a write-down to fair value less costs to sell according to IFRS 5.

(b) The situation is the same as in (a). However, assume that the discontinued operation was already sold in 01 and that there was no write-down. As a result of the sale, a loss of CU 2 was recognized.

Required

Present the discontinued operation in a simplified illustration of E's consolidated separate income statements for the periods 01 and 00. Furthermore, describe the presentation of the discontinued operation in E's consolidated statement of financial position. Ignore taxes.

Hints for solution

In particular Section 4.

Solution (a)

E's consolidated separate income statements for the periods 01 and 00 are presented as follows. The amounts for 01 and for the prior period 00 have to be presented in the section "discontinued operations" (IFRS 5.34).

	01	*00*
Continuing operations		
Revenue	X	X
Expenses	X	X
Profit from continuing operations	**X**	**X**
Discontinued operations		
Profit from discontinued operations	**7**	**2**
Profit	**X**	**X**

Comment: CU 7 = marginal revenue of CU 40 attributable to the discontinued operation – marginal expenses of CU 32 attributable to the discontinued operation – write-down in the amount of CU 1 to fair value less costs to sell (IFRS 5.33a).

Since the discontinued operation also constitutes a disposal group classified as "held for sale," separate presentation in the consolidated statement of financial position as at Dec 31, 01 is necessary (see Example 5). However, in the consolidated statement of financial position, reclassification or representation of the corresponding amounts as at Dec 31, 00 is prohibited (IFRS 5.40).

Solution (b)

	01	*00*
Continuing operations		
Revenue	X	X
Expenses	X	X
Profit from continuing operations	**X**	**X**
Discontinued operations		
Profit from discontinued operations	**6**	**2**
Profit	**X**	**X**

Comment: CU 6 = marginal revenue of CU 40 attributable to the discontinued operation – marginal expenses of CU 32 attributable to the discontinued operation – loss on the sale of CU 2 (IFRS 5.33a).

There are no reclassifications in the **consolidated statement of financial position**. This is because the carrying amounts have already been derecognized in 01.

IFRS 6 EXPLORATION FOR AND EVALUATION OF MINERAL RESOURCES

1 INTRODUCTION AND SCOPE

IFRS 6 specifies the financial reporting for the exploration for and evaluation of mineral resources (e.g. oil, natural gas, etc.). IFRS 6 is applied to exploration and evaluation expenditures that the entity incurs. However, IFRS 6 does not address other aspects of accounting by entities engaged in the exploration for and evaluation of mineral resources (IFRS 6.1–6.4).

Exploration and evaluation is the search for mineral resources after the receipt of the legal rights to explore in a specific area, as well as the determination of the technical feasibility and commercial viability of extracting the mineral resource (IFRS 6.Appendix A). An example of such activities would be test drillings.

IFRS 6 must not be applied to expenditures incurred before the exploration for and evaluation of mineral resources or after the technical feasibility and commercial viability of extracting a mineral resource are demonstrable (IFRS 6.5).

2 FINANCIAL REPORTING

Requirements with regard to the recognition and initial measurement of exploration and evaluation assets are included in IFRS 6 only to a minor degree. According to the general rules of IFRS, IAS 8.10–8.12 would have to be applied in order to close the regulatory gap. However, in the present case, **only IAS 8.10** has to be applied, which results in a lot of **discretion**. An entity that applies IFRS for the first time can generally continue to apply its previously applied principles (e.g. US GAAP) for the recognition and initial measurement of exploration and evaluation assets. It is not necessary to examine whether they correspond with the Conceptual Framework or with the individual standards of the IASB.

According to IFRS, it is for example possible to apply the principles that are applied in the USA in the oil industry and in the gas industry in order to determine if and to which extent there are exploration and evaluation assets. Hence, it is possible to choose between the following methods:

- **Full cost method**: According to this method all exploration costs (i.e. even unsuccessful attempts) in a particular country are capitalized. Therefore, the success of an exploration is not necessary for capitalization. Depreciation, amortization, and impairment losses with regard to the expenses capitalized are recognized on a country-specific basis.
- **Successful efforts method**: Only the costs associated with successful projects are capitalized. Costs that were preliminarily capitalized are recognized in profit or loss as soon as the success can no longer be expected.

- Methods, which constitute a **mix** of the full cost method and the successful efforts method.

At recognition, exploration and evaluation assets are **measured at cost** (IFRS 6.8). **After recognition**, they are **measured** either according to the **cost model** or according to the **revaluation model** (IFRS 6.12).

An exploration and evaluation asset is no longer classified as such when the technical feasibility and commercial viability of extracting a mineral resource are demonstrable. Exploration and evaluation assets have to be assessed for impairment – and any impairment loss recognized – before **reclassification** (IFRS 6.17).

Exploration and evaluation assets have to be assessed for impairment when facts and circumstances suggest that the carrying amount of an exploration and evaluation asset may exceed its recoverable amount. In this case, any resulting impairment loss generally has to be measured, presented, and disclosed according to IAS 36 (IFRS 6.18). Examples of such facts and circumstances are listed in IFRS 6.20. In order to identify an exploration and evaluation asset that may be impaired, IFRS 6.20 has to be applied rather than IAS 36.8–36.17 (IFRS 6.19).

An entity has to determine an accounting policy for allocating exploration and evaluation assets to CGUs or groups of CGUs for the purpose of assessing such assets for impairment. Each CGU or group of CGUs to which an exploration and evaluation asset is allocated must not be larger than an operating segment determined in accordance with IFRS 8 (IFRS 6.21–6.22).

3 STRIPPING COSTS IN THE PRODUCTION PHASE OF A SURFACE MINE

The Interpretation IFRIC 20 "Stripping Costs in the Production Phase of a Surface Mine" deals with a similar topic.[1] However, these activities are not part of the exploration and evaluation phase and hence they are **not in the scope of IFRS 6**. In surface mining operations, it may be necessary to remove mine waste materials (i.e. overburden) in order to gain access to mineral ore deposits. Such activities are referred to as "**stripping**" (IFRIC 20.1). The entity may **benefit** from stripping activities in one of the following ways (IFRIC 20.4):

- The overburden contains (to a minor extent) ore or minerals, which represent inventories.
- The entity gains improved access to further quantities of material that can be mined in the future.

IFRIC 20 specifies the **accounting treatment** of these two types of benefits and includes the following **core statements** (IFRIC 20.5–20.9):

- If the benefits are realized in the form of **inventory produced**, the costs of the stripping activities are accounted for according to **IAS 2**.

---

[1] *IFRIC 20 has to be applied in the financial statements as at Dec 31, 2013 (if the entity's reporting periods are identical with the calendar years). Earlier application is permitted by the IFRIC (IFRIC 20.A1). In the European Union, there has been no endorsement of IFRIC 20 as yet. The endorsement is expected to take place in the fourth quarter of 2012, at the time of writing.*

- To the extent the benefit is **improved access to mineable ore or minerals**, a **non-current asset** (referred to as the "stripping activity asset") is recognized, if **certain criteria** are met.

4 EXAMPLE WITH SOLUTION

Example

Scope of IFRS 6

(a) Entity E supposes that there is an oil well in region A. Until now, only geological pilot surveys have taken place. Test drillings and blasting operations could not be carried out yet because E had not yet received the necessary official authorization. However, E has already built an access road in conjunction with the activities.
(b) E carried out test drillings in region B. The technical feasibility and commercial viability of extracting the mineral resources are not yet demonstrable.
(c) In region C it has been determined that extracting the mineral resource is technically feasible and commercially viable. Consequently, E has planned and prepared drill holes and has removed the rock stratum. It is planned to build winding equipment in the next annual reporting period.

Required

Assess whether the items and activities described above are within the scope of IFRS 6 from E's perspective. If this is not the case, assess which other standard applies to them.

Hints for solution

In particular Section 1.

Solution (a)

The costs described are incurred before the exploration for and evaluation of mineral resources. Consequently, the **Conceptual Framework** is applicable to them (IFRS 6.BC10). However, costs incurred before the exploration for and evaluation of mineral resources might have to be regarded as part of the acquisition of an **intangible asset according to IAS 38** (right to explore in a specific area) with the consequence that they are capitalized as part of the intangible asset (IFRS 6.BC12). The expenditures for building the access road (infrastructure) are capitalized as an item of **property, plant, and equipment according to IAS 16** (IFRS 6.BC13).

Solution (b)

The technical feasibility and commercial viability of extracting the mineral resources are not yet demonstrable. Hence, the expenditures for the test drillings refer to the exploration and evaluation, meaning they are within the scope of **IFRS 6** (IFRS 6.Appendix A).

Solution (c)

The **Conceptual Framework** and **IAS 38** are important in this case (IFRS 6.10). The development of a mineral resource (e.g. planning and preparing drill holes, and removing the rock stratum) once the technical feasibility and commercial viability of extracting the mineral resource had been determined is an example of the development phase of an internal project. Hence, IAS 38.57 is relevant, which provides guidance regarding the recognition of an internally generated intangible asset (IFRS 6.BC27). The winding equipment, which will be built in the next annual reporting period, will represent **property, plant, and equipment according to IAS 16**. The **mineral resources must not be recognized as assets**.

IFRS 7 FINANCIAL INSTRUMENTS: DISCLOSURES[1]

1 INTRODUCTION

IFRS 7 requires **disclosures** in the **notes** about financial instruments that fall within the scope of this standard. Some of these disclosures may be made in the notes or alternatively in the statement of financial position or in the statement of comprehensive income.

2 SIGNIFICANCE OF FINANCIAL INSTRUMENTS FOR FINANCIAL POSITION AND PERFORMANCE

The disclosures specified in the section "significance of financial instruments for financial position and performance" of IFRS 7 can be roughly categorized and described as follows:

- The **carrying amounts** of each of the following **categories of financial assets or financial liabilities**, as specified in IFRS 9, have to be disclosed either in the statement of financial position or in the notes (IFRS 7.8). In the latter case, it is necessary to provide sufficient information to permit reconciliation to the line items presented in the statement of financial position (IFRS 7.6).
  - Financial assets measured at amortized cost.
  - Financial assets measured at fair value through other comprehensive income.
  - Financial assets measured at fair value through profit or loss, showing separately:
    - those designated as such upon initial recognition, and
    - those mandatorily measured at fair value according to IFRS 9.
  - Financial liabilities measured at amortized cost.
  - Financial liabilities at fair value through profit or loss, showing separately:
    - those designated as such upon initial recognition, and
    - those that meet the definition of held for trading in IFRS 9.
- Similar rules are set out with regard to the **net gains or net losses of the categories of financial instruments** as specified in IFRS 9 (IFRS 7.20a).
- Exercising of an **option to designate** financial assets or financial liabilities **as at fair value through profit or loss** (IFRS 7.9–7.11).
- **Investments in equity instruments** measured at **fair value through other comprehensive income** (e.g. which investments in equity instruments have been designated to be measured at fair value through other comprehensive income and the fair value of each such investment at the end of the reporting period) (IFRS 7.11A–7.11B).
- **Reclassification of financial assets** between the amortized cost category and the fair value category of IFRS 9 (IFRS 7.12B–7.12D and IFRS 9.4.4.1).
- **Offsetting financial assets and financial liabilities** (IFRS 7.13A–7.13F).

---

[1] *This chapter is based on financial instruments accounting according to IFRS 9 (as issued in Oct 2010), in line with the other chapters of the book.*

- Financial assets that the entity has pledged as **collateral** for liabilities or contingent liabilities (e.g. the carrying amount of these assets) (IFRS 7.14).
- **Allowance account for credit losses**: A reconciliation of changes in that account during the period for each class of financial assets has to be disclosed (IFRS 7.16).
- **Defaults and breaches of loans payable** (IFRS 7.18–7.19).
- **Accounting policies** (IFRS 7.21).
- **Hedge accounting** (e.g. description of each type of hedge, nature of the risks being hedged, etc.) (IFRS 7.22–7.24).
- **Fair values**: Among others, the fair value of each class of financial assets and financial liabilities has to be disclosed in a way that permits it to be compared with its carrying amount and the methods used in determining fair values have to be disclosed (IFRS 7.25–7.30).

3 NATURE AND EXTENT OF RISKS ARISING FROM FINANCIAL INSTRUMENTS

The entity has to disclose information that enables users of its financial statements to evaluate the nature and extent of risks arising from financial instruments to which the entity is exposed at the end of the reporting period. These risks typically include, but are not limited to, credit risk, liquidity risk, and market risk (IFRS 7.31–7.32). These risks are defined in the standard as follows (IFRS 7.Appendix A):

- **Credit risk** is the risk that one contracting party of a financial instrument will cause a financial loss for the other contracting party by failing to discharge an obligation.
- **Liquidity risk** is the risk that the reporting entity will encounter difficulty in meeting obligations associated with financial liabilities that are settled by delivering cash or another financial asset.
- **Market risk** is the risk that the fair value or the future cash flows of a financial instrument will fluctuate because of changes in market prices. Market risk comprises currency risk, interest rate risk, and other price risk.

With regard to **credit risk**, it is, among others, necessary to disclose the following information by class of financial asset (IFRS 7.37 and 7.Appendix A):

- An **analysis of the age** of financial assets that are **past due** as at the end of the reporting period **but not impaired**. A financial asset is past due when a counterparty has failed to make a payment when contractually due.
- An analysis of financial assets that are **individually determined to be impaired** as at the end of the reporting period, including the factors that were considered in determining that they are impaired.

With regard to **liquidity risk**, among others, a **maturity analysis** for non-derivative financial liabilities (including issued financial guarantee contracts) has to be disclosed. This maturity analysis shows how the contractual undiscounted future cash flows are divided up according to their remaining contractual maturities. When a counterparty has a choice of when an amount is paid it is allocated to the earliest period in which the entity can be required to pay. Therefore, **demand deposits** are included in the earliest time band (IFRS 7.39a, 7.B11C, and 7.B11D).

With regard to **market risk**, it is necessary to make the following disclosures (among others) (IFRS 7.40):

- **A sensitivity analysis** for each type of market risk to which the entity is exposed at the end of the reporting period. This sensitivity analysis has to show how profit or loss and equity would have been affected by changes in the relevant risk variable that were reasonably possible at the end of the reporting period.
- The methods and assumptions used in preparing the sensitivity analysis.

4 TRANSFERS OF FINANCIAL ASSETS

IFRS 7 requires quite a number of disclosures with regard to transfers of financial assets (IFRS 7.42A–7.42H).

5 EXAMPLES WITH SOLUTIONS

Example 1

Disclosure of the carrying amounts of the categories of financial instruments

The following line items of entity E's statement of financial position as at Dec 31, 01 represent financial assets or financial liabilities:[2]

- Non-current financial assets. This line item consists of the following items:
  - Shares of entity X (carrying amount: CU 900) which are measured at fair value through other comprehensive income (IFRS 9.5.7.1(b) and 9.5.7.5).
  - Shares of entity Y (carrying amount: CU 400) which have to be measured at fair value according to the classification rules of IFRS 9. E did not elect to present the fair value changes in OCI. Thus, they are presented in profit or loss.
  - A loan granted to entity Z (carrying amount: CU 100) which is measured at amortized cost.
  - A loan granted to entity A (carrying amount: CU 150) which has been designated as at fair value through profit or loss in order to eliminate an accounting mismatch (IFRS 9.4.1.5).
  - Derivative assets (carrying amount: CU 60) which have to be measured at fair value through profit or loss (IFRS 9.B4.1.9).
- Trade receivables (carrying amount: CU 800) which are held with the objective to collect contractual cash flows and are therefore measured at amortized cost according to IFRS 9 (IFRS 9.4.1.2).
- Cash and cash equivalents (carrying amount: CU 200).
- Non-current financial liabilities. This line item comprises loan payables (carrying amount: CU 400) which are measured at amortized cost.
- Trade payables (carrying amount: CU 500) which are measured at amortized cost.
- Short-term loan payables, which consist of the following items:
  - Borrowings (carrying amount: CU 170) resulting from hybrid contracts that have been designated as at fair value through profit or loss according to IFRS 9.4.3.5.
  - Borrowings (carrying amount: CU 40) that are measured at amortized cost.

[2] *See the chapter on IFRS 9/IAS 39 with regard to the classification of financial assets and financial liabilities into the appropriate (measurement) categories.*

- Short-term derivative liabilities (carrying amount: CU 200) that meet the definition of "held for trading" and are therefore measured at fair value through profit or loss (IFRS 9.4.2.1(a) and IFRS 9.Appendix A).

Required

Prepare a table for the notes to E's financial statements as at Dec 31, 01 that contains the disclosures required by IFRS 7.8 (carrying amounts of the categories of financial assets or financial liabilities) and IFRS 7.6 (reconciliation of these amounts to the line items presented in the statement of financial position).

Hints for solution

In particular Section 2.

Solution

	Financial assets at amortized cost	*Financial assets at fair value through OCI*	*Financial assets at fair value through P/L*		*Financial liabilities at fair value through P/L*		*Financial liabilities at amortized cost*	**Carrying amount by line item in the balance sheet**
			Fair value option	*Mandatorily measured at fair value*	*Fair value option*	*Held for trading*		
Non-current financial assets	100	900	150	460				**1,610**
Current financial assets								
Trade receivables	800							**800**
Cash and cash equivalents	200							**200**
Carrying amount by category	**1,100**	**900**	**150**	**460**				**2,610**
Non-current financial liabilities							400	**400**
Current financial liabilities								
Trade payables							500	**500**
Short-term loan payables					170		40	**210**
Short-term derivative liabilities						200		**200**
Carrying amount by category					**170**	**200**	**940**	**1,310**

Example 2

Liquidity risk

(a) On Jan 01, 01, Bank B issues a debt instrument which is subject to the following terms and conditions and which is measured at amortized cost (i.e. according to the effective interest method):

Issue price	CU 1,000
Date of maturity	Dec 31, 03
Redemption price	CU 1,331
Effective interest rate	10%
Carrying amount as at Dec 31, 01 (determined according to the effective interest method)	1,100

During the maturity of the debt instrument no interest has to be paid because the creditor's consideration is represented by the discount of CU 331. The owner of the debt instrument has no right to demand payment before the date of maturity.

(b) On Dec 31, 01, the demand deposits of B's customers amount to CU 300. B can be required to repay the deposits by its customers on demand.

Required

Describe how the debt instrument and the demand deposits are presented in the maturity analysis for non-derivative financial liabilities (including issued financial guarantee contracts) (IFRS 7.39a) that has to be disclosed in B's financial statements as at Dec 31, 01.

Hints for solution

In particular Section 3.

Solution

The carrying amount of the liabilities is not relevant to the maturity analysis. The maturity analysis shows the contractual undiscounted future cash flows (IFRS 7.B11D). When a counterparty has a choice of when an amount is paid it is allocated to the earliest period in which the entity can be required to pay. Therefore, the demand deposits are included in the earliest time band (IFRS 7.BllCa). The following table shows the maturity analysis. For simplification purposes only two time bands are presented:

	Remaining contractual maturities	
	1 year or less	*More than 1 year*
Debt instrument		1,331
Demand deposits	300	

IFRS 8 OPERATING SEGMENTS

1 INTRODUCTION

Segment reporting according to IFRS 8 aims at enabling users of financial statements to **see an entity through the eyes of its management**. Therefore, in the segment report, the entity has to report segments that correspond to internal management reports. Similarly, the amounts disclosed according to IFRS 8 are derived from internal management reports and therefore do not necessarily have to be determined in accordance with IFRSs.

2 SCOPE

IFRS 8 applies to the separate and consolidated financial statements of an entity whose debt or equity instruments are traded in a **public market** (a domestic or foreign stock exchange or an over-the-counter market including local and regional markets) or that files, or is in the process of filing, its financial statements with a securities commission or other regulatory organization for the purpose of issuing any class of instruments in a public market (IFRS 8.2). If a financial report contains both the consolidated financial statements of a parent (within the scope of IFRS 8) and the parent's separate financial statements, segment information is required only in the consolidated financial statements (IFRS 8.4).

IAS 34 includes disclosure requirements with regard to segment information in **interim financial reports** (IAS 34.16Ag).

3 OPERATING SEGMENTS AND CHIEF OPERATING DECISION MAKER

An operating segment is a component of an entity that meets all of the following criteria (IFRS 8.5 and IFRS 8.Appendix A):

- It engages in **business activities** from which it may earn **revenues** and incur **expenses** (including revenues and expenses relating to transactions with other components of the same entity).
- Its operating results are regularly reviewed by the entity's **chief operating decision maker (CODM)** in order to make decisions about resources to be allocated to the segment and assess its performance.
- **Discrete financial information** is available for it.

An operating segment may engage in **business activities** for which it has yet to earn revenues. For example, start-up operations may be operating segments before earning revenues (IFRS 8.5).

Not every part of an entity is necessarily an operating segment or part of an operating segment. For example, a corporate headquarters or some functional departments may not earn revenues or may earn revenues that are only incidental to the activities of the entity. Therefore, they do not represent operating segments (IFRS 8.6).

In the above definition of the term "operating segment," the term "**chief operating decision maker**" is used. The latter term identifies a function, not necessarily a manager with a specific title. That function is to allocate resources to and assess the performance of the entity's operating segments. Often the CODM is the entity's chief executive officer or chief operating officer. However, the CODM may also be a group of executive directors or others (IFRS 8.7).

Determination of the operating segments is **based on** the entity's **internal management reports**. Therefore, the segments presented in the financial statements may be based, for example, on product categories, geographical regions or customer groups or a mixed segmentation (e.g. product categories are presented as segments for one part of the entity, whereas customer groups are presented as segments for the remaining part of the entity) may be presented, provided that the same segmentation is also used in the entity's internal management reports.

Many entities, in particular multinational entities with diverse operations, organize and report financial information to the CODM in more than one way. As a result, identifying the appropriate operating segments **might not be obvious**. In such cases, judgment will be necessary in determining the operating segments and will depend on the individual facts and circumstances of the entity. In these situations, the operating segments are determined by reference to the **core principle** of IFRS 8, which requires the disclosure of information that enables users of an entity's financial statements to evaluate the nature and financial effects of the business activities in which the entity engages and the economic environments in which it operates. The following **additional factors** may identify the appropriate operating segments (IFRS 8.8–8.10):[1]

- The nature of the business activities of each component of the entity.
- The existence of managers responsible for the components of the entity.
- Information presented to the board of directors.
- Information provided to external financial analysts and on the entity's website.
- Information disclosed in the front/end of the financial statements, e.g. director's report.

Some entities use a **matrix organization** whereby business components are managed in more than one way. For example, there may be segment managers who are responsible for geographic regions as well as segment managers who oversee products and services. If the entity generates financial information about its business components based on both geography and products or services (and the CODM reviews both types of information, and both have segment managers), the appropriate operating segments are determined by reference to the core principle of IFRS 8 described above (IFRS 8.10).[2]

4 REPORTABLE SEGMENTS

4.1 Overview

It is necessary to **report** separately about each **operating segment** that (IFRS 8.11):

- has been **identified** in accordance with IFRS 8.5–8.10 (see Section 3) or results from the **aggregation** of two or more of those segments in accordance with IFRS 8.12 (see Section 4.2), and
- exceeds the **quantitative thresholds** in IFRS 8.13 (see Section 4.3).

---

[1] *See KPMG,* Insights into IFRS, *7th edition, 5.2.120.10–5.2.120.20.*

[2] *See KPMG,* Insights into IFRS, *7th edition, 5.2.130.10.*

Other situations in which separate information about operating segments may be reported or has to be reported are described in Section 4.4 (IFRS 8.14–8.19).

4.2 Aggregation of Operating Segments

Two or more operating segments may be **aggregated** into a single operating segment if all of the following criteria (**aggregation criteria**) are met (IFRS 8.12):

- Aggregation is consistent with the **core principle of IFRS 8** to disclose information that enables users of the entity's financial statements to evaluate the nature and financial effects of the business activities in which the entity engages and the economic environments in which it operates (IFRS 8.1).
- The operating segments have **similar economic characteristics**.
- The operating segments are **similar in each of the following respects**:
  - The nature of the products and services.
  - The nature of the production processes.
  - The class or type of customer for their products and services.
  - The methods used to distribute their products or provide their services.
  - If applicable, the nature of the regulatory environment (e.g. banking, insurance, or public utilities).

4.3 Quantitative Thresholds

It is necessary to separately report information about an operating segment that meets any of the following quantitative thresholds (IFRS 8.13):

- Its **revenue** (including both external and intersegment revenue) is 10% or more of the combined revenue (internal and external) of all operating segments.
- The absolute amount of its **profit or loss** is 10% or more of the greater, in absolute amount, of the following:
  - The combined profit of all operating segments that did not report a loss.
  - The combined loss of all operating segments that reported a loss.
- Its **assets** are 10% or more of the combined assets of all operating segments.

The measures of the segment amounts used for these tests are based on the amounts reported to the CODM.[3]

4.4 Remaining Operating Segments

Operating segments that do not meet any of the quantitative thresholds (see Section 4.3) may be **considered reportable** if management believes that information about the segment would be **useful** to users of the financial statements (IFRS 8.13).

Operating segments that do not meet the quantitative thresholds may be **combined to produce a reportable segment** if the operating segments have similar economic characteristics and share a majority of the aggregation criteria listed in IFRS 8.12 (IFRS 8.14).

If the total external revenue reported by operating segments is **less than 75% of the entity's revenue**, additional operating segments have to be identified as reportable segments until

---

[3] *See KPMG,* Insights into IFRS, *7th edition, 5.2.150.30.*

at least 75% of the entity's revenue is included in reportable segments (IFRS 8.15). Which segments are chosen is at the entity's discretion.

Other business activities and operating segments that are not reportable are combined in an "**all other segments**" **category** separately from other reconciling items in the reconciliations required by IFRS 8.28[4] (IFRS 8.16).

The entity should consider whether a **practical limit** to the number of reportable segments presented is reached when their number increases above 10. In that case, segment information may become too detailed (IFRS 8.19). However, that rule must not be used by the entity to depart from the mandatory requirements of IFRS 8 for determining reportable segments.

5 SEGMENT DISCLOSURES

5.1 Determination of the Amounts to be Disclosed

The **amount** of each segment item reported is based on **internal management reports**. More precisely, these amounts are the measures reported to the **CODM** for the purposes of making decisions about allocating resources to the segment and assessing its performance. If amounts are allocated to reported segment profit or loss, assets or liabilities, those amounts have to be allocated on a reasonable basis (IFRS 8.25).

If the CODM uses more than one measure of an operating segment's profit or loss, the segment's assets or the segment's liabilities, the reported measures are those that management believes are determined in accordance with the measurement principles most consistent with those used in measuring the corresponding amounts in the entity's financial statements (IFRS 8.26).

IFRS 8 **does not require the allocations** to reportable segments **to be symmetrical**. For example, depreciation expense may be taken into account when determining profit or loss of a particular segment, whereas the related depreciable assets are not allocated to that segment (IFRS 8.27f).

5.2 Disclosure Requirements

5.2.1 Segment Profit or Loss IFRS 8 requires the reporting of **a measure of segment profit or loss** (IFRS 8.23). The measure disclosed has to be the measure reported to the **CODM** for the purposes of making decisions about allocating resources to the segment and assessing its performance (IFRS 8.23 and 8.25). Hence, if the CODM does not use the same measure of segment profit or loss for all segments, the segment report according to IFRS 8 also includes different measures for the segments presented. If the CODM uses more than one measure of a segment's profit or loss, the reported measure is the one that management believes is determined in accordance with the measurement principles most consistent with those used in measuring the corresponding amounts in the entity's financial statements (IFRS 8.23 and 8.25–8.26). Examples of measures of segment profit or loss are revenue, gross profit, results of operating activities, EBIT, and EBITDA.

It is also necessary to disclose the following amounts about each reportable segment if they are included in the measure of segment profit or loss reviewed by the CODM, or are otherwise

[4] *See Section 5.2.3.*

regularly provided to the CODM even if they are not included in that measure of segment profit or loss (IFRS 8.23):

- Segment revenues from external customers
- Revenues from transactions with other segments of the same entity
- Interest revenue
- Interest expense
- Depreciation and amortization
- Material items of income and expense disclosed in accordance with IAS 1.97
- The entity's interest in the profit or loss of associates and joint ventures accounted for using the equity method
- Income tax expense or income
- Material non-cash items other than depreciation and amortization

The **measurement** of these amounts has to correspond with their measurement in the entity's internal management reports (IFRS 8.25).

Interest revenue has to be reported separately from **interest expense**. However, a segment's interest revenue may be reported net of its interest expense if (IFRS 8.23):

- a majority of the segment's revenues are from interest and the CODM relies primarily on net interest revenue to assess the performance of the segment and make decisions about resources to be allocated to the segment, and
- the entity discloses that it has reported these amounts on a net basis.

In addition, the amounts of **impairment losses** and **reversals of impairment losses** recognized in profit or loss and in other comprehensive income during the period have to be disclosed for each reportable segment (IAS 36.129).

5.2.2 Segment Assets and Segment Liabilities A measure of segment assets and segment liabilities has to be reported for each segment if such amounts are regularly provided to the CODM (IAS 8.23).

If the CODM uses only one measure of the segment's assets or the segment's liabilities in assessing segment performance and deciding how to allocate resources, the assets and liabilities are reported at those measures. If the CODM uses more than one measure of the segment's assets or the segment's liabilities, the reported measures are those that management believes are determined in accordance with the measurement principles most consistent with those used in measuring the corresponding amounts in the entity's financial statements (IFRS 8.26).

5.2.3 Reconciliations According to IFRS 8, an entity has to provide several reconciliations of the **total of the reportable segments' amounts** to the **amounts included in the financial statements**. For example, it is necessary to reconcile the total of the reportable segments' revenues to the entity's revenue or to reconcile the total of the reportable segments' measures of profit or loss to the entity's profit or loss before tax and discontinued operations. However, if the entity allocates to reportable segments items such as tax expense (tax income), the entity may reconcile the total of the segments' measures of profit or loss to the entity's profit or loss after those items (IFRS 8.28).

All material reconciling items have to be separately identified and described (IFRS 8.28). Information about other business activities and operating segments that are not reportable has to be combined and disclosed in an "**all other segments**" **category** separately from other reconciling items. The sources of the revenue included in that category have to be described (IFRS 8.16).

5.2.4 Other Disclosures The entity has to disclose the **factors used to identify its reportable segments** including the basis of organization. Moreover, the **types of products and services** from which each reportable segment derives its revenues have to be disclosed (IFRS 8.22).

IFRS 8 requires further disclosures, e.g. about the basis of accounting for any transactions between reportable segments and about the nature and effect of any asymmetrical allocations to reportable segments (IFRS 8.27).

6 ENTITY-WIDE DISCLOSURES

The entity-wide disclosures have to be made by **all entities subject to IFRS 8** including those entities that have a single reportable segment. However, they have to be provided only if they are not provided as part of the reportable segment information required by IFRS 8. These disclosure requirements have to be implemented, irrespective of whether the information is regularly provided to the CODM. The amounts reported are based on the financial information that is used to prepare the entity's financial statements (IFRS 8.31–8.34).

The entity has to report the **revenues from external customers** for each **product** and **service**, or each group of similar products and services, unless the necessary information is not available and the cost to develop it would be excessive (in which case that fact has to be disclosed) (IFRS 8.32).

The following **geographical information** has to be reported, unless the necessary information is not available and the cost to develop it would be excessive (in which case that fact has to be disclosed) (IFRS 8.33):

- **Revenues from external customers** (a) attributed to the entity's **country of domicile** and (b) attributed to **all foreign countries** in total from which the entity derives revenues. Moreover, if revenues from external customers attributed to an **individual foreign country** are **material**, they have to be disclosed separately. The basis for attributing revenues from external customers to individual countries also has to be disclosed.
- **Non-current assets** other than financial instruments, deferred tax assets, post-employment benefit assets, and rights arising under insurance contracts (a) located in the entity's country of domicile and (b) located in all foreign countries in total in which the entity holds assets. Moreover, if **assets in an individual foreign country** are **material**, those assets have to be disclosed separately.

If revenues from transactions with a single external customer amount to 10% or more of the entity's revenues (**major customer**), the entity has to disclose this fact, the total amount of revenues from each such customer, and the identity of the segment or segments reporting the revenues. To this end, a group of entities known to the reporting entity to be under common control has to be considered a single customer (IFRS 8.34).

7 EXAMPLES WITH SOLUTIONS

Example 1

Determining the reportable segments

The internal management reports of entity E and consequently also the segment report presented in E's financial statements are based on a mixed segmentation. The following table illustrates E's six operating segments resulting from that segmentation:

	Cars			*Trucks*	*Motorcycles*	*Mopeds*	
	Sales to individuals (Europe)	*Sales to individuals (USA)*	*Sales to companies*	*Sales to companies*	*Sales to individuals*	*Sales to individuals*	*Total*
External revenue	33.2	22.3	8.2	8.4	7.0	8.3	87.4
Intersegment revenue	8.9	6.0	1.2	0.0	0.0	0.0	16.1
Total segment revenue	42.1	28.3	9.4	8.4	7.0	8.3	103.5
Segment profit or loss	6.0	−0.7	−0.8	0.7	−0.1	0.6	5.7
Segment assets	80.1	69.4	20.0	21.0	14.1	14.4	219.0

Required

Determine E's reportable segments according to IFRS 8.

Hints for solution

In particular Sections 4.3 and 4.4.

Solution

In order to determine E's reportable segments, the following calculations are necessary (IFRS 8.13 and 8.15).

		Cars			*Trucks*	*Motorcycles*	*Mopeds*	
		Sales to individuals (Europe)	*Sales to individuals (USA)*	*Sales to companies*	*Sales to companies*	*Sales to individuals*	*Sales to individuals*	*Total*
External revenue	In CU	33.2	22.3	8.2	8.4	7.0	8.3	87.4
External revenue	In %	38.0%	25.5%	9.4%	9.6%	8.0%	9.5%	100.0%
Intersegment revenue	In CU	8.9	6.0	1.2	0.0	0.0	0.0	16.1
Total segment revenue	In CU	42.1	28.3	9.4	8.4	7.0	8.3	103.5
Total segment revenue	In %	40.7%	27.3%	9.1%	8.1%	6.8%	8.0%	100.0%
Segment profit or loss	In CU	6.0	−0.7	−0.8	0.7	−0.1	0.6	5.7
Segment loss	In CU		−0.7	−0.8		−0.1		−1.6
Segment profit	In CU	6.0			0.7		0.6	7.3
Segment profit or loss	In %	82.2%	9.6%	11.0%	9.6%	1.4%	8.2%	—
Segment assets	In CU	80.1	69.4	20.0	21.0	14.1	14.4	219.0
Segment assets	In %	36.6%	31.7%	9.1%	9.6%	6.4%	6.6%	100.0%

In the above table, segment profit or loss is always expressed as a percentage of the total of the segments' profits (because the total of the segments' profits is larger than the total of the segments' losses). The absolute amount of that percentage has to be compared with the 10% threshold (IFRS 8.13b).

The calculations above result in the following conclusions:

- The operating segments "cars – sales to individuals (Europe)," "cars – sales to individuals (USA)," and "cars – sales to companies" are reportable because each of them meets at least one of the quantitative thresholds specified in IFRS 8.13.
- The operating segments "trucks – sales to companies," "motorcycles – sales to individuals," and "mopeds – sales to individuals" are at first not considered reportable because they do not meet any of the quantitative thresholds specified in IFRS 8.13.

The total external revenue reported by the reportable segments "cars – sales to individuals (Europe)," "cars – sales to individuals (USA)," and "cars – sales to companies" represents 72.9% of E's consolidated revenue (i.e. of E's external revenue). Since that percentage is less than 75% of E's revenue, additional operating segments have to be identified as reportable until the 75% criterion is met (IFRS 8.15). Which segment is chosen ("trucks – sales to companies," "motorcycles – sales to individuals," and "mopeds – sales to individuals") is at E's discretion.

Example 2

Reconciliation of profit or loss

Entity E possesses the operating segments A, B, C, and D. The operating segments A, B, and C are reportable. The following information is available from E's internal management reports:

	A	*B*	*C*	*D*	*Headquarters*	*Total*
Depreciation charge (presented in E's internal management reports)	−20	−15	−10	−1	−20	−66
Depreciation charge (IFRS)	−15	−12	−9	−1	−18	−55
Intragroup profits and losses	−6	−4	7	3	0	0
EBIT	150	120	80	10	−60	300
Interest expense	−20	−10	−10	−5	−5	−50
Interest revenue	2	2	1	1	1	7

E uses EBIT as the measure of segment profit or loss in its internal management reports. In determining that measure, E deducts the depreciation charge (presented in its internal management reports) and not the depreciation expense determined according to IFRS. Moreover, intragroup profits and losses are not eliminated. For the rest, IFRSs are applied in E's internal management reports in the same way as in E's consolidated financial statements. The expense for recognizing a provision for litigation in the amount of CU 10 as well as the fair value gain on a financial asset that meets the definition of "held for trading" (IFRS 9.Appendix A) in the amount of CU 15 are not included in the amounts presented in the table above because they are not allocated to the individual segments.

Required

Prepare the reconciliation of profit or loss (IFRS 8.28b).

Hints for solution

In particular Section 5.2.3.

Solution

Before preparing the reconciliation of the total of the reportable segments' profits to E's profit (before tax and discontinued operations) (IFRS 8.28b), the following reconciliation between the internal segment data and the amounts included in the separate income statement is presented for a better understanding:

	A	*B*	*C*	*D*	*Headquarters*
EBIT	150	120	80	10	−60
Elimination of the depreciation charge presented in E's internal management reports	20	15	10	1	20
Depreciation charge (IFRS)	−15	−12	−9	−1	−18
Elimination of intragroup profits and losses	6	4	−7	−3	0
Adjusted EBIT	**161**	**127**	**74**	**7**	**−58**
Interest expense	−20	−10	−10	−5	−5
Interest revenue	2	2	1	1	1
Profit or loss before unallocated items	**143**	**119**	**65**	**3**	**−62**
Total	**268**				
Recognition of the provision for litigation	−10				
Fair value gain	15				
Profit before tax	**273**				

The reconciliation of profit or loss (IFRS 8.28b) (which is derived by combining amounts included in the table above) is presented as follows:

Total of the (unadjusted) EBITs of A, B, and C	**350**
Elimination of A's, B's, and C's depreciation charge presented in E's internal management reports	45
Depreciation expense according to IFRS (A, B, and C)	−36
Elimination of intragroup profits and losses (A, B, and C)	3
Interest expense (of A, B, and C)	−40
Interest revenue (of A, B, and C)	5
Recognition of the provision for litigation	−10
Fair value gain	15
Category "all other segments" (IFRS 8.16) (D and headquarters)	−59
Profit before tax	**273**

Example 3

Quiz

(a) Segment revenues are reported to the CODM of entity A for the purposes of making decisions about allocating resources to the segments and assessing their performance. It is currently discussed whether segment revenues have to be disclosed in A's segment report according to IFRS 8.

(b) Division X of entity B generates 80% of its total (internal and external) revenue by selling to other divisions of B. It is currently being discussed whether such a segment can become reportable according to IFRS 8.

(c) Entity C owns three operating segments (X, Y, and Z) that are reportable. C's CODM uses the results of operating activities as the measure of segment profit or loss for X and Y, whereas he uses gross profit for Z.

(d) The revenues of entity D stemming from transactions with entity Z amount to 15% of D's revenues. Z is an unrelated third party of D. Which of the following statements is/are correct?
   1. The situation described does not necessitate any additional disclosures.
   2. The total amount of revenues arising from sales to Z has to be disclosed.
   3. The identity of the major customer (i.e. of Z) has to be disclosed.
   4. The identity of the segment or segments reporting the revenues has to be disclosed.
   5. The amount of revenues generated by each reportable segment of D from sales to Z has to be disclosed.

Required

Describe the treatment of these issues in the segment reports of the entities according to IFRS 8.

Hints for solution

In particular Sections 3, 4.3, 5.2.1, and 6.

Solution

(a) Segment revenues have to be disclosed in the segment report according to IFRS 8 because they are used by the CODM for the purposes of making decisions about allocating resources to the segments and assessing their performance (IFRS 8.25–8.26).

(b) Segments that generate mainly internal revenue may also become reportable according to IFRS 8. Consequently, it has to be assessed (in the same way as for other components of entity B) whether division X has to be disclosed in B's segment report.

(c) The measure of segment profit or loss disclosed in C's segment report according to IFRS 8 has to be the measure used by the CODM. Hence, if the CODM does not use the same measure of segment profit or loss for all segments, the segment report according to IFRS 8 also includes different measures for the segments presented (i.e. the results of operating activities for X and Y and gross profit for Z) (IFRS 8.26).

(d) Statements (2) and (4) are correct (IFRS 8.34).

IFRS 9 FINANCIAL INSTRUMENTS AND IAS 39 FINANCIAL INSTRUMENTS: RECOGNITION AND MEASUREMENT

1 INTRODUCTION

IAS 39 sets out the requirements for recognizing and measuring financial assets and financial liabilities. However, the IASB is currently developing a new standard (**IFRS 9**) that will ultimately **replace IAS 39** in its entirety. The IASB divided that project to replace IAS 39 into **three main phases** (IFRS 9.IN1 and 9.IN5–9.IN6):

- Classification and measurement of financial assets and financial liabilities
- Impairment methodology
- Hedge accounting

As the IASB completes each phase, the relevant portions of IAS 39 will be deleted and new chapters will be created in IFRS 9 that replace the requirements in IAS 39.

In November 2009, the Board issued the chapters of IFRS 9 that relate to the **classification and measurement** of **financial assets**. In October 2010, the IASB added the requirements to IFRS 9 for classifying and measuring **financial liabilities**. At the same time, the requirements in IAS 39 related to the **derecognition** of financial assets and financial liabilities were carried forward unchanged to IFRS 9 (IFRS 9.IN7–IN8). By amending IFRS 9 in October 2010, the Board completed the first main phase of its project to replace IAS 39. However, currently the IASB intends to make limited modifications to the already existing rules of IFRS 9.

IFRS 9 (2010) has to be applied for annual periods beginning on or after Jan 01, **2015**. However **earlier application** is **permitted** (IFRS 9.7.1.1). In the **European Union**, new IFRSs have to be endorsed by the European Union before they can be applied. Since there has been no endorsement with regard to IFRS 9 until now, the new rules cannot be applied in the European Union at the moment.

The remaining part of this chapter of the book is subdivided as follows:

- In Section 2, financial instruments accounting is explained on the basis of IFRS 9 (as issued in October 2010) and its consequential amendments to IAS 39.
- In Section 3, the differences between financial instruments accounting prior to IFRS 9 and the requirements applicable when applying IFRS 9 (2010) early are illustrated.
- Each of these two sections closes with a subsection that includes examples.

2 FINANCIAL INSTRUMENTS ACCOUNTING ACCORDING TO IFRS 9 (AS ISSUED IN 2010) AND ITS CONSEQUENTIAL AMENDMENTS TO IAS 39

2.1 Scope[1]

Generally speaking, IFRS 9 (as issued in October 2010) is applied for **recognizing, derecognizing, and measuring financial assets and financial liabilities** (IFRS 9.2.1), whereas IAS 39 still sets out the requirements for **impairment testing and hedge accounting** that are not yet addressed by IFRS 9. Some aspects of financial instruments accounting are not covered by IFRS 9 and IAS 39. These are dealt with in the chapters on IAS 32 ("Financial Instruments: Presentation") and IFRS 7 ("Financial Instruments: Disclosures").

In the investor's consolidated financial statements, equity instruments are generally not in the scope of IFRS 9 if they are interests in subsidiaries, joint ventures or associates (IAS 39.2 and IFRS 9.2.1).

2.2 Initial Recognition

As a general principle, a financial asset or a financial liability is recognized in the statement of financial position when the entity becomes a **contracting party** (IFRS 9.3.1.1). As a consequence, positive and negative fair values of **financial derivatives** are recognized in that statement (IFRS 9.B3.1.1).

However, receivables and liabilities that are the result of a **firm commitment to purchase or sell goods or services** are generally not recognized until at least one of the parties has completed their side of the agreement. For example, an entity that receives an order generally does not recognize a trade receivable (and the entity that places the order does not recognize a trade payable) at the time of the commitment but, rather, delays recognition until the ordered goods or services have been shipped, delivered or rendered (IFRS 9.B 3.1.2b).

2.3 Measurement

2.3.1 Derivatives and Financial Instruments Held for Trading When discussing the measurement of financial instruments, it is first necessary to understand the terms "derivative" and "held for trading:"

- A **derivative** is a financial instrument or other contract within the scope of IFRS 9 that meets all three of the following criteria (IFRS 9.Appendix A):
  - Its value changes in response to the **change of an underlying**. Examples of underlyings are interest rates, financial instrument prices, commodity prices, foreign exchange rates, indices of prices or rates, credit ratings or credit indices. In the case of a **non-financial underlying** (e.g. weather conditions), the contract is only considered a derivative if the variable is **not specific to a party to the contract**. Non-financial variables that are not specific to a party to the contract include an index of earthquake losses in a particular region and an index of temperatures in a particular city. Non-financial variables specific to a party to the contract include the

[1] *The terms "financial instrument," "financial asset," "financial liability," and "equity instrument" are defined in IAS 32.11 (see the chapter on IAS 32, Section 1 and Example 1).*

occurrence or non-occurrence of a fire that damages or destroys an asset of a party to the contract (IFRS 9.BA5).
- No **initial net investment** is necessary or the initial net investment is **smaller** than would be required for other types of contracts that have a similar response to changes in market factors.
- **Settlement** is at a **future date**.

- A financial asset or financial liability meets the definition of **held for trading** if one of the criteria below is met (IFRS 9.Appendix A):
  - It is acquired or incurred principally for the purpose of **selling or repurchasing it in the near term** or it is part of a portfolio managed in this way.
  - It is a **derivative** that is neither a designated and effective hedging instrument nor a financial guarantee contract.

2.3.2 Initial Measurement Financial assets and financial liabilities are initially recognized at **fair value** (IFRS 9.5.1.1). This is the amount for which an asset could be exchanged or a liability settled between knowledgeable, willing parties in an arm's length transaction (IFRS 9.Appendix A).

Transaction costs are incremental costs that are directly attributable to the acquisition, issue or disposal of a financial asset or financial liability. The accounting treatment of transaction costs depends on the subsequent measurement[2] of the financial asset or financial liability (IFRS 9.5.1.1, IFRS 9.IG E.1.1, and IAS 39.9):

- If subsequent measurement is **at fair value through profit or loss**, transaction costs are immediately recognized in **profit or loss**.
- If subsequent measurement is **not at fair value through profit or loss**, transaction costs of a **financial asset** are **capitalized** and transaction costs of a **financial liability** are **deducted from the carrying amount** of the liability.

Transaction price is the fair value of the consideration given or received. Normally, the fair value of a financial instrument on initial recognition is the transaction price (IFRS 9.B5.1.1 and 9.B5.4.8). Hence, normally, measurement on initial recognition is actually at cost, when disregarding transaction costs.

2.3.3 Subsequent Measurement of Financial Assets With regard to financial assets, **IFRS 9** is based on a **mixed measurement model** in which some financial assets are measured at fair value and others at amortized cost after recognition. The distinction between the amortized cost and fair value category is **principle-based**.

IFRS 9 requires that financial assets are classified at initial recognition into the categories **"amortized cost" or "fair value"** which are relevant for the assets' subsequent measurement (IFRS 9.3.1.1 and 9.4.1.1–9.4.1.4). This classification is effected on the basis of both (IFRS 9.4.1.1):

- the entity's **business model** for managing the financial assets, and
- the **contractual cash flow characteristics** of the financial asset.

---

[2] *See Sections 2.3.3 and 2.3.4.*

A financial asset is classified into the category **"amortized cost"** if **both** of the following conditions are met (IFRS 9.4.1.2):

- **Subjective condition**: The objective of the **business model** for the group of assets to which the asset under review belongs is to hold assets **in order to collect contractual cash flows**.
- **Objective condition**: The contractual terms of the financial asset give rise on specified dates to cash flows which are **solely payments of interest and principal** on the principal amount outstanding.

If a financial asset does not meet both of these criteria it has to be measured at **fair value** (IFRS 9.4.1.4).

The **objective of the business model** is the objective determined by the entity's key management personnel within the meaning of IAS 24 (IFRS 9.B4.1.1).

The business model does not depend on management's intentions for an individual financial asset. This condition should be determined on a higher level of aggregation, i.e. for **portfolios of financial assets**. A single entity may have one or more such portfolio. For example, an entity may hold a portfolio of financial assets that it manages in order to collect contractual cash flows and another portfolio of financial assets that it manages in order to trade to realize fair value changes (IFRS 9.B4.1.2).

The objective of an entity's business model may be to hold financial assets in order to collect contractual cash flows, even though **not all of the assets are held until maturity**. However, if more than an infrequent number of sales are made out of a particular portfolio, it is necessary to assess whether and how such sales are consistent with an objective of collecting contractual cash flows (IFRS 9.B4.1.3 and 9.B4.1.4, Example 1).

The classification of a financial asset into the category "amortized cost" requires objectively that the contractual terms of the asset give rise on specified dates to cash flows that are **solely payments of interest and principal** on the principal amount outstanding (IFRS 9.4.1.2b). For the purpose of IFRS 9, interest is **consideration for the time value of money** (i.e. for the provision of money to another party over a particular period of time) and for the **credit risk** associated with the principal amount outstanding (IFRS 9.4.1.3), which may include a premium for liquidity risk (IFRS 9.BC4.22).

The assessment of this criterion is based on the currency in which the financial asset is denominated (IFRS 9.B4.1.8).

Leverage is a characteristic of the contractual cash flows of some financial assets. Leverage increases the variability of the contractual cash flows with the result that they do not have the economic characteristics of interest within the meaning of IFRS 9. Therefore, such contracts cannot be measured at amortized cost. Stand-alone options, forward and swap contracts are examples of financial assets that include leverage (IFRS 9.B4.1.9). A **variable interest rate** does not preclude contractual cash flows that are solely payments of interest and principal on the principal amount outstanding. However, the variable interest rate has to be consideration for the time value of money (i.e. for the provision of money to another party over a particular period of time) and for the credit risk associated with the principal amount outstanding (IFRS 9.B4.1.12).

In spite of the classification criteria described above, it is possible to designate a financial asset as measured at fair value through profit or loss (**fair value option**) at initial recognition. This requires that doing so eliminates or significantly reduces a measurement or recognition inconsistency (**accounting mismatch**) that would otherwise arise from measuring assets or liabilities or recognizing the gains and losses on them on different bases (IFRS 9.4.1.5).[3]

2.3.4 Subsequent Measurement of Financial Liabilities With regard to financial liabilities, **IFRS 9** is also based on a **mixed measurement model** in which some financial liabilities are measured at fair value and others at amortized cost after recognition.

Normally, financial liabilities are measured at **amortized cost**. Exceptions to this rule are, among others, financial liabilities at fair value through profit or loss (see below) and financial guarantee contracts[4] (IFRS 9.4.2.1).

The category "**financial liabilities at fair value through profit or loss**" consists of two sub-categories (IFRS 9.Appendix A):

- Financial liabilities that meet the definition of "**held for trading**."[5]
- Financial liabilities for which the **fair value option** is exercised, i.e. which are designated upon initial recognition by the entity as "at fair value through profit or loss." The fair value option may be exercised with respect to a financial liability if one of the following conditions is met (IFRS 9.4.2.2 and IFRS 9.4.3.5):
  - Exercising the option eliminates or significantly reduces an inconsistency (**accounting mismatch**).
  - **A group** of financial liabilities or financial assets and financial liabilities is **managed** and its performance is **evaluated** on a **fair value basis** according to a documented risk management or investment strategy and information about that group is provided internally on that basis to the entity's key management personnel.
  - Under certain circumstances, a contract that contains at least one embedded derivative (**hybrid or combined instrument**) may be designated as at fair value through profit or loss.

2.3.5 Measurement at Amortized Cost: Determining the Effective Interest Rate Measurement of financial assets or financial liabilities at **amortized cost** according to IFRS 9 means application of the **effective interest method** (IAS 39.9 and IFRS 9.4.2.1). Effective interest includes, for example, the contractual interest, premiums, discounts, and transaction costs. The **effective interest rate** is the rate that discounts the cash payments or receipts of the financial asset or financial liability to the net carrying amount of the asset or liability at initial recognition. When calculating the effective interest rate, the estimated future cash payments or receipts of the financial instrument through its expected life (or, when appropriate, a shorter period) are used. However, future credit losses are not included in this calculation (IAS 39.9).

[3] *Example 1 in Section 2.7.1 illustrates an accounting mismatch.*

[4] *See Section 2.6.*

[5] *See Section 2.3.1.*

2.3.6 Determining Fair Values After Recognition IFRS 9 establishes a **fair value hierarchy** (IFRS 9.5.4.1, 9.5.4.2, and IFRS 9.B5.4.1–9.B5.4.17):

- The best evidence of fair value is **quoted prices in an active market**.
- If there is **no active market**, fair value is determined on the basis of **recent transactions** or by reference to the current fair value of **another instrument that is substantially the same.**
- If it is not possible to determine fair value as described previously, **valuation models** are used (in particular discounted cash flow analysis and option pricing models).
- In the case of investments in unquoted equity instruments (and contracts on those investments that must be settled by delivery of the unquoted equity instruments) **cost** may be an appropriate estimate of fair value, in limited circumstances.

2.3.7 Presentation of Fair Value Gains and Losses Changes in fair value of financial assets or financial liabilities measured at their **fair values** and that are not part of a hedging relationship (see IAS 39.89–39.102) are **generally** recognized in **profit or loss.**

Exercising the **fair value option for financial assets**[6] means that the changes in fair value are presented in **profit or loss** (IFRS 9.4.1.5).

If the **fair value option** is exercised for **financial liabilities,**[7] fair value changes have to be presented as follows (IFRS 9.5.7.1 and 9.5.7.7–9.5.7.8):

- The amount of change in the fair value of the liability that is attributable to **changes in the liability's credit risk** is presented in **other comprehensive income.**
- The **remaining amount** of change in the fair value of the liability is presented in **profit or loss.**
- However, an exception is applicable if presentation of the changes in the liability's credit risk in other comprehensive income (see above) would **create or enlarge an accounting mismatch in profit or loss.** In such cases, **all fair value changes** of that liability (including the effects of changes in the liability's credit risk) have to be presented in **profit or loss.**

If the fair value option has been exercised for financial liabilities, amounts presented in other comprehensive income must not be subsequently transferred to profit or loss. However, the cumulative gain or loss may be transferred within equity, e.g. to retained earnings (IFRS 9.B5.7.9).

It is **possible** to recognize the **change in the fair value of an equity instrument** (e.g. a share) within the scope of IFRS 9 that is not held for trading in **other comprehensive income** instead of recognizing it in profit or loss. In order to avoid the so-called "cherry picking" (i.e. in order to avoid entities recognizing changes in fair value in profit or loss or in other comprehensive income selectively), this choice can only be made **at initial recognition** of the equity instrument and is **irrevocable** in the future (IFRS 9.5.7.5 and IFRS 9.BC5.25d).

---

[6] *See Section 2.3.3.*

[7] *See Section 2.3.4.*

Amounts presented in **other comprehensive income** for such equity instruments must **not be subsequently transferred to profit or loss**, i.e. not even when the equity instrument is derecognized. However, the entity may transfer the cumulative gain or loss within equity, e.g. to retained earnings (IFRS 9.B5.7.1).

2.3.8 Impairment Losses and Reversals of Impairment Losses In the case of financial assets measured at fair value, all fair value changes are recognized either in profit or loss or in other comprehensive income (IFRS 9.5.7.1). Amounts recognized in other comprehensive income must not be subsequently transferred to profit or loss (IFRS 9. B5.7.1). Consequently, according to the systematics of IFRS 9, assessing whether financial assets are impaired and recognizing impairment losses is **only necessary for financial assets carried at amortized cost**. In this respect, the rules of **IAS 39** apply because IFRS 9 does not yet contain such rules (IFRS 9.5.2.2).

At the end of each reporting period, it has to be assessed whether there is any **objective evidence of impairment** (**loss events**) in respect of financial assets measured at amortized cost (IAS 39.58). IAS 39 includes a list of examples of loss events that relate to financial difficulties of the debtor (e.g. it becoming probable that the borrower will enter bankruptcy) (IAS 39.59).

If there is **objective evidence** that an impairment loss on these financial assets has been incurred, the following amounts have to be compared with each other (IAS 39.63):

- The asset's **carrying amount** as at the end of the reporting period determined according to the effective interest method.
- The **present value** of the asset's estimated **future cash flows** (excluding future credit losses that have not been incurred). These cash flows are discounted at the financial asset's original effective interest rate (i.e. the effective interest rate computed at initial recognition).

If the asset's carrying amount exceeds its present value, an impairment loss is recognized in profit or loss (IAS 39.63). It is important to note that this present value does not correspond with fair value because the cash flows are not discounted at a market interest rate. This results in moderate impairment losses which reflect financial difficulties of the debtor, but **not market risks**.

An entity first assesses whether an impairment exists **individually** for financial assets that are individually significant. If there is objective evidence of impairment, the impairment loss has to be determined and recognized for the financial asset under review. Assessing impairment on the basis of a **group** of financial assets is **possible** for insignificant financial assets instead of an assessment on an individual basis. Moreover, assessment on a group basis is **necessary** in the case of financial assets tested individually for impairment, for which no impairment has been determined on an individual basis and for which statistical credit risks exist (IAS 39.64).

If the amount of an impairment loss recognized in a previous period decreases and the decrease can be related objectively to an event occurring after the impairment was recognized, a **reversal of the impairment loss** has to be recognized in profit or loss. The reversal must not result in a carrying amount of the asset that exceeds what the amortized cost would have been at the date the impairment is reversed had the impairment not been recognized (IAS 39.65).

2.4 Hybrid Contracts

2.4.1 Introduction **Hybrid or combined instruments** consist of a host contract (e.g. a bond) that is supplemented with additional rights or obligations. A simple example is a **convertible bond**. A convertible bond consists of a bond (**host**) which is redeemed at maturity if the conversion right is not exercised. However, if the conversion right (**embedded derivative**) is exercised, the holder of the convertible bond receives shares of the issuer instead of cash.

A derivative that is attached to a financial instrument but is contractually transferable independently of that instrument, or has a different counterparty is **not an embedded derivative, but a separate financial instrument** (IFRS 9.4.3.1).

If a hybrid contract contains a liability component as well as an equity component (e.g. in the case of a convertible bond from the perspective of the issuer), these components are separated according to the rules of **IAS 32** in the **issuer's financial statements** (IFRS 9.2.1, IAS 39.2d, and IAS 32.28–32.32) which differ from the rules of IFRS 9 illustrated in Sections 2.4.2 and 2.4.3 below.[8] However, the holder of such contracts classifies them in accordance with IFRS 9.

2.4.2 Hybrid Contracts with Financial Asset Hosts When the hybrid contract contains a **host** that is an asset **within the scope of IFRS 9**, the **hybrid contract** is classified either into the category "amortized cost" or into the category "fair value" in its **entirety** according to the **classification rules** of IFRS 9 (IFRS 9.4.3.2, 9.B5.2.1, and 9.4.1.1–9.4.1.5).

2.4.3 Other Hybrid Contracts A hybrid contract may contain a host that is not an asset within the scope of IFRS 9. In such a case it is necessary to determine whether the embedded derivative has to be separated from the host. **Separate accounting of an embedded derivative** under IFRS 9 is necessary if all of the following criteria are met (IFRS 9.4.3.3):

- The hybrid instrument is not measured at fair value through profit or loss.
- The economic characteristics and risks of the embedded derivative are not closely related to those of the host contract.
- A separate instrument with the same terms as the embedded derivative would meet the definition of a derivative.

If separation of an embedded derivative is necessary, the **host** is accounted for in accordance with the **appropriate IFRSs** (IFRS 9.4.3.4) and the **embedded derivative** is measured at **fair value** at initial recognition and subsequently (IFRS 9.B4.3.1).

If an entity is unable to determine reliably the fair value of an embedded derivative on the basis of its terms and conditions, the fair value of the embedded derivative is the difference between the fair value of the hybrid contract and the fair value of the host if those can be determined according to IFRS 9. If separate accounting of an embedded derivative from its host is necessary, but the entity is **unable to measure the embedded derivative separately** either at acquisition or at the end of a subsequent period, the entire hybrid contract has to be designated as at fair value through profit or loss (IFRS 9.4.3.6–9.4.3.7).

[8] *See the chapter on IAS 32, Section 3*

Assessment of whether an embedded derivative is required to be separated is made when the entity first becomes a party to the contract. **Subsequent reassessment** is prohibited unless there is a change in the terms of the contract that significantly modifies the cash flows, in which case reassessment is necessary (IFRS 9.B4.3.11–9.B4.3.12).

There is extensive case history with regard to embedded derivatives (IFRS 9.B4.3.1–9.B4.3.8 and IFRS 9.IG C.1–9.IG C.10). The **analysis may be complex** depending on the circumstances and the requirements may result in **less reliable measures** than measuring the entire instrument at fair value through profit or loss. Hence, it is possible to measure the entire hybrid instrument at fair value through profit or loss if certain criteria are met (IFRS 9.4.3.5 and 9.B4.3.9–9.B4.3.10).[9] If this form of the **fair value option** is exercised, separating the embedded derivative becomes unnecessary and is prohibited (IFRS 9.4.3.3c).

2.5 Derecognition of Financial Assets

IFRS 9 contains extensive rules relating to the issue of when and how a previously recognized financial asset has to be removed from the statement of financial position (derecognition) (IFRS 9.Appendix A). Apart from situations in which financial assets (e.g. receivables) are extinguished (e.g. statute of limitation or redemption) and apart from consolidation rules, the following chart applies (IFRS 9.B3.2.1):

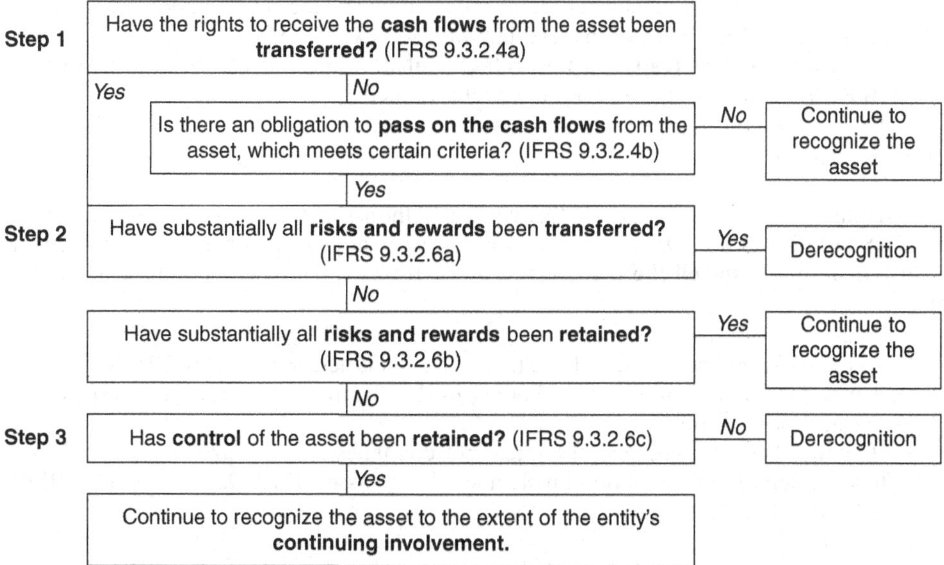

Remarks to Step 1

At first it is necessary to investigate whether the financial **asset** has been **transferred**. This is the case in each of the following situations:

[9] *See Section 2.3.4.*

- The rights to receive the **cash flows** have been **transferred** (IFRS 9.3.2.4a) (e.g. a receivable has been sold).
- The entity retains the contractual rights to **receive the cash flows** of the financial asset but assumes an obligation to **pay the cash flows** to one or more recipients in an arrangement that meets the conditions specified in IFRS 9.3.2.5 (IFRS 9.3.2.4b).

Remarks to Step 2

If the financial asset has been transferred (see Step 1), it is necessary to investigate whether the entity has retained or substantially transferred all the risks and rewards of ownership of the financial asset. In the case of receivables, the relevant risk is the credit risk, whereas in the case of securities, the relevant risk is the risk of fluctuations in market prices. Three situations are possible:

- The entity has **transferred substantially all the risks and rewards** (IFRS 9.3.2.6a). In this case, the financial asset has to be derecognized. Moreover, any rights and obligations created or retained in the transfer are recognized separately as assets or liabilities.
- The entity **retains substantially all the risks and rewards** (IFRS 9.3.2.6b). In this case, the financial asset continues to be recognized. If the entity has, for instance, sold a receivable and already received the consideration therefor, the receivable continues to be recognized in the statement of financial position and the consideration is recognized via the entry "Dr Cash Cr Financial liability" (IFRS 9.3.2.15).
- The entity **neither transfers nor retains substantially all the risks and rewards** (IFRS 9.3.2.6c). For this situation, we refer to Step 3.

Remarks to Step 3

Step 3 requires determination as to whether **control** of the asset has been retained (IFRS 9.3.2.9 and IFRS 9.B3.2.7–9.B3.2.9). This involves an assessment as to whether the **transferee** has the **practical ability to sell the transferred asset**. If this is the case, the transferor has lost control.

- If control has not been retained, the financial asset is derecognized (IFRS 9.3.2.6(c)(i)). Any rights and obligations created or retained in the transfer are recognized separately as assets or liabilities.
- If control has been retained, the transferor continues to recognize the financial asset to the extent of its continuing involvement in the asset (IFRS 9.3.2.6(c)(ii) and IFRS 9.3.2.16–9.3.2.21).

The **gain or loss on derecognition** of a financial asset is calculated on the basis of the carrying amount measured at the date of derecognition (IFRS 9.3.2.12, 9.3.2.13, and 9.3.2.20).

2.6 Financial Guarantee Contracts From the Issuer's Perspective

A financial guarantee contract is a contract that requires the issuer to make specified payments to reimburse the holder for a loss it incurs because a specified debtor fails to make payment when due in accordance with the original or modified terms of a debt instrument (IFRS 9.Appendix A). This chapter focuses on the typical accounting treatment of liabilities from co-signing in the financial statements of industrial and mercantile enterprises.

Under certain circumstances, a co-signer can apply IFRS 4. In other situations (these are the normal situations for industrial and mercantile enterprises) application of IFRS 9 is mandatory. Subsequently, only the accounting treatment according to IFRS 9 is illustrated.

Financial guarantees are measured **initially at fair value** (IFRS 9.5.1.1).

Two different types of financial guarantees that are issued against consideration have to be distinguished:

- The issuer receives a one-time payment in advance when issuing the guarantee.
- The issuer receives payments on an ongoing basis.

The remaining part of this section focuses on contracts with **ongoing payments**. In the case of such a contract, the initial fair value of the financial guarantee is the present value of the ongoing payments. In our view, in this case, the entry "Dr Receivable (right to receive commission payments) Cr Liability (obligation from co-signing)" is necessary at initial recognition.

Liabilities from co-signing against consideration are normally **measured subsequently** at amortized cost in the financial statements of industrial and mercantile enterprises. Two different situations have to be distinguished:

- A **default is not expected**: In this case, commission income is recognized over the duration of the obligation from co-signing. The entry is "Dr Liability (obligation from co-signing) Cr Commission income" (IFRS 9.4.2.1c). The receivable (right to receive commission payments) is reduced by the ongoing commission payments.
- A **default is expected**: If risk assessments deteriorate when the liability from co-signing is subsequently measured with the result that the amount of the liability from co-signing under IAS 37 exceeds the amount initially recognized and reduced by the appropriate amount of revenue, this higher amount is the new carrying amount of the liability (IFRS 9.4.2.1c). This means that the carrying amount is increased to the expected value of the obligation (which is the amount co-signed for, multiplied by the probability of default) ("Dr Expense Cr Liability"). Thereby, in our view, only the measurement rules and not the recognition rules of IAS 37 apply. This means that the liability is measured at expected value, even if the default risk is below 50%. This new carrying amount of the liability is amortized according to IAS 18 in subsequent periods. In the case of a deteriorated risk assessment, the carrying amount is again increased to the expected value of the obligation according to IAS 37.

2.7 Hedge Accounting

2.7.1 Introduction The application of IFRS 9 may lead to measurement or recognition inconsistencies (**accounting mismatches**). These are sometimes due to the fact that IFRS 9 is based on a mixed measurement model in which some financial assets and financial liabilities are measured at fair value and others at amortized cost after recognition.[10]

Example 1: Entity E is the creditor of a fixed interest rate loan. An increase (a reduction) in the market interest rate leads to a reduction (an increase) in fair value (calculated as present value) of the loan. Assume that E intends to hedge the risk of changes in fair value. Hence, E enters into an interest rate swap (derivative) under which E pays fixed interest and receives variable interest. This means that in essence, E receives variable interest on the loan instead of fixed interest due to the effect of the derivative. In other words, E receives variable interest from the combination of the loan and the swap, which means that E has eliminated the **risk of changes in fair value** (hedging strategy). This applies under the presumption that hedge effectiveness is 100%, i.e. if fair value of the loan decreases (increases) by CU 5, fair value of the derivative improves (deteriorates) by CU 5. If E measures the loan at amortized cost (i.e. according to the effective interest method), an increase in fair value above amortized cost must not be recognized in E's financial statements. Only decreases in fair value attributable to the debtor's credit risk (impairment losses) are recognized by E. By contrast, the interest rate swap has to be measured at fair value through profit or loss (IFRS 9.4.2.1(a) and IFRS 9.B4.1.9). Consequently, E has to recognize all changes in fair value of the swap in profit or loss. For example, if fair value of the loan increases by CU 5 above amortized cost, E must not recognize this increase in its financial statements. However, the corresponding deterioration of CU 5 in the fair value of the derivative has to be recognized. This results in an incorrect illustration of the hedging relationship in E's financial statements (inconsistency or accounting mismatch) because the loan and the derivative are measured on different bases, after recognition.

Example 2: Entity E is the creditor of a variable interest rate loan, which is measured at amortized cost. An increase (a reduction) in the market interest rate leads to an increase (a reduction) in the interest payments that E receives on the loan. Assume that E intends to hedge the risk of changes in interest payments. Hence, E enters into an interest rate swap (derivative) under which E receives fixed interest and pays variable interest. This means that in essence, E receives fixed interest on the loan instead of variable interest due to the effect of the derivative. In other words, E receives fixed interest from the combination of the loan and the swap, which means that E has eliminated the **risk of changes in cash flows** (hedging strategy). This applies under the presumption that hedge effectiveness is 100%. In this situation, applying the general requirements of IFRS 9 results in an inconsistency (accounting mismatch): the interest rate swap has to be measured at fair value through profit or loss (IFRS 9.4.2.1(a) and IFRS 9.B4.1.9). Consequently, E has to recognize all changes in fair value of the swap (present value of the future interest payments arising under the swap) in profit or loss. However, the future cash flows (i.e. the future interest payments) arising on the loan measured at amortized cost that are hedged must not be recognized by E (because they have not yet occurred). Consequently, an inconsistency arises because the hedging derivative affects E's financial statements, whereas the hedged position does not.

In order to avoid such inconsistencies, an entity may – under certain circumstances – (see Section 2.7.2) **depart from the general requirements of IFRS 9** and apply the **hedge accounting** rules of IAS 39 (IFRS 9.5.2.3 and 9.5.3.2). Basically, there are two different types of hedge accounting:

---

[10] *See Sections 2.3.3 and 2.3.4.*

- In the case of a **fair value hedge**, the accounting treatment of the hedged item (e.g. of the loan of a creditor) is changed so that the inconsistency is eliminated. This means that the hedged item is measured at fair value (with respect to the hedged risk) through profit or loss (which corresponds to the accounting treatment of the hedging derivative) instead of being measured at amortized cost. Thus, the effect of the changes in fair value of the hedged item and of the hedging derivative on profit or loss is zero (if hedge effectiveness is 100%). Consequently, reality is correctly portrayed in the financial statements, meaning the false presentation of results is avoided. In **Example 1**, application of the concept of fair value hedge would mean that changes in fair value of the loan (caused by changes in market interest rates) would also be recognized in profit or loss. For example, if fair value of the loan increases by CU 5 above amortized cost, this increase would be recognized in profit or loss. The corresponding deterioration of CU 5 in the fair value of the derivative would also be recognized in profit or loss. This results in a correct illustration of reality in E's financial statements.
- In the case of a **cash flow hedge**, the accounting treatment of the hedging derivative is changed. This means that the hedging derivative is measured at fair value through other comprehensive income instead of being measured at fair value through profit or loss. Thus, the effect of the hedging relationship on profit or loss is zero (if hedge effectiveness is 100%). This is because the future cash flows arising on the hedged item are not recognized by E (because they did not yet occur) and the fair value changes of the hedging derivative are generally recognized in other comprehensive income. This means that neither the future cash flows arising on the hedged item nor the hedging instrument affect profit or loss. Consequently, there is no inconsistency with regard to profit or loss. However, applying cash flow hedge accounting does not eliminate all inconsistencies in the financial statements because the fair value changes of the hedging derivative affect other comprehensive income (and consequently also equity), whereas the hedged future cash flows do not. These considerations can be applied to **Example 2**.

2.7.2 The Rules in More Detail As illustrated above, there may be different types of hedging strategies which are implemented in practice. In order to avoid inconsistencies, the hedge accounting rules allow an entity to depart from the general requirements of IFRS 9 if certain criteria are met (see next) in order to correctly present reality in the financial statements.

If a transaction, which has **already been recognized** in the financial statements, is hedged (e.g. a bond acquired by the entity), fair value hedge accounting (e.g. if a fixed interest rate loan is hedged against the risk of fair value changes with an interest rate swap) or cash flow hedge accounting (e.g. if a variable interest rate loan is hedged against the risk of changes in future interest payments with an interest rate swap) may be applied. Also a **firm commitment** can be hedged. A firm commitment is a binding agreement for the exchange of a specified quantity of resources on a specified future date or dates at a specified price (IAS 39.9). For example, entity E may enter into a contract in Nov 01 for the purchase of 10 tons of a specified raw material for 1 million CAD, which will be delivered on Feb 01, 02. On Dec 31, 01 (E's end of the reporting period 01) this transaction is a firm commitment. Generally, a hedge of a firm commitment is accounted for as a fair value hedge. However, a hedge of the **foreign currency risk of a firm commitment** may be also be accounted for as a cash flow hedge (IAS 39.87). A **forecast transaction** is an uncommitted but anticipated future transaction (IAS 39.9). In contrast to a firm commitment, no contract has been entered into in the current reporting period. Hedges of forecast transactions may only be accounted for as cash flow hedges.

Hedge accounting can only be applied if **restrictive criteria** are met. For example, hedge accounting can only be applied if the hedging instrument is a derivative. An exception to this rule only applies in the case of a hedge of the risk of changes in foreign currency exchange rates (IAS 39.9 and 39.72).

In addition to further restrictions, it is necessary that all of the following conditions are met (IAS 39.88):

- **Documentation** of the hedging relationship.
- **Hedge effectiveness** has to be demonstrated on a **retrospective basis** (i.e. relating to the past) as well as on a **prospective basis** (i.e. effectiveness is expected for the future).
- For cash flow hedges, the occurrence of a **forecast transaction** must be **highly probable**.

In some hedging relationships, hedge effectiveness is not 100%. For example, fair value of the hedging instrument may improve by CU 96 if fair value of the hedged item deteriorates by CU 100 due to the hedged risk. In this case, the changes are within the boundaries of 80% and 125%, prescribed by IAS 39,[11] which means that continuing hedge accounting is possible (96 : 100 = 96% and 100 : 96 = 104.17%), although the changes in value are not compensated by each other in full.

In the case of hedging relationships that are effective within the meaning of IAS 39, any **ineffectiveness** is treated as follows:

- In the case of *a fair value hedge,* the fair value changes of the hedging derivative and the fair value changes of the hedged item that are attributable to the hedged risk are recognized in profit or loss. Due to this procedure, any ineffectiveness is automatically recognized in profit or loss.
- In the case of a *cash flow hedge,* the hedged future cash flows (IAS 39.AG103) are not recognized in the financial statements in the current reporting period. The hedging derivative is measured at fair value through other comprehensive income. The last principle has to be stated more precisely (IAS 39.95–39.96):
  - First, the carrying amount of the hedging derivative is adjusted to fair value.
  - The separate component of equity (i.e. the amount of other comprehensive income accumulated in equity) relating to the hedging relationship at the balance sheet date is always the lower of the following amounts:
    - The cumulative gain or loss on the hedging derivative from inception of the hedge.
    - The cumulative change in fair value (present value) of the expected future cash flows on the hedged item from inception of the hedge.
  - After the change in the carrying amount of the hedging derivative and the appropriate amount of other comprehensive income have been recognized, the amount that has to be recognized in profit or loss is the remaining amount.

[11] *The boundaries of 80% and 125% apply when testing hedge effectiveness on a prospective, as well as on a retrospective basis (IAS 39.BC136–39.BC137).*

In the case of cash flow hedge accounting, there are two possibilities for the subsequent accounting treatment of the separate component of equity (hedging reserve) (i.e. the amount of other comprehensive income accumulated in equity):

(a) The associated gains and losses that were recognized in other comprehensive income are reclassified to profit or loss in the same period or periods during which the asset acquired or liability assumed affects profit or loss (such as in the periods that depreciation expense or cost of sales are recognized).
(b) The hedging reserve is derecognized and included in the initial carrying amount of the asset or liability.

If the forecast transaction subsequently results in the recognition of a non-financial asset (e.g. a machine or raw materials) or a non-financial liability, or a forecast transaction for a non-financial asset or non-financial liability becomes a firm commitment for which fair value hedge accounting is applied, then the entity applies either (a) or (b) above. In all other cases, alternative (a) is mandatory (IAS 39.97–39.100).

Among others, the entity has to **discontinue hedge accounting** prospectively if the criteria for applying hedge accounting (IAS 39.88 – see above) are no longer met. Moreover, an entity may discontinue hedge accounting voluntarily by revoking the designation (IAS 39.91 and 39.101).

2.8 Examples with solutions

Example 1

Financial assets: classification criterion "business model"

(a) Entity A holds a group of trade receivables which are held in order to collect contractual cash flows. A only sells receivables of this group if the third reminder has not been successful. This is a very seldom occurrence.
(b) Entity B holds a group of loans which are held in order to collect contractual cash flows. B never sells loans of this group. However, in some cases, B enters into interest rate swaps in order to convert the variable interest of some loans into fixed interest.
(c) Entity C holds a group of loans in order to collect contractual cash flows. C never sells loans of this group. However, C expects credit losses from some of these loans. Thus, C does not expect to receive all of the contractual cash flows.
(d) Entity D holds a group of receivables in order to realize fair value changes by selling them.

Required

Determine whether the objective of the business model is to hold the assets to collect contractual cash flows according to IFRS 9.4.1.2(a) in the above situations.

Hints for solution

In particular Section 2.3.3.

Solution

(a) Since A only sells receivables of this group if the third reminder has not been successful (which is a very seldom occurrence), the objective of A's business model is to hold the receivables in order to collect contractual cash flows (IFRS 9.B4.1.3 and 9.B4.1.4, Example 1).
(b) Irrespective of the interest rate swaps, the objective of B's business model is to hold the loans in order to collect contractual cash flows (IFRS 9.B4.1.4, Example 2).
(c) Irrespective of the expected losses, the objective of C's business model is to hold the receivables in order to collect contractual cash flows (IFRS 9.B4.1.4, Example 2).
(d) The objective of D's business model is *not* to hold the receivables in order to collect contractual cash flows. Instead, it is intended to realize fair value changes through the sale of the receivables (IFRS 9.B4.1.5 and 9.B4.1.6).

Example 2

Financial assets: classification criterion "contractual cash flow characteristics"

(a) An entity holds a loan with a stated maturity date. Payments of principal and interest on the principal amount outstanding are linked to an inflation index of the currency in which the loan is issued. The inflation link is not leveraged (i.e. for example, the payments are not adapted to the threefold of changes of the index) and the principal is protected.
(b) The amount of interest paid on a bond depends on the amount of profit or loss for the year generated by the debtor.
(c) A bond pays an inverse variable interest rate, i.e. the interest rate has an inverse relationship to the market interest rate. For example, if the market interest rate decreases by 50 bp, the interest rate of the bond increases by 50 bp.

Required

Determine whether the contractual terms of the financial assets described above give rise (on specified dates) to cash flows that are solely payments of principal and interest on the principal amount outstanding according to IFRS 9.4.1.2(b).

Hints for solution

In particular Section 2.3.3.

Solution

(a) Despite the link to the inflation index, A's loan gives only rise to payments of principal and interest on the principal amount outstanding within the meaning of IFRS 9 (IFRS 9.B4.1.13, Example A).
(b) In this case, the contractual cash flows are not payments of principal and interest on the principal amount outstanding within the meaning of IFRS 9. That is because the interest payments are not consideration for the time value of money and for the credit risk associated with the principal amount outstanding. There is variability in the contractual interest payments that is inconsistent with market interest rates (IFRS 9.4.1.2–9.4.1.3 and 9.B4.1.13, Example A).

(c) In this situation, the interest amounts are not consideration for the time value of money on the principal amount outstanding. Thus, there are not solely payments of principal and interest on the principal amount outstanding within the meaning of IFRS 9 (IFRS 9. B4.1.14, Example F).

Example 3

Measurement at fair value through other comprehensive income

On Oct 15, 01, entity E acquires shares. The purchase price of CU 99 as well as transaction costs (incremental costs that are directly attributable to the acquisition) of CU 1 are paid at the same date.

The stock market price of the shares develops as follows:

Version (a)

Dec 31, 01	110
Dec 31, 02	75
Dec 31, 03	70
Dec 31, 04	120

Version (b)

Dec 31, 01	97
Dec 31, 02	90
Dec 31, 03	85

Required

Prepare any necessary entries in the financial statements of E as at Dec 31 for the years 01–04 (version a) and for the years 01–03 (version b). Assume that the shares do not meet the definition of "held for trading" (IFRS 9. Appendix A) and that they are in the scope of IFRS 9. E always measures shares at fair value through other comprehensive income, if possible.

Hints for solution

In particular Sections 2.3.2, 2.3.3, and 2.3.7.

Solution (general remarks)

Shares do not meet the criterion "solely payments of principal and interest," which means that they have to be measured at fair value. Fair value changes of financial assets are generally recognized in profit or loss. However, it is also possible to recognize the fair value changes of the shares held by E in other comprehensive income, because the shares are equity instruments within the scope of IFRS 9 and they do not meet the definition of "held for trading." Such an election can only be made at initial recognition and is irrevocable (IFRS 9.4.1.2(b), 9.4.1.4, 9.5.7.1(b), and 9.5.7.5). Since the election is possible, E recognizes the fair value changes of the shares in other comprehensive income. This means that impairment losses are also recognized in other comprehensive income (fair value reserve) instead of profit or loss. The subsequent transfer of amounts recognized in other comprehensive income to profit or loss is prohibited (IFRS 9.B5.7.1). At initial measurement, the transaction costs of CU 1 are capitalized since measurement is not at fair value through profit or loss (IFRS 9.5.1.1).

Solution (a)

Oct 15, 01	Dr	Shares	100	
	Cr	Cash		100
Dec 31, 01	Dr	Shares	10	
	Cr	Other comprehensive income		10
Dec 31, 02	Dr	Other comprehensive income	35	
	Cr	Shares		35
Dec 31, 03	Dr	Other comprehensive income	5	
	Cr	Shares		5
Dec 31, 04	Dr	Shares	50	
	Cr	Other comprehensive income		50

Solution (b)

Oct 15, 01	Dr	Shares	100	
	Cr	Cash		100
Dec 31, 01	Dr	Other comprehensive income	3	
	Cr	Shares		3
Dec 31, 02	Dr	Other comprehensive income	7	
	Cr	Shares		7
Dec 31, 03	Dr	Other comprehensive income	5	
	Cr	Shares		5

Example 4

Financial assets held for trading

Required

Prepare any necessary entries for version (a) of Example 3, but presume that the shares meet the definition of "held for trading." Presume that increases and decreases in fair value of E's financial instruments held for trading are material.

Hints for solution

In particular Sections 2.3.2, 2.3.3, and 2.3.7.

Solution

The shares held for trading do not qualify for measurement at amortized cost because they do not meet the business model criterion (IFRS 9.4.1.2(a) and 9.B4.1.6) and because shares do not meet the criterion "solely payments of principal and interest" (IFRS 9.4.1.2(b)).

This means that the shares have to be measured at fair value (IFRS 9.4.1.4). The fair value changes (fair value gains and fair value losses) have to be presented in profit or loss because in the case of shares held for trading, fair value changes must not be presented in other comprehensive income (IFRS 9.5.7.1(b) and 9.5.7.5).

The transaction costs of CU 1 are recognized in profit or loss because subsequent measurement of the shares is at fair value through profit or loss (IFRS 9.5.1.1).

Oct 15, 01	Dr	Shares	99	
	Dr	Transaction costs (profit or loss)	1	
	Cr	Cash		100

Since increases and decreases in fair value of E's financial instruments held for trading are material, the gains and losses have to be presented separately (IAS 1.35).

Dec 31, 01	Dr	Shares	11	
	Cr	Fair value gain		11
Dec 31, 02	Dr	Fair value loss	35	
	Cr	Shares		35
Dec 31, 03	Dr	Fair value loss	5	
	Cr	Shares		5
Dec 31, 04	Dr	Shares	50	
	Cr	Fair value gain		50

Example 5

Effective interest method – introductory example (financial liability)

On Jan 01, 01, entity E takes up a loan. According to the loan, E receives CU 100 on the same date. No interest is explicitly stipulated with respect to the loan. However, E has to pay CU 121 on Dec 31, 02 in order to settle its obligations under the loan.

Required

Prepare any necessary entries in E's financial statements as at Dec 31 for the years 01 and 02. The loan is measured at amortized cost, i.e. according to the effective interest method.

Hints for solution

In particular Section 2.3.5.

Solution

Jan 01, 01	Dr	Cash	100	
	Cr	Liability		100

No interest is explicitly stipulated with respect to the loan. However, E has to pay an amount of CU 121 on Dec 31, 02 although E receives only CU 100 on Jan 01, 01. The difference of CU 21 is the consideration for E's creditor and E's cost for the loan. These costs have to be allocated by E over the years 01 and 02 according to the effective interest method.

The difference of CU 21 (from CU 121 and CU 100) corresponds to an effective interest rate of 10% p.a. (CU 121: 1.1^2 = CU 100 *or* CU 100 $\cdot$ 1.1^2 = CU 121). Thus, effective interest is CU 10 for 01 (= carrying amount as at Jan 01, 01 of CU 100 $\cdot$ 10%).

Dec 31, 01	Dr	Interest expense	10	
	Cr	Liability		10

On Jan 01, 02, the carrying amount of the liability is CU 110 (= CU 100 + CU 10). Thus, effective interest is CU 11 for 02 (= carrying amount as at Jan 01, 02 of CU 110 $\cdot$ 10%).

Dec 31, 02	Dr	Interest expense	11	
	Cr	Liability		11

On Dec 31, 02 (before derecognition of the liability), the carrying amount of the liability corresponds with redemption amount.

Dec 31, 02	Dr	Liability	121	
	Cr	Cash		121

Example 6

Effective interest method – financial liability

On Jan 01, 01, entity E takes up a loan. According to the loan agreement, E receives CU 100 on the same date. The maturity of the loan is two years. At the end of each year, E has to pay CU 56.

Required

Prepare any necessary entries in E's financial statements as at Dec 31 for the years 01 and 02. The loan is measured at amortized cost, i.e. according to the effective interest method.

Hints for solution

In particular Section 2.3.5.

Solution

Jan 01, 01	Dr	Cash	100	
	Cr	Liability		100

The effective interest rate is 7.90%:[12]

Date	*Cash inflow (+) and cash outflows (–)*	*Effective interest rate*
Jan 01, 01	100	7.9%
Dec 31, 01	–56	
Dec 31, 02	–56	

The amortization table is presented below. As in Example 5, effective interest results from multiplying the carrying amount as at Jan 01 by the effective interest rate. The amount presented in the column "redemption" is calculated by deducting the amount shown in the column "interest" from the amount presented in the column "installment." The amount shown in the column "redemption" reduces the carrying amount of the liability.

Year	*Carrying amount as at Jan 01*	*Installment*	*Interest*	*Redemption*	*Carrying amount as at Dec 31*
01	100.00	56.00	7.90	48.10	51.90
02	51.90	56.00	4.10	51.90	0.00
Total		**112.00**	**12.00**	**100.00**	

Dec 31, 01	Dr	Interest expense	7.90	
	Dr	Liability	48.10	
	Cr	Cash		56.00
Dec 31, 02	Dr	Interest expense	4.10	
	Dr	Liability	51.90	
	Cr	Cash		56.00

Example 7

Effective interest method – financial asset

On Jan 01, 01, entity E acquires a fixed interest rate bond for CU 89.69. The redemption amount, which is payable on Dec 31, 03, is CU 100. At the end of each year, E receives interest of 4% on the redemption amount.

Required

Prepare any necessary entries in E's financial statements as at Dec 31 for the years 01–03. Assume that the bond has to be measured at amortized cost according to IFRS 9.

Hints for solution

In particular Section 2.3.5.

[12] *The effective interest rate is calculated by applying the formula "IRR" in the English version of Excel to the payments shown below.*

Solution

Acquisition of the bond:

Jan 01, 01	Dr	Bond	89.69	
	Cr	Cash		89.69

At first, the financial asset has to be classified either into the category "amortized cost" or into the category "fair value." In this example, it is presumed that the bond has to be measured at amortized cost, according to the classification criteria (IFRS 9.4.1.1–9.4.1.4). Measurement at amortized cost according to IFRS 9 requires application of the effective interest method (IFRS 9.Appendix A refers to IAS 39.9 regarding the definition of the terms "amortized cost" and "effective interest method").

From the bond, E receives fixed interest of 4% p.a. Moreover, E receives additional consideration of CU 10.31 because it acquires the bond for CU 89.69 whereas the redemption amount is CU 100. Consequently, not only an amount of CU 4 (= CU 100 · 4%) is recognized as interest income in 01. Instead, effective interest income, which is a higher amount, has to be recognized. Effective interest income for 01 also includes an allocation of the additional consideration of CU 10.31. The effective interest rate is 8.00%:[13]

Date	*Cash inflows (+) and cash outflow (–)*	*Effective interest rate*
Jan 01 01	–89.69	8.0%
Dec 31, 01	4.00	
Dec 31, 02	4.00	
Dec 31, 03	104.00	

At first, the contractual interest of 4%, which is received on Dec 31, 01, is recognized:

Dec 31, 01	Dr	Cash	4	
	Cr	Interest income		4

However, it is necessary to recognize the effective interest income of CU 7.18 (= CU 89.69 · 8%) in 01, which also includes an allocation of the additional consideration of CU 10.31 and not only the contractual interest. Thus, the remaining amount of interest income of CU 3.18 (= CU 7.18 – CU 4.00) has to be additionally recognized.

E will receive the additional consideration of CU 10.31 on Dec 31, 03 (when the redemption amount of CU 100 is paid). Therefore, E has to recognize its right to receive this additional consideration in its statement of financial position to the extent that the additional consideration has been allocated to 01 (CU 3.18).

Dec 31, 01	Dr	Bond	3.18	
	Cr	Interest income		3.18

[13] *The effective interest rate is calculated by applying the formula "IRR" in the English version of Excel to the payments shown below.*

These considerations are useful in understanding the table and the entries below:

Year	*Carrying amount as at Jan 01*	*Effective interest*	*Contractual interest*	*Carrying amount as at Dec 31*
01	89.69	7.18	−4.00	92.87
02	92.87	7.43	−4.00	96.30
03	96.30	7.70	−4.00	100.00

Alternatively, the carrying amounts as at Dec 31 can also be explained as the present value of the future payments (e.g. CU 92.87 = CU 104 : 1.08^2 + CU 4 : 1.08 and CU 96.30 = CU 104: 1.08).

Dec 31, 02	Dr	Cash	4.00	
	Dr	Bond	3.43	
	Cr	Interest income		7.43
Dec 31, 03	Dr	Cash	4.00	
	Dr	Bond	3.70	
	Cr	Interest income		7.70
Dec 31, 03	Dr	Cash	100	
	Cr	Bond		100

Example 8

Effective interest method – impairment loss

The situation is the same as in Example 7. However, on Dec 31, 01, E expects that due to significant financial difficulties of the debtor, it will receive the redemption amount of CU 100 on Dec 31, 03 but will not receive the interest payments. In the following years, it turns out that this assumption was correct.

Required

Prepare any necessary entries in E's financial statements as at Dec 31 for the years 01–03. Assume that the bond has to be measured at amortized cost according to IFRS 9.

Hints for solution

In particular Sections 2.3.5 and 2.3.8.

Solution

The rules of IAS 39 relating to impairment losses still apply to financial assets accounted for at amortized cost in accordance with IFRS 9 (IFRS 9.5.2.2) because IFRS 9 does not yet contain its own rules in this respect.

In 01, the same entries are made as in Example 7. However, on Dec 31, 01, the significant financial difficulties of the debtor are an indication that the financial asset (bond) is impaired (IAS 39.59a). For this reason, E expects that it will not receive part of the payments and determines the amount of the impairment loss (IAS 39.58 and 39.63). The impairment loss is calculated as the difference between the carrying amount and the lower present value of the expected future cash flows, discounted by the original effective interest rate of 8% p.a.

(which is the interest rate determined at initial recognition of the asset, i.e. on Jan 01, 01, as illustrated in Example 7).

Carrying amount as at Jan 01, 01	89.69	Costs of purchase
Carrying amount as at Dec 31, 01 (before recognition of the impairment loss)	92.87	CU 104 : 1.08^2 + CU 4 : 1.08 *or* CU 89.69 · 1.08 – CU 4
Carrying amount as at Dec 31, 01 (after recognition of the impairment loss)	85.73	CU 100 : 1.08^2
Impairment loss	**7.14**	CU 92.87 – CU 85.73

Dec 31, 01	Dr	Impairment loss	7.14	
	Cr	Bond		7.14

In the following years, effective interest is recognized although E does not receive contractual interest (IAS 39.AG93). Effective interest for 02 is CU 6.86 (= CU 85.73 · 8% *or* carrying amount of CU 92.59 as at Dec 31, 02 – carrying amount of CU 85.73 as at Dec 31, 01 after recognition of the impairment loss). The increased carrying amount as at Dec 31, 02 results from the fact that the payment of CU 100 is only discounted for one period.

Carrying amount as at Dec 31, 01 (after recognition of the impairment loss)	85.73	CU 100 : 1.08^2
Carrying amount as at Dec 31, 02	92.59	CU 100 : 1.08 *or* CU 85.73 · 1.08

Dec 31, 02	Dr	Bond	6.86	
	Cr	Interest income		6.86

The above considerations are applied along the same lines for 03.

Carrying amount as at Dec 31, 02	92.59	CU 100 : 1.08 *or* CU 85.73 · 1.08
Carrying amount as at Dec 31, 03	100.00	Redemption amount of CU 100 *or* CU 92.59 · 1.08

Dec 31, 03	Dr	Bond	7.41	
	Cr	Interest income		7.41

Until Dec 31, 03, the carrying amount has been increased to CU 100, which corresponds to the redemption amount.

Dec 31, 03	Dr	Cash	100	
	Cr	Bond		100

Example 9

Effective interest method – reversal of an impairment loss

The situation is the same as in Example 8. However, on Dec 31, 02, the reason for the impairment does not exist anymore. E expects to receive the redemption amount as well as the last interest payment on Dec 31, 03. However, E does not expect to receive the interest payment for the year 02. Finally, it turns out that these assumptions were correct.

Required

Prepare any necessary entries in E's financial statements as at Dec 31 for the years 01–03. Assume that the bond has to be measured at amortized cost according to IFRS 9.

Hints for solution

In particular Sections 2.3.5 and 2.3.8.

Solution

The rules of IAS 39 relating to impairment losses and reversals of impairment losses still apply to financial assets accounted for at amortized cost in accordance with IFRS 9 (IFRS 9.5.2.2) because IFRS 9 does not yet contain its own rules in this respect.

In 01 and 02, the same entries are made as in Example 8. Hence, the carrying amount of the bond as at Dec 31, 02 is CU 92.59.

On Dec 31, 02, E expects to receive the redemption amount as well as the last interest payment on Dec 31, 03, i.e. an amount of CU 104 in total. Present value of these payments is CU 96.30 (= CU 104 : 1.08), which corresponds with the carrying amount of the bond as at Dec 31, 02 in Example 7 (in which no impairment loss occurs). The carrying amount of the bond is increased to this amount:

Dec 31, 02	Dr	Bond	3.71	
	Cr	Reversal of impairment losses		3.71

In 03, the same entries are made as in Example 7.

Example 10

Convertible bond

Entity E is creditor of a convertible bond, i.e. E may opt for conversion of the bond into shares of the debtor. Since E is granted a conversion right, interest on the bond is only 3% p.a. Without the conversion right, 6% would have been stipulated.

Required

Describe the accounting treatment of the convertible bond in E's financial statements.

Hints for solution

In particular Sections 2.3.3, 2.4.1, and 2.4.2.

Solution

The hybrid contract (i.e. the convertible bond) contains a host (the bond) which is an asset within the scope of IFRS 9. Therefore, the convertible bond has to be classified in its entirety either into the category "amortized cost" or into the category "fair value" for subsequent measurement according to the criteria of IFRS 9 (IFRS 9.4.3.2 and 9.2.1).

The interest rate does not reflect only consideration for the time value of money and the credit risk. Thus, the contractual cash flows are not payments of principal and interest on the principal amount outstanding. The return is also linked to the value of the equity of the issuer due to the conversion right. Consequently, the entire hybrid contract (i.e. the entire convertible bond) has to be measured at fair value (IFRS 9.4.1.1–9.4.1.4 and 9.B4.1.14, Example E).

Since the convertible bond does not represent an equity instrument, the option for recognizing the fair value changes in other comprehensive income (IFRS 9.5.7.1b and 9.5.7.5) is not available. This means that the fair value changes have to be recognized in profit or loss.

Example 11

Derecognition of financial assets – introductory example

Entity E is creditor of a bond. The carrying amount of the bond of CU 100 as at Jan 01,01 corresponds with its redemption amount. The redemption amount has to be paid on Dec 31, 01. The contractual interest rate and the effective interest rate are 7% p.a. Contractual interest for the year always has to be paid on Dec 31. On Jan 01, 01, E sells the bond to entity F at its fair value. On the same date, the market interest rate is 5% p.a.

Required

Prepare any necessary entries in E's financial statements as at Dec 31, 01. Assume that the bond is measured at amortized cost, according to IFRS 9.

Hints for solution

In particular Section 2.5.

Solution

Fair value of the bond is calculated by discounting the future cash flows of the bond by the current market interest rate. Thus, on Jan 01, 01, fair value is CU 101.90 (= CU 107 : 1.05). The bond is sold to F for this amount. On Jan 01, 01, the carrying amount of the bond (amortized cost) is CU 100 (= CU 107 : 1.07). The difference of CU 1.90 has to be recognized in profit or loss (IFRS 9.3.2.12).

Jan 01, 01	Dr	Cash	101.90	
	Cr	Bond		100.00
	Cr	Profit or loss		1.90

Example 12

Derecognition of financial assets – factoring

E owns a group of short-term receivables which are measured at amortized cost. Their carrying amount as at Dec 31, 01 is CU 80. E sells this group of receivables on

Dec 31, 01 to bank B for CU 70. The sales price is settled on the same date. After this sale, the debtors of the receivables are instructed to make their outstanding payments to B. Due to experience, credit losses of CU 8 are expected relating to this group of receivables. The following is stipulated:

(a) B assumes the risk of credit losses completely.
(b) E retains the risk of credit losses completely.
(c) E and B each bear 50% of the credit losses. There are no restrictions in respect of the transfer of the receivables to B. This means that B has the ability to resell or to pledge the receivables.
(d) E and B each bear 50% of the credit losses. There are restrictions relating to the transfer of the receivables to B. This means that B does not have the ability to resell or to pledge the receivables.

Required

Prepare any necessary entries in E's financial statements as at Dec 31, 01. E has already made its consolidation entries (IFRS 9.3.2.1 and 9.B3.2.1).

Hints for solution

In particular Section 2.5.

Solution

After the consolidation entries have been made (IFRS 9.3.2.1), it has to be determined whether the derecognition principles are applied to the whole group of receivables or to a part of the group of receivables (IFRS 9.3.2.2). In this example, all of the cash flows of the group of receivables are transferred to B. Hence, the derecognition principles are applied to the whole group of receivables.

The next question is whether the contractual rights to the cash flows from the group of receivables have expired (IFRS 9.3.2.3a). Although, E sells the group of receivables, the acquirer (B) is entitled to receive cash flows from the receivables because the receivables have not yet been settled, they have not yet become time-barred, etc. Consequently, the rights to the cash flows have not yet expired.

The next matter is whether E has transferred the contractual rights to receive the cash flows from the receivables (IFRS 9.3.2.4a). In this example, it is presumed that the transfer is irrevocable and unalienable and that the transfer is also valid in the case of bankruptcy. This is necessary for the existence of a transfer within the meaning of IFRS 9. Consequently, E has transferred the contractual rights to receive the cash flows.

In this situation, the accounting treatment of the receivables depends on the question to which extent the risks and rewards with respect to the receivables are transferred from E to B (IFRS 9.B3.2.1). In the case of receivables, the relevant risk is the risk of credit losses. When all of these risks are shared substantially by E and B (version (c) and (d) of this example), it is necessary to determine whether E has retained control of the group of receivables.

Version (a)

Since B assumes the risk of credit losses completely, substantially all risks and rewards are transferred from E to B. Hence, E has to derecognize the receivables (IFRS 9.3.2.6a and IFRS 9.B3.2.1):

Dec 31, 01	Dr	Cash	70	
	Dr	Profit or loss	10	
	Cr	Receivables		80

Version (b)

Credit losses of CU 8 are expected. E retains the risk of these credit losses completely. Therefore, E retains substantially all risks and rewards, which means that E continues to recognize the receivables (IFRS 9.3.2.6b, IFRS 9.B3.2.5e, and 9.B3.2.1). E has to recognize the consideration received of CU 70 as a financial liability (IFRS 9.3.2.15).

Dec 31, 01	Dr	Cash	70	
	Cr	Liability		70

Version (c)

In this version, E does not retain control of the receivables (IFRS 9.3.2.9 and 9.B3.2.7–9. B3.2.9). Hence, the receivables are derecognized (IFRS 9.3.2.6(c)(i) and 9.B3.2.1):

Dec 31, 01	Dr	Cash	70	
	Dr	Profit or loss	10	
	Cr	Receivables		80

The agreement that E has to bear 50% of the credit losses (remaining risk) is a guarantee that is measured at fair value of CU 4 (= 50% of CU 8) (IFRS 9.3.2.6(c)(i)):

Dec 31, 01	Dr	Profit or loss	4	
	Cr	Liability		4

Version (d)

In this version, E retains control of the receivables (IFRS 9.3.2.9 and IFRS 9.B3.2.7–9. B3.2.9). Hence, the receivables continue to be recognized to the extent of E's continuing involvement. This is to reflect E's continuing exposure to the risks and rewards of the receivables (IFRS 9.3.2.6(c)(ii), 9.B3.2.1, and 9.BCZ3.27). The receivables continue to be recognized to the extent of the maximum risk of CU 40 (= 50% of CU 80) and are derecognized to the extent of CU 40. Since receivables in the amount of CU 40 remain in E's statement of financial position, a liability has to be recognized to that extent. Moreover, a liability of CU 4 (= 50% of CU 8) has to be recognized for the part of the receivables already derecognized (IFRS 9.3.2.17):

Dec 31, 01	Dr	Cash	70	
	Dr	Profit or loss	14	
	Cr	Liability		44
	Cr	Receivables		40

Example 13

Co-signing

On Jan 01, 01, debtor D takes out a loan at bank B. The loan is to be redeemed on Dec 31, 02.

On Jan 01, 01, entity E co-signs D's loan. From E's perspective, D is an unrelated third party.

It is stipulated that E will receive consideration of CU 72.60 for co-signing on Dec 31, 01 as well as on Dec 31, 02.

From the end of 01 until Dec 31, 02, D's creditworthiness is excellent.

Required

Prepare any necessary entries in the co-signer's (i.e. in E's) financial statements as at Dec 31, for the years 01 and 02. The interest rate is 10% p.a.

Hints for solution

In particular Section 2.6.

Solution

On Jan 01, 01, E recognizes a liability (which represents E's obligation from co-signing), as well as a receivable (which represents E's right to receive commission payments). The present value of the ongoing commission payments is CU 126 (= CU 72.6 : 1.1 + CU 72.6 : 1.1^2).

Jan 01, 01	Dr	Receivable	126	
	Cr	Liability		126

On Dec 31, 01, the carrying amount of the liability and of the receivable are increased by the interest of CU 12.6 (= CU 126 · 10%) for 01.

Dec 31, 01	Dr	Interest expense	12.6	
	Cr	Liability		12.6
Dec 31, 01	Dr	Receivable	12.6	
	Cr	Interest income		12.6

After that, income of CU 72.6 is recognized. The liability is reduced by the same amount:

Dec 31, 01	Dr	Liability	72.6	
	Cr	Commission income		72.6

The carrying amount of the receivable has to be reduced because E receives a commission payment:

Dec 31, 01	Dr	Cash	72.6	
	Cr	Receivable		72.6

Thus, on Dec 31, 01, the carrying amounts of the liability and of the receivable are CU 66 each (CU 126 + CU 12.6 – CU 72.6). On Dec 31, 02, the carrying amount of the liability and of the receivable are increased by the interest of CU 6.6 (= CU 66 · 10%) for 02.

Dec 31, 02	Dr	Interest expense	6.6	
	Cr	Liability		6.6
Dec 31, 02	Dr	Receivable	6.6	
	Cr	Interest income		6.6
Dec 31, 02	Dr	Liability	72.6	
	Cr	Commission income		72.6
Dec 31, 02	Dr	Cash	72.6	
	Cr	Receivable		72.6

On Dec 31, 02, the carrying amounts of the liability and of the receivable are CU 0 each (CU 66 + CU 6.6 – CU 72.6).

Example 14

Hedge accounting – forecast transaction

Entity E's own currency is the CNY. On Nov 30, 03, E plans to purchase a machine in country Z on Mar 31, 04 for 10 m units of foreign currency F. It is highly probable that this purchase will take place. However, no contract of purchase has been entered into until the end of the reporting period 03.

On Nov 30, 03, E enters into a forward contract in order to hedge against the foreign exchange risk (currency risk) arising on the forecast transaction. Under this contract, E is obliged to buy 10 m units of foreign currency F on Mar 31, 04 at an exchange rate of 10 (1 unit of F = 10 CNY) from bank B.[14]

The following table shows the development of the exchange rate (1 unit of F = x CNY):[15]

Nov 30, 03	10
Dec 31, 03	8
Mar 31, 04	9

On Mar 31, 04, the machine is purchased, delivered, and paid. On Apr 01, 04, the machine is available for use. The machine's useful life is five years.

[14] *In this example the exchange rates are presented as "1 unit of foreign currency F = x CNY" (e.g. 1 unit of F = 10 CNY).*

[15] *For simplification purposes, differences between the spot exchange rate and the forward exchange rate are ignored in this example.*

Required

Prepare any entries in E's financial statements that are necessary from Nov 30, 03 until Dec 31, 04. E's reporting periods end on Dec 31. E applies the hedge accounting rules of IAS 39.

Hints for solution

In particular Section 2.7.

Solution

Measurement of the hedging derivative on *Dec 31, 03*:

Conversion of 10 m units of F into CNY:			
Fixed rate	10	100 m	$= 10m \cdot 10$
Rate on Dec 31, 03	8	80 m	$= 10m \cdot 8$
Fair value		**–20 m**	

The negative fair value of –20 m CNY results from the fact that E could purchase 10 m units of F for 80 m CNY without existence of the forward contract, but has to pay 100 m CNY due to the forward contract.

Conversely, fair value of the forecast transaction has improved. On Nov 30, 03, E would have had to pay 100 m CNY in order to buy the machine. On Dec 31, 03, E would have to pay only 80 m CNY. Hence, fair value of the forecast transaction is positive (+20 m CNY).

In reality, the fair value changes of the forecast transaction and of the derivative offset each other. However, on Dec 31, 03, the expected purchase of the machine cannot be recognized in the financial statements. Nevertheless, E would have to recognize the derivative at its negative fair value ("Dr Profit or loss Cr Liability 20 m CNY"). Consequently, profit or loss for 03 would deteriorate by –20 m CNY although the fair value changes actually offset each other. In order to avoid this, IAS 39 permits the application of cash flow hedge accounting.

Under the cash flow hedge accounting technique, the fair value change of the derivative of –20 m CNY is recognized in other comprehensive income (hedging reserve). Thus, neither the forecast transaction nor the hedging derivative affect profit or loss, i.e. the effect on profit or loss is zero. This corresponds with reality (see above).

Dec 31, 03	Dr	Other comprehensive income	20 m	
	Cr	Liability		20 m

The change in the hedging reserve during the period is presented in other comprehensive income (IAS 1.7e).

It should be noted that the cash flow hedge accounting technique avoids a distortion of profit or loss but not of other comprehensive income, total comprehensive income or equity as a whole.

Year 04

Measurement of the hedging derivative on *Mar 31, 04*:

Conversion of 10 m units of F into CNY:			
Fixed rate	10	100 m	*= 10 m · 10*
Rate on Mar 31, 04	9	90 m	*= 10 m · 9*
Fair value		**–10 m**	

The reduction in the carrying amount of the liability from –20 m CNY to –10 m CNY is recognized in other comprehensive income (hedging reserve):

Mar 31, 04	Dr	Liability	10 m	
	Cr	Other comprehensive income		10 m

On Mar 31, 04, the machine is purchased for 10 m units of F, converted at the current exchange rate (= 10 m units of F · 9 = 90 m CNY). Moreover, the forward contract (fair value as at Mar 31, 04 = –10 m CNY) is settled. Therefore, in total, an amount of 100 m CNY has to be paid. This corresponds with the purchase price that E intended to fix by securing the rate of 10 (10 m units of F · 10 = 100 m CNY).

Mar 31, 04	Dr	Machine	90 m	
	Dr	Liability	10 m	
	Cr	Cash		100 m

After this entry, the question arises of how to treat the carrying amount of the hedging reserve of –10 m CNY. A machine represents a non-financial asset. Consequently, IAS 39.98 has to be applied, which permits two different ways of treating the hedging reserve.

IAS 39.98(a): Derecognition of the hedging reserve is effected in the same periods during which the machine affects profit or loss. In 04, the machine is depreciated for nine months (90 m CNY : 5 years : 12 months · 9 months = 13.5 m CNY). Derecognition of the hedging reserve is effected to the same extent (10 m CNY : 5 : 12 · 9 = 1.5 m CNY).

Dec 31, 04	Dr	Depreciation expense	13.5 m	
	Cr	Machine		13.5 m
Dec 31, 04	Dr	Depreciation expense	1.5 m	
	Cr	Other comprehensive income		1.5 m

IAS 39.98(b): On Mar 31, 04, the hedging reserve is derecognized and included in the carrying amount of the machine. This entry does not affect E's OCI for the year 04.

Mar 31, 04	Dr	Machine	10 m	
	Cr	Hedging reserve (accumulated OCI)		10 m
Dec 31, 04	Dr	Depreciation expense	15 m	
	Cr	Machine		15 m

Example 15

Hedge accounting – firm commitment

Entity E's own currency is the CNY. On Nov 30, 03, E orders a machine in country Z for 10 m units of foreign currency F. The machine will be delivered on Mar 31, 04.

On Nov 30, 03, E enters into a forward contract in order to hedge against the foreign exchange risk (currency risk) arising from the firm commitment. According to this contract, E is obliged to buy 10 m units of foreign currency on Mar 31, 04 at an exchange rate of 10 (1 unit of F = 10 CNY) from bank B.[16]

The following table shows the development of the exchange rate (1 unit of F = x CNY):[17]

Nov 30, 03	10
Dec 31, 03	8
Mar 31, 04	9

On Mar 31, 04, the machine is delivered and paid. On Apr 01, 04, the machine is available for use. The machine's useful life is five years.

Required

Prepare any entries in E's financial statements that are necessary from Nov 30, 03 until Dec 31, 04. E's reporting periods end on Dec 31. E applies the hedge accounting rules of IAS 39. E treats hedges of foreign currency risks arising from firm commitments as fair value hedges (IAS 39.87).

Hints for solution

In particular Section 2.7.

Solution

Measurement of the hedging derivative on *Dec 31, 03*:

Conversion of 10 m units of foreign currency F into CNY:			
Fixed rate	10	100 m	$= 10m \cdot 10$
Rate on Dec 31, 03	8	80 m	$= 10m \cdot 8$
Fair value		**–20 m**	

The negative fair value of –20 m CNY results from the fact that E could purchase 10 m units of foreign currency for 80 m CNY without existence of the forward contract, but has to pay 100 m CNY due to the forward contract.

[16] *In this example the exchange rates are presented as "1 unit of foreign currency F = x CNY" (e.g. 1 unit of F = 10 CNY).*

[17] *For simplification purposes, differences between the spot exchange rate and the forward exchange rate are ignored in this example.*

Conversely, fair value of the firm commitment has improved. On Nov 30, 03, E would have had to pay 100 m CNY for the machine. On Dec 31, 03, E would have to pay only 80 m CNY. Hence, fair value of the firm commitment is positive (+20 m CNY).

In reality, the fair value changes of the firm commitment and the derivative offset each other. E has to recognize the negative fair value of the derivative ("Dr Profit or loss Cr Liability 20 m CNY"). However, the positive fair value of the firm commitment must not be recognized in the financial statements according to IFRS. Consequently, profit or loss for 03 would deteriorate by –20 m CNY, although the fair value changes actually offset each other. In order to avoid this, IAS 39 permits the application of fair value hedge accounting.

Under the fair value hedge accounting technique, the positive fair value of E's firm commitment is recognized as an asset. The fair value increase is recognized in profit or loss. Thus, the effect of the total of the fair value changes of the firm commitment and of the derivative on the amount of profit or loss for the year is zero. This corresponds with reality (see above).

Dec 31, 03	Dr	Profit or loss	20 m	
	Cr	Liability (derivative)		20 m
Dec 31, 03	Dr	Asset (firm commitment)	20 m	
	Cr	Profit or loss		20 m

Year 04

Measurement of the hedging derivative on *Mar 31, 04*:

Conversion of 10 m units of F into CNY:			
Fixed rate	10	100 m	$= 10m \cdot 10$
Rate on Mar 31, 04	9	90 m	$= 10m \cdot 9$
Fair value		**–10 m**	

Mar 31, 04	Dr	Liability (derivative)	10 m	
	Cr	Profit or loss		10 m

Fair value of the firm commitment deteriorates to +10 m CNY:

Mar 31, 04	Dr	Profit or loss	10 m	
	Cr	Asset (firm commitment)		10 m

The following entry shows the settlement of the derivative (fair value as at Mar 31, 04 = –10 m CNY):

Mar 31, 04	Dr	Liability (derivative)	10 m	
	Cr	Cash		10 m

Regarding the acquisition of the machine, the exchange rate as at Mar 31, 04 is relevant. The acquisition of the machine results in a payment of 90 m CNY (= 10 m units of F · 9):

Mar 31, 04	Dr	Machine	90 m	
	Cr	Cash		90 m

The positive fair value of the asset recognized relating to the firm commitment is derecognized and included in the carrying amount of the machine (IAS 39.94):

Mar 31, 04	Dr	Machine	10 m	
	Cr	Asset (firm commitment)		10 m

Thus, the machine is recognized at an amount of 100, which corresponds to the exchange rate, hedged on Nov 30, 03 (10 m units of F · 10 *or* 90 m CNY + 10 m CNY).

Finally, the machine is depreciated for nine months (100 m CNY : 5 years : 12 months · 9 months):

Dec 31, 04	Dr	Depreciation expense	15 m	
	Cr	Machine		15 m

3 FINANCIAL INSTRUMENTS ACCOUNTING PRIOR TO IFRS 9

This section generally describes financial instruments accounting prior to IFRS 9 only to the extent that it differs from IFRS 9 as issued in October 2010 (and its consequential amendments to IAS 39). Subsequently, references to IAS 39 refer to the "old" version of that Standard, i.e. to IAS 39 before any consequential amendments resulting from IFRS 9.

3.1 Scope[18]

IAS 39 sets out the requirements for recognizing and measuring **financial instruments**. However, the scope of IAS 39 does not include all financial instruments. For example, equity instruments are not within the scope of IAS 39 from the issuer's perspective. In the holder's consolidated financial statements, equity instruments are not in the scope of IAS 39 if they are interests in subsidiaries, joint ventures or associates (IAS 39.2).

3.2 Subsequent Measurement

IAS 39 is based on a **mixed measurement model** in which some financial assets and financial liabilities are measured at fair value and others at amortized cost after recognition. The method of subsequent measurement depends on the measurement category to which the financial asset or financial liability is assigned.

3.2.1 Assigning a Financial Asset or a Financial Liability to a Measurement Category

Loans and receivables This category comprises non-derivative financial assets with fixed or determinable payments that are not quoted in an active market (IAS 39.9). An active market is a market that meets all the following conditions (IAS 36.6):

- The items traded within the market are homogeneous.
- Willing buyers and sellers can normally be found at any time.
- Prices are available to the public.

[18] *The terms "financial instrument," "financial asset," "financial liability," and "equity instrument" are defined in IAS 32.11 (see the chapter on IAS 32, Section 1 and Example 1).*

Held-to-maturity investments This category includes non-derivative financial assets with fixed or determinable payments and fixed maturity. However, they have to be quoted in an active market (e.g. bonds quoted on the stock exchange). Moreover, classification into this category requires that the entity has the positive intention and ability to hold the financial assets to maturity.

In the case of sales of financial assets classified as "held to maturity" that do not meet specified conditions, the entity must not classify any financial assets into this category for a specified period of time. Moreover, any remaining financial assets of the category "held to maturity" have to be reclassified into the category "available for sale" (IAS 39.9 and 39.52).

Financial assets available for sale Available-for-sale financial assets represent primarily a residual category: All financial assets not falling into one of the other categories belong to this category (IAS 39.9).

Financial assets or financial liabilities at fair value through profit or loss This category includes financial assets as well as financial liabilities and consists of two sub-categories ("held for trading" and "fair value option").

- Financial assets or financial liabilities that meet the definition of "**held for trading**." The terms "held for trading" and "derivative" have the same meaning as in IFRS 9 (IFRS 9. Appendix A).[19]
- Financial assets or financial liabilities for which the **fair value option** is exercised (i.e. which are designated as at fair value through profit or loss). Exercising that option is possible if one of the following conditions (which correspond with the eligibility criteria for financial liabilities according to IFRS 9[20]) is met and the asset's or liability's fair value can be determined reliably (IAS 39.9 and 39.11 A):
  - Exercising the option **eliminates or significantly reduces an inconsistency (accounting mismatch)**. For example, an entity may own a fixed-interest bond (classified as "available for sale") that is refinanced by a fixed-interest financial liability (measured at amortized cost). Without exercising the option, fair value changes of the bond due to changes in the market interest rate would be recognized outside profit or loss and fair value changes of the financial liability due to changes in the market interest rate would not be recognized at all. Exercising of the option eliminates this inconsistency by recognizing the fair value changes of the asset as well as the fair value changes of the liability in profit or loss.
  - A **group** of financial assets, financial liabilities or both is **managed** and its performance is **evaluated** on a **fair value basis** according to a documented risk management or investment strategy and information about that group is provided internally on that basis to the entity's key management personnel.
  - Under certain circumstances (IAS 39.11 A), a contract that contains at least one embedded derivative **(hybrid or combined instrument)** may be designated as at fair value through profit or loss.

---

[19] *See Section 2.3.1.*

[20] *See Section 2.3.4.*

Financial liabilities measured at amortized cost **Normally**, financial liabilities are measured at amortized cost, i.e. according to the effective interest method.[21] Exceptions to this rule are, among others, financial liabilities at fair value through profit or loss (see previous) and financial guarantee contracts (IAS 39.47).

3.2.2 Gains and Losses and Technical Aspects Loans and receivables, held-to-maturity investments, and most financial liabilities are measured at amortized cost, i.e. according to the effective interest method (IAS 39.9 and 39.46–39.47).[22]

Available-for-sale financial assets are measured at **fair value**. Changes in fair value are generally recognized in **other comprehensive income** and accumulated in a separate component of equity (fair value reserve). However, in the case of **debt instruments** of this category, interest is first calculated using the effective interest method and recognized in profit or loss. Only the change in the difference between amortized cost calculated according to the effective interest method and fair value is recognized in other comprehensive income. Impairment losses arising from available-for-sale financial assets are recognized in profit or loss. When the financial asset is derecognized, the cumulative gain or loss previously recognized in other comprehensive income is reclassified to profit or loss. Impairment losses also lead to the derecognition of amounts previously recognized in other comprehensive income (IAS 39.46, IAS 39.55b, IAS 1.7, and 1.95).[23]

Financial assets and financial liabilities **held for trading** or for which the **fair value option** has been exercised are measured at their **fair values**. Changes in fair value are recognized in **profit or loss** (IAS 39.46–39.47 and 39.55a).

3.2.3 Determining Fair Values After Recognition For **debt instruments**, there is an **irrefutable presumption** that fair value can be measured reliably. By contrast, for **equity instruments** that do not have a quoted market price in an active market, there is a **presumption** which can be **rebutted** in certain cases that **fair value can be measured reliably**. If the presumption is rebutted in the case of equity instruments, they are measured **at cost**, less any **impairment losses**. There are also exceptions from fair value measurement for derivatives under certain circumstances (IAS 39.46, 39.66, and 39.AG80–39.AG81).

3.2.4 Impairment Losses and Reversals of Impairment Losses Financial assets at fair value through profit or loss are not tested for impairment because their fair value changes are recognized in profit or loss. However, all other financial assets are subject to review for impairment (IAS 39.46). This means that it has to be assessed at the end of each reporting period whether there is any **objective evidence of impairment (loss events)** (IAS 39.58).

IAS 39 includes a list of examples of loss events that relate to financial difficulties of the debtor (e.g. it becoming probable that the borrower will enter bankruptcy) (IAS 39.59).

---

[21] *See Section 2.3.5 with regard to the effective interest method.*

[22] *See Section 2.3.5 with regard to the effective interest method.*

[23] *Impairment losses and reversals of impairment losses from available-for-sale financial assets are discussed in Section 3.2.4 in more detail.*

In the case of **equity instruments** (e.g. shares), a **significant** or **prolonged** decline in fair value below cost is also objective evidence of impairment (IAS 39.61). We believe that it is appropriate to interpret the terms "significant" and "prolonged" as follows:

- A decline is **prolonged** if the market price of equity instruments – which are quoted in an active market – remains below cost for more than nine months. This criterion of nine months has to be applied retrospectively from the end of the reporting period.
- A decline is **significant** if the market price of equity instruments is at least 20% below cost. This applies irrespective of the change in value in a certain period of time before or after the end of the reporting period.

It is important to note that IAS 39.61 uses cost as reference point and not the carrying amount as at the end of the previous reporting period.

Three categories of financial assets have to be distinguished with regard to the calculation and accounting treatment of impairment losses and reversals of impairment losses.

Financial assets carried at amortized cost (i.e. loans and receivables as well as held-to-maturity investments)[24] The procedure is the same as for financial assets measured at amortized cost according to IFRS 9.[25]

Financial assets carried at cost If there is objective evidence that an equity instrument carried at cost instead of fair value (because its fair value cannot be reliably measured[26]) is **impaired**, the following amounts have to be compared (IAS 39.66):

- Carrying amount of the instrument.
- Present value of the estimated future cash flows discounted at the current market rate of return for a similar financial asset.

If present value is below the instrument's carrying amount, an impairment loss is recognized. In this category, impairment losses **must not be reversed** (IAS 39.66).

Available-for-sale financial assets If an equity instrument classified as "available for sale" is **impaired** for the first time, the following applies (IAS 39.67–39.68):

- The cumulative amount previously recognized in other comprehensive income (i.e. the fair value reserve) is derecognized.
- The asset's carrying amount is reduced to fair value.
- An impairment loss (being the difference between cost and fair value) is recognized in profit or loss.

Reversals of impairment losses for equity instruments classified as "available for sale" are recognized in other comprehensive income (IAS 39.69).

---

[24] *See Sections 3.2.1 and 3.2.2.*

[25] *See Section 2.3.8.*

[26] *See Section 3.2.3.*

3.3 Hybrid Contracts

According to the old version of IAS 39 the separation rules that apply to hybrid contracts with financial liability hosts under IFRS 9[27] applied to both hybrid contracts with financial asset hosts and hybrid contracts with financial liability hosts.

3.4 Examples with Solutions

Example 16

Solution of Example 3 according to the "old" version of IAS 39

The situation is the same as in Example 3. With regard to version (b), the following additional information is available in respect of the fair value changes:

Dec 31, 01	97	The stock market price is permanently below cost of CU 100 since Dec 01, 01
Dec 31, 02	90	The stock market price is permanently below cost of CU 100 since Mar 15, 02
Dec 31, 03	85	The stock market price is permanently below cost of CU 100 since Mar 15, *02* and permanently below CU 90 since Nov 01, *03*

Required

Prepare any necessary entries in E's financial statements as at Dec 31 for the years 01–04 (version a) and for the years 01–03 (version b). E still applies the "old" version of IAS 39. Assume that E classifies the shares as "available for sale" (IAS 39.9). With respect to impairment losses, E interprets the terms "significant" and "prolonged" (IAS 39.61) as described in Section 3.2.4.

Hints for solution

In particular Sections 3.2.1, 3.2.2, and 3.2.4.

Solution (a)

The shares are initially measured at fair value, which normally corresponds to the purchase price at that time. Since subsequent measurement of the shares is not at fair value through profit or loss (because the shares are classified as "available for sale"), transaction costs are capitalized (IAS 39.43).

Oct 15, 01	Dr	Shares	100	
	Cr	Cash		100

The shares classified as available for sale are subsequently measured at fair value. Fair value changes are generally recognized in other comprehensive income (IAS 39.46 and 39.55b).

Dec 31, 01	Dr	Shares	10	
	Cr	Other comprehensive income		10

[27] *See Section 2.4.3.*

The decline in fair value to CU 75 until Dec 31, 02 is significant within the meaning of IAS 39.61 because CU 75 is below CU 80 (20% below cost of CU 100). Hence, the shares are impaired. This means that the carrying amount of the shares decreases from CU 110 to CU 75 and that the fair value reserve previously recognized with respect to the shares is derecognized. Moreover, the reduction from CU 100 (cost of the shares) to fair value of CU 75 is recognized in profit or loss as an impairment loss.

Dec 31, 02	Dr	Other comprehensive income	10	
	Dr	Impairment loss	25	
	Cr	Shares		35

Since the decline to CU 75 in 02 was significant within the meaning of IAS 39.61, the further decrease from CU 75 to CU 70 is also significant, which means that it represents an impairment loss. That is because the decrease from CU 75 to CU 70 is a further decrease below the threshold of CU 80.

Dec 31, 03	Dr	Impairment loss	5	
	Cr	Shares		5

Reversals of impairment losses of equity instruments (e.g. shares) classified as "available for sale" must not be recognized in profit or loss (IAS 39.69). Consequently, the increase in the stock market price from CU 70 to CU 120 is recognized in OCI.

Dec 31, 04	Dr	Shares	50	
	Cr	Other comprehensive income		50

Solution (b)

Oct 15, 01	Dr	Shares	100	
	Cr	Cash		100

The decrease from CU 100 to CU 97 is not significant (because it is not a decrease below the threshold of CU 80 – see version (a)). The criterion "prolonged" is not met, either because on Dec 31, 01, the stock market price is below cost since one month and not since more than nine months. Thus, there is no impairment loss, which means that the decrease is recognized in other comprehensive income.

Dec 31, 01	Dr	Other comprehensive income	3	
	Cr	Shares		3

The decrease in the stock market price to CU 90 does not meet the criterion "significant." However, it is prolonged because on Dec 31, 02 the stock market price is below cost since it is more than nine months. Hence, the carrying amount of the shares is reduced from CU

97 to CU 90, the fair value reserve is derecognized, and the reduction from cost to fair value is recognized in profit or loss as an impairment loss.

Dec 31, 02	Dr	Impairment loss	10	
	Cr	Other comprehensive income		3
	Cr	Shares		7

The decrease in the stock market price to CU 85 does not meet the criterion "significant." However, it meets the criterion "prolonged." It is only relevant that the nine month criterion is met with regard to cost.

Dec 31, 03	Dr	Impairment loss	5	
	Cr	Shares		5

Example 17

Solution of Examples 4–15 according to the "old" version of IAS 39

Required

Determine whether the solution according to the "old" version of IAS 39 (i.e. according to IAS 39 before any consequential amendments as a result of IFRS 9) differs from the solution when applying IFRS 9 as issued in October 2010 (and its consequential amendments to IAS 39) for Examples 4–15 and describe the differences. It is not necessary to present the accounting entries.

Hints for solution

In particular Sections 2 and 3.

Solution (Example 4)

According to the "old" version of IAS 39, the shares that meet the definition of "held for trading" also have to be measured at fair value through profit or loss (IAS 39.9 and 39.55a). The transaction costs of CU 1 also have to be recognized in profit or loss because subsequent measurement of the shares is at fair value through profit or loss (IAS 39.43). Consequently, the accounting treatment is the same according to the old version of IAS 39.

Solutions (Examples 5 and 6)

The solutions of Examples 5 and 6 under the old version of IAS 39 are the same as according to IFRS 9 (and its consequential amendments). This is because IFRS 9 did not change the accounting treatment of financial liabilities, in general.

Solutions (Examples 7–9)

According to the old version of IAS 39, measurement of the bond depends on the category into which the bond is classified. If the bond had to be measured at amortized cost (effective interest method), the accounting treatment (including the impairment loss and the reversal of the impairment loss) would be the same as according to IFRS 9 (IFRS 9.5.2.2).

The category "available for sale" and its accounting rules only exist under the old version of IAS 39. With regard to the accounting treatment in the case of classification as "available for sale," we refer to Sections 3.2.2 and 3.2.4.

If it were possible to exercise the fair value option, the consequence would be measurement at fair value through profit or loss, both according to the old version of IAS 39 and according to IFRS 9.

Solution (Example 10)

E has to apply the rules of IAS 39 with respect to embedded derivatives because E is the creditor of the convertible bond. (By contrast, the debtor would have to apply the rules of IAS 32 (IAS 32.28 and 32.AG30).)

Under IAS 39, the economic characteristics and risks of the conversion right are not closely related to those of the bond. The bond is subject to interest rate risk, whereas the conversion right is subject to the risk of changes in the share price. Hence, the conversion right has to be accounted for separately from the bond if the convertible bond is not measured at fair value through profit or loss (IAS 39.11 and 39.AG30–39.AG31).

Solution (Example 11)

If the bond is also measured at amortized cost in accordance with the old version of IAS 39, the solution of this example is the same as according to IFRS 9.

Solution (Example 12)

If the receivables are also measured at amortized cost in accordance with the old version of IAS 39, the solution of this example is the same as according to IFRS 9.

Solution (Example 13)

IFRS 9 has not changed the accounting treatment of financial guarantees from the issuer's perspective. Consequently, the solution remains the same when applying the old version of IAS 39.

Solutions (Examples 14 and 15)

IFRS 9 has not yet changed the hedge accounting requirements of IAS 39. Thus, the solution remains the same when applying the old version of IAS 39.

IFRS 10 CONSOLIDATED FINANCIAL STATEMENTS

See the chapter on IAS 27/IFRS 10

IFRS 11 JOINT ARRANGEMENTS

See the chapter on IAS 31/IFRS 11

IFRS 12 DISCLOSURE OF INTERESTS IN OTHER ENTITIES

1 INTRODUCTION

IFRS 12 sets out the **disclosure requirements for interests in subsidiaries, joint arrangements, associates or unconsolidated structured entities**. In general, the standard only applies to the entity's consolidated financial statements (IFRS 12.6b). According to IFRS 12, the term "**interest in another entity**" refers to contractual and non-contractual involvement (e.g. through equity instruments) that exposes an entity to variability of returns from the performance of the other entity (IFRS 12.Appendix A and 12.B7).

The new standard has to be applied in the financial statements as at **Dec 31, 2013** (if the entity's reporting periods start on Jan 01 and end on Dec 31). **Earlier application** is **permitted** by the IASB (IFRS 12.C1). However, in the **European Union**, new IFRSs have to be endorsed by the European Union before they can be applied. There has been no endorsement of IFRS 12 as yet.

The **general objective** of IFRS 12 is to require an entity to disclose information that enables evaluation of (IFRS 12.1):

- the nature of, and risks associated with, its interests in other entities, and
- the effects of those interests on its financial position, financial performance, and cash flows.

In order to meet the objective, an entity has to disclose (IFRS 12.2):

- the significant judgments and assumptions the entity has made in determining the nature of its interest in another entity or arrangement, and in determining the type of joint arrangement in which it has an interest (see Section 3.1), and
- information about its interests in:
  - subsidiaries (see Section 3.2),
  - joint arrangements (i.e. joint operations or joint ventures)[1] and associates (see Section 3.3), and
  - unconsolidated structured entities (i.e. structured entities that are not controlled by the entity) (see Section 3.4).

2 THE TERM "STRUCTURED ENTITY"

IFRS 12 introduces the term "structured entity," which is used in different sections of the standard. Hence, it is necessary to explain this term before discussing the individual disclosure requirements of IFRS 12. A structured entity is defined as an entity that has been designed so

---

[1] *See the chapter on IAS 31/IFRS 11, Section 3.*

that **voting or similar rights are not the dominant factor in deciding who controls the entity** (such as when any voting rights relate to administrative tasks only and the relevant activities are directed by means of contractual arrangements) (IFRS 12.Appendix A and 12.B21). The relevant activities are the activities of the investee that significantly affect the investee's returns (IFRS 10.10 and 10.Appendix A).[2]

A structured entity **often** has **some or all** of the following **characteristics** (IFRS 12. B22):

- Restricted activities.
- A narrow and well-defined objective (e.g. to carry out research and development activities, effect a tax-efficient lease, provide a source of capital or funding to an entity or provide investment opportunities for investors by passing on risks and rewards associated with the assets of the structured entity to investors).
- Insufficient equity to permit the structured entity to finance its activities without subordinated financial support.
- Financing in the form of multiple contractually linked instruments to investors that create concentrations of credit or other risks (tranches).

The following are **examples** of entities that are regarded as structured entities (IFRS 12. B23):

- Securitization vehicles.
- Asset-backed financings.
- Some investment funds.

An entity that is controlled by voting rights is not a structured entity simply because, for example, it receives funding from third parties following a restructuring (IFRS 12.B24).

The IASB notes that the type of entity that is characterized by IFRS 12 as a structured entity is **unlikely to differ significantly from** an entity that SIC 12 described as **a special purpose entity (SPE)** (IFRS 12.BC82 and 12.BC84).[3]

3 THE INDIVIDUAL DISCLOSURE REQUIREMENTS OF IFRS 12

3.1 Significant Judgments and Assumptions

It is necessary to disclose information about significant judgments and assumptions the entity has made in **determining** (IFRS 12.7):

- **that it has control** of an investee according to IFRS 10,[4]
- **that it has joint control** of an arrangement according to IFRS 11[5] **or significant influence** over another entity according to IAS 28,[6] and

---

[2] *See the chapter on IAS 27/IFRS 10, Section 3.2.1.*
[3] *See the chapter on IAS 27/IFRS 10, Section 2.1 with regard to special purpose entities.*
[4] *See the chapter on IAS 27/IFRS 10, Section 3.2.*
[5] *See the chapter on IAS 31/IFRS 11, Section 3.2.*
[6] *See the chapter on IAS 28, Section 2.1.*

- **the type of joint arrangement** according to IFRS 11 (i.e. **joint operation or joint venture**)[7] when the arrangement has been structured through a separate vehicle.

In order to comply with these requirements, an entity has to disclose, for example, significant judgments and assumptions made in determining that (IFRS 12.9):

- it controls another entity even though it holds less than half of the voting rights of the other entity.
- it does not have significant influence even though it holds 20% or more of the voting rights of another entity.

3.2 Interests in Subsidiaries

It is necessary to disclose information that enables users of the entity's consolidated financial statements to understand the following (IFRS 12.10a):

- The **composition** of the group.
- The **interest that non-controlling interests have** in the group's activities and cash flows. For example, an entity is, among others, required to disclose the following for each of its subsidiaries that have non-controlling interests that are material to the reporting entity (IFRS 12.12):
  - The proportion of ownership interests and voting rights held by non-controlling interests.
  - The profit or loss allocated to non-controlling interests of the subsidiary during the reporting period.
  - Summarized financial information about the subsidiary (e.g. current assets, non-current liabilities, revenue, and total comprehensive income) which represents amounts before inter-company eliminations (IFRS 12.B10–12.B11).

It is also necessary to disclose information that enables users of the entity's consolidated financial statements to evaluate the following (IFRS 12.10b):

- The nature and extent of **significant restrictions** (e.g. contractual, statutory, and regulatory restrictions) on the entity's ability to access or use assets, and settle liabilities, of the group (e.g. those that restrict the ability of a parent or its subsidiaries to transfer cash or other assets to or from other entities within the group) (IFRS 12.13).
- The nature of (and changes in) the **risks** associated with interests in **consolidated structured entities**. Among others, the entity has to disclose the terms of any contractual arrangements that could require the parent or its subsidiaries to provide financial support to a consolidated structured entity, including events or circumstances that could expose the reporting entity to a loss (e.g. liquidity arrangements or credit rating triggers associated with obligations to purchase assets of the consolidated structured entity or provide financial support) (IFRS 12.14).
- The consequences of **changes in its ownership interest** in a subsidiary which **do not result in losing control**. In this context, a schedule has to be presented that shows the effects of these changes on the equity attributable to owners of the parent (IFRS 12.18).

[7] *See the chapter on IAS 31/IFRS 11, Section 3.3.*

- The consequences of a **loss of control** of a subsidiary during the reporting period. Among others, the gain or loss on deconsolidation[8] (IFRS 10.25 and 10.B98) has to be disclosed, as well as the line item(s) in profit or loss in which it has been recognized (IFRS 12.19).

3.3 Interests in Joint Arrangements and Associates

IFRS 12 requires the disclosure of information that enables users of the entity's financial statements to evaluate the following (IFRS 12.20):

- The **nature, extent, and financial effects of the entity's interests** in joint arrangements and associates, including the nature and effects of its contractual relationship with the other investors with joint control of joint arrangements, or significant influence over associates. Among others, the following disclosures are necessary in this respect:
  - For each **joint arrangement** and **associate** which is **material** to the reporting entity (IFRS 12.21a):
    - The proportion of ownership interest or participating share held by the entity and the proportion of voting rights held.
    - The nature of the entity's relationship with the associate or joint arrangement (by, for example, describing the nature of the activities of the associate or joint arrangement and whether they are strategic to the entity's activities).
  - For each **joint venture** and **associate** which is **material** to the reporting entity (IFRS 12.21b):
    - **Summarized financial information** about the joint venture or associate (including for example current assets, non-current liabilities, revenue, and total comprehensive income) (IFRS 12.B12–12.B13).
    - If the associate or joint venture is accounted for in accordance with the equity method, the **fair value** of its investment in the associate or joint venture, provided that there is a quoted market price for the investment.
  - The nature and extent of any **significant restrictions** on the ability of associates or joint ventures to transfer funds to the entity in the form of cash dividends, or to repay loans or advances made by the entity (IFRS 12.22a).
- The **nature of** (and changes in) **the risks** associated with the entity's interests in joint ventures and associates. Among others, it is necessary to disclose the following in this respect (IFRS 12.23):
  - **Total unrecognized commitments** the entity has made **relating to its interests in joint ventures** (including the entity's share of commitments made jointly with other investors with joint control of a joint venture). Commitments are those that may give rise to a future outflow of cash or other resources (IFRS 12.B18).
  - In accordance with IAS 37 (unless the probability of loss is remote) **contingent liabilities incurred relating to the entity's interests in associates or joint ventures** (including the entity's share of contingent liabilities incurred jointly with other investors with joint control of the joint ventures, or significant influence over the associates), separately from the amount of other contingent liabilities.

---

[8] *See the chapter on IAS 27/IFRS 10, Section 2.4.*

3.4 Interests in Unconsolidated Structured Entities

IFRS 12 requires the disclosure of information that enables users of the entity's financial statements (IFRS 12.24):

- To understand the **nature and extent of the entity's interests** in unconsolidated structured entities. In this respect, it is necessary to disclose qualitative and quantitative information about the entity's interests in unconsolidated structured entities, including (but not limited to) the nature, purpose, activities, and size of the structured entity and how the latter is financed (IFRS 12.26).
- To evaluate the **nature of** (and changes in) **the risks** associated with the entity's interests in unconsolidated structured entities. This also includes information about the entity's exposure to risk from involvement that it had with unconsolidated structured entities in previous periods (e.g. sponsoring the structured entity), even if the entity no longer has any contractual involvement with the structured entity at the reporting date (IFRS 12.25). Among others, a summary of the following has to be disclosed in tabular format (unless another format is more appropriate) (IFRS 12.29):
  - The carrying amounts of the assets and liabilities recognized in the entity's financial statements relating to its interests in unconsolidated structured entities, as well as the line items in its statement of financial position in which those assets and liabilities have been recognized.
  - The amount that best represents the entity's maximum exposure to loss from its interests in unconsolidated structured entities. If the entity cannot quantify this exposure, it has to disclose that fact and the reasons.
  - A comparison of the carrying amounts of the assets and liabilities of the entity that relate to its interests in unconsolidated structured entities and the entity's maximum exposure to loss from those entities.

4 EXAMPLES WITH SOLUTIONS

Example 1

Is the entity a structured entity?

Entity E establishes entity X. However, E does not hold any equity instruments of X. After the establishment of the new entity, E sells receivables to X. X issues equity instruments to unrelated third parties (of E and X) and uses the proceeds of the issue to pay the purchase price of the receivables. X collects the principal of and interest on the receivables and forwards the corresponding cash inflows (after deduction of the costs that X incurs for these activities) to the investors. E retains some part of the credit risk associated with the receivables by providing a guarantee. Collecting interest on and the principal of the receivables is the only business activity that X is allowed to conduct.

Required

E applies IFRS 10 and IFRS 12 early, in its consolidated financial statements. Assess whether X represents a structured entity in these statements.

Hints for solution

In particular Section 2.

Solution

The transaction described is an example of a transaction involving asset-backed securities. X represents a structured entity according to IFRS 12. This is because X's business activities are restricted and X has been established for a narrow and well-defined objective. For these reasons, X would have qualified as a special purpose entity (SPE) according to SIC 12 if E had not applied IFRS 12 early.

Example 2

Disclosures relating to structured entities

Entity E sells receivables to structured entity S, which has been established by E for this purpose. E issues guarantees relating to the receivables sold. In the worst case, E could be required to pay material amounts as a result of these guarantees. However, it is assumed that the probability that E has to pay material payments with regard to S is remote and that, therefore, E does not bear the majority of the risks relating to S. Consequently, the existence of control is negated, which means that S is not consolidated by E.

Required

List some disclosures that have to be presented in E's consolidated financial statements with regard to S according to IFRS 12. Assume that the negation of the existence of control is correct.

Hints for solution

In particular Section 3.4.

Solution

In E's consolidated financial statements, S represents an unconsolidated structured entity. Important disclosures, which have to be made in these statements with regard to S, are described in Section 3.4 (IFRS 12.24–12.31).

IFRS 13 FAIR VALUE MEASUREMENT

1 INTRODUCTION

IFRS 13 **defines fair value**, sets out a **framework for measuring fair value** (i.e. explains how to measure fair value for financial reporting), and requires **disclosures** about fair value measurements (IFRS 13.1 and 13.IN4).

The new standard has to be applied in the financial statements as at **Dec 31, 2013** (if the entity's reporting periods start on Jan 01 and end on Dec 31). **Earlier application** is **permitted** by the IASB (IFRS 13.C1). However, in the **European Union**, new IFRSs have to be endorsed by the European Union before they can be applied. There has been no endorsement with regard to IFRS 13 as yet.

Explaining fair value measurement in detail cannot be effected in only one chapter of a book. Instead, this would require writing a separate book. Consequently, in this chapter only the fundamentals of measuring fair value (and not every detail) are discussed.

Since the initial mandatory application of IFRS 13 applies to financial statements as at Dec 31, 2013 (see above), the other chapters of this book do not yet incorporate the consequential amendments of IFRS 13 to other standards.

2 SCOPE

The standard applies **when another IFRS permits or requires fair value measurements or disclosures about fair value measurements** (including measurements such as fair value less costs to sell, based on fair value, and disclosures about those measurements), except in specified circumstances. It does not require fair value measurements in addition to those already permitted or required by other IFRSs (IFRS 13.5, 13.IN2, and 13.IN4).

The definition of fair value focuses on assets and liabilities. In addition, IFRS 13 has to be applied to an entity's own equity instruments measured at fair value (IFRS 13.4).

There are two categories of **exemptions from the scope** of IFRS 13 (IFRS 13.6–13.7):

- Exemptions from the **disclosure requirements** of IFRS 13
- Exemptions from the **measurement and disclosure requirements** of IFRS 13:
  - Share-based payment transactions within the scope of IFRS 2
  - Leasing transactions within the scope of IAS 17
  - Measurements that have some similarities to fair value but are not fair value, such as value in use in IAS 36 or net realizable value in IAS 2.

The fair value measurement framework of IFRS 13 applies to **both initial and subsequent measurement** if fair value is permitted or required by other IFRSs (IFRS 13.8).

3 THE MEASUREMENT REQUIREMENTS OF IFRS 13

3.1 Definition of Fair Value

Fair value represents the price that would be received to sell an asset or paid to transfer a liability in an orderly transaction between market participants at the measurement date under current market conditions. This means that fair value represents an exit price from the perspective of a market participant that holds the asset or owes the liability (IFRS 13.2, 13.9, 13.Appendix A, and 13.B2).

It is clear from the above that fair value is a **market-based measurement** and **not an entity-specific measurement** (IFRS 13.2).

An **orderly transaction** is a transaction that assumes exposure to the market for a period before the measurement date to allow for marketing activities that are usual and customary for transactions involving such assets or liabilities. It does not represent a forced transaction (e.g. a forced liquidation or a distress sale) (IFRS 13.Appendix A).

3.2 The Asset or Liability

Since a fair value measurement is for a particular asset or liability, the entity has to take into account the **characteristics of the asset or liability** when measuring fair value if market participants would also take these characteristics into account. The effect of a particular characteristic on fair value measurement depends on how it would be taken into account by market participants. The following are examples of such characteristics (IFRS 13.11–13.12):

- Restrictions, if any, on the sale or use of the asset.
- The condition and location of the asset.

The asset or liability measured at fair value might be either of the following (IFRS 13.13):

- A **stand-alone asset or liability** (e.g. a financial liability or an item of property, plant, and equipment).
- A **group** of assets, a group of liabilities or a group comprising assets and liabilities (e.g. a cash-generating unit[1] or a business[2]).

Whether the asset or liability is a stand-alone asset or liability or a group (see above) as described above for recognition or disclosure purposes depends on its **unit of account**. The unit of account represents the level at which an asset or a liability is aggregated or disaggregated in an IFRS for recognition purposes. The unit of account for the asset or liability has to be determined according to the IFRS that requires or permits the fair value measurement, except as provided in this IFRS (IFRS 13.14 and IFRS 13.Appendix A).

---

[1] *See the chapter on IAS 36, Sections 1 and 4.*

[2] *See the chapter on IFRS 3, Section 1.*

3.3 The Transaction

Consistent with the definition of fair value,[3] a fair value measurement assumes that the asset or liability is exchanged in an orderly transaction between market participants to sell the asset or transfer the liability at the measurement date under current market conditions (IFRS 13.15).

When measuring fair value, it is presumed that the transaction takes place in the following market (IFRS 13.16, 13.18, and 13.Appendix A):

- In the **principal market** for the asset or liability (if a principal market exists). This presumption applies irrespective of whether the price in that market is directly observable or estimated using another valuation technique. The principal market is the market with the greatest volume and level of activity for the asset or liability.
- In the absence of a principal market, in the **most advantageous market** for the asset or liability. This is the market that maximizes the amount that would be received to sell the asset or minimizes the amount that would be paid to transfer the liability after taking into account transport costs and transaction costs. The latter two types of costs are defined as follows:
  - **Transport costs** represent the costs that would be incurred to transport an asset from its current location to its most advantageous (or principal) market.
  - **Transaction costs** are the costs to sell an asset or to transfer a liability in the most advantageous (or principal) market for the asset or liability that are directly attributable to the sale or the transfer. Transaction costs have to meet both of the following criteria:
    - They result directly from and are essential to that transaction.
    - They would not have been incurred by the entity if the decision to sell the asset or transfer the liability had not been made.

In the absence of evidence to the contrary, the market in which the entity would normally sell the asset or transfer the liability is presumed to be the principal market (or the most advantageous market) (IFRS 13.17).

At the measurement date, the entity must have **access** to the principal (or most advantageous) market. Different entities (and businesses within those entities) may have access to different markets. Thus, the principal (or most advantageous) market for the same asset or liability might be different for different entities (and businesses within those entities) according to IFRS 13. This means that market participants also have to be considered from the perspective of the entity. As a consequence, differences may arise among entities in this aspect. Although the entity must be able to access the market, it **need not be able to sell the asset or transfer the liability on the measurement date** in order to be able to measure fair value on the basis of the price in that market (IFRS 13.19–13.20).

If there is no observable market to provide pricing information about the sale or the transfer at the measurement date, it has to be assumed that a transaction takes place at that date, which has to be considered from the perspective of a market participant that holds the asset or owes

[3] *See Section 3.1.*

the liability. The **assumed transaction** serves as a basis for estimating the price to sell the asset or to transfer the liability (IFRS 13.21).

3.4 Market Participants

Market participants are buyers and sellers in the principal (or most advantageous) market[4] for the asset or liability that have all of the following **characteristics** (IFRS 13.Appendix A):

- They are **independent** of each other. This means that they are **not related parties**[5] as defined in IAS 24.[6]
- They are **knowledgeable**, having a **reasonable understanding** about the asset or liability and the transaction **using all available information**.
- They are **able to enter into a transaction** for the item.
- They are **willing to enter into a transaction** for the item. This means that they are motivated but not forced or otherwise compelled to do so.

The entity has to measure fair value using the **assumptions that market participants would use** when pricing the asset or liability assuming that market participants act in their **economic best interest**. In developing those assumptions, the entity need not identify specific market participants. Rather, the entity identifies characteristics that distinguish market participants generally, considering factors specific to all the following (IFRS 13.22–13.23):

- The asset or liability.
- The principal (or most advantageous) market for the asset or liability.
- Market participants with whom the entity would transact in that market.

3.5 The Price

Fair value is the **price** that would be received to sell an asset or paid to transfer a liability (i.e. an exit price) in an orderly transaction in the principal (or most advantageous) market at the measurement date under current market conditions irrespective of whether that price is directly observable or estimated using another valuation technique (IFRS 13.24 and 13.Appendix A).

The price used to measure the fair value of the asset or liability **must not be adjusted for transaction** costs.[7] This is because transaction costs do not represent a characteristic of an asset or a liability. Transaction costs have to be accounted for according to the appropriate IFRS. They do not include transport costs.[8] If location is a characteristic of the asset (as might be the case, for example, for a commodity), the price in the principal (or most advantageous) market has to be adjusted for the costs (if any) that would be incurred in order to transport the asset from its current location to that market (IFRS 13.25–13.26).

---

[4] *See Section 3.3 with regard to the definition of the terms "principal market" and "most advantageous market."*

[5] *See the chapter on IAS 24, Section 2.*

[6] *However, the price in a related party transaction may be used as an input to a fair value measurement, if there is evidence that the transaction was entered into at market terms (IFRS 13.Appendix A).*

[7] *See Section 3.3 with regard to the definition of the term "transaction costs."*

[8] *See Section 3.3 with regard to the definition of the term "transport costs."*

3.6 Application to Non-financial Assets

When measuring fair value of a non-financial asset, a market participant's ability to generate economic benefits by using the asset in its **highest and best use** or by selling it to another market participant that would use the asset in its highest and best use has to be taken into account. The highest and best use is the use of a non-financial asset by market participants that would **maximize the value** of the asset (or the group of assets and liabilities (e.g. a business) within which the asset would be used). The highest and best use takes into account the use of the asset that is **physically possible, legally permissible, and financially feasible** (IFRS 13.27–13.28 and 13.Appendix A).

It is clear from the above that the highest and best use is determined from the **perspective of market participants** even if the entity plans a different use. For example, the entity may acquire an intangible asset only with the intention to prevent others from using it and not with the intention to use the asset. Nevertheless, fair value has to be determined assuming the highest and best use of the asset by market participants (IFRS 13.29–13.30).

3.7 Application to Liabilities and the Entity's Own Equity Instruments

A fair value measurement assumes that a non-financial or financial liability or an entity's own equity instrument (e.g. equity interests issued as consideration in a business combination) is **transferred to a market participant** at the measurement date. The transfer assumes the following (IFRS 13.34):

- A **liability** would remain outstanding and the transferee (a market participant) would be required to fulfill the obligation. The liability would not be settled with the counterparty on the measurement date.
- **The entity's own equity instrument** would remain outstanding and the transferee (a market participant) would take on the rights and responsibilities associated with the instrument. The instrument would not be cancelled or otherwise extinguished on the measurement date.

There might be no observable market to provide pricing information about the transfer of a liability or the entity's own equity instrument (e.g. as a result of contractual or other legal restrictions with regard to transfers of such items). Nevertheless, there might be an **observable market** for such items **if they are held by other parties as assets** (IFRS 13.35).

In all cases, it is necessary to **maximize the use of observable inputs** and to minimize the use of unobservable inputs (IFRS 13.36).

When a **quoted price** for the transfer of an identical or a similar liability or entity's own equity instrument is **not available** and the identical item is (IFRS 13.37 and 13.40):

- **held by another party as an asset**, the fair value of the liability or equity instrument is measured from the perspective of a market participant that holds the identical item as an asset at the measurement date,
- ***not* held by another party as an asset**, the fair value of the liability or equity instrument is measured using a valuation technique from the perspective of a market participant that owes the liability or has issued the claim on equity.

The fair value of a liability has to reflect the effect of **non-performance risk,** which is the risk that the entity will not fulfill the obligation. Non-performance risk includes the entity's own credit risk and any other factors that might influence the likelihood that the obligation will or will not be fulfilled. Non-performance risk is assumed to be the same before and after the transfer of the liability (IFRS 13.42, 13.43, and 13.Appendix A).

3.8 Fair Value at Initial Recognition

The prices paid by entities to acquire assets may differ from the prices received for selling them. Similarly, entities do not necessarily transfer liabilities at the prices received to assume them (IFRS 13.57 and 13.Appendix A):

- When an asset is acquired or a liability is assumed in an exchange transaction for that asset or liability, the **transaction price** represents the price paid to acquire the asset or received to assume the liability (an **entry price**).
- By contrast, the **fair value** of the asset or liability represents the price that would be received to sell the asset or paid to transfer the liability (an **exit price**).

In many cases, the transaction price will equal the fair value at initial recognition (IFRS 13.58).

If another standard requires or permits measuring an asset or a liability at fair value at initial recognition and the transaction price differs from fair value, the resulting gain or loss (**day 1 gain or day 1 loss**) has to be recognized **in profit or loss unless that standard specifies otherwise** (IFRS 13.60).

3.9 Valuation Techniques

It is necessary to use valuation techniques that are appropriate in the circumstances and for which sufficient data are available to measure fair value, **maximizing** the use of relevant **observable inputs** and **minimizing** the use of **unobservable inputs** (IFRS 13.61).

Three widely used valuation techniques are the market approach, the income approach, and the cost approach (IFRS 13.62 and 13.Appendix A):

- The **market approach** is defined as a valuation technique that uses prices and other relevant information generated by market transactions involving identical or comparable (i.e. similar) assets, liabilities or a group of assets and liabilities (such as a business). For example, valuation techniques consistent with the market approach often use market multiples derived from a set of comparables (IFRS 13.B5–13.B6).
- The **income approach** comprises valuation techniques that convert future amounts (e.g. cash flows or income and expenses) to a single current (i.e. **discounted**) amount. The fair value measurement is based on current market expectations about the future amounts. The valuation techniques include, for example, the following (IFRS 13.B10–13.B11):
  - Present value techniques.
  - Option pricing models, such as the Black–Scholes–Merton formula or a binomial model (i.e. a lattice model),[9] which incorporate present value techniques and reflect both the time value and the intrinsic value of an option.

---

[9] *See Section 4.2.*

  - The multi-period excess earnings method, which is used to measure the fair value of some intangible assets.
- The **cost approach** represents a valuation technique that reflects the amount that would be required currently to **replace the service capacity** of an asset (often referred to as **current replacement cost**). This means that under this approach, fair value is based on the cost to a market participant buyer to acquire or construct a substitute asset of comparable utility, adjusted for obsolescence. Obsolescence comprises physical deterioration, functional (technological) obsolescence, and economic (external) obsolescence (IFRS 13.B8–13.B9).

The entity has to use valuation techniques that are consistent with one or more of these three approaches to measure fair value (IFRS 13.62).

3.10 Inputs to Valuation Techniques

Inputs are the **assumptions** that market participants would use when pricing the asset or liability, including assumptions about risk. Inputs can be categorized as follows (IFRS 13.Appendix A):

- **Observable inputs** are inputs that are developed using market data (such as publicly available information about actual events or transactions).
- **Unobservable inputs** are inputs for which market data are not available. They are developed using the best information available about the assumptions that market participants would use when pricing the item.

Valuation techniques used to measure fair value have to **maximize** the use of relevant **observable inputs** and **minimize** the use of **unobservable inputs** (IFRS 13.67). Examples of markets in which inputs might be observable for some assets and liabilities (e.g. financial instruments) are exchange markets, brokered markets, dealer markets, and principal-to-principal markets (IFRS 13.67–13.68 and 13.B34).

The entity has to select inputs that are **consistent with the characteristics of the item** that **market participants** would take into account in a transaction for the item. In some cases, these characteristics result in the application of an **adjustment**, such as a premium or discount (e.g. a control premium or a non-controlling interest discount). If there is a quoted price in an active market[10] (i.e. a Level 1 input[11]) for an asset or a liability, the entity generally has to use that price without adjustment when measuring fair value (IFRS 13.69).

3.11 Fair Value Hierarchy

IFRS 13 establishes a fair value hierarchy that categorizes the inputs to valuation techniques used to measure fair value into three levels (the hierarchy gives the highest priority to Level 1 inputs and the lowest priority to Level 3 inputs) (IFRS 13.72).

If the inputs used to measure the fair value of an asset or a liability are categorized within different levels of the fair value hierarchy, the fair value measurement is categorized in its

[10] *See Section 3.11.1.*

[11] *See Section 3.11.1.*

entirety in the same level as the lowest level input that is significant to the entire measurement (IFRS 13.73).

3.11.1 Level 1 Inputs Level 1 inputs are **quoted prices in active markets** for **identical assets or liabilities** that the entity can **access at the measurement date** (IFRS 13.76 and 13.Appendix A). An **active market** is a market in which transactions for the asset or liability take place with sufficient volume and frequency to provide pricing information on an ongoing basis (IFRS 13.Appendix A). In general, **no adjustment** is made to a quoted price (IFRS 13.77 and 13.79).

Some financial assets and financial liabilities, for which a Level 1 input is available, might be exchanged in **multiple active markets** (e.g. on different exchanges). Hence, the emphasis within Level 1 is on determining both of the following (IFRS 13.78):

- The **principal market** for the asset or liability or, in the absence of a principal market, the **most advantageous market** for the asset or liability.[12]
- Whether the entity **can enter into a transaction** for the asset or liability at the price in that market at the measurement date.

3.11.2 Level 2 Inputs Level 2 inputs are inputs other than quoted prices included within Level 1 that are observable for the asset or liability, either directly or indirectly. Level 2 inputs include the following (IFRS 13.81–13.82 and 13.Appendix A):

- Quoted prices for identical or similar assets or liabilities in inactive markets.
- Quoted prices for similar assets or liabilities in active markets.
- Inputs other than quoted prices that are observable for the asset or liability (e.g. interest rates observable at commonly quoted intervals and credit spreads).
- Market-corroborated inputs (i.e. inputs that are derived principally from or corroborated by observable market data by correlation or other means).

Adjustments to Level 2 inputs will vary depending on factors specific to the asset or liability, which include the following (IFRS 13.83):

- The location or condition of the asset.
- The extent to which inputs relate to items that are comparable to the item.
- The volume or level of activity in the markets in which the inputs are observed.

3.11.3 Level 3 Inputs Level 3 inputs are **unobservable inputs for the asset or liability** (IFRS 13.86 and 13.Appendix A). Unobservable inputs have to be used to measure fair value to the extent that relevant observable inputs are not available. Since fair value is a market-based measurement and not an entity-specific measurement,[13] unobservable inputs have to reflect the **assumptions that market participants would use** when pricing the item, including those about risk (IFRS 13.87). A fair value measurement has to include an **adjustment for risk** if market participants would include one when pricing the item. For example, it might be

[12] *See Section 3.3 with regard to the definition of the terms "principal market" and "most advantageous market."*

[13] *See Section 3.1.*

necessary to include a risk adjustment in the case of significant measurement uncertainty (IFRS 13.88).

4 ILLUSTRATION OF THE APPLICATION OF SELECTED VALUATION TECHNIQUES

4.1 Measuring Owner-occupied Items of Property, Plant, and Equipment

The measurement of owner-occupied items of property, plant, and equipment is generally based on the **cost approach** as described in Section 3.9.

4.2 Measuring American Options According to the Binomial Model

In this section, the measurement of **American call options on shares** according to the binomial model is illustrated. However, only the basics of the model are explained. An American option may be exercised on any trading day on or before expiry.

In practice, the binomial model is applied for measuring options within the scope of IFRS 9, as well as for measuring employee share options within the scope of IFRS 2. Although IFRS 13 does not apply to share-based payment transactions within the scope of IFRS 2 (IFRS 13.6a), the logic of the binomial model is the same irrespective of whether IFRS 13 applies or not.

Determining fair value of an option according to the binomial model involves the following steps:

- First, the **binomial price tree** is created. The price tree shows the changes in fair value of the shares that are possible. Fair value of the shares can move up or down by specific factors (the up factor (u) and the down factor (d)). The following applies with regard to these factors (whereby the last assumption is usually made, but does not have to be made): $u \geq 1; 0 < d \leq 1$ and $d = 1: u$.
- Next, the exercise price of the option is deducted from each of the possible fair values of the shares determined for the **expiration date**. This results in a number of different **intrinsic values** for the option. It is important to note that intrinsic value cannot become negative because, in this case, the holder of the option would simply not exercise it.
- In the next step, fair value of the option is determined by working back to the valuation date. This means that the intrinsic values at the time of expiration are multiplied pairwise by their so-called risk neutral probabilities. Thereby, p is the risk neutral probability of an up move and (1 – p) is the risk neutral probability of a down move. **Discounting** using the risk-free interest rate results in the possible values of the option as at the end of the prior period. This procedure is **repeated**, i.e. means that working back to the first node of the tree (the measurement date) is necessary where the calculated number is the fair value of the option.

4.3 Measuring a Brand According to the Relief from Royalty Method

In this section, the determination of the fair value of a **brand** according to the "**relief from royalty method**" is illustrated. According to this method the value of a brand is the present value of the royalty receipts that could be obtained from licensing the brand to another party (or alternatively, as the present value of the royalty payments that the owner of the brand saves because of not having to license the brand from a third party).

In any case, these hypothetical royalty receipts must not be reduced by the **costs of maintaining the brand** if the costs of maintaining the brand are paid by the hypothetical licensee. The reason for this is that the costs of maintaining the brand are already considered when fixing the royalty, in this case. An explicit deduction from the royalty would lead to these costs being accounted for twice.

4.4 The Tax Amortization Benefit

For many assets, depreciation or amortization is deductible for tax purposes, leading to a tax advantage (deductibility for tax purposes reduces taxable profit and consequently also taxes payable). Discounting the asset's future cash flows results in a present value that does not take this tax advantage into account. As noted above, fair value is an objective amount.[14] Thus, this tax advantage (which is called **tax amortization benefit**) has to be included when determining fair value, irrespective of whether the acquirer is able to realize the tax advantage.

The tax amortization benefit can be determined by multiplying the present value by the following formula:[15] $UL : (UL - PVIFA \cdot t) - 1$

The tax amortization benefit is characteristic of the income approach.[16] It is typically taken into account when fair value of intangible assets, investment properties or items of property, plant, and equipment (rented to others) is determined according to the income approach. However, when fair value is determined according to the market approach, it is presumed that the market price already includes the tax amortization benefit.

5 EXAMPLES WITH SOLUTIONS

Example 1

Measuring an American option according to the binomial model

On Jan 01, 01, entity E acquires one American call option to buy one share. The expiration date of the option is Dec 31, 02. The exercise price of the option is CU 9. On Jan 01, 01, fair value of one share is CU 10. The up factor (u) is 1.25 p.a. and the down factor (d) is 0.80 p.a. (= 1 : 1.25). The risk neutral probability of an up move (p) in fair value of the share is 0.40 (i.e. 40%). The risk-free interest rate is 10% p.a.

Required

Determine the fair value of the option as at Jan 01, 01, according to the binomial model.

[14] *See Section 3.1.*

[15] *UL = useful life for tax purposes; PVIFA = present value interest factor of annuity for the period UL and the interest rate i (corresponds with the present value of an annuity of CU 1 during the term UL, on the basis of the interest rate i); t = tax rate.*

[16] *See Section 3.9.*

Hints for solution

In particular Sections 4.2 and 3.9.

Solution

For reasons of simplification, the calculations in this example are effected on the basis of numbers that relate to an entire year. In practice, the calculations are normally made on a more detailed basis.

The assumed development of fair value of the shares is illustrated in the **price tree** presented below. The figures are determined on the basis of the up and down factors.

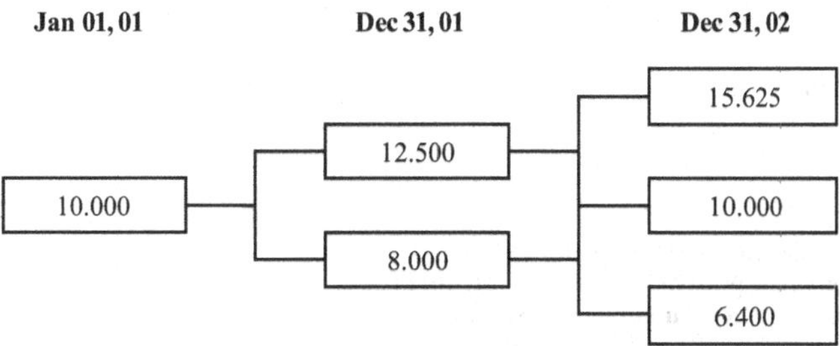

Next, the exercise price of the option (CU 9) is deducted from each of the possible fair values of the shares determined for the expiration date (Dec 31, 02). This results in a number of different intrinsic values for the option. An intrinsic value cannot become negative. Afterwards, the intrinsic values as at Dec 31, 02 are multiplied pairwise by their risk neutral probabilities. Discounting for one period results in the figures presented in the column "Dec 31, 01" in the table below.[17] This procedure is **repeated**, i.e. means that working back to the first node of the tree is necessary where the calculated number is the fair value of the option as at Jan 01, 01.

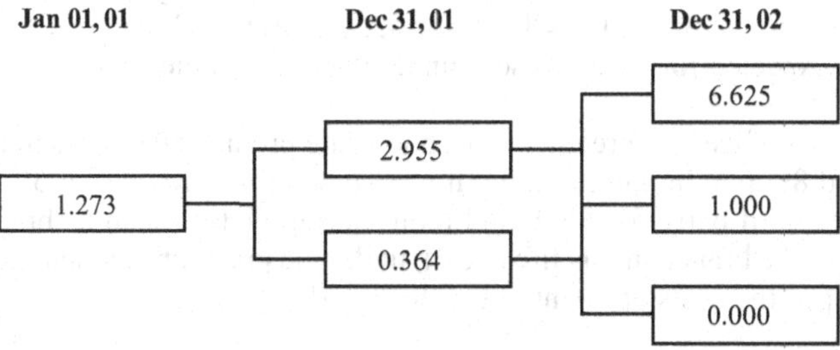

Hence, fair value of the option (rounded to two decimal figures) as at Jan 01, 01 is CU 1.27.

[17] *For example, the amount of CU 2.955 is determined as follows: [CU 6.625 · p + CU 1.000 · (1 – p)] : 1.1.*

Example 2

Measuring an owner-occupied item of property, plant, and equipment

On Dec 31, 10, entity E gains control of entity S. S owns a specialized building. The building was constructed by S at the beginning of the year 01. The costs of conversion were CU 10. Between the time of construction and Dec 31, 10, the appropriate price index increased by 20%. Originally the realistically estimated useful life was 30 years. On Dec 31, 10, the remaining useful life is 20 years.

Required

Determine the carrying amount (fair value) of the building in E's consolidated financial statements as at Dec 31, 10.

Hints for solution

In particular Sections 3.9 and 4.1.

Solution

Costs of conversion (incurred at the beginning of 01)	10
Increase in the appropriate price index (until Dec 31, 10) of 20%	2
Costs of conversion for a new building (Dec 31, 10)	**12**
Depreciation for the years 01–10 (= 12 : 30 · 10)	–4
Fair value	**8**

Example 3

Measurement of a brand according to the relief from royalty method (including the tax amortization benefit)

On Dec 31, 00, entity E acquires 100% of the shares of entity S. S produces body care products under a brand name that has been well known for many years. Annual inflation-adjusted revenues of CU 80 for 01, CU 88 for 02, CU 96 for 03, and of CU 104 p.a. from 04 onwards are expected for products sold under the brand name.

A database search on license agreements for body care products indicates that royalties are between 2% and 8% p.a. In this example, it is assumed that a royalty of 5% p.a. could be stipulated with a third party for S's brand (considering factors such as brand awareness, the positioning of the brand, and its life cycle), under the presumption that the hypothetical licensee would pay the costs of maintaining the brand.

For measurement purposes, a risk-adjusted and inflation-adjusted discount rate of 10% p.a. is appropriate. In the future, high costs of maintaining the brand are planned in order to be able to use the brand for an indefinite period of time.

Required

Determine the carrying amount of the brand (fair value) on the date of acquisition of S in E's consolidated statement of financial position according to the relief from royalty method. The tax rate is 25%. Assume that the brand's statutory useful life for tax purposes is 15 years.

Hints for solution

In particular Sections 4.3 and 4.4.

Solution

According to the **relief from royalty method**, fair value of the brand is determined on the basis of the present value of the future royalty receipts that could be obtained from licensing the brand to another party.

In this example, the royalty receipts must not be reduced by the **costs of maintaining the brand** because these costs are paid by the hypothetical licensee and have already been considered when fixing the royalty. A deduction from the royalty receipts would lead to the costs of maintaining the brand being accounted for twice.

The present value of the hypothetical future royalty receipts is determined as follows:[18]

		01	*02*	*03*	*04 onwards*
Annual revenue		80.0	88.0	96.0	104.0
Royalty (before tax)	5%				
Hypothetical royalty receipts (before tax)		4.0	4.4	4.8	5.2
Taxes	25%	−1.0	−1.1	−1.2	−1.3
Hypothetical royalty receipts (after tax)		3.0	3.3	3.6	3.9
Discount rate	10%				
Present values		2.7	2.7	2.7	29.3
Total of the present values		**37.4**			

The **tax amortization benefit** is calculated by multiplying the total of the present values of CU 37.4 by the formula "UL : (UL – PVIFA · t) – 1:"[19]

Useful life for tax purposes (in years)	15	
Interest rate	10%	
PVIFA[20]	7.60608	Present value of an annuity of CU 1 during the term UL and on the basis of the interest rate i: $1 : 1.1 + 1 : 1.1^2 + \ldots$ until the end of the period UL (formula "PV" in Excel).
Tax amortization benefit	**5.4**	37.4 · (15 : (15 – 7.60608 · 0,25) –1)

Therefore, the **fair value** of the brand as at Dec 31, 00 (i.e. on the acquisition date) is CU 42.8 (= CU 37.4 + CU 5.4).

[18] *The present value for 04 onwards is determined as follows: first, the present value as at Jan 01, 04 of a perpetual annuity has to be calculated: CU 3.9 : 0.1 = CU 39. This result has to be discounted for three periods from Jan 01, 04 to Dec 31, 00 with a discount rate of 10% p.a.*

[19] *UL = useful life for tax purposes; PVIFA = present value interest factor of annuity for the period UL and the interest rate i (corresponds with the present value of an annuity of CU 1 during the term UL, on the basis of the interest rate i); t = tax rate.*

[20] *PVIFA = present value interest factor of annuity.*

INDEX

Printed in the United States
By Bookmasters